MENTAL CAPACITY ACT

D1579396

MENTAL CAPACITY ACT MANUAL

SEVENTH EDITION

by

RICHARD M. JONES M.A. (Kent and Brunel)
Solicitor, C.Q.S.W.
Consultant, Blake Morgan Solicitors
Honorary Professor of Law, Cardiff University

SWEET & MAXWELL

THOMSON REUTERS

First edition 2005
Second edition 2007
Third edition 2008
Fourth edition 2010
Fifth edition 2012
Sixth edition 2014
Seventh edition 2016

Published in 2016 by Thomson Reuters (Professional) UK Limited trading as
Sweet & Maxwell, Friar's House, 160 Blackfriars Road, London, SE1 8EZ
(Registered in England & Wales, Company No 1679046.
Registered Office and address for service:
2nd floor, 1 Mark Square, Leonard Street, London EC2A 4EG)

For further information on our products and services, visit
www.sweetandmaxwell.co.uk

Typeset by Servis Filmsetting Ltd, Stockport, Cheshire, SK2 5AJ
Printed and bound by CPI Group (UK) Ltd, Croydon, CR0 4YY

British Library Cataloguing in Publication Data

A CIP catalogue record for this book
is available from the British Library

ISBN 978-0-41405-750-0

*No natural forests were destroyed to make this product; only farmed
timber was used and re-planted*

PREFACE

In the preface to the previous edition of this Manual reference was made to the recommendation of the House of Lords Select Committee on the Mental Capacity Act contained in its 2014 report, "Mental Capacity Act 2005: post-legislative scrutiny" that the deprivation of liberty safeguards be the subject of a comprehensive review as they were "not fit for purpose". Partly as a response to this recommendation and partly as a result of the decision of the Supreme Court in the *Cheshire West* case which resulted in a 10-fold increase in applications for deprivation of liberty authorisations, the Department of Health decided to fund the Law Commission to undertake a fundamental review of the deprivation of liberty legislation.

The Law Commission published a consultation paper "Mental Capacity and Deprivation of Liberty" in July 2015. The key proposal in the consultation is the replacement of the safeguards with a new scheme called "protective care", which would apply to a wider range of individuals than the current scheme. The new scheme would be sub-divided into "supportive care" which is intended to provide protection for mentally incapacitated people who are in a vulnerable position but who are not yet subject to the second element of the scheme which is "restrictive care and treatment".

Although the consultation paper is an impressive document, the proposed new scheme can be criticised for being unnecessarily complex and for the significant demand that it would make on increasingly scarce resources, a demand which has been estimated as being 13 times the cost of the current scheme.

The current scheme is itself resource intensive which has resulted in resources being diverted to it from the provision of social care services. Ann Coffey, the MP for Stockport, gave an example of the cost of the current scheme in Parliament:

> "Deprivation of liberty assessments are costing Stockport Council £1.2 million this year, as a result of the Cheshire West judgment. Not one single penny of that is providing social care" (*Hansard*, Vol.607, col.1359).

The current scheme can also be criticised for its bewildering legal complexity. This has resulted in the judges handing down very lengthy judgments which occasionally betray an ignorance of the practical pressures facing social care practitioners. It has also led to a disproportionate amount of money being spent on legal costs. Some years ago, Lord McCluskey famously predicted that the Human Rights Act would prove to be "a pain in the neck for judges and legislators and a goldmine for lawyers". It is unfortunately the case that a similar prediction could have accurately been made about the deprivation of liberty legislation.

The Department of Health required the Law Commission to adopt an approach in its review that would be rooted in the Mental Capacity Act. Given the potential futility of attempting to tinker with a scheme which has proved to be dysfunctional, has the time come to look afresh at the issue of how society can best safeguard the interests of mentally incapacitated individuals who are being deprived of their liberty? In particular, should fresh consideration be given to replacing the current scheme with a modified form of Mental Health Act guardianship? This was one of the options identified by the Government in its consultation following the decision of the European Court of Human Rights in the *Bournewood* case. Although this option did not find favour at the time, a guardianship-based scheme would have the significant advantage of avoiding the need for a separate system of legal adjudication for a particular group of mentally incapacitated individuals who are being deprived of their liberty. Such a scheme would also be cost effective, would be familiar to both legal and social care practitioners, would eradicate the complex legislative interface issues that bedevil the current scheme, and would utilise the existing Mental Health Act tribunal system which provides for the local administration of justice.

I have attempted to state the law on the basis of material that was available to me on May 1, 2016.

Richard Jones
email: richard.m.jones@blakemorgan.co.uk

CONTENTS

Contents

TABLE OF CASES

Table of Cases

Table of Cases

PART 1

MENTAL CAPACITY ACT 2005

(2005 C.9)

ARRANGEMENT OF SECTIONS

SECTION

PART 1

PERSONS WHO LACK CAPACITY

The principles

PART 2

THE COURT OF PROTECTION AND THE PUBLIC GUARDIAN

PART 3

MISCELLANEOUS AND GENERAL

An Act to make new provision relating to persons who lack capacity; to establish a superior court of record called the Court of Protection in place of the office of the Supreme Court called by that name; to make provision in connection with the Convention on the International Protection of Adults signed at the Hague on 13th January 2000; and for connected purposes. [7th April 2005]

BACKGROUND TO THE ACT

1–002   The Mental Capacity Act 2005 (the Act) is a measure which is likely to touch the lives of everyone because, at some point, all adults will probably be affected by a lack of capacity to make decisions relating to their everyday lives, either personally, or through contact with people who are unable to make decisions for themselves. As the Government noted:

"a wide range of conditions can result in incapacity to take decisions. In some cases, the capacity to take decisions is never attained (for example in the case of some people with a learning disability). In other cases, capacity is attained but is subsequently lost. This may occur for a number of reasons, including medical disorders or traumatic injury. The loss of capacity may be temporary for example during a toxic confusional state, which might result from an illness, or use of drugs. In some cases, capacity may fluctuate during periods when they are well, but may lose it during periods of illness. Finally, the loss of capacity may be permanent, as for example in some cases of dementia or the persistent vegetative state" (*Who Decides? Making Decisions on Behalf of Mentally Incapacitated Adults*, Cm. 3803, para.2.1).

The following factors can be said to have driven the process that cumulated in the passing of the Act: the legal context, demographic tends and improvements in healthcare, the community care policy, and the protection of human rights.

The legal context

As is pointed out below, the legal context that confronted the Law Commission when it commenced its investigation into the adequacy of legal procedures for decision-making on behalf of mentally incapacitated adults was most unsatisfactory. It was described as "one of incoherence, inconsistency and historical accident" (Law Comm. No.231, para.2.45). The High Court had attempted to respond to this situation by using the doctrine of necessity and the declaratory jurisdiction to determine the legality of action proposed to be taken in respect of a mentally incapacitated person, but this approach, which is aimed at responding to individual problems, was ill-suited to developing a coherent legal framework. It was clear that the law did not offer sufficient protection either for the mentally incapacitated, or for those who looked after them.

1–003

Demographic trends and improvements in healthcare

The number of elderly people is rising steadily in the population. The mental faculties of the elderly often decline with age and the number of persons suffering from dementia, which leads to a progressive loss of mental capacity, is increasing markedly. The House of Lords Select Committee on Economic Affairs estimated that the proportion of the population aged 65 or over as a percentage of those aged 16–64 would be 24.4 per cent in 2000, 32.8 per cent in 2025, and 39.2 per cent in 2050 (Session 2002–03, 4th Report, *Aspects of the Economics of an Ageing Population*, Vol.1, p.10). The House of Commons Library report on "Key Issues for the New Parliament 2015" states in the chapter on "The ageing population" at p.50:

1–004

"Vastly improved life expectancy, one of the great triumphs of the last century, looks set to be one of great challenges of this one. Between 2015 and 2020, over a period when the general population is expected to rise 3%, the numbers aged over 65 are expected to increase by 12% (1.1 million); the numbers aged over 85 by 18% (300,000); and the number of centenarians by 40% (7,000)."

Medical advances, in particular the development of antibiotics, have saved the lives of many people who would in earlier times have died from disease or trauma. Some of those who survive will do so with impaired mental capacity or even, exceptionally, lapse into a vegetative state. In the case of Tony Bland, a young man who as a result of being crushed at the Hillsborough disaster was in a vegetative state, Lord Browne-Wilkinson expressed his concern about the "scale of the problem that is presented by modern technological developments" and said that it seemed to him "imperative that the moral, social and legal issues raised by this case should be considered by Parliament" (*Airedale NHS Trust v Bland* [1993] 1 All E.R. 821 at 878, 879, HL). Also, as the Law Commission noted:

"the achievements of medical science have also created difficult dilemmas about the appropriate measure of medical care which should be given at the end of life, particularly where unconscious or incapacitated people have, in advance, indicated an unwillingness to be kept alive once their health has deteriorated" (Law Comm. No.231, para.2.38).

A further concern in the medical context was the recognition that certain procedures involving the mentally incapacitated were almost certainly unlawful. The most prevalent example was the practice of carrying out research on a person who was mentally incapable of consenting to participating in it, and where that person would receive no benefit from the results of the research.

The community care policy

1–005   The community care policy comprised two distinct threads. The first related to the policy of discharging mentally disordered people from large, isolated long stay hospitals into community based provision. This lead to significant changes to the ways in which such people are cared for. The second thread focused on the manner in which social care needs of the population should be assessed and provided for. The White Paper *Caring for People: Community Care in the Next Decade and Beyond* (1989) Cm. 849, stated at para.1.1:

> "Community care means providing the services and support which people who are affected by problems of ageing, mental illness, mental handicap or physical or sensory disability need to be able to live as independently as possible in their own homes, or in 'homely' settings in the community."

The combination of these two policy initiatives has lead to a decrease in reliance on institutional care for the mentally disabled. Institutional care tends to encourage a paternalistic approach to meeting patient/resident needs, while community based care increases the opportunities for mentally disabled individuals to make many of the decisions that occur in everyday life either by themselves or with support. Some of the decisions that may be required to be taken might raise the question of whether the person concerned possesses the required level of mental capacity to make the decision in question.

The protection of human rights

1–006   The Act is indicative of a growing shift in attitude toward those who, for whatever reason, lack the mental capacity to make key decisions for themselves. In particular, there has been a growing international recognition of the unacceptability of discrimination against the mentally disabled which started in 1971 with the United Nations "Declaration of the Rights of Mentally Retarded Persons". Despite its dated terminology, the Declaration represented an important milestone in that it established some important rights, in particular the person with a learning disability has "the same rights as other human beings" (para.1) which cannot be restricted without due process that "must contain proper legal safeguards against every form of abuse" (para.7). The Law Commission paid "careful regard" to aspects of the Declaration when it made its final report (Law Comm. No.231, para.2.27).

The United Nations Convention on the Rights of Persons with Disabilities was adopted by the General Assembly on December 13, 2006. The UK Government ratified the Convention on June 8, 2009. The European Union ratified the Convention on December 23, 2010. Although the Convention has been referred to by Sales J. as "an unincorporated international treaty [which] does not have direct effect in English law (*R. (on the application of NM v London Borough of Islington* [2012] EWHC 414 (Admin) at para.98), in *AH v West London MHT* [2011] UKUT 74 (AAC) the Upper Tribunal, presided over by Carnwath L.J., said at para.16:

> "The CRPD provides the framework for Member States to address the rights of persons with disabilities. It is a legally binding international treaty that comprehensively clarifies the human rights of persons with disabilities as well as corresponding obligations on state parties. By ratifying a Convention, a state undertakes that wherever possible its laws will conform to the norms and values that the Convention enshrines."

This approach was approved by the Court of Appeal in *Burnip v Birmingham City Council* [2012] EWCA Civ 629, where Maurice Kay L.J. said that the Convention has "the potential to illuminate our approach to both discrimination and justification" (para.22).

In her judgment in *P v Cheshire West and Chester Council* [2014] UKSC 19 at para.36, Baroness Hale described the status of the Convention in the following terms:

"The whole point about human rights is their universal character. The rights set out in the European Convention are to be guaranteed to 'everyone' (article 1). They are premised on the inherent dignity of all human beings whatever their frailty or flaws. The same philosophy underpins the United Nations Convention on the Rights of Persons with Disabilities (CRPD), ratified by the United Kingdom in 2009. Although not directly incorporated into our domestic law, the CRPD is recognised by the Strasbourg court as part of the international law context within which the guarantees of the European Convention are to be interpreted."

Among those covered by the Convention are people "who have long term . . . mental [or] intellectual . . . impairments which in interaction with various barriers may hinder their full and effective participation in society on an equal basis with others" (art.1). There is a tension between s.4 of the Act, which provides for the making of decisions for P (substituted decision-making), and art.12 of the Convention which focuses on the right of individuals to make their own decisions with appropriate support (supported decision-making) given that art.12(2) requires States to "recognize that persons with disabilities enjoy legal capacity on an equal basis with others in all aspects of life". The approach that should be adopted where, even with the assistance of extensive support, the past or present wishes and feelings of a mentally incapacitated person (P) regarding the decision that has to be made cannot be ascertained is not addressed in art.12. Supported decision-making is promoted by the Act at ss.1(3), 3(2) and 4(4). The Convention is considered by Phil Fennell and Urfan Khaliq in "Conflicting or complementary obligations? The UN Disability Rights Convention on Human Rights and English Law", *European Human Rights Law Review*, 2011, 6, 662–674 and by Peter Bartlett in "The United Nations Convention on the Rights of Persons with Disabilities and Mental Health Law", (2012) 75(5) M.L.R. 752–778. The House of Lords Select Committee on the Mental Capacity Act 2005 concluded that it would "not be prudent [for the Committee] to make specific recommendations concerning the Act's compatibility or otherwise with the Convention, and any legislative changes that may or may not be necessary". However, the Committee took the view that although "the issue of compatibility cannot be resolved at present it will be relevant in future, and we have therefore taken the view that better alignment [of the Act with the Convention] in practice should be regarded as a reasonable aim" (para.53). The compatibility of the Act with the Convention is examined by the Essex Autonomy Project in "Achieving CRPD Compliance" (2014) which can be accessed at: http://autonomy.essex.ac.uk/uncrpd-report.

The only international instrument against which UK law can be judicially tested is the European Convention on Human Rights. The Human Rights Act 1998 (HRA) makes Convention rights enforceable in domestic courts. The Joint Committee on Human Rights said that the provisions of the Draft Mental Incapacity Bill:

"engage a wide range of [Convention] rights, including the right to respect for family life, the right to property, and the right to be free of degrading treatment. In our view, however, the safeguards built into the Draft Bill are sufficient to ensure that there is no significant risk of the implementation of the Draft Bill leading to an incompatibility with any of them" (Session 2002–03, 15th Report, *Scrutiny of Bills and Draft Bills: Further Progress Report* (HL 149 / HC 1005), para.4.7).

Further reports of the Joint Committee were more questioning of whether particular provisions of the Bill risked violating either arts 2, 3, 5, or 8 of the Convention. Generally speaking, the Committee was satisfied with the responses that it received from the Government either in terms of amendments to the Bill, or from assurances the it received regarding the contents of the Code of Practice (Session 2004–05, 4th Report (HL 26/HC 224), Ch.4).

In *G v E* [2010] EWCA Civ 822 at para.86, the Court of Appeal said that the Act generally, and the deprivation of liberty procedures set out in Sch.A1 in particular, are compliant with art.5 of the Convention and that there is therefore no additional need for the criteria set out by the European Court of Human Rights in *Winterwerp v Netherlands* (1979–80) 2 E.H.R.R. 387 to be satisfied if the Sch.A1 procedures are to be utilised.

A combination of s.15(1)(c) and 47(1) of the Act and ss.7(1)(b) and 8(1) of the HRA provide the Court of Protection with jurisdiction to make declarations as to whether the Convention rights of a relative of P have been contravened by a public authority and to award damages under the HRA for breaches of the Convention rights of P or a relative of P (*YA(F) v A Local Authority* [2010] EWHC 2770 (Fam)). With regard to the awarding of damages, see *A Local Authority v Mrs D* [2013] EWHC B34 (COP) which is noted under s.15(1)(c).

THE LEGISLATIVE PROCESS

1–007   The Law Commission's Fourth Programme of Law Reform (1989, Law Com. No.185) proposed an investigation into the adequacy of legal and other procedures for decision-making on behalf of mentally incapacitated adults. There followed an extensive consultation exercise in the course of which the Commission published the following consultation papers:

- Mentally Incapacitated Adults and Decision-Making: An Overview (CP No.119)
- Mentally Incapacitated Adults and Decision-making: A New Jurisdiction (CP No.128)
- Mentally Incapacitated Adults and Decision-Making: Medical Treatment and Research (CP No.129)
- Mentally Incapacitated and Other Vulnerable Adults: Public law Protection (CP No.130).

The current state of the law was described by the Commission at para.1.1 of its Final Report "Mental Incapacity" (Law Com. No.231) which was published in March 1995:

"It is widely recognised that, in this area, the law as it now stands is unsympathetic and full of glaring gaps. It does not rest on clear or modern foundations of principle. It has also failed to keep up with developments in our understanding of the rights and needs of those with mental disability."

The Report sought to provide:

"A new set of coherent answers to a single question. The question, put simply, is 'who decides?' Although it may be asked in a variety of situations and for a variety of reasons, it arises whenever a person lacks the mental capacity to make a legally effective decision for himself or herself. There are various supplementary questions which must then be put. 'On what basis?' and 'with what formalities?' are examples of these. The types of decision which may be called for can be divided into three broad categories: 'personal welfare' decisions, 'health care' decisions and 'financial' decisions" (para.2.1).

A draft "Mental Incapacity Bill" was appended to the Report. This was intended to "provide a unified and comprehensive scheme within which people can make decisions for themselves" (para.3.1).

Lord Mackay, the Lord Chancellor, announced in January 1996 that the "Government has decided not to legislate on the basis of the Law Commission's proposals in their current form and has also concluded that it would be inappropriate to make any proposals to Parliament in the absence of full public consultation" (Lord Chancellor's Department, Press Notice, January 16,1996).

The incoming Labour Government issued a consultation paper "Who Decides? Making Decisions on Behalf of Mentally Incapacitated Adults", Cm.3803 (1997) which was based on the Commission's proposals. It also took into account the report of the House of Lords Select Committee on Medical Ethics (HL Paper 21-1) which had considered the issue of advance statements about healthcare. The consultative paper sought views on a possible framework for providing protection for mentally incapacitated adults and those who look after them, and for providing an organised framework of law to manage the welfare and affairs of mentally incapacitated adults. The consultation resulted in over 4,000 responses being received. The Government's response to the consultation was published in October 1999 as "Making Decisions: The Government's proposals for making decisions on behalf of mentally incapacitated adults", (Cm.4465). The proposals were largely based on the Law Commission's recommendations. The Lord Chancellor, Lord Irvine, announced in November 1999 that the Government had decided to bring forward legislation "to empower mentally incapacitated adults, so far as can safely be allowed, to make provision for the care they want before they lose capacity, and to ensure that when decisions come to be made about their care and welfare, they contain adequate safeguards and protection, they are made consistently and in line with each individual's particular best interests" (speech to the Law Society's Conference on Mental Incapacity, November 10, 1999).

A "Draft Mental Incapacity Bill" (Cm.5859-1) was presented to Parliament in June 2003. In July 2003, the House of Commons and House of Lords appointed a Joint Committee to scrutinise the Draft Bill. The Joint Committee's Report, which contained 99 recommendations and was mainly supportive of the principles underlying the draft Bill, was published in two volumes in November 2003 (HL Paper 189-1, 2; HC 1083-1, 2). The Government's response to the report was published in February 2004 (Cm.6121). The great majority of the Joint Committee's recommendations were accepted by the Government.

Several witnesses to the Joint Committee suggested that the title "Mental Incapacity Bill" was inappropriate and had negative connotations and preferred "Mental Capacity Bill" which they saw as a more accurate description of the Bill, as well as being more positive and reassuring. The Joint Committee considered that the Bill "should avoid the pejorative implications of incapacity and instill confidence in those it is intended to serve" and recommended "that consideration should be given to changing the Bill's title to 'Mental Capacity Bill' " (paras 362–364). The Government accepted this recommendation.

The objectives of the legislation, which has the general aim of seeking to strike a balance between respect for individual autonomy and the need to protect the vulnerable, were explained by the Secretary of State for Constitutional Affairs and Lord Chancellor, Lord Falconer, when he moved the second reading of the Bill:

"The Bill seeks to do six main things. First, it allows adults to take as many decisions as they can for themselves and, in any event, to put them at the centre of the decision-making process about themselves.

Secondly, when adults fear that they may not be able to take decisions about their medical treatment in the future, it allows them, if they wish, and subject to effective safeguards, to make decisions in advance of incapacity about whether treatment should be carried out or continued.

Thirdly, where adults cannot make decisions and have not made any decision in advance about their own personal welfare or other property or affairs, the Bill ensures that the decisions which are made for them are made in their best interests.

Fourthly, where an adult lacks capacity to make a decision for himself about serious medical treatment, accommodation in a hospital or care home, or other residential accommodation, and they have no friends or family to be consulted, the Bill will require the relevant NHS body or local authority to appoint an independent [mental capacity advocate] to support the person in these most difficult decisions.

Fifthly, the Bill will provide protection against subsequent legal liability for those carers who have honestly and reasonably sought to act in the best interests of the person for whom they have cared.

Finally, the Bill will provide clarity and safeguards around the carrying out of research in relation to people who lack capacity" (*Hansard*, HL Vol.668, col.12).

Ten years elapsed between the publication of the Law Commission's Mental Incapacity Bill on February 28, 1995 and the Mental Capacity Act receiving its Royal Assent on April

7, 2005. This delay can be partly explained by the sensitivity of successive Governments to concerns that had been expressed by a number of bodies about the prospect of the provisions on advance decisions enabling euthanasia to be introduced "by the backdoor". This concern, which was a recurring issue throughout the parliamentary debates on the Bill, led to the enactment of s.62.

The Mental Health Act 2007 made substantial amendments to the Act to provide for a procedure that can be used to authorise the deprivation of liberty of a mentally incapacitated person. The amendments are considered in Part 2.

The House of Lords Select Committee on the Mental Capacity Act 2005

1–008   The Select Committee was established in May 2013 to conduct post-legislative scrutiny of the Act. Its task "was to answer the question of whether the Act is working as Parliament intended" (p.6). The main themes that emerged from the evidence that the Committee received is set out at paras.12 to 19 of Chapter 1 of its Report "Mental Capacity Act: post-legislative scrutiny", HL Paper 139, March 13, 2014:

> "The vast majority of our witnesses considered that the Act was a very significant and progressive piece of legislation, with the potential to transform lives. Its principles remained appropriate and relevant. It provides empowerment for those who may lack capacity; a structure for decision-making for those who do lack capacity; and protection for carers, families and professionals.

> However, the overwhelming theme of the evidence was that the Act was not well implemented. The principles of the Act, which govern the empowering ethos, are not widely embedded. The processes outlined in the Act—how capacity is to be assessed, how a best interests decision is to be made—are not widely known, and not adequately or consistently followed. In general, the evidence suggested that these problems were greater in health care than in social care settings.

> Poor implementation appeared to be a function of low awareness combined with poor understanding of the Act: this was a consistent theme identified across professions, families, carers and the wider public. Health and social care professionals continue to struggle with how to apply the core principles in practice. Greater levels of awareness and better understanding will be required to deliver the 'quiet revolution in public attitudes and practice' which the Act was expected to usher in.

> A consistent theme in the evidence was the tension between the empowerment which the Act was designed to deliver, and the tendency of professionals to use the Act for safeguarding purposes. Prevailing professional cultures of risk aversion and paternalism have inhibited the aspiration of empowerment from being realised.

> The presumption of capacity as set out in the Act—a person must be assumed to have capacity unless it is established that he does not—is widely misunderstood. At times, it is used to justify non-intervention by health or social care services, either erroneously or, in some cases, deliberately.

> A further theme is the lack of consistent monitoring of implementation of the Act. Limited data are collected, and from those data that are available only limited inferences can be drawn about the operation of the Act. There is insufficient monitoring of how the Act affects Black and Minority Ethnic communities.

> Ministers are ultimately accountable for the successful implementation of the Act. The present arrangements are unsatisfactory: there are many organisations involved, but none has overall responsibility for implementation. The lack of co-ordination of activities of the various organisations by a single body is reflected in the patchy implementation of the Act. To address this we recommend that a single independent body be given overall responsibility for the implementation of the Act. This independent body could be free-standing or be located within an existing organisation.

The most significant exception to the overall finding that the Act was considered to be a good piece of legislation was the evidence on the Deprivation of Liberty Safeguards. Criticism of the safeguards is widespread and, unlike the rest of the Act, the criticism is not confined to implementation. The Deprivation of Liberty Safeguards were considered to be poorly drafted and poorly implemented. Our principal recommendation to address this is to replace the safeguards with new legislative provisions."

The Committee made 39 recommendations. Its principal recommendation "to address the failure to embed the Act in every day practice" is "that overall responsibility for implementation of the Mental Capacity Act be given to a single independent body" (p.6 and para.114). The Committee's other "key recommendation" is that "the Government undertake a comprehensive review of the DoLS legislation with a view to replacing it with provisions that are compatible in style and ethos with the Mental Capacity Act" (p.7 and para.258). In the Committee's final evidence session "Lord McNally, then Minister of State for Justice, conceded that while getting the Act onto the statute book had been a success, ensuring that it was fully implemented and understood was "work in progress" (para.9). However, the Committee noted that "there was no evidence of how, or indeed whether, the Government sought to assess progress against the criteria identified for success" (para.34). The Committee's Report can be accessed at: *www.publications. parliament.uk/pa/ld201314/ldselect/ldmentalcap/139/13902.htm*. The Government published its response to the Committee's recommendations on June 10, 2014. The response can be accessed at: *www.gov.uk/government/uploads/system/uploads/attachment_data/ file/318730/cm8884-valuing-every-voice.pdf*.

Territorial extent

The Act only extends to England and Wales, apart from the two exceptions set out in s.68(5).   **1–009**

ABBREVIATIONS

"ANH": artificial nutrition and hydration.   **1–010**

"*Code of Practice*": the *Code of Practice* laid before Parliament in draft in February 2007, pursuant to ss.42 and 43 of the Act, and approved in April 2007.

"CPR 2007": the Court of Protection Rules 2007 (SI 2007/1744).

"EPA": Enduring Powers of Attorney.

"Explanatory Notes": Explanatory notes on the Mental Capacity Bill prepared by the Department for Constitutional Affairs and the Department of Health.

"House of Lords Select Committee": The Report of the Select Committee on the Mental Capacity Act 2005, "Mental Capacity Act: post-legislative scrutiny", HL Paper 139, March 13, 2014.

"IMCA": independent mental capacity advocate.

"Joint Committee": House of Lords, House of Commons, Joint Committee on the Draft Mental Incapacity Bill, Session 2002–3.

"LPA": lasting power of attorney.

"Oral and written evidence": House of Lords, House of Commons, Joint Committee on the Draft Mental Incapacity Bill, Session 2002–3, Volume II: Oral and written evidence, HL Paper 189-II, HC 1083-II.

"the Bill": the Mental Capacity Bill.

"the court": the Court of Protection.

"the 1983 Act": the Mental Health Act 1983 (c.20).

"the 1985 Act": Enduring Powers of Attorney Act 1985 (c.29).

Throughout the Act, the capital letter "P" is used to refer to a person who lacks capacity or is believed to lack capacity to make a decision about a particular matter, and the capital letter "D" is used to refer to a person exercising powers in relation to P.

PART 1

PERSONS WHO LACK CAPACITY

The principles

The principles

1-011   **1.**—(1) The following principles apply for the purposes of this Act.

(2) A person must be assumed to have capacity unless it is established that he lacks capacity.

(3) A person is not to be treated as unable to make a decision unless all practicable steps to help him to do so have been taken without success.

(4) A person is not to be treated as unable to make a decision merely because he makes an unwise decision.

(5) An act done, or decision made, under this Act for or on behalf of a person who lacks capacity must be done, or made, in his best interests.

(6) Before the act is done, or the decision is made, regard must be had to whether the purpose for which it is needed can be as effectively achieved in a way that is less restrictive of the person's rights and freedom of action.

GENERAL NOTE

1-012   The Joint Committee recommended that a statement of principles should appear on the face of the Act. The Committee believed "that such a statement inserted as an initial point of reference could give valuable guidance to the courts, as well as helping non-lawyers to weigh up difficult decisions" (para.43). The principles apply to all actions and decisions taken under the Act by both lay and professional people and the judiciary. The provisions of s.2(3) can be added to the principles contained in this section.

The status of this section is that decisions and actions carried out under the Act should be tested against the principles which act as benchmarks for decision makers. Although there is no duty placed on persons or bodies to apply the principles, a failure to do so could be cited in legal proceedings.

The principles "set the context in which the case before the Court of Protection proceeds but do not strictly govern its case management or other decisions under the Court of Protection Rules 2007" (*Re AB* [2013] EWHC B39 (COP), per DJ Batten at para.63).

Although the principles apply "for the purposes of this Act" (subs.(1)), they are integral to the definition of capacity in s.2 which is imported as the test of capacity in the Civil Procedure Rules 1998 Pt 21 (as inserted by SI 2007/2204). Importing the definition therefore imports the principles into Part 21 (*Saulle v Nouvet* [2007] EWHC 2902 (QB) at para.46).

Subsection (2)

1-013   This provision establishes the fundamental principle that persons over the age of 16 (s.2(5)) are assumed to be mentally capable of making their own decisions. This assumption of personal autonomy can only be overridden if the person concerned is assessed as lacking the mental capacity to make a particular decision for him or herself at the relevant time. Thus, in the absence of a capacity assessment, any doubts have to be resolved in favour of capacity.

The consent of a mentally capable person to care or treatment provides the carer or clinician with legal authority to provide the care or treatment. Such a person's refusal of care or treatment must be respected even though the refusal might have drastic consequences, including death, for that person: see *Airedale NHS Trust v Bland* [1993] 1 All E.R. 821, per Lord Goff at 866. However, the presumption of capacity should not prevent a capacity assessment from being undertaken in a situation where a person's decisions are clearly contrary to his or her interests.

The House of Lords Select Committee found that:

"The presumption of capacity, in particular, is widely misunderstood by those involved in care. It is sometimes used to support non-intervention or poor care, leaving vulnerable adults exposed to risk of harm. In some cases this is because professionals struggle to understand how to apply the principle in practice. In other cases, the evidence suggests the principle has been deliberately misappropriated to avoid taking responsibility for a vulnerable adult" (para.105).

If a person is assessed as being mental incapable of making a decision that has long term consequences for that person, the assessment should be confirmed at regular intervals: see *Stanev v Bulgaria* (2012) E.H.R.R. 22 at para.156, where the European Court of Human Rights held that a gap in assessments of over two years in a case where a person had been assessed as being mentally incapable of agreeing to enter a care home was excessive.

The approach to be taken when making the assessment is set out in ss.2 and 3. In legal proceedings, the burden of proof will fall on the person who asserts that capacity is lacking.

Subsection (3)

This principle, which is aimed at maximising the decision making capacity of individuals, is expanded upon in s.3(2). The House of Lords Select Committee said that the principle is "generally referred to as supported decision-making making, and is intended to enable P as much as necessary to be able to make a decision". The evidence that the Committee received suggested "that this is rare in practice" (para.79).

1–014

The nature of the help provided will depend upon the condition of the person, the available resources and the nature and urgency of the decision to be taken. Family and legal and medical advisers could be involved where appropriate to "ensure that [the person] has proper explanations of information required for the decision, and that he takes decisions when he is in the right frame of mind to do so" (*Saulle v Nouvet*, above, at para.48). The Joint Committee said that such steps "might include using specific communication strategies, providing information in [a] more accessible form, or treating an underlying mental disorder to enable a person to regain capacity" (para.70). The Explanatory Notes suggest that "all practicable steps" could include "making sure the person is in an environment in which he is comfortable or involving an expert in helping him express his views" (para.20). Providing information over time may allow a person to assimilate information more completely, thereby maximising their actual understanding. Consideration could be given to postponing the decision if it is felt that the person might regain capacity over time. Chapter 3 of the *Code of Practice* considers the steps that can be taken to help people make their own decisions.

It is important not to equate "practicable" with "possible" (*Owen v Crown House Engineering* [1973] 3 All E.R. 618 at 622 NIRC). In *Dedman v British Building and Engineering Appliances Ltd* [1974] 1 W.L.R. 171 at 179, CA, Scarman L.J. said:

"The word 'practicable' is an ordinary English word of great flexibility: it takes its meaning from its context. But, whenever used, it is a call for the exercise of common sense, a warning that sound judgment will be impossible without compromise. Sometimes the context contemplates a situation rarely to be achieved though much to be desired: the word then indicates one must be satisfied with less than perfection . . . [S]ometimes . . . what the context requires may have been possible, but may not for some reason have been 'practicable'. Whatever its context, the quality of the word is that there are circumstances in which we must be content with less than 100 per cent: and it calls for judgment to determine how much less."

During the second reading debate on the Bill in the House of Lords, Lord Brennan cited a dramatic example of the impact that appropriate help can have on the ability of a disabled person to communicate:

"[A] client whom I represented had for 12 years, while being able to walk and grunt but not talk, been treated as a zombie, because his family did not believe that he was capable of any cognitive function. After obtaining a judgment on liability and getting an interim payment, at the second meeting with a speech therapist who knew about communication my client was able to converse with her. When challenged by me in conference, he readily spelt the word 'encyclopaedia'. Yet his family—his carers—were convinced for 12 years that his life was pretty well worthless" (*Hansard*, HL Vol.668, col.84).

In *AK (Adult Patient) (Medical Treatment: Consent), Re* [2001] 1 F.L.R. 129, a patient who had lost the use of virtually all his muscles, apart from those in one of his eyelids, through motor neurone disease was assisted to communicate by means of a device known as an "E transport" which involved the painstaking spelling out of words letter by letter by a process linked to the line of sight.

Although all practicable steps must be taken to help a person make a decision, those assisting the person must beware of subjecting the person to undue influence. Undue influence can apply to any person regardless of his or her mental capacity. In the context of consent to medical treatment, Lord Donaldson M.R. said in *T (Adult: Refusal of Treatment), Re* [1992] 4 All E.R. 649 at 662 that while it is acceptable for the patient to receive advice or for the patient to have been subject to the strong persuasion of others in reaching a decision, such persuasion must not "overbear the independence of the patient's decision". His Lordship identified the real question in each case as being: "does the patient really mean what he says or is he merely saying it for a quiet life, to satisfy someone else or because the advice and persuasion to which he has been subjected is such that he can no longer think and decide for himself? In other words, is it a decision expressed in form only, not in reality?" His Lordship identified two aspects of the effect of outside influence that could be of "crucial importance": the strength of will of the patient and the relationship of the "persuader" to the patient. With regard to the former, a patient who is "very tired, in pain or depressed will be much less able to resist having his will overborne than one who is rested, free from pain and cheerful". With regard to the relationship between the persuader and the patient, his Lordship spoke of the potential strength of the parental and marital relationship, especially with regard to arguments based on religious belief. Munby J. pointed out in *SA (Vulnerable Adult with Capacity: Marriage), Re* [2005] EWHC 2942 at para.78, that:

". . . where the influence is that of a parent or other close and dominating relative, and where the arguments and persuasions are based upon personal affection, or duty, religious beliefs, powerful social or cultural conventions, or asserted social, familial or domestic obligations, the influence may . . . be subtle, insidious, pervasive and powerful. In such cases . . . very little pressure may suffice to bring about the desired result."

Other outside influences that could vitiate a person's consent include fraud, misrepresentation and duress. The fact that a person is vulnerable to exploitation does not by itself mean that that person lacks capacity: see *Lindsay v Wood* [2006] EWHC 2895 (QB) which is noted in the General Note to s.3.

For a consideration of the application of art.12(4) of the Convention on the Rights of Disabled Persons to the concept of undue influence, see *Re GW* [2014] EWCOP B23 where Senior Judge Lush said at para.32:

"In its General Comment No 1 (2014), published on 11 April 2014, the Committee on the Rights of Persons with Disabilities stated, at paragraph 18, that:

'All people risk being subject to "undue influence" yet this may be exacerbated for those who rely on the supports of others to make decisions. Undue influence is characterized where the quality of the interaction between the support person and the person being supported includes signs of fear, aggression, threat, deception or manipulation. Safeguards for the exercise of legal capacity must include protection against undue influence—however the protection must also respect the rights, will and preferences of the person, including the right to take risks and make mistakes.'"

A useful summary of the law of presumed undue influence can be found in the judgment of Silber J. in *V Hackett v CPS* [2011] EWHC 1170 (Admin). Undue influence in the context of financial transactions was considered by the House of Lords in *Royal Bank of Scotland v Etridge* [2001] UKHL 44; [2001] 4 All E.R. 449.

Research into the decision-making capabilities of persons with learning disabilities has shown that the presentation of information in a user-friendly manner makes it possible to move some people from being assessed as incapable to being assessed as capable (M.J. Gunn et al., "Decision-making capacity" (1999) 7(3) Med. L. Rev. 269). Confirmation that capacity is not static, even among patients who have engaged in self-harm, is contained in a study which found that the number of patients judged to have capacity increased significantly following the presentation of an information sheet about the specific treatment being proposed, together with a verbal explanation (R. Jacob et al., "Self-Harm, Capacity, and Refusal of Treatment: Implications for Emergency Medical Practice" (2005) 22 *Emergency Medical Journal* 799). For a publication which offers practical help in assisting with communication, see N. Grove and B. McIntosh, "Communication for Person Centred Planning" (2006) *Foundation for People with Learning Disabilities*.

Subsection (4)

This principle underpins the right to personal autonomy by preserving the right of a **1–015** person to make an irrational, capricious, spiteful or eccentric decision which, viewed objectively, is not in that person's best interests without the person being treated as being mentally incapable by virtue of that decision alone. In *A Local Authority v FG* [2011] EWHC 3932 (COP) at para.11, Hedley J. suggested that this principle is "likely to have less weight" with a young person. The House of Lords Select Committee found that "across the evidence, the balance between empowerment and protection emerged as the key challenge to the implementation of the empowering ethos of the Act, and this seems most clear in relation to unwise decision-making. The right to make an unwise decision runs counter to the prevailing cultures in health and social care, which present barriers to implementation" (para.84). In *Re P (Statutory Will)* [2009] EWHC 163 (Ch), Lewison J. said at para.42:

> "I would add that, although the fact that P makes an unwise decision does not on its own give rise to any inference of incapacity (s.1(4)), once the decision-making power shifts to a third party (whether carer, deputy or the court) I cannot see that it would be a proper exercise for a third party decision-maker consciously to make an unwise decision merely because P would have done so. A consciously unwise decision will rarely, if ever, be made in P's best interests."

As the use of the term "merely" indicates, this provision does not prevent a capacity assessment being undertaken in respect of a person who makes an unwise decision, a series of unwise decisions, a decision that puts that person at risk, or who makes a decision which does not appear to reflect that person's values, beliefs or approach to risk-taking. The Joint Committee "considered carefully the dilemma created when a person with apparent capacity was making repeatedly unwise decisions that put him/her at risk or resulted in preventable suffering or disadvantage". While the Committee recognised that "the possibility of over-riding such decisions would be seen as unacceptable to many user groups", they suggested that "such a situation might trigger the need for a formal assessment of capacity" (Vol.1, para.78).

In the words of Davis L.J.:

> "It is, of course, of the essence of humanity that adults are entitled to be eccentric, entitled to be unorthodox, entitled to be obstinate, entitled to be irrational. Many are. But the decided authorities show that there can be no power of public intervention simply because an adult proposes to make a decision, or to tolerate a state if affairs, which most would consider neither wise nor sensible" (*DL v A Local Authority* [2012] EWCA Civ 253 at para.76).

Also note the following remarks of Hedley J. in *A NHS Trust v P* [2013] EWHC 50 (COP) at para.10:

"The intention of the Act is not to dress an incapacitous person in forensic cotton wool but to allow them as far as possible to make the same mistakes that all other human beings are at liberty to make and not infrequently do."

In *PC v City of York Council* [2013] EWCA Civ 478, McFarlane L.J. said at para.54:

"Mr Bowen correctly submits that there is a space between an unwise decision and one which an individual does not have the mental capacity to take and he powerfully argues that it is important to respect that space, and to ensure that it is preserved, for it is within that space that an individual's autonomy operates."

Paragraph 4.30 of the *Code of Practice* states:

"It is important to acknowledge the difference between

- unwise decisions . . . and
- decisions based on a lack of understanding of risks or inability to weigh up the information about a decision.

Information about decisions the person has made based on a lack of understanding of risks or inability to weigh up the information can form part of a capacity assessment— particularly if someone repeatedly makes decisions that put them at risk or result in harm to them or someone else."

This statement was confirmed by Parker J. in *YLA v PM* [2013] EWHC 4020 (COP) who said at para.43(e):

"Unwise decisions are different from decisions based on a lack of understanding of risks or inability to weigh up the information about a decision."

In *CC v KK* [2012] EWHC 2136 (COP) at para.65, Baker J. said that "in evaluating capacity the court must recognise that different individuals may give different weight to different factors. There is, I perceive, a danger that professionals, including judges, may objectively conflate a capacity assessment with a best interests analysis and conclude that the person under review should attach greater weight to the physical security and comfort of a residential home and less importance to the emotional security and comfort that the person derives from being in their own home. . . . These considerations underpin the cardinal rule, enshrined in statute, that a person is not to be treated as unable to make a decision merely because she makes what is perceived as being an unwise one". Baker J. returned to this theme in *A NHS Trust v Dr A* [2013] EWHC 2442 (COP) at para.34, where he said that "there is a risk that all professionals involved with treating and helping a person - including of course a Judge in the Court of Protection - may feel drawn towards an outcome that is more protective of the adult and thus, in certain circumstances, fail to carry out the appropriate assessment of capacity that is both detached and objective".

That the nature of the decision taken might be indicative of a lack of capacity on the part of the decision maker was emphasised by Kennedy L.J. in *Masterman-Lister v Brutton & Co* [2002] EWCA Civ 1889 at para.54, where his Lordship said that although the role of the court was the investigation of capacity not outcomes, outcomes "can often cast a flood of light on capacity".

In the context of consent to medical treatment, Lord Donaldson M.R. said:

"Prima facie every adult has the right and capacity to decide whether or not he will accept medical treatment, even if a refusal may risk permanent injury to his health or even lead to premature death. Furthermore, it matters not whether the reasons for the refusal were rational or irrational, unknown or even non-existent. This is so notwithstanding the very strong public interest in preserving the life and health of all citizens" (*T (Adult: Refusal of Treatment), Re* [1992] 4 All E.R. 649 CA, at 664).

Butler-Sloss P., in confirming that a mentally competent person is entitled to refuse treatment even if she does not give good reasons for doing so, said that "there is a point at which refusal and irrationality, as others might see it, tips the usually competent person over into a situation where the person, for however long or short a period, is actually unable to see through the consequences of the act, because that capacity to see through those consequences is inhibited by the panic situation in which the patient finds [her]self" (*Bolton Hospitals NHS Trust v O* [2003] 1 F.L.R. 824 at para.15).

There is a tension between this provision, which allows for a person to make an irrational decision without that decision on its own leading to a conclusion that the person is mentally incapable of making the decision, and the fact that the courts have been prepared to accept that an irrational decision can be evidence of incapacity. In *D v R (the Deputy of S)* [2010] EWHC 2405 (COP) at para.40, Henderson J., having confirmed a person's freedom to act in an unwise, capricious or spiteful manner, said:

"The significance of section 1(4) must not, however, be exaggerated. The fact that a decision is unwise or foolish may not, without more, be treated as conclusive, but it remains in my judgment a relevant consideration for the court to take into account in considering whether the criteria of inability to make a decision for oneself in section 3(1) are satisfied. This will particularly be the case where there is a marked contrast between the unwise nature of the impugned decision and the person's former attitude to the conduct of his affairs at a time when his capacity was not in question."

The approach taken in this provision is consistent with the finding of the European Court of Human Rights in *Winterwerp v Netherlands* (1979–80) 2 E.H.R.R. 387 at para.37, that Art.5 of the European Convention on Human Rights does not permit the detention of a person "simply because his views or behaviour deviate from the norms prevailing in a particular society".

Subsection (5)

The best interest principle, which must guide all actions done for or decisions made under the Act on behalf a person who lacks capacity, is expanded upon in s.4. The principle "calls for a sensible decision, not the pursuit of perfection" (*Re A and B* [2014] EWCOP 48 at para.14 per Peter Jackson J.).   **1–016**

A public law decision of a local authority relating to the provision of community care services under s.47 of the NHS and Community Care Act 1990 is not a decision "made . . . for or on behalf" of P. Such a decision is for the local authority to take, with due regard for P's welfare. It is therefore not a decision which is determined by the best interests of P (*R.(on the application of Chatting) v Viridian Housing* [2012] EWHC 3595 (Admin), para.100: also see *Re MN (Adult)* [2015] EWCA Civ 411 which is noted in the General Note to s.16).

A clinician who follows a valid and applicable advance decision (see ss.24–26) is not acting "for or on behalf of a person who lacks capacity"; he or she is acting on the instructions of a capacitated individual. It follows that the best interests principle does not apply to such decisions and healthcare professionals must comply with a valid and applicable advance decision, even though they do not consider that it would be in the patient's best interests to do so.

Subsection (6)

"Section 1(6) operates as a brake on excessive use of the powers vested in local authorities and the court" (*RB v Brighton and Hove City Council* [2014] EWCA Civ 561, per Jackson L.J. at para.51). In *Re GM* [2011] EWHC 2778 (COP) at para.18, Hedley J. said that "section 1(6) . . . is a principle of minimum intervention consistent with best interests" and in *Heart of England NHS Foundation Trust v JB* [2014] EWHC 342 (COP) at para.6, Peter Jackson J. said that this provision "acknowledges that people who lack capacity still have rights and that their freedom of action is as important to them as it is to anyone else".

Someone making a decision or acting on behalf of a mentally incapacitated person must consider whether it is possible to decide or act in a way that would interfere less with the   **1–017** person's rights and freedom of action, or whether there is a need to act at all. Put another way, the intervention should be proportional to the particular circumstances of the case. As only "regard" must be had to this principle, an option which is not the least restrictive option can still be in the person's best interests (*C v A Local Authority* [2011] EWHC 1539 (Admin) at para.61). In other words, the best interests principle takes priority (*Havering L.B.C. v LD* [2010] EWHC 3876 (COP) at para.9).

With regard to P's rights under the European Convention on Human Rights, in *A Local Authority v TZ* [2014] EWHC 973 (COP), Baker J. said that in applying this principle "and generally, the Court must have regard to [P's] human rights, in particular his rights under art.8 of ECHR to respect for private and family life. As the European Court of Human Rights observed in *Niemitz v Germany* (1993) 16 EHRR 97 at para 29, 'private life' includes, inter alia, the right to establish relationships with other human beings. . . . There is a positive obligation on the state to take measures to ensure that his private life is respected, and the European Court has stated that 'these obligations may involve the adoption of measures designed to secure respect for private life even in the sphere of the relations of individuals between themselves': *Botta v Italy* (1998) 26 EHRR 241 para.33".

The Parliamentary Under-Secretary of State for Constitutional Affairs gave the following example of an approach that would satisfy this principle: "A care assistant might be worried about residents with dementia wandering into the kitchen of the establishment unsupervised in case they come into contact with cleaning fluids. However, to steer them away from the kitchen would be unnecessary if staff ensured that all dangerous liquids were locked in a cupboard. That would not interfere with the freedom of action of the person suffering from dementia" (St.Comm.A, col.25).

The study by Dr I.C.H. Clare and her colleagues "found little evidence of a consideration of less restrictive alternatives such as environmental modifications that might limit the extent to which restrictions might need to be placed on a patient's freedom of movement" (*Understanding the interface between the Mental Capacity Act's Deprivation of Liberty Safeguards (MCA-DOLS) and the Mental Health Act (MHA)*, University of Cambridge, 2013, p.iii). The House of Lords Select Committee concluded that "the least restrictive option is not routinely or adequately considered" (para.104).

Preliminary

People who lack capacity

1–018   **2.**—(1) For the purposes of this Act, a person lacks capacity in relation to a matter if at the material time he is unable to make a decision for himself in relation to the matter because of an impairment of, or a disturbance in the functioning of, the mind or brain.

(2) It does not matter whether the impairment or disturbance is permanent or temporary.

(3) A lack of capacity cannot be established merely by reference to—

(a) a person's age or appearance, or

(b) a condition of his, or an aspect of his behaviour, which might lead others to make unjustified assumptions about his capacity.

(4) In proceedings under this Act or any other enactment, any question whether a person lacks capacity within the meaning of this Act must be decided on the balance of probabilities.

(5) No power which a person ("D") may exercise under this Act—

(a) in relation to a person who lacks capacity, or

(b) where D reasonably thinks that a person lacks capacity, is exercisable in relation to a person under 16.

(6) Subsection (5) is subject to section 18(3).

DEFINITIONS
"enactment": s.64(1).

GENERAL NOTE

This section sets out the Act's definition of a person (i.e. a person over the age of 16 (subs.(5)) who lacks capacity, bearing in mind the assumption is that a person has capacity (s.1(2)). The definition applies for "the purposes of this Act" only (subs.(1)). Schedule 6 makes consequential amendments to other statutes to ensure that the definition contained in the Act is used in relation to relevant proceedings. Common law definitions of capacity, such as the capacity to make a will (*Banks v Goodfellow* (1869-70) L.R. 5 Q.B. 549), are not affected. However, when cases come before the court, judges can adopt the definition of capacity contained in this section and s.3 if they think it is appropriate: see para.4.33 of the *Code of Practice* and *Local Authority X v MM and KM* [2007] EWHC 2003 (Fam) at para.80, where Munby J. explained that "appropriate" in para.4.33 means appropriate "having regard to the existing principles of common law".

An assessment should take place whenever there is a concern that an individual might lack the mental capacity to make the proposed decision. The assessor should first evaluate the capacity of the individual to make the decision in question using the formula set out in s.3. If the conclusion reached is that the person lacks the ability to make the decision, the assessor must then decide whether this is due to the fact that the person satisfies the "diagnostic test" set out in this section. If the person fails to satisfy the diagnostic test, there can be no finding of incapacity for the purposes of the Act: see *PC v City of York Council* [2013] EWCA Civ 478 which is noted in the General Note to s.3. In *Seaton v Seddon* [2012] EWHC 735 (Ch), Roth J. said that because "of the implications of a finding of mental incapacity for an individual's freedom of action, the thrust of the 2005 Act is to safeguard against a ready finding of lack of capacity" (para.108).

J. Beckett and R. Chaplin report that the capacity of patients with schizophrenia has been extensively studied and has shown a broad range from the significantly impaired to full capacity in both the acute and chronic stages of the illness, and that patients with depression have shown relatively unimpaired capacity. Their own study found that many patients hospitalised with mania have capacity to make an informed choice regarding treatment even when compulsorily detained ("Capacity to consent to treatment in patients with acute mania" (2006) 30 *Psychiatric Bulletin* 419). In a similar vein, T. Grisso and P. Appelbaum have pointed out that a "patient may be psychotic, seriously depressed, or in a moderately advanced stage of dementia, yet still found competent to make some or all decisions" (*Assessing Competence to Consent to Treatment* (1998) p.18).

European Convention on Human Rights

A decision that a person lacks capacity can infringe their right for respect for their private life under art.8 of the Convention (*Shtukaturov v Russia* (2012) 54 E.H.R.R. 27 at para.83).

Subsection (1)

AT THE MATERIAL TIME. Capacity is therefore time specific (*A Local Authority v TZ* [2013] EWHC 2322 (COP) at para.50).

BECAUSE OF. See para.58 of *PC v City of York Council* which is reproduced in the General Note to s.3.

IMPAIRMENT OF, OR A DISTURBANCE IN THE FUNCTIONING OF, THE BRAIN OR MIND. A wide range of conditions can result in incapacity to make decisions. In some cases, the capacity to take decisions is never attained (for example a person born with a severe learning disability). In other cases, capacity is attained but is subsequently lost, either on a temporary or permanent basis. The Explanatory Notes state that the diagnostic test contained in this provision could "cover a range of problems, such as psychiatric illness, learning disability, dementia, brain damage or even a toxic confusional state, as long as it has the necessary effect on the functioning of the mind or brain, causing the person to be unable to make the decision" (para.22). It also covers "the symptoms of alcohol or drug use" (*Code of Practice*, para.4.12). The test will "clearly also apply to patients with grave physical illnesses, which, by reason of vital organ failure and consequent biochemical disturbances, will cause either confusion or impairment of consciousness" (Dr Fiona Randall, "Oral and written evidence", Ev 301). It could also cover people who are suffering from the effects of pain, shock or exhaustion (*T (Adult: Refusal of Treatment), Re* [1992] 4 All E.R. 649), or whose mind is completely dominated by fear (*MB (Medical Treatment), Re* [1997] 2 F.L.R. 426) or an irrational thought process (*KB (Adult) (Mental Patient: Medical Treatment), Re* (1994) 19 B.M.L.R. 144). A person who is rendered unconscious will clearly satisfy the test. There is no requirement for the impairment or disturbance to be identified as a diagnosis recognised in ICD-10 or DSM-V.

Although medical evidence supporting a conclusion that the test has been satisfied is not required, it would be advisable for the assessor to seek such evidence in difficult or controversial cases: see further, the General Note to s.3.

Subsection (2)

1–023   The temporary nature of P's incapacity matters for the purposes of decision making because a decision should be delayed if the person's mental capacity might return and the delay would be consistent with the person's best interests (see s.4(3)). Temporary loss of capacity could be caused by the effect of excessive alcohol consumption, the misuse of drugs, the nature of a person's mental disorder, the effect of prescribed medication or an emotional crisis.

Subsection (3)

1–024   This provision is aimed at preventing unjustified assumptions being made about a person's mental capacity. It "gives further emphasis to the Bill's principle that everyone should be assumed to have capacity until it is shown that they do not. For example, it is not acceptable to say, on the assumption that someone has a learning disability, that he cannot or will not want to make decisions about where to live", per Baroness Andrews (*Hansard*, HL Vol.670, col.1319).

Subsection (4)

1–025   "The balance of probability standard means that a court is satisfied an event occurred if the court considers that, on the evidence, the occurrence of the event was more likely than not", per Lord Nicholls in *H (Minors) (Sexual Abuse: Standard of Proof), Re* [1996] A.C. 563 at 586.

Subsections (5) and (6)

1–026   Although the powers under the Act only generally arise where the person lacking capacity is 16 or over, powers in relation to property might be exercised in relation to a younger person who has disabilities which will cause the incapacity to last into adulthood (see s.18(3)). Any overlap with the jurisdiction under the Children Act 1989 (c.41) can be dealt with under the Mental Capacity Act 2005 (Transfer of Proceedings) Order (SI 2007/1899) which is reproduced in Part 3. Further exceptions to the general rule that the Act applies to those who are 16 and over are:

1. A lasting power of attorney can only be made be a person who has reached 18 (s.9(2) (c)).
2. An advance decision can only be made by a person who reached 18 (s.24(1)).
3. The standard and urgent authorisation procedure in Sch.A1 only applies to a person who has reached 18 (Sch.A1, para.13).
4. The offence of ill-treatment or neglect of a mentally incapacitated person established by s.44 has no age limit.

Inability to make decisions

3.—(1) For the purposes of section 2, a person is unable to make a decision for   **1–027**
himself if he is unable—

(a) to understand the information relevant to the decision,

(b) to retain that information,

(c) to use or weigh that information as part of the process of making the decision, or

(d) to communicate his decision (whether by talking, using sign language or
any other means).

(2) A person is not to be regarded as unable to understand the information relevant to a decision if he is able to understand an explanation of it given to him in
a way that is appropriate to his circumstances (using simple language, visual aids
or any other means).

(3) The fact that a person is able to retain the information relevant to a decision
for a short period only does not prevent him from being regarded as able to make
the decision.

(4) The information relevant to a decision includes information about the reasonably foreseeable consequences of—

(a) deciding one way or another, or

(b) failing to make the decision.

GENERAL NOTE

This section, which is based on the common law test of capacity ("there is no relevant   **1–028**
distinction" between them: *Local Authority X v MM and KM* [2007] EWHC 2003 (Fam)
at para.74, per Munby J.), sets out the test for determining whether a person is "unable to
make a [particular] decision" (subs.(1)). In *IM v LM* [2014] EWCA Civ 37, the Court of
Appeal said that

> "every single issue of capacity which falls to be determined under Part 1 of the Act
> must be evaluated by applying s 3(1) in full and considering each of the four elements
> of the decision making process that are set out at (a) to (d). . . . The extent to which, on
> the facts of any individual case, there is a need either for a sophisticated, or for a more
> straightforward, evaluation of any of these four elements will naturally vary from case
> to case and from topic to topic" (para.73).

A helpful summary of the law relating to the assessment of capacity is provided by
MacDonald J. in *Kings College NHS Foundation Trust v C* [2015] EWCOP 80 at paras
25 to 39.

In *PC v City of York Council* [2013] EWCA Civ 478 Macfarlane L.J., giving the lead
judgment, said that if the conclusion reached by the assessor is that the person lacks the
ability to make the decision, the assessor must then decide whether this is due to the fact
that the person satisfies the "diagnostic test" set out in s.2. His Lordship gave his rationale
for this approach at para.58:

> "There is . . . a danger in structuring the decision by looking to s 2(1) primarily as requir-
> ing a finding of mental impairment and nothing more and in considering s 2(1) first before
> then going on to look at s 3(1) as requiring a finding of inability to make a decision. The
> danger is that the strength of the causative nexus between mental impairment and inabil-
> ity to decide is watered down. That sequence—'mental impairment' and then 'inability to
> make a decision'—is the reverse of that in s 2(1)—'unable to make a decision . . . *because
> of* an impairment of, or a disturbance in the functioning of, the mind or brain' [emphasis
> added]. The danger in using s 2(1) simply to collect the mental health element is that the
> key words 'because of' in s 2(1) may lose their prominence and be replaced by words
> such as those deployed by Hedley J.: 'referable to' or 'significantly relates to'."

Commenting on this aspect of the judgment in *NCC v PB* [2014] EWCOP 14 at paras 89 and 90, Parker J. said:

"[Counsel submitted] that Dr Khalifa approached the test [of capacity] the wrong way round. They submit that the Code of Practice stipulates that the first step is to decide whether there is a disturbance of mind, and the second to decide on capacity whereas McFarlane LJ in *PC v City of York* . . . stated that this should be considered in reverse order. In my view MacFarlane LJ did not purport to lay down a different test: nor did he take the questions in the reverse order, but simply stressed that there must be a causative nexus between the impairment and the incapacity.

I do not consider that it matters what order the expert addressed the issues so long as she or he observes the causative nexus."

The approach adopted by MacFarlane L.J. in *PC* was followed by MacDonald J. in *Kings College NHS Foundation Trust v C* [2015] EWCOP 80.

In *PC* the Court of Appeal confirmed that the determination of capacity under the Act is "decision" specific, rather than being "person" or "act" specific. McFarlane L.J. said at paras 35 and 37:

"Some decisions, for example agreeing to marry or consenting to divorce, are status or act specific. Some other decisions, for example whether P should have contact with a particular individual, may be person specific. But all decisions, whatever their nature, fall to be evaluated within the straightforward and clear structure of MCA 2005, ss.1 to 3 which requires the court to have regard to 'a matter' requiring 'a decision'. There is neither need nor justification for the plain words of the statute to be embellished. . . .

The central provisions of the MCA 2005 have been widely welcomed as an example of plain and clear statutory language. I would therefore deprecate any attempt to add any embellishment or gloss to the statutory wording unless to do so is plainly necessary. In this context the reference within the Official Solicitor's argument to 'domains' of decision-making is unwelcome and unnecessary. The court is charged, in relation to 'a matter', with evaluating an individual's capacity 'to make a decision for himself in relation to the matter' (s.2(1)); no need has been identified for grouping categories of 'matter' or 'decision' into domains, save where to do so has been established by common law or by the express terms of the MCA 2005 (for example, capacity to marry)."

In making this finding, the court confirmed the approach taken at first instance by Hedley J. who said:

"[I]t seems to me that what the statute requires is the fixing of attention upon the actual decision in hand. It is the capacity to take a specific decision, or a decision of a specific nature, with which the Act is concerned" (*CYC v PC* (COP No.12015615) at para.19).

The approach taken by the Court of Appeal reflects the "functional" approach to capacity which relates to the ability of the person to make a particular decision at a particular moment in time, not on the person's ability to make decisions generally. The functional approach can be contrasted with the "outcome" approach which uses the consequence of the decision-making process as the criterion for determining capacity, and the "status" or "diagnostic" approach under which a person's capacity is determined by his or her membership of a specific population, such as those who have been detained under the Mental Health Act 1983.

In *PC and NC,* above, the court rejected the "outcome" approach in the following terms:

"[T]he court's jurisdiction is not founded upon professional concern as to the 'outcome' of an individual's decision. There may be many women who are seen to be in relationships with men regarded by professionals as predatory sexual offenders. The Court of Protection does not have jurisdiction to act to 'protect' these women if they do not lack the mental capacity to decide whether or not to be, or continue to be, in such a relationship. The individual's decision may be said to be 'against the better judgment' of the woman concerned, but the point is that, unless they lack mental capacity to make that judgment, it is against their better judgment. It is a judgment that they are entitled to make. The statute respects their autonomy so to decide and the Court of Protection has no jurisdiction to intervene" (para.53).

In *C v V* [2008] EWHC B16 (Fam) at para.53, Judge Marshall Q.C. said that under the functional approach a person "may not have sufficient capacity to be able to make complex, refined or major decisions but may still have the capacity to make simpler or less momentous ones, or to hold genuine views as to what he wants to be the outcome of more complex decisions or situations." A striking example of a situation where a person was found to be capable of making a decision in relation to one matter, but not in relation to another is the deceased who on the same day was found by Karminski J. to have had capacity to marry (*Park, In the Estate of* [1954] P. 89), and by Pearce J. and a jury not to have had capacity to make a will (*Park, Culross v Park* (1950) *The Times*, December 2, 1950) (cited by Munby J. in *Sheffield City Council v E*, below, at para.25). In *T (Adult: Refusal of Treatment), Re* [1992] 4 All E.R. 649 at 661 Lord Donaldson held that the required capacity to consent to medical treatment is the capacity which is "commensurate with the gravity of the decision" which the person is purporting to make. Thus the more serious the decision, the greater the level of capacity required. This issue is considered by A. Buchanan in "Mental capacity, legal competence and consent to treatment", *Journal of the Royal Society of Medicine* 2004; 97: 415–420.

The appropriateness of adopting the functional approach has been confirmed by research that has shown that people with mild intellectual disabilities may have the capacity to make some financial decisions but not others (W.M.I. Suto et al., "Capacity to make financial decisions among people with mild intellectual disabilities", *Journal of Intellectual Disability Research* (2005) 49, 199–209). However, as Mary Donnelly has pointed out, "the conceptual attractions of the MCA's approach come at a price. Under a functional approach, once the possibility of incapacity arises, the person's capacity has to be assessed in respect of each individual decision. It would be administratively impossible to carry out a formal judicial assessment of capacity in each case. Unsurprisingly, therefore, the MCA framework involves the use of alternative, non-judicial, assessors. Reliance on these assessors can only be justified, however, if the assessor has the skills and knowledge necessary to carry out the task. Otherwise, administrative convenience may be purchased at an unacceptable cost to the overall goals of the legislation". Although the research evidence on how assessments operate in practice is limited, Donnelly concludes that "the available information suggests that any presumption that capacity is assessed by a legally aware, fully informed and value-neutral assessor must be questioned" ("Capacity assessment under the Mental Capacity Act 2005: Delivering on the functional approach?" (2009) *Legal Studies* 29:3, 464–491 at 465 and 480).

In *Sheffield City Council v E* [2004] EWHC 2808 (Fam) at para.144, Munby J. said:

"We must be careful not to set the test of capacity to marry too high, lest it operate as an unfair, unnecessary and indeed discriminatory bar against the mentally disabled".

This statement was applied by Baker J. in *PH v A Local Authority* [2011] EWHC 1704 (Fam) who said at para.16(xi):

"Although that observation concerned the capacity to marry, I agree with the submission made by Miss Morris on behalf of the Official Solicitor in this case that it should be applied to other questions of capacity. In other words, courts must guard against imposing too high a test of capacity to decide issues such as residence because to do so would run the risk of discriminating against persons suffering from a mental disability. In my judgement, the carefully drafted detailed provisions of the 2005 Act and the Code of Practice are consistent with this approach."

In *PH*, at para.16(xii), Baker J. rejected a submission made on behalf of the Official Solicitor that a finding of a lack of capacity should only be made where the quality of the evidence in support of such a finding is "compelling". His Lordship also rejected a submission that the test set out in this section should be construed "narrowly" and said that the question of incapacity must be construed in accordance with the statutory test—"no more and no less".

In *CC v KK* [2012] EWHC 2136 (COP) at para.25, Baker J. said:

"There is a further point, to which I alluded in an earlier decision in *PH v A Local Authority, Z Ltd and R* [2011] EWHC 1704 (Fam). In assessing the evidence, the court must be aware of the difficulties which may arise as a result of the close professional relationship between the clinicians and professionals treating and working with, P. In *PH*, I drew attention to a potential risk, identified by Ryder J in *Oldham MBC v GW and PW* [2007] EWHC 136 (Fam), another case brought under Pt IV of the Children Act 1989, that the professionals and the court may be unduly influenced by what Ryder J called the 'child protection imperative', meaning "the need to protect a vulnerable child" that, for perfectly understandable reasons, may influence the thinking of professionals involved in caring for the child. Equally, in cases of vulnerable adults, there is a risk that all professionals involved with treating and helping that person—including, of course, a judge in the Court of Protection—may feel drawn towards an outcome that is more protective of the adult and thus, in certain circumstances, fail to carry out an assessment of capacity that is detached and objective. On the other hand, the court must be equally careful not to be influenced by sympathy for a person's wholly understandable wish to return home."

In *B (Consent to Treatment: Capacity), Re* [2002] EWHC 429 (Fam) at para.100, Butler-Sloss P. stressed the importance of distinguishing between capacity and best interests in the context of consent to medical treatment:

"If there are difficulties in deciding whether the patient has sufficient mental capacity, particularly if the refusal may have grave consequences for the patient, it is most important that those considering the issue should not confuse the question of mental capacity with the nature of the decision made by the patient, however grave the consequences. The view of the patient may reflect a difference in values rather than an absence of competence and the assessment of capacity should be approached with this firmly in mind. The doctors must not allow their emotional reaction to or strong disagreement with the decision of the patient to cloud their judgment in answering the primary question whether the patient has the mental capacity to make the decision."

1–029   As s.1(2) of the Act establishes a presumption of capacity in respect of persons over the age of 16, a capacity assessment by a potential decision maker should only be undertaken if there is evidence to suggest that the presumption might be rebutted. Although, strictly speaking, this section requires a fresh capacity assessment to be undertaken in respect of every decision that the person might be required to make, with a person who is profoundly mentally incapacitated this could result in a large number of separate capacity assessments having to be made by different people during the course of a single day. For routine decisions such as what clothes the person should wear, what food he or she should eat, or whether he or she should go for an accompanied walk, it is likely that the capacity assessment, if it happens at all, will be undertaken in a perfunctory manner. It would be appropriate for the approach that paid carers should adopt in relation to such matters to be incorporated into the person's care plan. It is suggested that formal capacity assessments should be undertaken in respect of significant, complex or controversial decisions, decisions which would involve placing the incapacitated person at risk, or where the mental capacity of the person is disputed. In *A Local Authority v E* [2012] EWHC 1639 (COP), a case where a severely anorexic patient was attempting to refuse potentially life-saving treatment by making an advance decision, Peter Jackson J. said, at para.65, that "a full, reasoned and contemporaneous assessment evidencing mental capacity to make such a momentous decision would in my view be necessary".

Given the number of decisions that might have to be made in respect of P, "judges have pointed out that, for pragmatic reasons, it is not possible for every individual decision made by the person to be the subject of a determination under the MCA: see *IM v LM* [2014] EWCA Civ 37 at para.77" (*RB v Brighton and Hove City Council* [2014] EWCA Civ 561 at para.56, per Jackson L.J.).

If there is any doubt as to whether a person lacks capacity, this should be decided on a balance of probabilities (s.2(4)). Prior to reaching a conclusion that a person lacks the capacity to make a particular decision, all practicable steps must be taken to help him or her to make the decision (s.1(3)). A person who wishes to challenge a finding of capacity can, if the matter cannot be resolved by discussion, mediation or the provision of a second opinion, make an application to the Court of Protection for a declaration (s.15(1)(a)).

In *RB v Brighton and Hove City Council*, above, at para.65, Jackson L.J. said:

"There appear to be innumerable 'capacity' cases out there in the law reports and on the websites. I have only referred to those authorities which one or other counsel regard as relevant. There are many others. If lawyers are going to trawl through previous cases looking for factual similarities or analogies and then debate these in their skeleton arguments, that will involve a substantial waste of costs and time."

Capacity assessments (also see the notes on s.15(1)(a))

In *Re P* [2014] EWHC 119 (COP) at para.26, Cobb J. referred to the difficulties that can be encountered by a capacity assessor if the patient is either unwilling or unable to engage in the assessment:

1–030

"It is right to observe . . . that assessments of capacity can undoubtedly be rendered more difficult where the patient deliberately avoids engaging or co-operating with the process. In that regard, it seems to me that a patient's lack of engagement or co-operation with the assessment may contribute in itself to a conclusion that a patient is unable to 'understand the information relevant to the decision' (s.3(1)(a)), and/or (perhaps more significantly, if the patient is shown to understand) 'unable . . . to use or weigh that information as part of the process' (s.3(1)(c)). In this case, the lack of capacity is demonstrated clearly by P's inability to use or weigh the information which has been personally conveyed to him many times by clinicians, that he may be suffering from a life-threatening condition."

In *Re SB* [2013] EWHC 1417 (COP), Holman J. dealt with the problem of how to approach an assessment of the capacity of a person who suffers from a delusional disorder. At paras 41 and 44 he said:

"What weighs most significantly with me is that even if the patient has some skewed thoughts and paranoid or delusional views with regard to her husband and his attitude toward her and his behaviour, she gives many other reasons for desiring a termination. . . . It seems to me therefore that even if aspects of the decision making are influenced by paranoid thoughts in relation to her husband and her mother, she is nevertheless able to describe, and genuinely holds, a range of rational reasons for her decision. When I say rational, I do not necessarily say they are good reasons nor do I indicate whether I agree with her decision, for s.1(4) of the Act expressly provides that someone is not be treated as unable to make a decision simply because it is an unwise decision".

The person who is required to assess an individual's capacity is the person who is proposing to make the decision in respect of, or to act on behalf of, the person in question. Although this person may seek professional assistance (see below), the responsibility to make the decision about capacity cannot be delegated. The *Code of Practice* states at para.4.38:

"The person who assesses an individual's capacity to make a decision will usually be the person who is directly concerned with the individual at the time the decision needs to be made. This means that different people will be involved in assessing someone's capacity to make different decisions at different times. For most day-to-day decisions, this will be the person caring for them at the time a decision must be made. For example, a care worker might need to assess if the person can agree to being bathed. Then a district nurse might assess if the person can consent to have a dressing changed."

Evidence to the House of Lords Select Committee "revealed confusion over who was responsible for making a decision in a best-interests process" (para.97). The Committee also received evidence that "families were surprised to discover that they were not the decision-maker on behalf of their relative". The Committee stated that this evidence "is borne out by research cited by Compassion in Dying, which indicated that 53% of the public wrongly believe they have the legal right to make end of life treatment decisions for their next of kin" (para.95).

If a professional, such as a psychiatrist or a psychologist, is brought in to assist the potential decision-maker with an assessment of the person's capacity to make a complex or serious decision, the ultimate decision about capacity is that of the potential decision-maker and not the psychiatrist or psychologist whose role is that of an advisor.

The *Code of Practice*, at para.4.53, suggests that:

"Professional involvement [in a capacity assessment] might be needed if:

- the decision that needs to be made is complicated or has serious consequences
- an assessor concludes a person lacks capacity, and the person challenges the finding
- family members, carers and/or professionals disagree about a person's capacity
- there is a conflict of interest between the assessor and the person being assessed
- the person being assessed is expressing different views to different people—they may be trying to please everyone or telling people what they think they want to hear
- somebody might challenge the person's capacity to make the decision—either at the time of the decision or later (for example, a family member might challenge a will after a person has died on the basis that the person lacked capacity when they made the will)
- somebody has been accused of abusing a vulnerable adult who may lack capacity to make decisions that protect them
- a person repeatedly makes decisions that put them at risk or could result in suffering or damage."

The Act does not establish any formal procedure for the assessment of capacity and no statutory form confirming incapacity needs to be completed. Neither is there a requirement for a particular professional, such as a psychologist or a psychiatrist, to be involved in the assessment. In contrast, a person who carries out a capacity assessment under the deprivation of liberty procedure set out in Sch.A1 must be an experienced professional who has received special training (SI 2008/1858, regs 4 to 6). In the context of decision making by multi-disciplinary care teams, it is not sufficient for a decision to be categorised as a "team decision": the person who has professional accountability for a decision relating to an individual who may lack capacity must be identified, and it is that person who must undertake the capacity assessment: see para.4.40 of the *Code of Practice*. Note, however, that the guidance given in para.4.40 does not fit comfortably with that given in para.5.11 of the *Code*.

In *Re MM* [2011] 1 F.L.R. 712 at para.18, Judge Moir said:

"Where . . . capacity is in issue and if it has been determined that a medical opinion is necessary before taking any action or steps in respect of determining either the Article 8 rights or the best interests of [a] person, then it is incumbent on the Local Authority to act with all expediency in securing the determination of that capacity."

In *MM*, it was held that the local authority's unacceptable delay in arranging for a capacity assessment to be undertaken in respect of P breached the art.8 rights of both P and her cohabitee who was seeking access to P at the care home where she resided.

1–031   It is a striking fact that during the Parliamentary debates on the Bill no-one questioned the ability of professionals, let alone lay people, to assess mental capacity. The available evidence suggests that professional competence in this area is poor (see the studies cited below). In the context of medical practice, T. Grisso and P. Appelbaum suggest that doctors approach the issue of capacity assessments intuitively:

"Whether they recognise it or not, most clinicians assess their patients' decision-making abilities as part of every encounter. Ordinarily, this occurs unconsciously, as clinicians take notice of patients' dress, demeanour, communicative skills, intelligence, ability to attend to a conversation, apparent understanding, and ability to reach a decision. Since we all assume, appropriately, that people with whom we deal are competent to make decisions about their own lives—indeed the law makes a similar assumption—only when our unconscious monitoring detects something unexpected do we attend to it directly" (*Assessing Competence to Consent to Treatment* (1998) p.61).

The authors suggest that the following factors alert clinicians to the need for a capacity assessment: abrupt changes in patients' mental states, patients' refusal of recommended treatment, patients' consent to specially invasive or risky treatment, and the presence of one or more risk factors to impaired decision making, such as diagnosis or age (pp.62–76).

In *G v E* [2010] EWCA Civ 822, the Court of Appeal held that, when hearing an applica-   **1–032**
tion under s.16(2)(a), it is sufficient for the court to be satisfied on credible expert evidence, which need not be that of a psychiatrist, that the individual concerned lacks capacity. Also note Judge Marshall's comment in *F, Re* [2009] M.H.L.R. 196 at para.44, that the Act "is meant to operate in a simple and practical way, and to facilitate any necessary determination about P's capacity if there is doubt. It is clearly intended at least that general medical practitioners and health professionals other than mental capacity specialists should be able to supply evidence which will enable the Court of Protection to decide whether it can or should intervene, and if so, how". An assessment of capacity undertaken by a social worker was commended by the judge in *A Local Authority v SY* [2013] EWHC 3485 (COP), which is noted under s.15(1)(a).

In *Re SB* [2013] EWHC 1417 (COP), Holman J. reached a different overall conclusion as to capacity of a mentally disordered patient to consent to an abortion from that of two psychiatrists in a case in which the patient herself positively and strongly asserted, and gave evidence, that she had the required capacity. His Lordship said at para.44:

"[I]t would be a total affront to the autonomy of this patient to conclude that she lacks capacity to the level required to make this decision. It is of course a profound and grave decision, but it does not necessarily involve complex issues. It is a decision that she has made and maintains; and she has defended and justified her decision against challenge. It is a decision which she has the capacity to reach".

The evidence of the patient's wife was preferred to the medical evidence in *Lindsay v Wood* [2006] EWHC 2895 (QB), largely because of the "difference between 'real life', as it is described, and the artificial conditions of medical assessment" (para.49). Stanley Burnton J. said at para.18:

"When considering the question of capacity, psychiatrists and psychologists will normally wish to take into account all aspects of the personality and behaviour of the person in question, including vulnerability to exploitation. However, vulnerability to exploitation does not of itself lead to the conclusion that there is a lack of capacity. Many people who have full capacity are vulnerable to exploitation, or more so than most other people. Many people make rash and irresponsible decisions, but are of full capacity. The issue is . . . whether the person concerned has the mental capacity to make a rational decision".

In *A Local Authority v TZ* [2014] EWHC 973 (COP) at para.27, Baker J. confirmed that "the court must consider all the evidence, not merely the views of the independent expert".

The Act requires judgments to be made about a person's mental capacity by people without a clinical background who will probably have had no training or experience in making such assessments. There must be a very considerable doubt as to their ability to do this. Similar doubts can be expressed about the competence of some medical practition-ers to undertake this task. In its evidence to the Joint Committee, the Alzheimer's Society emphasised the need for a skilled capacity assessment. One of its members wrote of her experiences:

"As a former nurse, my mother was extremely good at covering up her problems and was extremely plausible. Her doctor reacted with shocked amazement at our suggestion that my mother had dementia.—'There's nothing wrong with your mother. I saw her only the other day and had a conversation with her. She's fine.' This was at a time when my mother was putting the electric kettle on the gas ring, entertaining phantom meetings of teachers in her front room, turning up at the hairdressers at 2 a.m. and living on a diet of biscuits having forgotten how to cook" (Oral and Written Evidence, Ev 384).

Fluctuating mental capacity

1–033   Although the test set out in this section is easily understandable and, perhaps, gives the impression that the assessment of a person's mental capacity is a relatively straightforward task, the reality is that the assessment can sometimes be extremely difficult, especially when the person's capacity appears to fluctuate. Baroness Finlay of Llandaff gave evidence to the Joint Committee on this point:

"If I can give you two specific and very common instances, one where patients have been anxious, which is understandable because they are facing dying, and where the benzodiazepine group of drugs such as Midazolam are used to remove the churning drive of anxiety without sedating the patients so they can still function but they are relieved in part of this desperate feeling of anxiety, butterflies and churning inside. With some of these patients you can have a conversation and they appear to under-stand everything that is said and have recall. The following day they have no recall whatsoever of that conversation. It may have been a few hours later in some patients. Another situation which arises is where patients' calcium goes up and that occurs in about ten per cent of all cancer patients. They become confused. That is a gradual onset and the outset is difficult to diagnose. They may appear to be arguing rationally but when their calcium level has been brought down and is treated they then are behaving differently and they have no recall of that previous conversation or the direction that they were trying to give in expressing what they wanted. Also they may completely change their mind which is a terribly important situation for a clinician. The difficulty is in judging whether they have capacity or not because at any one point in time the conversation appears to be logical and consequential. There are lots of other situations which arise, particularly with patients on steroids where the steroids may have created a very mild steroid psychosis which can be difficult to diagnose and just presents as emotional immobility. Again, their thinking and perception is distorted" (Oral and Written Evidence, Ev 126).

In *A,B and C v X, Y and Z* [2012] EWHC 2400 (COP), Hedley J. dealt with the issue of responding to a person's fluctuating mental capacity by making "qualified" declarations regarding X's capacity to make a will and to create an enduring power of attorney. With respect to the latter, his Lordship said at para.38:

"I am unwilling to make, on the evidence, a general declaration that he lacks capacity, but qualify that immediately by saying that the exercise of such a power, unless accom-panied by contemporary medical evidence of capacity, would give rise to a serious risk of challenge or of refusal to register. It seems to me, for exactly the same reasons as I endeavoured to set out in relation to testamentary capacity, that X's capacity is likely to diminish in the future and there will be times when undoubtedly he lacks capacity, just as there will be times when he retains it."

Also see *G (An Adult) (Mental Capacity: Court's Jurisdiction), Re* [2004] EWHC 222 (Fam Div), a case under the inherent jurisdiction which is noted under s.15(1)(c).

Research and related publications

It has been noted that competency is rarely questioned when the patient consents to **1–034** treatment (B. Hoffman and J. Srinivasan, "A study of competence to consent to treatment in a psychiatric hospital" (1992) 37 *Canadian Journal of Psychiatry* 179). Also see R. Cairns et al., "Reliability of mental capacity assessments in psychiatric in-patients" (2005) 187 *British Journal Psychiatry* 372, where the researchers found a probable bias towards judging a patient as having capacity if they made the apparently "correct" decision of agreeing to treatment. A review of the research on capacity undertaken by P. Lepping concluded that clinicians regularly overestimate patients' capacity to make decisions ("Overestimating patients' capacity" (2011) *British Journal of Psychiatry* 199, 355–356). Some of the difficulties inherent in capacity assessments made by clinicians are examined by Mary Donnelly in "Capacity assessments under the Mental Capacity Act 2005: Delivering on the functional approach?" (2009) 29 *Legal Studies* 464. For an account of establishing the mental capacity of a person who was suffering from a devastating condition, see S. Carrington and J. Birns, "Establishing capacity in a patient with incomplete locked-in syndrome", *Progress in Neurology and Psychiatry*, Nov/Dec 2012, pp.18–20.

For an extensive analysis of the assessment of capacity from a psychological perspective, see "Assessment of Capacity in Adults: Interim Guidance for Psychologists" (2006) *British Psychological Society*. The Society has also published an "Audit Tool for Mental Capacity Assessments" (2010) which aims to "provide standards and examples of good practice in assessing mental capacity" (p.9). Also see, *Assessment of Mental Capacity: A Practical Guide for Doctors and Lawyers* (2009) BMA/Law Society, and M. Church and S. Watts, "Assessment of mental capacity: a flow chart guide" Psychiatric Bulletin (2007), 31: 304–307.

Empowerment Matters has published "Making Financial Decisions: Guidance for assessing, supporting and empowering specific decision-making" which focuses primarily on how to assess an individual's capacity in relation to financial decision-making and gives practical suggestions about how to support someone to manage their money and financial decisions. The guidance can be accessed at: *http://www.empowermentmatters.co.uk.*

Capacity to consent to medical treatment

In *Re T (Adult: Refusal of Treatment)* [1993] Fam. 95 at 102, Lord Donaldson observed **1–035** that:

> "An adult patient who . . . suffers from no mental incapacity has an absolute right to choose whether to consent to medical treatment, to refuse it or to choose one rather than another of the treatments being offered . . . This right of choice is not limited to decisions which others might regard as sensible. It exists notwithstanding that the reasons for making the choice are rational, irrational, unknown or even non-existent."

In *Heart of England NHS Foundation Trust v JB* [2014] EWHC 342 (COP), Peter Jackson J. said at para.7:

> "The temptation to base a judgement of a person's capacity upon whether they seem to have made a good or bad decision, and in particular upon whether they have accepted or rejected medical advice, is absolutely to be avoided. That would be to put the cart before the horse or, expressed another way, to allow the tail of welfare to wag the dog of capacity. Any tendency in this direction risks infringing the rights of that group of persons who, though vulnerable, are capable of making their own decisions. Many who suffer from mental illness are well able to make decisions about their medical treatment, and it is important not to make unjustified assumptions to the contrary."

His Lordship further stated that there "is a danger that in a difficult case . . . the patient is regarded as capable of making a decision that follows medical advice but incapable of making one that does not" (para.27). His Lordship held that the evidence confirmed that the patient's "schizophrenia is relevant to the way in which she decides, and not to her capacity to decide. Her tendency at times to be uncommunicative or avoidant and to minimise the risks of inaction are understandable human ways of dealing with her predicament and do not amount to incapacity" (para.39): also see the studies noted under *Research and related publications*, above.

In *Kings College NHS Foundation Trust v C* [2015] EWCOP 80, MacDonald J. said at para.30:

"[T]he fact that a decision not to have life saving medical treatment may be considered an unwise decision and may have a fatal outcome is not of itself evidence of a lack of capacity to take that decision, notwithstanding that other members of society may consider such a decision unreasonable, illogical or even immoral, that society in general places cardinal importance on the sanctity of life and that the decision taken will result in the certain death of the person taking it. To introduce into the assessment of capacity an assessment of the probity or efficacy of a decision to refuse life saving treatment would be to introduce elements which risk discriminating against the person making that decision by penalising individuality and demanding conformity at the expense of personal autonomy in the context of a diverse, plural society which tolerates a range of views on the decision in question (see *Mental Incapacity* (1995) (Law Comm No 231) (HC 189), para 3.4)."

Paragraphs 1.11 and 1.12 of the *Reference guide to consent for examination or treatment* (Department of Health 2009) state:

"Once it has been determined that a person has the capacity to make a particular decision at a particular time, a further requirement (under the common law) for that consent to be valid is that it must be given voluntarily and freely, without pressure or undue influence being exerted upon them.

When people are seen and treated in environments where involuntary detention may be an issue, such as prisons and mental hospitals, there is a potential for treatment offers to be perceived coercively, whether or not this is the case. Coercion invalidates consent, and care must be taken to ensure that the person makes decisions freely. Coercion should be distinguished from providing the person with appropriate reassurance concerning their treatment, or pointing out the potential benefits of treatment for the person's health. However, threats such as withdrawal of any privileges, loss of remission of sentence for refusing consent or using such matters to induce consent may well invalidate the consent given, and are not acceptable."

The nature of undue influence is further considered in the note on s.1(3).

A person's ambivalence about whether to receive medical treatment is only relevant to the issue of capacity "if, and only if, the ambivalence genuinely strikes at the root of the mental capacity of the patient", per Butler-Sloss P. in *B (Consent to Treatment: Capacity), Re* [2002] EWHC 429 (Fam) at para.35.

If there is concern or doubt about the mental capacity of a person to consent to medical treatment, that doubt should be resolved as soon as possible, by doctors within the hospital or NHS trust or by other normal medical procedures. In the meantime, while the question of capacity is being resolved, the person must be cared for in accordance with the judgment of the doctors as to the person's best interests. In the rare case where disagreement still exists about competence, it is of the utmost importance that the person is fully informed of the steps being taken, such as enlisting independent outside expertise, and made part of the process. Those in charge must not allow a situation of deadlock or drift to occur. If all appropriate steps to seek independent assistance from medical experts outside the hospital have failed, the hospital should not hesitate to make an application to the Court of Protection or seek the advice of the Official Solicitor (*X NHS Trust v T (Adult Patient: Refusal of Medical Treatment)* [2004] EWHC 1279 (Fam).

In *Montgomery v Lanarkshire Health Board* [2015] UKSC 11, the Supreme Court comprehensively reviewed the case law on a doctor's obligation to warn a patient of the risks of treatment. The substantive judgment was given by Lords Kerr and Reed who held that the correct position is that:

"87. . . . An adult person of sound mind is entitled to decide which, if any, of the available forms of treatment to undergo, and her consent must be obtained before treatment interfering with her bodily integrity is undertaken. The doctor is therefore under a duty to take reasonable care to ensure that the patient is aware of any material risks involved in any recommended treatment, and of any reasonable alternative or variant treatments. The test of materiality is whether, in the circumstances of the particular case, a reasonable person in the patient's position would be likely to attach significance to the risk, or the doctor is or should reasonably be aware that the particular patient would be likely to attach significance to it.

88. The doctor is however entitled to withhold from the patient information as to a risk if he reasonably considers that its disclosure would be seriously detrimental to the patient's health. The doctor is also excused from conferring with the patient in circumstances of necessity, as for example where the patient requires treatment urgently but is unconscious or otherwise unable to make a decision. It is unnecessary for the purposes of this case to consider in detail the scope of those exceptions."

Their Lordships said that three further points should be made: first, assessing the significance of a risk is fact-sensitive and cannot be reduced to percentages. Second, in order to advise, the doctor must engage in dialogue with her patient. Third, the therapeutic exception is limited, and should not be abused (paras 89 – 91).

In *Heart of England NHS Foundation Trust v JB*, above, a case concerning a patient's capacity to consent to an amputation of her leg, Peter Jackson J. said at paras 24 and 25:

"[W]hat is in my view required is that [JB] should understand the nature, purpose and effects of the proposed treatment, the last of these entailing an understanding of the benefits and risks of deciding to have or not to have one or other of the various kinds of amputation, or of not making a decision at all.

What is required here is a broad, general understanding of the kind that is expected from the population at large. JB is not required to understand every last piece of information about her situation and her options: even her doctors would not make that claim. It must also be remembered that common strategies for dealing with unpalatable dilemmas—for example indecision, avoidance or vacillation—are not to be confused with incapacity. We should not ask more of people whose capacity is questioned than of those whose capacity is undoubted."

In *An NHS Trust v The Patient* [2014] EWCOP 54 (Fam), Holman J. said at para.22 that information about an impending operation should be give even if the patient is incapacious:

"My own view is that even in the case of incapacitous or very incapacitous patients (leaving aside those who lack consciousness) it remains extremely important in any civilised society that they are not subjected to anaesthesia or invasive surgery without, as a minimum, being informed in sensitive and appropriate language as to what is about to be done to them before it is done."

His Lordship confirmed that it was acceptable in this case for the patient to be sedated before he was given the information in an attempt to prevent him going berserk as his sister had predicted.

Capacity to consent to sexual relations

"[W]hen determining the question of sexual capacity under the MCA the relevant information as referred to in s.3(1)(a) comprises an awareness of the following elements on the part of P: **1–036**

(i) the mechanics of the act; and

(ii) that there are health risks involved; and
(iii) in following the judgment of Hedley J. in *H*, below, that he or she has a choice and can refuse" (*London Borough of Tower Hamlets v TB* [2014] EWHC 4295 (COP) at para.41, per Mostyn J.).

In *A Local Authority v TZ* [2013] EWHC 2322 (COP), Baker J. held that that "capacity to consent to sexual relations is act specific and has to be assessed in relation to the particular kind of sexual activity in question" (para.24). With regard to gay or lesbian people his Lordship held that:

> "[I]n the case of a person in respect of whom it is clearly established that he or she is homosexual—gay or lesbian—it is ordinarily unnecessary to establish that the person has an understanding or awareness that sexual activity between a man and a woman may result in pregnancy" (para.31).

In *A Local Authority v H* [2012] EWHC 49 (COP), Hedley J. held that the person concerned must be able to understand that the health risks associated with sexual relations can be reduced by precautions such as a condom (para.23). His Lordship further held that although the moral aspect of human sexual relations can have no specific role in a test of capacity (para.24), the person whose capacity is in question must understand that they have a choice and that they can refuse (para.25).

The authorities were extensively reviewed by the Court of Appeal in *IM v LM* [2014] EWCA Civ 37 which confirmed that the test for capacity to consent to sexual relationships is general and issue specific, rather than person or event specific (para.79). The court said that as the process of decision-making is "largely visceral rather than cerebral . . . the ability to use and weigh information is unlikely to loom large in the evaluation of capacity to consent to sexual relations". The information typically "regarded by persons of full capacity as relevant to the decision whether to consent to sexual relations is relatively limited. The temptation to expand that field of information in an attempt to simulate more widely informed decision-making is likely to lead to . . . both paternalism and a derogation from personal autonomy" (paras 80 to 82). The court identified the policy reason for its decision at para.77:

> "[I]t would be totally unworkable for a local authority or the Court of Protection to conduct an assessment every time an individual over whom there was doubt about his or her capacity to consent to sexual relations showed signs of immediate interest in experiencing a sexual encounter with another person. On a pragmatic basis, if for no other reason, capacity to consent to future sexual relations can only be assessed on a general and non-specific basis."

Where a person lacks the mental capacity to consent to sexual relations, "the relevant local authority must undertake the very closest supervision of that individual to ensure, to such extent as is possible, that the opportunity for sexual relations is removed" (para.1).

In *Derbyshire CC v AC* [2014] EWCOP 38, Cobb J. held that while P lacked the capacity to decide whether to have contact with others, she had capacity to decide whether to engage in sexual relations. Given that engaging in sexual relations involves contact with another, this finding is perplexing.

Capacity to consent to marriage

1–037 In *A Local Authority v AK* [2012] EWHC B29 (COP), Bodey J. examined pre-Act authority, in particular the decision of Munby J. in *Sheffield City Council v E* [2004] EWHC 2808 (Fam), when identifying the test for capacity to marry. His Lordship said at paras 17 to 19:

> "[In *Sheffield*], after a far-ranging review of case law on this topic, Munby J propounded the following: (i) that it is not enough that someone appreciates that he or she is taking part in a marriage ceremony or understands the words; (ii) that he or she must understand the nature of the marriage contract; (iii) that this means that he or she must be mentally capable

of understanding the duties and responsibilities which normally attach to marriage; and (iv) that the contract of marriage is in essence a simple one which does not require a high degree of intelligence to comprehend. Munby J laid down further that the issue is whether the individual had the capacity to understand the nature of the contract of marriage 'full stop'; not the implications of a particular marriage to a particular person. Otherwise the necessary distinction between capacity and 'best interests' would be compromised.

At paragraph 132 of *Sheffield,* Munby J set out in a non-exhaustive list the information which an individual needs to have the ability to understand in order to have capacity to marry: 'One must be mentally capable of understanding the duties and responsibilities that normally attach to marriage . . . marriage, whether civil or religious, is a contract formally entered into. It confers on the parties the status of husband and wife, the essence of the contract being an agreement between a man and a woman to live together and to love one another as husband and wife to the exclusion of all others. It creates a relationship of mutual and reciprocal obligations, typically involving the sharing of a common home and a common domestic life and the right to enjoy each other's society, comfort and assistance.' At para.56 of *X City Council -v- MB, NB and MAB* [2006] EWHC 168 (Fam) Munby J added to the requirements for capacity to marry a need for capacity to consent to sexual relations (a point which had not arisen in *Sheffield*) because a sexual relationship is generally implicit in marriage.

In *Local Authority X -v- MM and KM* [2007] EWHC 2003 (Fam) Munby J repeated what he had said at paragraph 134 of *Sheffield*, restating how the s.3 test for capacity (which was then about to come into force) fits with *Sheffield*. He explained that the test of being able to 'understand, retain and weigh up' under s.3 is just as applicable where the question is whether an individual has the capacity to marry as it is where the question is whether he or she has the capacity to take any other decision: '. . . it is simply that such a refined analysis is probably not necessary where the issue is as simple as the question whether someone has the capacity to marry, or to consent to sexual relations.' In other words, because for most people, marriage is to be regarded as a fairly straightforward concept (compared for example with litigating, or with many medical procedures) one would not normally need to spend too much time on assessing an individual's ability to 'understand, retain, use and weigh' the information about marriage which is referred to in *Sheffield*. Nevertheless, there will occasionally be cases where the degree and/or nature of the individual's impairments does make it necessary to do so, because for him or her a decision about marrying is not actually a simple one."

In *PC v City of York Council* [2013] EWCA Civ 478 at para.23, McFarlane L.J. said that he saw

"no reason not to accept Munby J's conclusion [in *Sheffield*], based as it is upon established authority, that capacity to marry is to be assessed in general and as a matter of principle, and not by reference to any particular prospective marriage. It is, as Mostyn J neatly put it in *D Borough Council v B* [2012] Fam 36; [2011] EWHC 101 (Fam), status-specific and not spouse-specific. The subsequent implementation of the MCA 2005 does not establish any basis for questioning the continued applicability of a general and non-specific approach to capacity to marry in proceedings under the Act".

Also see the discussion on *Forced or arranged marriages* in the General Note to s.15.

Capacity to consent to contraception
In *A Local Authority v A* [2010] EWHC 1549 (Fam) at para.64, Bodey J. held that with **1–038** regard to the capacity required to consent to contraception, the woman had to "understand and weigh up the immediate medical issues surrounding contraceptive treatment . . . including:
(i) the reason for contraception and what it does (which includes the likelihood of pregnancy if it is not in use during sexual intercourse);

(ii)   the types available and how each is used;
(iii) the advantages and disadvantages of each type;
(iv) the possible side-effects of each and how they can be dealt with;
(v)   how easily each type can be changed; and
(vi) the generally accepted effectiveness of each."

His Lordship said: "I do not consider that questions need to be asked as to the woman's understanding of what bringing up a child would be like in practice; nor any opinion attempted as to how she would be likely to get on; nor whether any child would be likely to be removed from her care".

Bodey J.'s decision was applied by Cobb J. in *Mental Health Trust v DD* [2015] EWCOP 4 at para.64 et seq.

Capacity of a person with learning disabilities to make deeply personal decisions

1–039   In *An NHS Trust v P* [2013] EWHC 50 (COP), Hedley J. said at para.16:

"It is, as I said, very important to bear in mind, particularly in the field of those with significant learning difficulties who may well be unable to function independently in the community in every aspects of their life, that they may very well retain capacity to make deeply personal decisions about how they conduct their lives. One has in mind the question of choice of partners; the extent to which they wish to be sexually active; the extent to which they may wish to make permanent relationships by way of marriage or indeed civil partnership; the extent to which they may wish to be able to make decisions about their own medical care, including, as in this case, the continuation or termination of a pregnancy. It cannot be the case that merely because a person has significant difficulties in functioning in the community, it can be presumed that they lack capacity to make profoundly personal decisions. They may in fact do so but that has to be assessed on an individual basis."

Capacity to consent to a gift

1–040   The criteria for capacity to make a gift were considered in *Beaney (Deceased), Re* [1978] 2 All E.R. 595. Martin Nourse QC, sitting as a Deputy Judge of the High Court, said at 601:

"The degree or extent of understanding required in respect of any instrument is relative to the particular transaction which it is to effect. Thus, at one extreme, if the subject-matter and value of a gift are trivial in relation to the donor's other assets, a low degree of understanding will suffice. But, at the other, if its effect is to dispose of the donor's only asset of value and thus, for practical purposes, to pre-empt the devolution of his estate under [the donor's] will or intestacy, then the degree of understanding required is as high as that required for a will, and the donor must understand the claims of all potential donees and the extent of the property to be disposed of."

In *Kicks v Leigh* [2014] EWHC 3926 (Ch), Stephen Morris QC, sitting as a deputy High Court judge, held at para.63 that "the correct approach to a post-MCA inter vivos gift is to apply the common law principles in *Re Beaney* rather than those set out in s.2 and 3 MCA 2005". However, the judge did not consider that there was any difference between the two approaches (at para.66).

Capacity to conduct litigation

1–041   The issue of whether a person has capacity to litigate is separate from the question of whether that person has the capacity to make the decision in question. The test of litigation capacity is to be found in *Masterman-Lister v Brutton & Co* [2002] EWCA Civ 1889 (approved by the Supreme Court in *Dunhill v Burgin* [2014] UKSC 18 at para.13). The test is whether or not a party to the legal proceedings is capable of understanding, with the assistance of such proper explanation from legal advisers and experts in other disciplines as the case requires, the issue on which his consent or decision is likely to be necessary in the course of the proceedings. He needs to be able to understand the relevant issues and be able to give instructions thereon. In *Masterman-Lister,* Kennedy L.J. cited with approval a passage from the judgment of Boreham J. in *White v Fell* Unreported November 12, 1987:

> "To have that capacity she requires first the insight and understanding of the fact that she has a problem in respect of which she needs advice . . . Secondly, having identified the problem, it will be necessary for her to seek an appropriate adviser and to instruct him with sufficient clarity to enable him to understand the problem and to advise her appropriately . . . Finally she needs sufficient mental capacity to understand and to make decisions based upon, or otherwise give effect to, such advice as she may receive."

At paras 38 and 39 of *Sheffield City Council v E* [2005] Fam. 236, Munby J. said:

> "[T]he capacity to litigate is not something to be determined in the abstract. One has to focus on the particular piece of litigation in relation to which the issue arises. The question is always whether the litigant has capacity to litigate in relation to the particular proceedings in which he is involved. . . . Someone may have the capacity to litigate in a case where the nature of the dispute and the issues are simple, whilst at the same time lacking the capacity to litigate in a case where either the nature of the dispute or the issues are more complex."

In *D v R (the Deputy of S)* [2010] EWHC 2405 (COP), Henderson J. had to consider whether Mr S had the necessary mental capacity to decide whether an action in the Chancery Division of the High Court, regarding gifts that he had given to his carer, should be discontinued or compromised. His Lordship held that if a gift is to be set aside or recovered, some vitiating factor such as fraud, misrepresentation or undue influence has to be established; and if the donor is to decide whether or not to pursue a claim, he needs to understand, at least in general terms, the nature of the vitiating factor upon which he may be able to rely, and to weigh up the arguments for and against pursuing the claim. Provided that the donor is equipped with this information, and provided that he understands it and takes it into account in reaching his decision, it will not matter if his decision is an imprudent one, or one which would fail to satisfy the "best interests" test in s.4. His Lordship said that the need for an understanding of the nature of the claim is particularly pronounced where the claim is founded on a rebuttable presumption of undue influence, and where the relationship which arguably gave rise to the claim is still in existence. If a donor is to decide whether or not to pursue such a claim, he must understand (at least in the simple terms envisaged by s.3(2)):

(i)   the nature and extent of the relationship of trust and confidence arguably reposed by him in the donee;
(ii) the extent to which it may be said that the gifts cannot readily be accounted for by the ordinary motives of ordinary people in such a relationship; and
(iii) the nature of the evidential burden resting on the donee to rebut any presumption of undue influence.

It is possible in a rare case for a person to lack subject matter capacity whilst still having litigation capacity: see, for example, *Sheffield City Council v E*, above.

Capacity to make a will

The test for testamentary capacity (the capacity required to make a will) was set out by the Court of Appeal in *Banks v Goodfellow* (1870) L.R. 5 Q.B. 549:   **1–042**

> "It is essential that a testator shall understand the nature of the act and its effects; shall understand the extent of the property of which he is disposing; shall be able to comprehend and appreciate the claims to which he ought to give effect; and, with a view to the latter object, that no disorder of mind shall poison his affections, pervert his sense of right, or prevent the exercise of his natural faculties—that no insane delusion shall influence his will in disposing of his property and bring about a disposal of it which, if the mind had been sound, would not have been made."

In *Perrins v Holland* [2009] EWHC 1945 (Ch) at para.40, Lewison J. said, obiter and without explanation, that the test of capacity in *Banks v Goodfellow* has been "superseded" by the Act. This remark was not referred to at the Court of Appeal ([2010] EWCA Civ 840). And in *Scammell v Farmer* [2008] EWHC 1100 (Ch) at para.24, Stephen Smith QC, sitting as a deputy High Court judge, said that there

> "was a large measure of agreement between counsel that the test of mental capacity under s.3 of the 2005 Act is a modern restatement of the test propounded in *Banks v Goodfellow* ... There is, however, an obvious difference between the position at common law and the position under the 2005 Act, in that the onus of proof of incapacity under the 2005 Act (s.1(2)) is from the outset, and remains, on the complainant. At common law, the position is different."

These cases were cited in *Walker v Badmin* [2014] All E.R. (D) 258 where, Mr N Strauss QC, sitting as a deputy High Court judge, said the he did not agree with the agreement reached by counsel in *Scammell* or the comment made by Lewison J. and held that while one of the purposes of the Act is to govern the making of a will by the court on behalf of a person without capacity in his lifetime, it is not intended to affect a retrospective decision by a court as to whether a testator had capacity to make his own will where the correct and only test is the test set out in *Banks v Goodfellow*.

Subsection (1)

1–043   The use of the word "or" in para.(c) demonstrates that the individual incapacities set out in this subsection are not cumulative. A person lacks capacity if any one of subss.(a) to (d) applies (*RT and LT v A Local Authority* [2010] EWCA (Fam) 1910 at para.40).

Subsection (1) para.(a)

1–044   Although identifying the decision that needs to be taken can be straightforward, understanding the "information relevant to [that] decision" can be challenging: see, for example, *D v R (Deputy of S)* [2010] EWHC 2405 (COP) at paras 43 and 142. The *Code of Practice* stresses that "it is important not to assess someone's understanding before they have been given relevant information about a decision" (para.4.16). "Relevant information" is said to include "what the likely consequences of a decision would be (the possible effects of deciding one way or another)—and also the likely consequences of making no decision at all" (para.4.19).

The nature of understanding is considered by T. Grisso and P. Appelbaum in *Assessing Competence to Consent to Treatment* (1998) , at p.38:

> "As basic as the concept of understanding may seem, the psychological process related to it are not easily defined. A person's accurate assimilation of information involves a complex series of events. First the information must be received as presented, a process that is influenced not only by sensory integrity, but also by perceptual functions such as attention and selective awareness. Whatever is received then undergoes cognitive processing and is encoded in a manner consistent with the person's existing fund of information and concepts, which in turn influences how, and how well, the message is recorded and stored in the memory."

The authors point out that many medical conditions, as well as chronic mental disorders and disabilities, can "have a substantial negative influence on these functions" (p.39).

In the context of an individual's capacity to execute an instrument, it has been held that the degree or extent of the understanding required is relative to the particular transaction which it is to effect (*Beaney (deceased) Re* [1978] 2 All E.R. 595).

The information provided must include the information specified in subs.(4). As the information must be "relevant to the decision", the person should be able to comprehend the salient details; "it is not necessary for the person to comprehend all peripheral detail" per Macur J. in *LBL v RYJ* [2010] EWHC 2665 (COP) at para.24. Her Ladyship noted that "it is recognised that different individuals may give different weight to different factors" (ibid.). All practicable steps should be taken to assist the person to understand the information (s.1(3)), with account being taken of any cultural or religious factors relating to the person which might inhibit communication.

For case law on the provision of information relating to medical treatment, see *Capacity to consent to medical treatment*, above.

Subsection (1) para.(b)
RETAIN. See subs.(3).   **1–045**

Subsection (1) para.(c)
In *Kings College NHS Foundation Trust v C* [2015] EWCOP 80, MacDonald J. said at para.35 that a person seeking to prove that another lacks capacity has to show that the person lacks the capacity to both use <u>and</u> weigh the relevant information.

In *IM v LM* [2014] EWCA Civ 37, the court said at para.52:   **1–046**

> "It is important to emphasise that s.3(1)(c) of the Act refers to the ability to use or weigh information as part of the process of making the decision. In some circumstances, having understood and retained relevant information, an ability to use it will be what is critical; in others, it will be necessary to be able to weigh competing considerations."

In *PCT v P, AH and The Local Authority* [2009] C.O.P.L.R. Con. Vol. 956 at para.35, Hedley J. described the ability to use and weigh information as "the capacity actually to engage in the decision making process itself and to be able to see the various parts of the argument and to relate one to another".

It "is not necessary for a person to use and weigh every detail of the respective options available to them in order to demonstrate capacity, merely the salient factors (see *CC v KK and STCC* [2012] EWHC 2136 (COP) at [69]). Even though a person may be unable to use and weigh some information relevant to the decision in question, they may nonetheless be able to use and weigh other elements sufficiently to be able to make a capacitous decision (see *Re SB* [2013] EWHC 1417 (COP))" (*Kings College NHS Foundation Trust v C*, above, at para.36).

The ability to use or weigh the information involves having "the capacity actually to engage in the decision-making process itself and to be able to see the various parts of the argument and to relate the one to the other" (*The PCT v P* [2009] EW Misc 10 (COP), per Hedley J. at para.35). Only the "salient details" need to be comprehended and weighed as part of this process (*LBL v RYJ* [2010] EWHC 2665 (COP) at para.58). In using the information, the person can be assisted by relevant professional advice (*Masterman-Lister v Brutton & Co* [2003] 3 All E.R.162 CA), and by support from the person's care network. The *Code of Practice*, at para.4.22, offers the following examples of persons who able to understand, but not "use or weigh" the information:

> "For example, a person with the eating disorder anorexia nervosa may understand information about the consequences of not eating. But their compulsion not to eat might be too strong for them to ignore. Some people who have serious brain damage might make impulsive decisions regardless of information they may have been given or their understanding of it."

In *A Local Authority v E* [2012] EWHC 1639 (COP), a case concerning a severely anorexic patient, Peter Jackson J. said at para.49:

> "[T]here is strong evidence that E's obsessive fear of weight gain makes her incapable of weighing the advantages and disadvantages of eating in any meaningful way. For E, the compulsion to prevent calories entering her system has become the card that trumps all others. The need not to gain weight overpowers all other thoughts."

His Lordship acknowledged, at para.53, that "a person with severe anorexia may be in a Catch 22 situation regarding capacity: namely, that by deciding not to eat, she proves that she lacks capacity to decide at all".

With regard to the application of this paragraph to people who have deeply held religious beliefs, Mostyn J. said in *Nottinghamshire Healthcare NHS Trust* [2014] EWHC 1317 (COP) at paras 34 and 35:

"This aspect of the test of capacity must be applied very cautiously and carefully when religious beliefs are in play. In his essay John Stuart Mill speaks of the prohibition in Islam on the eating of pork. He describes how Muslims regard the practice with 'unaffected disgust'; it is 'an instinctive antipathy'. There can be no circumstances where a Muslim could 'weigh' the merit of eating pork. It is simply beyond the pale. So too, it would appear, when it comes to Jehovah's Witnesses and blood transfusions. But it would be an extreme example of the application of the law of unintended consequences were an iron tenet of an accepted religion to give rise to questions of capacity under the MCA.

I therefore place little emphasis on the fact that a tenet of RC's religious faith prevents him from weighing the advantages of a blood transfusion should his medical circumstances indicate that one is necessary."

In assessing capacity it is inappropriate to start with a "blank canvas". In the context of a person making a choice between staying in a care home and going home, the choice which the person "should be asked to weigh up is not between the nursing home and a return to the bungalow with no or limited support, but rather between staying in the nursing home and a return home with all practicable support" (*CC v KK* [2012] EWHC 2136 (COP) at para.68, per Baker J.).

In order to "use or weigh" information, the person must not be prevented by mental disorder from believing the information because "the specific requirement of belief is subsumed in the more general requirements of understanding and of ability to use and weigh information" (*Local Authority X v MM and KM* [2007] EWHC 2003 (Fam) at para.81, per Munby J.). In *B v Croydon HA* (1994) 22 B.M.L.R. 13 at 20, Thorpe J. said that in the context of consent to medical treatment there is a difference between outright disbelief (due to mental disorder) which meant being "impervious to reason, divorced from reality, or incapable of adjustment after reflection", and "the tendency which most people have when undergoing medical treatment to self assess and then puzzle over the divergence between medical and self assessment". In *R. (on the application of B) v Dr SS, Dr AC and the Secretary of State for Health* [2005] EWHC 86 (Admin) at paras 188, 190, Charles J. found that the patient was refusing treatment because he did not accept or believe that he is, or may be, mentally ill. It therefore followed that the patient lacked capacity because he "does not believe or accept a cornerstone of the factors to be taken into account in considering the information he has been given about his proposed treatment and therefore is not able to use and weigh in the balance the relevant information as to his proposed treatment in reaching a decision to agree to it or to refuse it".

In *MB (Medical Treatment), Re* [1997] 2 F.L.R. 426 the court said that if a compulsive disorder or phobia from which the patient suffers dominates her thinking, the decision may not be a true one. In this case the patient's phobia to needles induced such panic in her that "at that moment the needle or mask dominated her thinking and made her quite unable to consider anything else" (at 431). *MB, Re*, was applied in *Trust A v H (An Adult Patient), Re*, [2006] EWHC 1230 (Fam) where Potter P. said, at para.22, that "a compulsive disorder or phobia may prevent the patient's decision from being a true one, particularly if conditioned by some obsessional belief or feeling which so distorts the judgment as to render the decision invalid". Similar considerations apply if the patient's thinking is dominated by factors such as confusion, shock, fatigue, pain or drugs (*T (Adult: Refusal of Treatment), Re*, [1992] 4 All E.R. 649).

A person who is subject to the undue influence of another would be unable to give a valid consent: see the notes on s.1(3).

Subsection (1) para.(d)

1–047   The rationale for this provision is explained in the Explanatory Memorandum at para.27:

"This is intended to be a residual category and will only affect a small group of persons, in particular some of those with the very rare condition of 'locked-in syndrome'. It seems likely that people suffering from this condition can in fact still understand, retain and use information and so would not be regarded as lacking capacity under subs.(1) (a)-(c). Some people who suffer from this condition can communicate by blinking an eye, but it seems that others cannot communicate at all. [This provision] treats those who are completely unable to communicate their decisions as unable to make a decision. Any residual ability to communicate (such as blinking an eye to indicate 'yes' or 'no' in answer to a question) would exclude a person from this category."

As well as affecting people with "locked-in syndrome", this provision "clearly covers people with physical disorders of the brain, for example head injuries or strokes, which prevent them communicating as well as people with disorders of the mind which have the same effect" (*R v C* [2009] UKHL 42 at para.29, per Lady Hale). It will be rare for such people to be unable to communicate their decision by any means.

This provision is concerned with people who are "unable" to communicate their decision; it does not encompass people who are unwilling to communicate their decision. If a person falls into the latter category, he or she must be assumed to be mentally capable unless the decision-maker assesses that person as lacking the capacity to make the decision in question (s.1(2)). If the failure of the person to communicate is assessed as being the consequence of "an impairment of, or a disturbance in the functioning of, [that person's] mind or brain" (s.2(1)), the decision-maker must consider whether the identified impairment or disturbance results in a failure of the person to satisfy the requirements of paras (a),(b) or (c). If there is such a failure, the person will lack the capacity to make the decision. Also see *Re P* [2014] EWHC 119 (COP) which is noted under *Capacity assessments* in the General Note to this section.

Subsection (2)

This provision, which expands upon the principle set out in s.1(3), was added at the third reading of the Bill so that there "is no longer any doubt: no one should be labelled incapable merely because insufficient efforts have been made to help him understand and communicate", per the Parliamentary Under-Secretary of State (*Hansard*, HC Vol.428, col.1632). **1–048**

AN EXPLANATION. The explanation must be sufficiently specific to enable the person to use or weigh the information as required by subs.(1)(c).

Subsection (3)

This provision allows for situations where the person's mental capacity fluctuates, with the person being able to make a decision during a lucid interval. **1–049**

SHORT PERIOD. The person must be able to retain the information for the time that it takes to make the decision. Most decisions will therefore require the information to be retained for a brief period only. Significant or difficult decisions might require the person to retain the information over a number of days before a decision is made.

In "Summing up—a Judge's Perspective", [2006] Crim. L.R. 817, Judge Nic Madge makes reference to Professor Robert H. Margolis's review of the literature that shows that patients retain about 50 per cent of the information provided to them by health care professionals. Of the information recalled, about half is remembered incorrectly, i.e. patients remember correctly only about a quarter of what they are told. An equally disturbing finding is that patients often forget their own medical diagnoses. Information presented in a simple, easy to understand format is remembered better than information presented in a more complex manner. The more information presented, the lower the proportion that is recalled by the patient. When verbal presentation is supplemented by written explanations, recall can be significantly enhanced.

Subsection (4)

1–050   In *A Local Authority v A*, which is considered in the note on *Capacity to Consent to Contraception*, above, Bodey J. held that "the reasonably foreseeable consequences" of a decision by a woman about the need for contraception did not extend to understanding about what bringing up a child would be like.

Best interests

1–051   **4.**—(1) In determining for the purposes of this Act what is in a person's best interests, the person making the determination must not make it merely on the basis of—

(a) the person's age or appearance, or

(b) a condition of his, or an aspect of his behaviour, which might lead others to make unjustified assumptions about what might be in his best interests.

(2) The person making the determination must consider all the relevant circumstances and, in particular, take the following steps.

(3) He must consider—

(a) whether it is likely that the person will at some time have capacity in relation to the matter in question, and

(b) if it appears likely that he will, when that is likely to be.

(4) He must, so far as reasonably practicable, permit and encourage the person to participate, or to improve his ability to participate, as fully as possible in any act done for him and any decision affecting him.

(5) Where the determination relates to life-sustaining treatment he must not, in considering whether the treatment is in the best interests of the person concerned, be motivated by a desire to bring about his death.

(6) He must consider, so far as is reasonably ascertainable—

(a) the person's past and present wishes and feelings (and, in particular, any relevant written statement made by him when he had capacity),

(b) the beliefs and values that would be likely to influence his decision if he had capacity, and

(c) the other factors that he would be likely to consider if he were able to do so.

(7) He must take into account, if it is practicable and appropriate to consult them, the views of—

(a) anyone named by the person as someone to be consulted on the matter in question or on matters of that kind,

(b) anyone engaged in caring for the person or interested in his welfare,

(c) any donee of a lasting power of attorney granted by the person, and

(d) any deputy appointed for the person by the court, as to what would be in the person's best interests and, in particular, as to the matters mentioned in subsection (6).

(8) The duties imposed by subsections (1) to (7) also apply in relation to the exercise of any powers which—

(a) are exercisable under a lasting power of attorney, or

(b) are exercisable by a person under this Act where he reasonably believes that another person lacks capacity.

(9) In the case of an act done, or a decision made, by a person other than the court, there is sufficient compliance with this section if (having complied with the requirements of subsections (1) to (7)) he reasonably believes that what he does or decides is in the best interests of the person concerned.

(10) "Life-sustaining treatment" means treatment which in the view of a person providing health care for the person concerned is necessary to sustain life.

(11) "Relevant circumstances" are those—

(a) of which the person making the determination is aware, and

(b) which it would be reasonable to regard as relevant.

DEFINITIONS

    "treatment": s.64(1)

    "lasting power of attorney": s.64(1)

    "deputy": s.64(1)

    "the court": s.64(1)

1–052

GENERAL NOTE

Section 1(5) establishes the principle that "an act done, or decision made, under the Act for or on behalf of a person who lacks capacity must be done, or made, in his best interests". Any person or body (including the court) that intervenes on behalf of P must therefore believe that their act or decision is in that person's best interests and that belief will have to be reasonable (subs.(9)).

1–053

This section sets out a checklist of factors which must be considered before the decision is made, or the act is carried out. In effect, the checklist establishes the course of action that should be followed in order to reach a determination whether a decision is in the person's best interests, a term which is not defined in the Act. In other words, it deals with the process of acquiring evidence, rather than specifying the criteria of best interests. The nature of the checklist grants considerable latitude to the decision-maker when reaching a reasonable belief as to where P's best interests lie. The best interests test applies to all decisions made or actions taken under the Act, ranging from a decision of the Court of Protection to a minor decision made by an informal carer. It is unrealistic to imagine that the process established by this section will be followed in respect of every minor decision that will need to be taken on behalf of P. It is also surely unrealistic to think that, on occasions, informal cares might not be permitted to give priority to their own interests.

In *Re AK (Gift Application)* [2014] EWHC B11 (COP), a case where the court considered whether a substantial gift (£150,000) should be made from the damages award of an eleven-year-old boy to his parents, Senior Judge Lush said that where P is profoundly disabled and has lacked capacity from birth the application of the best interests' checklist in this section is not always conclusive because of its strong emphasis on supported decision making and substituted judgment. Given the limitations of the checklist, Judge Lush applied a "balance-sheet" approach, setting out the advantages and disadvantages of the proposal.

It is the best interests of P that must be determined; not the best interests of another. In *Local Authority X v MM and KM* [2007] EWHC 2003 (Fam) at para.108, Munby J. said:

"Parental rights and responsibilities, and the rights and responsibilities of partners and other carers, have in the final analysis to give way to the best interests of a vulnerable adult."

Determining what is in the best interests for P by applying this section is not the same deciding, albeit with the best of intentions, what is best for P (*A Local Authority v WMA* [2013] EWHC 2580 (COP)).

In *Aintree University Hospitals NHS Foundation Trust v James* [2013] UKSC 67, Lady Hale said:

"The purpose of the best interests test is to consider matters from the patient's point of view. That is not to say that his wishes must prevail, any more than those of a fully capable patient must prevail. We cannot always have what we want. Nor will it always be possible to ascertain what an incapable patient's wishes are. Even if it is possible to determine what his views were in the past, they might well have changed in the light of the stresses and strains of his current predicament" (para.45).

There is a tension between this passage and the judgment of Munby J. in *Re M*, below in that Lady Hale seems to assume that the patient's wishes and feelings are the most important factor to consider in a best interests assessment, whereas Munby J. states that although there is no hierarchy between the various factors that comprise the assessment, P's wishes and feelings will always be a "significant factor" in the determination: see the notes on subs.6(a). Lady Hale confirmed at para.24 that the test in this section is "a 'best interests' rather than a 'substituted judgment' test, but one which accepts that the preferences of the person concerned are an important component in deciding where his best interests lie".

In *Re SK* [2013] All E.R. D 12 (Jul), Bodey J. held this section is concerned with the P's present best interests, choosing between currently available or reasonably foreseeable options. His Lordship said at para.10:

"That much appears both from common sense and from s.4(1) of the Act, which is stated in the present tense." (Also see the note on "best interests" in s.16(3)).

As well as being in the person's best interests, the decision should also aim to satisfy the least restrictive option principle set out in s.1(6) "which, in effect, is a principle of minimum intervention consistent with best interests" (*FP v GM* [2011] EWHC 2778 (COP), para.18, per Hedley J.). Having gone through the structured process set out in this section, the decision maker must form an objective value judgement giving effect to the statutory imperative (*Re MM (An Adult), A Local Authority v MM* [2007] EWHC 2003 (Fam) at paras 34–35). This judgment must not amount to a violation of P's rights under art.8 of the ECHR (*K v LBX* [2012] EWCA Civ 79). Decision makers should not be risk averse. As Munby J. commented in *MM* at para.120 (see further the note on *Best interests and living arrangements*, below):

"The emphasis must be on sensible risk appraisal not striving to avoid all risk, whatever the price, but instead seeking a proper balance and being willing to tolerate management of acceptable risks as the price appropriately to be paid in order to achieve some other good - in particular to achieve the vital good of the elderly or vulnerable person's *happiness*. What good is it making someone safer if it merely makes them miserable?"

In *ZH v Metropolitan Police Commissioner* [2013] EWCA Civ 69 at para.49, the Court of Appeal held that the Act

"does not impose impossible demands on those who do acts in connection with the care or treatment of others. It requires no more than what is reasonable, practicable and appropriate. What that entails depends on all the circumstances of the case. . . . what is reasonable, practicable and appropriate where there is time to reflect and take measured action may be quite different in an emergency or what is reasonably believed to be an emergency." (per Lord Dyson M.R.)

In *Re M* [2009] EWHC 2525 (Fam); [2010] 3 All E.R. 682 at para.32, Munby J. made three points arising from the experience in other jurisdictions which seemed to his Lordship to be of equal application to the statutory scheme under ss.1 and 4 of the Act and which, in particular, inform a proper understanding of how to evaluate the significance and weight to be attached to P's "wishes and feelings" under subs.(6)(a):

"1. The first is that the statute lays down no hierarchy as between the various factors which have to be borne in mind, beyond the overarching principle that what is determinative is the judicial evaluation of what is in P's 'best interests'.

2. The second is that the weight to be attached to the various factors will, inevitably, differ depending upon the individual circumstances of the particular case. A feature or factor which in one case may carry great, possibly even preponderant, weight may in another, superficially similar, case carry much less, or even very little, weight.

3. The third, following on from the others, is that there may, in the particular case,

be one or more features or factors which, as Thorpe LJ has frequently put it, are of 'magnetic importance' in influencing or even determining the outcome: see, for example, *Crossley v Crossley* [2007] EWCA Civ 1491, [2008] 1 F.L.R. 1467, at para.[15] (contrasting 'the peripheral factors in the case' with the 'factor of magnetic importance') and *White v White* [1999] Fam 304 (affirmed, [2001] 1 A.C. 596) where at page 314 he said 'Although there is no ranking of the criteria to be found in the statute, there is as it were a magnetism that draws the individual case to attach to one, two, or several factors as having decisive influence on its determination.' Now that was said in the context of section 25 of the Matrimonial Causes Act 1973 but the principle, as it seems to me, is of more general application."

In *Re G(TJ)* [2010] EWHC 3005 (COP) at para.35, Morgan J. said that "the word 'interests' in the phrase 'best interests' is not confined to matters of self interest or, putting it another way, a court could conclude in an appropriate case that it is in the interests of P for P to act altruistically". Also see the note on subs.(6)(c).

The practical effect of subs.(6) is to attempt to ascertain what P's subjective preference would have been had he or she been mentally capable. However, the effect of this is not to require the decision-maker to make a form of substituted judgment on behalf of P as the matters itemised in subs.(6) must merely be considered by the decision-maker who may come to a decision which P would not have wanted. For example, "if someone had a life-long aversion to needles, a decision could still be taken to give them the necessary injection when they were unconscious after a car crash", per the Parliamentary Under-Secretary of State, St.Comm. A, col.73. Although subs.(6) involves "an element of substituted judgment being taken into account . . . it is absolutely clear that the ultimate test for the court is the test of best interests and not the test of substituted judgment" (*Re G(TJ)*, above, at para.55). The Explanatory Notes state at para.28:

"Best interests is not a test of 'substituted judgment' (what the person would have wanted), but rather it requires a determination to be made by applying an objective test as to what would be in the person's best interests."

The provisions of subss.(3)–(7), which are not prioritised (*Re M*, above), do not provide an exhaustive list of factors that need to be taken into account as the decision maker must consider "all the relevant circumstances" (subs.(2)). The assessment of a P's best interests is clearly going to be influenced by either the personal or professional relationship that the decision-maker has with P. If P's incapacity is likely to be temporary, it might be possible for the decision to be postponed until capacity is regained: see subs.(3).

The best interest determination is made by the person or body who has the power to make the decision in respect of P. There is a widespread belief that the "next of kin" of P have the power to make decisions in respect of P solely because of their relationship with P. This is not the case: see, for example, *Re MM* [2011] 1 F.L.R. 712.

When making a best interest decision in relation to P, it is important to be confident that the correct issue is being addressed. For example, in a study of people with a learning disability who have cancer it was found that late diagnosis was common as complaints about physical pain were often attributed to attention-seeking behaviour (Tuffrey-Wijne et al. (2009) "People with learning difficulties who have cancer: an ethnographic study", Br. J. of General Practice, 59: 503-510). The following anecdote of Lord Adebowale, speaking during a debate on the Bill that became the Mental Health Act 2007, is also instructive:

"Mr S, who has a severe learning difficulty, autism and communication difficulties, lives in a residential setting. He was detained under the [Mental Health Act 1983] because he was becoming increasingly agitated and exhibited aggressive behaviour, banging his head against a wall. It was later discovered—this is shocking but true——that Mr S had a small twig in his ear, which was causing him distress, as it would most people, and which he expressed in his agitated behaviour. This scenario shows how the distress of a person with a learning disability can be automatically attributed to a mental disorder without paying sufficient attention to physical factors. This is about not just lazy diagnosis but making false assumptions" (*Hansard,* HL Vol.668, col.66).

A caution against lawyers adopting a precedent based approach to the determination of best interests was given by Hedley J. in *GC, Re* [2008] EWHC 3402 (Fam) at para.15:

"It is an almost irresistible temptation to lawyers, schooled in common law tradition, to seek to bring a case within other decided cases. In my view, at least, it is generally a temptation to be resisted. Each human being is unique and, thus, best interests decisions are unique to that human being. In almost every case, it should be enough to test the facts of the case against the relevant statutory provisions in order to ascertain the unique solution to that particular case."

If someone disagrees with the best interests determination that has been made, the Department of Constitutional Affairs Consultation Paper CP 10/06, at pp.10–11, identifies the following options that may be explored:

- involving an advocate, who is independent of all the parties, to work with the person who lacks capacity and help them understand the situation or act as an advocate of their best interests;
- getting a second opinion in cases where the decision relates to medical treatment;
- holding a formal or informal case conference if the decision relates to medical treatment or social care;
- using the informal or formal complaints processes if the decision in question is to be taken by the health, social or other welfare services; or
- participating in mediation or other forms of dispute resolution. This may be most appropriate to decisions on the day-to-day care or welfare of a person.

If all attempts to resolve a dispute fail, it may be appropriate to apply to the Court of Protection for a ruling on what particular decision or course of action is in P's best interests. However, the court will not entertain an application that is academic (*AVS v A NHS Foundation Trust* [2011] EWCA Civ 7 at para.39).

The "balance sheet" approach

1–054   The use of the "balance sheet" approach in medical cases, which was identified by Thorpe L.J. in *A (Mental Patient: Sterilisation), Re* [2000] 1 F.L.R. 549 at 560, was endorsed by Wood J. in *Ealing LBC v KS* [2008] EWHC 636 at para.71, as an appropriate approach to adopt when considering best interest determinations under this section: also see *Re G(TJ)* noted under subs.(6). However, in *Gloucestershire CCG v AB* [2014] EWCOP 49, Baker J. said at para.17(viii) that where a patient is in a vegetative state, "the balance sheet approach is not normally appropriate because all the factors that are relevant normally fall on one side of the scale". In *A, Re*, Thorpe L.J. said at 560:

"[T]he first instance judge with the responsibility to make an evaluation of the best interests of a claimant lacking capacity should draw up a balance sheet. The first entry should be of any factor or factors of actual benefit Then on the other sheet the judge should write any counterbalancing dis-benefits to the applicant Then the judge should enter on each sheet the potential gains and losses in each instance making some estimate of the extent of the possibility that the gain or loss might accrue. At the end of that exercise the judge should be better placed to strike a balance between the sum of the certain and possible gains against the sum of the certain and possible losses. Obviously, only if the account is in relatively significant credit will the judge conclude that the applicant is likely to advance the best interests of the claimant."

This approach was used by Cobb J. in *Mental Health Trust v DD* [2015] EWCOP 4 where his Lordship said at para.112:

"While I have adopted the 'balance sheet' approach . . . and consider it helpful, it does not of itself resolve the issues; my final determination is ultimately informed by the *weight* put upon the various factors in favour of or against the proposed course of action that are identified therein."

In *M v Mrs N* [2015] EWCOP 76, Hayden J. said at para.46:

"The balancing exercise is qualitative rather than merely numerical. The point is made in the deft analogy of McFarlane LJ in: *Re F (A Child) (International Relocation Cases)* [2015] EWCA Civ 882 at para 52:

'Finally I wish to add one further observation relating to paragraph 29 of Ryder LJ's judgment where my Lord suggests that it may be helpful for judges facing the task of analysing competing welfare issues to gain assistance by the use of a 'balance sheet'. Whilst I entirely agree that some form of balance sheet may be of assistance to judges, its use should be no more than an aide memoire of the key factors and how they match up against each other. If a balance sheet is used it should be a route to judgment and not a substitution for the judgment itself. A key step in any welfare evaluation is the attribution of weight, or lack of it, to each of the relevant considerations; one danger that may arise from setting out all the relevant factors in tabular format, is that the attribution of weight may be lost, with all elements of the table having equal value as in a map without contours'".

If a patient is in a vegetative state, the balance sheet approach does not apply as there is no balancing exercise to be performed (*A Hospital v SW* [2007] Med. L.R. 273 at para.28).

In *A NHS Trust v MB* [2006] 2 F.L.R. 319, Holman J. suggested that the exercise of creating a "Benefits/Disadvantages Table" should be part of "the standard preparation of a case" and that the list can always be added to or amended in the light of evidence as it evolves.

'Wishes' and 'best interests' should never be conflated, they are entirely separate matters which may ultimately weigh on different sides of the balance sheet (*Sheffield Teaching Hospitals NHS Foundation Trust v TH* [2014] EWCOP 4 at para.56, per Hayden J.).

Recording best interests decisions
The *Code of Practice* states at para.5.15:

1–055

"Any staff involved in the care of a person who lacks capacity should make sure a record is kept of the process of working out the best interests of that person for each relevant decision, setting out:

- how the decision about the person's best interests was reached
- what the reasons for reaching the decision were
- who was consulted to help work out best interests, and
- what particular factors were taken into account.

This record should remain on the person's file."

This guidance could prove to be a bureaucratic nightmare if it applied to every decision made on behalf of P as there would be a real danger of staff being submerged with paperwork and diverted from their caring role if it was applied indiscriminately. It is suggested that the potential significance of the decision to P and/or others should determine whether a formal record of the decision should be made. For example, a decision to allow P unescorted access to the grounds of the care home would not require a formal record to made on every occasion when it was granted if such access posed no risk either to P or to others. If, however, P had a history of being aggressive to fellow residents when given access to the grounds, a risk assessment should be made before unescorted leave access is granted and a record along the lines suggested by the *Code of Practice* made. Routine decisions that need to be taken in respect of P could be recorded in a care plan.

Guidance on the conduct of formal best interests meetings can be found in Section 3 of *Best Interests: Guidance on determining the best interests of adults who lack the capacity to make a decision (or decisions) for themselves*, British Psychological Society, undated.

Best interests and medical treatment

1–056   In *Aintree University Hospitals NHS Foundation Trust v James* [2013] UKSC 67, Lady Hale, with whom all the other Justices of the Supreme Court agreed, held that:

1. In considering the best interests of a particular patient at a particular time, decision-makers must look at his welfare in the widest sense, not just medical but social and psychological; they must consider the nature of the medical treatment in question, what it involves and its prospects of success; they must consider what the outcome of that treatment for the patient is likely to be; they must try and put themselves in the place of the individual patient and ask what his attitude to the treatment is or would be likely to be; and they must consult others who are looking after him or interested in his welfare, in particular for their view of what his attitude would be (para.39).
2. The purpose of the best interests test is to consider matters from the patient's point of view. Insofar as it is possible to ascertain the patient's wishes and feelings, his beliefs and values or the things which were important to him, it is those which should be taken into account because they are a component in making the choice which is right for him as an individual human being (para.45).
3. A treatment may bring some benefit to the patient even though it has no effect upon the underlying disease or disability (para.43). The benefit could be the resumption of a quality of life which P regarded as worthwhile (para.44).

Her Ladyship confirmed that although a patient cannot order a doctor to give a particular form of treatment, he may refuse it, and that the court's position is no different (para.18). *Aintree* is also considered under *Best interests and the withholding of treatment which would sustain life*, below.

In *DH NHS Foundation Trust v PS* [2010] EWHC 1217 (Fam), a hysterectomy was in the best interests of P who had agreed on previous occasions to undergo the operation, but had been overcome on the day by fear and needle phobia. The President made an order which approved a plan which included provision for covert sedation at the patient's home with a sedative drug mixed with a soft drink. There was also provision in the order for the use of force if necessary to sedate P and convey her to hospital. This case was followed in *A NHS Trust v K* [2012] EWHC 2922 (COP) where Holman J. held that as it was in the overall best interests of P to have an operation, it would be lawful, and in her best interests, to sedate her to enable it to take place, and lawful to do so before she is told, after sedation but before anaesthesia, what is planned.

In *Y (Mental Patient: Bone Marrow Donation), Re* [1996] 2 F.L.R. 787, Connell J. held that it was in the best interests of an incompetent patient to donate bone marrow to her gravely ill sister. Having heard evidence that the death of the sister would have a particularly adverse effect upon the mother, with whom the patient enjoyed a very close relationship, and, in particular, would significantly handicap her ability to visit the patient, his Lordship held that the procedure would be to the patients "emotional, psychological and social benefit".

Although, in the absence of an appropriate lasting power of attorney, the next of kin of a mentally incapable patient has no legal right either to consent or to refuse treatment on behalf of the patient, it is not necessarily undesirable for such consent to be sought if the interests of the patient will not be adversely affected by any consequential delay. This is because "contact with the next of kin may reveal that the patient has made an anticipatory choice which, if clearly established and applicable in the circumstances—two major 'ifs'—would bind the practitioner" (*T (Adult Patient: Refusal of Medical Treatment)* [1992] 4 All E.R. 649, per Lord Donaldson M.R. at 649).

Best interests and the withholding of treatment which would sustain life

1–057   [Also see the notes on *Patients in a Vegetative State* and *Patients in a Minimally Conscious State* in s.15(1)(c).]

In *Aintree University Hospitals NHS Foundation Trust v James* [2013] UKSC 67, the Supreme Court addressed the question of how doctors and courts should decide when it is in the best interests of P to be given, or not to be given, treatments necessary to sustain life. Lady Hale, with whom all the other Justices agreed, held that:

1. The starting point is a strong presumption that it is in a person's best interests to stay alive. Nevertheless, there are cases where it will not be in a patient's best interests to receive life-sustaining treatment. Every patient, and every case, is different and must be decided on its own facts (paras 35, 36). The question for the court is whether it is in the patient's best interests to give the treatment, rather than on whether it is in his best interests to withhold or withdraw it. If the treatment is not in his best interests, the court will not be able to give its consent on his behalf and it will follow that it will be lawful to withhold or withdraw it (para.22).
2. The judge at first instance had been correct when he considered whether the proposed treatments would be futile in the sense of being ineffective or being of no benefit to the patient. He was also correct to see the assessment of the medical effects of the treatment as only part of the equation. Regard had to be had to the patient's welfare in the widest sense, and great weight to be given to P's family life which was "of the closest and most meaningful kind" (para.40). Where the patient is close to death, the object may properly be to make his dying as comfortable and as dignified as possible, rather than to take invasive steps to prolong his life for a short while. Resuming a quality of life which the patient would regard as worthwhile is more readily applicable in the case of a patient with permanent disabilities. It is not for others to say that a life which the patient would regard as worthwhile is not worth living (para.44).
3. The judge was right to be cautious about making declarations in circumstances which were not fully predictable or fluctuating (para.41).

The *Code of Practice* deals with decisions about life-sustaining treatment at paras.5.31 to 5.33. The following statement is to be found at para.5.31:

"All reasonable steps which are in the person's best interests should be taken to prolong their life. There will be a limited number of cases where treatment is futile, overly burdensome to the patient or where there is no prospect of recovery. In circumstances such as these, it may be that an assessment of best interests leads to the conclusion that it would be in the best interests of the patient to withdraw or withhold life-sustaining treatment, even if this may result in the person's death. The decision-maker must make a decision based on the best interests of the person who lacks capacity. They must not be motivated by a desire to bring about the person's death for whatever reason, even if this is from a sense of compassion. Healthcare and social care staff should also refer to relevant professional guidance when making decisions regarding life-sustaining treatment."

This was accepted by Lady Hale as "an accurate statement of law" (para.29).

Given the decision in *Aintree*, hospitals might consider that an application to the court for a declaration would not be appropriate in a situation where (1) all of the clinicians involved in the treatment of a patient considered that life-sustaining treatment should not be offered to the patient, and (2) their stance was confirmed by an independent expert who was also unwilling to provide such treatment. In such a situation there is, in effect, no best interests decision to be taken as there is no treatment option that is available for the patient. *Aintree* confirmed that a refusal to provide treatment cannot be challenged in the Court of Protection.

Aintree was applied in *An NHS Foundation Trust v VT* [2103] EWHC B26 (Fam) where Hayden J. granted a declaration relating to lawfulness of withholding certain intensive care treatments from a patient who was in a minimally conscious state but not close to death in a situation where, for religious reasons, the patient's family wanted every effort to be made to preserve the patient's life. His Lordship held that "to require the team to treat VT in Intensive Care would be wholly futile, in that it would be:

(i) Likely to cause distress, discomfort and probably pain.
(ii) Unable to achieve any positive medical benefit.

(iii)   Life-threatening, in and of itself.
(iv)   To further compromise VT's vital organs, and therefore medically harmful" (para.28).

In *St George's Healthcare NHS Trust v P* [2015] EWCOP 42, Newton J. highlighted the decision of Baker J. in *W v M (adult patient) minimally conscious state: withdrawing treatment* [2012] 1 W.L.R. 1653 where it was stated that standardised testing is always necessary before the application is made to the court:

"[I]t is of the utmost importance that every step should be taken to diagnose the patient's true condition before any application is made to the court. In future no application for an order authorising the withdrawal of ANH from a patient in a vegetative state or a minimally conscious state should be made unless a SMART assessment or similarly validated equivalent has been carried out to provide a diagnosis of the patient's disorder of consciousness and in the case of the patient thereby diagnosed as being in the minimally conscious state a series of WHIM assessments have been carried out over time with a view to tracking the patient's progress and recovery if any through the minimally conscious state".

Newton J. ended his judgment with the following cautionary words at para.49:

"Therefore in all cases where there is any question of doubt about diagnosis, in order to eliminate mistakes or potential tragedies it is essential that those assessments are carried out in good time so that the diagnosis is clear before the court, then the court can conduct its own enquiry and balance".

With regard to P's wishes and feelings, values and beliefs, Newton J. said at para.38:

"The quality of life should be judged not by the values of others but from the particular perspective of the patient. In considering what the patient himself might regard as worthwhile P's prior statement and behaviours as they can be discerned from his family, his wishes, his beliefs, his feelings and his values are all relevant."

That the sanctity of life is a fundamental principle when treating patient was emphasised by Lord Goff said in *Airedale NHS Trust v Bland* [1993] 1 All E.R. 821 at 865–866:

". . . the fundamental principle is the principle of the sanctity of human life - a principle long recognised not only in our own society but also in most, if not all, civilised societies throughout the modern world, as is indeed evidenced by its recognition both in Art.2 of the European Convention on Human Rights and in Art. 6 of the International Covenant on Civil and Political Rights

But this principle, fundamental though it is, is not absolute We are concerned with circumstances in which it may be lawful to withhold from a patient medical treatment or care by means of which his life may be prolonged. But here too there is no absolute rule that the patient's life must be prolonged by such treatment or care, if available, regardless of the circumstances."

This approach is illustrated by the case of *D (Medical Treatment: Mentally Disabled Patient), Re* [1998] 2 F.L.R. 22 where Sir Stephen Brown P. granted a declaration that "notwithstanding the [patient's] inability to consent to or refuse medical treatment, it is lawful as being in the best interests of the patient that the [NHS Trust] do not impose haemodialysis upon him in circumstances in which, in the opinion of the medical practitioners responsible for such treatment, it is not reasonable practicable so to do". This was a case where it had proved to be impossible to treat a gravely ill, physically protesting, mentally incompetent patient. The doctors had sought a declaration to protect themselves from any liability arising from a failure to carry out the treatment.

In *W Healthcare NHS Trust v H* [2004] EWCA Civ 1324, Brooke L.J. said at para.30:

"English law, as it stands at present, places a very heavy burden on those who are advocating a course which would lead inevitably to the cessation of a human life."

In *R. (on the application of Burke) v The General Medical Council* [2005] EWCA Civ 1003, Lord Phillips M.R. said at para.33:

"The courts have accepted that where life involves an extreme degree of pain, discomfort or indignity to a patient, who is sentient but not competent and who has manifested no wish to be kept alive, these circumstances may absolve the doctors of the positive duty to keep the patient alive. Equally the courts have recognised that there may be no duty to keep alive a patient who is in a persistent vegetative state. In each of these examples the facts of the individual case may make it difficult to decide whether the duty to keep the patient alive persists."

Where there is no alternative treatment available for a mentally incapacitated patient and the disease is progressive and fatal, it is reasonable to consider experimental treatment with unknown benefits and risks, but without significant risks of increased suffering to the patient, in cases where there is some chance of benefit to the patient (*Simms v Simms* [2002] EWHC 2734 (Fam)). Butler-Sloss P. said at para.57: "A patient who is not able to consent to pioneering treatment ought not to be deprived of the chance in circumstances where he would be likely to consent if he had been competent". Her Ladyship stressed that in such cases the views of the family of the patient about the proposed treatment would carry great weight in the wider considerations of the best interests test (para.64).

The Lord Chancellor said at the second reading of the Bill in the House of Lords that "in some cases it will be in the best interests of the person to withhold treatment or to give palliative care that might incidentally shorten life" (*Hansard*, HL Vol.668, col.15). In support of this approach, he quoted from the Roman Catholic Archbishop of Cardiff who had said:

". . . it is not the church's position that life must be sustained at all costs. On the contrary, one can quite reasonably, and consistently with one's responsibilities for oneself and others, decide to refuse treatment—even life sustaining treatment—which one judges burdensome or futile, knowing that forgoing the treatment will shorten one's life."

The BMA, the Resuscitation Council (UK) and the Royal College of Nursing have published joint guidance on "Decisions relating to cardiopulmonary resuscitation", 3rd edn (2014) which can be accessed at: *www.resus.org.uk/pages/dnacpr.htm*.

Best interests and the force feeding of a gravely ill patient suffering from anorexia nervosa **1–058**
In *The NHS Trust v L* [2012] EWHC 2741 (COP), Eleanor King J. made declarations which were predicted on the basis that the patient was in the closing stages of her life and that force feeding was not in her best interests. They were aimed at alleviating the patient's distress and pain and allowing her to die with dignity (para.65). After noting that the strong presumption to preserve life is not absolute, her Ladyship said at paras 68 to 70:

"In my judgment this is one of those few cases where the only possible treatment, namely force feeding under sedation, is not to be countenanced in Ms L's best interests: to do so would be futile, carrying with it a near certainty that it would cause her death in any event. Such a course would be overly burdensome in that every calorie that enters her body is an enemy to Ms L.

Ms L would I am satisfied be appallingly distressed and resistant to any suggestion that she was to be force fed and to what purpose? Her poor body is closing down, organ failure has begun, she can no longer resist infection and she is, at all times in imminent danger of cardiac arrest. Even if she could, by some miracle, agree to some miniscule increase in her nutrient intake her organ failure is nevertheless irreversible and her anorexia so severe and deep rooted that there could be no real possibility of her maintaining her co-operation. Ms L on occasion shows some small spark of insight – she said on the 1st August that she was frightened as she cannot help herself from 'messing with the tube'.

In all the circumstances therefore I have concluded that it is in Ms L's best interests for me to make declarations in the terms set out in the agreed draft. The draft allows for the faint hope that even now Ms L may 'turn the corner' but recognises and addresses the far more likely outcome."

In this case the patient, who had expressed a wish to live, had virtually no chance of survival. In *A Local Authority v E* [2012] EWHC 1639 (COP) the force feeding of an anorexic patient was authorised in a situation where the prospects of recovery of the patient, who had expressed a wish to be allowed to die, were estimated to be 20 per cent. In this case, Peter Jackson J. said at paras 137 to 140:

"We only live once—we are born once and we die once—and the difference between life and death is the biggest difference we know. E is a special person, whose life is of value. She does not see it that way now, but she may in future.

I would not overrule her wishes if further treatment was futile, but it is not. Although extremely burdensome to E, there is a possibility that it will succeed. Services and funding will now be provided that were not available before, and it would not be right to turn down the final chance of helping this very vulnerable young woman. . . .

I am also influenced by the fact that those who know E best are not in outright opposition to treatment taking place, however sceptical they justifiably feel.

The competing factors are, in my judgment, almost exactly in equilibrium, but having considered them as carefully as I am able, I find that the balance tips slowly but unmistakably in the direction of life-preserving treatment. In the end, the presumption in favour of the preservation of life is not displaced."

A declaration that it would be lawful for an NHS Trust not to compel treatment on a patient who was suffering from a severe form of anorexia nervosa and alcohol dependence that had caused irreversible liver damage was granted by Cobb J. in *A NHS Trust v Ms X* [2014] EWCOP 35. His Lordship said at para.42:

"Medical treatment is invariably designed to achieve the protection and preservation of life. But there is a paradox in this case: that if I were to compel treatment, I may (and the doctors argue strongly that I would) be doing no more than facilitating or accelerating the termination of her life. I have no jurisdiction to make 'best interests' decisions about Ms X's drinking; that remains wholly within her power. Any treatment for her anorexia (particularly if that is in-patient and compelled) is likely—on past experience—to provoke subsequent increased, sustained and dangerous alcohol consumption which will (in the medical view) hasten Ms X's death."

Best interests and the imminent possibility of death

1–059   In *A NHS Trust v DU* [2009] EWHC 3504 (Fam), the family of an 86-year-old Nigerian woman (DU) with serious medical needs wished her to be returned to Nigeria. Although concerns were raised about whether DU could be adequately cared for there, the family were given permission to return DU to Nigeria. Hedley J, in para.10 of his judgment, said:

"It is an integral part of the concept of best interests when dealing with a person of this age that the court recognises the imminent possibility of death and the importance of making arrangements so as to secure that the experience of death may be in a context which is the most congenial and peaceful that can be devised. Also implicit in the concept of best interests is the importance of the country and culture of origin and the whereabouts of the family. They will often take precedence over, for example, the question of risk avoidance or the exact quality of care that may be available."

Best interests in cases where a pregnant woman lacks capacity to make decisions about her obstetric care

1–060   In *NHS Trust v FG* [2014] EWCOP 30, Keehan J. was invited by the Official Solicitor to give guidance on the steps to be taken when a local authority and/or medical professionals are concerned about and dealing with a pregnant woman who has mental health problems and, potentially lacks capacity to litigate and to make decisions about her welfare or medical treatment. The guidance is reproduced at Appendix B. Among the observations made by Keehan which underpin the guidance are:

1. "The Guidance should not be read as applying to every pregnant woman with a diagnosed mental health illness. No doubt in the vast majority of such cases it will not be necessary to make an application to the Court of Protection or to the Family Division of the High Court" (para.82).

2. "The Guidance is intended: (i) to prevent the need for urgent applications to be made to the out of hours judge; and (ii) to ensure trusts do not rely inappropriately on the provisions of s.5 of the MCA" (para.83).

3. "Urgent applications to the out of hours judge must be limited to those rare and few cases where a genuine medical emergency has arisen and an immediate court order is necessary. I do not consider a failure to plan appropriately and/or a failure to identify a case where an application to the court may be required constitutes a genuine medical emergency" (para.84).

4. Although, in "the vast majority of these cases obstetric care will be provided to P under [s.5 of] the MCA" (para.88), obstetric "care may be provided under [s.63 of] the Mental Health Act. There may be circumstances where delivery of P's baby may be undertaken earlier than term to enable effective treatment of P's severe mental illness" (para.85).

5. "The distinction between actions which amount to restraint only, and those which become a deprivation of liberty might be difficult, but is of critical legal significance because s.4A(1) prevents clinicians performing acts which amount to a deprivation of liberty as part of the care and treatment under s.5" (para.93).

6. "It will commonly be the case that when at the acute hospital P: (i) will have obstetric and midwifery staff constantly present throughout her labour and delivery; (ii) will be under the continuous control of obstetric and midwifery staff who, because she lacks capacity to make decisions about her medical case, will take decisions on her behalf in her best interests; (iii) will often not be permitted to leave the delivery suite (para.96). These "factors may, when applying the acid test [set out in *P v Cheshire West* [2014] UKSC 19], lead to a conclusion that P is or will suffer a deprivation of her liberty when at the acute hospital. If the Trusts are to deprive P of her liberty, they have a duty not to do so unlawfully: s6 HRA 1998" (para.97). "The Trusts must, therefore, plan how P is to receive obstetric care in sufficient detail to identify whether there is potential for a deprivation of liberty to arise. When trusts identify there is a real risk that P will suffer an additional deprivation of her residual liberty during transfer to and from the acute hospital and/or when present at the acute hospital, the Trusts must take steps to ensure the deprivation of liberty is authorised in accordance with the law . . . " (para.98). "Where the Trusts identify there is a real risk that P will suffer a deprivation of liberty in these circumstances it is for them to decide whether the same is achieved by a standard authorisation under Schedule A1 of the MCA, by an application to the court or under another lawful jurisdiction" (para.98).

7. If "the need for the deprivation of liberty in relation to the proposed obstetric care was foreseeable but the Trusts omit to seek a standard authorisation, the use of an urgent authorisation may be unlawful: see paragraphs 6.2 and 6.3 of Deprivation of Liberty Safeguards Code of Practice . . ." (para.101(ii)).

8. The "mere fact that a deprivation of liberty could be authorised under Schedule A1 does not absolve the Trusts from making an application to the court where the facts of the individual case would otherwise merit the same" (para.101(iii)).

9. Applications should be made by the Trusts treating P to obtain permissive orders relating to P's obstetric care in the following circumstances:

   i. "the interventions proposed by the Trust(s) probably amount to serious medical treatment within the meaning of COP Practice Direction 9E, irrespective of whether it is contemplated that the obstetric treatment would otherwise be provided under the MCA or MHA; or

ii. there is a real risk that P will be subject to more than transient forcible restraint; or

iii. there is a serious dispute as to what obstetric care is in P's best interests whether as between the clinicians caring for P, or between the clinicians and P and/or those whose views must be taken into account under s 4(7) of the MCA; or

iv. there is a real risk that P will suffer a deprivation of her liberty which, absent a Court order which has the effect of authorising it, would otherwise be unlawful (i.e. not authorised under s 4B of or Schedule A1 to the MCA)" (para.103).

Best interests and sterilisation as a method of contraception

1–061   *A NHS Trust v DE* [2013] EWHC 2562 (Fam) is the first reported case in which the court has found that it was in the best interests of a mentally incapacitated learning disabled adult to have a vasectomy as a means of contraception. The judge was strongly influenced by the knowledge that DE, who had fathered one child, had a clear and consistent desire not to have more children. Also of importance was the fact that the procedure would allow DE to regain his independence by resuming his long standing relationship with a female who also had a learning disability.

The test to ascertain a woman's capacity to consent to contraception is set out in *A Local Authority v A* [2010] EWHC 1549 which is considered in the General Note to s.3.

Best interests and third party interests, e.g. needlestick accidents

1–062   In *A (Mental Patient: Sterilisation), Re* [2000] I F.L.R. 549, the question whether third party interests, such as the interests of potential sexual partners of the patient, should ever be considered in a case concerned with the best interests of a patient was left open. During the Bill's passage through Parliament, the BMA sought assurances that it would be possible to conduct a diagnostic test on an incapacitated person primarily for the benefit of a family member in the case of genetic diseases, or to a nurse or doctor if a needlestick accident had occurred during the person's treatment. The Minister of State responded to these concerns as follows:

"[T]he Bill will allow for acts whose primary purpose is to benefit a third party, provided that those acts are in P's best interests. I reassure the House that the interpretation of best interests could be broader than P's medical best interests. I can confirm that the Bill will not prevent a genetic test for a familial cancer, for example, that might not be essential to P's medical care but would provide considerable benefit to some other family member. Similarly, HIV testing would be lawful if there were a needlestick injury to a nurse involved in P's care and if a timely diagnosis of HIV status would be in P's best interests, so that treatment could be started. There is the ability for a medical professional in those circumstances—if they reasonably think that a person might have HIV/AIDS or hepatitis C and they might have been affected by it—to request a test so that treatment of P could start" (*Hansard*, HC Vol.428, col.1601).

The following question and answer were given in the House of Lords on March 13, 2013:

"To ask Her Majesty's Government what is their policy on testing for HIV in patients lacking capacity to give consent following a needlestick injury to a healthcare worker. [HL5920]

The Parliamentary Under-Secretary of State, Department of Health (Earl Howe): Where a person lacks capacity to consent their rights are protected by the Mental Capacity Act 2005, which determines that decisions on behalf of such a person have to be made in their best interests.

The department's view is that both the taking of samples and the testing of samples previously obtained from a patient who lacks capacity to consent are therefore acts that may only be undertaken if they are in the best interests of the patient. This would include testing a patient for a serious communicable disease such as HIV following a needlestick injury to a healthcare worker.

The department's view is that determining whether it is in the best interests of a patient who lacks capacity to take and test samples for the purpose of determining what treatment, if any, to offer a healthcare worker with a needlestick injury is a stringent test to pass. It involves assessment of the individual circumstances of the patient on a case-by-case basis."

The best interests principle, which is not confined to P's best medical interests (see para.5.48 of the *Code of Practice*), would not be satisfied in a situation where the procedure in question resulted in no tangible or intangible benefit to P. It could be argued in a situation where the primary purpose of the intervention is to benefit a third party that an intangible benefit would be the desire of P, had he or she been capable, to be seen to be "a normal decent person, acting in accordance with contemporary standards of morality" (*C (Spinster and Mental Patient), Re* [1991] 3 All E.R. 866 at 870, per Hoffmann J.). See further L.A. Burrows and A. Padkin, "A survey of the management of needlestick injuries from incapacitated patients in intensive care units", *Anaesthesia*, 2010, 65, 880–884, together with the associated editorial at 875–879.

Best interests and living arrangements

While the law requires a "significant harm" test to be satisfied before a child can be **1–063** removed from the family home against parental wishes (Children Act 1989 s.31(2)), the court can order the removal of a mentally incapable adult from the family home under the Act on the sole ground that removal would be in the adult's best interests.

Apart from "very rare" situations, "any significant issue of principle such as residence, type of care, treatment and such like" should be made by the court rather that a personal welfare deputy (*MK v JK* [2013] EWHC 4334 (COP) at para.30, per D.J. Ralton). In *A (child), Re and C (adult), Re* [2010] EWHC 978, Munby J. said at para.75:

"[If] there is objection to the steps it is proposing to take, either from the vulnerable adult or from relatives, partners, friends or carers, it seems to me that a local authority needs to enlist the assistance of the court—either the High Court or the Court of Protection—*before* it embarks upon any attempt to regulate, control, compel, restrain, confine or coerce a vulnerable adult. Only if the person is compliant and there is no objection from those concerned with his welfare is a local authority probably going to be justified in having resort without judicial assistance to the doctrine of necessity. And even where the person appears to be compliant a local authority needs to act with considerable caution before attempting even to regulate or control, let alone to restrain or coerce, a vulnerable adult. One cannot conflate absence of objection with consent. And to equate helpless acquiescence with consent when a person is confronted with the misuse or misrepresentation of non-existent authority by an agent of the State is both unprincipled and, indeed, fraught with potential danger"

In relation to a dispute regarding what should be included in information relevant to a decision regarding accommodation, in *LBX v K* [2013] EWHC 3230 (Fam) at para.43 Theis J. agreed with the following analysis submitted by the Official Solicitor:

1. What the two options are, including information about what they are, what sort of property they are and what sort of facilities they have.
2. In broad terms, what sort of area the properties are in (and any specific known risks beyond the usual risks faced by people living in an area if any such specific risks exist).
3. The difference between living somewhere and visiting it.
4. What activities P would be able to do if he lived in each place.
5. Whether and how he would be able to see his family and friends if he lived in each place.

6. In relation to the proposed placement, that he would need to pay money to live there, which would be dealt with by his appointee, that he would need to pay bills, which would be dealt with by his appointee, and that there is an agreement that he has to comply with the relevant lists of "do's" and "don't's", otherwise he will not be able to remain living at the placement.
7. Who he would be living with at each placement.
8. What sort of care he would receive in each placement in broad terms, in other words, that he would receive similar support in the proposed placement to the support he currently receives, and any differences if he were to live at home.
9. The risk that his father might not want to see him if P chooses to live in the new placement.

The following factors were found not to be relevant: "firstly, the cost of the placements and the value of money; secondly, the legal nature of the tenancy agreement or licence; and, thirdly, what his relationship with his father might be in 10 or 20 years' time if [P] chooses to live independently now" (para.33).

In the context of a person making a choice between staying in a care home and going home, Baker J. said that the person should be provided with "a detailed analysis of the effects of the decision either way, which in turn necessitates identifying the best ways in which option would be supported. In order to understand the likely consequences of deciding to return home, KK should be given full details of the care package that would or might be available" (*CC v KK* [2012] EWHC 2136 (COP) at para.68).

In *S (Adult Patient) (Inherent Jurisdiction: Family Life), Re* [2002] EWHC 2278 (Fam); [2003] 1 F.L.R. 292 at para.48, Munby J. said:

"I am not saying that there is in law any presumption that mentally incapacitated adults are better off with their families: often they will be; sometimes they will not be. But respect for our human condition, regard for the realities of our society and . . . common sense . . ., surely indicate that the starting point should be the normal assumption that mentally incapacitated adults will be better off if they live with a family rather than in an institution—however benign and enlightened the institution may be, and however well integrated into the community—and the mentally incapacitated adults who have been looked after within their family will be better off if they continue to be looked after within the family rather than by the State."

His Lordship returned to this issue in *Local Authority X v MM* [2007] EWHC 2003 (Fam), where he said:

1. There is a need "to be conscious of the limited ability of public authorities to improve on nature. We need to be careful not to embark upon 'social engineering'" (para.116).
2. If the State is to justify removing "vulnerable adults from their relatives, partners, friends or carers it can only be on the basis that the State is going to provide a *better* quality of care than that which they have hitherto been receiving" (para.117).
3. The court is entitled to intervene to protect a vulnerable adult from the risk of future harm "so long as there is a real possibility, rather than a merely fanciful risk of such harm. But the court must adopt a pragmatic, common sense approach to the identification, evaluation and management of perceived risk" (para.119). The "emphasis must be on a sensible risk appraisal, not striving to avoid all risk, whatever the price, but instead seeking a proper balance and being willing to tolerate manageable or acceptable risks as the price appropriately to be paid in order to achieve some other good—in particular to achieve the vital good of the elderly or vulnerable person's *happiness*. What good is it making someone safer if it merely makes them miserable?" (para.120).

Peter Jackson J. followed the approach advocated by Munby J. in *Re M (Best Interests: Deprivation of Liberty)* [2013] EWHC 3456 (COP) where he held that it would be in the best interests of P, who had very significant health needs which were being successfully catered for in a care home, to return to her home with a care package. His Lordship said at para.38:

> "In the end, if M remains confined in a home she is entitled to ask 'What for?' The only answer that could be provided at the moment is 'To keep you alive as long as possible.' In my view that is not a sufficient answer. The right to life and the state's obligation to protect it is not absolute and the court must surely have regard to the person's own assessment of her quality of life. In M's case there is little to be said for a solution that attempts, without any guarantee of success, to preserve for her a daily life without meaning or happiness and which she, with some justification, regards as insupportable".

In *GC, Re* [2008] EWHC 3402 (Fam) at para.18, Hedley J. said that in applying the principle of least intervention in a case where there would be an unwilling entry into state care, the court "must really conclude that a return to private life is inconsistent with the welfare of the person with whose best interests it is concerned, before it considers the alternatives." When making this judgment in respect of an elderly person, the "emotional component" associated with the family setting "rates extremely highly" (para.27). His Lordship said at para.21:

> ". . . GC is a man in the 83rd year of his life and my concern is to ask myself: how will he most comfortably and happily spend the last years that are available to him? Secondly I have approached this case on the basis that his primary need is for emotional warmth, emotional security and the commitment of human relationship. That has been a huge feature of his life to date and one that is not readily to be set aside. Next it seems to me that for the elderly there is often an importance in place which is not generally recognised by others; not only physical place but also the relational structure that is associated with a place . . .".

With regard to the possibility of a trial placement at GC's home, his Lordship said at para.24:

> "[I]t seems to me that it would be wrong not to try, even with a degree of pessimism, a placement with a package of support that has now been advanced . . ."

A similar approach was adopted by McFarlane J. in *LLBC v TG, JG and KR* [2007] EWHC 2640 (Fam); [2007] M.H.L.R. 203, where his Lordship said at paras 30, 33,

> ". . . the fact that the assessment of the option of a family placement was not given priority is a matter of concern. Placement in the family should be at the top of any priority list before alternative non-family placements are considered. . . .
>
> Before a local authority seeks to invoke the court's powers to compel a family to place a relative in a residential care home, the court is entitled to expect that the authority will have made a genuine and reasonable attempt to carry out a full assessment of the capacity of the family to meet the relative's needs in the community."

The significance to be attached to P's family life was also emphasised by Peter Jackson J. in *Hillingdon LBC v Neary* [2011] EWHC 1377 (COP) at para.24:

> "Decisions about incapacitated people must always be determined by their best interests, but the starting point is their right to respect for their family life where it exists. The burden is always on the State to show that an incapacitated person's welfare cannot be sustained by living with and being looked after by his or her family, with or without outside support."

Living arrangements and art.8 of the European Convention on Human Rights

1–064

Where there is a conflict between P's right to respect for private and family life under art.8 of the European Convention on Human Rights and the art.8 rights of a relative who is caring for P, P's art.8 rights take precedence if intervention is necessary to ensure the protection of such rights (*S (Adult Patient) (Inherent Jurisdiction; Family Life), Re* [2002] EWHC 2278; [2003] 1 F.L.R. 292).

In cases where P is ready to be discharged from hospital and the choice is one of either institutional care or care at home, "the starting point has to be the question: why should [P] not return to the family home?": see *FP v GM and A Health Board* [2011] EWHC 2778 (COP) at para.25, per Hedley J. In this case, his Lordship said at para.20:

"Everybody accepts that Article 8 of the European Convention on Human Rights [(ECHR) which states that everyone has the right to respect for his private and family life] is engaged in this case, principally so far as [P] is concerned, but to some extent in relation to FP [with whom he lived at the family home]. The effect of that is that the court is not to deprive a person of family life unless such deprivation can be justified under Article 8(2) of the Convention. The European jurisprudence has rather established that Article 8(2) and a broad welfare test in relation to children are compatible, the one with the other, and making a child's rights decisive is also compatible with the observance of the Article 8(1) rights. I see no reason at all why that parity of reasoning is not implied into the Court of Protection which, in effect, is faced with very similar tasks."

In *K v LBX* [2012] EWCA 79, the Court of Appeal had to decide whether or not art.8 of the ECHR requires the court in determining issues under the Act to afford a priority to the placement of an incapacitated adult in their family or whether family life is simply one of "all the relevant circumstances" which the court must consider under s.4. It was held that when determining issues under the Act, a judge should first ascertain the best interests of an incapacitated adult by applying the checklist of factors in s.4, then ask whether the resulting conclusion amounted to a violation of the person's rights under art.8 and whether that violation was necessary and proportionate.

The procedural safeguards associated with art.8 include the right of the family or long term carers of P to be appropriately involved in the decision making process (*G v E* [2010] EWHC 621 (Fam) at paras 83 to 90).

If P is living in a care home and access to her is being demanded by a friend, carer of relative, the art.8 rights of both P and that person could be violated if there is an unacceptable delay in resolving the issue: see *Re MM* [2011] 1 F.L.R. 712, noted in the General Note to s.3.

Best interests and the marriage of a mentally incapacitated person

1–065   See the General Note to s.15 under the heading "Forced or arranged marriages".

Subsection (1)

1–066   Although the Government resisted an amendment to insert an anti-discrimination principle in s.1 for technical reasons and because it "would be inconceivable that giving someone less favourable treatment because of his disability, sex, age, race or sexual orientation could ever be considered to be in his best interests" (per the Parliamentary Under-Secretary of State (*Hansard*, HL Vol.668, col.1194)), the question of including some form of anti-discrimination or equal consideration provision in the Bill was a recurrent theme in the Parliamentary debates. The Government's response to this concern was to amend this provision at report stage in the House of Lords to "make sure that no one began a best interests determination with unjustified assumptions or prejudices. [The provision now] makes it clear that decision-making must start from a blank slate. People cannot say, 'She is very old so it is not necessary to give her this treatment' or, 'He has very severe physical disabilities, so it is obviously not in his best interests to have an operation'. Instead there must be a full and objective best interests assessment in every situation", per Baroness Andrews (*Hansard*, HL Vol.670, col.1320).

A PERSON'S BEST INTERESTS.   The best interests criterion does not apply to advance decisions: see the note on s.1(5).

MERELY. All relevant factors must be considered.

APPEARANCE. This covers "visible medical problems, disabilities, the colour of someone's skin, religious dress, and so on", per Baroness Andrews, above.

CONDITION. The condition, which might relate to either a mental or physical disorder, could be temporary.

UNJUSTIFIED ASSUMPTIONS. Some assumptions can be justified assumptions.

Subsection (2)

This provision requires the decision-maker to follow the decision making process set out in this section.　　　　　　　　　　　　　　　　　　　　　　　　　　　**1–067**

ALL THE RELEVANT CIRCUMSTANCES. See subs.(11). In *Re M* [2009] EWHC 2525 (Fam); [2010] 3 All E.R. 682 at para.36, Munby J. pointed out that material which falls outside the defined provisions of subs.(6) and (7) may still be a "relevant circumstance" within the meaning of this provision. For example, "the use of the words "engaged in caring" in s.4(7)(b), which would seem to connote only someone who is currently caring and to exclude someone whose caring has come to an end, does not mean that the views of a past carer are irrelevant. The effect of s.4(7)(b) may be to limit the decision-maker's duty to consult to current carers, but the views of a past carer if known are nonetheless part of the circumstances which have to be taken into account under s.4(2)".

None of the considerations set out in the indicative "checklist" contained in subs. (3)–(7) take precedence over any other consideration. However, some features or factors might be of "magnetic importance" in influencing or even determining the outcome (*Re M*, above). The Government's view was that "any prioritising of factors within the best interests checklist would have the effect of unnecessarily fettering the application of all factors in the checklist. We believe that the checklist as it is in the draft Bill is sufficiently flexible to allow the factors to be applied to any particular individual in their particular circumstances" (*The Government Response to the Scrutiny Committee's Report on the draft Mental Incapacity Bill*, (Cm.6121)).

"All the relevant circumstances" includes a consideration of P's rights under art.8 of the European Convention on Human Rights: see *K v LBX* [2012] EWCA 79 which is noted under the heading "Best interests and living arrangements", above.

Subsection (3)

If the person is likely to regain his or her capacity at some point in the future, the deci-　**1–068**
sion should be postponed until then if such a delay is consistent with the person's best interests. Paragraph 5.28 of the *Code of Practice* identifies "some factors which may indicate that a person may regain or develop capacity in the future". They

"are:

- the cause of the lack of capacity can be treated, either by medication or some other form of treatment or therapy
- the lack of capacity is likely to decrease in time (for example, where it is caused by the effects of medication or alcohol, or following a sudden shock)
- a person with learning disabilities may learn new skills or be subject to new experiences which increase their understanding and ability to make certain decisions
- the person may have a condition which causes capacity to come and go at various times (such as some forms of mental illness) so it may be possible to arrange for the decision to be made during a time when they do have capacity
- a person previously unable to communicate may learn a new form of communication."

Subsection (4)

1–069   This provision complements the principle contained in s.1(3). The decision-maker might wish to seek the help of others when complying with this obligation to involve the person to the fullest practicable extent in both the decision-making process and the consequences of the decision.

REASONABLY PRACTICABLE.   This is an objective requirement. "[T]here will always be cases where, for urgent or non-emergency reasons, it would be inappropriate and not in a person's best interests to delay acting, which is why the words 'reasonably practicable' are in clause 4(4). It is also unrealistic to expect all people affected by the Bill to be able to participate in decisions. The Bill applies to people in a coma, as well as to those who are seriously distressed or who need urgent care. While in some cases it would be possible to wait until the person is capable of making the decision themselves, in other cases it clearly would not", per the Parliamentary Under-Secretary of State, St. Comm. A, col.92.

In *A NHS Trust v K* [2012] EWHC 2922 (COP) at para.37, Holman J. held that it was not reasonably practicable to comply with this provision in a situation where P's relatives would have to be "economical with the truth" in order to ensure that P would undergo a potentially life-saving operation for an grave illness that she did not believe she suffered from. In this case, a declaration was made that "it can be lawful, and in her best interests, to sedate [P] to enable [the operation] to take place, and lawful to do so before [P] is told, after sedation but before anaesthesia, what is planned" (para.43).

IMPROVE HIS ABILITY TO PARTICIPATE.   Using communication support where this is appropriate.

Subsection (5)

1–070   This provision was inserted at the committee stage in the House of Lords in an attempt to respond to the concern of those who considered that decisions concerning life-sustaining treatment could lead to euthanasia by omission. Its purpose is to "make it absolutely clear that no person, whether doctor, attorney, deputy or court, can, when making a best interests determination, have the motive of causing death, regardless of what would be in his best interests" (Joint Committee on Human Rights, Fourth Report, Session 204–2005, Appendix 4, para.41). The Joint Committee expressed its concern that proving the motive of a person making a best interests determination will in practice "be extremely difficult" (para.4.42). This concern was shared by some members of the House of Lords who drew a distinction between intent, which can be objectively identified by examining the act, and motive, which is a state of mind which cannot be objectively verified: see, for example, Lord St John of Fawsley at *Hansard*, HL Vol.668, cols 1167–1170.

The Parliamentary Under-Secretary of State said that this provision "does not change the law as it stands at the moment. But it does put it beyond doubt. All that matters is that the decision-maker considers the range of treatment options available and the patient's objective best interests in respect of those treatments. [Subsection (5)] cannot be interpreted to mean that doctors are under an obligation to provide, or to continue to provide, life-sustaining treatment where that treatment is not in the best interests of the patients. That is the case even when the patient's death is foreseen" (*Hansard*, HC Vol.670, cols 1293–1294). Medical treatment that is judged to be in the best interests of P because, for example, it would provide effective pain control can therefore be given even if one of the adverse consequences of the treatment would be to shorten P's life. The *Code of Practice* states at para.5.31:

"All reasonable steps which are in the person's best interests should be taken to prolong their life. There will be a limited number of cases where treatment is futile, overly burdensome to the patient or where there is no prospect of recovery."

If there is any ambiguity in either an advance decision or a lasting power of attorney about a purported refusal of life-sustaining treatment, the treatment should be provided:

see s.11(8) and *HE v A Hospital NHS Trust* [2003] EWHC 1017 (Fam), noted under s.24.

The scope of this provision in the context of the sanctity of life doctrine is considered by J. Coggon in "Ignoring the moral and intellectual shape of the law after *Bland*: the unintended side effect of a sorry compromise", *Legal Studies* 27 (2007) 110–125.

LIFE-SUSTAINING TREATMENT.   Is defined in subs.(10).

Subsection (6)
The factors set out in this provision cannot determine the decision: they must be con- **1–071** sidered by the decision-maker and weighed against other factors. Whether information is "reasonably ascertainable" will depend upon its accessibility and the urgency of the situation. The *Code of Practice* states, at para.5.6, that the "checklist" contained in this provision "is only the starting point: in many cases, extra factors will need to be considered". No guidance is provided as to the weighting that should be given to the various factors. In the absence of a written record, it may be difficult to establish whether the decision-maker has complied with this provision.

In *Re G(TJ)* [2010] EWHC 3005 (COP) at para.37, Morgan J. said:

"The provisions of s.4(6)(b) and (c) extend beyond the actual wishes of P. They refer to the matters which P would be likely to consider if he were able to make the relevant decision. P would be likely to consider any relevant beliefs and values and all other relevant factors. Therefore, the matters which the court must consider under these paragraphs of s.4(6) involve the court in drawing up the balance sheet of factors which P would be likely to draw up if he were able to do so. Of course, the ultimate question for the court is: what is in the best interests of P? The court will necessarily draw up its own balance sheet of factors and that may differ from P's notional balance sheet. The court is not obliged to give effect to the decision which P would have arrived at, if he had capacity to make the decision for himself. Indeed, s.4(6) does not expressly require the court to reconstruct the decision which P, acting reasonably or otherwise, would have reached. Nonetheless, if the court considers the balance sheet of factors which would be likely to influence P, if P had capacity, the court is likely to be able to say what decision P would be likely to have reached. The court is not obliged to give effect to the decision which P, acting reasonably, would have made (the test of 'substituted judgment') but s.4(6) appears to require the court to consider what P would have decided (or, at least, the balance sheet of factors which P would be likely to have considered). My provisional view is that, in an appropriate case, a court could conclude that it is in the best interests of P for the court to give effect to the wishes which P would have formed on the relevant point, if he had capacity."

In *Ashan v University Hospitals Leicester NHS Trust* [2006] EWHC 2624 (QB), Judge Hegarty QC held that a patient who has been left in a persistent vegetative state following elective surgery should be cared for at home by her family rather than at a specialist private nursing and rehabilitation centre funded by the Trust. The patient's "immediate family are devout Muslims. They firmly believe that she should be cared for at home in a Muslim environment where they could pray together in her presence and ensure the proper observance of Muslim traditions and practices" (para.43). The judge concluded that "the wishes and beliefs of [the patient's] family and, so far they can properly be attributed to her, those which she herself would have held had she continued to have the capacity to do so, are factors which can and should be taken into account in determining whether it is reasonable for her to be cared for at home, even though no tangible benefits, whether physical or emotional, are likely to flow from a recognition of those wishes and beliefs in view of her profound mental incapacity and lack of awareness" (para.56). The judge said, at para.54, that this approach "appears to be entirely consistent" with this provision and subs.(7)(b).

Paragraph (a)

"Wishes and feelings" about a particular issue can be expressed orally, in writing, or through behaviour such as facial expressions. Bearing in mind that P's past or present wishes and feelings might not always be grounded in reality (e.g. a wish to be cared for by a spouse who is no longer alive) and that P might not have or had wishes and feelings about the matter at issue, P's wishes and feelings would normally carry substantial weight in the determination of that person's best interests, especially if they are well thought out, written down and signed: see the note on "Relevant written statement", below. The *Code of Practice*, at para.5.42, states:

"Section 4(6)(a) places special emphasis on written statements the person might have made before losing capacity. These could provide a lot of information about a person's wishes."

In *Re Treadwell* [2013] EWHC 2409 (COP), Senior Judge Lush said:

"In the context of someone's property and financial affairs, I can think of no written statement that is more relevant or more important than a will, and when testators make a will, they have a reasonable expectation that their wishes will be respected" (para.88).

The House of Lords Select Committee noted that:

"The general lack of awareness of the provisions of the Act has allowed prevailing professional practices to continue unchallenged, and allowed decision-making to be dominated by professionals, without the required input from families and carers about P's wishes and feelings" (para.107).

In *Re M* [2009] EWHC 2525 (Fam), Munby J. made the following observations at para.35:

"1. First, P's wishes and feelings will always be a significant factor to which the court must pay close regard: see *MM, Re; Local Authority X v MM (by the Official Solicitor) and KM* [2007] EWHC 2003 (Fam), [2009] 1 FLR 443, at paras [121]-[124].

2. Secondly, the weight to be attached to P's wishes and feelings will always be case-specific and fact-specific. In some cases, in some situations, they may carry much, even, on occasions, preponderant, weight. In other cases, in other situations, and even where the circumstances may have some superficial similarity, they may carry very little weight. One cannot, as it were, attribute any particular a priori weight or importance to P's wishes and feelings; it all depends, it must depend, upon the individual circumstances of the particular case. And even if one is dealing with a particular individual, the weight to be attached to their wishes and feelings must depend upon the particular context; in relation to one topic P's wishes and feelings may carry great weight whilst at the same time carrying much less weight in relation to another topic. Just as the test of incapacity under the 2005 Act is, as under the common law, 'issue specific', so in a similar way the weight to be attached to P's wishes and feelings will likewise be issue specific.

3. Thirdly, in considering the weight and importance to be attached to P's wishes and feelings the court must of course, and as required by s.4(2) of the 2005 Act, have regard to *all* the relevant circumstances. In this context the relevant circumstances will include, though I emphasise that they are by no means limited to, such matters as:

i. the degree of P's incapacity, for the nearer to the borderline the more weight must in principle be attached to P's wishes and feelings: *MM, Re; Local Authority X v MM (by the Official Solicitor) and KM* [2007] EWHC 2003 (Fam), [2009] 1 F.L.R. 443, at para [124];

ii. the strength and consistency of the views being expressed by P;

iii. the possible impact on P of knowledge that her wishes and feelings are not being" given effect to: see again *MM, Re; Local Authority X v MM (by the Official Solicitor) and KM* [2007] EWHC 2003 (Fam), [2009] 1 F.L.R. 443, at para [124];

iv. the extent to which P's wishes and feelings are, or are not, rational, sensible, responsible and pragmatically capable of sensible implementation in the particular circumstances; and

v. crucially, the extent to which P's wishes and feelings, if given effect to, can properly be accommodated within the court's overall assessment of what is in her best interests."

Also see the decision of Lewison J. in *Re P* [2009] EWHC 163 (Ch) as summarised by H.H. Judge Behrens in *NT v FS* [2013] EWHC 684 (COP) which is noted under s.18(1)(i).

Peter Jackson J. provided the following analysis of the weight to be given to P's wishes and feelings in *Wye Valley NHS Trust v Mr B* [2015] EWCOP 60:

"10. Where a patient lacks capacity it is . . . of great importance to give proper weight to his wishes and feelings and to his beliefs and values. [I]n this case, [the Trust] submitted that the views expressed by a person lacking capacity were in principle entitled to less weight than those of a person with capacity. This is in my view true only to the limited extent that the views of a capacitous person are by definition decisive in relation to any treatment that is being offered to him so that the question of best interests does not arise. However, once incapacity is established so that a best interests decision must be made, there is no theoretical limit to the weight or lack of weight that should be given to the person's wishes and feelings, beliefs and values. In some cases, the conclusion will be that little weight or no weight can be given; in others, very significant weight will be due.

11. This is not an academic issue, but a necessary protection for the rights of people with disabilities. As the Act and the European Convention make clear, a conclusion that a person lacks decision-making capacity is not an 'off-switch' for his rights and freedoms. To state the obvious, the wishes and feelings, beliefs and values of people with a mental disability are as important to them as they are to anyone else, and may even be more important. It would therefore be wrong in principle to apply any automatic discount to their point of view.

12. In this case, the Trust and the Official Solicitor consider that a person with full capacity could quite reasonably decide not to undergo the amputation that is being recommended to Mr B, having understood and given full thought to the risks and benefits involved. However, the effect of their submissions is that because Mr B himself cannot balance up these matters in a rational way, his wishes and feelings are outweighed by the presumption in favour of life. It is, I think, important to ensure that people with a disability are not—by the very fact of their disability—deprived of the range of reasonable outcomes that are available to others. For people with disabilities, the removal of such freedom of action as they have to control their own lives may be experienced as an even greater affront that it would be to others who are more fortunate."

Wye Valley was cited by Mostyn J. in *A Hospital Trust v CD* [2015] EWCOP 74 who said at para.28 that "it is vital that wishes and feelings are strictly confined to the best interests analysis and do not act subtly to undermine a capacity assessment. Where, as here, there is no doubt about incapacity then the wishes and feelings of the protected person cannot alter that fact even if they happen to align exactly with a rational, 'capacitous', decision".

In the context of a case where the court sanctioned the withdrawal of treatment to a patient who was in a Minimally Conscious State, Hayden J. said:

"[W]here the wishes, views and feelings of P can be ascertained with reasonable confidence, they are always to be afforded great respect. That said, they will rarely, if ever, be determinative of P's 'best interest's'. Respecting individual autonomy does not always require P's wishes to be afforded predominant weight. Sometimes it will be right to do so, sometimes it will not. The factors that fall to be considered in this treatment, how intrusive such treatment might be and crucially what the outcome of that treatment maybe for the individual patient. Into that complex matrix the appropriate weight to be given to P's wishes will vary. What must be stressed is the obligation imposed by statute to inquire into these matters and for the decision maker fully to consider them. Finally, I would observe that an assessment of P's wishes, views and attitudes are not to be confined within the narrow parameters of what P may have said. Strong feelings are often expressed non-verbally, sometimes in contradistinction to what is actually said. Evaluating the wider canvass may involve deriving an understanding of P's views from what he may have done in the past in circumstances which may cast light on the strength of his views on the contemplated treatment" (*M v Mrs N* [2015] EWCOP 76 at para.28).

In *M v Mrs N*, above, Hayden J., having considered the provisions in this Act relating to advance decisions to refuse treatment contained in ss.24 to 26, said at para.32:

"Perhaps the most significant impact of these provisions is that they illustrate that the presumption of life, predicated on what is often referred to as the 'sanctity of life' or the 'intrinsic value of life', can be rebutted (pursuant to statute) on the basis of a competent adult's cogently expressed wish. It follows, to my mind, by parity of analysis, that the importance of the wishes and feelings of an incapacitated adult, communicated to the court via family or friends but with similar cogency and authenticity, are to be afforded no less significance than those of the capacitous."

1–073   In *GC, Re* [2008] EWHC 3402 (Fam) at para.23, Hedley J. said:

"Where a person is in a position to express views, however limited their horizons, those are views which carry weight. The greater their appreciation of the horizons, the greater the weight those views must carry and they can, of course, by definition never be decisive."

If a person falls just below the borderline of capacity, "the more weight must in principle be attached to her wishes and feelings, because the greater the distress, the humiliation and indeed it may be the anger she is likely to feel the better she is able to appreciate that others are taking on her behalf decisions about matters which vitally affect her—matters, it may be, as here, of an intensely private and personal nature" (*Local Authority X v MM and KM* [2007] EWHC 2003 (Fam) at para.124, per Munby J.).

In *Newcastle upon Tyne Hospitals Foundation Trust v LM* [2014] EWHC 454 (COP), LM was a Jehovah's Witness who, when mentally capable, had refused a potentially life-saving blood transfusion at the hospital where she was being treated. On granting a declaration that it would be lawful for doctors treating LM to withhold blood transfusions, Peter Jackson J. said that if LM had not made a valid and applicable advance decision, he would have granted the declaration on the basis that to order a transfusion would not be in her best interests. His Lordship said at para.23:

"Applying s.4(6) in relation to the specific issue of blood transfusion, her wishes and feelings and her long-standing beliefs and values carried determinative weight."

In *R. (on the application of Wilkinson) v Broadmoor Special Hospital Authority* [2001] EWCA Civ 1545 at para.64, Hale L.J. said:

"The wishes and feelings of the incapacitated person will be an important element in determining what is, or is not, in his best interests. Where he is actively opposed to a course of action, the benefits which it holds for him will have to be carefully weighed against the disadvantages of going against his wishes, especially if force is required to do this."

There will clearly be occasions when, having undertaken the consultations set out in subs.(7), it would be difficult for the decision-maker to establish whether the person's past expression of wishes and feelings as reported by others represent that person's actual wishes and feelings expressed at that time. This situation could occur when the reporter has a vested interest in the decision. It is also important for the decision-maker to be alert to the possibility of the person's expression of his or her past or present wishes and feelings having been subject to the undue influence of another (see the note on s.1(3)).

The context within which the wishes and feelings were expressed should be carefully examined, e.g. a person might have expressed a desire not to live at a time when he or she was clinically depressed or was ignorant about the true prognosis of an illness or of the treatment that could be offered. The person might also have been misinformed about a crucial component of an issue that was being considered. It is also the case that a person's wishes and feelings can undergo dramatic shifts due to a change of personal perspective. One disabled witness to the Joint Committee wrote that she had had a settled wish that she wanted to die "that lasted about ten years, and during the first five of those years I made serious suicide attempts several times. I was saved only because my friends refused to accept my view that my life had no value, and made sure I received emergency treatment in hospital, which was given against my will. Then I was extremely angry with them; now I am eternally grateful. What has changed is not my medical condition, but my outlook on life. If advance decisions had been legally binding then, I have no doubt that I would have written one" (Alison Davis, Oral and written evidence, Ev 359).

RELEVANT WRITTEN STATEMENT.   The purpose of the words in parenthesis "is to clarify that if someone with capacity has written down their wishes and feelings in respect of a matter, including positive preferences, those must be explicitly taken into account in a best- interests determination", per the Parliamentary Under-Secretary of State (*Hansard*, HC Vol.670, col.1442). A decision-maker who does not follow a written statement should record the reasons for his decision (*Code of Practice*, para.5.43). In *RGB v Cwm Taf Health Board* [2013] EWHC B23 (COP), Moor J. said that a "clearly articulated" advance statement made by P which set out her strong wish not to have contact with her husband was "absolutely central" to the matter and that there "would have to be some extremely compelling reason to go against such clearly expressed wishes" (para.39).

In the context of medical treatment, where someone has sought to make a written advance decision that does not qualify under ss.24 and 25, but there is a reasonable belief that the written statement is an expression of the person's wishes, it must be taken into account under this provision. Also see the note on "advance statements" in the General Note to s.24.

Paragraph (b)

Beliefs and values may be evidenced by factors such as the person's cultural back-ground, religious and/or political affiliation, memberships of societies, subscriptions to charitable causes and known past behaviour and expressions of conviction: also see the Code of Practice at para.5.46.

1–074

Paragraph (c)

OTHER FACTORS.   Such as emotional bonds, family obligations or concern for others: see para.5.48 of the *Code of Practice*. They would also include any relevant professional advice received by the decision-maker and factors which were not present when P made an expression of his or her wishes regarding a particular matter.

1–075

If P has never had capacity, it will be extremely difficult to ascertain what "other factors" he or she would be likely to consider. In this situation, it is suggested that an assumption should be made that P would be "a normal decent person, acting in accordance with con-temporary standards of morality" (*C (Spinster and Mental Patient), Re* [1991] 3 All E.R. 866 at 870, per Hoffmann J.). In *Re G(TJ)* [2010] EWHC 3005 (COP), Morgan J. observed at para.35 that:

". . . the words 'interests' in the phrase 'best interests' is not confined to matters of self interest or, putting it another way, a court could conclude in an appropriate case that it is in the interests P for P to act altruistically."

His Lordship also said that "in most cases the court will be able to determine what decision it is likely that P would have made, if he had capacity. In such a case, in my judgment, P's balance sheet of factors and P's likely decision can be taken into account by the court. This involves an element of substituted judgment being taken into account, together with anything else which is relevant. However, it is absolutely clear that the ultimate test for the court is the test of best interests and not the test of substituted judgment. Nonetheless, the substituted judgment can be relevant and is not excluded from consideration. As Hoffmann L.J. said in the *Bland* case, the substituted judgment can be subsumed within the concept of best interests. That appeared to be the view of the Law Commission also" (para.55).

Subsection (7)

1–076   The purpose of the consultation is to seek information which would assist the decision-maker in making the best interests determination; it is not to ask the consultees what decision they would make. The decision-maker must consider consulting the persons listed. Such persons may be able to assist with providing information relevant to the issues set out in subs.(6). The consultations might also disclose the existence of an advance decision made by P. As the procedure set out in this section has to be followed in respect of every decision that is taken on behalf of an incapacitated person, it is likely that the decision-maker would conclude that it would not be "appropriate" to consult where trivial decisions have to be made.

The mental incapacity of consultees does not mean that their views should be discounted: see *An NHS Trust v Mr and Mrs H* [2012] EWHC B18, where Peter Jackson J. said at para.16:

> "Parents who lack capacity may still make telling points about welfare and it would be wrong to discount the weight to be attached to their views simply because of incapacity. It is the validity of the views that matter, not the capacity of the person that holds them."

Where consideration is being given to making a major decision relating to P, consultation must be undertaken at a time when the proposal is still formative, with sufficient reasons given for the proposal to allow for intelligent consideration and response (*R. (on the application of W) v London Borough of Croydon* [2011] EWHC 696 (Admin)).

The decision-maker must bear in mind P's right to confidentiality when undertaking the consultation(s). Disclosure in confidence can be made to someone who has a proper interest in having the information in question (*R. (on the application of S) v Plymouth City Council* [2002] EWCA Civ 388 at para.49) if such disclosure is the best interests of P. It is likely that appropriate consultees would have such an interest.

If there is no-one apart from a paid carer in the categories set out in this provision with whom it would be appropriate to consult about P's best interests, an independent mental capacity advocate must be consulted in the situations set out in ss.37–39.

A decision-maker must be able to justify a decision that it was not "practicable and appropriate" to consult someone identified in this provision. It is important not to equate "practicable" with "possible" (*Owen v Crown House Engineering* [1973] 3 All E.R. 618, 622 NIRC). In *Dedman v British Building and Engineering Appliances Ltd* [1974] 1 W.L.R. 171 at 179, CA, Scarman L.J. said:

> "The word 'practicable' is an ordinary English word of great flexibility: it takes its meaning from its context. But, whenever used, it is a call for the exercise of common sense, a warning that sound judgment will be impossible without compromise. Sometimes the context contemplates a situation rarely to be achieved though much to be desired: the word then indicates one must be satisfied with less than perfection . . . [S]ometimes . . . what the context requires may have been possible, but may not for some reason have been 'practicable'. Whatever its context, the quality of the word is that there are circumstances in which we must be content with less than 100 per cent: and it calls for judgment to determine how much less."

Given this interpretation, although reasonable steps should be taken in an attempt to make contact with the persons named in this provision, the decision-maker would not be required either to act as a private detective in order to discover a person's whereabouts or to use a disproportionate amount of time in the attempt.

If it is both practicable and appropriate to consult then in the absence of some other compelling reason against consultation, the decision to place on the patient's clinical record a notice to the effect that cardio-pulmonary resuscitation should not be attempted (DNACPR) would be procedurally flawed as it would not meet the requirements of this provision and would accordingly not be in accordance with the law for the purposes of art.8 of the European Convention on Human Rights (*Winspear v City Hospitals Sunderland NHS Foundation Trust* [2015] EWHC 3250 (QB) at para.47).

Whether it is "appropriate" to undertake the consultation will depend upon a number of factors including the urgency and nature of the decision, and the relationship that the potential consultee has had with P. For example, it is unlikely that it would be "appropriate" to consult with a person who has a history of ill-treating or neglecting P, or to consult at all if the decision to be taken is trivial.

In *Allen, Re* July 21, 2009, Senior Judge Lush said:

> "[The arguments of the objector] raise interesting issues regarding the extent to which any attorney should be reasonably be expected to consult with someone who, in all reality, will treat every single issue upon which he is likely to be consulted as a bone of contention or stumbling-block. In such circumstances, the process of consultation would become both burdensome and futile.
>
> The first line of section 4(7) provides that any best interests decision-maker 'must take into account, if it is practicable and appropriate to consult them, the views of' various categories of individuals. In my judgment, where any attempt at consultation will inevitably be unduly onerous, futile, or serve no useful purpose, it cannot be in P's best interests, and it would be neither practicable nor appropriate to embark on that process in the first place."

The weight to be given to the views expressed by the consultees will depend on a number of factors including the extent of their knowledge of P, the amount of contact that they have with P, whether they have a vested interest in the decision to be taken and their relationship with P.

It should be noted that studies have shown that relatives' perception of the patient's likely views often differ substantially from the patient's own wishes: see, for example, A.B. Seckler et al, "Substituted judgment: how accurate are proxy predictions?"(1991) 115(9) Ann. Intern. Med. 92–8. Studies on social comparison processes suggest that "we are not particularly good at assessing other people's opinions, abilities, or future behaviour" and that the "dominant view is that we tend to be egocentric", i.e. people judge others in the same way that they judge themselves (N. Harvey et al., "Making Decisions for other People: The Problem of Judging Acceptable Levels of Risk" (Jan, 2006) 7(1) *Forum: Qualitative Social Research* (On-line Journal) Art.26, para.21). Also see R. Dresser, 'Missing Persons: Legal Perceptions of Incompetent Patients' (1994) 46 *Rutgers Law Review* 609.)

Paragraph (b)

Carers UK in its evidence to the Joint Committee expressed concern that this provision gives "equal decision-making weight to both professionals and to carers" (Oral and written evidence, Ev 338). It should be noted in this context that there have been occasions when the sustained opposition of family carers to the firmly held views of professionals about the care needs of an incapacitated person has been proved to have been correct: see, for example, the "Report on an Investigation into Complaint No.02/C/17068 against Bolton Metropolitan Borough Council" (November 2004).

1–077

INTERESTED IN HIS WELFARE. The decision-maker should consider the nature of the interest before consulting persons in this category. The Parliamentary Under-Secretary of State for Constitutional Affairs said that an advocate could fall into this category (St. Comm. A, col.100). A donee of a lasting power of attorney executed by P would clearly be interested in P's welfare.

ANYONE ENGAGED IN CARING FOR THE PERSON. It is suggested that the approach that should be adopted when determining whether a person qualifies as a carer under this provision should mirror the approach that the Court of Appeal took in *D (Mental patient: habeas corpus), Re* [2000] 2 F.L.R. 848 when explaining the meaning of the term "cared for" in s.26(4) of the Mental Health Act 1983. Having described the phrase as containing clear and everyday words, the court held that in order to justify a finding that a relative is caring for the patient, the services provided must be more than minimal and they need not have been provided in the long term. The court was asked to consider the situation of a relative who assisted the patient in managing his financial affairs, checked whether he was eating appropriately and took away his soiled clothing and bed clothes. In finding that the relative was caring for the patient, the court said that there "was more than sufficient evidence to pass the 'cared for' test, wherever one sets the threshold of services amounting to 'cared for'. In other words, the services were not merely minimal. They were services which were substantial and sustained". It is clear from this case that a person may be engaged in caring for P even if they do not share the same residence.

Paragraph (d)

1–078   When an experienced professional deputy has gone through the checklist of factors in this section and has considered all the relevant circumstances and has concluded a particular course of action is in P's best interests, the court should be reluctant to interfere with his decision unless it is plainly wrong (*David Ross v A* [2015] EWCOP 46 at para.40).

Subsection (8)

1–079   This applies the duties contained in this section to the following situations: (1) any decision made by a donee acting under a lasting power of attorney; and (2) where the person concerned does not in fact lack capacity but where the decision-maker reasonably believes the person lacks capacity.

Subsection (9)

1–080   If the decision-maker, having satisfied the requirements of subss.(1)–(7) reasonably believes that what has been done or decided is in the best interests of the P, he or she will have complied with this section. Reasonable belief is an objective test and the decision-maker will therefore need to identify objective reasons to support the contention that he or she believed that the decision was in the P's best interests.

Subsection (10)

1–081   The definition of life sustaining treatment, which applies throughout this Act (s.64(1)), was subject to a Government amendment to delete the word "his" before "life" because "in the case of a pregnant woman we want to ensure that the life of the baby, not only the life of the mother, must be considered", per the Parliamentary Under-Secretary of State (*Hansard*, HL Vol.668, col.1184).

The nature of life sustaining treatment is considered in the *Code of Practice* at para.5.30:

> "Whether a treatment is 'life-sustaining' depends not only on the type of treatment, but also on the particular circumstances in which it may be prescribed. For example, in some situations giving antibiotics may be life-sustaining, whereas in other circumstances antibiotics are used to treat a non-life-threatening condition. It is up to the doctor or healthcare professional providing treatment to assess whether the treatment is life-sustaining in each particular situation."

Subsection (11)

This provision recognises that the decision-maker might not be aware of all of the cir- **1–082**
cumstances of P, or of the decision in question.

[Restriction on deprivation of liberty

4A.—(1) This Act does not authorise any person ("D") to deprive any other **1–083**
person ("P") of his liberty.

(2) But that is subject to—

(a) the following provisions of this section, and

(b) section 4B.

(3) D may deprive P of his liberty if, by doing so, D is giving effect to a relevant
decision of the court.

(4) A relevant decision of the court is a decision made by an order under section
16(2)(a) in relation to a matter concerning P's personal welfare.

(5) D may deprive P of his liberty if the deprivation is authorised by Schedule
A1 (hospital and care home residents: deprivation of liberty).]

AMENDMENT

This section was inserted by the Mental Health Act 2007 s.50(2). **1–084**

DEFINITIONS

"deprivation of liberty": s.64(5), (6). **1–085**
"the court": s.64(1).

GENERAL NOTE

This section prohibits the deprivation of the liberty of a person under the Act other **1–086**
than in the following situations: first, where the court has made an order under s.16(2)(a);
second, where it is authorised for life-sustaining or other emergency treatment (s.4B); and,
third where the authorisation procedure set out in Sch.A1 is used. It follows that a deprivation of liberty cannot take place on the authority of s.5, or through the actions of the donee
of an LPA or a court appointed deputy. The detaining authority can be either a public or a
private body (s.65(6)). In *A Local Authority v PB* [2011] EWHC 2675 (COP), Charles J.
said at para.64(v):

"[T]he approach of s.4A(3) and (4) which refer to 'giving effect to an order made under
s.16(2)(a)' recognises that the crucial issue is the best interests issue and not the question
whether there is, or is not, a deprivation of liberty."

As an authorisation under Sch.A1 can only apply to the detention of a person in a
hospital or a care home, an application must be made to the Court of Protection if detention takes place elsewhere. Detention under the Act does not entitle the institution to do
anything other than detain the patient or resident for the purposes of the order or authorisation. An account of the deprivation of liberty procedure set out in Sch.A1 is contained
in Part 2. The procedure authorises detention, but does not require it.

Deprivations of liberty in emergency situations

If an emergency occurs which requires the immediate use of a level of restraint which **1–087**
constitutes a deprivation of P's liberty, it is submitted that the common law doctrine of
necessity will provide a defence to those exercising the restraint if:

(i) no other statutory power is available to authorise the deprivation (e.g. s.5(2) or (4)
of the Mental Health Act 1983);

(ii) it was not practicable to seek the assistance of the Court of Protection prior to the
emergency occurring;

(iii) the restraint is required to prevent serious harm to P; and

(iv)   authority to authorise the deprivation of liberty is sought at the earliest opportunity if the deprivation continues after the immediate emergency has been resolved.

[Deprivation of liberty necessary for life-sustaining treatment etc

1–088   **4B.**—(1) If the following conditions are met, D is authorised to deprive P of his liberty while a decision as respects any relevant issue is sought from the court.

(2) The first condition is that there is a question about whether D is authorised to deprive P of his liberty under section 4A.

(3) The second condition is that the deprivation of liberty—

(a)   is wholly or partly for the purpose of—

(i)   giving P life-sustaining treatment, or

(ii)   doing any vital act, or

(b)   consists wholly or partly of—

(i)   giving P life-sustaining treatment, or

(ii)   doing any vital act.

(4) The third condition is that the deprivation of liberty is necessary in order to—

(a)   give the life-sustaining treatment, or

(b)   do the vital act.

(5) A vital act is any act which the person doing it reasonably believes to be necessary to prevent a serious deterioration in P's condition.]

AMENDMENT

1–089   This section was inserted by the Mental Health Act 2007 s.50(2).

DEFINITIONS

1–090   "deprivation of liberty": s.64(5), (6).

"the court": s.64(1).

"life-sustaining treatment": ss.4(1), 64(1).

GENERAL NOTE

1–091   This section enables a person to be deprived of his liberty for the purpose of providing him with emergency medical treatment for either a physical or mental disorder while a decision as respects "any relevant issue" is sought from the court. In order for the deprivation to be lawful, the conditions set out in subss.(2) to (4) must be satisfied.

If reliance is put on this section to justify a deprivation of liberty of P, the relevant decision maker must consider it and the tests that it contains at that time (*A County Council v MB* [2010] EWHC 2508 (COP)).

This section cannot be invoked if P is ineligible within the meaning of Sch.1A, i.e. he comes within a category where the Mental Health Act 1983 must be used. This is because the court cannot make an order under s.16(2)(a) if P is ineligible (s.16A).

Acts in connection with care or treatment

1–092   **5.**—(1) If a person ("D") does an act in connection with the care or treatment of another person ("P"), the act is one to which this section applies if—

(a)   before doing the act, D takes reasonable steps to establish whether P lacks capacity in relation to the matter in question, and

(b)   when doing the act, D reasonably believes—

(i)   that P lacks capacity in relation to the matter, and

(ii)   that it will be in P's best interests for the act to be done.

(2) D does not incur any liability in relation to the act that he would not have incurred if P—

(a) had had capacity to consent in relation to the matter, and

(b) had consented to D's doing the act.

(3) Nothing in this section excludes a person's civil liability for loss or damage, or his criminal liability, resulting from his negligence in doing the act.

(4) Nothing in this section affects the operation of sections 24 to 26 (advance decisions to refuse treatment).

GENERAL NOTE

The aim of this section is to clarify aspects of the common law doctrine of necessity   **1–093** which enable decisions to be taken for people who lack capacity. It does not create any new powers of intervention or duties to act, but offers protection against civil and criminal liability for certain acts done in connection with the care or treatment of P and which would normally require that persons consent. In particular, this section does not authorise a local authority to remove P from his or her home against the wishes of P's family. As a large number of people are unlikely to have made provision for their incapacity through creating lasting powers of attorney, the "operational reality of [this section] is likely to be crucial" (Joint Committee, para.103). In *Re NRA* [2015] EWCOP 76, Charles J. said at para.40 that the underlying purpose of this section "shows that Parliament intended that when possible welfare issues and decisions should be left to those who, on a day to day basis, are caring for and supporting P". In their evidence to the House of Lords Select Committee, Professor Phil Fennell and Dr Lucy Series said that the general defence contained in this section provides "tremendous discretionary power" which was "not subject to any routine monitoring" (para.98).

"Section 5 acts", which could be performed by a range of professional and lay people, are not limited to "day to day" or emergency situations, as they could include, for example, performing a serious planned operation on P. Without the protection of this section, such acts could amount to civil wrongs, such as trespass, or crimes, such as assault. The authority for undertaking "section 5 acts" is to be found in the common law doctrine of necessity: see *JO v GO* [2013] EWHC 3932 (COP) where Sir James Munby P. said at para.18:

> "Put shortly, what the doctrine of necessity requires is a decision taken by a relative or carer which is reasonable, arrived at in good faith and taken in the best interests of the assisted person. There is, in my judgment, nothing in the 2005 Act to displace this approach. Sections 4 and 5, after all, pre-suppose that such actions are not unlawful per se; they merely, though very importantly, elaborate what must be done and provide, if certain conditions are satisfied, a statutory defence against liability".

At para.20, the President said:

> "Of course, the doctrine of necessity is not a licence to be irresponsible. It will not protect someone who is an officious busybody. And it will not apply where there is bad faith or where what is done is unreasonable or not in the best interests of the assisted person."

The requirement of reasonableness was emphasised by the Court of Appeal in *ZH v Metropolitan Police Commissioner* [2013] EWCA Civ 69 at para.49, where Lord Dyson MR said that the Act "does not impose impossible demands on those who do acts in connection with the care or treatment of others. It requires no more than what is reasonable, practicable and appropriate. What that entails depends on all the circumstances of the case. . . . [W]hat is reasonable, practicable and appropriate where there is time to reflect and take measured action may be quite different in an emergency or what is reasonably believed to be an emergency".

Liability for negligent acts is unaffected (subs.(3)). Subject to subs.(4) and the limitations set out in s.6, this section enables steps to be taken on behalf of P by family members, carers, and health and care professionals without the need for any formal authority or involvement of the Court of Protection as long as the steps are in the P's best interests.

Some decisions cannot be made without the involvement of an independent mental capacity advocate (see s.35 et seq.) and certain medical procedures cannot be provided without the authority of the court (see below). Section 27 lists those decisions that can never be made on behalf of a person who lacks capacity.

The person who undertakes the s.5 act (D) can only act on a reasonable belief that P lacks capacity, and having concluded that there are reasonable grounds for believing that the decision or act is in P's best interests. The steps taken to establish the reasonableness of the belief and the reasonableness of the grounds will reflect the status of the decision-maker and the significance of the decision being taken: a healthcare professional would be expected to adopt a more rigorous approach than a lay carer, and a routine care intervention would require less investigation than a serious medical decision. It will also be the case that the urgency of the action required, for example, the provision of emergency medical treatment, will dictate the extent of the steps that can be taken.

The *Code of Practice*, at para.4.44, states that carers "(whether family carers or other carers) and care workers do not have to be experts in assessing capacity". It follows that professionals who act as assessors should be held to a higher standard than non-professionals: see Mary Donnelly, "Capacity assessment under the Mental Capacity Act 2005: Delivering on the functional approach?", (2009) *Legal Studies* 29:3, 464–491 at 471. In practice, formal assessments of capacity will rarely be required with most day to day decisions, but D must be able to identify objective reasons to explain why he or she believes P lacks capacity. A formal capacity assessment should be undertaken where a decision is either contentious, significant or is likely to be challenged. Professional assistance should be sought by a lay carer in these circumstances. The starting point is a presumption of capacity (s.1(2)). The other relevant principles set out in s.1 should also be applied.

This section cannot be used to justify steps amounting to a deprivation of liberty such as circumventing the provisions of the Mental Health Act 1983 by removing a person from their home in order for a mental health assessment to be undertaken at a hospital. In *R. (on the application of Sessay) v South London and Maudsley NHS Foundation Trust* [2011] EWHC 2617 (QB), the Divisional Court endorsed the following declaration which had been agreed by the parties:

> "Sections 135 and 136 of the Mental Health Act 1983 are the exclusive powers available to police officers to remove persons who appear to be mentally disordered to a place of safety. Sections 5 and 6 of the Mental Capacity Act 2005 do not confer on police officers authority to remove persons to hospital or other places of safety for the purposes set out in sections 135 and 136 of the Mental Health Act 1983."

The protection provided by this section will apply in any setting where P is being cared for or where services are being provided to him or her, e.g. at P's home, a care home, a day centre or a hospital. As one person does not have power to act to the exclusion of others, it is likely that a number of persons will be acting under the powers contained in this section during the course of a day. It is surely unrealistic to expect lay carers, the majority of whom are unlikely to have received any training on the Act, to undertake a capacity assessment and a best interests determination in respect of the decisions that they need to make in respect of P. These expectations are confirmed by the *Code of Practice* at paras 6.27 and 6.28.

The established common law position that no-one has the power to make decisions on behalf of a mentally incapacitated person is unchanged (*F v West Berkshire HA* [1989] 2 All E.R. 545, HL) as this section does not confer power on anyone to make substitute decisions on behalf of the person or to give substitute consent. Despite the clarity of the legal position, there appears to be a continuing belief that a close relative or "next of kin" of P has a legal right to make decisions on his or her behalf: see, for example, *Re MM (Mental Capacity: Contact)* [2011] 1 F.L.R. 712.

If P is subject to guardianship under the Mental Health Act 1983, D cannot make a decision, including a decision about where P should reside, which conflicts with that of the guardian (ibid. s.8(1)).

A decision made by either a donee under a lasting power of attorney or a deputy appointed by the court will take priority over any action that might be taken under this section (s.6(6)). This means that a donee or a deputy can refuse as well as consent to medical treatment relating to P as long as such decisions are within the scope of their authority.

The point at which it would be unwise to rely on the protection provided by this section, and when an application should be made to the Court of Protection for an order or to have a deputy appointed is unclear. Certain categories of medical treatment must be referred to the court for a decision: see the note on s.15(1)(c). In *G v E* [2010] EWHC 2512 (COP) at para.57, Baker J. said:

"The Act and Code [of Practice] are . . . constructed on the basis that the vast majority of decisions concerning incapacitated adults are taken informally and collaboratively by individuals or groups of people consulting and working together. It is emphatically not part of the scheme underpinning the Act that there should be one individual who as a matter of course is given a special legal status to make decisions about incapacitated persons. Experience has shown that working together is the best policy to ensure that incapacitated adults . . . receive the highest quality of care. . . . Where there is disagreement about the appropriate care and treatment, (which cannot be resolved by the methods suggested in Chapter 15 [of the Code]) or the issue is a matter of particular gravity or difficulty, the Act and Code provide that the issue should usually be determined by the court. The complexity and/or seriousness of such issues are likely to require a forensic process and formal adjudication by an experienced tribunal."

This provision does not provide any procedural safeguards aimed at preventing the inappropriate use of "section 5 acts". If there is concern about the manner in which P is being cared for, consideration could be given to invoking the multi-agency adult protection procedure. In extreme cases, the offence of ill-treatment or wilful neglect might be committed under s.44. Where allegations are made about the abuse of a mentally incapacitated adult in civil cases, the burden of proving each allegation is upon the maker, and the requisite standard of proof is the balance of probability (*Ealing LBC v KS* [2008] EWHC 636 (Fam) at para.49).

Tenancy agreements

Guidance on "Applications to the Court of Protection in relation to tenancy agreements" **1–094** is reproduced at Appendix A.

Subsection (1)

Paragraph (a) emphasises the Act's "ethos of empowerment and personal autonomy, **1–095** and the key obligation of all carers to support and maximise the decision-making capacity of the person who lacks capacity", per the Parliamentary Under-Secretary of State for Constitutional Affairs, St. Comm. A, col.107.

The *Code of Practice*, at para.6.5, states that actions that might be covered by this section include:

"Personal care

- helping with washing, dressing or personal hygiene
- helping with eating and drinking
- helping with communication
- helping with mobility (moving around)
- helping someone take part in education, social or leisure activities
- going into a person's home to drop off shopping or to see if they are alright
- doing the shopping or buying necessary goods with the person's money
- arranging household services (for example, arranging repairs or maintenance for gas and electricity supplies)
- providing services that help around the home (such as homecare or meals on wheels)

- undertaking actions related to community care services (for example, day care, residential accommodation or nursing care). . .
- helping someone to move home (including moving property and clearing the former home).

Healthcare and treatment

- carrying out diagnostic examinations and tests (to identify illness, condition or other problem)
- providing professional medical, dental and similar treatment
- giving medication
- taking someone to hospital for assessment or treatment
- providing nursing care (whether in hospital or in the community)
- carrying out any other necessary medical procedures (for example, taking a blood sample) or therapies (for example, physiotherapy or chiropody)
- providing care in an emergency."

A healthcare professional is not authorised under this section to provide medical treatment to P if he or she is aware that the treatment in question is specified in a valid and applicable advance decision that has been made by P (subs.(4)).

A PERSON.   Including a person who instructs another to act. The Act does not specify who has the authority to take a particular decision or to undertake a particular act.

CARE.   This term is not defined. Payment for something that is arranged for P's care or treatment is provided for by s.8.

TREATMENT.   Includes a diagnostic or other procedure (s.64(1)).

LACKS CAPACITY. IN RELATION TO THE PARTICULAR DECISION THAT NEEDS TO BE MADE.

BEST INTERESTS.   The checklist contained in s.4 must be followed, and the least restrictive principle contained in s.1(6) should be considered. The amount of time devoted to ascertaining the best interests of P will, in non-urgent cases, depend upon the significance of the decision under consideration.

Subsection (3)

1–096   Consent is not a defence to a claim in the tort of negligence and there are some criminal offences, such as manslaughter, which depend on a finding of negligence as defined in civil law. This provision therefore makes it clear that liability for negligence is unaffected by this section.

Subsection (4)

1–097   A valid and applicable advance decision relating to the person's healthcare is unaffected by this section which gives no protection from liability if the decision is not followed.

Section 5 acts: limitations

1–098   **6.**—(1) If D does an act that is intended to restrain P, it is not an act to which section 5 applies unless two further conditions are satisfied.

(2) The first condition is that D reasonably believes that it is necessary to do the act in order to prevent harm to P.

(3) The second is that the act is a proportionate response to—

(a) the likelihood of P's suffering harm, and

(b) the seriousness of that harm.

(4) For the purposes of this section D restrains P if he—

    (a)   uses, or threatens to use, force to secure the doing of an act which P resists, or

    (b)   restricts P's liberty of movement, whether or not P resists.

(5) [*Repealed by the Mental Health Act 2007 s.50(4)(a)*]

(6) Section 5 does not authorise a person to do an act which conflicts with a decision made, within the scope of his authority and in accordance with this Part, by—

    (a)   a donee of a lasting power of attorney granted by P, or

    (b)   a deputy appointed for P by the court.

(7) But nothing in subsection (6) stops a person—

    (a)   providing life-sustaining treatment, or

    (b)   doing any act which he reasonably believes to be necessary to prevent a serious deterioration in P's condition,

while a decision as respects any relevant issue is sought from the court.

DEFINITIONS

1–099

"the Human Rights Convention": s.64(1)
"public authority": s.64(1)
"lasting power of attorney": s.64(1)
"deputy": s.64(1)
"the court": s.64(1)
"life-sustaining treatment": ss.4(10), 64(1)

GENERAL NOTE

1–100

This section sets two important limitations to the protection from liability given to "section 5 acts".

Restraint

1–101

The first (subss.(1) to (4)) relates to restraint, which is defined in subs.(4). Restraint can only be used when: (1) the person using it reasonably believes that it is necessary to prevent harm to P and (2) its use is proportionate both to the likelihood and seriousness of the harm. The restraint, which can include restraint on those who are the subject of a deprivation of liberty authorisation granted under Sch.A1, must also be in P's best interests (s.1(5)). Restraint that does not meet these conditions is not protected by s.5. The practical result of this is that only the minimum amount of restraint for the shortest duration should be used to prevent the harm occurring: see the note on "proportionate response" in subs.(3). This reflects the "least restrictive option" principle in s.1(6).

    This section, together with s.5, provides authority for taking P to hospital and providing P with treatment at the hospital, even if taking P to the hospital and the subsequent treatment involves restricting P's liberty (subs.(4)(b)). The use of restraint which results in P being deprived of his or her liberty would constitute a violation of P's rights under art. 5 of the European Convention of Human Rights: see *R. (on the application of Sessay) v South London and Maudsley NHS Foundation Trust* [2011] EWHC 2617 (QB), noted under s.5. A deprivation of P's liberty can only be authorised under the Act in the situations set out in s.4A. If an emergency occurs which requires the immediate use of a level of restraint which constitutes a deprivation of P's liberty, see the note on *Deprivations of Liberty in emergency situations* in s.4A. The nature of a "deprivation of liberty" is considered in Part 2.

    Although this provision does not provide for the restraint of P in order to prevent harm to others, such action is authorised under common law powers to prevent a breach of the peace. In *Albert v Lavin* [1981] 3 All E.R 878, the House of Lords confirmed that under common law "every citizen in whose presence a breach of the peace is being, or reasonably appears to be about to be, committed has the right to take reasonable steps to make the person who is breaking or threatening to break the peace refrain from doing so; and those reasonable steps in appropriate cases will include detaining him against his will" (per Lord Diplock at 880). A breach, which can take place in public or on private property, occurs when "harm is actually done or is likely to be done to a person or in his presence to his property or a person is in fear of being so harmed through an assault, an affray, a riot, an unlawful assembly or other disturbance" (*R. v Howell* [1981] 3 All E.R. 383 at 389, per Watkins L.J.). Restraining P from causing harm to others could be justified under this provision if it was considered that P's actions would provoke a reaction that would cause harm to P. If there is concern about the manner in which a donee of a lasting power of attorney or a court appointed deputy is restraining P, a complaint may be made to the Public Guardian (s.58(1)(h)).

In *AJ v A Local Authority* [2015] EWCOP 5, Baker J. agreed with the following submission made by counsel for the Official Solicitor at para.25:

"[I]n any case in which physical restraint is used in the care of an incapacitated adult, any physical intervention, whether considered to amount to 'restraint' or not, should be recorded in the care plan maintained by the service provider and monitored by the statutory body responsible for commissioning the person's care. Furthermore, precise details of all physical interventions should be ascertained and documented as part of the Deprivation of Liberty Safeguards process or indeed any best interest assessment from direct discussion with care staff implementing the interventions."

Decisions by donees or deputies

1–102 The second limitation to the protection from liability given to "section 5 acts" is that under subss.(6) and (7) a valid decision by a donee or a deputy takes priority over any action which might be taken under s.5. There is an important proviso to this limitation. If there is a dispute as to whether a decision of a donee or deputy either prevents life-sustaining treatment being given to P or might cause a serious deterioration of Ps condition, action can be taken to sustain life or prevent serious deterioration while the dispute is referred to the Court of Protection.

Subsection (1)

1–103 RESTRAIN. Acts of restraint could include steadying P's shaking arm to enable an injection to be given safely, using reasonable force to take P to hospital to receive necessary treatment, using barriers to prevent P from falling out of bed, preventing P from running into the road, putting a car seatbelt on P, telling P that he will be restrained if he persists in a particular activity, securing the external doors of a care home to prevent P from leaving, assisting P to undress, and preventing P from harming himself. Sedating P in order to control behaviour also constitutes restraint. However, a disproportionate use of sedation, for example, the inappropriate use of neuroleptic drugs for people with dementia, could constitute a deprivation of P's liberty: see further, Geraldine Boyle, *Controlling behaviour using neuroleptioc drugs: the role of the Mental Capacity Act 2005 in protecting the liberty of people with dementia,* Disability and Society 23, no.7: 759–771. It is a matter of concern that the research by Dr I.C.H. Clare and her colleagues found that the "use of restraint was also almost invariably viewed as a deprivation of liberty" (*Understanding the interface between the Mental Capacity Act's Deprivation of Liberty Safeguards (MCA-DOLS) and the Mental Health Act (MHA)*, University of Cambridge, 2013, para.3.7.19).

In *YB v BCC* [2010] EWHC 3355 (COP) at para.39, Mostyn J. said:

"To suggest that taking steps to prevent [P] attacking others amounts to 'restraint' signifying confinement is untenable."

Restrictions on P's liberty are not confined to emergency situations as P could be subjected to restrictions of his or her liberty for an indefinite period without such restrictions constituting a deprivation of his or her liberty. The Government did not adopt the recommendation of the Joint Committee on Human Rights that the use or threat of force or other restrictions of liberty of movement be expressly confined to emergency situations for the following reason:

"Sometimes it is not always in a person's best interests for matters to be left until it is an urgent situation. For example, restraint may be necessary in order to undertake a diagnostic procedure. If such a procedure is left until there is an urgent need or an emergency, then the resulting harm to the person may be worse. If a person needs treatment for a bad tooth, it will generally be in that person's best interests to be restrained, and to have the tooth treated, rather than to wait until it is so bad as to count as an emergency requiring intervention" (Letter from the Parliamentary-Under Secretary of State to the Chair of the Committee, December 16, 2004, Annex, para.4).

The Department of Health has published "Positive and Proactive Care: reducing the need for restrictive interventions" (2014) which "provides guidance on the delivery of services together with key actions that will ensure that people's quality of life is enhanced and that their needs are better met, which will reduce the need for restrictive interventions and promote recovery" (para.5).

The use of restraint to ensure that mentally incapacitated patients are provided with artificial nutrition and hydration is considered by G.M. Sayers and S.M. Gabe in "Restraint in order to feed: justifying a lawful policy for the UK", *European Journal of Health Law* 14 (2007) 3–20.

Subsection (2)

REASONABLY BELIEVES. D must be able to identify objective reasons to justify the **1–104** necessity of acting to prevent P from suffering harm.

HARM. This term, which is not defined, is not confined to physical harm. It could include preventing P from causing financial harm to him or her self by, for example, restraining P from ripping up bank notes or from spending money recklessly. It could also include the prevention of psychological harm by, for example, restraining P from acting in a manner which could result in him or her suffering verbal abuse from members of the public.

The *Code of Practice*, at para.6.45, provides the following examples of harmful situations:

"• a person with learning disabilities might run into a busy road without warning, if they do not understand the dangers of cars
• a person with dementia may wander away from home and get lost, if they cannot remember where they live
• a person with manic depression might engage in excessive spending during a manic phase, causing them to get into debt
• a person may also be at risk of harm if they behave in a way that encourages others to assault or exploit them (for example, by behaving in a dangerously provocative way)."

Subsection (3)

PROPORTIONATE RESPONSE. In terms of both the degree and duration of the restraint. It **1–105** follows that (a) the minimum amount of restraint should be used in order to prevent harm occurring, and (b) the level of restraint used should diminish as the risk of harm diminishes. The *Code of Practice* provides the following example at para.6.47:

"[A] carer may need to hold a person's arm while they cross the road, if the person does not understand the dangers of roads. But it would not be a proportionate response to stop the person going outdoors at all. It may be appropriate to have a secure lock on a door that faces a busy road, but it would not be a proportionate response to lock someone in a bedroom all the time to prevent them from attempting to cross the road."

In the context of restraint used in the provision of medical treatment, the following pre-Act decisions remain relevant:

1. The extent of force or compulsion that may become necessary in ensuring that medical treatment is provided to a mentally incapacitated patient can only be judged in each individual case and by health professionals. It may become for them a balance between continuing treatment that is forcibly opposed and deciding not to continue with it (*MB (Medical Treatment), Re* [1997] 2 F.L.R. 426 CA, at 439).

2. It is lawful "to overcome non-co-operation of a resisting patient by sedation and a moderate and reasonable use of restraint" in order to provide treatment if such treatment "is in the patient's best interests. The lawfulness of such restraint has to be carefully considered when assessing the balance of benefit and disadvantage in the giving of the proposed medical treatment and where the best interest of the patient truly lies. A patient . . . has . . . the right not to be subjected to degrading treatment under article 3 of the European Convention on Human Rights" (*Trust A v H (an Adult patient)* [2006] EWHC 1230 at para.27, per Sir Mark Potter P.).

3. In *R. (on the application of Wilkinson) v The Responsible Medical Officer Broadmoor Hospital* [2001] EWCA 1545 at para.64, Hale L.J. said that where a mentally incapacitated patient is "actively opposed to a course of action, the benefits which it holds for him will have to be carefully weighed against the disadvantages of going against his wishes, especially if force is required to do this."

Subsection (4)

1–106   The definition contained in this provision includes verbal restraint, such as threatening P with the use of force, and locking P in a room even if P does not indicate any objection to the confinement.

Subsection (6)

1–107   If a carer or doctor wishes to challenge a decision made by a donee or deputy on the ground that the decision of the donee or deputy is not in P's best interests, either a complaint could be made to the Public Guardian or an application could be made to the Court of Protection to determine the issue. In the absence of such action, the decision of the donee or deputy which is within the scope of his or her authority must be respected as a failure to do so would be unlawful.

DOES AN ACT.   It is submitted that this phrase includes an instruction to another to do an act.

Subsection (7)

1–108   This provision does not apply where a complaint has been made to the Public Guardian under s.58(1)(h) about the decision of the donee or deputy.

LIFE-SUSTAINING TREATMENT.   Is defined in s.4(10).

Payment for necessary goods and services

1–109   **7.**—(1) If necessary goods or services are supplied to a person who lacks capacity to contract for the supply, he must pay a reasonable price for them.

(2) "Necessary" means suitable to a person's condition in life and to his actual requirements at the time when the goods or services are supplied.

GENERAL NOTE

1–110   In general, a contract entered into by a person who lacks capacity (P) is voidable and can be set aside if the other person knew or must be taken to have known of the lack of capacity. Under s.3(2) of the Sale of Goods Act 1979 (c.54), this rule does not apply if "necessaries" are supplied and P must pay a "reasonable price" for the goods. There is also a matching common law rule about "necessary" services. This section combines these rules to set out a single statutory rule to cover "necessary" goods and services. Subsection (2) repeats the established legal definition of what is "necessary". Thus, for example, a cleaner who carries on cleaning the house of P, who has a progressive dementia, can expect to be paid. As P lacks the capacity both to order or to pay for necessaries, ss.5 and 8 allows for a carer to do both.

At the committee stage in the House of Lords, the Government resisted an amendment to extend the existing powers to set aside a contract made by a person who lacks capacity to a situation where: (1) the other party was not aware of the incapacity and (2) the contract can be set aside without loss to the other party, or where the person lacking capacity has been persuaded to enter into a plainly disadvantageous contract. However, the Government committed itself "to carrying out scoping research work to assess whether there is a problem arising from the current law and, if so, the extent of that problem. This will take into account people who lack capacity and the broader group of vulnerable consumers more generally. The Department of Constitutional Affairs [now the Ministry of Justice] will also commit to working with the Department of Trade and Industry as part of the implementation strategy of the Bill to ensure that policy on consumer strategy, credit and indebtedness is sensitive to the needs of consumers who lack capacity", per the Parliamentary Under-Secretary of State (*Hansard*, HL Vol.670, cols 1471–1472).

In *Wychavon District Council v EM (HB)* [2012] UKUT 12 (AAC), UT Judge Mark said that he doubted whether the term "services" in the section is wide enough to cover the provision of accommodation. However, he held that the common law rules as to the supply of necessities as exemplified in *Re Rhodes* (1890) 44 Ch D 94 survives and that the provision of accommodation is an obvious necessity. Judge Mark said at para.31:

> "The suggestion by the local authority that such matters ought to be dealt with through the Court of Protection may well be appropriate in many cases, and was adopted in the present case, but that does not mean that pending the hearing of any application, which currently takes many months, a person without capacity should be left without necessaries, including accommodation, which can only be supplied in the confidence that they will be paid for. Nor does it mean that if, as will normally be the case, nobody does bring the matter before the Court of Protection, a person under disability will at any stage be able to deny liability for a reasonable sum in appropriate circumstances when necessaries are provided to that person."

In *Aster Healthcare Ltd v Estate of Shafi* [2014] EWHC 77 (QB); [2014] 3 All E.R. 283, Andrews J. confirmed that this section mirrors the common law rule on "necessities" and said that it does not come into play where it was not intended by the supplier that the recipient should pay for the goods and services (para.55). Her Ladyship said at paras 59 and 60:

> "It follows that s.7 of the Mental Capacity Act is not, and cannot be engaged in circumstances in which the services in question are being provided to the mentally incapacitated individual pursuant to an arrangement made by the service provider with a local authority exercising its statutory duty under Part III of the [National Assistance Act 1948]. In those circumstances, even if an arrangement is in place under s 26(3A), it is never intended that the individual will be indebted to the service provider for those services. The debt, if any, is owed by the individual or his Estate to the local authority. That is the position even if the local authority has a right to recoupment of 100% of the costs. There is no unfairness in this. Indeed it would be invidious if the statutory scheme under the 1948 Act and the [NHS and Community Care Act 1990] [now see the Care Act 2014] could be bypassed by a direct claim in debt against the individual concerned merely because he suffers from a mental incapacity. Matters would be different if the local authority had no obligation to pay; in those circumstances it is still possible that the service provider could recover under s.7 of the Mental Capacity Act, provided that he could establish, on the balance of probabilities, that it was his intention at the time of

making the arrangements for the supply of the services that the individual should pay the fees if the local authority had no obligation to do so.

If the services are not being provided under an agreement with the Local authority exercising its duties under s.21 [of the 1948 Act], but pursuant to an arrangement made with a third party, then the question whether s.7 of the Mental Capacity Act is engaged will depend on the facts and circumstances and in particular whether the arrangement made with the third party contemplated that payment would be made by that person (and possibly recouped by him or her in due course under s.8 of that Act) or by the person under the incapacity."

Andrew's J.'s reasoning was approved by the Court of Appeal at [2014] EWCA Civ 1350.

Guidance on "Applications to the Court of Protection in relation to tenancy agreements" is reproduced at Appendix A. The Office of Fair Trading has published "Mental capacity— OFT guidance for creditors" (September 2011).

Subsection (2)

1–111   In *Aster*, above, Andrews J. said that so "far as the position as between the supplier of the necessaries and the incapacitated recipient is concerned, *Re Rhodes* makes it clear that the right to a reasonable price only arises in cases where the supplier 'intends to be repaid' (for the supply) and 'to constitute a debt' against the person who is incapacitated. The rule does *not* cover supplies which are, vis a vis the recipient, gratuitous" (para.51). Her Ladyship held that specialist residential accommodation came within the scope of this provision because the "services were suitable to [P's] condition in life, being specialist services having regard both to his dementia and to his other physical disabilities, and fulfilled the requirements for care and accommodation to which his physical and mental condition gave rise. The definition relates only to the nature of the services themselves. The word 'require-ments' does not extend to the recipient's subjective wishes, however reasonable, as to the location at which those necessary services are to be provided" (para.54).

CONDITION IN LIFE.   This means the living circumstances of P, in particular the standard of life that P enjoys. The *Code of Practice* states, at para.6.58, that the aim of this provision "is to make sure that people can enjoy a similar standard of living and way of life to those they had before lacking capacity. For example, if a person who now lacks capacity previously chose to buy expensive designer clothes, these are still necessary goods—as long as they can still afford them. But they would not be necessary for a person who always wore cheap clothes, no matter how wealthy they were". Deciding whether goods and services are "necessary" can therefore depend upon a identifying a number of subtle factors that shape a person's lifestyle.

Expenditure

1–112   **8.**—(1) If an act to which section 5 applies involves expenditure, it is lawful for D—

(a) to pledge P's credit for the purpose of the expenditure, and

(b) to apply money in P's possession for meeting the expenditure.

(2) If the expenditure is borne for P by D, it is lawful for D—

(a) to reimburse himself out of money in P's possession, or

(b) to be otherwise indemnified by P.

(3) Subsections (1) and (2) do not affect any power under which (apart from those subsections) a person—

(a) has lawful control of P's money or other property, and

(b) has power to spend money for P's benefit.

DEFINITIONS
   "property": s.64(1)   **1–113**

GENERAL NOTE

If D, acting under s.5, arranges something for P's care or treatment that costs money then   **1–114** D can either promise that P will pay (i.e. D may pledge the credit of P), use money which P has in his possession, pay himself back from P's money in his possession or consider himself owed by P. Nothing in this section allows D to gain access to P's funds where they are held by a third party such as a bank or building society. Such funds cannot be accessed until formal steps are taken, such as registering a relevant power of attorney, or making an application to the Court of Protection for a deputy to be appointed or for a single order to be made. This section does not authorise D to sell any of P's property or to gain access to any of P's assets other than cash that is in P's possession.

D cannot make a decision that conflicts with a decision made by either a donee of a lasting power of attorney ("LPA") or a deputy (s.6(6)).

D could be appointed under reg.33 of the Social Security (Claims and Payments) Regulations 1987 (SI 1987/1968) to be the "appointee" to act on behalf of P. Appointeeship is considered in the General Note to s.18.

Although there is no requirement placed on D to keep records of the financial transactions undertaken on behalf of P, given the potential for allegations of financial abuse to be made it would clearly be sensible for D to do so.

Subsection (2)

INDEMNIFIED. If D cannot be compensated by cash that is in the possession of P, an   **1–115** application should be made to the court if it is not possible to claim reimbursement from a donee of an LPA or a deputy who has been granted appropriate powers by the court.

Subsection (3)

This recognises that people may have control over P's money or property by other   **1–116** routes, for example by virtue of being appointed as P's appointee. A donee or a deputy appointed by the court could also have lawful control over P's money.

Lasting powers of attorney

Lasting powers of attorney

9.—(1) A lasting power of attorney is a power of attorney under which the   **1–117** donor ("P") confers on the donee (or donees) authority to make decisions about all or any of the following—

   (a) P's personal welfare or specified matters concerning P's personal welfare, and

   (b) P's property and affairs or specified matters concerning P's property and affairs, and which includes authority to make such decisions in circumstances where P no longer has capacity.

(2) A lasting power of attorney is not created unless—

   (a) section 10 is complied with,

   (b) an instrument conferring authority of the kind mentioned in subsection (1) is made and registered in accordance with Schedule 1, and

   (c) at the time when P executes the instrument, P has reached 18 and has capacity to execute it.

(3) An instrument which—

   (a) purports to create a lasting power of attorney, but

   (b) does not comply with this section, section 10 or Schedule 1,

confers no authority.

(4) The authority conferred by a lasting power of attorney is subject to—

(a) the provisions of this Act and, in particular, sections 1(the principles) and 4 (best interests), and

(b) any conditions or restrictions specified in the instrument.

DEFINITIONS

1–118   "property": s.64(1)

GENERAL NOTE

1–119   A power of attorney is a legal document under which one person (the "donor") empowers another person (the "attorney" or "donee") or persons to act in his or her stead, either generally or for specific purposes. An act done by an attorney or donee can be treated as an act done by the donor, so as to affect the donor's relations with third parties. Prior to the Enduring Powers of Attorney Act 1985 (c.29), a power of attorney would be automatically revoked if the donor lost mental capacity. That Act introduced enduring powers of attorney ("EPA") which enabled donors to continue to act on behalf of the donor's property and affairs after the donor ceased to have capacity if certain formalities were satisfied. This section, together with ss.10–14, creates a new form of power of attorney, a "lasting power of attorney" ("LPA"). These replace the EPA and the 1985 Act is repealed by Sch.7. A key distinction between an EPA and an LPA is that the former were confined to the donor's property and affairs, while the latter can also extend to personal welfare matters, which can include health care decisions (s.11(7)(c)). The legal effect of existing EPAs is preserved and integrated into the scheme of the Act by s.66(3) and Sch.4. A person with mental capacity who has made an EPA before the Act comes into force can either destroy it and then make an LPA, or can do nothing. An EPA cannot be made after October 1, 2007 (s.66(3)). The power to make an ordinary power of attorney under the Powers of Attorney Act 1971(c.27) is unaffected by the Act.

A LPA can only be executed by a mentally capable adult (subs.(2)(c)), and it will only be valid if it complies with s.10, and the instrument conferring the authority is made in the form prescribed by the Lasting Powers of Attorney, Enduring Powers of Attorney and Public Guardian Regulations 2007 (SI 2007/1253), *and* it is registered with the Public Guardian in accordance with Sch.1 (subss.(2)(a)(b), (3)) and Part 2 of SI 2007/1253. There is nothing to prevent a person who is detained under the Mental Health Act 1983 from executing an LPA as long as he or she has the capacity to do so. The Public Guardian is required to establish and maintain a register of LPAs (s.58(1)(a)), and will receive reports from donees (s.58(1)(f)). The Public Guardian has published Practice Notes for the guidance of attorneys and deputies on various matters. They can be accessed on the website of the Office of Public Guardian.

Decisions made by the donee must be in P's best interests and they cannot extend beyond the scope of the Act (see ss.27–29). The donee must act in accordance with the principles set out in s.1 (subs.(4)(a)). The donee must also comply with any conditions or restrictions that P has put in the LPA (subs.(4)(b)). If the donee is granted the power to refuse consent to life sustaining treatment, his or her decision must not be motivated by a desire to bring about the donor's death (ss.4(5),11(8)). The donee, who acts as the agent of P (see the General Notes to s.10), is subject to the restrictions on restraint set out in s.6 (s.11(1)–(6)), and to any advance decision made by P (s.11(7)(b); but see s.25(2)(b)). Although the Public Guardian has no obligation to supervise donees, he can investigate a complaint about the way in which a donee is exercising his or her powers (s.58(1)(h)). This function can be discharged in co-operation with other persons who are involved in the care of treatment of P (s.58(2)). The Public Guardian can direct a Court of Protection Visitor to investigate the complaint and report to him (s.58(1)(d)). The Public Guardian could then report to the court which could decide to revoke the LPA (s.22(4)(b)). The court can also interpret the terms of an LPA or give directions as to its exercise (s.23), but it does not have power to extend or amend the terms of the LPA as granted by the donor.

By making an LPA, the donor (P), confers on the donee or donees authority to make decisions about P's personal welfare and/or property and affairs or specified matters concerning those areas. The authority to make decisions includes, where appropriate, the authority to act on decisions made (s.64(2)). The LPA must include authority for the donee/s to make decisions when P no longer has capacity to make those decisions (subs.(1)).

If P wishes, an LPA relating to P's property and affairs can operate as an "ordinary" power of attorney while P has mental capacity as long as it will continue to have effect after P loses capacity. Section 11(7)(a) prevents a personal welfare LPA having similar effect: it can only be used once the donor has lost capacity.

Separate LPAs can be created for welfare and financial matters. It is not possible for a single LPA to cover both matters. In her evidence to the Joint Committee, the Health Minister acknowledged the need, in some cases, to appoint different donees in relation to different types of decision:

"From the health care side it may be that people might want different attorneys for different decisions. Somebody that you trust with your finances may not be the same as somebody that you wanted to make decisions about your health and welfare" (Q754).

The Public Guardian has published a paper on "Avoiding Invalid Provisions in your LPA" (2013). Its introductory paragraph states:

"Every month the Public Guardian makes a large number of applications (usually over a hundred) to the Court of Protection to 'sever' invalid provisions from LPAs which have been sent in for registration. These applications create a large workload for the court and for the Office of the Public Guardian (OPG), which would be reduced if people making LPAs (the "donors") and their professional advisers were more aware of the problem. This paper aims to explain how to avoid the need for severance, which delays registration and can cause annoyance and frustration to donors and attorneys."

An LPA cannot contain provisions that limit the rights of the Public Guardian or the Court of Protection (*The Public Guardian v VT* [2014] EWCOP 52).

The Law Society has issued a Practice Note on lasting powers of attorney (2011). Paragraph 6.2 states that there "may be circumstances where an LPA may not be appropriate, and a later application to the Court of Protection for deputyship, with oversight of the Office of the Public Guardian, may be preferable. This may be advisable, for example:

- where there are indications of persistent family conflicts suggesting that an LPA may be contested, or
- where the assets are more substantial or complex than family members are accustomed to handle, or
- in cases where litigation may lead to a substantial award of damages for personal injury."

Financial abuse

1–120 The Joint Committee expressed its concern about evidence that it has received "indicating that financial abuse occurs in approximately 10–15% of cases involving EPAs. Further evidence estimated that that abuse was as high as 20%" (para.138). These figures relate to unethical conduct. It is estimated that 2–3 per cent of cases involve criminal conduct (Oral and written evidence, Ev 188). The Act attempts to reduce the risk of financial abuse by requiring an LPA to be executed and registered before it can be used (see subs.(2)), thereby reducing the difficulties associated with the monitoring of EPAs. A report prepared for the Public Guardianship Office, "The role of the Public Guardianship Office in safeguarding vulnerable adults against financial abuse" (undated) by Hilary Brown et al, suggests that further action will be required to tackle the financial abuse of incapacitated persons who are subject to LPAs. The powers of the Court of Protection in relation to LPAs are set out in ss.22 and 23. They include the power to revoke an LPA if the donee is not acting in P's best interests (s.22(3)(4)). The Public Guardian can receive reports from donees (s.58(1)(f)).

Baroness Andrews outlined the manner in which the Act can be utilised to prevent financial abuse by donees:

"[D]onors of financial LPAs will be advised that they can, if they so choose, stipulate in their financial LPA that they wish the [donee] to provide annual accounts to the Public Guardian or to any other third party for checking. That is a front-line defence. Therefore, the Public Guardian can check accounts not only if he is asked to do so but also if someone raises a concern. Concerns can be raised by different sorts of objectors at all stages. If an objector raises concerns about a prospective [donee] at the registration stage, the Court may add a requirement for the [donee] to lodge accounts if that would alleviate the concerns of the objector. That is a second line of defence.

Anyone can raise a concern with the Office of the Public Guardian if they fear that [a donee] of a registered LPA is not acting properly. The Court will then be able to direct that the [donee] should lodge accounts. We believe that is robust. They could be 'one-off' accounts or annual accounts. They could be lodged with the Court, a solicitor, an accountant or, indeed, a third party.

In the broader context the *Code of Practice* makes it clear to financial [donees] that they should keep accounts. We intend to issue guidance to reinforce that message" (*Hansard*, HL Vol.669, cols 771–772).

In *R. v TJC* [2015] EWCA Crim 1276, the Court of Appeal held that a donee of an LPA can be guilty of abuse of position under s.4 of the Fraud Act 2006 where there is evidence of a "general deficiency" in the donee's management of the donor's affairs.

Guidance to financial institutions and others

1–121   See the General Note to s.18.

Subsection (1)

1–122   DONOR.   See subs.(2)(c). Only individuals can make LPAs. There is no provision for joint LPAs to be made by, for example, a husband and wife. The donor is not required to live in England or Wales.

AUTHORITY TO MAKE DECISIONS.   A donee will be provided with protection by ss.5 and 6 for acts done outside the scope of the LPA.

Subsection (1)(a)

1–123   PERSONAL WELFARE.   The donee has no power to act under the authority of a welfare LPA if the donor has the mental capacity to make the decision in question (s.11(7)(a)).

The *Code of Practice*, at para.7.21, states that personal welfare LPAs might include decisions about:

"• where the donor should live and who they should live with
• the donor's day-to-day care, including diet and dress
• who the donor may have contact with
• consenting to or refusing medical examination and treatment on the donor's behalf
• arrangements needed for the donor to be given medical, dental or optical treatment
• assessments for and provision of community care services
• whether the donor should take part in social activities, leisure activities, education or training
• the donor's personal correspondence and papers
• rights of access to personal information about the donor, or
• complaints about the donor's care or treatment."

A welfare LPA which gives general powers to the donee would include all of the above powers. A welfare LPA which is not drafted in general terms can either specify the powers that the donee is granted, or can specify the types of decisions that the donee is not empowered to make. Those involved in caring for P should read the LPA, if it is available, in order to confirm the extent of the donee's power.

There is a potential overlap between financial and welfare LPAs. For example, a decision that it would be in the best interests of P to live in a care home, which is a welfare decision, would require a financial decision to be made in that the care home fees would need to be paid. If the LPA provides for separate donees for financial and welfare matters, this could lead to the decision of the welfare donee being thwarted by the refusal of the financial donee to pay the fees. In such a situation, both donees must act in the best interests of P. If the dispute cannot be resolved, a complaint should be made to the Public Guardian who can require a Court of Protection Visitor to report to him on the matter (s.58(1)(d)).

The implications of providing healthcare decision making powers to a donee are considered in the General Note to s.11.

Subsection (1)(b)

PROPERTY AND AFFAIRS. Subject to any restrictions contained within it, the donee of a **1–124** financial LPA can act under it as soon as it has been registered with the Public Guardian. The term "property and affairs" means "business matters, legal transactions and other dealing of a similar kind" (*F v WEST BERKSHIRE HA* [1989] 2 All E.R. 545, HL, per Lord Brandon at 554). The *CODE OF PRACTICE*, at para.7.36, states that financial LPAs might include decisions about:

"• buying or selling property
• opening, closing or operating any bank, building society or other account
• giving access to the donor's financial information
• claiming, receiving and using (on the donor's behalf) all benefits, pensions, allowances and rebates (unless the Department for Work and Pensions has already appointed someone and everyone is happy for this to continue)
• receiving any income, inheritance or other entitlement on behalf of the donor
• dealing with the donor's tax affairs
• paying the donor's mortgage, rent and household expenses
• insuring, maintaining and repairing the donor's property
• investing the donor's savings
• making limited gifts on the donor's behalf . . .
• paying for private medical care and residential care or nursing home fees
• applying for any entitlement to funding for NHS care, social care or adaptations
• using the donor's money to buy a vehicle or any equipment or other help they need
• repaying interest and capital on any loan taken out by the donor."

A financial LPA may grant the donee general powers, in which case the donee will be authorised to undertake any of the acts set out above. As an alternative, the donor might wish to grant the donee specific powers, or could specify the types of decisions the donee is not empowered to make.

Subsection (2)(b)

REGISTERED. The donor could either register the instrument straight away, or could **1–125** leave it with the proposed donee with a request that it be registered when he or she believes that the donor has lost the capacity to make the decision to register. In both cases, the LPA cannot be used until the Public Guardian has registered it.

Subsection (2) (c)

REACHED 18. This ensures that there is no overlap with the Children Act 1989 or the **1–126** wardship jurisdiction of the High Court.

CAPACITY. The donor must have the capacity to execute the instrument at the time when it is executed. The fact that a capacious donor is detained under the Mental Health Act 1983 does not disqualify him or her from executing an LPA. In *K, Re F, Re* [1998] 1

All E.R. 358, a case on the 1985 Act, Hoffmann J. held that the donor should be able to understand:

1. If such be the terms of the power, that the donee will be able to assume complete authority over the donor's affairs.
2. If such be the terms of the power, that the donee will in general be able to do anything with the donor's property which he himself could have done.
3. That the authority will continue if the donor should be or become mentally incapable.
4. That if he should be or become mentally incapable, the power will be irrevocable without confirmation by the court.

This test, which was described by Sir Christopher Staughton in the Court of Appeal in *W, Re* [2001] 4 All E.R. 88 at 92, as a "sound indication of what the donor must understand if the power is to be valid", is a broader test than that set out in Sch.1, para.2(1)(e).

In *Re Collis* (COP) Oct.27, 2010, Senior Judge Lush held that:

1. As mental capacity is "issue specific", the capacity required to create an LPA is not the same as the capacity to manage one's property and financial affairs generally.
2. Under the terms of s.3(4), the potential donor must be provided with:
    (i) information specifically relevant to the execution of an LPA which includes the prescribed information about the purpose of the instrument and the effect of an LPA which is contained in the LPA form itself (Sch.1, para.2(1)(a)); and
    (ii) information about the consequences of not executing an LPA.

If there is a dispute about the donor's capacity, it has been said that "there is a strong body of opinion to support the view that a solicitor is in a better position than a medical practitioner to assess a client's capacity to enter into a specific juristic act . . ." (*Heywood and Massey: Court of Protection Practice*, para.11–037). In *Re Collis*, above, the Senior Judge preferred the evidence of capacity provided by a solicitor which was both issue and time specific to that of an experienced medical practitioner whose evidence was neither time specific nor issue specific.

Subsection (3)

1–127 CONFERS NO AUTHORITY. Note, however, that the court can declare an instrument that is not in the prescribed form to be treated as if it were, if it is satisfied that the person executing the instrument intended it to create an LPA (Sch.1, para.3(2)).

Subsection (4)

1–128 BEST INTERESTS. The donee must therefore apply the s.4 check list before any decision is made on behalf of P.

ANY CONDITIONS OR RESTRICTIONS. Even if the condition or restriction, viewed objectively, does not serve the best interests of P. The scope of a donee's power is also limited by the fact that he or she acts as the agent of P: see the General Note to s.10.

Appointment of donees

1–129 **10.**—(1) A donee of a lasting power of attorney must be—
(a) an individual who has reached 18, or
(b) if the power relates only to P's property and affairs, either such an individual or a trust corporation.

(2) An individual who is bankrupt [or is a person to whom a debt relief order is made] may not be appointed as donee of a lasting power of attorney in relation to P's property and affairs.

(3) Subsections (4) to (7) apply in relation to an instrument under which two or more persons are to act as donees of a lasting power of attorney.

(4) The instrument may appoint them to act—

(a) jointly,

(b) jointly and severally, or

(c) jointly in respect of some matters and jointly and severally in respect of others.

(5) To the extent to which it does not specify whether they are to act jointly or jointly and severally, the instrument is to be assumed to appoint them to act jointly.

(6) If they are to act jointly, a failure, as respects one of them, to comply with the requirements of subsection (1) or (2) or Part 1 or 2 of Schedule 1 prevents a lasting power of attorney from being created.

(7) If they are to act jointly and severally, a failure, as respects one of them, to comply with the requirements of subsection (1) or (2) or Part 1 or 2 of Schedule 1—

(a) prevents the appointment taking effect in his case, but

(b) does not prevent a lasting power of attorney from being created in the case of the other or others.

(8) An instrument used to create a lasting power of attorney—

(a) cannot give the donee (or, if more than one, any of them) power to appoint a substitute or successor, but

(b) may itself appoint a person to replace the donee (or, if more than one, any of them) on the occurrence of an event mentioned in section 13(6)(a) to (d) which has the effect of terminating the donee's appointment.

AMENDMENT

The words in square brackets in subs.(2) were inserted by SI 2012/2404 art.3(2), Sch.1, para.53(2). **1–130**

DEFINITIONS

"lasting power of attorney": s.64(1) **1–131**

"property": s.64(1)

"trust corporation": s.64(1)

"bankrupt": s.64(3)

GENERAL NOTE

This section sets out requirements relating to the appointment of donees and how **1–132** they should act. The maximum number of donees that a donor of an LPA may specify is five (Lasting Powers of Attorney, Enduring Powers of Attorney and Public Guardian Regulations 2007 (SI 2007/1253), reg.6). An individual donee must be an adult and, if the LPA relates to property and affairs, not be a bankrupt or a person in relation to whom a debt relief order is made (subss.(1)(a),(2)). A trust corporation, as well as an individual, can be appointed as donee to an LPA that relates only to property and affairs (subs.(1)(b)). Apart from where a trust corporation is appointed, the appointment of a donee is personal. If an individual is appointed, it is important for the donor to be confident that the chosen donee would be likely to act in his or her best interests when performing functions under the Act. The Act does not prescribe the personal attributes of a donee and does not place an obligation on a donee to accept appointment.

A donee acts as the agent of the donor. Under the law of agency, an act of an agent done within the scope of his authority binds his principal, in this case P. As an agent the donee is bound by a number of common law duties toward P, including the duty to act with due care and skill, to act in good faith, not to delegate his or her functions to another, to keep the donor's affairs confidential apart from where the disclosure of information is allowed by the LPA or is otherwise required, to keep accounts of monies received and paid on P's behalf, to keep money belonging to P separate from his or her own funds and not to permit his or her own interests to conflict with the duties owed to P. The duties of an agent are described in the *Code of Practice* at paras 7.58–7.68. For a comprehensive account of the law of agency, see Peter Watts and Francis M.B. Reynolds, *Bowstead and Reynolds on Agency*, 20th edn (London: Sweet & Maxwell, 2014). In *Re Harcourt* (COP), July 31, 2012, Senior Judge Lush said at para.39:

"The common law of agency imposes a number of fiduciary duties on attorneys, including two that relate specifically to their accountability. First, an attorney is expected to keep and be constantly ready to produce correct accounts of all his dealings and transactions on the donor's behalf: *Gray v Haig* (1855) 20 Beav 219. And secondly, the attorney has a duty to produce to the donor, or to anyone appointed by the donor, all books and documents he has relating to the donor's affairs: *Dadswell v Jacobs* (1887) 34 Ch D 278."

With regard to the responsibilities of a donee when investing the donor's funds, Judge Lush gave the following guidance in *Re Buckley* (2013) EWHC 2965 (COP) at para.41:

"Until such time as the Office of the Public Guardian issues its own guidance to attorneys and deputies on the investment of funds, I would suggest that, as they have fiduciary obligations that are similar to those of trustees, attorneys should comply with the provisions of the Trustee Act as regards the standard investment criteria and the requirement to obtain and consider proper advice. I would also recommend that attorneys and their financial advisers have regard to the criteria that were historically approved by the court and the antecedents of the OPG in *Investing for Patients*, albeit with some allowance for updating, as suggested in paragraph 37 above."

Judge Lush said at para.36:

"Generally speaking, attorneys acting under an LPA should ensure that any investment products or services they acquire on a donor's behalf are provided by individuals or firms who are regulated by the Financial Services Authority."

With regard to the prohibition against delegation, para.7.10 of the Law Society's Practice Note on lasting powers of attorney (2011) states:

"There are exceptions to this general rule and, like any other agent, an attorney acting under an LPA has an implied power in certain circumstances to delegate:

- any functions which are of a purely administrative nature and do not involve or require the exercise of discretion;
- any functions which the donor would not expect the attorney to attend to personally; or
- through necessity or unforeseen circumstances;

Any wider power of delegation must be expressly provided for in the LPA itself." (Also see paras 7.61 and 7.62 of the *Code of Practice*.)

The relationship of the donee to the patient is that of a fiduciary and like all fiduciaries the donee should not benefit from the relationship (*Bunting v W* [2005] EWHC 1274 (Ch) at para.31). The donee also has a duty to act within the scope of the LPA (s.9(4)(b)) although he or she has implied authority to do what is necessary for or incidental to the effective execution of the powers granted. The donee also has a duty to act in the donor's best interests, to be guided by the principles set out in s.1, to have regard to the *Code of Practice* (s.42(4)(a)), and to comply with any directions that the Court of Protection might make. References to making decisions, in relation to a donee, include, where appropriate, acting on decisions made (s.64(2)).

A donee or proposed donee can disclaim his or her appointment by completing the prescribed form (LPA005) which must be sent to the donor and copied to the Office of the Public Guardian and any other donee(s) appointed under the power.

Any concerns about the way in which the donee in undertaking his or her functions, including a concern that the donee might lack mental capacity, should be reported to the Public Guardian or, if criminal behaviour is suspected, the police. The Public Guardian may decide to direct a Court of Protection Visitor to visit P and/or the donee (s.58(1)(d)). In serious cases, the Public Guardian will refer the matter to the court (see reg.43 of Lasting Powers of Attorney, Enduring Powers of Attorney and Public Guardian Regulations 2007 (SI 2007/1253)) which has the power to revoke the LPA if it finds that the donee is either contravening his or her authority or is not acting in P's best interests (s.22(4)(b)). Also see the note on adult protection procedures in s.44.

The *Code of Practice*, at para.7.70, states that signs that a donee may be exploiting the donor (or failing to act in the donor's best interests) include:

"• stopping relatives or friends contacting the donor – for example, the attorney may prevent contact or the donor may suddenly refuse visits or telephone calls from family and friends for no reason
• sudden unexplained changes in living arrangements (for example, someone moves in to care for a donor they've had little contact with)
• not allowing healthcare or social care staff to see the donor
• taking the donor out of hospital against medical advice, while the donor is having necessary medical treatment
• unpaid bills (for example, residential care or nursing home fees)
• an attorney opening a credit card account for the donor
• spending money on things that are not obviously related to the donor's needs
• the attorney spending money in an unusual or extravagant way
• transferring financial assets to another country."

A number of witnesses to the Joint Committee expressed their concern about the situation that could arise when a donee who is a close relative of P appears not to be acting in the best interests of the P because of a conflict of interest. This difficulty was said to be "not common but neither is it rare" (Oral and written evidence, Ev 472). An example of how such a conflict can arise has been given by Baroness Finlay:

"A lady aged 59 was very ill. Her family appeared to be very concerned about her pain and constantly asked for her diamorphine to be increased. However, we remained unconvinced that her pain was really that severe. In fact, the patient declined increasing doses of diamorphine. Her 60th birthday arrived and was passed with minimal celebration, after which the family visited very little. She became depressed and spoke to one of the night nurses, explaining that the problem was that on her 60th birthday, her fixed-term life insurance policy expired. The family would not now inherit what they thought they would if she had died, and if her drugs had been duly increased" (*Hansard*, HL Vol.642, col.766).

Donees who are close relatives might not accurately reflect P's wishes as studies have shown that relatives' perception of the patient's likely views often differ substantially from the patient's own wishes; see, for example, A.B. Seckler et al, "Substituted judgment: how accurate are proxy predictions?" (1991) 115(9) Ann. Intern. Med. 92–98; also see the studies cited in R Schiff et al, "Living wills and the Mental Capacity Act: a postal questionnaire survey of UK geriatricians" (2006) 35 *Age and Ageing* 116 and the notes to s.4(7).

Subsection (1)

Paragraph (a)
There is no provision comparable to s.19(2) that permits the donor of an LPA to appoint an office holder to be his or her donee.

1–133

INDIVIDUAL. In *Re Mckenna* (COP), February 1, 2011, Senior Judge Lush, the donor purported to appoint a replacement attorney who, at the date the donor signed the instrument, was 16 years old. The donor added the following restriction; "My replacement attorney shall only act if she is over the age of 18". On the application of the Public Guardian the appointment of the replacement attorney was severed as it contravened this paragraph.

A professional donee, such as an accountant or a solicitor, must be referred to by name. For example, it is not possible to refer to "a partner in Sue, Grabit and Run".

Paragraph (b)

1–134   TRUST CORPORATION. Is defined in the Trustee Act 1925 (c.19), s.68(1) as "the Public Trustee or a corporation either appointed by the court in any particular case to be a trustee, or entitled by rules made under s.4(3) of the Public Trustee Act 1906 (c.55), to act as custodian trustee". A trust corporation is "often parts of banks or other financial institutions" (*Code of Practice*, para.7.9).

Subsection (2)

1–135   The Parliamentary Under-Secretary of State announced that the Government had "decided that the Office of the Public Guardian will check to see if prospective financial attorneys are bankrupt when an LPA is registered" (*Hansard*, HL Vol.668, col.1417). As only one donee was found to have been bankrupt at the point of registration during the period April 1, 2010 to March 31, 2011, the Government decided to cease this practice (*Hansard* Written Answer from the Parliamentary Under-Secretary of State for Justice, October 18, 2011, Col.64WS). If the donee is bankrupt or is a person to whom a debt relief order is made, then the LPA will be invalid. There is nothing to prevent such a person from being appointed to act as a donee of a welfare LPA.

Subsection (4)

1–136   This provides that where two or more people are appointed as donees, they may be appointed either to act jointly (so that they must all join together in any decision), or to act jointly and severally (which means that they can act either independently or all together) or to act jointly in respect of some matters and jointly and severally in respect of others. The donor therefore "has all possible options when wanting to appoint more than one donee", per the Parliamentary Under-Secretary of State (*Hansard*, HL Vol.670, col.1473). If the donor does not specify, it will be assumed that the donees were appointed jointly (subs.(5)).

It is not possible for a donor to appoint a donee to act jointly with a person who is not a donee (*Re Reading* Unreported June 25, 2009 (COP, Senior Judge Lush)). In *Miles and Beattie v The Public Guardian* [2015] EWHC 2960 (Ch), Nugee J. held that there is nothing in the Act that prevents a donor from appointing A and B to act as donees, and if one of them was unable or unwilling to act to appoint the remaining donee as sole donee, and only if both of the original donees were unable or unwilling to act to appoint a replacement donee, C, under subs.(8)(b).

The Public Guardian has published a paper on "Avoiding Invalid Provisions in your LPA" (2013) which can be accessed at: *www.justice.gov.uk/downloads/protecting-the-vulnerable/mca/avoiding-invalid-lpas.pdf*.

Subsection (6)

1–137   For joint donees, any breach by one of them of the requirements concerning how LPAs are made will prevent an LPA from being created.

Subsection (7)

1–138   Where donees are appointed jointly and severally, a breach by one of them of the requirements concerning how LPAs are made will only prevent the appointment taking affect in his or her case; a valid LPA is created in respect of the other donee(s).

Subsection (8)

This enables a donor to provide in the LPA for the replacement of the donee(s) on the occurrence of an event mentioned in s.13(6)(a)–(d) which would normally terminate a donee's powers. One of these events is the death of the donee. It would therefore be possible, for example, for a donor to appoint his spouse as donee, but nominate his child as a replacement donee. Under para.(a), a donee cannot be given power by the LPA to choose a successor.

1–139

This provision does not enable a donor of an LPA to appoint a replacement donee to succeed another replacement donee; a replacement donee can only replace an original donee (*Public Guardian v Boff* [2013] W.T.L.R. 1349). Senior Judge Lush noted some of the practical problems that arise with the appointment of replacement donees (Judge Lush uses the term "attorneys") at para.51:

"(1) When the donor or an attorney makes an application to register an LPA, the named persons are not informed of the identity of any replacement attorneys on form LPA 001; they are only given the names and addresses of the original attorneys.

(2) There is no formal registration process for replacement attorneys and no facility whereby a named person, donor or co-attorney can object to the appointment of a replacement attorney, either when the original application is made to register the instrument, or when an event under section 13(6) of the Mental Capacity Act 2005 activates the replacement.

(3) Replacement attorneys are really only viable where the donor appoints a sole original attorney or more than one original attorney to act jointly and severally.

(4) Although a replacement attorney can replace an original attorney who has been appointed to act jointly, the outcome is unlikely to be what the donor intended. For example, if the donor appointed A and B to act jointly, and C to act as a replacement attorney, A's bankruptcy, death or disclaimer would terminate A and B's joint appointment, and C would become the sole attorney, rather than act jointly with B. Although the OPG guidance refers to this at the foot of page 19 of LPA 112, the prescribed form itself does not warn donors of the implications of appointing a replacement attorney where they have appointed their original attorneys to act jointly, or jointly for some decisions, and jointly and severally for other decisions".

There is nothing in para.(b) to displace the fundamental principle that the survivor of joint attorneys cannot act. Where one of the original joint attorneys can no longer act, the replacement(s) will step in and act alone, to the exclusion of the surviving original attorney (*Re Druce* (COP) May 31, 2011, Senior Judge Lush).

Lasting powers of attorney: restrictions

11.—(1) A lasting power of attorney does not authorise the donee (or, if more than one, any of them) to do an act that is intended to restrain P, unless three conditions are satisfied.

1–140

(2) The first condition is that P lacks, or the donee reasonably believes that P lacks, capacity in relation to the matter in question.

(3) The second is that the donee reasonably believes that it is necessary to do the act in order to prevent harm to P.

(4) The third is that the act is a proportionate response to—

(a) the likelihood of P's suffering harm, and

(b) the seriousness of that harm.

(5) For the purposes of this section, the donee restrains P if he—

(a) uses, or threatens to use, force to secure the doing of an act which P resists, or

(b) restricts P's liberty of movement, whether or not P resists,

or if he authorises another person to do any of those things.

(6) [*Repealed by the Mental Health Act 2007 s.50(4)(b)*]

(7) Where a lasting power of attorney authorises the donee (or, if more than one, any of them) to make decisions about P's personal welfare, the authority—

    (a) does not extend to making such decisions in circumstances other than those where P lacks, or the donee reasonably believes that P lacks, capacity,

    (b) is subject to sections 24 to 26 (advance decisions to refuse treatment), and

    (c) extends to giving or refusing consent to the carrying out or continuation of a treatment by a person providing health care for P.

(8) But subsection (7)(c)—

    (a) does not authorise the giving or refusing of consent to the carrying out or continuation of life-sustaining treatment, unless the instrument contains express provision to that effect, and

    (b) is subject to any conditions or restrictions in the instrument.

DEFINITIONS

1–141   "lasting power of attorney": s.64(1)
"the Human Rights Convention": s.64(1)
"treatment": s.64(1)
"life-sustaining treatment": s.64(1)

GENERAL NOTE

1–142   As subsections (1)–(5) place restrictions on the use of restraint by donees similar to those that apply to "section 5 acts" (see s.6) and deputies (see s.20), reference should be made to the notes on s.6. A donor of an LPA does not have power to authorise her donees to consent to the deprivation of her liberty in the absence of a court order or going through the deprivation of liberty authorisation procedures contained in Sch.A1 (*Re Stewart* (COP) November 9, 2011, Senior Judge Lush).

A donee has no power to bring or defend legal proceedings on behalf of the donor. The authority of the court could be sought for the donee to act as the donor's litigation friend.

Under subs.(7), a personal welfare LPA:

    (i) can only take effect after P loses capacity. Decision making will therefore fluctuate between the donor and donee in cases where the donor has fluctuating capacity. It is also the case that P could be capable of making some simple personal welfare decisions, but not other, more complex, decisions. This could give rise to considerable practical difficulties. A healthcare professional who is proposing to provide medical treatment for P must also assess P's capacity. Any dispute between donee and the professional about the assessment of P's capacity that remains unresolved should be referred to the Court of Protection for a declaration under s.15(1)(a);

    (ii) is generally subject to any advance decision that P has made: see the note on subs.(7)(b), below; and

    (iii) can authorise the donee to give or refuse consent to the carrying out or continuation of health care for P. This power is subject to any conditions or restrictions in the LPA and to subs.(8) which prohibits the donee from refusing life-sustaining treatment for P unless the LPA expressly allows for this. A LPA does not provide the donee with a power to demand that a specific form of medical treatment be provided to P.

In order to make a healthcare decision on behalf of P, the donee should have received the same information about the nature of the treatment being proposed and its consequences as P would have received had he or she had been mentally capable. An application to the Court of Protection should be made if the donee is asked to consent to a non-therapeutic treatment, such as an organ donation, if such treatment is not specified in the LPA.

The fact that the donee has the power to refuse medical treatment on behalf of P represents a significant change in the doctor patient relationship in that a non-medical donee can override the doctor's clinical judgment as to what treatment his or her patient should receive. If a doctor wishes to challenge a decision made by a donee not to consent to treatment for P, the doctor could consider making an application to the court for on order overriding the donee's decision on the ground that the donee was not acting in P's best interests. But as the briefing note on the Mental Capacity Bill by the Catholic Bishops' Conference of England and Wales (July 2004, at para.24) notes, how many doctors "will have the time, energy and motivation to ask a court to override a[donee] whose determination of best interests appears to them to be defective or questionable?" If the decision of the donee to refuse treatment either stops the doctor from providing life-sustaining treatment or would be likely to lead to a serious deterioration in P's condition, the treatment can continue until the decision of the court is made (s.6(6), (7)). A donee's decision must not be motivated by a desire to bring about P's death (s.4(5)).

A donee cannot refuse the provision of basic care for P, such as the provision of hydration and nutrition by non-artificial means and keeping P clean, because the cessation of such care would never be in P's best interests.

A healthcare professional who treats P despite the existence of an LPA which provides for a donee to make the decision in question will be protected from legal liability by virtue of s.5 unless, at the time, he or she is satisfied that such an LPA exists. If an urgent healthcare decision needs to be taken in respect of P and there is no time to contact the donee, the healthcare professional should proceed to treat P in his or her best interests and then report to the donee.

If P is subject to guardianship under the Mental Health Act 1983, the donee cannot make a decision, including a decision about where P should reside, which conflicts with that of the guardian (ibid. s.8(1)).

Subsection (7)
MAKE DECISIONS.   See s.64(2).   **1–143**

Subsection (7) para.(a)
The physical incapacity of the donor cannot bring a welfare LPA into effect (*Azancot,*   **1–144**
Re, (COP) May 27, 2009, Senior Judge Lush).

REASONABLY BELIEVES.   The donee must be able to satisfy this objective test by identifying the grounds that he or she had for believing that P lacked capacity.

Subsection (7) para.(b)
Generally, an LPA is subject to the terms of an advance decision. However, if the LPA is   **1–145**
made after the advance decision it overrides the advance decision if it confers on the donee the power to refuse treatments specified in the advance decision (s.25(2)(b)).

Subsection (7) para.(c)
The LPA does not provide a donee with the power to require that a particular medical   **1–146**
treatment be given to P. Nor does it provide authority for the donee to make decisions about treatments for mental disorder which are regulated by the Mental Health Act 1983. For the provision of life-sustaining treatments, see subs.(8).

Subsection (8)
The power of a donee to prevent life-sustaining treatment to be given to P, which is   **1–147**
subject to the restriction contained in s.4(5), was the subject of considerable criticism during the Bill's passage through Parliament. For example, Earl Howe said:

"In very many cases—perhaps the majority—the doctor and the [donee] will be in agreement about what is in the patient's best interests, and no problem will therefore arise. The problems arise when doctor and [donee] are in disagreement.

Both of them are required under the Bill to work in the patient's best interests. But the interpretation of 'best interests' is open to difference. What the Bill is saying is that, in the worst case, [a donee] with no medical knowledge whatever can take it on himself to gainsay a doctor whose professional advice is that the patient whose life is at stake should receive certain treatment. It might be perfectly possible for the [donee] to maintain, with some justification, that his decision to refuse consent was taken in the best interests of P. But the doctor, who had close knowledge and experience of the treatment, might not think that a fair and reasonable view of best interests.

What happens then? The Bill allows the doctor to seek a ruling from the Court [of Protection] where there is such disagreement. But let us take the example of a doctor who has no previous knowledge of the patient and who is confronted by a [donee] with no medical expertise and articulates his views plausibly and forcefully. Are we going to imagine that every doctor in that position will have the strength of purpose and the degree of self-belief to refer the matter to the Court? I find that unlikely. Doctors are professional people, but they are also human. I very much fear that some will be browbeaten into agreeing to a course of action that runs contrary to their better judgment" (*Hansard*, HL Vol.670, col.1484).

In *Re Spaas* (COP), April 2, 2013, the donor of a welfare LPA included the following provision: "If I become completely mentally or physically incapable for example being unable to recognise my daughter then I wish steps to be taken to end my life as quickly and painlessly as possible. It that was not possible, I would wish the minimum medical intervention possible. I would not want my life unnecessarily prolonged". On the application of the Public Guardian the words from "steps to be taken" to "I would wish" were severed. Senior Judge Lush said that the donor may have been envisaging assisted suicide, which is unlawful (see *Re Gardner* (COP) July 6, 2011) or even expressing a wish for her life to be terminated by others in circumstances which would involve a criminal offence.

This provision is compatible with art.2 of the European Convention on Human Rights which provides for a "right to life" because the donee is chosen by a competent adult and can only act under the Act in the best interests of that person.

Scope of lasting powers of attorney: gifts

1–148   **12.**—(1) Where a lasting power of attorney confers authority to make decisions about P's property and affairs, it does not authorise a donee (or, if more than one, any of them) to dispose of the donor's property by making gifts except to the extent permitted by subsection (2).

(2) The donee may make gifts—

(a) on customary occasions to persons (including himself) who are related to or connected with the donor, or

(b) to any charity to whom the donor made or might have been expected to make gifts,

if the value of each such gift is not unreasonable having regard to all the circumstances and, in particular, the size of the donor's estate.

(3) "Customary occasion" means—

(a) the occasion or anniversary of a birth, a marriage or the formation of a civil partnership, or

(b) any other occasion on which presents are customarily given within families or among friends or associates.

(4) Subsection (2) is subject to any conditions or restrictions in the instrument.

DEFINITIONS

1–149   "lasting power of attorney": s.64(1)
"property": s.64(1)

GENERAL NOTE

This section limits the power of a donee of a financial LPA to dispose of P's property by **1–150** making gifts. Only gifts coming within the categories set out in subs.(2) are allowed even if the donor had indicated otherwise (*Sykes, Re* (COP) July 9, 2009, Senior Judge Lush). The donee must also act in accordance with any conditions or restrictions on his or her power to make gifts which are specified in the LPA, and satisfy the best interests criterion (s.9(4) (a)). If the donee wishes to make a gift which exceeds his or her authority under the LPA, an application should be made to the Court of Protection under s.18(1)(b). The court has power to authorise gifts otherwise than in accordance with subs.(2) if satisfied that these would be in P's best interests (s.23(4)).

In *Re GM* [2013] EWHC 2966 (COP) at para.54, Senior Judge Lush offered the following guidance to both donees and deputies on the making of gifts:

"It is important that deputies and attorneys should:

(a)   realise that they have only a very limited authority to make gifts;
(b)   understand why their authority is limited; and
(c)   be aware that, in an appropriate case, they may apply to the Court of Protection for more extensive gift-making powers" (see *Re Buckley*, noted under s.23, where Judge Lush made findings with regard to *de minimis* payments).

Judge Lush said that the

"first and paramount consideration must be whether the gift is in P's best interests, and other circumstances to which regard should be given, in addition to the size of P's estate, include, but are not limited to, the following:

- the extent to which P was in the habit of making gifts or loans of a particular size or
- nature before the onset of incapacity;
- P's anticipated life expectancy;
- the possibility that P may require residential or nursing care and the projected cost of such care;
- whether P is in receipt of aftercare pursuant to section 117 of the Mental Health Act 1983 or NHS Continuing Healthcare;
- the extent to which any gifts may interfere with the devolution of P's estate under his or her will or intestacy; and
- the impact of Inheritance Tax on P's death" (para.67).

The Public Guardian has issued Practice Note No. 02/2012 on "Gifts: Deputies and EPA/ LPA Attorneys" which can be accessed on the website of the Office of the Public Guardian.

Subsection (2)

In *Public Guardian v GB* [2015] EWCOP 6 at para.32, Senior Judge Lush said:

"The reason why attorneys have only a limited authority to make gifts was discussed by the Law Commission in its report *The Incapacitated Principal*, [1983] EWLC 122, which was published in 1983 and led to the enactment of the Enduring Powers of Attorney Act 1985. At paragraph 4.24, the Law Commission stated:

'An unlimited authority to make gifts might tempt the attorney to abuse his position especially if he himself fell on hard times and persuaded himself that the donor, if capable, would have wanted him to benefit in this way. And the unscrupulous attorney might persuade a semi-capable donor that such an authority was standard practice and perfectly safe.'"

CHARITY. Donations to a political party do not fall within this provision (*Re Rider* (COP) Feb. 20, 2013)

NOT UNREASONABLE. This is for the donee to determine having regard to all the **1–151** circumstances. In *Re GM* [2013] EWHC 2966 (COP) at para.73, Judge Lush said that

that "the threshold at which the value of a gift made by a deputy or attorney could be considered as 'not unreasonable' is likely to be low". In *Re Treadwell* [2013] EWHC 2409 (COP) at para.67, Judge Lush agreed with a submission made on behalf of the Public Guardian that "it is not possible to lay down any general rule as to the amounts a deputy may give away, as each case will turn on its own facts". Judge Lush confirmed that "after the death of the person to whom the proceedings relate, the court no longer has jurisdiction to ratify any gifts made by their former deputy" (para.78). The donee is not required to obtain consent from anyone before making the gift. The authorisation of the court should be obtained if it is proposed to make a substantial gift in order to reduce P's tax liability.

Estate. This should be construed as meaning the totality of P's current and anticipated income and capital, expenditure and debts (*Re GM,* above, para.66).

Subsection (3)

1–152   Any other occasion. Taking into account P's past and present wishes and feelings (s.4(6)(a)).

Revocation of lasting powers of attorney etc
1–153   13.—(1) This section applies if—
  (a) P has executed an instrument with a view to creating a lasting power of attorney, or
  (b) a lasting power of attorney is registered as having been conferred by P,
and in this section references to revoking the power include revoking the instrument.

(2) P may, at any time when he has capacity to do so, revoke the power.

(3) P's bankruptcy [, or the making of a debt relief order (under Part 7A of the Insolvency Act 1986) in respect of P,] revokes the power so far as it relates to P's property and affairs.

(4) But where P is bankrupt merely because an interim bankruptcy restrictions order has effect in respect of him [or where P is subject to an interim debt relief restrictions order (under Schedule 4ZB of the Insolvency Act 1986)], the power is suspended, so far as it relates to P's property and affairs, for so long as the order has effect.

(5) The occurrence in relation to a donee of an event mentioned in subsection (6)—
  (a) terminates his appointment, and
  (b) except in the cases given in subsection (7), revokes the power.

(6) The events are—
  (a) the disclaimer of the appointment by the donee in accordance with such requirements as may be prescribed for the purposes of this section in regulations made by the Lord Chancellor,
  (b) subject to subsections (8) and (9), the death or bankruptcy of the donee [or the making of a debt relief order (under Part 7A of the Insolvency Act 1986) in respect of the donee] or, if the donee is a trust corporation, its winding-up or dissolution,
  (c) subject to subsection (11), the dissolution or annulment of a marriage or civil partnership between the donor and the donee,
  (d) the lack of capacity of the donee.

(7) The cases are—
  (a) the donee is replaced under the terms of the instrument,

(b) he is one of two or more persons appointed to act as donees jointly and severally in respect of any matter and, after the event, there is at least one remaining donee.

(8) The bankruptcy of a donee [or the making of a debt relief order (under Part 7A of the Insolvency Act 1986) in respect of a donee] does not terminate his appointment, or revoke the power, in so far as his authority relates to P's personal welfare.

(9) Where the donee is bankrupt merely because an interim bankruptcy restrictions order has effect in respect of him [or where the donee is subject to an interim debt relief restrictions order (under Schedule 4ZB of the Insolvency Act 1986),] his appointment and the power are suspended, so far as they relate to P's property and affairs, for so long as the order has effect.

(10) Where the donee is one of two or more appointed to act jointly and severally under the power in respect of any matter, the reference in subsection (9) to the suspension of the power is to its suspension in so far as it relates to that donee.

(11) The dissolution or annulment of a marriage or civil partnership does not terminate the appointment of a donee, or revoke the power, if the instrument provided that it was not to do so.

AMENDMENTS

The words in square brackets in subss.(3), (4), (6)(b), (8) and (9) were inserted by SI 2012/2404 art.3(2), Sch.1, para.53(3). **1–154**

DEFINITIONS

"lasting power of attorney": s.64(1) **1–155**
"property": s.64(1)
"bankrupt": s.64(3)
"bankruptcy restrictions order": s.64(4)
"debt relief order": s.64(3A)
"debt relief restrictions order": s.64(4A)
"trust corporation": s.64(1)

GENERAL NOTE

This section identifies the way in with an LPA can be revoked, whether before or after registration. A donor who has revoked the LPA must follow the procedure set out in the Lasting Powers of Attorney, Enduring Powers of Attorney and Public Guardian Regulations 2007 (SI 2007/1253) reg.21. The death of the donor revokes the LPA (reg.22). **1–156**

P can revoke an LPA at any time while he or she has capacity to do so (subs.(2)). P's bankruptcy or him being subject to a debt relief order will revoke an LPA that relates to P's property and affairs, but not a personal welfare LPA or that part of an LPA giving authority to make personal welfare decisions (subs.(3)). An interim bankruptcy restrictions order or an interim debt relief restrictions order merely suspends a financial LPA (subs.(4)).

The events relating to the donee which are set out in subs.(6) terminate his or her appointment and also revoke the LPA, apart from when the terms of the LPA replace the donee or where the donee is acting jointly and severally with others and, after the event, there is at least one remaining donee (subs.(7)).

The Public Guardian should be informed if an LPA is revoked as this would enable him to cancel the registration (Sch.1, para.17).

Subsection (2)

P might have the capacity to revoke the power by, for example, saying "I don't want X deciding things for me any more", but not have the capacity to make the decision in question. This power can be exercised during a period of temporary capacity. In *S, Re* **1–157**

Unreported, March 13, 1997, Master Lush held that in order to revoke an EPA, a donor should have the capacity to understand who the attorneys are; what authority they have; why it is necessary of expedient to revoke the power; and the foreseeable consequences of revoking the power.

Subsection (4)

1–158   BANKRUPTCY RESTRICTIONS ORDERS. These are provided for in Sch.4A of the Insolvency Act 1986 (c.45).

Subsection (6)

1–159   In *Re Harcourt* (COP), July 31, 2012, Senior Judge Lush said at para.66:

"[S]urprisingly, a finding of the court that an attorney is behaving in a way that contravenes his authority or is not in the donor's best interests is not, in fact, an event that would trigger the appointment of a replacement attorney under section 13(6) of the Act."

A replacement donee may only act on the occurrence of an event mentioned in this provision: see, for example, *Jenkins, Re* (COP) September 2, 2008, Senior Judge Lush.

DISCLAIMER OF THE APPOINTMENT. The procedure set out in SI 2007/1253 reg.20 must be followed.

BANKRUPTCY OF THE DONEE. But see subss.(8)–(10).

DISSOLUTION OR ANNULMENT OF A MARRIAGE, OR CIVIL PARTNERSHIP. But see subs.(11).

LACK OF CAPACITY OF THE DONEE. Although the matter is not free from doubt, it is submitted that a temporary incapacity of the donee would not revoke the LPA.

Protection of donee and others if no power created or power revoked

1–160   **14.**—(1) Subsections (2) and (3) apply if—
  (a) an instrument has been registered under Schedule 1 as a lasting power of attorney, but
  (b) a lasting power of attorney was not created,
whether or not the registration has been cancelled at the time of the act or transaction in question.

(2) A donee who acts in purported exercise of the power does not incur any liability (to P or any other person) because of the non-existence of the power unless at the time of acting he—
  (a) knows that a lasting power of attorney was not created, or
  (b) is aware of circumstances which, if a lasting power of attorney had been created, would have terminated his authority to act as a donee.

(3) Any transaction between the donee and another person is, in favour of that person, as valid as if the power had been in existence, unless at the time of the transaction that person has knowledge of a matter referred to in subsection (2).

(4) If the interest of a purchaser depends on whether a transaction between the donee and the other person was valid by virtue of subsection (3), it is conclusively presumed in favour of the purchaser that the transaction was valid if—
  (a) the transaction was completed within 12 months of the date on which the instrument was registered, or
  (b) the other person makes a statutory declaration, before or within 3 months after the completion of the purchase, that he had no reason at the time of the transaction to doubt that the donee had authority to dispose of the property which was the subject of the transaction.

(5) In its application to a lasting power of attorney which relates to matters in addition to P's property and affairs, section 5 of the Powers of Attorney Act 1971 (c. 27) (protection where power is revoked) has effect as if references to revocation included the cessation of the power in relation to P's property and affairs.

(6) Where two or more donees are appointed under a lasting power of attorney, this section applies as if references to the donee were to all or any of them.

DEFINITIONS
"lasting power of attorney": s.64(1)   **1–161**
"purchaser": s.64(1)
"property": s.64(1)

GENERAL NOTE
This section provides legal protection to donees and others who act on invalid LPAs.   **1–162**
Subsection (1) outlines the situations to which subss.(2) and (3) apply. It gives protection to donees and others who rely on registered LPAs which later turn out to be invalid. The protection applies whether or not the registration has been cancelled. Broadly, both donees and third parties will be protected from legal liability if they were unaware that the LPA was invalid.

Subsections (4) and (5) deal with property. If either para.(a) or (b) of sub.(4) is satisfied, a purchaser of property from a donee of an invalid LPA will be protected unless the purchaser was aware of the invalidity.

General powers of the court and appointment of deputies

Power to make declarations
15.—(1) The court may make declarations as to—   **1–163**
(a) whether a person has or lacks capacity to make a decision specified in the declaration;
(b) whether a person has or lacks capacity to make decisions on such matters as are described in the declaration;
(c) the lawfulness or otherwise of any act done, or yet to be done, in relation to that person.
(2) "Act" includes an omission and a course of conduct.

DEFINITIONS
"the court": s.64(1)   **1–164**

GENERAL NOTE
This section provides the Court of Protection with the power to make declarations about   **1–165**
whether an individual has mental capacity, and whether an act or proposed act was or would be lawful. In *Aintree University Hospitals NHS Foundation Trust v James* [2013] UKSC 67 at para.18, Lady Hale said that the Act is concerned with enabling the court to do for the patient what he could do for himself if of full capacity, but it goes no further. A patient cannot order a doctor to give a particular form of treatment, although he may refuse it. The court's position is no different.

In *Re MN (Adult)* [2015] EWCA Civ 411, Sir James Munby P. said at para.91:

". . . it might be thought that, unless the desired order clearly falls within the ambit of section 15, orders are better framed in terms of relief under section 16 and that, if non-compliance or interference with the arrangements put in place by the Court of Protection is thought to be a risk, that risk should be met by extracting appropriate undertakings or, if suitable undertakings are not forthcoming, granting an injunction."

A declaration that a particular course of action is lawful does not have the effect of requiring a party to follow that course of action. An injunction would have to be granted in order to achieve this objective. In *MASM v MMAM* [2015] EWCOP 3, Hayden J. confirmed that acting in a way that is not compatible with a best interests declaration, rather than an injunction, does not expose an individual to contempt proceedings.

A declaration may be refused on the ground that no such declaration is needed. For example, in *H (Mental Patient: Diagnosis), Re* (1993) 1 F.L.R. 28, it was held that a C.T. scan for a schizophrenic patient with a suspected brain tumour was not one of those cases where it was either necessary or desirable to grant a declaration.

The power to make declarations regarding a person's capacity is likely to be exercised where: (a) healthcare professionals cannot resolve a dispute about a person's capacity to make a serious decision regarding the provision of medical treatment; or (b) there is a dispute as to whether a person was mentally capable when either an advance decision or a lasting power of attorney was made. Declarations regarding the lawfulness of an act are likely to be made most frequently in cases involving controversial or particularly serious decisions regarding the provision of care or medical treatment for the incapacitated person. Subsection (2) confirms that the Court of Protection can be asked to make declarations on an omission to act (for example, the withholding or withdrawing of medical treatment), as well as on a course of conduct. The court has the same powers as the High Court, including the power to grant injunctive relief (s.47(1)) and the power to call for reports (s.49). Chapter 15 of the *Code of Practice* identifies options that are available for settling disputes without recourse to the court.

A summary of the principles which should be applied to a fact finding hearing in the court was provided by Baker J. in *A Local Authority v M* [2014] EWCOP 33 at paras 82 to 90: see the General Note to s.16.

The inherent jurisdiction

Although the Court of Protection cannot develop its "own inherent jurisdiction" which permits it to go outside its statutory powers (*XCC v AA* [2012] EWHC 2183 (COP) at para.49), the inherent jurisdiction of the High Court to grant declaratory and injunctive relief relating to adults is not ousted by the Act (*DL v A Local Authority*, below). Key cases under the inherent jurisdiction are summarised in the notes to subs.(1)(c). The purpose of the High Court's inherent jurisdiction was explained by Sir Thomas Bingham M.R. in *S (Hospital Patient: Court's Jurisdiction) (No.1), Re* [1996] Fam. 1 at 18:

> "[I]n cases of controversy and cases involving momentous and irrevocable decisions, the courts have treated as justicable any genuine question as to what the best interests of a patient require or justify. In making these decisions the courts have recognised the desirability of informing those involved whether a proposed course of conduct will render them criminally or civilly liable; they have acknowledged their duty to act as a safeguard against malpractice, abuse and unjustified action; and they have recognised the desirability, in the last resort, of decisions being made by an impartial independent tribunal."

The nature of the High Court's inherent jurisdiction over mentally incompetent adults was reviewed by Munby J. in *A (A Patient) v A Health Authority* [2002] EWHC 18 (Fam Div/Admin). His Lordship held that:

  (i) the jurisdiction could be invoked by anyone whose past or present relationship with the incompetent adult, whether formal or informal, gave him or her a genuine and legitimate interest in obtaining a decision, rather than being a stranger or officious busybody. Thus proceedings can be brought by a relative, a carer, a local authority or a NHS Trust;
 (ii) the jurisdiction may regulate all that conduces to the incompetent adult's welfare and happiness, including companionship and his or her domestic and social environment;
(iii) the jurisdiction, which extended no further than the *parens patriae* jurisdiction in relation to children, extended not merely to declaratory relief but also to the grant of

injunctive relief—at least interlocutory injunctive relief to preserve or regulate the status quo; and

(iv) if the task facing the judge was to come to a decision for and on behalf of an incompetent adult then the welfare of that person had to be the paramount consideration. If the task of the judge was to review the decision of the public authority taken in the exercise of some statutory power then the governing principles were those of public law.

The court has jurisdiction to grant whatever relief in declaratory form is necessary to safeguard and promote the incapacitated adult's welfare and interests (*S (Adult Patient) (Inherent Jurisdiction: Family Life), Re* [2002] EWHC 2278 at para.50). This can include injunctive relief, including interlocutory injunctive relief, the making of tipstaff orders (location orders, collection orders and passport orders) and orders enabling third parties to take protective steps in relation to an incapacitated adult: see *SA Re*, below, paras 84–95. The court also has the power to make a range of orders, similar to those available to the Family Division in child abduction cases, aimed at the location and recovery of an abducted incapacitated adult (*PM v KH* [2010] EWHC 870 (Fam)).

Although this section does not provide for the making of declarations as to whether or not circumstances amount to a deprivation of liberty, it may be that the court's power to make such declarations arises under the inherent jurisdiction: see *BB v AM,* noted under subs.1(c).

In *Re SA (Vulnerable Adult with Capacity: Marriage)* [2005] EWHC 2942 (Fam); [2006] 1 F.L.R. 867, Munby J. held that in certain circumstances the inherent jurisdiction can be exercised for the protection of vulnerable adults who do not lack capacity to make the decision in question. His Lordship said at para.79:

"The inherent jurisdiction can be invoked wherever a vulnerable adult is, or is reasonably believed to be, for some reason deprived of the capacity to make the relevant decision, or disabled from making a free choice, or incapacitated or disabled from giving or expressing a real and genuine consent. The cause may be, but is not for this purpose limited to, mental disorder or mental illness. A vulnerable adult who does not suffer from any kind of mental incapacity may nonetheless be entitled to the protection of the inherent jurisdiction if he is, or is reasonably believed to be, incapacitated from making the relevant decision by reason of such things as constraint, coercion, undue influence or other vitiating factors."

His Lordship elaborated by stating that (1) "constraint" involved "some significant curtailment of the freedom to do those things which in this country free men and women are entitled to do"; (2) undue influence occurs "where a vulnerable adult's capacity or will to decide has been sapped or overborne by the improper influence of another"; and (3) other disabling circumstances include "circumstances that may so reduce a vulnerable adult's understanding and reasoning powers as to prevent him from forming or expressing a real and genuine consent, for example, the effects of deception, misinformation, physical disability, illness, weakness (physical, mental or moral), tiredness, shock, fatigue, depression, pain or drugs" (para.78). A vulnerable adult is "someone who, whether or not mentally incapacitated, and whether or not suffering from any mental illness or mental disorder, is or may be unable to take care of him or herself, or unable to protect him or herself against significant harm or exploitation, or who is deaf, blind or dumb, or who is substantially handicapped by illness, injury or congenital deformity. This, I emphasise, is not and is not intended to be a definition. It is descriptive, not definitive; indicative rather than prescriptive" (para.82). His Lordship said, at para.96, that when exercising the inherent jurisdiction, it is "elementary that the court exercises its powers by reference to the incompetent adult's best interests".

SA was applied by Sir Nicholas Wall P. in *A Local Authority v DL* [2010] EWHC 2675 (Fam), a case where, in contrast to the situation in *SA*, the adults had the capacity to take legal proceedings.

Confirmation that the Act has not displaced the High Court's inherent jurisdiction to act as a safety net to protect vulnerable adults was given by the Court of Appeal in *DL v A Local Authority* [2012] EWCA Civ 253. McFarlane L.J., who gave the lead judgment, said at para.54:

> "The jurisdiction . . . is in part aimed at enhancing or liberating the autonomy of a vulnerable adult whose autonomy has been compromised by a reason other than mental incapacity because they are (to adopt the list in paragraph 77 of *Re SA*):
>
> a) Under constraint; or
> b) Subject to coercion or undue influence; or
> c) For some other reason deprived of the capacity to make the relevant decision or disabled from making a free choice, or incapacitated or disabled from giving or expressing a real and genuine consent."

His Lordship endorsed, at para.62, the following description of the jurisdictional relationship between the statutory scheme and the inherent jurisdiction given by Roderic Wood J. in *Westminster Council v C* [2008] EWCA Civ 198 at first instance ([2007] EWHC 3096 (Fam)):

> "[W]here it is necessary, lawful and proportionate I consider that this court can exercise its inherent jurisdiction in relation to mentally handicapped adults alongside, as appropriate, the Mental Capacity Act 2005. Consistent with long-standing principle, the terms of the Statute must be looked to first to see what Parliament has considered to be the appropriate statutory code, and the exercise of the inherent jurisdiction should not be deployed so as to undermine the will of Parliament as expressed in the Statute or any supplementary regulatory framework."

In terms of the manner in which the jurisdiction should be exercised, his Lordship expressly commended, at para.67, the facilitative, rather than dictatorial, approach described by Macur J. in *LBL v RYJ and VJ* [2010] EWHC 2665 (COP) at para.62.

As there is no provision in the Act to make declarations in respect of a non-recognition of a marriage, the court, of its own motion, invoked the inherent jurisdiction to make such a declaration in *XCC v AA* [2012] EWHC 2183, above, where Parker J. held that as the provisions of the Act were not to be imported in to the inherent jurisdiction evaluation, the decision was not dictated only by considerations of best interests but public policy considerations were also relevant (see paras 56–57 and 71–76). A declaration of non-marriage was made under the inherent jurisdiction in *A Local Authority v SY* [2013] EWHC 3485 (COP) where Keehan J. said that there are "compelling reasons of public policy why sham 'marriages' are declared non-marriages" (para.50).

Cases involving vulnerable adults who do not lack the mental capacity to make the decision in question will be heard in High Court under the inherent jurisdiction, not the Court of Protection.

The Official Solicitor has published a Practice Note on "Appointment in family proceedings and proceedings under the Inherent Jurisdiction in relation to adults" (March 2013) which is mainly concerned with the appointment of the Official Solicitor as a litigation friend.

Without notice applications

1–166   Guidance on the making of without notice applications to the court was provided by Charles J. in *B Borough Council v Mrs S and Mr S (by the Official Solicitor)* [2006] EWHC 2584 (Fam) at paras 38–43, 158. This guidance was applied and supplemented by Theis J. in *KY v DD* [2011] EWHC 1277 (Fam) and by McFarlane J. in *LLBC v TG, JG and TR* [2007] EWHC 2640 (Fam) at paras 52–55. In the latter case, his Lordship said at para.54:

> "The general approach of the court . . . is to evaluate as best it can the degree of urgency, the risks of intervening by way of making an order and the risks of not intervening at that stage."

In *A Local Authority v C* [2013] EWHC 4036 (Fam), C had long-standing mental health problems which had resulted in her two children being removed from her. Parker J. made an anticipatory declaration under the inherent jurisdiction on a without notice application that it was lawful for C's third baby to be removed immediately upon delivery, in order to safeguard the child's interests, on the understanding that the local authority would apply for an emergency protection order or an interim care order at the first possible moment. No evidence was heard from C, and a litigation friend was not appointed, in order to avoid C being informed of the proceedings.

Subsection (1) para.(a)

WHETHER A PERSON HAS OR LACKS CAPACITY. In *YLA v PM* [2013] EWHC 4020 (COP), **1–167**
Parker J. concluded that:

1. While this section is framed in discretionary terms, she did not have "true 'discretion' or choice" as to whether to make a declaration of capacity (para.116).
2. Respect for private and family life comes into the best interests test: it is not an invasion of private or family life to declare that a person lacks capacity in any particular respect (para.117).
3. The purpose of a declaration of capacity is to engage the powers of the Court of Protection: the question of whether it is in the best interests of P is not a relevant consideration in deciding whether to make such a declaration (para.119).

Her Ladyship agreed with the following comment made by Ryder J in *Oldham MBC v GW and PW* [2007] EWHC 136 (Fam):

"A judge in the Court of Protection – may feel drawn towards an outcome that is more protective of the adult and thus, in certain circumstances, fail to carry out an assessment of capacity that is detached and objective. On the other hand, the court must be equally careful not to be influenced by sympathy for a person's wholly understandable wish to return home."

The court will apply the tests set out in ss.2 and 3 at the date when it is considering the question (*CC v KK* [2012] EWHC 2136 (COP) at para.20). In *Masterman-Lister v Brutton & Co* [2002] EWCA Civ 1889 at para.29, Kennedy L.J. said that the "conclusion that in law capacity depends on time and context means that inevitably a decision as to capacity in one context does not bind a court which has to consider the same issue in a different context". This case is also authority for the proposition that although the final decision as to capacity rests with the court, in almost every case "the court will need medical evidence to guide it". However, capacity is a legal concept, not medical. In *CC v KK*, above, the court received evidence from KK herself to assist in determining the question of capacity, not only in a written statement but also orally in court. This procedure was described by Baker J. at para.44 as being unusual, but not unique. His Lordship said, at para.24, that "the court must consider all the evidence, not merely the views of the independent expert. In many cases, perhaps most cases, the opinion of the expert will be confirmed by the other evidence, but inevitably there will be cases where the court reaches a different conclusion. When taking evidence from P herself, the court must plainly be careful about assessing the capacity to understand, retain and use and weigh up information, but, whilst acknowledging the important role for expert evidence, the assessment is ultimately a matter for the court". In this case, Baker J. rejected the unanimous opinion of the medical experts that KK lacked capacity to make decisions about her residence and care. A similar finding with regard to a person's capacity to consent to an abortion was made by Holman J. in *Re SB* [2013] EWHC 1417 (COP) at para.36. The importance of the judge hearing evidence in an appropriate case from the person who is said by the medical experts to lack the required mental capacity is also illustrated by the finding of Baker J. in *A Local Authority v TZ* [2013] EWHC 2322 (COP). Rule 88 of the CPR 2007 allows for the attendance of P at court.

Those judges who decide not to meet P should bear in mind that in *Shtukaturov v Russia* (2012) 54 E.H.R.R. 27 at para.73, the European Court of Human Rights said:

"The applicant was indeed an individual with a history of psychiatric problems. From the materials of the case, however, it appears that despite his mental illness he had been a relatively autonomous person. In such circumstances it was indispensable for the judge to have at least a brief visual contact with the applicant, and preferably to question him. The Court concludes that the decision of the judge to decide the case on the basis of documentary evidence, without seeing or hearing the applicant, was unreasonable and in breach of the principle of adversarial proceedings enshrined in Article 6 § 1".

And in *X and Y v Croatia* (App.No.5193/09), the Court said at para.84:

"The Court considers that judges adopting decisions with serious consequences for a person's private life, such as those entailed by divesting someone of legal capacity, should in principle also have personal contact with those persons."

In *Sykora v Czech Republic* [2013] M.H.L.R. 283, the ECtHR held that although national authorities have a margin of appreciation in assessing somebody's mental capacity, the margin is reduced where the court does not hear from P.

In *CC v KK*, Baker J. said that when "assessing the evidence, the court must be aware of the difficulties which may arise as a result of the close professional relationship between the clinicians and professionals treating and working with, P . . . [I]n cases of vulnerable adults, there is a risk that all professionals involved with treating and helping that person—including, of course, a judge in the Court of Protection—may feel drawn towards an outcome that is more protective of the adult and thus, in certain circumstances, fail to carry out an assessment of capacity that is detached and objective. On the other hand, the court must be equally careful not to be influenced by sympathy for a person's wholly understandable wish to return home" (para.25).

There is no power to order an individual to co-operate with a capacity assessment: see *Baker Tilly v Maker* [2013] EWHC 759 (QB), where Sir Raymond Jack said at para.15:

"The absence of medical evidence cannot be a bar to a finding of lack of capacity but where most unusually circumstances arise in which medical evidence cannot be obtained, the court should be most cautious before concluding that the probability is that there is a disturbance of the mind. . . . Such a finding is a serious step for both parties. It takes away the protected party's right to conduct their litigation. It may constitute, and here would constitute, a serious disadvantage to the other party."

Paragraph 8.16 of the *Code of Practice* states:

"Applications concerning a person's capacity are likely to be rare – people can usually settle doubts and disagreements informally. But an application may be relevant if:

- a person wants to challenge a decision that they lack capacity

- professionals disagree about a person's capacity to make a specific (usually serious) decision

- there is a dispute over whether the person has capacity (for example, between family members)."

Practice Direction 9A specifies that the court must have evidence of capacity in the prescribed form, which is Form COP3. In *A Local Authority v SY* [2013] EWHC 3485 (COP), Keehan J. said at paras 21 and 22:

"The assessment of capacity (COP 3) was completed by SY's social worker, NU. It is a full, detailed and helpful assessment of SY's capacity to make decisions as to her residence, contact with others, her care needs and to enter into a contract of marriage.

I am told by counsel that it is more usual for the assessment of capacity to be undertaken by a medical practitioner or a psychiatrist. The assessment in this case demonstrates that an appropriately qualified social worker is eminently suited to undertake such capacity assessments. I commend the practice which I hope will be followed in appropriate future cases."

It should be noted that the courts have been criticised for exhibiting an excessive degree of deference to medical professionals; see, for example, Lord Woolf, "Are the courts excessively deferential to the medical profession?" ((2001) 9 *Medical Law Review* 1.

In *Re KGB*, noted at para.4.6.3 of the Annual Report, April 1, 2009 to March 31, 2010, of the Official Solicitor and Public Trustee, Roderic Wood J. held that the Court of Protection does not have jurisdiction to make decisions concerning a person's capacity to litigate proceedings in other courts.

Subsection (1) para.(c)

A declaration cannot be used to authorise what would otherwise be unlawful, nor can it **1–168** render unlawful that which would otherwise be lawful (*R. (on the application of Burke) v General Medical Council* [2005] EWCA Civ 1003 at para.71). As an alternative to making a declaration under this provision, the court could make a decision under s.16: see *Re MN (Adult)* noted in the General Note to this section. Under s.4A, a personal welfare order under s.16(2)(a) is the mechanism that the court must use to order the deprivation of P's liberty. However, if the court is prevented by s.16A from making such an order, the High Court has the power under its inherent jurisdiction to make a declaration and order authorising the treatment of an incapacitated adult that includes the provision for the deprivation of his liberty provided that the order complies with art.5 of the European Convention on Human Rights (ECHR) (*A NHS Trust v Dr A* [2013] EWHC 2442 (COP)).

In *City of Sunderland v PS* [2007] EWHC 623 (Fam) at para.22, Munby J. said that "proper compliance with s.6 of the Human Rights Act 1998 requires the judges to mould and adapt the inherent jurisdiction so that it is compatible with the requirement of art.5, as well as art.8". Applying this principle to cases where it was in the best interests of mentally incapable adults to be detained in care homes, his Lordship said, at para.23, that the following minimum requirements must be satisfied in order to comply with art.5:

1. The detention must be authorised by the court on application made by the local authority and before the detention commences.
2. Subject to the exigencies of urgency or emergency the evidence must establish unsoundness of mind of a kind or degree warranting compulsory confinement. In other words, there must be evidence establishing at least a prima facie case that the individual lacks capacity and that confinement of the nature proposed is appropriate.
3. Any order authorising detention must contain provision for an adequate review at reasonable intervals, in particular with a view to ascertaining whether there still persists unsoundness of mind of a kind or degree warranting compulsory confinement. Further guidance on the nature of the review process was given by his Lordship in *BJ, Re* [2008] EWHC 1097 (Fam), paras 40 and 44, and in *Salford City Council v BJ* [2009] EWHC 3310 (Fam), paras 23 and 24 where his Lordship said that reviews did not necessarily require an oral hearing and that the regime laid down in Sch.A1 provides important guidance as to the nature, intensity and frequency of review.

The Court of Protection has jurisdiction to make a declaration as to whether the ECHR rights of P or a family member of P have been contravened, and to award damages for breaches of such rights (*YA(F) v A Local Authority* [2010] EWHC 2770 (Fam)). In *A Local Authority v Mrs D* [2013] EWHC B34 (COP), a case where the court approved an agreed order compromising a claim for remedies under s.8 of the Human Rights Act 1998, which included a sum in damages for alleged breaches of a party's rights under arts 5 and 8 of the ECHR, DJ Mainwaring-Taylor said that remedies under ECHR are "*vindicatory* rather than restitutionary in their nature" (para.48). The judge said that the decision of the Supreme Court in *R (on the application of Faulkner) v Secretary of State for Justice* [2013] UKSC 23

"clarifies (at para 13) that given the present stage of the development of the remedy of damages under section 8 of the HRA 1998:

'3. . . . . courts should be guided, primarily by any clear and consistent practice of the European court.

4. In particular, the quantum of awards under section 8 should broadly reflect the level of awards made by the European court in comparable cases brought by applicants from the UK or other countries with a similar cost of living . . .

6. Where it is established on a balance of probabilities that a violation of article 5(4) has resulted in the detention of a prisoner beyond the date when he would otherwise have been released, damages should ordinarily be awarded as compensation for the resultant detention.

7. The appropriate amount to be awarded in such circumstances will be a matter of judgment, reflecting the facts of the individual case and taking into account such guidance as is available from awards made by the European court, or by domestic courts under section 8 of the 1998 Act, in comparable cases."

On the basis of case law under the inherent jurisdiction, the *Code of Practice* states, at para.8.18, that cases involving any of the following decisions should be brought before the court:

"• decisions about the proposed withholding or withdrawal of artificial nutrition and hydration (ANH) from patients in a permanent vegetative state (PVS)
• cases involving organ or bone marrow donation by a person who lacks capacity to consent
• cases involving the proposed non-therapeutic sterilisation of a person who lacks capacity to consent to this (e.g. for contraceptive purposes) and
• all other cases where there is a doubt or dispute about whether a particular treatment will be in a person's best interests."

Paragraph 2.27 of the *Reference guide to consent for examination or treatment* (Department of Health 2009) states:

"Other cases likely to be referred to the court include those involving ethical dilemmas in untested areas (such as innovative treatments for variant CJD), or where there are otherwise irresolvable conflicts between healthcare staff, or between staff and family members."

The first three examples in the list set out in para.8.18 of the *Code of Practice* are reproduced in Practice Direction 9E ("Applications relating to Serious Medical Treatment") as cases which should be referred to the court. Other examples of "serious medical treatment" are set out in para.6 of the Practice Direction:

"(a) certain terminations of pregnancy in relation to a person who lacks capacity to consent to such a procedure;
(b) a medical procedure performed on a person who lacks capacity to consent to it, where the procedure is for the purpose of a donation to another person;
(c) a medical procedure or treatment to be carried out on a person who lacks capacity to consent to it, where that procedure or treatment must be carried out using a degree of force to restrain the person concerned;
(d) an experimental or innovative treatment for the benefit of a person who lacks capacity to consent to such treatment; and
(e) a case involving an ethical dilemma in an untested area."

Whether or not other procedures are to be regarded as serious medical treatments which should be referred to the court "will depend on the circumstances and the consequences for the patient" (para.7).

In *AVS v A NHS Foundation Trust* [2011] EWCA Civ 7 at para.35, Ward L.J. said:

"It is trite that the court will not order medical treatment to be carried out if the treating physician/surgeon is unwilling to offer that treatment for clinical reasons conscientiously held by that medical practitioner."

Healthcare decisions involving children under the age of 16 will come before the High Court, not the Court of Protection.

Patients in a vegetative state
[Also see the note on *Best interests and the withholding of treatment which would keep*   **1–169**
P alive in the General Note to s.4.]
In *Re AW (Permanent Vegetative State)* [2013] EWHC 78 (COP) at paras 16 and 17, Peter Jackson J. identified the distinction between a vegetative state (VS) and a permanent vegetative state (PVS):

"The vegetative state has been described as an absence of awareness of one's self and one's environment, a sleep/wake cycle, no demonstration of purposeful movement, no experience of suffering and no evidence of comprehension. Behaviours are limited to reflexive activities indicating no cortical involvement.

The permanent vegetative state has been defined as a vegetative state persisting for more than six months as a result of non-traumatic brain damage, or six months as the result of traumatic brain damage."

The leading case on the withdrawal of life sustaining treatment, including artificial hydration and nutrition (ANH), on a patient in a PVS is the decision of the House of Lords in *Airedale NHS Trust v Bland* [1993] 1 All E.R. 821. Decisions on this issue now have to be made by reference to both s.4 and the decision in *Bland*. In *Re M* [2011] EWHC 2443 (Fam) at para.65, Baker J. identified the key principle to be drawn from Lord Goff's speech in *Bland*:

"(1) the principle of the sanctity of life is fundamental; (2) that principle is not, however, absolute and may yield in certain circumstances, for example to the principle of self-determination; (3) a decision whether ANH treatment should be initiated or withdrawn must be determined by what is in the best interests of the patient; (4) in the great majority of cases the best interests of the patient were likely to require that the treatment should be given; (5) there was a category of case in which the decision whether to withhold treatment would be made by weighing up relevant and competing considerations, but (6) such an approach was inappropriate in the case of Anthony Bland as the treatment had no therapeutic purpose and was 'futile' because he was unconscious and had no prospects of recovery."

With regard to principle (6), Baker J. said, at para.35, that in PVS cases the balancing exercise required by s.4 "falls in one direction every time – in favour of withdrawal [of medical treatment]".
The importance of diagnosing P's condition before the application is made was emphasised by Newton J. in *Cwm Taf University Health Board v F* [2015] EWHC 2533 (Fam). His Lordship said at para.13:

"The important distinction of diagnosis (between minimally conscious state and vegetative states) so far as the court is concerned self evidently dictates a different path, with different considerations and vastly different outcomes. In relation to a permanent vegetative state it may mean that the life sustaining treatment is futile, whereas in a minimally conscious state the court takes an holistic balance sheet approach. . . . The Court must examine therefore diagnosis with some considerable degree of care."

The significance of the requirement to refer PVS cases to the Court is underlined by the following case which is referred to in the Preface to the Annual Report, April 1, 2009 to March 31, 2010, of the Official Solicitor:

"We wish to draw particular attention to one disturbing case in which the Official Solicitor acted as litigation friend in the Court of Protection during the year. The case concerned Y, a 22 year old man who sustained a severe head injury in a road traffic accident, who had been in what appeared to be a state of deep unconsciousness for over 4 years. His treating consultant in rehabilitation medicine diagnosed him as being in the persistent vegetative state (PVS). He obtained the agreement of Y's parents to withdraw nutrition. The Mental Capacity Act 2005: Code of Practice and Rules of the Court of Protection provide that decisions about the removal of artificial nutrition from a person in PVS should be brought to the Court of Protection for determination. However, in this case the treating consultant withdrew artificial nutrition without a court order. When the NHS Trust was alerted to this several weeks later, it immediately applied to the Court of Protection. By this time Y had been without nutrition for 3 weeks. The Trust acknowledged that the consultant had acted improperly in withdrawing artificial nutrition without a court order but expressed concern that it was not in Y's best interests to resume feeding. The Official Solicitor was invited to act for Y. Advice was immediately taken by the Official Solicitor from a leading expert in Rehabilitation Medicine. The expert advocated the immediate resumption of artificial nutrition and the reduction in the amount of sedation Y was being given. This was to allow an opportunity for Y's diagnosis to be thoroughly assessed before any final decision was made about the withdrawal of artificial nutrition and hydration. The NHS trust opposed both the resumption of feeding and the reduction in sedation arguing that Y's diagnosis was well established and that the sedation being given to Y was medically necessary to control his epilepsy and to prevent distressing physical symptoms and did not suppress Y's awareness in any way. The Official Solicitor and his experts took the view that feeding could be safely resumed and that the reduction in sedation could be safely undertaken and that without such a reduction any assessment of Y's awareness would be unreliable and potentially flawed. The court on an interim basis ordered a resumption of feeding. Before the final hearing the Trust withdrew its application and agreed its clinicians would keep under review whether Y was in PVS and whether further assessments were appropriate. It is understood that Y was subsequently found not to be in PVS and that he is currently undergoing rehabilitation treatment which so far has allowed him to sit up and which may in time allow him to both drink and feed orally, and to speak."

The Royal College of Physicians has published *Prolonged disorders of consciousness: National clinical guidelines* (2013). The importance of applicants complying with these guidelines and of providing the court with adequate evidence and analysis was emphasised by Newton J. in *St George's Healthcare NHS Trust v P* [2015] EWCOP 42, which is noted under *Best interest and the withholding of treatment which would sustain life* in the General Note to s.4.

Patients in a minimally conscious state

1–170   [Also see the note on *Best interests and the withholding of treatment which would keep P alive* in the General Note to s.4.]

In *Re M* [2011] EWHC 2443 (Fam), the applicant's case was summarised by Baker J. at para.34:

"Medical science has developed from the 1990s when the concept of persistent or permanent vegetative state (originally 'PVS' but now more commonly 'VS') was first considered in the English courts. Since then medical science has recognised the concept of the minimally conscious state ('MCS'), which is a state just above that of vegetative state, but which also involves extremely significant limitations on consciousness with a quality of life that many would find impossible to accept were they able to consistently express themselves with full competence. The court has jurisdiction to decide what treatment patients in a minimally conscious state should receive. The issue in this case is whether M continuing to have medical treatment in the form of ANH is truly in her best interests, as defined in s.4 of the Mental Capacity Act 2005."

His Lordship made the following findings:

1. All decisions about the proposed withholding or withdrawal of ANH from a person

in a PVS or MCS should always be brought to the court before a High Court judge (paras 82 and 257).

2. It is of the utmost importance that every step should be taken to diagnose the patient's true condition before an application is made to the court (para.259).

3. The burden of establishing that discontinuance of treatment is in a person's best interests is always on those who assert that life-sustaining treatment be withdrawn (para.73).

4. In a number of respects, including the provisions concerning advance decisions, the Act has refined the previous law concerning the withdrawal of life-sustaining treatment. The basic principles, however, remain unchanged (para.85).

5. The Official Solicitor's argument that withdrawal of ANH can never be in the best interests of a clinically-stable MCS patient was rejected in favour of the usual "balance sheet" approach to best interests, although clinical stability is an important factor to be taken into account (paras 101–103).

6. The principle of the right to life carries very great weight in the balancing exercise. (para.222). It was the decisive factor in this case (para.249).

7. A best interests assessment, properly conducted under English law in accordance with established principles, is fully compliant with the ECHR, and it is unnecessary and inappropriate to deploy any additional arguments based on the individual articles of the Convention as a separate test of the legitimacy of the proposal to withdraw ANH. "Best interests "is a wide enough test to encompass all relevant factors in articles 2, 3 and 8 of the ECHR.

8. Given the importance of the sanctity of life, and the fatal consequences of withdrawing treatment, and the absence of an advance decision that complied with the requirements previously specified by the common law and now under statute, it would be wrong to attach significant weight to general statements made by the patient prior to her collapse concerning her wish not to live a life dependent on others (paras 223–230).

With regard to point 8, a greater reliance on general relevant comments that had been made by an MCS patient as to what she would wish in the event of a road traffic accident was made by Pauffley J. in *United Lincolnshire Hospitals NHS Trust v N* [2014] EWCOP 16. Her Ladyship made the following declarations relating to the patient:

"The critical decision is whether it is in N's best interests to continue invasive, risk laden, medical care as would be involved in a further attempt at artificial feeding. I am utterly convinced that it would not. Accordingly, I declare that it is lawful and in her best interests for the clinicians (a) not to make any further attempt to secure a means of providing artificial nutrition; (b) to withdraw the provision of intravenous fluids and dextrose; and (c) to provide such palliative care and related treatment (including pain relief) as considered appropriate to ensure she suffers the least distress and retains the greatest dignity until such time as her life comes to an end" (para.66).

M v Mrs N [2015] EWCOP 76 is the first case in which the court expressly sanctioned the withdrawal of clinically assisted nutrition and hydration from a person who was in an MCS.

Patients who might require a non-therapeutic sterilisation

[Also see the note on *Best interests and sterilisation as a method of contraception* in the   **1–171** General Note to s.4]

In *A Local Authority v K* [2013] EWHC 242 (COP) at paras 36 and 37, Cobb J. gave guidance as to the practice and procedure that should be followed in cases involving non-therapeutic sterilisation:

"Referral to the Court of Protection in a case such as this could and should always be considered at the earliest moment in accordance with the Rules (see in particular *Practice*

Direction 9E to the *Court of Protection Rules 2007*, and *Para.6.18* and *Paras.8.18–8.29* of the *Mental Capacity Act 2005 Code of Practice*). I take this opportunity to remind medical (and, where relevant, legal) practitioners of the Court of Protection's role in considering a question of non-therapeutic sterilisation. Such a treatment decision is so serious that the Court has to make it. In particular I advise that particular note is made of the process as follows:

(a) The decision of whether someone who lacks capacity to consent should have a non-therapeutic sterilisation is a question involving 'serious medical treatment' (see *Practice Direction E (PD9E)*—Applications relating to serious medical treatment). Non-therapeutic sterilisation is specifically identified in this category (see *Paragraph 5(c)*);

(b) A question concerning non-therapeutic sterilisation of a person who lacks capacity to give consent '*should be brought to the court*' (*Para.5* ibid.);

(c) Where a question arises as to non-therapeutic sterilisation of a person who lacks capacity to consent, the proposed applicant (whether it be carer, local authority or trust), can (indeed I suggest should) usefully discuss the application with the Official Solicitor's department before the application is made (see *PD9E para.8*): such cases should be addressed to a family and medical litigation lawyer at the Office of the Official Solicitor,

(d) The organisation which is, or will be, responsible for providing clinical or caring services to P should usually be named as a respondent in the application form (where it is not already the applicant in the proceedings);

(e) Proceedings of this kind must be conducted by a judge of the Court of Protection who has been nominated as such by virtue of section 46(2)(a) to (c) of the Act (i.e. the President of the Family Division, the Chancellor or a puisne judge of the High Court) (*Para.12 PD9E*);

(f) At the first hearing of the application the Court will consider
  (i) whether P should be joined as party to the proceedings, and give directions to that effect;
  (ii) if P is to be joined as a party to the proceedings, decide whether the Official Solicitor should be invited to act as a litigation friend or whether some other person should be appointed as a litigation friend;
  (iii) identify anyone else who has been notified of the proceedings and who has filed an acknowledgment and applied to be joined as a party to proceedings, and consider that application; and
  (iv) set a timetable for the proceedings including, where possible, a date for the final hearing.

(g) Note that the hearing will generally be in public, given the nature of the application, although the Court will ordinarily make an order pursuant to *Rule 92* that restrictions be imposed in relation to publication of information about the proceedings.

Where a declaration is needed, the order sought should be in the following or similar terms:

(a) That P lacks capacity to make a decision in relation to the [proposed medical treatment or procedure]. e.g. 'That P lacks capacity to make a decision in relation to sterilisation by [named procedure]'; and

(b) That, having regard to the best interests of P, it is lawful for the [proposed medical treatment or procedure] to be carried out by [proposed healthcare provider]; or

(c) That it is not in the best interests of P to undergo [the proposed medical treatment or procedure]."

Declarations under the High Court's inherent jurisdiction were applied for in a number of cases where it was proposed to sterilise a mentally incompetent patient. The test for making an application for a declaration in such cases was established by Sir Stephen Brown P. in *GF (Medical Treatment), Re* [1992] 1 F.L.R. 293, when he said at 294:

"I take the view that no application for leave to carry out [a sterilisation] operation need be made in cases where two medical practitioners are satisfied that the operation is (1) necessary for therapeutic purposes, (2) in the best interests of the patient, and (3) there is no practicable, less intrusive means of treating the condition."

In *LC (Medical Treatment: Sterilisation), Re* [1997] 2 F.L.R. 258, Thorpe J. held that leave to perform the sterilisation operation could not be justified upon the basis of some vague and unsubstantiated fear that the patient would be exposed to the risks of pregnancy from which she is presently protected. A similar approach was taken in *S (Medical Treatment: Adult Sterilisation, Re* [1998] 1 F.L.R. 944, where Johnson J. refused to grant a declaration on an application by the patient's mother in "the absence of any risk [of pregnancy] that can be called identifiable rather than speculative". A sterilisation can be in the best interests of the patient even if the risk of pregnancy is small (*W (An Adult: Mental Patient) (Sterilisation), Re* [1993] 1 F.L.R. 381).

Forced or arranged marriages

In *XCC v AA* [2012] EWHC 2183 (COP), Parker J. held the High Court could exercise **1–172** its inherent jurisdiction of its own motion to refuse to recognise a marriage celebrated abroad where one party was unable to consent to the marriage. Her Ladyship was satisfied that once "a matter is before the Court of Protection, the High Court may make orders of its own motion, particularly if such orders are ancillary to, or in support of, orders made on application. Since the inherent jurisdiction of the High Court in relation to adults is an aspect of the parens patriae jurisdiction, the court has particularly wide powers to act on its own motion" (para.85). As her Ladyship was "exercising inherent jurisdiction powers and not making an order under the MCA 2005, then the provisions of Part 1 of the Act (entitled 'Persons who lack capacity') which are specifically expressed to apply 'for the purposes of this Act' are not imported into the inherent jurisdiction evaluation" (para.56). Granting a non-recognition declaration "is not a welfare or best interests decision" (para.61), although "welfare may be relevant to the decision" (para.62).

Her Ladyship further held that "a marriage with an incapacitated person who is unable to consent is a forced marriage within the meaning of the Forced Marriage Act 2007" and that " 'force' in the context of a person who lacks capacity must include inducing or arranging for a person who lacks capacity to undergo a ceremony of marriage, even if no compulsion or coercion is required as it would be with a person with capacity". (para.30). Her Ladyship provided the following guidance (taken from an earlier judgment) to health and social care professionals:

"[I]n my view it is the duty of a doctor or other health or social work professional who becomes aware that an incapacitated person may undergo a marriage abroad, to notify the learning disabilities team of Social Services and/or the Forced Marriage Unit if information comes to light that there are plans for an overseas marriage of a patient who has or may lack capacity. The communities where this is likely to happen also need to be told, loud and clear, that if a person, whether male or female, enters into a marriage when they do not have the capacity to understand what marriage is, its nature and duties, or its consequences, or to understand sexual relations, that that marriage may not be recognised, that sexual relations will constitute a criminal offence, and that the courts have the power to intervene" (para.96).

In *YLA v PM* [2013] EWHC 4020 (COP), Parker J. confirmed her opinion that an incapacious marriage is a forced marriage within the meaning of the 2007 Act, provided guidance on when a Forced Marriage Protection Order might be applied for in order to protect P, and commented upon the guidance that the Registrar General provides to Registrars in such cases.

If it has not been possible to prevent an arranged marriage involving a mentally incapacitated person taking place abroad, the relevant local authority should bring the case before the Court of Protection: see, for example, *Sandwell M.B.C v RG* [2013] EWHC

2373 (COP) where Holman J. refused to annul the marriage of RG on the ground that it was not in his best interests to disturb the status quo.

Section 121 of the Anti-social Behaviour, Crime and Policing Act 2014 makes forced marriage a criminal offence.

DNA tests

1–173   In *LG v DK* [2011] EWHC 2453 (COP), the court held that it has jurisdiction to exercise the power under s.21(4) of the Family Law Reform Act 1969, but not under this section or s.16, to bring about a scientific test on P in order to determine parentage if such action is deemed to be in P's best interests. This is the case notwithstanding the absence of a specific application within the proceedings on this issue. The President said that it would "require unusual facts for [P's] best interests to depart from the ascertainment of truth or the interests of justice" (para.55). Section 21(4) states:

> "A bodily sample may be taken from a person who lacks capacity (within the meaning of the Mental Capacity Act 2005) to give his consent, if consent is given by the court giving the direction under section 20 or by –
>
> (a) a donee of an enduring power of attorney or lasting power of attorney (within the meaning of that Act), or
>
> (b) a deputy appointed, or any other person authorised, by the Court of Protection,
>
> with power in that respect."

It was also held that it is not necessary for litigants to invoke s.55A of the Family Law Act 1986 which allows any person to apply to the High Court, a county court or a magistrates' court (but not to the Court of Protection) for a declaration as to whether or not a person named in the application is or was the parent of another person so named (*LG v DK* [2011] EWHC 2453 (COP)).

Healthcare decisions involving children under the age of 16 will come before the High Court, not the Court of Protection.

Pre-Act cases decided on the inherent jurisdiction

Termination of pregnancy

1–174   In *An NHS Trust v D* [2003] EWHC 2793 (Fam), Coleridge J. considered the following question: when should an NHS Trust make an application to the High Court for a declaration that the proposed termination of the pregnancy of a mentally incapacitated patient is lawful? His Lordship held that where there is any doubt as to either the mental capacity of the patient or whether the termination would be in her best interests, an application to the court should be made. In particular, the following circumstances would ordinarily warrant the making of an application:

1. Where there is a dispute as to capacity, or where there is a realistic prospect that the patient will regain capacity, following a response to treatment, within the period of her pregnancy or shortly thereafter;
2. Where there is a lack of unanimity amongst the medical professionals as to the best interests of the patient;
3. Where the procedures under s.1 of the Abortion Act 1967 (c.87) have not been followed (i.e. where two medical practitioners have not provided a certificate);
4. Where the patient, members of her immediate family, or the foetus's father have opposed, or expressed views inconsistent with, a termination of the pregnancy; or
5. Where there are other exceptional circumstances (including where the termination may be the patient's last chance to bear a child).

His Lordship said that if any case is considered to fall anywhere near the boundary line in relation to any of the above criteria, it should for the avoidance of doubt be referred to the court.

The guidance provided in this pre-Act case received the endorsement of Hedley J. in *A NHS Trust v P* [2013] EWHC 50 (COP).

It is essential for protocols to be put in place to deal with the possible termination of the pregnancy of patients in psychiatric hospitals. Such protocols should be designed to address the issue in good time and should ensure that the patient is referred at an early stage to independent legal advice whether from the Official Solicitor or from the solicitor who represented her at the Mental Health Review Tribunal (*SS (Medical Treatment: Late Termination), Re* [2002] 1 F.L.R. 445).

Emergency medical treatment

In *NHS Trust v T (Adult Patient: Refusal of Medical Treatment)* [2004] EWHC 1279 **1–175** (Fam); [2005] 1 All E.R. 387, Charles J. confirmed that an interim declaration could be made pursuant to CPR Part 25.1(1)(b). His Lordship said, at para.45, that when the court is faced with an emergency situation where treatment cannot be delayed because of an imminent high risk to life the court should make every effort to ensure that the person who it is proposed should be treated in reliance of any declaration has an opportunity to make representations (either directly or indirectly) to the court (and thus in cases of emergency out of hours to the Duty Judge). It would then be for the Judge to decide on capacity and then if appropriate on best interests by applying the normal civil standard on the best evidence then available. It is submitted that in extreme emergencies where there is no time to seek the assistance of the court, any doubt that may exist about the patient's capacity must be resolved in favour of society's interest in upholding the concept that all human life is sacred and that it should be preserved if at all possible.

Threatened criminal acts of another

In *A Local Authority v Z* [2004] EWHC 2817 (Fam), Hedley J. considered the extent of **1–176** the duty owed by a local authority when the welfare of a vulnerable adult (who may or may not be mentally incapacitated) in their area is threatened by the criminal (or other wrongful) act of another. In this case a husband was intending to assist his severely disabled wife in her desire to commit suicide. Assisting the suicide of another is a crime (Suicide Act 1961 (c.60), s.2(1)). His Lordship held that in such a case the local authority incurred the following duties:

1. To investigate the position of a vulnerable adult to consider what was her true position and intention.
2. To consider whether she was legally competent to make and carry out her decision and intention.
3. To consider whether any other (and if so, what) influence may be operating on her position and intention and to ensure that she has all the relevant information and knows all the available options.
4. To consider whether to invoke the inherent jurisdiction of the High Court so that the question of competence could be judicially investigated and determined.
5. In the event of the adult not being competent, to provide all such assistance as may be reasonably required both to determine and give effect to her best interests.
6. In the event of the adult being competent, to allow her in any lawful way to give effect to her decision although that should not preclude the giving of advice or assistance in accordance with what are perceived to be in her best interests.
7. Where there are reasonable grounds to suspect that the commission of a criminal offence may be involved, to draw that to the intention of the police.
8. In very exceptional circumstances, to invoke the jurisdiction of the court under s.222 of the Local Government Act 1972 (c.70) in order to seek an injunction to restrain a criminal act.

Fluctuating mental capacity

1–177   In *G (An Adult) (Mental Capacity: Court's Jurisdiction), Re* [2004] EWHC 2222 (Fam), an incapacitated young woman had been made the subject of interim declarations to protect her from the actions of her father. The evidence was that after a period of being subject to the interim declarations the daughter would regain her mental capacity and her mental health would improve, but that once the protection of the court was withdrawn the daughter's mental health would deteriorate and she would lose her mental capacity. Bennett J. held that in these circumstances he had jurisdiction to make declarations to ensure that the continuing protection of the court was not withdrawn simply because the daughter had regained her mental capacity, given the likely consequences if the court withdrew its protection. The judge said, at para.104, that if the declarations sought were in the daughter's best interests, the court, by intervening, far from depriving her of her right to make decisions, will be ensuring that her now stable and improving mental health is sustained, that she has the best possible chance of continuing to be mentally capable, and of ensuring a quality of life that prior to the court's intervention she was unable to enjoy.

Publication of reports

1–178   Butler-Sloss P. invoked the inherent jurisdiction to grant an injunction to prevent the publication of a report that had been prepared by a local authority subsequent to its decision to remove a number of foster children and vulnerable adults from the home of their foster mother (*Local Authority v Health Authority (Disclosure: Restriction on Publication*) [2003] EWHC 2746 (Fam). Her Ladyship found that the publication of the report would be "deeply damaging and detrimental" to the welfare of the mentally incapacitated adults.

Future disputes

1–179   In *Wyatt Re,* [2005] EWHC 2293 (Fam), Hedley J. held that, in exceptional circumstances, a declaration can be used to resolve a future dispute which can be clearly identified and reasonably anticipated. This finding was upheld on appeal, although the Court of Appeal expressed reservations about judges making open-ended declarations which they may have to re-visit if circumstances change (*Wyatt v Portsmouth Hospital NHS Trust* [2005] EWCA Civ 1181 at para.118).

Powers to make decisions and appoint deputies: general

1–180   **16.**—(1) This section applies if a person (P) lacks capacity in relation to a matter or matters concerning—

(a)   P's personal welfare, or

(b)   P's property and affairs.

(2) The court may—

(a)   by making an order, make the decision or decisions on P's behalf in relation to the matter or matters, or

(b)   appoint a person (a deputy) to make decisions on P's behalf in relation to the matter or matters.

(3) The powers of the court under this section are subject to the provisions of this Act and, in particular, to sections 1 (the principles) and 4 (best interests).

(4) When deciding whether it is in P's best interests to appoint a deputy, the court must have regard (in addition to the matters mentioned in section 4) to the principles that—

(a)   a decision by the court is to be preferred to the appointment of a deputy to make a decision, and

(b)   the powers conferred on a deputy should be as limited in scope and duration as is reasonably practicable in the circumstances.

(5) The court may make such further orders or give such directions, and confer

on a deputy such powers or impose on him such duties, as it thinks necessary or expedient for giving effect to, or otherwise in connection with, an order or appointment made by it under subsection (2).

(6) Without prejudice to section 4, the court may make the order, give the directions or make the appointment on such terms as it considers are in P's best interests, even though no application is before the court for an order, directions or an appointment on those terms.

(7) An order of the court may be varied or discharged by a subsequent order.

(8) The court may, in particular, revoke the appointment of a deputy or vary the powers conferred on him if it is satisfied that the deputy—

(a) has behaved, or is behaving, in a way that contravenes the authority conferred on him by the court or is not in P's best interests, or

(b) proposes to behave in a way that would contravene that authority or would not be in P's best interests.

DEFINITIONS

"property": s.64(1)   **1–181**
"the court": s.64(1)

GENERAL NOTE

This section sets out the core jurisdiction of the Court of Protection, which is to make **1–182** substitute decisions for persons lacking the required mental capacity to make decisions for themselves about either their personal welfare or their property and affairs, or to appoint a deputy to do so if this is in their best interests. Sections 17 and 18 indicate to extent of the court's powers with regard to the personal welfare and the property and affairs of P, and s.16A limits the extent to which the court can authorise the deprivation of P's liberty. A decision of the court, which is limited to those decisions that could have been made by P, is to be preferred to the appointment of a deputy who, if appointed, should be granted powers as limited in scope and duration as is reasonable practicable (subs.(4)). A deputy's appointment can be revoked or his or her powers varied if the court considers that the deputy's past, present or future actions will not serve P's best interests (subs.(8)). The court has power to act on its "own motion" to make whatever order is in P's best interests (subs. (6)), and can vary or discharge existing orders (subs.(7)). When exercising this jurisdiction, the court must adhere to the principles set out in s.1 and must make decisions which are in the best interests of the P (subs.(3)). The court can make any order or appointment which is in the best interests of P, regardless of the nature of the application made to it.

In *Re MN (Adult)* [2015] EWCA Civ 411, the Court of Appeal held that the function of the Court of Protection is to take, on behalf of adults who lack capacity, the decisions which, if they had capacity, they would take themselves. Sir James Munby P. said at para.80:

"The Court of Protection has no more power, just because it is acting on behalf of an adult who lacks capacity, to obtain resources or facilities from a third party, whether a private individual or a public authority, than the adult if he had capacity would be able to obtain himself. . . . The Court of Protection is thus confined to choosing between available options, including those which there is good reason to believe will be forthcoming in the foreseeable future."

At para.81, Sir James said:

"The Court of Protection, like the family court and the Family Division, can explore the care plan being put forward by a public authority and, where appropriate, require the authority to go away and think again. Rigorous probing, searching questions and persuasion are permissible; pressure is not. And in the final analysis the Court of Protection cannot compel a public authority to agree to a care plan which the authority is unwilling to implement. I agree with the point Eleanor King J made in her judgment (para 57):

'In my judgment, such discussions and judicial encouragement for flexibility and negotiation in respect of a care package are actively to be encouraged. Such negotiations are however a far cry from the court embarking on a 'best interests' trial with a view to determining whether or not an option which has been said by care provider (in the exercise of their statutory duties) not to be available, is nevertheless in the patient's best interest.'"

At para.82, Sir James elaborated on the reasoning for this approach:

"First, it is not a proper function of the Court of Protection (nor, indeed, of the family court or the Family Division in analogous situations), to embark upon a factual inquiry into some abstract issue the answer to which cannot affect the outcome of the proceedings before it. Secondly, it is not a proper function of the Court of Protection (nor of the family court or the Family Division) to embark upon a factual inquiry designed to create a platform or springboard for possible future proceedings in the Administrative Court. Thirdly, such an exercise runs the risk of confusing the very different perspectives and principles which govern the exercise by the Court of Protection of its functions and those which govern the exercise by the public authority of its functions—and, in consequence, the very different issues which arise for determination in the Court of Protection in contrast to those which arise for determination in the Administrative Court. Fourthly, such an exercise runs the risk of exposing the public authority to impermissible pressure."

In *North Yorkshire CC v MAG* [2016] EWCOP 5 at para.37, Cobb J. held that *Re MN* applies across all welfare determinations, including those which involve deprivation of liberty.

The Public Guardian is required to establish and maintain a register of orders appointing deputies, and to supervise deputies (s.58(1)(b) and (c)), and will receive reports from deputies (s.58(1)(f)). The Public Guardian can investigate a complaint about the way in which a deputy is exercising his or her powers (s.58(1)(h)). Ultimately the matter could be referred to the court which has power to either discharge the order appointing the deputy or to vary the deputy's powers (subs.(7)). The supervision and investigatory functions of the Public Guardian can be discharged in co-operation with other persons who are involved in the care of treatment of P (s.58(2)). The Public Guardian has no equivalent obligation to supervise donees acting under a lasting power of attorney.

In *Re HM* (COP) November 4, 2011, Judge Marshall held that the court has the power to authorise the creation of a trust—in particular a personal injury trust—of P's assets as the means of administering those assets for him, rather than appointing a deputy for him under this section. Although each case is fact sensitive, deputyship should be taken to be the norm for the due administration of P's assets, and authorisation of a settlement under s.18(1)(h) must therefore be justified as a departure from this norm. Judge Marshall said at para.35:

"Deputyship will . . . be the usual course where some formal scheme for managing P's assets is needed at all. However, if the court is satisfied that P's best interests are better served, in the particular case, by the authorisation of a settlement rather than the appointment of a deputy, that will prevail. The key is that the test is a relative one, namely, in all the particular circumstances, are P's best interests *better* served by taking that course?"

The following comment on this case was made by Martin Terrell in the November 2011 issue of the 39 Essex Street Court of Protection Newsletter:

"The difficulty with this case is that it was decided on its very particular facts and despite the decision to approve the creation of a trust, it should not be seen as a green light for trusts to be created as a matter of course where there is a personal injury award. A party proposing a trust must complete a detailed analysis of the costs and benefits of a trust compared to a deputyship and show that the former will be more cost effective without prejudicing the safety of the trust assets. Evidence would need to be produced of the professional trustee's charges and commitment to a charging policy as well as to the lay trustee's competence. The Official Solicitor will need to be instructed and there is no guarantee the Court will agree. This process alone will add risk and cost to any application and will deter all but the most determined (and well founded) applications."

In *Re M (Best Interests: Deprivation of Liberty)* [2013] EWHC 3456 (COP), Peter Jackson J. endorsed the approach taken at an earlier stage of the proceedings when the District Judge visited M in her care home. His Lordship said:

"A careful written record was made and placed with the papers. The visit has therefore had the dual purpose of informing the court of M's views and of making M feel connected to the proceedings without putting her into the stressful position of having to come to court in person. I commend this as an approach that may be of value in other cases of this kind" (para.42).

Fact finding hearings

In *Re S (Adult's Lack of Capacity: Care and Residence)* [2003] EWHC 1909 (Fam), **1–183** [2003] 2 F.L.R. 1235 at para.13, Wall J. said that, unlike in the case of care proceedings in relation to a child, there is no requirement to establish a "threshold" in the case of proceedings in relation to an adult, whether the proceedings are brought in the High Court under the inherent jurisdiction or in the Court of Protection. His Lordship went on to point out (para.15) that the absence of any threshold criteria equivalent to those contained in s.31 of the Children Act 1989, "raises the question as to the extent to which (if at all) it is necessary, for the purposes of exercising the jurisdiction and deciding which course of action is in the best interests of S, to make findings of fact relating in particular to disputed historical issues." His answer was as follows:

"18 . . . I agree that there must be good reason for local authority intervention in a case such as the present. Equally, if there are disputed issues of fact which go to the question of Mr S's capacity and suitability to care for S, the court may need to resolve them if their resolution is necessary to the decision as to what is in S's best interests. Findings of fact against Mr S on the two issues identified in paragraph16 would plainly reflect upon his capacity properly to care for S. But it does not follow, in my judgment, that the proceedings must be dismissed simply because the factual basis upon which the local authority instituted them turns out to be mistaken, or because it cannot be established on the balance of probabilities. What matters (assuming always that mental incapacity is made out) is which outcome will be in S's best interests. There will plainly be cases which are very fact specific. There will be others in which the principal concern is the future, and the relative suitability of the plans which each party can put forward for both the short and long-term care of the mentally incapable adult. The instant case, in my judgment, is one of the cases in the latter category. . . .

21 Whilst I acknowledge that in a relatively untried jurisdiction there are dangers in too relaxed an approach to historical issues, I am unable to accept the proposition that the approach to best interests is fettered in any way beyond that which applies to any judicial decision, namely that it has to be evidence based; that it excludes irrelevant material; and that it includes a consideration of all relevant material. In a field as complex as care for the mentally disabled, a high degree of pragmatism seems to me inevitable. But in each case it seems to me that the four essential building blocks are the same. First, is mental incapacity established? Secondly, is there a serious, justiciable issue relating to welfare? Thirdly, what is it? Fourthly, with the welfare of the incapable adult as the court's paramount consideration, what are the balance sheet factors which must be drawn up to decide which course of action is in his or her best interests?"

This analysis was endorsed by Sir James Munby in *Re AG* [2015] EWCOP 78 at para.31.

His Lordship said that the decisions in *TT* and *DP*, below, had to be read in the context of the "overarching principles" articulated by Wall J.

In *LBX v TT* [2014] EWCOP 24, Cobb J. found in deciding whether to conduct a fact finding hearing, the following check list of considerations identified by McFarlane J. in *A County Council v DP* [2005] EWHC 1593 (Fam) to be useful:

1. The interests of the child [i.e. P] (which are relevant but not paramount).
2. The time that the investigation will take.
3. The likely cost to public funds.
4. The evidential result.
5. The necessity or otherwise of the investigation.
6. The relevance of the potential result of the investigation to the future care plans for the child.
7. The impact of any fact finding process upon the other parties.
8. The prospects of a fair trial on the issue.
9. The justice of the case.

An account of the principles which should be applied to a fact finding hearing was provided by Baker J. in *A Local Authority v M* [2014] EWCOP 33 at paras 82 to 90. In summary they are:

1. The burden of proof lies with the body bringing the proceedings.
2. The standard of proof is the balance of probabilities.
3. Findings of fact must be based on evidence.
4. The court must take into account all the evidence and, furthermore, consider each piece of evidence in the context of all the other evidence.
5. Whilst appropriate attention must be paid to the opinion of medical experts, those opinions need to be considered in the context of all the other evidence.
6. In assessing the expert evidence, one important consideration is that the court must be careful to ensure that each expert keeps within the bounds of their own expertise and defers where appropriate to the expertise of others.
7. Where it is relevant, the evidence of the parents is of the utmost importance.
8. It is not uncommon for witnesses in contested cases to tell lies, both before and during the hearing. The court must be careful to bear in mind that a witness may lie for many reasons—such as shame, misplaced loyalty, panic, fear and distress—and the fact that a witness has lied about some matters does not mean that he or she has lied about everything.

Subsection (1)

1–184   LACKS CAPACITY IN RELATION TO A MATTER OR MATTERS.   The court "must deal with the issue of capacity before it embarks on any enquiry into welfare" (*London Borough of Haringey v FG (No.1)* [2011] EWHC 3932 (COP) at para.2, per Hedley J.). The court has no power to act in relation to a matter in respect of which P has capacity: see further s.20(1).

Subsection (2)(a)

1–185   Section 16A prevents the court from making an order under this provision authorising the deprivation of P's liberty if P is ineligible to be deprived of his liberty within the meaning of Sch.1A (see below under *Deprivations of liberty*).

In *London Borough of Hillingdon v Neary* [2011] EWHC 1377 (COP); [2011] 4 All E.R. 584 at para.33, Jackson J. said:

"Significant welfare issues that cannot be resolved by discussion should be placed before the Court of Protection, where decisions can be taken as a matter of urgency where necessary."

The *Code of Practice* states at paras 8.27–8.28:

"In some cases, the court must make a decision, because someone needs specific author-ity to act and there is no other route for getting it. These include cases where:

- there is no EPA or property and affairs LPA in place and someone needs to make a financial decision for a person who lacks capacity to make that decision (for example, the decision to terminate a tenancy agreement), or
- it is necessary to make a will, or to amend an existing will, on behalf of a person who lacks capacity to do so.
- Examples of other types of cases where a court decision might be appropriate include cases where:
- there is genuine doubt or disagreement about the existence, validity or applicability of an advance decision to refuse treatment . . .
- there is a major disagreement regarding a serious decision (for example, about where a person who lacks capacity to decide for themselves should live)
- a family carer or a solicitor asks for personal information about someone who lacks capacity to consent to that information being revealed (for example, where there have been allegations of abuse of a person living in a care home)
- someone suspects that a person who lacks capacity to make decisions to protect themselves is at risk of harm or abuse from a named individual (the court could stop that individual contacting the person who lacks capacity)."

The House of Lords Select Committee said at para.236:

"We are concerned that the responsibility of public authorities to initiate proceedings in cases of dispute is not widely known or adhered to. We also share the concerns of Professor Fennell and Dr Series regarding the ability of the person concerned to chal-lenge decision-making when all others are in agreement."

Where, in accordance with an order made under this provision, a person has been author-ised to carry out a transaction for a person who lacks capacity, the Public Guardian has the functions set out in reg.45 of the Lasting Powers of Attorney, Enduring Powers of Attorney and Public Guardian Regulations 2007 (SI 2007/1253).

Orders of the court must be obeyed. It is submitted that, by analogy with the position that obtains with regard to decisions of the First-tier Tribunal (Mental Health), in cases of great urgency professionals can only take a different course of action if subsequent to the court's decision they have formed the "reasonable and bona fide opinion" that they have information which was not known to the court and which "which put a significantly dif-ferently complexion on the case as compared with that before the [court]": see *R. (on the application of Von Brandenburg) v East London and the City Mental Health NHS Trust* [2003] UKHL 58 at para.10, per Lord Bingham. If this course of action is taken, the matter should be referred to the court at the earliest opportunity.

The powers of the court under this provision and subs.(5) are very broad. They include the power to force entry into P's home, to restrain and sedate her, and to remove her to hospital in order for her to undergo surgery (*Mental Health Trust v DD* [2014] EWCOP 11 and [2015] EWCOP 4). They also include the power to allow a third party, such as a local authority social worker, to gain access to P. In "When protection matters", NLJ, 15&22 April 2011, pp.537, 538, Robert Eckford describes how the court made orders to allow a local authority to undertake works on a property for the sole purpose of allowing P to maintain his tenancy. P was suffering from a paranoid delusional disorder which led him to refuse permission to the local authority landlord to undertake annual gas inspections, thus placing himself, his neighbours and the property at risk. The order made by the court authorised contractors to enter the property and to undertake works, required P to reside in a care home for seven days, and permitted the local authority to use reasonable and proportionate force, if necessary, to effect P's removal to the care home. Similar use of the court's power could be used in a situation where P is living in domestic squalor.

Making orders under this provision will frequently require the court to undertake a risk appraisal. The following passage from Munby J.'s judgment in *MM (An Adult), Re* [2007] EWHC 2003 (Fam) at para.120, is apposite:

"The fact is that all life involves risk, and the young, the elderly and the vulnerable, are exposed to additional risks and to risks they are less well equipped than others to cope with. But just as wise parents resist the temptation to keep their children metaphorically wrapped up in cotton wool, so too we must avoid the temptation always to put the physical health and safety of the elderly and the vulnerable before everything else. Often it will be appropriate to do so, but not always. Physical health and safety can sometimes be bought at too high a price in happiness and emotional welfare. The emphasis must be on sensible risk appraisal, not striving to avoid all risk, whatever the price, but instead seeking a proper balance and being willing to tolerate manageable or acceptable risks as the price appropriately to be paid in order to achieve some other good - in particular to achieve the vital good of the elderly or vulnerable person's happiness. What good is it making someone safer if it merely makes them miserable?"

See further, the cases noted under *Best interests and living arrangements* in the General Note to s.4.

In *C v Blackburn and Darwen Borough Council* [2011] EWHC 3321 (COP) at para.37, Peter Jackson J. made the following comments about disputes relating to P's place of residence:

"[I]t is not in my view appropriate for genuinely contested issues about the place of residence of a resisting incapacitated person to be determined either under the guardianship regime [of the Mental Health Act 1983] or by means of a standard authorisation under the DOLS regime. Substantial decisions of that kind ought properly to be made by the Court of Protection, using its power to make welfare decisions under s16 MCA."

His Lordship held, at para.39, that the Court of Protection lacks jurisdiction to determine the place of residence of P while a guardianship residence requirement made under s.8(1)(a) of the 1983 Act remains in effect.

What approach should the court take when a public authority seeks to interfere with the rights of family members under art.8 of the European Convention on Human Rights (ECHR) by preventing or imposing restrictions on contact with P because of safeguarding concerns? This question was considered by Hedley J. in *LBB v JM*, February 5, 2010 (COP), paras 7 and 8:

"The local authority took the view that since the intervention of the court would engage a potential breach of the Article 8 rights of the parties, that it may be incumbent upon them to establish on a factual basis why it was that the court's jurisdiction should be exercised. Broadly speaking, I would endorse that approach and recognise that where an Article 8.2 justification is required then the case should not be dealt with purely as a welfare case if there are significant factual issues between the parties which might bear on the outcome of the consideration under Article 8.2 as to whether state intervention was justified.

The Mental Capacity Act does not contain provisions equivalent to the threshold provisions under s.31 of the Children Act. Nor should any such provisions be imported in it as clearly Parliament intended that they should not be, but an intervention with parties' rights under Article 8 is a serious intervention by the state which requires to be justified under Article 8.2. If there is a contested factual basis it may often be right, as undoubtedly it was in this case, that that should investigated and determined by the court."

His Lordship also confirmed, at para.13, that the burden of proof in establishing factual allegations lies on the public authority, and that the standard of proof is the balance of probabilities.

The issues that need to be considered when the court is imposing visiting restrictions were identified by Judge Marin in *WCC v GS* [2011] EWHC 2244 (COP) at para.53:

"When considering the types of conditions to impose both generally and in this case, the court needs to have the following considerations in mind. First, that there should be appropriate reviews of the conditions. Nothing should be set in stone and either the court should review the conditions and/or there should be a review by the local authority. Second, given the medical evidence, an end of life plan should be put in place. The health of elderly people can deteriorate quickly and it may come to a point when even members of a family who have been excluded from contact should be able to spend time with their parent or relative. Obviously there will be exceptional cases where the level of harm or potential for harm by a family member against a vulnerable person is such that even in an end of life scenario contact would not be appropriate, but these will be very exceptional and rare cases. Third, the length to which the conditions should address each step of a contact session. Thus, in some cases there will be a need for conditions to manage every step of the way from the arranging of the visit to the arrival of the family member at the home until his departure. In other cases, a more general approach can be appropriate. Fourth, the dates and times of visits will need to be set out clearly in a contact schedule. Fifth, whether a plan is needed to address problems, for example, the family member cannot get to the home on a particular day due to an emergency. Sixth, whether it is appropriate for financial assistance to be made available by a local authority or other relevant third party to the relative for travelling to and from a care home. Seventh, if the visit is to be supervised, who is to supervise and what level of supervision is required. In some cases the supervision may take the form of detailed note taking by an independent person; in other cases it may be a cursory check-up by a member of the care home staff; in yet other cases, the allocated social worker may attend to just keep a watching brief. Eighth, a right for the home or contact supervisor to cancel the visit if circumstances deem it appropriate, either before the visit or during the visit. Ninth, the ability to shorten or lengthen a visit if, for example, the visit is not going well or if the relative has become sick. Tenth, regulation of behaviour. Conditions may include provision that the family member not be rude to or harass staff or other residents, the point of entry and exit to and from the care home, the fact that other residents need to be left alone, that their care should not be interfered with, restrictions as to what food and drink can be brought into the home and the venue in the home for contact. Eleventh, a record of the visit. The level of formality will depend on the situation. In more serious cases every word may need to be recorded and in other cases a note will simply be taken that the visit passed without incident and everything went well."

Article 8 may impose on a local authority not merely the power but in appropriate circumstances the duty to apply to the court for an order if that is necessary to protect a vulnerable adult from possible harm at the hands of his family. In *S (Adult Patient) (Inherent Jurisdiction; Family Life), Re* [2002] EWHC 2278 at para.39, Munby J. said:

"[A]s *Botta v Italy* [(1998) 26 E.H.R.R. 241] shows, the State, even in this sphere of relations between purely private individuals, may have positive obligations to adopt measures which will ensure effective respect for the son's private life. Thus the State, in the form of the local authority, may have a positive obligation to intervene, even at the risk of detriment to the father's family life, if such intervention is necessary to ensure respect for the son's Article 8 rights. And the State, in the form of the High Court, has a positive obligation to act in such a way as to ensure respect for those rights."

In *A local Authority v PB and P* [2011] EWHC 502 (COP) at para.46, Charles J. said that in most welfare cases, a direction along the following lines should be given:

"(1) (a) the facts that he/she/it is asking the court to find, (b) the disputed facts that he/she/it asserts the court need not determine, and (c) the findings that he/she/it invites the court to make by reference to the facts identified in (a);

(2) With sufficient particularity the investigations he/she/it has made of the alternatives for the care of P and as a result thereof the alternatives for the care of P that

he/she/it asserts should be considered by the court and in respect of each of them how and by whom the relevant support and services are to be provided;

(3)   By reference to (1) and (2) the factors that he/she/it asserts the court should take into account in reaching its conclusions;

(4)   The relief sought by that party and by reference to the relevant factors the reasons why he/she/it asserts that those factors, or the balance between them, support the granting of that relief; and

(5)   The relevant issues of law."

Deprivations of liberty

1–186   The court can make an order the effect of which is to deprive P of his or her liberty (s.4A(3),(4)), apart from situations where P is ineligible within the meaning of Sch.1A (s.16A). Such an order does not require the deprivation of the P's liberty, but rather permits the deprivation of liberty in certain circumstances and mitigates liability in terms of potential breaches of art.5 of the ECHR. Applications to the court to authorise a deprivation of liberty, which should be made before the deprivation commences (*R. (on the application of C) v A Local Authority* [2011] EWHC 1539 (Admin)), are governed by Practice Direction 10A which is reproduced in the note to r.82A of the CPR 2007. It is submitted that such an order should contain directions which replicate the essential safeguards contained in Sch. A1. It should also provide for regular reviews, which may take the form of a review on the papers, if the deprivation is likely to be long term (see *GJ, NJ and BJ (Incapacitated Adults), Re* [2008] EWHC 1097 (Fam); [2008] 2 F.L.R. 1295 and *Salford City Council v BJ* [2009] EWHC 3310 (Fam)). In *GJ v Foundation Trust* [2009] EWHC 2972 (Fam) at para.23, Charles J. said that the provisions in Sch.A1 relating to the suspension (Part 6) and review (Part 8) of a standard authorisation "are matters that the Court of Protection should take into account in determining whether (a) it should make an order authorising the deprivation of P's liberty, and if so (b) the extent and period of such an authorisation and in particular whether, and/or for how long, it should continue after P is placed in a hospital or care home having regard to, for example, the authorities relating to the need for review of a deprivation of liberty based on the exercise of the inherent jurisdiction". In *A PCT v LDV* [2013] EWHC 272 (Fam) at para.29, Baker J. said that although "the court is not, strictly speaking, bound by the provisions of Sch.A1 when deciding whether or not to make an order depriving a person of their liberty, I accept . . . that the appropriate course in these circumstances is for the court to approach the question as if it was considering the 'mental capacity requirement' under para.15 [of Sch.A1]".

In *G v E* [2010] EWCA Civ 822; [2010] 4 All E.R. 579, the Court of Appeal held that:

(i)   art.5 of the ECHR does not place distinct threshold conditions regarding the warranting of compulsory confinement, in particular the criteria established in *Winterwerp v Netherlands* (1979–1980) 2 E.H.R.R. 387, which have to be satisfied before a person accepted to be lacking capacity can be detained under the Act in his or her best interests [NB This finding appears to be inconsistent with the decision of the European Court of Human Rights in *Stanev v Bulgaria* (2012) 55 E.H.R.R. 22, where the Court said, at para.145, that an individual cannot be deprived of his liberty unless the *Winterwerp* criteria are satisfied.];

(ii)   the court is merely empowered under this provision to make a decision in the individual's best interests, although in exercising that power it must comply with art.5 (and other provisions of the ECHR); and

(iii)   it is sufficient for the court to be satisfied on credible expert evidence, which need not be that of a psychiatrist, that the individual concerned lacks capacity.

At first instance ([2010] EWHC 621 (Fam) at para.106), Baker J. held that a failure to make an application to the court before the detention commences does not deprive the court of the power to sanction a future deprivation and render it lawful by making an order under either this provision or s.48.

In *North Yorkshire CC v MAG* [2016] EWCOP 5 at para.37, Cobb J. held that the decision of the Court of Appeal in *Re MN* , which is considered above, applies across all welfare determinations, including those which involve deprivation of liberty. In this case, it was held that:

1. Deprivation of liberty is a binary concept; either a person is, or is not, deprived of liberty.
2. If there was an agreement that there was only one available residential option for P and that it was in his best interests to reside there, the next stage is to consider whether the deprivation of liberty is a proportionate response to the risk. The court also had to consider whether the accommodation provided to P was so unsuitable as to be unlawfully so provided, breaching his rights under art.5 of the ECHR which is a high threshold that needs to be crossed.
3. The engagement of P's art.5 rights did not impose a positive obligation on the local authority to seek out alternative accommodation for P.

The fact that a deprivation of liberty could be authorised under Sch.A1 does not absolve the supervisory body from making an application to the court where the facts would otherwise merit it (*NHS Trusts 1 and 2 v FG*) [2014] EWCOP 30 at para.101(iii)).

Should P be a party to proceedings seeking welfare orders to authorise a deprivation of liberty?

In *Re NRA* [2015] EWCOP 76, Charles J. was faced with contradictory obiter dicta on **1–187** the issue whether P must be a party to such proceedings. On the one hand, the President concluded that in a non-controversial case a streamlined procedure was possible under which P was not joined as a party and this is contained in Practice Direction 10AA to the Court of Protection Rules (see *Re X* [2014] EWCOP 25 and 37). On the other hand, the Court of Appeal concluded that in all applications for welfare orders that will authorise a deprivation of liberty P must be made a party and so a litigation friend must be appointed for P (see *Re X (Court of Protection Practice)* [2015] EWCA Civ 599). His Lordship ended his judgment by summarising his conclusions at para.269:

"(1) P does not have to be a party to all applications for welfare orders sought to authorise, and which when they are made will authorise, a deprivation of P's liberty caused by the implementation of the care package on which the welfare order is based.

(2) In two of the test cases before me I have made orders that reflect that conclusion and my conclusion that the procedural safeguards required by Article 5 are (and are best) provided in those cases by appointing a parent of P as P's Rule 3A [of the Court of Protection Rules] representative. As such, that parent as a continuation of the dedicated and devoted support given by P's family to P and directed to promoting P's best interests, in a balanced way, can best provide (a) the court with the information it requires about the care package and P, and (b) P's participation in the proceedings. Also, that parent can and in my view will monitor the implementation of the care plan and so initiate any challenge to it or review of it that the parent considers should be made in P's best interests.

(3) I do not have a test case before me in which (a) P has not been joined as a party and the Official Solicitor has not agreed to act as P's litigation friend, and (b) the appointment of a family member or friend as P's Rule 3A representative without joining P as a party is not an available option. Such a test case or cases should be listed for hearing.

(4) In contrast to the Court of Appeal in *Re X* and subject to further argument in such a test case or cases, I consider that the way in which the Court of Protection can at present best obtain further information and P's participation in such cases is for it to exercise its investigatory jurisdiction to obtain information through obtaining s.49 reports or through the issue of a witness summonses. This keeps the matter under the control of the court rather than invoking the necessity of appointing a litigation

friend with the problems and delays that history tells us this entails and will entail and I have concluded is, or shortly will be, not fit for purpose.

(5) I do not for a moment suggest that absent further resources being provided there will not be problems and delays in taking the course referred to in paragraph (4). Also, and importantly, I recognise that it would be focused on Article 5(1) and would not provide for monitoring on the ground until it is repeated from time to time for that purpose. But, the appointment of a litigation friend will also not provide that monitoring.

(6) In such cases the argument advanced by the Secretary of State before me that a Rule 3A representative identified by the local authority be appointed shows that if this was a practically available option it would replicate the input that I have decided can be provided by an appropriate family member or friend and so satisfy the procedural safeguards required by Article 5 and common law fairness in non-controversial cases without joining P as a party.

(7) That replication is an obvious solution that will provide the necessary safeguards more efficiently and at less expense than either

    i. the making of orders for s.49 reports and the issuing of witness summonses perhaps coupled with more frequent reviews, or

    ii. joining P as a party.

(8) So I urge the Secretary of State and local authorities to consider urgently, and in any event before a test case or cases of this type are before the court, how this solution can be provided on the ground."

In a sequel to this case, *Re JM* [2016] EWCOP 15, Charles J. agreed "with the primary submission of the Secretary of State in *NRA* and in these cases, that the *Re X* streamlined procedure does not meet the minimum procedural requirements but a procedure in which P was not joined as a party and there was no hearing would do so if a Rule 3A representative is appointed for P" (para.23). His Lordship said that the primary responsibility to provide a resource that enables the Court of Protection either to make Rule 3A appointments or to otherwise meet the minimum procedural requirements in these test cases falls on the Secretary of State, or on the Secretary of State together with the applicant local authorities (para.24). His Lordships decided that in cases in which there is no appropriate family member or friend who could be appointed as a Rule 3A representative he would

"make an order:

    i) joining both the MoJ and the DoH as parties (but if I receive an assurance that neither will seek to argue that the Crown is divisible and it is the other who should act; I will join only the MoJ),

    ii) inviting the parties to take steps to either:

        a) identify a suitable person who is ready, willing and able to accept immediate appointment as P's Rule 3A representative, or

        b) identify an alternative procedure that is actually available to the COP to take to meet the minimum procedural requirements in the case, and so for example a short term solution for the case (and possibly others in the class represented by the four test cases),

    iii) staying the applications pending the identification of a practically available procedure that enables the COP to adopt a procedure that meets the minimum procedural requirements in that case, and

    iv) giving all the parties liberty to apply to lift the stay and generally" (para.25).

His Lordship further stated that "this is an order that can and should be made by the COP in other cases in the class represented by these test cases" (para.26).

In the linked case of *Re VE* [2016] EWCOP 16, Charles J. suggested an "Explanatory Note for a Family Member or Friend Appointed as a Rule 3A Representative."

Children

In *Liverpool City Council v SG* [2014] EWCOP 10, Holman J. made an order which **1–188** recorded "that the court does consider that neither the Children's Homes Regulations 2001 nor the joint guidance issued by the President of the Court of Protection and OFSTED dated 12th February 2014 prevent the Court of Protection from authorising under the Mental Capacity Act 2005 that a person who is an adult (viz. over the age of 18) may be deprived of his liberty in premises which are a children's home" (para.51). In the *Liverpool* case, the court did not have cause to consider the National Minimum Standards National Minimum Standards for Children's Homes issued by the Department of Education in April 2011. The Standards were considered by Holman J. in *Barnsley MBC v GS* [2014] EWCOP 46 who confirmed, in disagreeing with the reasoning in para.6 of the guidance, that there "is nothing in either the legislation, or the regulations, or the National Minimum Standards which has the effect that a children's home, which is not an approved secure children's home, is 'unable' to deprive a person of his liberty" (para.23). [NB The joint guidance referred to by Holman J. in the *Liverpool* case was withdrawn in 2015.]

Subsection (2)(b)

The *Code of Practice* states at paras 8.38–8.39: **1–189**

"Deputies for personal welfare decisions will only be required in the most difficult cases where:

- important and necessary actions cannot be carried out without the court's authority, or
- there is no other way of settling the matter in the best interests of the person who lacks capacity to make particular welfare decisions.

Examples include when:

- someone needs to make a series of linked welfare decisions over time and it would not be beneficial or appropriate to require all of those decisions to be made by the court. For example, someone (such as a family carer) who is close to a person with profound and multiple learning disabilities might apply to be appointed as a deputy with authority to make such decisions
- the most appropriate way to act in the person's best interests is to have a deputy, who will consult relevant people but have the final authority to make decisions
- there is a history of serious family disputes that could have a detrimental effect on the person's future care unless a deputy is appointed to make necessary decisions
- the person who lacks capacity is felt to be at risk of serious harm if left in the care of family members. In these rare cases, welfare decisions may need to be made by someone independent of the family, such as a local authority officer. There may even be a need for an additional court order prohibiting those family members from having contact with the person."

APPOINT A PERSON (A DEPUTY). In *SBC v PBA* [2011] EWHC 2580 (Fam); [2011] COPLR Con. Vol. 1095 at para.67, Roderic Wood J. said that the "unvarnished" words of this section set down the test for the appointment of deputies, and that the *Code of Practice* at para.8.38, with its reference to "most difficult" health and welfare cases, did not compel the court to be satisfied that the circumstances were difficult or unusual before a deputy could be appointed. The appointment of deputies is governed by s.19. In *MK v JK* [2013] EWHC 4334 (COP) at para.30, DJ Ralton said that apart from "very rare" situations, "any significant issue of principle such as residence, type of care, treatment and such like" should be made by the court rather that a personal welfare deputy.

In *Re M* (COP) January 28, 2013 at para.35, Senior Judge Lush said that he disagreed "with those who have suggested that any authorities predating the Mental Capacity Act are best consigned to history". These authorities had established the following "order of preference" for the appointment of deputies:

"● P's spouse or partner;
● any other relative who takes a personal interest in P's affairs
● a close friend;
● a professional adviser, such as the family's solicitor or accountant;
● a local authority's social services department; and finally
● a panel deputy, as deputy of last resort" (para.37).

Judge Lush said at paras 39 and 40:

"The court prefers to appoint a family member or close friend, if possible, as long as it is in P's best interests to do so. This is because a relative or friend will already be familiar with P's affairs, and wishes and methods of communication. Someone who already has a close personal knowledge of P is also likely to be better able to meet the obligation of a deputy to consult with P, and to permit and encourage him to participate, or to improve his ability to participate, as fully as possible in any act done for him and any decision affecting him. And, because professionals charge for their services, the appointment of a relative or friend is generally preferred for reasons of economy.

There are, of course, cases in which the court would not countenance appointing a particular family member as deputy. For example, if there had been physical or financial abuse; if there is a conflict of interests; if the proposed deputy has an unsatisfactory track record in managing his own financial affairs; and if there is ongoing friction between various family members that is likely to interfere with the administration of P's affairs. This list is not exhaustive."

"Another exception to strict adherence to the order of preference is in cases where P has received a substantial award of damages for personal injury or clinical negligence, and the quantum of damages has been expressly calculated on the basis that a professional deputy will act" *Re ES* [2014] EWHC B6, per Senior Judge Lush, at para.42).

In *Re P* [2010] EWHC 1592 (COP) at para.9, Hedley J. suggested that "the court ought to start from the position that, where family members offer themselves as deputies, then, in the absence of family dispute or other evidence that raises queries as to their willingness or capacity to carry out those functions, the court ought to approach such an application with considerable openness and sympathy".

After the appointment, the Public Guardian must determine the level of supervision required by s.58(1)(c) and the level of fee as set out in the Schedule to the Public Guardian (Fees, etc) Regulations 2007 (SI 2007/2051) is payable accordingly. The levels of supervision are set out in reg.8(3) of SI 2007/2051; see further the General Note to s.19.

A deputy's power to make decisions on behalf of P is limited to the matters specified by the court. Where possible, the court will seek to make a single order (subs.(4)(a)). Given the terms of s.5, the appointment of a deputy to make personal welfare decisions in relation to P is rarely made: see subs.(4).

The need for a deputy to be appointed to manage the person's property and affairs is likely to arise when property needs to be sold or if the person has financial resources that the court considers requires management by a deputy.

Subsection (3)

1–190   In *Re SK* [2013] All E.R. D 12 (Jul), Bodey J. held that s.4 is concerned with the P's present best interests, choosing between currently available or reasonably foreseeable options. His Lordship said at para.10:

"That much appears both from common sense and from s.4(1) of the Act, which is stated in the present tense. Of course there will also be cases where the court looks forward to the future as part of deciding about present best interests and where it may wish to retain a measure of oversight and control; but such an approach has to be proportionate and adopted only where there is a reasonable foreseeability of the court being able to take a further decision at a subsequent hearing within a reasonably finite period of time."

This approach is consistent with the finding of the Supreme Court in *Aintree University Hospitals NHS Foundation Trust v James* [2013] UKSC 67, where Lady Hale said at para.18:

"This Act is concerned with enabling the court to do for the patient what he could do for himself if of full capacity, but it goes no further. On an application under this Act, therefore, the court has no greater powers than the patient would have if he were of full capacity."

Aintree and *SK* were applied by Eleanor King J. in *ACCG v ACC* [2013] EWHC 3859 (COP) who said at para.73:

"The law, as I have found it to be presently stated, is that the court may choose only between the available options in the same way as a person would if of full capacity. It may be, that in certain rare circumstances, a court may choose to hear a best interests argument, (as for example Bodey J did in *Re SK* where there was a possibility of a third party providing funds). Another example is in cases where there is a properly pleaded case showing a credible argument that a provider, in failing to agree to fund a package of care, has in doing so, breached or might breach the human rights of one or more of the parties to the proceedings."

Her Ladyship confirmed that judicial review in the Administrative Court "remains the proper vehicle through which to challenge unreasonable or irrational decisions made by 'care providers' and other public authorities" (para.86(ii)). Any jurisdictional issues need to be flagged up well before the case comes on for a full hearing (*A Local Authority v PB* [2011] EWHC 502 (COP) at para.31).

Subsection (4)
This subsection is consistent with the least restrictive principle set out in s.1(6). In **1–191** *Havering L.B.C. v LD* [2010] EWHC 3876 (COP) at para.42, Judge Turner QC (sitting as a judge of the High Court) said:

"The authors of 'Mental Capacity: A guide to the new law' (second edition) rightly noted, in my judgment, the application of the principle in section 16(4)(a) 'suggests that there is little scope for the appointment of deputies on a general basis effectively to act as if they were donees of a general power under an LPA.' Later, they continued that 'it is expected that a deputy will be appointed to take personal welfare decisions in only the most extreme cases and the court will usually seek to make an order in respect of a decision, rather than confer an ongoing power on a deputy.' That, I have concluded, is a proper summary of the position and reflects the desirable approach. Section 16(4) seems to me to be intended specifically to minimise the scope and duration of control. Specific decisions of the court are to be preferred to the ongoing appointment of a deputy and when a deputy must be appointed it is to be for the narrowest scope and the shortest time reasonably practicable in the circumstances."

This passage was cited in *G v E* [2010] EWHC 2512 (COP) where Baker J. said at para.58 that it "will usually be the case that decisions about complex and serious issues are taken by a court rather than any individual. In certain cases, as explained in paras 8.38 and 8.39 of the Code, it will be more appropriate to appoint a deputy or deputies to make these decisions. But because it is important that such decisions should wherever possible be taken collaboratively and informally, the appointments must be as limited in scope and duration as is reasonably practicable in the circumstances".

Subsection (4) para. (b)
LIMITED IN SCOPE AND DURATION. This provision reflects the fact that many disabled **1–192** people have capacity to take many day-to-day decisions and would only require the assistance of a deputy in relation to a limited range of matters. Also see the note on s.19(5).

Subsection (5)

1–193   If a deputy considers that the powers conferred by the court are insufficient to carry out the necessary duties toward the person lacking capacity, he or she should apply to the court either to vary the powers in the order of appointment, or for the court to make a particular decision itself. The court "will be able to grant powers to the deputy on condition that it first obtains the Public Guardian's consent for certain actions. It is important that deputies are, of course, properly supervised, but it would be disproportionately burdensome and costly to require them to apply to the court all the time for authority to act. That supervisory role should properly be undertaken by the Public Guardian", per the Parliamentary Under-Secretary of State (*Hansard*, HL Vol.670, col.1474).

This provision can be used by the court to authorise forced entry into P's home, to restrain P and to take P to hospital: see *Mental Health Trust v DD* [2015] EWCOP 4 (noted under subs.(2)(a)) where Cobb J. said that this provision "endows the court with a wide jurisdiction, limited essentially by what is lawful, necessary and proportionate, to support its essential orders" (para.133). It has also been used to limit the assets over which a deputy is given powers, so as to minimise the risk to P of default or negligence: see *Baker v H* [2009] EWHC B31 (Fam) at paras 61–63.

Subsection (7)

1–194   See s.18(5).

A decision under this provision to discharge an order appoint a person as P's deputy and to replace him with another can only be made if the decision is in P's best interests (*Re Rodman* [2012] EWHC 347 (Ch)).

Subsection (8)

1–195   This provides the court with similar powers to those it has with respect to donees: see s.22(3), (4).

In *EB v RC* [2011] EWHC 3805 (COP) at para.43, Senior Judge Lush said that apart from this provision there is no modern authority in English Law that considers the criteria to be applied by the court when considering applications for the removal of a deputy for property and affairs purposes. However, various guidelines were set out by the Court of Appeal of New South Wales in *Holt v The Protective Commissioner* (1993) 31 N.S.W.L.R. 227 and these have generally been applied by judges of the Court of Protection in the past. Judge Lush set down the following summary of the guidelines set out in *Holt* at para.46:

(1) An application for the removal of a deputy may be made by any interested person, including P himself.

(2) The burden of proof is on the person seeking a change in the *status quo*.

(3) It is normally necessary for the person seeking the change to show some reason why the court should remove the existing deputy and appoint someone else in his or her place.

(4) Where it is shown that the existing deputy is unsuitable to be P's deputy for property and affairs (perhaps because he or she is incompetent, or has acted unlawfully or improperly, or is not acting in P's best interests), the court will terminate the appointment and appoint some other suitable person as deputy.

(5) If, however, the unsuitability of the existing deputy is not an issue, or if the applicant fails to prove that the existing deputy is unsuitable, it must be shown forensically that P's best interests will in some way be advanced or promoted by discharging the existing deputy and appointing someone else in his or her place.

(6) The standard of proof is the usual civil standard, namely "the balance of probabilities". It does not have to be "clear and convincing" or "compelling". Section 2(4) of the Act provides that "In proceedings under this Act or any other enactment, any question whether a person lacks capacity within the meaning of this Act must be decided on the balance of probabilities."

(7) In deciding what is in P's *best interests* the court will have regard to all the circumstances. Section 4(2) of the Act states that "The person making the determination must consider all the relevant circumstances and, in particular, take the following steps," which are listed in subss (3) to (11).

[Section 16 powers: Mental Health Act patients etc

16A.—(1) If a person is ineligible to be deprived of liberty by this Act, the court   **1–196** may not include in a welfare order provision which authorises the person to be deprived of his liberty.

(2) If—

(a) a welfare order includes provision which authorises a person to be deprived of his liberty, and

(b) that person becomes ineligible to be deprived of liberty by this Act,

the provision ceases to have effect for as long as the person remains ineligible.

(3) Nothing in subsection (2) affects the power of the court under section 16(7) to vary or discharge the welfare order.

(4) For the purposes of this section—

(a) Schedule 1A applies for determining whether or not P is ineligible to be deprived of liberty by this Act;

(b) "welfare order" means an order under section 16(2)(a).]

AMENDMENT

This section was inserted by the Mental Health Act 2007 s.50(3).   **1–197**

DEFINITIONS

"deprivation of liberty": s.64(5),(6).   **1–198**
"the court": s.64(1).

GENERAL NOTE

This section prevents the court from making an order under s.16(2)(a) authorising the   **1–199** deprivation of P's liberty if P is ineligible to be deprived of his liberty within the meaning of Sch.1A, i.e. he comes within a category where the Mental Health Act 1983 must be used. It also, in subs.(2), provides that an existing order under s.16(2)(a) authorising P to be deprived of his or her liberty ceases to have effect on P becoming ineligible. In *A NHS Trust v Dr A* [2013] EWHC 2442 (COP), Baker J. held that if the patient is ineligible and therefore cannot be treated under the 1983 Act for physical disorder that does not come within the scope of s.63 of that Act, the High Court has the power under its inherent jurisdiction to make a declaration and order authorising the medical treatment of an incapacitated adult that includes the provision for the deprivation of his liberty provided that the order complies with art.5 of the European Convention on Human Rights. His Lordship said at para.96:

> "Unless and until this court or another court clarifies the interpretation of section 16A of the MCA, it will therefore be necessary, in any case in which a hospital wishes to give treatment to a patient who is ineligible under section 16A, for the hospital to apply for an order under the inherent jurisdiction where the treatment (a) is outside the meaning of medical treatment of the MHA 1983 and (b) involves the deprivation of a patient's liberty."

The reasoning in this case was followed by Hayden J. in *Great Western Hospitals NHS Foundation Trust v AA* [2014] EWHC 132 (Fam) where a declaration was granted to enable a caesarean section to undertaken on a mentally incapacitated patient who was detained under the 1983 Act, using restraint if necessary.

Section 16 powers: personal welfare

1–200   17.—(1) The powers under section 16 as respects P's personal welfare extend in particular to—

(a) deciding where P is to live;

(b) deciding what contact, if any, P is to have with any specified persons;

(c) making an order prohibiting a named person from having contact with P;

(d) giving or refusing consent to the carrying out or continuation of a treatment by a person providing health care for P;

(e) giving a direction that a person responsible for P's health care allow a different person to take over that responsibility.

(2) Subsection (1) is subject to section 20 (restrictions on deputies).

DEFINITIONS

1–201   "treatment": s.64(1)

"deputy": s.64(1)

GENERAL NOTE

1–202   This section sets out in subs.(1) the types of personal welfare matters that, under s.16, the Court of Protection may either determine itself or appoint a deputy to make decisions about on P's behalf. The power of deputies to make decisions is subject to the restrictions set out in s.20 (subs.(2)) and is limited to the matters specified by the court (s.16(2)(b)).

The list in subs.(1) which is indicative, not exhaustive, is based on matters that have been dealt with by the High Court in the exercise of its inherent jurisdiction to make declarations. It is not a list of decisions that must always go the court for determination; rather it provides examples of decisions that could go to the court for determination if it would be appropriate to do so. Further examples are given in the note on s.16(2)(a).

In *PB v RB* [2013] EWCOP B41, Judge Altman noted that this section distinguished "deciding what contact, if any P, is to have with any specified person" (para.(b)) and "making an order prohibiting a named person from having contact with P" (para.(c)). The latter was not within the power of a deputy by virtue of s.20(2)(a) MCA 2005. As 'prohibiting contact' did not mean a permanent ban on contact, how could the seven day ban which the deputy was permitted to impose be distinguished from the prohibition of contact? The judge found that the difference between the two provisions was determined by asking if the period without contact could be part and parcel and an incident of an on-going management and monitoring of contact in a flexible way for a proportionate period of time and as a proportionate adjustment to the arrangements that would otherwise have taken effect in the particular family, or would it be more of a specific response, standing alone, to a situation with the consequence of a set pattern of no contact probably for a more substantial period of time commensurate with an application to court (para.24)? In the instant case, it was within the scope of the deputy's powers to prevent contact between RB and PB for up to seven days at a time as part of the day-to-day management of contact without having to refer back to the court, the court having determined itself the limit to the cessation of contact but allowing the deputy to exercise his discretion in deciding whether to cease contact for short periods within that framework. The deputy had not been given a power to prohibit contact within the meaning of s.20(2)(a).

In *London Borough of Redbridge v G* [2014] EWCOP 17, Russell J. held that she had the power under this section to require carers to leave P's house. The decision was made on P's behalf "in relation to a matter concerning her personal welfare as provided for in s 16(1) (a) and s 16(2) (a) and s 47 (1)" (para.93).

For applications in cases where a pregnant woman lacks capacity to make decisions about her obstetric care, see *NHS Trust v FG* [2014] EWCOP 30 which is noted under *Best interests in cases where a pregnant woman lacks capacity to make decisions about her obstetric care* in s.4.

Subsection (1) (a)

This power enables a judge to prevent P from being taken to another country if this would be contrary to his or her health and welfare (*KC v City of Westminster Social and Community Services Department*) [2008] EWCA Civ 198 at para.13). **1–203**

As the court only has power to make any decision that P could have made, this power cannot be used to require a local authority to fund a particular care home placement for P. The appropriate vehicle for challenging the authority's decision on P's placement is judicial review.

Subsection (1) (c)

A restraining order could be made where the named person presents a risk of abuse, or where continued contact with that person will harm or distress P. The power restrain a named person cannot extend to any interference with other rights of that person, such as the right to occupy property. Where appropriate, a penal notice can be attached to a restraining order: see s.47(1). In *London Borough of Hammersmith and Fulham v MW* Unreported, July 29, 2012, the fact that H.H. Judge Horowitz proceeded on the basis that P lacked the capacity "to make his own decision as to the boundaries of contact with an important person in his life" (para.63) suggests that the test of capacity in contact cases is person specific, rather than issue specific. **1–204**

Subsection (1) (d)

By virtue of s.26(1), the court cannot make an order which is inconsistent with the terms of a valid and applicable advance decision. **1–205**

In the consultation paper *"Who Decides"* (Cm.3803 at 7.26), the Government expressed its concern that a deputy "might have less prior knowledge of a patient's wishes regarding treatment than the patient's doctor". The fact that a deputy has the power to refuse treatment on behalf of P represents a significant change in the doctor patient relationship in that a non-medical deputy can override the doctor's clinical judgment as to what medical treatment his or her patient should receive: see further the General Note to s.11. This power is subject to the limitation set out in s.20(5).

The deputy does not have the power to direct that a different person should take over responsibility for P's health care (s.20(2)(b)). Neither does the deputy have the power to require a doctor to provide treatment which is not considered to be in P's best interests. This is because if P were capable, he or she would not have such a power.

Subsection (1) (e)

This allows for the court to order that the responsibility for P's healthcare be transferred to another doctor where P's doctor has a conscientious or clinical objection to a treating P. **1–206**

Section 16 powers: property and affairs

18.—(1) The powers under section 16 as respects P's property and affairs extend in particular to— **1–207**

(a) the control and management of P's property;

(b) the sale, exchange, charging, gift or other disposition of P's property;

(c) the acquisition of property in P's name or on P's behalf;

(d) the carrying on, on P's behalf, of any profession, trade or business;

(e) the taking of a decision which will have the effect of dissolving a partnership of which P is a member;

(f) the carrying out of any contract entered into by P;

(g) the discharge of P's debts and of any of P's obligations, whether legally enforceable or not;

(h) the settlement of any of P's property, whether for P's benefit or for the benefit of others;

(i) the execution for P of a will;

(j) the exercise of any power (including a power to consent) vested in P whether beneficially or as trustee or otherwise;

(k) the conduct of legal proceedings in P's name or on P's behalf.

(2) No will may be made under subsection (1)(i) at a time when P has not reached 18.

(3) The powers under section 16 as respects any other matter relating to P's property and affairs may be exercised even though P has not reached 16, if the court considers it likely that P will still lack capacity to make decisions in respect of that matter when he reaches 18.

(4) Schedule 2 supplements the provisions of this section.

(5) Section 16(7) (variation and discharge of court orders) is subject to paragraph 6 of Schedule 2.

(6) Subsection (1) is subject to section 20 (restrictions on deputies).

DEFINITIONS

1–208   "property": s.64(1)

GENERAL NOTE

1–209   This section, which is supplemented by Sch.2, provides a non-exhaustive, indicative list of the matters relating to P's property and affairs that come within the jurisdiction of the Court of Protection under s.16. The court may either determine the matter itself or appoint a deputy to make decisions on P's behalf. The power of deputies to make decisions is subject to the restrictions set out in s.20 (subs.(6)) and is limited to the matters specified by the court (s.16(2)(b)).

Like s.17, subs.(1) does not contain a list of matters which must always be referred to the court; it provides an indication of the types of order the court might make if an application is made.

In *Re X, Y and Z* [2014] EWHC 87 (COP) at para.45, Baker J. considered the question of whether the court had the power to make orders for payment for the benefit of P's children:

"I accept that the court has power under the 2005 Act to approve payments for the maintenance or other benefit of members of P's family, notwithstanding the absence of an express provision to that effect in the Act, provided such payments are in P's best interests. Such payments might be called altruistic, but are more characterised as falling within the broad meaning of the concept of 'best interests' under the Act. Where a parent loses mental capacity at a time when she is still responsible for her children, those responsibilities are part of her 'interests' which have to be addressed by those making decisions on her behalf, and payments to meet the reasonable needs of those children are manifestly capable of being described as in her 'best interests'. As set out above, the powers available to the court and the deputy under s.18 when acting in her best interests include the power to discharge any of P's obligations, 'whether legally enforceable or not' and the settlement of any of P's property, whether for P's benefit or for the benefit of others. Whether or not such payments are in her best interests depends on all the circumstances, applying the criteria in the Act."

In *Peters v East Midlands Area Health Authority* [2009] EWHC Civ 145, the court held that if P is awarded compensation in a personal injury action which is awarded to cover P's care costs, there is no obligation placed a deputy to claim public funding for such care. The deputy's responsibilities in such a case were explained by Dyson L.J. at paras 64 and 65:

"Mrs Miles has offered an undertaking to this court in her capacity as Deputy for the claimant that she would (i) notify the senior judge of the Court of Protection of the outcome of these proceedings and supply to him copies of the judgment of this court and that of Butterfield J; and (ii) seek from the Court of Protection (a) a limit on the authority of the claimant's Deputy whereby no application for public funding of the claimant's care under section 21 of the National Assistance Act can be made without further order, direction or authority from the Court of Protection and (b) provision for the defendants to be notified of any application to obtain authority to apply for public finding of the claimant's care under section 21 of the National Assistance Act and be given the opportunity to make representations in relation thereto.

In our judgment, this is an effective way of dealing with the risk of double recovery in cases where the affairs of the claimant are being administered by the Court of Protection. It places the control over the Deputy's ability to make an application for the provision of a claimant's care and accommodation at public expense in the hands of a court. If a Deputy wishes to apply for public provision even where damages have been awarded on the basis that no public provision will be sought, the requirement that the defendant is to be notified of any such application will enable a defendant who wishes to do so to seek to persuade that the Court of Protection should not allow the application to be made because it is unnecessary and contrary to the intendment of the assessment of damages. The court accordingly accepts the undertaking that has been offered."

Peters was considered by Senior Judge Lush in *Re Mark Reeves* (COP) January 5, 2010 who said:

"Notwithstanding the undertaking that was approved in *Peters* and other undertakings of a similar nature, I am of the view that the Court of Protection is no longer really the appropriate forum to adjudicate on matters of this kind. Its primary function is to act in the best interests of a protected beneficiary and, even though it would strive to be impartial, there may be a perception of bias for this reason. Furthermore, the close links which the court had with personal injury litigants generally were effectively severed when the Mental Capacity Act 2005 came into force on 1 October 2007, and the court's approval was no longer required in cases involving settlements out of court on behalf of incapacitated claimants. Additionally, the court no longer supervises deputies: that is one of the functions of the Office of the Public Guardian.

In the absence of any order of the Court of Protection restricting the authority of a claimant's deputy from applying for public funding of the claimant's care under s.21 of the National Assistance Act [now see Care Act 2014], the correct procedure would seem to be for the deputy to apply to the local authority and, if he is dissatisfied with the response he receives, to consider the merits of an application for judicial review."

With regard to the powers of a deputy, Senior Judge Lush said:

"In most cases, since the Mental Capacity Act 2005 came into force, the Court of Protection's order appointing a deputy for property and affairs confers on the deputy general authority to take possession or control of all of the protected beneficiary's property and financial affairs and to exercise the same powers of management and investment as he has as the beneficial owner, subject to any restrictions or conditions set out in the order. Accordingly, a deputy for property and affairs on whom this general authority has been conferred can apply for social security benefits and to a local authority for a care needs assessment without having to obtain specific authorisation from the court to do these things. It was implicit in the judgment in *Peters* that a deputy has such authority, and the purpose of the undertaking in *Peters* was 'to place the control over the deputy's ability to make an application for the provision of a claimant's care and accommodation in the hands of a court'."

In *PJV v The Assistant Director of Adult Social Care Newcastle City Council* [2015] EWCOP 87, Charles J. considered the role of the Court of Protection in connection with applications to the Criminal Injuries Compensation Authority (CICA). His Lordship held at paras 81 and 82 that:

"There is no need for an application to the Court of Protection to finalise an award that CICA, in the proper exercise of its powers under the relevant scheme, decides should be held on trust and so requires to be paid to trustees on trusts that include and do not conflict with terms that CICA is so entitled to require.

A deputy appointed by the Court of Protection can be authorised to negotiate and finalise the terms of such an award and so of the trust and to enter into the 'Acceptance of Final Award' or the equivalent document for an interim award on behalf of P and thereby finalise the claim."

It is submitted that the court may make an order if the provisions of a financial LPA do not enable P's best interests to be satisfied: see *C Re*, Unreported, January 23, 1996, Rattee J.

Use of the inherent jurisdiction

1–210   In *City of Sunderland v PS* [2007] EWHC 623 (Fam), Munby J. held that the power under s.37 of the Senior Courts Act 1981 for the court to appoint a receiver could be invoked by the court in the exercise of the inherent jurisdiction even though there was an available statutory remedy under Pt VII of the Mental Health Act 1983 (now see this Act). His Lordship said at para.34:

"It is necessary for PS's interests for her income and savings to be put under proper control, but it would be an unnecessary burden and, in my judgment, wholly disproportionate to the very modest amounts involved, to condemn the parties to the trouble and expense of separate proceedings in the Court of Protection. In the circumstances it seemed to me that the appropriate course was for me to appoint an appropriate officer of the local authority to be PS's receiver."

Tenancy agreements

1–211   Guidance on "Applications to the Court of Protection in relation to tenancy agreements" is reproduced at Appendix A.

Appointees

1–212   If an incapacitated person has little capital and receives income only from certain state benefits, the necessary financial arrangements can be made under reg.33 of the Social Security (Claims and Payment) Regulations 1987 (SI 1987/1968) which provides that the Secretary of State may appoint someone aged 18 or over (the "appointee") to act on behalf of the claimant. The appointee is usually a close member of the claimant's family, but can be a friend or an officer of a local authority. The appointee has no power to deal with the claimant's capital but can:

(i)   exercise any rights and duties that the claimant has under the social security legislation;

(ii) receive any benefits payable to the claimant; and

(iii) deal with the money received on the claimant's behalf in the interests of the claimant or his or her dependants.

The Court of Protection has no jurisdiction to dismiss an appointee or to replace an appointee with someone else (*LBL v RYJ and VJ* [2010] EWHC 2665 (COP), para.69)

Concern has been expressed about the nature of the enquiries conducted before appointments are made, and about the absence of regular supervision or monitoring of the performance of appointees: see R. Lavery and L. Lundy "The Social Security Appointee System" (1994) *Journal of Social Welfare and Family Law* 313.

The Government resisted amendments to the Bill which would have brought the appointee system under the jurisdiction of the Court of Protection. However, Baroness Andrews, speaking during the committee stage in the House of Lords, said:

"The Bill has enabled us to take stock of the arrangements for appointees and to improve them in the light of the Bill's principles. Officials and Ministers from the Department for Constitutional Affairs and Department for Work and Pensions have been discussing how they can use the Bill to improve the appointeeship system . . .

During the process a DWP official—a benefits official—will visit the person lacking capacity and the prospective appointee. The official needs to be sure that the person does in fact lack the capacity to look after their own benefits, and that the appointee will act in their best interests. That process will be enhanced by the Bill and the code of practice. For example, it will be useful for the officials carrying out those visits to have the benefit of the extra advice on assessing capacity. DWP and DCA officials will work together to ensure that DWP guidance reflects the principles of the Bill and places best interests at its heart. In addition DWP acknowledges that the question of monitoring needs to be addressed, and it will look at options for introducing a monitoring system. With half a million appointees, that is not going to be easy; but it is clearly important, and there will be visits, paper reviews, targeted monitoring—all those sorts of things can be looked at in the light of the Bill. DWP will act quickly to revoke appointments where allegations of mismanagement are made" (*Hansard,* HL Vol.668, col.1463).

The appointee should carry out his or her functions in accordance with the provisions of the Act, in particular ss.1 to 4.

The DWP has produced an "Agents, Appointees and Receivers Guide" which can be accessed on its website (see Appendix B).

Guidance for financial institutions and others
"Guidance for people wanting to manage a bank account for someone else" (2013) **1–213** can be downloaded from a number of websites, including those of the British Bankers Association and the Building Societies Association. The Lloyds Banking Group and the Alzheimer's Society have jointly published a "Dementia-friendly financial services charter" which is designed to help financial services organisations recognise, understand and respond to the needs of customers living with dementia and their carers. The charter can be accessed at: *www.alzheimers.org.uk/site/scripts/download_info. php?fileID=1983.*

The Law Society has published a "Financial Abuse Practice Note" (2013) which is aimed at "solicitors who advise clients that are or may be at risk of financial abuse, in particular those conducting private client work involving financial planning, execution of wills or LPAs" (para.1.1). It can be accessed at: *www.lawsociety.org.uk/advice/practice-notes/financial-abuse/#fa11.*

For guidance on providing services to people with mental health problems to financial institutions, see "Good Practice Guidelines: For consumers with Mental Health Problems and Debt", Money Advice Liaison Group (2009) which can be accessed at: *www.rcpsych. ac.uk/pdf/MALG%202009.pdf.* "Banking on good decisions", Mental Health Foundation (2008) provides guidance for the customers of a bank, building society or post office who have mental health problems.

A Lending Code, which includes guidance on debt and mental health, published by the British Bankers' Association, the Building Societies Association and the UK Cards Association came into force on November 1, 2009 (accessed at www.lendingstandards-board.org.uk/docs/lendingcode.pdf).

Subsection (1)
This largely reproduces the list which applied to the Court of Protection under s.96 of the **1–214** Mental Health Act 1983. The term "property and affairs" is not defined. The same term as it

appeared in the 1983 Act was construed "as including only business matters, legal transactions and other dealings of a similar kind" (*F v West Berkshire Health Authority* [1989] 2 All E.R. 545 at 554, per Lord Brandon).

Paragraph (a)

1–215   PROPERTY.   This includes papers held by the Official Solicitor in an action in which he acts as the patient's litigation friend: see *E (Mental Health Patient), Re* [1985] 1 All E.R. 609 CA where the court held that the parents of a patient had no absolute right to see such papers, although they were the patient's property, but must obtain the authority of the Court of Protection to order disclosure of them as necessary or expedient for the benefit of the patient.

Paragraph (b)

1–216   GIFT.   The Public Guardian has issued Practice Note No. 02/2012 on "Gifts: Deputies and EPA/LPA Attorneys" which can be accessed on the website of the Office of Public Guardian.

In *Re G (TJ)* [2010] EWHC 3005 (COP), Morgan J. adopted the balance sheet approach when assessing whether it was in P's best interests to make a lifetime gift. The relevant extract from the judgment is reproduced in the note on s.4(6). His Lordship suggested, at para.62, that a cautious approach should be taken to ensure that sufficient funds remain available for P for the rest of his or her life.

In *KGS v JDS* [2012] EWHC 302 (COP), a case where an application had been made to make a gift to mitigate the incidence of Inheritance Tax on P's death, Senior Judge Lush said at para.34:

> "[I]n in my judgment, in most cases where an individual's assets derive exclusively from a damages award for personal injury, when determining whether making an *inter vivos* gift is in his or her best interests, the factor of magnetic importance is likely to be the purpose for which the compensation was awarded and the assumptions upon which it was based. This is not confined to the multiplicands and multipliers that have been applied in a specific case, but extends to the fundamental principles that underlie personal injury and clinical negligence litigation generally."

Judge Lush said at para.39 that "it is not the function of the court to anticipate, ring-fence or maximise any potential inheritance for the benefit of family members on the death of a protected party, because this is not the purpose for which the compensation for personal injury was intended".

DISPOSITION OF P'S PROPERTY.   Provisions relating to the preservation of interests in property disposed of on behalf of P are contained in paras 8 and 9 of Sch.2.

Paragraph (h)

1–217   The settlement of any of P's property is a decision which must be made by the court itself, and cannot be entrusted to a deputy (s.20(3)(a)).

Paragraphs 5 and 6 of Sch.2 are concerned with the making of settlements on behalf of P. Settlements are likely to be created, with or without the appointment of a deputy, where P has been awarded substantial damages for personal injury. A personal injury trust was authorised in *Re HM* which is noted in the General Note to s.16.

In *L (WJG), Re* [1966] Ch. 135 at 144 and 145, Cross J. considered the approach to be adopted by a judge in determining whether and how he should exercise his discretion in regard to the making of a settlement where one of the objects of the exercise was to save death duties. His Lordship said: "As the state had maintained [P] free of charge for many years, it would be a little shabby to deprive it of the chance of recouping some of that expenditure by way of death duties".

Paragraph (i)

The execution of a will for P is a decision which must be made by the court itself, and **1–218** cannot be entrusted to a deputy (s.20(3)(b)). Any decision to authorise, or not to authorise, a statutory will must be made in P's best interests (s.1(5)). In the context of s.4, the wishes and feelings to be considered are those of P, and not those of what a reasonable person in that person's position might think (*Aintree University Hospitals NHS Trust v James* [2013] UKSC 67 at para.45, per Lady Hale).

Paragraphs 2 to 4 of Sch.2 apply to the making of a will on behalf of P. Paragraph 4(3) provides that a will made under the Act has the same effect as a will made by a competent testator. The will must be executed in accordance with para.3(2). An example form of statutory will is set out in the Annex to Practice Direction 9F.

An application for a statutory will can be made without the permission of the court by any of the persons specified in s.50 and rr.51(1) and 52(4) of the CPR 2007. The procedure for making an application, including an urgent application, is considered in Ch.20 of *Heywood and Massey: Court of Protection Practice*, (London: Sweet and Maxwell). The areas that should be covered in evidence to the court are set out in Practice Direction 9F. P must be an adult before a will can be made (subs.(2)).

The following authorities were helpfully summarised by HH Judge Behrens in *NT v FS* [2013] EWHC 684 (COP): *Re P* [2009] EWHC 163 (Ch); [2009] 2 All E.R. 1198, *Re M* [2009] EWHC 2525 (Fam); [2010] 3 All E.R. 682, *Re G(TJ)* [2010] EWHC 3005 (COP), and *Re J(C)* [2012] W.T.L.R. 121 (reference should also be made to the notes on s.4). His Honour said at para.8:

"1. The 2005 Act marks a radical change in the treatment of persons lacking capacity. The overarching principle is that any decision made on behalf of P must be in P's best interests. This is not the same as inquiring what P would have decided if he or she had had capacity. It is not a test of substituted judgment but requires the Court to apply an objective test of what would be in P's best interests. [*Re P* paragraphs 36–38]

2. The Court must follow the structured decision making process laid down by the 2005 Act. Thus the Court must consider all relevant circumstances and in particular must consider and take into account the matters set out in sections 4(6) and 4(7) . . . .

3. The Court must then make a value judgment giving effect to the paramount statutory instruction that the decision must be made in P's best interests. [See *Re P* paragraph 39].

4. As Munby J pointed out [*Re M* paragraph 32] the 2005 Act contains no hierarchy between the various factors which have to be borne in mind. The weight to be attached to different factors will inevitably differ depending on the individual circumstances of the particular case. There may however in a particular case be one or more features which, in a particular case, are of 'magnetic importance' in influencing or even determining the outcome.

5. The authorities contain a discussion of the weight to be attached to P's wishes and feelings. In paragraph 40 of *Re P* Lewison J cited at length from the decision of Judge Marshall QC in Re S [2009] WTLR 315. In paragraph 55 of her judgment she had said that the views and wishes of P in regard to decisions made on his behalf are to carry great weight. Her reasons, expressed in paragraph 56 were:

'The Act does not of course say that P's wishes are to be paramount, nor does it lay down any express presumption in favour of implementing them if they can be ascertained. Indeed the paramount objective is that of P's best interests. However, by giving such prominence to the above matters, the Act does in my judgment recognise that having his views and wishes taken into account and respected is a very significant aspect of P's best interests. Due regard should therefore be paid when doing the weighing exercise of determining what is in P's best interests in all the circumstances of the case.'

She went on in paragraph 57 to suggest that there was a presumption in favour of implementing those wishes. Lewison J did not wholly agree with this reasoning. In paragraph 41 of *Re P* he said:

'I agree with the broad thrust of this, although I think that HH Judge Marshall QC may have slightly overstated the importance to be given to P's wishes. First, section 1 (6) is not a statutory direction that one "must achieve" any desired objective by the least restrictive route. Section 1 (6) only requires that before a decision is made *'regard* must be had' to that question. It is an important question, to be sure, but it is not determinative. The only imperative is that the decision must be made in P's best interests. Second, although P's wishes must be given weight, if, as I think, Parliament has endorsed the 'balance sheet' approach, they are only one part of the balance. I agree that those wishes are to be given great weight, but I would prefer not to speak in terms of presumptions. Third, any attempt to test a decision by reference to what P would hypothetically have done or wanted runs the risk of amounting to a 'substituted judgment' rather than a decision of what would be in P's best interests. But despite this risk, the Act itself requires some hypothesising. The decision maker must consider the beliefs and values that would be likely to influence P's decision if he had capacity and also the other factors that P would be likely to consider if he were able to do so. This does not, I think, necessarily require those to be given effect.'

In paragraph 34 of *Re M* Munby J agreed with the broad thrust of Lewison J and Judge Marshall's views. He amplified his views in paragraph 35:

'I venture, however, to add the following observations:

i)   First, P's wishes and feelings will always be a significant factor to which the court must pay close regard: see *Re MM; Local Authority X v MM (by the Official Solicitor) and KM* [2007] EWHC 2003 (Fam), [2009] 1 FLR 443, at paras [121]–[124].

ii)   Secondly, the weight to be attached to P's wishes and feelings will always be case-specific and fact-specific. In some cases, in some situations, they may carry much, even, on occasions, preponderant, weight. In other cases, in other situations, and even where the circumstances may have some superficial similarity, they may carry very little weight. One cannot, as it were, attribute any particular *a priori* weight or importance to P's wishes and feelings; it all depends, it must depend, upon the individual circumstances of the particular case. . .'

6.   Differing views are expressed in the authorities as to relevance to the decision maker of P 'having done the right thing' by his will and being remembered for that after his death. Both Lewison J and Munby J took the view that this was a relevant matter to be placed in the balance sheet. However Morgan J and Senior Judge Lush have expressed doubts. [See paragraphs 52–53, 64 of *Re G(TJ)* and paragraph 54 of *Re JC*.] As Morgan J pointed out the making of the gift and/or the terms of the will are not being made by P but by the Court. Furthermore insofar as there is a dispute between family members the unsuccessful members are not likely to think that he had done the right thing. For my part I think there is force in Morgan J's views on the facts of this case with the result that I do not intend to place any weight on this factor."

With regard to point 6, HHJ Hodge said in *Re Meek* [2014] EWCOP 1 at para.34:

"Speaking for myself, I do not consider that either Lord Justice Lewison, or the present President of the Court of Protection, were oblivious to the considerations identified by Mr Justice Morgan in the case of *Re G (TJ)* [2010] EWHC 3005 (COP). In my judgment, what Mr Justice Lewison referred to as 'the right thing' is to be judged from the perspective, not of any relatives or friends who may be competing for a share of the incapacitous person's testamentary bounty, but rather from the perspective of the well-informed, and disinterested, objective bystander. Nevertheless, 'the right thing' is to be judged, as Baroness Hale's recent speech makes clear, by reference to the standards of the incapacitous person himself, and not by what the reasonable incapacitous person might be thought to think. Further, in my judgment, the concept of being remembered 'as having done the right thing' still has relevance even if, because of the lack of testamentary capacity, the right thing has to be done for the testator by the Court of Protection."

Judge Hodge endorsed the "balance sheet" approach to the making of statutory wills at para.35.

It is submitted that following comment made by Megarry VC in *D(J), Re* [1982] 2 All E.R. 37 at 49 about the evidence presented to the judge in a statutory will case has continuing relevance:

"I hope that in future cases . . . more attention will be paid to setting out what may be called the hard facts of the case. Those who seek to have a will made for a patient should at least provide reasonably detailed information as to the size of the estate, the income, and the expenses of maintaining the patient. A person making a will, whether for himself or anyone else, ought to have a reasonable knowledge of what there is, and what there is likely to be, for disposal under the will. The financial and other circumstances of all those who claim to receive benefits under a will ought also to be made clear. Many a testator will discriminate between those who are well provided for and those who are needy. Some idea should also be given of the nature of the patient while still of testamentary capacity, even if only to state the negative of the patient being ordinary in every way and having no relevant prejudices or the like."

The Court of Protection has no jurisdiction to determine the validity of an existing will and, in particular, whether P had the required mental capacity when he made it (*Re M*, [2009] EWHC 2525 (Fam)). However, the court has authorised the execution of a statutory will as a means of circumventing possible later disputes about the validity of a will over which substantial doubt has been cast: see *Re D (Statutory Will)* [2010] EWHC 2159 (Ch).

Paragraph (k)   **1–219**
This provision has been used to obtain an order appointing a deputy to conduct litigation on behalf of P in the employment tribunal: see the May 2013 issue of the 39 Essex Street Court of Protection Newsletter at p.16.

The conduct of legal proceedings need not be confined to proceedings relating either to P's personal welfare or his property and affairs *(W (EEM), Re* [1971] Ch.123).

Subsection (3)   **1–220**
The purpose of this provision "is to enable the Court of Protection to appoint a deputy who can take a long-term view where a child has been awarded substantial compensation for personal injury or clinical negligence and it is unlikely that the child will have the capacity to manage the award when they attain adulthood" (*Re AK* [2014] EWHCB11 (COP), per Senior Judge Lush at para.4).

Appointment of deputies   **1–221**
19.—(1) A deputy appointed by the court must be—
(a) an individual who has reached 18, or
(b) as respects powers in relation to property and affairs, an individual who has reached 18 or a trust corporation.
(2) The court may appoint an individual by appointing the holder for the time being of a specified office or position.

(3) A person may not be appointed as a deputy without his consent.

(4) The court may appoint two or more deputies to act—

(a) jointly,

(b) jointly and severally, or

(c) jointly in respect of some matters and jointly and severally in respect of others.

(5) When appointing a deputy or deputies, the court may at the same time appoint one or more other persons to succeed the existing deputy or those deputies—

(a) in such circumstances, or on the happening of such events, as may be specified by the court;

(b) for such period as may be so specified.

(6) A deputy is to be treated as P's agent in relation to anything done or decided by him within the scope of his appointment and in accordance with this Part.

(7) The deputy is entitled—

(a) to be reimbursed out of P's property for his reasonable expenses in discharging his functions, and

(b) if the court so directs when appointing him, to remuneration out of P's property for discharging them.

(8) The court may confer on a deputy powers to—

(a) take possession or control of all or any specified part of P's property;

(b) exercise all or any specified powers in respect of it, including such powers of investment as the court may determine.

(9) The court may require a deputy—

(a) to give to the Public Guardian such security as the court thinks fit for the due discharge of his functions, and

(b) to submit to the Public Guardian such reports at such times or at such intervals as the court may direct.

DEFINITIONS

1–222
"deputy": s.64(1)
"the court": s.64(1)
"property": s.64(1)
"trust corporation": s.64(1)
"Public Guardian": s.64(1)

GENERAL NOTE

1–223
A deputy appointed by the Court of Protection must be an adult who consents to the appointment, with the exception that a trust corporation can be appointed in respect of P's property and affairs (subss.(1) and (3)). The order of preference for the appointment of a deputy is considered in the notes on s.16(2)(6). More than one deputy can be appointed for P (subs.(4)). When appointing a deputy, the court will exercise its discretion so as to satisfy the best interests of P (s.1(5)). A deputy will not be appointed if the court can satisfactorily deal with the matter itself by making an order (s.16(4); and see the notes thereto). The court will decide the extent of the powers to be conferred on the deputy (s.16(5)) and the deputy can only act in accordance with such powers. References to making decisions, in relation to a deputy, include, where appropriate, acting on decisions made (s.64(2)).The deputy can be provided with the power to deal with all matters concerning the control and management of P's property, including being able to invest (subs.(8)). The court is able to require a deputy to give the Public Guardian security against misbehaviour and to direct the deputy to file reports with the Public Guardian at specified intervals (subs.(9)). The Public Guardian has no role to play in determining the extent of the deputy's powers; only the court can

do this. A deputy has no power to act if he or she believes that P has the capacity to make the proposed decision (s.20(1)). The powers of the deputy will also be subject to the other restrictions contained in s.20. The deputy's powers can be varied by the court, which can also revoke the appointment (s.16(8)). A deputy will be provided with protection by ss.5 and 6 for acts done outside the scope of the appointment. There is no time limit attached to the appointment. Where a deputy is appointed in relation to P and P then dies, the powers of the deputy cease (*Re G(TJ)* [2010] EWHC 3005 (COP) at para.17).

Those applying to become deputies would need to demonstrate why an appointment is necessary. There is no requirement for the court to be satisfied as to the suitability of an individual for appointment by, for example, investigating any actual or potential conflict of interest, although the Public Guardian is required to supervise deputies (see below). Unlike a donee under a lasting power of attorney, the deputy can be the holder of a specified office, such as a Director of Adult Services (subs.(2)).

Senior Judge Lush set out the court's approach to the appointment of a deputy in *Re BM* [2014] EWCOP B20 at paras. 46 to 49:

"No one has an automatic right to be appointed as deputy. The Court of Protection has a discretion as to whom it appoints and, as I have said before in other judgments, tradition-ally the court has preferred to appoint a relative or friend as deputy (if it is satisfied that it is in P's best interests to do so), rather than appoint a complete stranger.

This is because a relative or friend is usually familiar with P's affairs and aware of their wishes and feelings. Someone with a close personal knowledge of P is also likely to be in a better position to meet the obligation of a deputy to consult with P, and to permit and encourage them to participate, or to improve their ability to participate, as fully as pos-sible in any act or decision affecting them. And, because professionals charge for their services, the appointment of a relative or friend is preferred for reasons of economy.

There are, however, cases in which the court wouldn't contemplate appointing a particu-lar family member or friend as deputy. These include situations where:

(a) the proposed deputy has physically, psychologically, financially or emotionally abused P;

(b) there is a need to investigate dealings with P's assets prior to the matter being brought to the court's attention, and the proposed deputy's conduct is the subject of that investigation;

(c) there is a real conflict of interests;

(d) the proposed deputy has an unsatisfactory track record in managing his or her own financial affairs; and

(e) there is ongoing friction between various family members, which is likely to interfere with the proper administration of P's affairs.

For a completely different set of reasons . . . the court generally prefers to appoint an independent, professional deputy, rather than a family member, in cases where P has been awarded substantial compensation for personal injury or clinical negligence."

In *Re GW* [2014] EWCOP B23 at para.29, Judge Lush said that there is one matter he did not mention in *Re BM* which is the need to ensure that P is not subjected to undue influence: also see *Re PAW* [2015] EWCOP 57 at para.26.

Some of the advantages in having a local authority act as deputy were identified by Senior Judge Lush in *Suffolk CC v JU* [2014] EWCOP 21 at para.43. They include:

"(a) considerable hands-on experience in dealing with the property and financial affairs of adults who lack capacity to manage their own affairs;

(b) more rigorous checks and balances against financial misconduct and other forms of abuse than are possible in cases where a lay deputy is appointed;

(c) membership of a professional association, the Association of Public Authority Deputies ('APAD'), which provides guidance on professional ethics and best practice; and

(d) a greater awareness of:

> (i)   the provisions of the Mental Capacity Act 2005;
> (ii) the application of the principles in section 1 of the Act;
> (iii) the requirement, where necessary, to assess the person's capacity to make a particular decision at a particular time;
> (iv) the criteria and procedure for making a best interests decision;
> (v)   the contents of the Mental Capacity Act Code of Practice, particularly relating to the duties of a deputy; and
> (vi) the ongoing case law emanating from judgments such as this."

Judge Lush identified how the court could manage conflicts of interests in *Re JW* [2015] EWCOP 82.

The fact that someone lives outside the jurisdiction should not be an impediment to their appointment as a deputy if, in all other respects, they are the most suitable candidate to be appointed and their appointment is in P's best interests (*DGP Law v DGHP* [2015] EWCOP 58).

Where there is more than one deputy, they can be appointed to act either jointly or jointly and severally, i.e. they must either act together with the agreement of all donees (jointly), or each donee can act independently of the other (severally). As an alternative, the donees can be appointed to act jointly in respect of some matters and jointly and severally in respect of others (subs.(4)). When making the appointment, the court has the power to appoint a successor or successors to the original appointee(s) and to specify the circumstances under which this could occur (subs.(5)). The *Code of Practice* states at para.8.44:

"Appointment of a successor deputy might be useful if the person appointed as deputy is already elderly and wants to be sure that somebody will take over their duties in the future, if necessary."

A deputy can claim reasonable expenses and, if the court directs, the deputy can be paid for his or her services: see CPR 2007, r.167. Both expenses and the payments will be made out of P's property (subs.(7)). The expenses of an officer of a local authority who applies to the court for appointment as a deputy may be defrayed by the authority (National Assistance Act 1948, s.49).

Although case law established that receivers appointed by the Court of Protection under Pt VII of the Mental Health Act 1983 are statutory agents of the person who lacks capacity (*EG, Re* [1914] 1 Ch. 927), it was considered "helpful to make statutory provision to that effect in relation to deputies" (Explanatory Notes, para.73). This is done in subs.(6). An act of an agent, done within the scope of his authority binds his principal, in this case P. As an agent the deputy is bound by a number of common law duties toward P, including the duty to act with due care and skill, to act within the scope of the authority granted by the court, to act in good faith, not to delegate his or her functions to another without authority (but see paras 8.61 and 8.62 of the *Code of Practice*), to keep the affairs of P confidential, to keep accounts of monies received and paid on P's behalf, and not to permit his own interests to conflict with his duties to P. The duties of an agent are set out in the *Code of Practice* at paras 8.55–8.67. In addition to these duties, the deputy is required to act in P's best interests (s.20(6)), to apply the principles set out in s.1 and to have regard to the *Code of Practice* (s.42(4)(b)). *EG, Re* is authority for the propositions that the property of P does not vest in the deputy (at 933), and that the deputy is not personally liable for the costs of those he or she employs in the course of acting for P (at 935). The deputy should notify any third party with whom he is dealing of the fact that he is acting as deputy for P, as it is a general principle of the law of agency that an agent is personally liable on any contract made in his own name on behalf of a principal where the name or existence of the principal (P) is undisclosed at the time of contracting. Also see the comment on the law of agency in the General Note to s.10.

Any concerns about the manner in which a deputy is performing his or her functions should be reported to the Public Guardian who is responsible for supervising the activities of deputies (s.58(1)(c)). The levels of supervision that Deputies will receive are set out in reg.8(3) of the Public Guardian (Fees, etc) Regulations 2007 (SI 2007/2051). The Public Guardian may decide to direct a Court of Protection Visitor to visit P and/or the deputy. Allegations of serious criminal conduct, such as physical or sexual abuse, should be reported directly to the police, and the Public Guardian informed. Also see the note on adult protection procedures in s.44.

The levels of supervision that Deputies will receive are set out in reg.8(3) of the Public Guardian (Fees, etc) Regulations 2007 (SI 2007/2051). In December 2014, the Office of the Public Guardian submitted a "Fundamental Review of the Supervision of Court Appointed Deputies by the Public Guardian" to Parliament.

References to making decisions, in relation to a deputy, include, where appropriate, acting on decisions made (s.64(2)).

The Public Guardian has published Practice Note 01/2016 on "Local authority deputyship responsibilities". Practice Note 02/2016 sets out the OPG's approach to solicitor client accounts where the solicitor is acting as a deputy.

Subsection (1)

APPOINTED BY THE COURT.   An application for the appointment of a deputy is made by   **1–224**
using the procedure set out in Part 9 of the CPR 2007. For a detailed analysis, see Ch.8 of *Heywood and Massey: Court of Protection Practice*, Sweet and Maxwell.

Subsection (4)

JOINTLY AND SEVERALLY.   In *P, Re* [2010] EWHC 1592 (Fam) at para.29, Hedley J.   **1–225**
said that

> "the difficulty generally in granting powers to act severally, is to lay the seeds of possible dispute where you have a number of deputies. I think that is a problem that the court simply needs to recognise without having to be able to do very much about it. The very limited experience of the operation of this Act so far suggests that, where deputies disagree, one or more of them will in fact notify either the court or the public guardian of the existence of disagreement, and therefore the matter is able to be addressed. It seems to me that it would be unduly complicated to provide conditions as to when deputies were able to act severally in a case like this, where many, many decisions, many of them wholly unpredictable at the present time, will arise for consideration".

Subsection (5)

In *Re H* [2015] EWCOP 52, Senior Judge Lush said at paras 1 and 4:   **1–226**

> "There are two provisions in the Mental Capacity Act 2005 ('MCA') that seem to contradict each other. Section 16(4)(b) envisages that a deputyship appointment will be of limited duration, whereas section 19(5) facilitates an appointment that could last for decades. . . . When it comes to the crunch, section 16(4)(b) trumps section 19(5) because it is a principle to which the court must have regard when deciding whether it in P's best interests to appoint a deputy, while section 19(5) is simply a discretion conferred upon the court, once it has decided to appoint a deputy."

In this case, there was an application to appoint successive deputies for a young woman, H, aged 26. The appointment was allowed, the judge saying that "[t]he factor of magnetic importance [in the balance sheet approach] is that the appointment of successive deputies will give H's parents peace of mind' (para.51).

Subsection (6)

"A key principle governing deputies is that they cannot do more than the person could   **1–227**
do if he or she had capacity", per the Parliamentary Under-Secretary of State, St. Comm. A, para.191.

Subsection (7)

1–228   This subsection relates solely to the functions performed by the deputy as a deputy, rather than to the functions performed by him in any other capacity, such as a carer or case manager. The court has broader powers under ss.16(5) and 18(1), which enable it to set a level of remuneration for carer or case management services (*Re HNL* EWCOP 77, per Senior Judge Lush at paras 41 and 42).

Subsection (9)(a)

1–229   The Public Guardian has issued Practice Note No. 03/2012 on "Surety Bonds: Statement of Expectations of the Public Guardian" which can be accessed on the website of the Office of the Public Guardian.

The purpose of a security is to protect P and his or her resources from the consequences of negligence or default (such as misappropriation) by the deputy. In *Baker v H* [2009] EWHC B31 (Fam) at para.106, Judge Marshall QC set out the approach that should be taken in considering the setting up of security and its interplay with the terms of appointment of a deputy:

"(1) If the Court has real doubts about whether a deputy can be trusted with P's assets, then it must consider not appointing him as a deputy. Alternatively (if this will largely allay such doubts) the court can and should consider imposing limits on the funds under the deputy's control and, in particular, should consider whether the general words of the order appointing the deputy should be narrowed to prevent his having any authority to deal with any property occupied by P as his home, (or any interest of P therein) without further order of the court.

(2) The court should then consider the amount of funds that are to be placed in the deputy's hands or under his control, and envisage the costs and/or loss to P if there were to be a total default by the deputy.

(3) The court should then consider whether the deputy carries professional indemnity insurance which would be effective to replace P's assets in his hands in the event of such a total default. This will include reviewing such matters as the level of aggregation of assets in the hands of a single deputy relative to his insurance.

(4) In the absence of adequate insurance cover then the starting point will be the value of the assets in or passing through the deputy's hands. This consideration may lead back to a review of the terms of the deputyship order with a view to limiting the value of the vulnerable assets.

(5) Where the deputy apparently has adequate and effective professional indemnity insurance, then the court
    (i) should require him to deposit a copy of this with the OPG and inform the OPG/ the court immediately if its level is reduced, and
    (ii) should aim to set a level of security which will provide adequate resources to meet P's immediate expenditure needs for a period related to the time it may take to settle the insurance claim (perhaps up to 2–3 years), the costs of making such a claim, and an allowance in case immediate debts of P may have been left unpaid, applying a suitable margin for error.

[(6)] Having formed the above provisional view as to the appropriate level of security, the court should finally consider the level of premium and whether this would cause P undue financial hardship, or would otherwise in all the circumstances (including the apparent status of the deputy) appear to be an unjustifiable or wasteful use of P's resources, when balanced against the benefit of having that security. Special circumstances (eg husband/wife deputyships, or lay deputies of obvious stature, or situations in which the real risk would appear to be merely negligence rather than total default) may mitigate this, but must provide some real justification for taking the view that such a level of security is not reasonably necessary. The court will then decide whether it is in P's best interests to maintain the level of security originally assessed, or to reduce it to any extent."

Judge Marshall said, at paras 54, 55, that it is "the *real and realistic* degree and quantum of risk to P, in the particular circumstances, which must provide the starting point for fixing an appropriate level of security. Simply taking the value of P's estate without further examination, or even taking that value and applying some arbitrary fraction, is simplistic and incorrect. . . . [T]he following factors will fall to be considered . . . :

(1) The value and vulnerability of the assets which are under the control of the deputy.
(2) How long it might be before a default or loss is discovered.
(3) The availability and extent of any other remedy or resource available to P in the event of a default or loss.
(4) P's immediate needs in the event of a default or loss.
(5) The cost to P of ordering security, and the possibilities and cost of increasing his protection in any other way.
(6) The gravity of the consequences of loss or default for P, in his circumstances
(7) The status, experience and record of the particular deputy."

In *Re Meek* [2014] EWCOP 1, Judge Hodge held that:

1. The "best interests" principle applies to a decision by the court whether to call in a security bond provided by a defaulting deputy (para.41); and
2. The appropriate course the Court of Protection should take in cases of default by a deputy is to call in the security bond almost as a matter of course (para.93).

Also see CPR 2007 r.200 and the Lasting Powers of Attorney, Enduring Powers of Attorney and Public Guardian Regulations 2007 (SI 2007/1253) regs 33 to 37.

Subsection (9)(b)
SUBMIT TO THE PUBLIC GUARDIAN . . . REPORTS. See regs 38 to 40 of SI 2007/1253. **1–230**

Restrictions on deputies

20.—(1) A deputy does not have power to make a decision on behalf of P in **1–231** relation to a matter if he knows or has reasonable grounds for believing that P has capacity in relation to the matter.

(2) Nothing in section 16(5) or 17 permits a deputy to be given power—
(a) to prohibit a named person from having contact with P;
(b) to direct a person responsible for P's health care to allow a different person to take over that responsibility.

(3) A deputy may not be given powers with respect to—
(a) the settlement of any of P's property, whether for P's benefit or for the benefit of others,
(b) the execution for P of a will, or
(c) the exercise of any power (including a power to consent) vested in P whether beneficially or as trustee or otherwise.

(4) A deputy may not be given power to make a decision on behalf of P which is inconsistent with a decision made, within the scope of his authority and in accordance with this Act, by the donee of a lasting power of attorney granted by P (or, if there is more than one donee, by any of them).

(5) A deputy may not refuse consent to the carrying out or continuation of life-sustaining treatment in relation to P.

(6) The authority conferred on a deputy is subject to the provisions of this Act and, in particular, sections 1 (the principles) and 4 (best interests).

(7) A deputy may not do an act that is intended to restrain P unless four conditions are satisfied.

(8) The first condition is that, in doing the act, the deputy is acting within the scope of an authority expressly conferred on him by the court.

(9) The second is that P lacks, or the deputy reasonably believes that P lacks, capacity in relation to the matter in question.

(10) The third is that the deputy reasonably believes that it is necessary to do the act in order to prevent harm to P.

(11) The fourth is that the act is a proportionate response to—

(a)   the likelihood of P's suffering harm, [and]

(b)   the seriousness of that harm.

(12) For the purposes of this section, a deputy restrains P if he—

(a)   uses, or threatens to use, force to secure the doing of an act which P resists, or

(b)   restricts P's liberty of movement, whether or not P resists,

or if he authorises another person to do any of those things.

(13) [*Repealed by the Mental Health Act 2007 s.50(4)(c)*]

AMENDMENT

1–232   The word in square brackets in subs.(11) was substituted by the Mental Health Act 2007 s.51.

DEFINITIONS

1–233   "deputy": s.64(1)

"property": s.64(1)

"lasting power of attorney": s.64(1)

"life-sustaining treatment": s.64(1)

"the Human Rights Convention": s.64(1)

"public authority": s.6(1)

GENERAL NOTE

1–234   This section sets out a number of limitations on the powers of deputies, who must always act in P's best interests (subs.(6)).

Subsection (1) specifies that a deputy cannot act where P is able to act for himself. The Explanatory Notes state at para.75:

"In some cases the person may have fluctuating capacity, for example as a result of mental health problems, and it is not acceptable for a deputy to carry on making substitute decisions when the person concerned has in fact recovered."

As it can be sometimes difficult to determine whether a person with fluctuating mental capacity is enjoying a lucid interval, the deputy should consider seeking professional assistance if he or she suspects that P is able to act for himself.

Subsections (2) and (3) list matters which must always be dealt with by the court, not a deputy.

Subsection (4) provides that a deputy cannot be given power to override a valid decision made by a donee under P's LPA. If there is concern or a dispute about the way the donee is carrying on his or her responsibilities under the LPA, the court must use its powers under ss.22 and 23 rather than seeking to appoint a deputy.

Subsection (5) prevents deputies from refusing consent to the carrying out or continuation of life-sustaining treatment.

Subsections (7)–(12) impose limitations on a deputy's power to restrain P. They match those imposed in relation to "section 5 acts" by s.6 and on donees by s.11, and reference should be made to the notes on s.6. The deputy will have to be acting within the scope of an authority expressly conferred on him by the court (subs.(8)).

If P is subject to guardianship under the Mental Health Act 1983, a deputy cannot make a decision, including a decision about where P should reside, which conflicts with that of the guardian (ibid. s.8(1)).

Subsection (2)(a)

In *PB v RB* [2013] EWCOP B41, Judge Altman held that the deputy had not been given **1–235** a power to prohibit contact in a situation where the court had authorised the deputy to prevent contact between RB and PB for up to seven days at a time as part of the day-to-day management of contact without having to refer back to the court. The court had determined itself the limit to the cessation of contact and allowed the deputy to exercise his discretion in deciding whether to cease contact for short periods within that framework. Also see the note on this case in the General Note to 17.

If a deputy is concerned about someone's conduct toward P, he or she can apply to the court for a relevant order to be made, or apply for a non-molestation order under Pt IV of the Family Law Act 1996 (c.27) as P's litigation friend.

Subsection (6)

All deputies, both professional and lay, will need to be familiar with the principles set **1–236** out in s.1 and with the "checklist" approach used in best interest determinations made under s.4.

Transfer of proceedings relating to people under 18

21.—[(1)] The [Lord Chief Justice, with the concurrence of the Lord Chancellor] **1–237** may by order make provision as to the transfer of proceedings relating to a person under 18, in such circumstances as are specified in the order—

(a) from the Court of Protection to a court having jurisdiction under the Children Act 1989 (c. 41), or

(b) from a court having jurisdiction under that Act to the Court of Protection.

[(2) The Lord Chief Justice may nominate any of the following to exercise his functions under this section—

(a) the President of the Court of Protection;

(b) a judicial office holder (as defined in section 109(4) of the Constitutional Reform Act 2005).]

AMENDMENTS

The amendments to this section were made by SI 2006/1016 art.2, Sch.1, para.31. **1–238**

GENERAL NOTE

Generally speaking, the Act is concerned with people aged 16 and over who lack capac- **1–239** ity (s.2(5); but see s.18(3)), while the Children Act 1989 is mainly concerned with people under the age of 18. This section deals with any overlap between the two jurisdictions by providing the Lord Chancellor with a power to make transfer of proceedings orders. The Parliamentary Under-Secretary of State gave the following example of the need for a transfer:

"[I]f the parents of a 17 year-old who has profound learning difficulties are in dispute with each other about residence or contact, it might be more appropriate for the Court of Protection to deal with that, since a s.8 order made under the Children Act 1989 would expire on the child's eighteenth birthday at the latest" (*Hansard*, HL Vol.668, col.1485).

Subsection (1)

MAY BY ORDER. See the Mental Capacity Act 2005 (Transfer of Proceedings) Order **1–240** 2007 (SI 2007/1899) which is reproduced in Pt 3.

Powers of court in relation to Schedule A1

1–241   **21A.**—(1) This section applies if either of the following has been given under Schedule A1—

(a)   a standard authorisation;

(b)   an urgent authorisation.

(2) Where a standard authorisation has been given, the court may determine any question relating to any of the following matters—

(a)   whether the relevant person meets one or more of the qualifying requirements;

(b)   the period during which the standard authorisation is to be in force;

(c)   the purpose for which the standard authorisation is given;

(d)   the conditions subject to which the standard authorisation is given.

(3) If the court determines any question under subsection (2), the court may make an order—

(a)   varying or terminating the standard authorisation, or

(b)   directing the supervisory body to vary or terminate the standard authorisation.

(4) Where an urgent authorisation has been given, the court may determine any question relating to any of the following matters—

(a)   whether the urgent authorisation should have been given;

(b)   the period during which the urgent authorisation is to be in force;

(c)   the purpose for which the urgent authorisation is given.

(5) Where the court determines any question under subsection (4), the court may make an order—

(a)   varying or terminating the urgent authorisation, or

(b)   directing the managing authority of the relevant hospital or care home to vary or terminate the urgent authorisation.

(6) Where the court makes an order under subsection (3) or (5), the court may make an order about a person's liability for any act done in connection with the standard or urgent authorisation before its variation or termination.

(7) An order under subsection (6) may, in particular, exclude a person from liability.]

AMENDMENT

1–242   This section was inserted by the Mental Health Act 2007 s.50(7), Sch.9, Pt.1, para.2.

DEFINITION

1–243   "the court": s.64(1).

GENERAL NOTE

1–244   This section gives the court jurisdiction for the purposes of art.5(4) of the European Convention on Human Rights to review the authorisation of a person's detention under the procedure set out in Sch.A1 and to terminate the authorisation if it is not lawful. It also provides the court with the power to determine key issues relating to the authorisation, to vary the authorisation, and to order either the supervisory body (for standard authorisations) or the managing authority (for urgent authorisations) to either vary or terminate the authorisation. The scope of the powers contained in this section were considered in *Re UF* [2013] EWHC 4289 (COP) and in *CC v KK* [2012] EWHC 2136 (COP). In *Re UF*, Charles J. said at paras 34 and 42:

"It seems to me that the combination of s. 21A (2)(b) and (3)(a) and (b), s. 47 and s. 48 and paragraph 61(2) of Schedule A1 of the MCA empowers the Court of Protection to vary an existing standard authorisation by extending (or shortening) it and that if and when it exercises that power it would normally be sensible for the court to give consideration to whether it should then exercise its powers under ss. (6) and (7) or give directions concerning its future exercise of those powers. . . .

[However], the elasticity of the language of s. 21A does not extend to the revival of an authorisation which has ended and been substituted by the continuation of an authorisation under court order, or to the making by the Court or the supervisory body on the direction of the court of a new standard authorisation".

In *CC v KK,* Baker J. said at para.16:

"When a standard authorisation has been made by a supervisory body, s. 21A(2) empowers the Court of Protection to determine any questions relating to, inter alia, whether P meets one or more of the qualifying requirements. In particular, once the court determines the question, it may make an order varying or terminating the standard authorisation: s. 21A(3)(a). But once an application is made to the Court under s. 21A, the Court's powers are not confined simply to determining that question. Once its jurisdiction is invoked, the court has a discretionary power under s. 15 to make declarations as to (a) whether a person has or lacks capacity to make a decision specified in the declaration; (b) whether a person has or lacks capacity to make decisions on such matters as are described in the declaration, and (c) the lawfulness or otherwise of any act done, or yet to be done, in relation to that person. Where P lacks capacity, the court has wide powers under s. 16 to make decisions on P's behalf in relation to matters concerning his personal welfare or property or affairs."

In *TA v AA* [2013] EWCA Civ 1661 at para.75, Moses L.J. speaking obiter said:

"I need only emphasise that due and proper consideration of an appeal under s.21A may not require any lengthy consideration. A full hearing is not necessarily a lengthy, time consuming or expensive hearing."

In *A County Council v MB* [2010] EWHC 2508 (COP) at para.100, Charles J. said:

"Applications can be made to the court under s.21A in respect of authorisations that have been granted and the section specifies the limited extent of the relief that can be given thereunder. It is unlikely that s.21A will be applicable where the problem is that an authorisation or a further authorisation cannot be given. But then, and in other circumstances, an order that authorises a deprivation of liberty can be sought under ss.4A, 16, 47 and 48 from the court. If they are urgent, such applications to the court can be brought before the High Court Judge in the Family Division designated to hear urgent applications in and out of court hours. Supervisory bodies and managing authorities should take steps (i) to bring the statutory provisions relating to applications to the court to the notice of their decision makers, and (ii) to ensure that they are aware that pending a court decision they can either:

i) rely on s.4B, and that to do so they should expressly address the test set out therein and record their reasoning as to why they believe it is satisfied, or
ii) seek an interim order from the court to authorise a continuation of an existing detention."

Once an application is made to the court under this section, "the court's powers are not confined simply to determining that question. In particular, once the court determines the question, it may make an order varying or terminating the standard authorisation: s.21(3) (a). In addition, once its jurisdiction is evoked under s.21A the court has a discretionary power under s.15 to make a declaration as to whether P lacks capacity to make any decision. Once such a declaration is made, the court has wide powers under section 16 to make decisions on P's behalf in relation to matters" (*PH v A Local Authority* [2011] EWHC 1704 (Fam) at para.15, per Baker J.).

In *Re A* [2011] EWHC 727 (COP) at para.15, the President said that where the only person objecting to an authorisation is P, "the court cannot simply act as a rubber stamp, however beneficial the arrangements may appear to be for the individual concerned".

In *AB v LCC* [2011] 3151 (COP) at para.38, Mostyn J. held that that there is no impediment to a relevant person's representative (RPR) who has been appointed under Pt 10 of Sch.A1 acting as a litigation friend to P in a s.21A application provided that:

(i)   the RPR is not already a party to the proceedings;
(ii) the RPR fulfils the CPR 2007 r.140 conditions;
(iii) the RPR can and is willing to act as litigation friend in P's best interests; and
(iv) the procedure as set out in CPR 2007 r.143 is complied with.

His Lordship said that in "relation to s.21A MCA applications there may often be (but not always) a paid RPR. . . . [T]here does not appear to be any good reason, considering the overall statutory scheme, why the Court cannot, on its own initiative, pursuant to r.143, invite the RPR to be appointed as litigation friend and if he or she consents, to be so appointed. The Court would need to be satisfied that the RPR satisfies the conditions set out . . . above. This would require evidence" (para.42).The court was informed that the Official Solicitor has adopted a policy whereby he will act as litigation friend for P when there is no-one else willing and able to act. The role and responsibilities of the RPR as identified by Mostyn J. in this case are set out in Part 2 under *The appointment of representatives.*

If the court makes an order, it may also make an order about a person's liability for any act done before the variation or termination of the authorisation, and this includes an order excluding a person from liability (subss.(6),(7)).

A less expensive and time consuming alternative to making an appeal under this section is for a qualified person or body to demand that the supervisory body reviews the deprivation of liberty under Pt.8 of Sch.A1.

Applications

1–245   For applications under this section, see r.82A of the CPR 2007, together with the associated Practice Direction on "Deprivation of Liberty Applications". In *AB v LCC*, above, at para.30, Mostyn J. said that it "would appear that anyone" can make an application under this section, and that the persons identified in s.50(1), (1A) do not need permission to do so. His Lordship commented that the "test for the grant of permission does not appear unduly high in practice" (para.31). The court was informed that in many cases where the RPR makes an application, the court often appears to assume the RPR is doing so only on behalf of the detained person and as such he ceases to be a party. His Lordship said: "Properly understood the RPR may be a party in his or her own right and it is submitted by Mr McKendrick that the Court should not automatically appoint the detained person as the Applicant and end the role of the RPR (which appears often to take place in practice). I tend to agree" (para.35). His Lordship further stated that "there appear in practice to be few cases where the RPR acts as the applicant to s21A applications. Should the applicant be a paid RPR appointed by the supervisory body it may be the Court would want to encourage such RPRs remaining as such, as envisaged by the statutory scheme. If, however, the RPR is a family member, the Court will need to consider whether P's interests are properly represented before the Court. In circumstances where a family member RPR is the applicant, the Court may feel it necessary to make P a respondent and to appoint the Official Solicitor (or another person) as the litigation friend" (para.46).

An IMCA who has been instructed by the supervisory body under s.39D is required "to take such steps as are practicable to help P to exercise the right to apply to court, if it appears to the advocate that P . . . wishes to exercise that right" (s.39D(8)(a)).

Those who are concerned with the manner in which a deprivation of liberty authorisation has been implemented could consider making a complaint to the Local Government and/or

Health Service Ombudsman as an alternative to making an application to the Court whose primary focus is forward-looking.

Powers of the court in relation to lasting powers of attorney

Powers of court in relation to validity of lasting powers of attorney

22.—(1) This section and section 23 apply if—

1–246

   (a) a person (P) has executed or purported to execute an instrument with a view to creating a lasting power of attorney, or

   (b) an instrument has been registered as a lasting power of attorney conferred by P.

(2) The court may determine any question relating to—

   (a) whether one or more of the requirements for the creation of a lasting power of attorney have been met;

   (b) whether the power has been revoked or has otherwise come to an end.

(3) Subsection (4) applies if the court is satisfied—

   (a) that fraud or undue pressure was used to induce P—

   (i) to execute an instrument for the purpose of creating a lasting power of attorney, or

   (ii) to create a lasting power of attorney, or

   (b) that the donee (or, if more than one, any of them) of a lasting power of attorney—

   (i) has behaved, or is behaving, in a way that contravenes his authority or is not in P's best interests, or

   (ii) proposes to behave in a way that would contravene his authority or would not be in P's best interests.

(4) The court may—

   (a) direct that an instrument purporting to create the lasting power of attorney is not to be registered, or

   (b) if P lacks capacity to do so, revoke the instrument or the lasting power of attorney.

(5) If there is more than one donee, the court may under subsection (4)(b) revoke the instrument or the lasting power of attorney so far as it relates to any of them.

(6) "Donee" includes an intended donee.

DEFINITIONS

   "lasting power of attorney": s.64(1)

   "the court": s.64(1)

1–247

GENERAL NOTE

   This section and s.23 set out the powers of the Court of Protection where a person has drawn up a document (an "instrument") which is either intended to be registered as a lasting power of attorney (LPA) at some time in the future, or has already been registered as an LPA. The court is provided with a power to determine questions about the validity and revocation of LPAs (subs.(2)), and can direct that the instrument should not be registered, or where it has been registered and P lacks capacity, that it should be revoked if any of the grounds in subs.(3) are satisfied (subs.(4)). Although this section does not provide the court with the power to override a valid decision of a donee, the court can revoke the power if it determines that the donee is not acting in P's best interests (subs.(3)(b)). This section also provides that where there is more than one donee, the court may revoke the instrument or the LPA so far as it relates to any of them provided that P lacks capacity (subss.(5), (6)).

   The court must direct the Public Guardian to cancel the registration of the LPA if it has

1–248

either made a relevant determination under subs.(2)(a) or (b) or has exercised its power of revocation under subs.(4)(b) (Sch.1, para.18).

An application for an order under this section should be made using the procedure set out in Pt 9 of the CPR 2007.

Subsection (3)

1–249   IS SATISFIED. The burden of proof is placed on the person who is challenging the validity of the LPA.

Paragraph (a)

1–250   FRAUD. In the context of the tort of deceit, fraud has been defined as follows:

> "Fraud is proved when it is shown that a false representation has been made (i) knowingly, (ii) without belief in its truth, or (iii) recklessly, careless whether it be true or false. Although I have treated the second and third as distinct cases, I think that the third is but an instance of the second, for one who makes a statement under such circumstances can have no real belief in the truth of what he states. To prevent a false statement from being fraudulent, there must, I think, always be an honest belief in its truth" (*Derry v Peek* (1889) 14 App.Cas. 337 at 374 per Lord Herschell; also see *Clerk and Lindsell on Torts*, 19th edn (London: S&M, 2009), paras 18–17 et seq).

Apart from evidence of false representation, there must also be evidence that the representation induced P to create an LPA.

UNDUE PRESSURE. The meaning of this phrase in the context of an objection to the registration of an EPA, was considered by Master Lush in *G, Re* (Unreported, October 11, 2001). The Master held that:

> "To use 'pressure' means to behave in a manner whereby the will of the donor is overborne by the will of another person, so that in creating the power the donor is not acting of his or her own free will.

> Pressure can assume various forms. It can be physical, psychological, emotional, financial, and even pharmacological, though I would not venture to suggest that this list is exhaustive.

> Physical pressure constitutes any act or rough treatment directed towards the donor, whether or not actual physical injury results, and includes hitting, slapping and the misuse of restraints.

> Psychological or emotional pressure includes any behaviour that may diminish the donor's sense of identity, dignity and self-worth, including humiliation, intimidation, verbal abuse, threats, infantilisation and isolation. For example 'sign here, or I will put you in an old folks' home', or 'sign this, or I won't let you see your grandchildren.'

> Financial pressure includes the deliberate denial of the donor's access to his or her money or property. Excessive medication or the intentional withholding of medication would constitute pharmacological pressure.

> The meaning of 'undue' has been considered judicially in the context of hardship and delay. For example in *Liberian Shipping Corporation v A King & Sons Ltd* [1967] 1 All E.R. 934, 938, CA. Lord Denning M.R. said:

>> "'Undue' simply means excessive. It means greater hardship than the circumstances warrant.'

> In other words, the means should be proportionate to the end: the end being, in this instance the creation of a form of agency which will enable the donor's property and financial affairs to be managed lawfully and effectively whilst she is mentally incapacitated.

It may come as a surprise to note that by implication the Enduring Powers of Attorney Act assumes that some donors will be put under pressure to sign an instrument, but the Act is only concerned to invalidate those powers that have been created under pressure which can be qualified by the adjective 'undue'.

This principle of proportionality leaves a great deal to the discretion of the court, and generally speaking the court will not intervene unless there has been a clear and obvious infringement of the principle and it is satisfied that the creation of the power was not ultimately for the benefit of the donor."

This decision reflects the case law on the separate concept of "undue influence": see the note on s.1(3).

Paragraph (b)
In *Re F* [2004] 3 All E.R. 277, Patten J. said at 284:   **1–251**

"It seems to me that to remove a chosen attorney because of hostility from a sibling or other relative, in the absence of any effective challenge to his competence or integrity, should require clear evidence either that the continuing hostility will impede the proper administration of the estate or will cause significant distress to the donor which would be avoided by the appointment of a receiver."

The behaviour referred to in this provision is not confined to the behaviour of a donee when purporting to act under the authority of an LPA; it can include other behaviour that is not in P's best interests (*London Borough of Redbridge v G* [2014] EWCOP 17 at para.95, Russell J.). This finding is consistent with the decision in *Re J* [2011] Con. Vol. 716, where HHJ Marshall said at para.75:

"In my judgment, the key to giving proper effect to the distinction between an attorney's behaviour and his behaviour in any other capacity lies in considering the matter in stages. First, one must identify the allegedly offending behaviour or prospective behaviour. Second, one looks at all the circumstances and context and decide whether, taking everything into account, it really does amount to behaviour which is not in P's best interests, or can be fairly characterised as such. Finally, one must decide whether, taking everything into account including the fact that it is behaviour in some other capacity, it also gives good reason to take the very serious step of revoking the LPA."

At para.77, Judge Marshall held that "on a true construction of s.22(3), the court can consider any past behaviour or apparent prospective behaviour by the attorney, but, depending on the circumstances and the gravity of any offending behaviour found it can then take whatever steps it regards as appropriate in P's best interests (this only arises if P lacks capacity), to deal with the situation, whether by revoking the power or by taking some other course."

BEST INTERESTS. A consciously unwise decision will rarely if ever be made in P's best interests (*Re P (Statutory Will)* [2009] EWHC 163 (Ch) at para.42, per Lewison J.). That the decision to revoke an LPA must be in the best interests of P was confirmed by Senior Judge Lush in *Re Harcourt* (COP), July 31, 2013.

Subsection (4)
REVOKE. In *Public Guardian v JM* [2014] EWHC B4 (COP), Senior Judge Lush said   **1–252**
at para.29:

"To be able to revoke an LPA on the basis of the attorney's past performance, the court needs to be satisfied that:
(1) the attorney has contravened his authority; or
(2) the attorney has not acted in the donor's best interests; and
(3) the donor lacks capacity to revoke the LPA."

Powers of court in relation to operation of lasting powers of attorney

1–253   **23.**—(1) The court may determine any question as to the meaning or effect of a lasting power of attorney or an instrument purporting to create one.

(2) The court may—

(a) give directions with respect to decisions—

    (i) which the donee of a lasting power of attorney has authority to make, and

    (ii) which P lacks capacity to make;

(b) give any consent or authorisation to act which the donee would have to obtain from P if P had capacity to give it.

(3) The court may, if P lacks capacity to do so—

(a) give directions to the donee with respect to the rendering by him of reports or accounts and the production of records kept by him for that purpose;

(b) require the donee to supply information or produce documents or things in his possession as donee;

(c) give directions with respect to the remuneration or expenses of the donee;

(d) relieve the donee wholly or partly from any liability which he has or may have incurred on account of a breach of his duties as donee.

(4) The court may authorise the making of gifts which are not within section 12(2) (permitted gifts).

(5) Where two or more donees are appointed under a lasting power of attorney, this section applies as if references to the donee were to all or any of them.

DEFINITIONS

1–254   "the court": s.64(1)

"lasting power of attorney": s.64(1)

GENERAL NOTE

1–255   This section provides the Court of Protection with powers to decide any questions about the "meaning or effect" of an LPA or an instrument purporting to create one (subs. (1)), to give directions to donees where P lacks capacity (subs.(2)(a)), and to give any consent or authorisation which P might have given had he or she not lacked capacity (subs.(2)(b)). If P is incapacitated, the court also has power to give the donee directions in relation to producing reports, accounts, records and information, determining a donee's remuneration and expenses, and relieving a donee from some or all of the liabilities arising from a breach of his or her duties as donee (subs.(3)). The Court may also authorise the making of gifts beyond the scope of what is permitted by s.12(2) (subs. (4)). Certain determinations will require the Public Guardian to cancel the registration of the LPA (Sch.1, para.19).

In *Re MRJ* [2014] EWHC B15 (COP) at paras 38 and 39, Senior Judge Lush said that the combined effect of subs.(3)(b) and (4)(b) of this section

"is that the court may revoke an LPA, if it is satisfied that:

(a) the attorney (or, if more than one, any of them) has behaved, or is behaving in a way that contravenes his authority or is not in the donor's best interests; and

(b) the donor lacks the capacity to revoke the LPA.

The use of the word 'may' in [subs.](4)(b) means that revocation is not mandatory in these circumstances and that the court exercises a discretion when deciding whether or not to revoke an LPA. This discretion is subject to the provisions of the Act and, in particular, s.1 (the principles) and s.4 (best interests)."

In *Re Buckley* (2013) EWHC 2965 (COP) at para.43, Senior Judge Lush, said that "subject to a sensible *de minimis* exception, where the potential infringement is so minor that it would be disproportionate to make a formal application to the court, an application must be made to the court for an order under [this section] in any of the following cases:

(a) gifts that exceed the limited scope of the authority conferred on attorneys by section 12 of the Mental; Capacity Act;
(b) loans to the attorney or to members of the attorney's family;
(c) any investment in the attorney's own business;
(d) sales or purchases at an undervalue; and
(e) any other transactions in which there is a conflict between the interests of the donor and the interests of the attorney".

With regard to gifts, in *Re GM* [2013] EWHC 2966 (COP), noted under s.12, Judge Lush said that although *Re Buckley* involved a Lasting Power of Attorney, the same principle would apply to a deputyship, where the wording of the order appointing the deputies is virtually identical to that in s.12. Judge Lush made the following finding with regard to *de minimis* payments:

"Being both proportionate and pragmatic, and to prevent the court from being over-whelmed with applications, with which it does not have the resources to cope, this *de minimis* exception can be construed as covering the annual IHT exemption of £3,000 and the annual small gifts exemption of £250 per person, up to a maximum of, say, ten people in the following circumstances:

(a) where P has a life expectancy of less than five years;
(b) their estate exceeds the nil rate band for Inheritance Tax ('IHT') purposes, currently £325,000;
(c) the gifts are affordable having regard to P's care costs and will not adversely affect P's standard of care and quality of life, and
(d) there is no evidence that P would be opposed to gifts of this magnitude being made on their behalf.

The *de minimis* exception referred to in the preceding paragraph does not apply to potentially exempt transfers, or to the use of the normal expenditure out of income exemption, where the authorisation of the court is required under section 18(1)(b), section 23(4) and paragraph 16(2)(e) of Schedule 4 to the Mental Capacity Act 2005" (paras 89, 90).

An application for an order under this section should be made using the procedure set out in Pt 9 of the CPR 2007.

Human Rights Act 1998

In *Re MRJ*, above, at para.40, Senior Judge Lush said: **1–256**

"Unless such interference is warranted under art.8(2) [of the European Convention on Human Rights], the revocation by the Court of Protection of an LPA, which a donor executed when they had capacity and in which they chose a family member to be their attorney, would be a violation of their art.8(1) right to respect for their private and family life: *Re Harcourt* [2013] COPLR 69. The same applies to an order under s.23(2)(a) of the Mental Capacity Act suspending the attorney's authority."

Subsection (1)

MEANING OR EFFECT. This gives the court power to determine any point of construction **1–257** arising on the LPA, and whether a donee has power to carry out a particular act.

For the duty of the Public Guardian to make an application under this provision where it appears to him that an LPA contains an invalid provision, see para.11 of Sch.1.

Subsection (2)

Pursuant to para.(a), the court may direct the donee to make no decisions at all and **1–258** thereby suspend his or her authority to act under the LPA (*Re MRJ*, above, per Judge Lush at para.37).

The purpose of para.(b) was explained by the Parliamentary Under-Secretary of State:

"[Donees] are in law regarded as agents and are therefore affected by the law of agency as well as the provisions of the Bill. [Under the law of agency] it is sometimes necessary for the [donee] to give the consent or authorisation of the donor before they can act. The obvious example is where the donee would like to purchase the donor's property. The donor would make it a condition of the power of attorney that the [donee] must get their consent. In other words, if I wanted to buy the house of someone for whom I acted as [donee], I would need to get their consent to do so. However, if they lack capacity, I cannot get their consent. Yet, it would be wrong for me to purchase their house without consent. In those circumstances, the court would step in and give the consent. So, it is a protection, but a protection in circumstances where the law of agency applies" (*Hansard*, HL Vol.668, col.1426).

Subsection (3) para.(a)

1–259   As, generally speaking, the court will not exercise any supervision over the conduct of a donee, the giving of directions relating to the production of reports etc is likely to be triggered by concerns being raised by persons who are in close contact with P. In *Re Harcourt* [2013] C.O.P.L.R. 69, Senior Judge Lush said at para.39:

"Essentially, the Lasting Powers of Attorney scheme is based on trust and envisages minimal intervention by public authorities. Even where a donor lacks the capacity to ask the attorney to provide accounts and records, the court would not normally exercise its supervisory powers under section 23, unless it had reason to do so, possibly because of concerns raised by the [Office of the Public Guardian]. The court's powers in this respect simply duplicate those of a capable donor."

Paragraph 7.67 of the *Code of Practice* states:

"Property and affairs attorneys must keep accounts of transactions carried out on the donor's behalf. Sometimes the Court of Protection will ask to see accounts. If the attorney is not a financial expert and the donor's accounts are relatively straightforward, a record of the donor's income and expenditure (for example, through bank statements) may be enough. The more complicated the donor's affairs, the more detailed the accounts may need to be."

Subsection (3) para.(c)

1–260   REMUNERATION.   The directions could override a provision for remuneration contained in the LPA.

Subsection (3) para.(d)

1–261   ANY LIABILITY.   Note the breath of this power. Unlike the power to relieve trustees from breaches of trust under s.61 of the Trustee Act 1925, there is no requirement for the donee to have acted "honestly and reasonably".

Subsection (4)

1–262   This provision could be used to authorise gifts for tax planning purposes. Also see s.18(1)(b).

Subsection (5)

1–263   The effect of provision is that, where donees have been appointed to act jointly and severally, the court can revoke the appointment of just one of them (*Re MRJ*, above, at para.40).

Advance decisions to refuse treatment

Advance decisions to refuse treatment: general

24.—(1) "Advance decision" means a decision made by a person (P), after he   **1–264**
has reached 18 and when he has capacity to do so, that if—

(a)   at a later time and in such circumstances as he may specify, a specified treatment is proposed to be carried out or continued by a person providing health care for him, and

(b)   at that time he lacks capacity to consent to the carrying out or continuation of the treatment,

the specified treatment is not to be carried out or continued.

(2) For the purposes of subsection (1)(a), a decision may be regarded as specifying a treatment or circumstances even though expressed in layman's terms.

(3) P may withdraw or alter an advance decision at any time when he has capacity to do so.

(4) A withdrawal (including a partial withdrawal) need not be in writing.

(5) An alteration of an advance decision need not be in writing (unless section 25(5) applies in relation to the decision resulting from the alteration).

DEFINITIONS
"treatment": s.64(1)   **1–265**

GENERAL NOTE

Sections 24–26 deal with advance decisions to refuse medical treatment. They broadly   **1–266**
"seek to codify and clarify the current common law rules" relating to advance directives
(Explanatory Notes, para.84). An advance directive made before the commencement of
the Act will take effect as an advance decision if it complies with the relevant provisions
of the Act.

The Government's cautious approach to legislating in this area is illustrated by the following extract from "*Who Decides? Making Decisions on Behalf of Mentally Incapacitated Adults*" (Cm.3803):

"The Government recognises the strength of feeling on this subject. This was the area of the Law Commission's work which aroused the greatest public concern, and it is clear that this is a matter on which many have deep rooted personal, moral, religious and ethical views. The Government does not believe that it would be appropriate to reach any conclusions in this area in the absence of fresh consultation—not just on the detailed plans put forward by the Law Commission, but also on the need for and the merits of legislation in this area generally" (para.4.2).

To a certain extent, this caution was, to a certain extent, explained by the conclusion of the House of Lords Select Committee on Medical Ethics which had commended the development of advance directives, but decided that "it could well be impossible to give advance directives in general greater legal force without depriving patients of the benefit of the doctor's professional expertise and of new treatments and procedures which may have become available since the directive was signed" ((1993–94) HL Paper 21–1, para.185).

The House of Lords Select Committee noted that:

"Advance decisions to refuse treatment are an essential means of allowing individuals to determine their care in the event that they lose capacity. As with other aspects of the Act, the general public cannot benefit from this opportunity if they are not made aware of it. Similarly, advance decisions that are not recorded and shared with relevant public bodies are likely to be ineffective. Poor understanding among health and care staff needs to be addressed in order to promote the benefits of advance decisions to patients, as well as to ensure that they are followed when valid and applicable" (para.199).

Advance decisions

1–267   This section defines an advance decision, sometimes referred to as a "living will". The person making the advance decision need not refer to it as such. An advance decision can only be made by a mentally capable person aged 18 or over and the decision must specify the treatment that is being refused. The decision could have been made a considerable time before the coming into force of the Act. The effect of an advance decision is to enable the person to refuse the specified treatment when that person loses the capacity to give or refuse consent to that treatment. In other words, an advance decision which is valid and applicable (s.25) is as effective as a contemporaneous decision made by a mentally capable person in that healthcare professionals and the Court of Protection are bound by it (s.26), even if they or the patient's relatives or carers consider the decision to be unwise (s.1(4)).

An advance decision can be overridden by the operation of Pt IV of the Mental Health Act 1983 (see s.28), so that a decision that refuses a specific treatment for a mental disorder will be rendered ineffective if a person is detained under a section of the 1983 Act which comes within the scope of Pt IV. An exception to this general rule is s.58A of the 1983 Act which is concerned with the administration of electro-convulsive therapy.

Although this section is concerned with refusals of medical treatments and cannot be used to require a doctor to provide a particular form of medical treatment (*R. (on the application of Burke) v The General Medical Council* [2005] EWCA Civ 1003), the person making the advance decision could attempt to achieve this objective by refusing all but the preferred method of treatment for a particular disorder.

The advance decision can specify particular circumstances in which the refusal may apply. Both the treatment and the circumstances may be specified in lay (i.e. non-medical) terms. Section 25(5) and (6) comes into play if the person wishes the advance decision to apply to a refusal of life sustaining treatment. An advance decision cannot be used to give effect to an unlawful act such as euthanasia, which is a deliberate intervention with the express aim of ending life (s.62).

The best interests criterion does not apply to the application of an advance decision as the person concerned has identified his or her best interests when making the advance decision: see the General Note to s.26.

Apart from an advance decision that relates to life-sustaining treatment, the Act does not establish any procedures or formalities that must be followed for an advance decision to be made. The advance decision can be oral or written and there is no procedure that must be followed to establish that the person was mentally capable at the time when the advance decision is made. The advanced decision need not be witnessed and can be made without the benefit of professional advice. A written advance decision could be supplemented by a video recording of the person's verbal confirmation of their decision. There is no provision requiring the advance decision to be reviewed over time, although this is clearly desirable. A written advance decision can be withdrawn or altered orally. The *Code of Practice* states, at para.9.19, that it would be helpful for the following information to be included in a written advance decision:

"• full details of the person making the advance decision, including date of birth, home address and any distinguishing features (in case healthcare professionals need to identify an unconscious person, for example)
• the name and address of the person's GP and whether they have a copy of the document
• a statement that the document should be used if the person ever lacks capacity to make treatment decisions
• a clear statement of the decision, the treatment to be refused and the circumstances in which the decision will apply
• the date the document was written (or reviewed)
• the person's signature (or the signature of someone the person has asked to sign on their behalf and in their presence)

- the signature of the person witnessing the signature, if there is one (or a statement directing somebody to sign on the person's behalf)."

To avoid possible legal challenge, it would be sensible for advanced decisions to be written, witnessed and to contain a statement that, in the opinion of the witness, the person was mentally capable of making the decision at the time when it was made, together with a confirmation that the medical consequences of the decision have been explained to the person by a named doctor. An example of an advance decision form can be downloaded at *www.adrtnhs.co.uk*. The Royal College of Physician's publication *Prolonged disorders of consciousness: National clinical guidelines* (2013) is accompanied by a template Advance Decision to Refuse Treatment. This can be accessed at: *http://www.rcplondon.ac.uk/sites/default/files/annex_4c_template_for_an_adrt.pdf.*

It might be very difficult for a treating doctor to be confident that a patient who is said to have made an oral advance decision during the course of a conversation with a relative had the mental capacity to make the decision at that time (the presumption of capacity set out in s.1(2) will apply) and was provided with sufficient information to enable an informed decision to be made (it is difficult to see how appropriate information could be provided without the involvement of a healthcare professional). It might also be difficult to establish whether the person was subject to the undue influence of the relative at the relevant time (see the note on s.1(3)), or had subsequently revoked the advance decision. Indeed, it may be difficult to establish whether the reported conversation took place at all. Disputes about the existence, validity or applicability of an advance decision can be referred to the Court of Protection (s.26(4)). In *HE v A Hospital NHS Trust* [2003] EWHC 1017 (Fam) Munby J. said at para.34:

"The absence of anything in writing goes only to the practicability of proof. For it may be difficult to establish the existence of a binding oral advance directive given, first, the need for clear and convincing proof founded on convincing and inherently reliable evidence and, secondly, the need to demonstrate that the patient's expressed views represented a firm and settled commitment and not merely an offhand remark or informally expressed reaction to other people's problems."

The Minister assured members of the Standing Committee which considered the Bill that "including oral decisions does not mean that any casual statement would count as an advance decision. There would be a world of difference between someone remarking casually to a friend that they would never like to be kept alive artificially and someone with Alzheimer's discussing with a doctor charged with their care how they might expect the condition to progress and making an oral decision to refuse certain interventions as their condition worsens. I remind the Committee that the Bill requires tough tests to be passed if an advance decision is to apply. The decision must be specific and made with capacity to be valid and applicable to the treatment in question. Where there is any doubt, a clinician can safely treat someone and receive protection from liability for a claim for damages, tort, criminal liability or assault [see s.26(2)]", per the Parliamentary Under-Secretary of State, St. Comm. A, para.225.

With regard to oral advance decisions made to a member of the patient's healthcare team, the *Code of Practice* suggests, at para.9.23, that the following information be included in the patient's medical notes:

"• a note that the decision should apply if the person lacks capacity to make treatment decisions in the future
- a clear note of the decision, the treatment to be refused and the circumstances in which the decision will apply
- details of someone who was present when the oral advance decision was recorded and the role in which they were present (for example, healthcare professional or family member), and
- whether they heard the decision, took part in it or are just aware that it exists."

1–268   If healthcare professionals are alerted to the possibility that a patient might have made an advance decision, reasonable efforts, such as contacting relatives of the patient and the patient's GP, should be made to establish whether this is the case. Treatment should not be delayed while attempts are made to establish whether an advance decision has been made if the delay would prejudice the patient's health.

Healthcare professionals who have a conscientious objection to respecting a patient's valid and applicable advance directive should ensure that the care of the patient is transferred to the care of another healthcare professional. The following extract from correspondence between the Parliamentary Under-Secretary of State for Health and the Opposition spokesperson on health was read into the record during the report stage of the Bill in the House of Lords at *Hansard*, HL Vol.670, col.1306:

"I promised to check GMC and BMA guidance on provisions for when a doctor does not want to carry out treatment. Doctors are entitled to have their personal beliefs respected and will not be pressured to act contrary to those beliefs. As I stated during the Committee, where a doctor has a conscientious objection they may withdraw from the care of the patient. In doing so however they must ensure, without delay, that arrangements have been made for another suitably qualified colleague to take over their role, so that the patient's care does not suffer. The individual doctor does not necessarily have to arrange personally for a transfer of care, provided there are alternative means of doing so. However, the doctor must not abandon the patient or otherwise cause their care to suffer."

Also of relevance in this context is the following guidance given by Butler-Sloss P. in *B (Consent to Treatment: Capacity), Re* [2002] EWHC 429 (Fam) at para.100(viii):

"If there is no disagreement about competence but the doctors are for any reason unable to carry out the wishes of the patient, their duty is to find other doctors who will do so."

Guidance on conscientious objection is given in the *Code of Practice* at paras 9.61–9.63. Freedom of thought, conscience and religion is provided for in art.9 of the European Convention on Human Rights.

As an alternative to making an advance decision, the person could either leave decision making in the hands of healthcare professionals, make an advance statement (see below), or appoint someone to act as their donee under a lasting power of attorney. A personal welfare LPA does not take effect until the donor loses capacity (s.11(7)(a)).

The provisions of the Bill relating to advance decisions caused considerable controversy, particularly because of evidence that suggested that well people tend not to make the same decisions as sick people: see further, the notes to s.25(4)(c).

For an analysis of advance directives/advance decisions under common law and under the Act, see Sabine Michalowski, "Advance Refusals of Life-Sustaining Medical Treatment: The Relativity of an Absolute Right" (2005) 68(6) M.L.R. 948.

Advance statements

1–269   Unlike an advance decision, an advance statement is a non-legally binding document which may identify a person's views and preferences on a large range of medical and other issues. Under s.4(6)(a), such a statement would need to be taken into account when decisions are made subsequent to the patient's mental incapacity. The Making Decisions Alliance briefing document on the second reading debate on the Bill states, at p.19, that

"advance statements would enable an individual to express their views and preferences on a large range of issues, including:

- domestic arrangements
- treatment preferences
- financial arrangements
- childcare arrangements

- clarification of who to disclose information to, and the limits of what can be discussed
- dietary requirements."

The literature is replete with examples of a failure to appreciate the distinction between advance directives and advance statements: see the studies cited by T. Exworthy in "Psychiatric advance decisions—an opportunity missed" (September 2004) *Journal of Mental Health Law* 129, 132.

Subsection (1)

DECISION. A decision can only be made after full consideration of all relevant matters, including the consequences for the patient if the treatment is not given (*W Healthcare NHS Trust v H* [2004] EWCA Civ 1324; [2005] 1 W.L.R. 834 at para.17). This information can be given in to the patient in broad terms: see the note on s.3(1)(a). **1–270**

Subsection (1) para.(a)

SUCH CIRCUMSTANCES AS HE MAY SPECIFY. For example, the treatment is not to be given if there is no realistic prospect of P ever regaining mental capacity. **1–271**

SPECIFIED TREATMENT. Care should be taken to ensure that there can be no doubt about the identity of the particular treatment that is being refused. In *W Healthcare NHS Trust v H*, above, at para.21, the Court of Appeal found that a statement made by the patient that she would not wish "to be kept alive by machines" was not "an advance directive which was sufficiently clear to amount to a direction that she preferred to be deprived of food and drink for a period of time which would lead to her death in all circumstances". General statements indicating a desire not to be treated, such as "I should not be given any treatment that is likely to prolong my life", would also be invalid. "Treatment" is defined very widely in s.64(1). It can include the provision of nutrition and hydration to the patient by artificial means (*Airedale NHS Trust v Bland* [1993] 1 All E.R. 821, HL). The Joint Committee on Human Rights expressed its concern that the "classification of artificial nutrition and hydration as 'treatment' may not be well known to lay people" (23rd Report, para.2.46).

The Act distinguishes between "treatment" and "care": see, for example, s.5(1). The provision of "basic care" such as feeding and hydration which is not medically assisted, and care to maintain bodily cleanliness cannot be categorised as treatment and can therefore not be subject to an advance decision.

AT THAT TIME HE LACKS CAPACITY. The patient's capacity at that time must be presumed unless there is evidence to suggest that the presumption can be rebutted (s.1(2)). The burden of proof rests upon "those who seek to establish the existence and continuing validity and applicability of an advance directive" (*HE v A Hospital NHS Trust* [2003] EWHC 1017 (Fam) at para.46(v), per Munby J.). The standard of proof is the civil standard of a balance of probabilities: see s.2(4). In *A Local Authority v E* [2012] EWHC 1639 (COP), Peter Jackson J. said:

"[F]or an advance decision relating to life-sustaining treatment to be valid an applicable, there should be clear evidence establishing on the balance of probability that the maker had capacity at the relevant time. Where the evidence of capacity is doubtful or equivocal it is not appropriate to uphold the decision" (para.55).

Section 2(2) states that "it does not matter" if the patient's incapacity is temporary or permanent. This provision will cause difficulty in cases where P has made an advance decision refusing treatment, P becomes incapacitated and P's capacity could be restored if P was treated with that treatment. It is likely that s.25(4)(c) would apply in such a situation.

Situations can arise when it will only become apparent that a seemingly incapable person is, in fact, perfectly capable of making the decision in question if considerable time and trouble is taken in an attempt to communicate with that person. In a power-ful and moving speech on the second reading of the Bill (*Hansard*, HC Vol.425, cols 64–67), Mrs Claire Curtis-Thomas MP recounted how her mother, who had been hos-pitalised after having suffered a massive stoke which had left her paralysed, was con-sidered to be mentally incapable and was not being fed. Mrs Curtis-Thomas's mother had made an advance directive refusing treatment subsequent to her recovery from a previous stoke. Mrs Curtis-Thomas's attempts to communicate with her mother, which lasted a number of weeks, eventually succeeded and her mother was able to blink out "I want to live". This had the effect of revoking the advance directive. Mrs Curtis-Thomas said: "If my mother had not had me, all I believe would have happened is that she would have starved to death. I do not think that anybody would have taken the time or known her well enough to realise that she was actually present and capable of making deci-sions". The principle contained in s.1(3) is applicable to the situation described by Mrs Curtis-Thomas.

THE SPECIFIED TREATMENT IS NOT TO BE CARRIED OUT. An advance decision cannot be used to require that a patient be provided with any form of treatment that he might consider to be in his own best interests. However, s.4 requires an invalid advance decision of this nature to be taken into account when considering what is in the best interests of a patient if it is clear that the patient was attempting to refuse a particular treatment: see s.5(6)(a) and *R. (on the application of Burke) v The General Medical Council* [2005] EWCA Civ 1003 at para.57.

Subsection (2)

1–272
Lay terms can be used as long as the use of such terms does not lead to any ambiguity about the identity of the treatment that is being refused.

Subsection (3)

1–273
There is no procedure for withdrawing or altering an advance decision. A simple oral statement by a mentally capable person such as, "I no longer wish my advance decision to stand", would be sufficient to withdraw a decision. An alteration has to be in writing, and the formalities set out in s.25(6) complied with, if the decision relates to a life-sustaining treatment (subs.(5)).

Subsection (4)

1–274
This provision enables a capable patient to withdraw a written advance decision imme-diately before an anaesthetic is administered, even if the treatment refused is life-sustaining treatment.

Validity and applicability of advance decisions

1–275
25.—(1) An advance decision does not affect the liability which a person may incur for carrying out or continuing a treatment in relation to P unless the decision is at the material time—

    (a)   valid, and

    (b)   applicable to the treatment.

(2) An advance decision is not valid if P—

    (a)   has withdrawn the decision at a time when he had capacity to do so,

    (b)   has, under a lasting power of attorney created after the advance decision was made, conferred authority on the donee (or, if more than one, any of them) to give or refuse consent to the treatment to which the advance deci-sion relates, or

    (c)   has done anything else clearly inconsistent with the advance decision remaining his fixed decision.

(3) An advance decision is not applicable to the treatment in question if at the material time P has capacity to give or refuse consent to it.

(4) An advance decision is not applicable to the treatment in question if—

(a) that treatment is not the treatment specified in the advance decision,

(b) any circumstances specified in the advance decision are absent, or

(c) there are reasonable grounds for believing that circumstances exist which P did not anticipate at the time of the advance decision and which would have affected his decision had he anticipated them.

(5) An advance decision is not applicable to life-sustaining treatment unless—

(a) the decision is verified by a statement by P to the effect that it is to apply to that treatment even if life is at risk, and

(b) the decision and statement comply with subsection (6).

(6) A decision or statement complies with this subsection only if—

(a) it is in writing,

(b) it is signed by P or by another person in P's presence and by P's direction,

(c) the signature is made or acknowledged by P in the presence of a witness, and

(d) the witness signs it, or acknowledges his signature, in P's presence.

(7) The existence of any lasting power of attorney other than one of a description mentioned in subsection (2)(b) does not prevent the advance decision from being regarded as valid and applicable.

DEFINITIONS

"advance decision": s.64(1)

"treatment": s.64(1)

"lasting power of attorney": s.64(1)

"life-sustaining treatment": s.64(1)

1–276

GENERAL NOTE

This section states that a person shall not be legally liable for providing treatment to a patient who has made an advance decision unless the decision is both valid and applicable. It then proceeds to define both "valid" and "applicable".

1–277

Establishing whether an advance decision is both valid and applicable could lead to a significant increase in the workload of medical practitioners: see the study by Schiff, noted below. As the Law Commission pointed out, the existence of a formal document is no guarantee of either validity or applicability, nor is the absence of such a document any guarantee that a valid and applicable advance decision has not been made (Law Com No.231, para.5.29).

An advance decision is not valid if P has withdrawn the decision while he or she had the mental capacity to do so, has made a subsequent lasting power of attorney (LPA) which confers the necessary authority on the donee, or has acted in a manner which is clearly inconsistent with the terms of the decision (subs.(2)). In addition, an advance decision will not be valid if it was made either by a child or by an adult who lacked capacity (s.24(1)). Although an adult should be assumed to have been mentally capable at the time when the decision was made (s.1(2)), the medical practitioner should investigate any factors that suggest that this assumption could be rebutted: see the note on s.24(1)(a). It submitted that an advance decision will also not be valid if, at the time when it was made, P did not have adequate information to assess the consequences of the decision.

An advance decision will not be applicable if P is capable of making the treatment decision at the time the treatment is proposed (subs.(3)). It will also not be applicable to treatments not specified in the decision, if the circumstances specified in the decision are absent, or if there are reasonable grounds for believing that that the current circumstances were not anticipated by P and, if they had been anticipated they would have affected P's decision (subs.(4)). Finally, an advance decision is not applicable to life-sustaining treatment unless P has specified in writing that it should be, and the decision is signed and witnessed (subss.(5) and (6)).

A valid and applicable advance decision to refuse treatment will be as legally effective as a contemporaneous refusal of consent. It cannot be overridden by the Court of Protection, a deputy appointed by the court, the donee of an LPA made before the advance decision was made, or a person acting under s.5 (s.5(4)). Although the court may make declarations as to the existence, validity and applicability of an advance decision (s.15(1)(c)), it has no power to override a valid and applicable advance decision on the ground that it would not serve P's best interests. Life sustaining treatment or action to prevent a serious deterioration of the patient's condition may be provided while a decision is being sought from the court (s.26(5)).

In addition to the legal formalities required by this section, cases where the implementation of an advance decision would lead to P's death require "a full, reasoned and contemporaneous assessment evidencing mental capacity to make such a momentous decision" (*A Local Authority v E* [2012] EWHC 1639 (COP) at para.65, per Peter Jackson J.).

In *X Primary Care Trust v XB* [2012] EWHC 1390 (Fam), a case on the validity of an advance decision, Theis J. made the following general comments at paras 33 to 35:

> "Firstly, in the event that there is an issue raised about an advance decision, it is important it is investigated by the relevant health authorities or relevant bodies as a matter of urgency. This will clarify issues at an early stage. It will enable relevant primary evidence to be gathered (for example, by taking statements) and, if required, an application made to this court. . . .

> Secondly, there is no set form for advance decisions, because the contents will inevitably vary, depending on the person's wishes and situation. The Mental Capacity Code includes guidance on what should be included in an advanced decision at paragraphs 9.10 to 9.23. . . .

> Thirdly, there are number of pro forma advance decisions available on the internet. One of the difficulties in this case was the inclusion in the pro forma of a 'valid until' date. Those organisations that have such terms in their pro formas may want to look again at the necessity for that being in the pro forma form. It is clearly in the interests of the person who has made the advance decision, his or her family, and those who have responsibility for providing or withholding treatment that there is clarity in relation to what the terms of the advance decision are."

In a survey of UK geriatricians, advice concerning the validity of "living wills" was sought by 44 per cent, most frequently from hospital lawyers (R. Schiff et al. "Living wills and the Mental Capacity Act: a postal questionnaire survey of UK geriatricians" (2006) 35 *Age and Ageing* 116).

Advance decisions refusing life-sustaining treatment made before October 1, 2007

1–278   Article 5 of the Mental Capacity Act 2005 (Transitional and Consequential Provisions) Order 2007 (SI 2007/1898) gives effect, in certain circumstances, to advance decisions refusing life-sustaining treatment, notwithstanding that they do not comply with all of the requirements of this section. Article 5 states:

"Advance decisions to refuse life-sustaining treatment

1–279   **5.**—(1) An advance decision refusing life-sustaining treatment shall be treated as valid and applicable to a treatment and does not have to satisfy the requirements mentioned in paragraph (3) if the conditions in paragraph (2) are met.

(2) The conditions that must be met are that—

   (a) a person providing health care for a person ("P") reasonably believes that—

      (i) P has made the advance decision refusing life-sustaining treatment before 1 October 2007, and

      (ii) P has lacked the capacity to comply with the provisions mentioned in paragraph (3) since 1 October 2007;

(b) the advance decision is in writing;

(c) P has not—

    (i) withdrawn the decision at a time when he had capacity to do so, or

    (ii) done anything else clearly inconsistent with the advance decision remaining his fixed decision;

(d) P does not have the capacity to give or refuse consent to the treatment in question at the material time;

(e) the treatment in question is the treatment specified in the advance decision;

(f) any circumstances specified in the advance decision are present; and

(g) there are no reasonable grounds for believing that circumstances exist which P did not anticipate at the time of the advance decision and which would have affected his decision had he anticipated them.

(3) The requirements that do not have to be satisfied are as follows—

(a) the requirement for the decision to be verified by a statement by P to the effect that the advance decision is to apply to that treatment even if life is at risk (section 25(5)(a) of the Act); and

(b) the requirement for a signed and witnessed advance decision (section 25(6)(b) to (d) of the Act).

(4) In this article, "advance decision" has the meaning given in section 24(1) of the Act."

A person who has made an advance directive refusing life-sustaining treatment and who has capacity on or after October 1, 2007, should make an advance decision that complies with subss.(5) and (6).

Subsection (1)

The healthcare professional must be aware of the existence of the advance decision if he or she is to incur legal liability for providing the treatment (s.26(2)). If the healthcare professional has knowledge of the advance directive, the treatment can proceed if the professional considers that it is either invalid and/or not applicable to the treatment. **1–280**

Subsection (2) para.(a)

A written advance decision can be withdrawn orally. In the absence of evidence to the contrary, the healthcare professional should assume that the patient was capable of withdrawing the decision (s.1(2)). **1–281**

Patients can change their minds about having treatment at a very late stage. The difficulties of relying on an advance decision that has not been revoked can be seen from the following clinical example given by Baroness Finlay to the Joint Committee concerning a patient who had taken a massive overdose of paracetamol:

"He did not want to come to hospital but was persuaded to. He flatly refused any intervention or any treatment. Two psychiatrists spent a lot of time negotiating with him for several days and explained absolutely everything that might happen to him in graphic detail and he was adamant he wanted no treatment. They warned him of every scenario, including coughing up blood as he started to haemorrhage to death. When he started vomiting blood, he changed his mind and requested treatment. He ended up being transferred to King's [College Hospital] for a liver transplant" (Oral and Written Evidence, Ev 131).

If this patient had lost capacity at the point where he started to vomit blood, the doctors would have been bound by his advance decision (which, subsequent to the implementation of the Act, would have to comply with subss.(5),(6)) and the patient would have died.

Subsection (2) para.(b)

An LPA is not "created" until it is registered by the Public Guardian (s.9(2)(b)): see *Re E* [2014] EWCOP 27. **1–282**

It would be sensible for the advance decision to be withdrawn if an LPA of this nature is created as there could be a danger of the healthcare professional being unaware of the LPA. Also see the note on s.11(7)(b).

Subsection (2) para.(c)

1–283   The inconsistent behaviour would indicate that P has had a change of mind. An example of such behaviour is to be found in *HE v A Hospital NHS Trust* [2003] EWHC 1017 (Fam), where the patient, when a Jehovah's Witness, had made an advance directive refusing blood. Subsequent to this she had become betrothed to a Muslim man upon condition that she would revert to being a Muslim, and had ceased attending Jehovah's Witness meetings. The judge held that the advance directive was founded entirely on the patient's faith and could not survive the abandonment of that faith.

In *A Local Authority v E* [2012] EWHC 1639 (COP) at para.63, Peter Jackson J. said that an instruction in an advanced decision that "If I exhibit behaviour seemingly contrary to this advanced directive this should not be viewed as a change of decision" could not be binding in the light of this provision.

Although this provision does not exclude the inconsistent behaviour of a mentally incapable patient, judicial elaboration of the nature of "clearly inconsistent" behaviour would be helpful given that s.24(3) does not allow a mentally incapacitated patient to withdraw an advance decision.

Subsection (4) para.(a)

1–284   As an advance decision is a refusal of a specific treatment, a suicide note written by a capable person which does not specify a treatment that should not be given in the event of a suicide attempt that leads to mental incapacity is not an advance decision. Neither is a general statement such as: "If I become mentally incapacitated I do not wish my life to be sustained".

Subsection (4) para.(b)

1–285   The advance decision should be specific about the circumstances where it is to apply as a generally written decision could give rise to a situation where the decision applies in unintended circumstances.

Subsection (4) para.(c)

1–286   It is anticipated that this paragraph will be frequently invoked as it is unlikely that patients will have been able to precisely predict the circumstances that they will be in subsequent to the onset of their mental incapacity. In order to determine whether the unanticipated circumstances "would", rather than "may" have affected P's decision, the health care professional will need to step into P's shoes by effectively making a substituted judgment on behalf of P. An example of a relevant change in circumstances is where P made an advance decision refusing a particular type of treatment because of the severe side effects associated with that treatment prior to the development of a version of the same type of treatment which has far less severe side effects. A more problematic example is where P concluded that as the onset of a particular illness would be likely to cause him distress and unhappiness, he would make an advance decision refusing potentially life saving treatment. However, the reality is that P, who is now suffering from that illness, appears to be both content and free of pain. It is submitted that this situation would constitute a change in circumstances for the purposes of this provision as the feared consequences of the illness, which prompted the making of the advance decision, are absent. A significant change in P's family and/or personal circumstances could also be a relevant consideration.

Patients' views about the medical treatment that they would wish to receive are not fixed; they adapt to circumstances. In particular, healthy patients tend not make the same choices as sick ones as they may not fully comprehend what the future might hold for them should they become mentally incapacitated. It has been argued that patients need to experience a situation to know how they would feel about it and hence how they wish to be treated (Dr David Kingsley, Oral and written evidence, Ev 322). Many people adapt to their new situation, finding meaning and value in a life they would previously have considered unbearable (Kampman et al., "'I can do things now that people thought were impossible, actually things that I thought were impossible': A meta-synthesis of the qualitative findings on posttraumatic growth and severe physical injury", (2015) Canadian Psychology——Psychologie Canadienne, 56(3), 283–294). In *MB (Caesarean Section), Re* [1997] 2 F.L.R. 426 CA at 436 in a case concerning the mental capacity of a patient who was refusing to be anaesthetised in order to have a caesarean section, Butler-Sloss L.J. said that a "feature of some of the cases to which we have referred has been the favourable reaction of the patient who refused treatment to the subsequent medical intervention and successful outcome." A number of witnesses to the Joint Committee gave examples of patients who had made advance directives refusing life-prolonging treatment and had subsequently agreed to such treatment (see, for example, Dr Fiona Randall, Oral and written evidence, Ev 303). In her evidence to the Joint Committee, Baroness Finlay said:

"It is a feature of people who are suddenly facing the reality that they are dying that they could not preconceive how they would feel at the time. That is also a situation that one sees in people who are very seriously ill" (Oral and written Evidence, Ev 127).

These issues should be considered by those who make advance decisions and by those who advise them. In particular, those who have made advance decisions should review them at regular intervals to ensure that they reflect their current view.

Subsection (5)

This provision and subs.(6) were moved by the Government at the committee stage in **1–287** the House of Lords to meet concerns that had been raised by Parliamentarians, outside bodies, and the Joint Committee on Human Rights. They are aimed at tipping "the balance of advance decisions even further in favour of preserving life", per the Parliamentary Under-Secretary of State (*Hansard*, HL Vol.668, col.1486).

In *Newcastle upon Tyne Hospitals Foundation Trust v LM* [2014] EWHC 454 (COP), Peter Jackson J. said that LM had made a valid and applicable advance decision refusing a potentially life-saving blood transfusion even though the decision was not in the form required by this provision and subs.(6). For a discussion of this case, see the March 2014 issue of the 39 Essex Street "Mental Capacity Law Newsletter" at pp.11–14.

If there is a dispute about the validity and/or applicability of an advance decision that relates to life sustaining treatment, P can be treated until the issue is determined by the court (s.26(5)). Any doubt as to the validity and/or applicability of an advance decision to refuse life-sustaining treatment should be resolved by the court in favour of preserving life (*HE v A Hospital NHS Trust* [2003] EWHC 1017 (Fam)).

LIFE-SUSTAINING TREATMENT. The reference to "life" includes the life of an unborn child: see the note on s.4(10). A woman of child-bearing age should therefore consider whether she would want the advance decision to apply to her unborn child. If she did not wish it to apply to her unborn child, the terms of the decision should reflect this.

It might be difficult to identify whether a treatment is a "life-sustaining treatment" in those cases where, for example, drugs do not have single, targeted effects. Treatments may be life-sustaining in some circumstances, and in others not. This concern has been addressed by the requirement that P must verify that the decision is to apply to the specified treatment "even if life is at risk". In other words, life-sustaining treatment is treatment that is needed to keep P alive.

With regard to artificial nutrition and hydration (ANH), "there can be no doubt that ANH constitutes life-sustaining treatment. Thus, if a person has not specified that the refusal is still to apply where ANH is necessary to sustain life then ANH (if in the person's best interests) will have to be given" (Letter from the Parliamentary-Under Secretary of State to the Chair of the Joint Committee on Human Rights, December 16, 2004, Annex, para.28).

1–288   For the validity of advance directives made before the implementation of the Act on October 1, 2007, see art.5 of the Mental Capacity Act 2005 (Transitional and Consequential Provisions) Order 2007 (SI 2007/1898) which is reproduced above.

Given the difficulties that can arise when determining the validity and/or applicability of oral advance decisions, it is suggested that the general approach set out in this provision be adopted for all advance decisions.

IN WRITING.   There is no statutory form: see the General Note to s.24. "I want to make it clear what 'in writing' can mean. It means that an advance decision can be written by a family member or recorded in medical notes by a doctor or healthcare professional, and it can include electronic records", per the Parliamentary Under-Secretary of State (*Hansard*, HL Vol.668, col.1487).

IS SIGNED.   The decision can be signed in P's presence and by his or her direction. This is to ensure that there is "no discrimination against people who, for whatever reason, are unable to write but have the capacity to make decisions", ibid.

Effect of advance decisions

1–289   26.—(1) If P has made an advance decision which is—

(a)   valid, and

(b)   applicable to a treatment,

the decision has effect as if he had made it, and had had capacity to make it, at the time when the question arises whether the treatment should be carried out or continued.

(2) A person does not incur liability for carrying out or continuing the treatment unless, at the time, he is satisfied that an advance decision exists which is valid and applicable to the treatment.

(3) A person does not incur liability for the consequences of withholding or withdrawing a treatment from P if, at the time, he reasonably believes that an advance decision exists which is valid and applicable to the treatment.

(4) The court may make a declaration as to whether an advance decision—

(a)   exists;

(b)   is valid;

(c)   is applicable to a treatment.

(5) Nothing in an apparent advance decision stops a person—

(a)   providing life-sustaining treatment, or

(b)   doing any act he reasonably believes to be necessary to prevent a serious deterioration in P's condition,

while a decision as respects any relevant issue is sought from the court.

DEFINITIONS

1–290   "advance decision": s.64(1)

"treatment": s.64(1)

"the court": s.64(1)

"life-sustaining treatment": s.64(1)

GENERAL NOTE

1–291   If an advance decision is both valid and applicable as defined in s.25, it has the same effect as a contemporaneous refusal of treatment by a person with capacity (subs.(1)). Subject to subs.(5), this means that the treatment specified in the decision cannot lawfully be given. If the treatment is given, the patient would be able to claim damages for the tort of battery and the person who provided the treatment could face criminal liability for assault. However, a treatment provider will be protected from legal liability unless satisfied that there is a valid and applicable advance decision (subs.(2)); and a treatment provider may safely withhold or withdraw treatment as long as he or she has reasonable grounds for believing that there is a valid and applicable advance decision (subs.(3)). The responsibility for determining whether an advance directive is both valid and applicable is that of the healthcare professional who would be responsible for providing the treatment specified in the decision.

A clinician who follows a valid and applicable advance decision is not acting "for or on behalf of a person who lacks capacity" for the purposes of s.1(5); he or she is acting on the instructions of a capacitated individual. Such a decision must therefore be complied with even if it conflicts with an objective evaluation of the patient's best interests. This is the case even if complying with the decision would lead to the patient's death. The principle of the sanctity of human life must yield to the principle of patient self-determination as long as the terms of s.25(5) and (6) are satisfied.

Any dispute about the existence, validity or applicability of an advance decision can be determined by the court (subs.(4)). However, action may be taken to prevent the death of the person concerned, or a serious deterioration to his or her condition, whilst a ruling is sought (subs.(5)). The court has no power to determine that a valid and applicable advance decision is not in P's best interests.

The *Code of Practice* states at para.9.60:

"Some situations might be enough in themselves to raise concern about the existence, validity or applicability of an advance decision to refuse treatment. These could include situations when:

- a disagreement between relatives and healthcare professionals about whether verbal comments were really an advance decision
- evidence about the person's state of mind raises questions about their capacity at the time they made the decision
- evidence of important changes in the person's behaviour before they lost capacity that might suggest a change of mind.

In cases where serious doubt remains and cannot be resolved in any other way, it will be possible to seek a declaration from the court."

Subsection (2)

SATISFIED. In order to be satisfied that an advance decision is both valid and applicable, **1–292** the clinician would need to make enquiries about (1) any doubts that might exist about the patient's mental capacity at the time when the purported advance decision was made; (2) the information that the patient received about the consequences of his or her decision; (3) the circumstances surrounding the making of the purported advance decision; (4) the possible effect of undue influence on the patient's decision; and (5) whether the purported advance decision is applicable to the proposed treatment and was intended to apply in the circumstances that have arisen. It is likely that few oral statements made by patients to lay people that are said to constitute advance decisions would survive such scrutiny, especially if the statements were made a considerable time ago. It is submitted that this provision would provide a clinician with a defence in an action for battery if the clinician made a mistaken assumption that the patient lacked capacity when making the purported advance decision, as long as the mistake was made on reasonable grounds. If the clinician is satisfied that no valid and applicable advance decision has been made, the treatment can be given. However, it would be advisable to ask the court to determine the issue in cases where the argument in favour of the existence of a valid and applicable advance decision is finely balanced or where there is a dispute between the clinician and the patient's family about whether such an advance decision has been made.

If the purported advance decision is invalid but it is clear that P was attempting to refuse a particular treatment, the decision should be treated as if it were an expression of the patient's wishes for the purpose of s.4(6)(a).

Subsection (3)

1–293   REASONABLY BELIEVES.   This is an objective standard. The healthcare professional's belief must be supported by evidence.

Subsection (4)

1–294   In *X Primary Care Trust v XB* [2012] EWHC 1390 (Fam) at para.33, Theis J. said:

"[I]n the event that there is an issue raised about an advance decision, it is important it is investigated by the relevant health authorities or relevant bodies as a matter of urgency. This will clarify issues at an early stage. It will enable relevant primary evidence to be gathered (for example, by taking statements) and, if required, an application made to this court. The judges who sit in the Court of Protection are experienced in dealing with urgent applications, as this case has demonstrated."

Subsection (5)

1–295   As this provision is only available in respect of an "apparent" advance decision, it arguable that it cannot be invoked if the doctor is satisfied that the advance decision is both valid and applicable (subs.(2)). However if the validity or applicability of the advance decision is being challenged and the challenge is neither frivolous nor vexatious, the doctor should invoke this provision and seek the guidance of the Court of Protection.

Excluded decisions

Family relationships etc

1–296   **27.**—(1) Nothing in this Act permits a decision on any of the following matters to be made on behalf of a person—

  (a)   consenting to marriage or a civil partnership,

  (b)   consenting to have sexual relations,

  (c)   consenting to a decree of divorce being granted on the basis of two years' separation,

  (d)   consenting to a dissolution order being made in relation to a civil partnership on the basis of two years' separation,

  (e)   consenting to a child's being placed for adoption by an adoption agency,

  (f)   consenting to the making of an adoption order,

  (g)   discharging parental responsibilities in matters not relating to a child's property,

  (h)   giving a consent under the Human Fertilisation and Embryology Act 1990 (c. 37).

  [(i)   giving a consent under the Human Fertilisation and Embryology Act 2008].

(2) "Adoption order" means—

  (a)   an adoption order within the meaning of the Adoption and Children Act 2002 (c. 38) (including a future adoption order), and

  (b)   an order under section 84 of that Act (parental responsibility prior to adoption abroad).

AMENDMENT

1–297   In subs. (1), para (i) was inserted by the Human Fertilisation and Embryology Act 2008 s.56, Sch.6, Pt 1, para.40.

This section lists decisions that can never be made by the Court of Protection, a deputy **1–298** appointed by the court, the donee of an LPA, or a person acting under s.5 on behalf of a person who lacks capacity. It does not preclude the Court from making a declaration under s.15 with regard to P's capacity to consent to the matters set out in subs.(1). Also see s.29.

Subsection (1)(g)

By virtue of reg.65 the Special Educational Needs and Disability Regulations 2014 **1–299** (SI 2014/1530), regs 63 and 64 of the regulations which are concerned with parents and young people who lack mental capacity to take the decisions or actions required under the regulations "have effect in spite of section 27(1)(g) of the Mental Capacity Act 2005". The regulations supplement the procedural framework assessing a child or young person with special educational needs, and the procedure for making, reviewing, amending and ceasing to maintain an EHC plan (i.e. an assessment of the educational, health care and social care needs of the child or young person), set out in Pt 3 of the Children and Families Act 2014. They require local authorities to notify the child's parent or the young person of decisions within certain timescales, as well as notifying them of any right to appeal such decision.

Mental Health Act matters

28.—(1) Nothing in this Act authorises anyone— **1–300**

(a)   to give a patient medical treatment for mental disorder, or

(b)   to consent to a patient's being given medical treatment for mental disorder,

if, at the time when it is proposed to treat the patient, his treatment is regulated by Part 4 of the Mental Health Act.

[(1A) Subsection (1) does not apply in relation to any form of treatment to which section 58A of that Act (electro-convulsive therapy, etc.) applies if the patient comes within subsection (7) of that section (informal patient under 18 who cannot give consent).]

[(1B) Section 5 does not apply to an act to which section 64B of the Mental Health Act applies (treatment of community patients not recalled to hospital).]

(2) "Medical treatment", "mental disorder" and "patient" have the same meaning as in that Act.

AMENDMENTS

Subs.(1A) was inserted by the Mental Health Act 2007 s.28(1), and subs.(1B) was **1–301** inserted by s.35(5) of that Act.

DEFINITION

"Mental Health Act": s.64(1) **1–302**

GENERAL NOTE

If a mentally disordered patient who is also mentally incapacitated has been detained **1–303** under the long term provisions of the Mental Health Act 1983, the patient is subject to the regulatory regime for the treatment of his or her mental disorder which is set out in Pt IV of that Act. With the exception of the situation covered by subs.(1A), this section ensures that the provisions of the Act do not apply to any treatment given to a patient which is provided under the authority of Pt IV of the 1983 Act. In other words, the consent to treatment provisions contained in Pt IV will "trump" the provisions of the Act. This means that: (1) treatment for the patient's mental disorder cannot be given under the authority of the Act; (2) neither a donee of an LPA nor a deputy appointed by the court can either consent to or refuse treatment for mental disorder on the patient's behalf; and (3) with the exception of treatments regulated by s.58A of the 1983 Act, an advance decision made by the patient that refuses treatment for mental disorder is not binding on the treating psychiatrist.

Treatment decisions relating to mentally incapacitated patients which fall outside the scope of Pt IV, such as the treatment of community treatment order patients who have not been recalled to hospital, decisions about whether the patient should receive treatment for a physical disorder and treatments given to patients detained under the emergency provisions of the 1983 Act, are governed by the Act. This section does not prevent a treatment which is regulated by s.58 or s.58A of the 1983 Act being provided to a mentally incapacitated patient who has not been detained under that Act.

Subsection (1A)

1–304   This provides that the exclusion set out in subs.(1) does not apply in relation to treatments provided under s.58A of the 1983 Act (currently electro-convulsive therapy (ECT)) if the patient comes within s.58A(7). Section 58A(7) states:

"This section shall not by itself confer sufficient authority for [an informal patient under the age of 18 years to be given a treatment regulated by s.58A] if he is not capable of understanding the nature, purpose and likely effects of the treatment (and cannot therefore consent to it)."

This means that if the child is informal and incapable of consenting to ECT, the treatment is provided under the authority of s.5 for children over the age of 16 and by virtue of parental consent for younger children.

Subsection (1B)

1–305   Where treatment for mental disorder is being provided to an adult community patient under s.64B of the 1983 Act (treatment of incapacitated adult patient subject to a community treatment order), this provision prohibits the treatment from being provided under s.5. It does not preclude treatment decisions authorised by a donee or a court deputy.

Subsection (2)

1–306   Under s.145(1) of the 1983 Act, "medical treatment" is defined as including "nursing, psychological intervention and specialist mental health habilitation, rehabilitation and care", and "patient" is defined as "a person suffering or appearing to be suffering from mental disorder". "Mental disorder" is defined in s.1 of that Act as meaning "any disorder or disability of mind".

Voting rights

1–307   **29.**—(1) Nothing in this Act permits a decision on voting at an election for any public office, or at a referendum, to be made on behalf of a person.

(2) "Referendum" has the same meaning as in section 101 of the Political Parties, Elections and Referendums Act 2000 (c. 41).

GENERAL NOTE

1–308   This section excludes decisions on voting at an election for public office, or at a referendum, from the remit of the Act. It follows that a deputy or a donee of an LPA cannot vote on behalf of P.

Research

Research

1–309   **30.**—(1) Intrusive research carried out on, or in relation to, a person who lacks capacity to consent to it is unlawful unless it is carried out—

(a) as part of a research project which is for the time being approved by the appropriate body for the purposes of this Act in accordance with section 31, and

(b) in accordance with sections 32 and 33.

(2) Research is intrusive if it is of a kind that would be unlawful if it was carried out—

(a) on or in relation to a person who had capacity to consent to it, but

(b) without his consent.

(3) A clinical trial which is subject to the provisions of clinical trials regulations is not to be treated as research for the purposes of this section.

[(3A) Research is not intrusive to the extent that it consists of the use of a person's human cells to bring about the creation *in vitro* of an embryo or human admixed embryo, or the subsequent storage or use of an embryo or human admixed embryo so created.

(3B) Expressions used in subsection (3A) and in Schedule 3 to the Human Fertilisation and Embryology Act 1990 (consents to use or storage of gametes, embryos or human admixed embryos etc) have the same meaning in that subsection as in that Schedule.]

(4) "Appropriate body", in relation to a research project, means the person, committee or other body specified in regulations made by the appropriate authority as the appropriate body in relation to a project of the kind in question.

(5) "Clinical trials regulations" means—

(a) the Medicines for Human Use (Clinical Trials) Regulations 2004 (S.I. 2004 / 1031) and any other regulations replacing those regulations or amending them, and

(b) any other regulations relating to clinical trials and designated by the Secretary of State as clinical trials regulations for the purposes of this section.

(6) In this section, section 32 and section 34, "appropriate authority" means—

(a) in relation to the carrying out of research in England, the Secretary of State, and

(b) in relation to the carrying out of research in Wales, the National Assembly for Wales.

AMENDMENT

Subsections (3A) and (3B) were inserted by the Human Fertilisation and Embryology Act 2008 s.65, Sch.7, para.25.   **1–310**

GENERAL NOTE

The provisions in the Act that deals with research attempt to "balance the importance of   **1–311** properly conducted research into the treatment and care of people who lack capacity with the need to protect their interests and respect their current and previously expressed wishes and feelings", per Lord Hunt of Kings Heath, *Hansard*, HL Vol.689, col.GC107.

The Joint Committee recommended, at para.289, that the Bill

"should set out the key principles governing research, such as those enshrined by the World Medical Association [in the Helsinki Declaration]. Those key principles should include the following:

- research involving people who may be incapacitated must be reviewed by a properly established and independent ethics committee and can only proceed if ethical permission is granted.
- where a person has the capacity to consent then his decision whether or not to partake in research must be respected.
- considerable care should be taken to ensure that under these circumstances consent to participate was freely given and not a consequence of coercion.
- the inclusion of people in research, who lacked the capacity to consent, must only

occur when such research has the potential for direct benefit to those with that particular problem and could not have been done through the involvement of those with capacity.

- those undertaking research involving people lacking the capacity to consent must respect any indications that a person did not wish to participate (i.e. was dissenting). any discomfort or risk involved in the research must be, at the most, minimal."

The Government agreed that "key principles are important" and stated that it would "explore the extent to which these need be in statute, or whether they are already covered by existing Good Practice Guidance". Those carrying out research under the Act are required to act in accordance with the principles set out in s.1 and to have regard to the guidance contained in the *Code of Practice* (s.42(4)(c)).

This section, together with ss.31 to 34, make provision for "intrusive" research to be lawfully carried out on, or in relation to a person who lacks the capacity to consent to it, where the research is part of a research project which has been approved by the "appropriate body", as defined in subs.(4), and is carried out in accordance with the conditions set out in ss.32 and 33 (subs.(1)). Research covered by these provisions is not limited to research undertaken within NHS organisations or other public bodies. Intrusive research is research that would require consent if it involved a person with capacity (subs.(2)). Research is not intrusive if it comes within the scope of subs.(3A). Intrusive research undertaken on people who lack capacity which does not satisfy the requirements of the Act is unlawful. In addition to the obligations placed on them by the Act, researchers must also comply with their wider legal obligations such as their duties under the data protection and health and safety legislation.

If a person with capacity has consented to his involvement in research, the fact that he subsequently loses capacity does not mean that he has to be withdrawn from the research, in so far as it relates to the matter that he has consented to, because the fact that he given his consent means that the research is not intrusive (see subs.(2)). Baroness Andrews said: "The Bill does not apply to research during temporary incapacity, such as general anaesthesia during surgery, providing that consent was obtained in advance. Consent endures the temporary loss of capacity" (*Hansard*, HL Vol.670, col.1521). However, if the research is a continuing project rather than a one-off event, any further research would be research undertaken without consent and would therefore be intrusive research that would trigger the procedures set out in ss.31–33. For example, if the person consents to a sample of blood being taken as part of a research project, the sample can be taken even if the person loses capacity before that point. The taking of any further samples would constitute intrusive research because of the absence of the person's consent. Transitional provisions are contained in s.34.

Clinical trials that are regulated by the Medicines for Human Use (Clinical Trials) Regulations 2004 (SI 2004/1031) are excluded (subss.(3) and (5)) because the regulations already make provision for trials involving participants who lack capacity. The 2004 Regulations were amended by the Medicines for Human Use (Clinical Trials) Amendment (No.2) Regulations 2006 (SI 2006/2984) which are aimed at making the regulations consistent with the Act in so far as they relate to emergency research conducted on mentally incapacitated patients.

Paragraph 11.7 of the *Code of Practice* states:

"There are circumstances where no consent is needed to lawfully involve a person in research. These apply to all persons, whether they have capacity or not:

- Sometimes research only involves data that has been anonymised (it cannot be traced back to individuals). Confidentiality and data protection laws do not apply in this case.
- Under the Human Tissue Act 2004, research that deals only with human tissue that has been anonymised does not require consent . . . This applies to both those who have capacity and those who do not. But the research must have ethical approval, and the tissue must come from a living person.

- If researchers collected human tissue samples before 31 August 2006, they do not need a person's consent to work on them. But they will normally have to get ethical approval.
- Regulations made under section 251 of the NHS Act 2006 (formerly known as section 60 of the Health and Social Care Act 2001) allow people to use confidential patient information without breaking the law on confidentiality by applying to the Patient Information Advisory Group for approval on behalf of the Secretary of State."

The ethical and legal issues arising from medical research on mentally incompetent adults are considered by M.J. Gunn et al., in "Medical Research and Incompetent Adults" (2000) *Journal of Mental Health Law* 60. Practical issues are addressed by C. Dobson in *Conducting research with people not having capacity to consent to their participation*, British Psychological Society, 2008. For the application of these Regulations to emergency medicine, see T.J. Coats, "Consent for emergency care research: the Mental Capacity Act 2005" (2006) 23 *Emergency Medical Journal* 893.

Research that began before October 1, 2007

Sections 30 to 34 come into force in England on October 1, 2008 in respect of any research which (a) began before October 1, 2007; and (b) was approved before October 1, 2007 by a committee established to advise on, or on matters which include, the ethics of research in relation to people who lack capacity to consent to it (Mental Capacity Act 2005 (Commencement No.1) Order 2006 (SI 2006/2814) reg.4 (as amended by SI 2006/3473, art.2)). **1–312**

Subsection (1)

PERSON WHO LACKS CAPACITY. A capacitated person who consents to research which will be undertaken during a period of incapacity, such as when the person has been anaesthetised, is not a person who lacks capacity for the purpose of this provision. **1–313**

Subsection (2)

This definition is not limited to research that is physically invasive; it applies to any research where the consent of the person concerned would be legally required if he or she had capacity. An undated "Fact Sheet for Social Scientists" on the Act prepared by the Department of Health states that the definition "is wide ranging and covers all primary data collection, apart from that which involves the collection of anonymised, or effectively pseudonymised, data where there is no breach of the Data Protection Act (DPA) or the common law duty of confidence. **It is not limited to medical or biomedical research that is physically invasive** (e.g. the collection of tissue samples)" (para.2.2). **1–314**

Research undertaken with approval under s.251 of the National Health Service Act 2006 is not "intrusive" within the meaning of this provision because, if the person in question had capacity, his consent would not be a prerequisite for such research to be carried out. Section 251 enables the Secretary of State to make regulations enabling "prescribed patient information" to be processed for medical purposes, which includes medical research but not other forms of research: see the Health Service (Control of Patient Information) Regulations 2002 (SI 2002/1438).

Subsection (4)

By virtue of reg.2 of the Mental Capacity Act 2005 (Appropriate Body) (England) Regulations 2006 (SI 2006/2810) (as amended), the appropriate body in England for the purpose this section, s.31 and s.33 is a research ethics committee, i.e. **1–315**

"a committee—

    (a)   established to advise on, or on matters which include, the ethics of intrusive research in relation to people who lack capacity to consent to it; and

(b) recognised by that purpose by the Secretary of State in exercise of the powers in section 2 of the National Health Service Act 2006".

SI 2006/2810 came into force on July 1, 2007 for the purposes of enabling applications for ethical approval of research to be made and determined under the Act, and on October 1, 2007 for all other purposes (ibid., art.1, as amended by SI 2006/3474 art.2). A similar definition of appropriate body is made for Wales, with the same commencement dates, by the Mental Capacity Act 2005 (Appropriate Body) (Wales) Regulations 2007 (SI 2007/833 (W.71)) with the exception that the committee has to be recognised by the National Assembly for Wales (now the Welsh Ministers, see below).

The national Social Care Research Ethics Committee is the appropriate body under this provision: see the website of the Health Research Authority.

Subsection (5)

1–316 The 2004 Regulations, which came into force on May 1, 2004, implement European Clinical Trials Directive 2001/20/EC on "the approximation of the laws, regulations and administrative provisions of the Member States relating to the implementation of good clinical practice in the conduct of clinical trials on medicinal products for human use". The Regulations define "clinical trials" as meaning:

"any investigation in human subjects, other than a non-interventional trial, intended —

(a) to discover or verify the clinical, pharmacological or other pharmacodynamic effects of one or more medicinal products,
(b) to identify any adverse reactions to one or more such products, or
(c) to study absorption, distribution, metabolism and excretion of one or more such products

with the object of ascertaining the safety or efficacy of those products" (reg.2(1)).

Part 5 of Sch.1 to the regulations contains conditions and principles which apply to incapacitated adults.

Subsection (6) para.(b)

1–317 The functions of the National Assembly for Wales are performed by the Welsh Ministers (Government of Wales Act 2006 s.162, Sch.11, para.30).

Requirements for approval

1–318 **31.**—(1) The appropriate body may not approve a research project for the purposes of this Act unless satisfied that the following requirements will be met in relation to research carried out as part of the project on, or in relation to, a person who lacks capacity to consent to taking part in the project (P).

(2) The research must be connected with—

(a) an impairing condition affecting P, or

(b) its treatment.

(3) "Impairing condition" means a condition which is (or may be) attributable to, or which causes or contributes to (or may cause or contribute to), the impairment of, or disturbance in the functioning of, the mind or brain.

(4) There must be reasonable grounds for believing that research of comparable effectiveness cannot be carried out if the project has to be confined to, or relate only to, persons who have capacity to consent to taking part in it.

(5) The research must—

(a) have the potential to benefit P without imposing on P a burden that is disproportionate to the potential benefit to P, or

(b) be intended to provide knowledge of the causes or treatment of, or of the care of persons affected by, the same or a similar condition.

(6) If the research falls within paragraph (b) of subsection (5) but not within paragraph (a), there must be reasonable grounds for believing—

(a) that the risk to P from taking part in the project is likely to be negligible, and

(b) that anything done to, or in relation to, P will not—

(i) interfere with P's freedom of action or privacy in a significant way, or

(ii) be unduly invasive or restrictive.

(7) There must be reasonable arrangements in place for ensuring that the requirements of sections 32 and 33 will be met.

DEFINITIONS

"appropriate body": s.30(4)   1–319

GENERAL NOTE

This section sets out the requirements that must be satisfied before the appropriate   1–320
body (see s.30(4)) can approve a research project involving people who lack capacity. It does not preclude either observational or epidemiological research being undertaken. The research does not have to be undertaken in healthcare settings. Paragraph 11.2 of the *Code of Practice* states:

"The Act does not have a specific definition for 'research'. The Department of Health and National Assembly for Wales publications *Research governance framework for health and social care* both state:

'research can be defined as the attempt to derive generalisable new knowledge by addressing clearly defined questions with systematic and rigorous methods'.

Research may:

- provide information that can be applied generally to an illness, disorder or condition
- demonstrate how effective and safe a new treatment is
- add to evidence that one form of treatment works better than another
- add to evidence that one form of treatment is safer than another, or
- examine wider issues (for example, the factors that affect someone's capacity to make a decision)."

Research that can be undertaken under this provision includes "research on a person—involving direct contact with that person" and "research in relation to a person—indirect research on tissues, materials, data or information otherwise collected from the person" (Explanatory Memorandum to the Mental Capacity Act 2005 (Appropriate Body) (England) Regulations 2006 para.2).

There is a clear tension between the nature of some research contemplated by this section and the best interests principle established in s.1(5). This tension is illustrated by subss.(5) and (6) which contemplate research being undertaken which would be inconsistent with s.1(5). The Parliamentary Under-Secretary of State said that "the research procedures provide an alternative to a best interests determination" (*Hansard*, HL Vol.669, col.135). The Minister of State described the application of the best interests principle to research as being "difficult" (St. Comm. A, col.278), and that the principle is "interpreted slightly differently" when applied to research (*Hansard*, HC Vol.428, col.1604). At the third reading of the Bill, she said:

"[I]t is always difficult to prove that [research] can be in someone's best interests. We can only say that it is of potential benefit to that person, or might benefit him or her in the longer term, or might benefit him or her indirectly once more research has been done, or might benefit others with the same condition now or in the future" (*Hansard*, HC Vol.428, col.1603).

The Parliamentary Under-Secretary of State said:

"The purpose of [sections] 30 to 33 is to make provision for acts in connection with research that cannot necessarily be shown precisely to coincide with the person's best interests. It may be that the research procedure involves different or additional approaches to a person's care, which might not meet a narrow assessment of best interest" (*Hansard*, HL Vol.669, col.135).

The Joint Committee on Human Rights concluded that the "nature of the benefit from the research required in [subs.(5)] has the effect of lowering the threshold of when research will be permissible compared with the standards contained in the Convention" (23rd Report, para.2.60). The Government responded to this comment as follows:

"We have taken careful note of the Oviedo Convention [Council of Europe Convention on Human Rights and Biomedicine (ETS No.164)], but are conscious that it does not appear to extend across the breadth of research activities that we wish to cover. For example, Arts.15–17 of the Oviedo Convention are concerned with research 'on a person', which is further clarified in the Explanatory memorandum as 'research on human beings' and in the Additional Protocol which refers to 'research activities in the health field involving interventions on human beings'. We wished to cover wider aspects of research that would not normally require consent from a person with incapacity, including research into medical records, or observation of P in a social care setting. We hope that this helps to explain why, in some cases, we have departed from the language used in the Oviedo Convention" ("Memorandum submitted to the Joint Committee on Human Rights in response to their letter of 18 November 2004 as published in their 23rd Report", paras 59 and 60).

Subsections (2) and (3)

1–321   These provisions identify the scope of the research that can be undertaken. Baroness Andrews explained:

"The emphasis is now more clearly on the requirement that the research must be connected to an impairing condition that the person has. It concedes that the relationship between the impairing condition and the impairment of, or disturbance in, the functioning of the mind or brain is sometimes not perfectly understood. It makes it clearer that it may be valid to conduct properly designed research to see whether the condition and the impairment or the disturbance are linked.

The amendment makes it clear that research, for example, to prevent kidney failure in a person in a coma following a car accident or heart attack would be permissible if the other safeguards are met. The impairing condition would be the trauma or shock following the sudden crash or heart attack. The research ethics committee would have to be satisfied that there was a good case for believing that the research into kidney failure was connected to the impairing condition, or its treatment" (*Hansard*, HL Vol.670, col.1500).

IMPAIRMENT OF, OR DISTURBANCE IN THE FUNCTIONING OF THE MIND OR BRAIN.   See the note to s.2(1).

Subsection (4)

1–322   This provision was subject to a Government amendment to bring it closer to the wording of art.17.1 iii of the Oviedo Convention which states that "research of comparable effectiveness cannot be carried out on individuals capable of giving consent".

Subsection (5) para.(a)

POTENTIAL TO BENEFIT P.   If something is done which is intended to be of direct benefit   **1–323**
to P, it would constitute treatment rather than research.

BURDEN THAT IS DISPROPORTIONATE.   "By 'burden' we mean the risk or inconvenience
of a trial. For example, researchers might submit a proposal to use an MRI scanner to
understand the brain structures of people with dementia or schizophrenia. It might be
of potential benefit to their treatment. But if the use of an MRI scanner required long
confinement—we know that people with mental capacity or those suffering from cancer
or claustrophobia can be very vulnerable to extreme worry in these situations—or
perhaps regular and frequent scans, an ethics committee might decide that the research
would simply not bring enough benefit to justify the extra scans or trauma that might be
involved", per Baroness Andrews (*Hansard*, HL Vol.669, col.154).

Subsection (5) para.(b)

The Explanatory Notes state, at para.98, that this category or research "might include   **1–324**
indirect research on medical notes, or on tissue already taken for other purposes. It may
also include interviews or questionnaires with carers about health or social-care services
received by the person or limited observation of the person. And it could include taking
samples from the person, e.g. blood samples, specifically for the research project". It would
also include research into how the incapacity, and the medical and other complications that
are associated with it, might impact upon the care regime for the mentally incapacitated.
Note that s.33(3) states that the "interests of the person must be assumed to outweigh those
of science and society".

TREATMENT.   This provision allows for research into diagnostic procedures: see
s.64(1).

Subsection (6)

Paragraphs 11.18 and 11.19 of the *Code of Practice* state: **1–325**

"Any risk to people involved in this category of research must be 'negligible' (minimal).
This means that a person should suffer no harm or distress by taking part. Researchers
must consider risks to psychological wellbeing as well as physical wellbeing. This is
particularly relevant for research related to observations or interviews.

Research in this category also must not affect a person's freedom of action or privacy
in a significant way, and it should not be unduly invasive or restrictive. What will be
considered as unduly invasive will be different for different people and different types
of research. For example, in psychological research some people may think a specific
question is intrusive, but others would not. Actions will not usually be classed as unduly
invasive if they do not go beyond the experience of daily life, a routine medical examination or a psychological examination".

Consulting carers etc

32.—(1) This section applies if a person (R)—   **1–326**
   (a)   is conducting an approved research project, and
   (b)   wishes to carry out research, as part of the project, on or in relation to a
          person (P) who lacks capacity to consent to taking part in the project.
(2) R must take reasonable steps to identify a person who—
   (a)   otherwise than in a professional capacity or for remuneration, is engaged
          in caring for P or is interested in P's welfare, and
   (b)   is prepared to be consulted by R under this section.
(3) If R is unable to identify such a person he must, in accordance with guidance issued by the appropriate authority, nominate a person who—

(a)   is prepared to be consulted by R under this section, but

(b)   has no connection with the project.

(4) R must provide the person identified under subsection (2), or nominated under subsection (3), with information about the project and ask him—

(a)   for advice as to whether P should take part in the project, and

(b)   what, in his opinion, P's wishes and feelings about taking part in the project would be likely to be if P had capacity in relation to the matter.

(5) If, at any time, the person consulted advises R that in his opinion P's wishes and feelings would be likely to lead him to decline to take part in the project (or to wish to withdraw from it) if he had capacity in relation to the matter, R must ensure—

(a)   if P is not already taking part in the project, that he does not take part in it;

(b)   if P is taking part in the project, that he is withdrawn from it.

(6) But subsection (5)(b) does not require treatment that P has been receiving as part of the project to be discontinued if R has reasonable grounds for believing that there would be a significant risk to P's health if it were discontinued.

(7) The fact that a person is the donee of a lasting power of attorney given by P, or is P's deputy, does not prevent him from being the person consulted under this section.

(8) Subsection (9) applies if treatment is being, or is about to be, provided for P as a matter of urgency and R considers that, having regard to the nature of the research and of the particular circumstances of the case—

(a)   it is also necessary to take action for the purposes of the research as a matter of urgency, but

(b)   it is not reasonably practicable to consult under the previous provisions of this section.

(9) R may take the action if—

(a)   he has the agreement of a registered medical practitioner who is not involved in the organisation or conduct of the research project, or

(b)   where it is not reasonably practicable in the time available to obtain that agreement, he acts in accordance with a procedure approved by the appropriate body at the time when the research project was approved under section 31.

(10) But R may not continue to act in reliance on subsection (9) if he has reasonable grounds for believing that it is no longer necessary to take the action as a matter of urgency.

DEFINITIONS

1–327   "appropriate authority": s.30(6)

"lasting power of attorney": s.64(1)

"deputy": s.64(1)

"appropriate body": s.30(4)

GENERAL NOTE

1–328   This section provides that before any decision is taken to involve P in approved research, the researcher (R) must take reasonable steps to identify either an unpaid carer or a person who is interested in P's welfare in a non-professional capacity who is prepared to be consulted about P's involvement in the research (subss.(1), (2)). This person could be a deputy or a donee of a lasting power of attorney as long as that person is not acting in a paid or professional capacity (subs.(7)). If there is no such person, R must nominate (in accordance with guidance issued by the appropriate authority) a person who is willing to be consulted, but has no connection with the project (subs.(3)). This person could have a professional relationship with P, for example, his GP. The role of the consultee is to provide information to R; he or she does not provide consent for the research to proceed.

Subsection (4) identifies the purpose of the consultation. If the consultee advises R that, in his or her opinion, P would have been likely to decline to take part if he or she had capacity, P cannot be involved in the research, or if it is already underway P must be withdrawn from it (subs.(5)). However, if P has been receiving treatment as part of the research it should not be withdrawn if to do so would place P's health at significant risk (subs.(6)).

Subsections (8) and (9) allow for cases where P is being, or is about to be, provided with urgent treatment, research into that treatment must also be undertaken as a matter of urgency, and it is not reasonable practicable for R to consult. R may proceed to involve P in the research if he or she has the agreement of a doctor who is not concerned in the organisation or conduct of the research project, or, if there is no time to do this, he follows an approved procedure. R cannot continue to use these provisions if there is no longer an urgent need to act (subs.(10)). The Explanatory Notes, at para.104, state that examples of this type of research "may involve action by a paramedic or doctor to make measurements in the first few minutes following a serious head injury or stroke".

Guidance

"Guidance on nominating a consultee for research involving adults who lack capacity to consent", was issued by the Secretary of State and the Welsh Ministers in February 2008. It sets out the principles to which researchers must adhere in nominating a consultee and provides advice on ways of meeting this requirement in different research settings, including emergency research.

1–329

Subsection (2)

A PERSON.   Such as a family member, advocate or friend.

1–330

ENGAGED IN CARING FOR.   See the note on "anyone engaged in caring for the person" in s.4(7)(b).

Subsection (3)

GUIDANCE.   See above.

1–331

CONNECTION WITH THE PROJECT.   This phrase "would certainly include someone involved with, or connected to, either the study itself or a member of the research team. It would also cover wider connections, such as someone with a direct link to funding decisions for the study, for example, or who was involved with the research ethics committee" per Baroness Andrews (*Hansard*, HL Vol.670, col.1515).

Subsection (4)

Paragraph (b) requires R to ask the consultee to exercise a substituted judgment on behalf of P. This will be an almost impossible task to perform if the consultee has had no previous contact with P. Professor Coats argues that in this situation the consultee "will simply reason that most people wish to improve medical treatment and for most trials, most of the patients approached agree to participate in research projects. Therefore, the incapacitated patient would probably agree to be included in the trial. Without any prior knowledge of the patient the 'consultee' will therefore always agree to patient entry. . ." (T.J. Coats, "Consent for emergency care research: the Mental Capacity Act 2005" (2006) 23 *Emergency Medical Journal* 893).

1–332

Subsection (5)

1–333 If P is withdrawn part way through the project, this provision does not provide that information collected with respect to P up to that point must be disregarded for the purposes of the project.

Subsection (7)

1–334 DEPUTY. "[W]e will amend the *Code of Practice* to make it clear that if a deputy has no relationship to, or knowledge of, P before their appointment, they should not be consulted on the question of P's participation in research", per the Minister of State (*Hansard*, HC Vol.428, col.1605).

Subsection (9)

1–335 MAY TAKE THE ACTION. i.e. involve P in the research.

REGISTERED MEDICAL PRACTITIONER. The doctor to be consulted may be involved in the treatment of P. Baroness Andrews said:

> "We want provide that a doctor who can be consulted may well be a consultant surgeon or even a GP whose patient suffers a sudden cardiac arrest or goes into septic shock, for example.

> If the emergency happens in the community—outside the hospital—it is perfectly possible that a person's GP can be involved and give approval for research to be initiated by, for example, a paramedic attending the person at home. It is important to think that research in such a case may simply be the taking of a blood sample. As I hope is clear, those doctors are usually best placed to advise the researcher, as they are familiar with the patient's medical history" (*Hansard*, HL Vol.670, col.1501).

Additional safeguards

1–336 **33.**—(1) This section applies in relation to a person who is taking part in an approved research project even though he lacks capacity to consent to taking part.

(2) Nothing may be done to, or in relation to, him in the course of the research—

    (a) to which he appears to object (whether by showing signs of resistance or otherwise) except where what is being done is intended to protect him from harm or to reduce or prevent pain or discomfort, or

    (b) which would be contrary to—

        (i) an advance decision of his which has effect, or

        (ii) any other form of statement made by him and not subsequently withdrawn,

of which R is aware.

(3) The interests of the person must be assumed to outweigh those of science and society.

(4) If he indicates (in any way) that he wishes to be withdrawn from the project he must be withdrawn without delay.

(5) P must be withdrawn from the project, without delay, if at any time the person conducting the research has reasonable grounds for believing that one or more of the requirements set out in section 31(2) to (7) is no longer met in relation to research being carried out on, or in relation to, P.

(6) But neither subsection (4) nor subsection (5) requires treatment that P has been receiving as part of the project to be discontinued if R has reasonable grounds for believing that there would be a significant risk to P's health if it were discontinued.

GENERAL NOTE   **1–338**

This section provides that P's involvement in research must cease without delay if it appears that he or she objects to what is being done (this requirement is subject to the exceptions contained in subs.(2)(a)), if what is being done is contrary to either an advance decision made by P or to some other statement made by P, or if P indicates that he wishes to be withdrawn from the research (subss.(2),(4)). These provisions are subject to the principle that the interests of P must be assumed to outweigh those of science and society (subs.(3)). P must also be withdrawn from the research if the person conducting the research believes that one or more of requirements for approval is no longer met (subs.(5)). Subsection (6) makes it clear that any withdrawal from research does not require beneficial treatment to be halted.

Researchers have a duty to have regard to the guidance contained in the *Code of Practice* (s.42(4)(c)).

Subsection (3)   **1–339**

This principle is taken from section A.5 of the World Medical Association's Declaration of Helsinki on Ethical Principles for Medical Research Involving Human Subjects.

Loss of capacity during research project

34.—(1) This section applies where a person (P)—   **1–340**

  (a) has consented to take part in a research project begun before the commencement of section 30, but

  (b) before the conclusion of the project, loses capacity to consent to continue to take part in it.

(2) The appropriate authority may by regulations provide that, despite P's loss of capacity, research of a prescribed kind may be carried out on, or in relation to, P if—

  (a) the project satisfies prescribed requirements,

  (b) any information or material relating to P which is used in the research is of a prescribed description and was obtained before P's loss of capacity, and

  (c) the person conducting the project takes in relation to P such steps as may be prescribed for the purpose of protecting him.

(3) The regulations may, in particular,—

  (a) make provision about when, for the purposes of the regulations, a project is to be treated as having begun;

  (b) include provision similar to any made by section 31, 32 or 33.

GENERAL NOTE   **1–342**

The purpose of this section was explained by the Baroness Andrews:

"[This section establishes] a transitional regulation-making power to cover ongoing research and provides for the necessary flexibility in the provisions for approval of research by a research ethics committee, with consultation of carers and additional safeguards. Why do we need transitional regulations? Primarily because it is necessary to smooth the transition for researchers from the current common law position to the new statutory safeguards for research involving those who lose capacity. We need them to avoid stopping ongoing and essential research

We already have the flexibility to cater for the majority of those in the ordinary powers for making transitional provisions in [s.65], but we need to provide for more comprehensive regulation-making powers to cover projects that enrol people with capacity who go on to lose capacity during the research projects

Our aim is to ensure that a research project can continue in relation to samples or data obtained from people before they lost capacity, subject to certain specified safeguards" (*Hansard*, HL Vol.670, cols 1520–1522).

The Mental Capacity Act 2005 (Loss of Capacity during Research Project) (England) Regulations 2007 (SI 2007/679), which are reproduced in Part 3, have been made under this section (for Wales, see SI 2007/837 (W.72)). They only apply where a person has consented to take part in a research project which started before October 1, 2007, but before the end of the project loses capacity. The person's consent to take part in the project must be given before March 31, 2008. The regulations allow the researcher to continue to use information or material obtained with consent *before* the loss of capacity. They do not apply to situations where the researchers wish to go back to a person who lacks capacity in order to obtain more information or material. Such projects will need to have approval under s.30. The regulations will have a long-term effect. The Minister gave the following example: "[A] person could join an existing study in October 2007 or January 2008 and lose capacity in the 2020s, and, if the study is continuing, the regulations would apply" (*Hansard*, HL Vol.689, col.GC108).

REGULATIONS. Regulations made under this power are subject to the affirmative resolution procedure (s.65(4)).

Independent mental capacity advocate service

Appointment of independent mental capacity advocates

1–343   **35.**—(1) The [responsible authority] must make such arrangements as it considers reasonable to enable persons (independent mental capacity advocates) to be available to represent and support persons to whom acts or decisions proposed under sections 37, 38 and 39 relate [or persons who fall within section 39A, 39C or 39D].

(2) The appropriate authority may make regulations as to the appointment of independent mental capacity advocates.

(3) The regulations may, in particular, provide—

(a)   that a person may act as an independent mental capacity advocate only in such circumstances, or only subject to such conditions, as may be prescribed;

(b)   for the appointment of a person as an independent mental capacity advocate to be subject to approval in accordance with the regulations.

(4) In making arrangements under subsection (1), the [responsible authority] must have regard to the principle that a person to whom a proposed act or decision relates should, so far as practicable, be represented and supported by a person who is independent of any person who will be responsible for the act or decision.

(5) The arrangements may include provision for payments to be made to, or in relation to, persons carrying out functions in accordance with the arrangements.

(6) For the purpose of enabling him to carry out his functions, an independent mental capacity advocate—

(a) may interview in private the person whom he has been instructed to represent, and
(b) may, at all reasonable times, examine and take copies of—
   (i) any health record,
   (ii) any record of, or held by, a local authority and compiled in connection with a social services function, and
   (iii) any record held by a person registered under Part 2 of the Care
Standards Act 2000 (c.14) [or Chapter 2 of Part 1 of the Health and
Social Care Act 2008],

which the person holding the record considers may be relevant to the independent
mental capacity advocate's investigation.

[(6A) In subsections (1) and (4), "the responsible authority" means—
(a) in relation to the provision of the services of independent mental capacity
advocates in the area of a local authority in England, that local authority,
and
(b) in relation to the provision of the services of independent mental capacity
advocates in Wales, the Welsh Ministers.

(6B) In subsection (6A)(a), "local authority" has the meaning given in section
64(1) except that it does not include the council of a county or county borough in
Wales.]

(7) In this section, section 36 and section 37, "the appropriate authority"
means—
(a) in relation to the provision of the services of independent mental capacity
advocates in England, the Secretary of State, and
(b) in relation to the provision of the services of independent mental capacity
advocates in Wales, the National Assembly for Wales.

AMENDMENTS
   The amendments to this section were made by the Mental Health Act 2007 s.50(7), **1–344**
Sch.9, para.3, SI 2010/813 art.17(2), and the Health and Social Care Act 2012 s.55(2),
Sch.5, para.134.

GENERAL NOTE
   Sections 35–41 create a scheme designed to provide the input of an independent mental **1–345**
capacity advocate (IMCA) who will act as a representative and supporter of particularly
vulnerable persons who lacks capacity where certain decisions need to be taken. Such
people "may include older people with dementia who have lost contact with all friends
and family, or people with severe learning disabilities or long term mental health problems who have been in residential institutions for long periods and lack outside contacts"
(Explanatory Notes, para.109). The IMCA will become involved where there is no person,
other than a professional or paid carer, to be consulted with about P's best interests. An
IMCA will not become involved if one of the persons set out in s.40 can be consulted about
P's best interests. The Minister of State said:

"We estimate that about 20 per cent of people in England and Wales who lack capacity
when major decisions are being taken about their living arrangements, care or treatment,
have no friends or family to consult. The [IMCA] safeguard will provide the person with
someone who is on their side so that there is never a closed relationship between the
decision maker and the person lacking capacity.

. . . The [IMCA] will clearly have the right to talk to the person lacking capacity and a
right of access to relevant records. They will find out as much as they possibly can about

the likely wishes of the person and explore a range of possible outcomes that may be open to that individual. We want to give the person those powers so that they can take a broad view of what will eventually be in the best interests of the individual, which they can then recommend to the decision maker" (St. Comm. A, cols 314 and 315).

This section places a duty on the Secretary of State for Health and the Welsh Ministers to make arrangements for the provision of an IMCA service (subss.(1)–(4) and (7)) and provides the IMCA with the power to interview a mentally incapacitated person (P) in private and to examine relevant records (subs.(6)). The requirements set out in regulations made under subs.(2) must be satisfied before a person can be appointed to act as an IMCA. The IMCA, who could be remunerated for his or her services (subs.(5)), will act in P's best interests (ss.1(5)). However, as the role of the IMCA is to support and represent the person lacking capacity, he or she will not make the best interests judgment on P's behalf (subs. (1)). The involvement of the IMCA will cease if P regains mental capacity. The particular functions of IMCAs are set out in regulations (s.36). If the decision maker decides not to accept the advice proffered, the IMCA will need to consider whether take the matter further by, for example, using the NHS or local authority complaints procedure or, if the matter is particularly serious, seeking permission to refer the matter to the Court of Protection. Paragraphs 10.37 to 10.39 of the *Code of Practice* state:

"IMCAs may use complaints procedures as necessary to try to settle a disagreement—and they can pursue a complaint as far as the relevant ombudsman if needed. In particularly serious or urgent cases, an IMCA may seek permission to refer a case to the Court of Protection for a decision. The Court will make a decision in the best interests of the person who lacks capacity.

The first step in making a formal challenge is to approach the Official Solicitor (OS) with the facts of the case. The OS can decide to apply to the court as a litigation friend (acting on behalf of the person the IMCA is representing). If the OS decides not to apply himself, the IMCA can ask for permission to apply to the Court of Protection. The OS can still be asked to act as a litigation friend for the person who lacks capacity.

In extremely serious cases, the IMCA might want to consider an application for judicial review in the High Court. This might happen if the IMCA thinks there are very serious consequences to a decision that has been made by a public authority. There are time limits for making an application, and the IMCA would have to instruct solicitors—and may be liable for the costs of the case going to court. So IMCAs should get legal advice before choosing this approach. The IMCA can also ask the OS to consider making the claim."

In their evidence to the House of Lords Select Committee, Professor Phil Fennell and Dr Lucy Series argued that it was "far from clear in the legislation when an IMCA should challenge decision-making. They were concerned in particular by the suggestion that IMCAs would challenge decisions only when they judged them not to be in P's best interests: 'The right to obtain access to a court to air disputes under the MCA should not rest on the IMCA's judgment call as to best interests, but the person's own opposition to some measure which interferes with his ECHR rights and which is premised upon his 'incapacity' " (para.167). The Social Care Institute for Excellence has published *Commissioning and monitoring of Independent Mental Capacity Advocacy (IMCA) services, Guide 31* (2010) which can be accessed at: *www.scie.org.uk/publications/guides/guide31/*. Also see the report of the Royal College of Psychiatrists on "Independent advocacy for people with mental disorder" (CR171, Feb. 2012).

There is a potential for the overlap of duties between IMCAs and independent advocates who represent and support individuals under the Care Act 2014: see s.67 of that Act.

Subsection (1)

1–346   RESPONSIBLE AUTHORITY.   See subss.(6A), (6B).

Subsection (2)

See reg.5 of the Mental Capacity Act 2005 (Independent Mental Capacity Advocates **1–347** (General) Regulations 2006 (SI 2006/1832) which is reproduced in Part 3. Provision for the appointment of IMCAs in Wales is made by the Mental Capacity Act 2005 (Independent Mental Capacity Advocates) (Wales) Regulations 2007 (SI 2007/852 (W.77)) reg.5.

Under reg.5(3) of SI 2006/1832 and reg.5(8) of SI 2007/852 (W.77), enhanced criminal record certificates are required in determining whether a person meets the appointment requirements as to good character. An enhanced disclosure is not confined to checking the Police National Computer; it also includes a check of local police force records for information considered relevant to the position applied for. Applicants are also required to be checked against the disclosure and barring scheme established by the Safeguarding of Vulnerable Groups Act 2006.

Subsection (4)

So FAR AS PRACTICABLE.   It is important not to equate "practicable" with "possible": see **1–348** the note on s.4(7).

INDEPENDENT OF ANY PERSON.   Paragraph 10.19 of the *Code of Practice* states that people

"cannot act as IMCAs if they:

- care for or treat (in a paid or professional capacity) the person they will be representing (this does not apply if they are an existing advocate acting for that person), or

- have links to the person instructing them, to the decision-maker or to other individuals involved in the person's care or treatment that may affect their independence."

Subsection (6) para.(a)

The responsibility for determining the mental capacity of the person who is the subject **1–349** of the decision is that of the decision-maker, not the IMCA.

Subsection (6) para.(b)

It is the responsibility of the record holder to determine whether a record is "relevant" **1–350** to the IMCA's investigation. The record holder should therefore examine the record and ensure that the IMCA only has access to relevant material. The disclosure of irrelevant material to the IMCA would constitute a breach of P's right to confidentiality and to respect for private life under art.8 of the European Convention on Human Rights. If the IMCA is denied access to records that he or she considers are relevant to the investigation, a complaint should be made to the body that holds the record. Ultimately the IMCA could apply to the court for the record to be disclosed. The IMCA is subject to a duty of confidentiality in respect of information that is disclosed under this provision.

Subsection (7) para.(b)

The functions of the National Assembly for Wales are performed by the Welsh Ministers **1–351** (Government of Wales Act 2006 s.162, Sch.11, para.30).

Functions of independent mental capacity advocates

36.—(1) The appropriate authority may make regulations as to the functions of **1–352** independent mental capacity advocates.

(2) The regulations may, in particular, make provision requiring an advocate to take such steps as may be prescribed for the purpose of—

(a) providing support to the person whom he has been instructed to represent (P) so that P may participate as fully as possible in any relevant decision;

(b) obtaining and evaluating relevant information;

(c) ascertaining what P's wishes and feelings would be likely to be, and the beliefs and values that would be likely to influence P, if he had capacity;

(d) ascertaining what alternative courses of action are available in relation to P;

(e) obtaining a further medical opinion where treatment is proposed and the advocate thinks that one should be obtained.

(3) The regulations may also make provision as to circumstances in which the advocate may challenge, or provide assistance for the purpose of challenging, any relevant decision.

DEFINITIONS

1–353   "appropriate authority": s.35(7)
"independent mental capacity advocate": s.64(1)
"prescribed': s.64(1)

GENERAL NOTE

1–354   This section enables the Secretary of State and the Welsh Ministers to make regulations as to the functions of IMCAs. The primary function of the IMCA is to advocate on behalf of P in respect of decisions that require an IMCA involvement. The Mental Capacity Act 2005 (Independent Mental Capacity Advocates) (General) Regulations 2006 (SI 2006/1832) have been made under this section: see Part 3. They apply not only where the IMCA is instructed under ss.37 to 39 but also where he or she is instructed under regulations made under s.41. Regulation 6 sets out the steps an IMCA must take once he or she has been instructed to act in a particular case. Note that the IMCA is only required to carry out the functions identified in reg.6(4)(b) and (c) "to the extent that it is practicable and appropriate to do so". The meaning of "practicable" is considered in the note to s.4(7). For Wales, see the Mental Capacity Act 2005 (Independent Mental Capacity Advocates) (Wales) Regulations 2007 (SI 2007/852 (W.77)) reg.6, which contains the same terminology.

By virtue of reg.2 of the Mental Capacity Act 2005 (Independent Mental Capacity Advocates) (Expansion of Role) Regulations 2006 (SI 2006/2883), the role of the IMCA has been expanded to enable IMCAs to be appointed in the circumstances specified in reg.3 or 4 of the regulations, i.e. reviewing arrangements where P has been placed in either NHS or local authority accommodation and adult protection cases. SI 2006/2883 is reproduced in Part 3. The equivalent provision for Wales is the Mental Capacity Act 2005 (Independent Mental Capacity Advocates) (Wales) Regulations 2007 (SI 2007/852 (W.77)) regs 8 and 9.

Subsection (2) para.(c)

1–355   WOULD BE LIKELY TO BE.   As this provision would require the IMCA to make a substituted judgment on behalf of P, the IMCA should beware of the danger of expressing an opinion which merely reflects his or her views about the matter in question.

Subsection (3)

1–356   Under reg.7 of SI 2006/1832, above, once a decision has been made about P in a matter where an IMCA has been instructed, the IMCA "has the same rights to challenge the decision as he would have if he were a person (other than an IMCA) engaged in caring for P or interested in his welfare" (for Wales, see SI 2007/852 (W.77), reg.7). Paragraph 7.8 of the Explanatory Memorandum states that "it is intended that IMCAs will use existing complaints mechanisms to resolve disputes locally as far as possible, before making use of statutory procedures. In certain cases the IMCA may want to apply to the Court of Protection and he will be able to do this". Challenges can include a challenge to the decision that the person lacks capacity.

Provision of serious medical treatment by NHS body

37.—(1) This section applies if an NHS body—   **1–357**

(a) is proposing to provide, or secure the provision of, serious medical treatment for a person (P) who lacks capacity to consent to the treatment, and

(b) is satisfied that there is no person, other than one engaged in providing care or treatment for P in a professional capacity or for remuneration,

whom it would be appropriate to consult in determining what would be in P's best interests.

(2) But this section does not apply if P's treatment is regulated by Part 4 [or 4A] of the Mental Health Act.

(3) Before the treatment is provided, the NHS body must instruct an independent mental capacity advocate to represent P.

(4) If the treatment needs to be provided as a matter of urgency, it may be provided even though the NHS body has not been able to comply with subsection (3).

(5) The NHS body must, in providing or securing the provision of treatment for P, take into account any information given, or submissions made, by the independent mental capacity advocate.

(6) "Serious medical treatment" means treatment which involves providing, withholding or withdrawing treatment of a kind prescribed by regulations made by the appropriate authority.

(7) "NHS body" has such meaning as may be prescribed by regulations made for the purposes of this section by—

(a) the Secretary of State, in relation to bodies in England, or

(b) the National Assembly for Wales, in relation to bodies in Wales.

AMENDMENT

In subs.(2), the words in square brackets were inserted by the Mental Health Act 2007   **1–358**
s.35(6).

DEFINITIONS

"treatment": s.64(1)   **1–359**
"Mental Health Act": s.64(1)
"independent mental capacity advocate": s.64(1)

GENERAL NOTE

This section applies where "serious medical treatment" (apart from treatment regulated   **1–360**
under Pt 4 or 4A of the Mental Health Act 1983 (subs.(2)) is to be provided, withheld or
withdrawn (subs.(6)) by the NHS for a person who lacks capacity and there is no-one apart
from a professional or paid carer for the treatment-provider to consult in determining what
would be in P's best interests (subs.(1)). In this situation, unless a person mentioned in s.40
is available to be consulted, the treatment-provider must instruct an IMCA to represent P
and any information given, or submissions made, by the IMCA must be taken into account
when decisions are made about treating P (subs.(3),(5)). Such consultation is not required
if the need for the treatment is urgent (subs.(4)). The particular types of treatment that
will trigger the involvement of an IMCA have been prescribed by SI 2006/1832 and SI
2007/852 (W.77): see subs.(6).

Proper records should be taken by the treatment-provider of how the IMCA's representations has been taken into account and, where relevant, the reasons for disagreeing
with or ignoring those representations. Where a disagreement arises, every effort must
be made to resolve the disagreement at the earliest possible stage, where necessary using
the authority's dispute resolution or complaint's procedure. If an unresolved disagreement
relates to doubts over P's mental capacity or whether the proposed treatment is in P's best

interests, consideration should be given to referring the matter to the court. Under reg.7 of SI 2006/1832 once a decision has been made about P in a matter where an IMCA has been instructed, the IMCA "has the same rights to challenge the decision as he would have if he were a person (other than an IMCA) engaged in caring for P or interested in his welfare".

An IMCA can obtain a further medical opinion regarding P's condition (SI 2006/1832 regs 6(4)(d),(5)(d)), and a request for such an opinion can also be made by a deputy or donee if the making of such a request comes within the scope of their authority.

Subsection (1)

1–361   NHS BODY.   See subs.(7). Paragraph 10.9 of the *Code of Practice* states:

"For decisions about serious medical treatment, the responsible body will be the NHS organisation providing the person's healthcare or treatment. But if the person is in an independent or voluntary sector hospital, the responsible body will be the NHS organisation arranging and funding the person's care, which should have arrangements in place with the independent or voluntary sector hospital to ensure that an IMCA is appointed promptly."

Subsection (1) para.(a)

1–362   SECURE THE PROVISION OF.   The duty under this section will arise if the NHS is funding P's treatment in the private sector.

PERSON.   The obligation to appoint an IMCA applies if P is in prison (*Code of Practice*, para.10.73).

Subsection (1) para.(b)

1–363   APPROPRIATE TO CONSULT.   It is for the responsible body to decide whether there is anyone who comes within this category. The fact that a person might disagree with what is proposed does not mean that it is inappropriate to consult that person (*Code of Practice*, para.10.79). It is unlikely to be appropriate to consult with a person who:

(a) has a history of abusing or ill-treating P;
(b) is likely to be the cause of distress to P if P was aware of the consultation;
(c) is not available to be consulted with;
(d) could only be consulted with if a disproportionate amount of time was used in an attempt to contact that person;
(e) only has very limited knowledge of P;
(f) is unwilling to be a consultee;
(g) is suffering from a mental disorder which disables him or her from performing the role of a consultee; or
(h) would gain some material benefit as a result of a particular outcome.

Subsection (2)

1–364   Treatments regulated by Pts 4 and 4A of the Mental Health Act 1983 are excluded because that Act provides its own safeguards for patients.

Subsection (3)

1–365   MUST INSTRUCT.   This requirement will not be satisfied in the absence of a very wide range of staff being aware of the NHS body's duty to instruct an IMCA.

Subsection (4)

1–366   An IMCA would need to be instructed for any serious medical treatment that follows the emergency treatment (*Code of Practice*, para.10.46).

Subsection (6)

By virtue of reg.4 of the Mental Capacity Act 2005 (Independent Mental Capacity Advocates) (General) Regulations 2006 (SI 2006/1832) (for Wales, see the Mental Capacity Act 2005 (Independent Mental Capacity Advocates) (Wales) Regulations 2007 (SI 2007/852 (W.77)) reg.4), serious medical treatment "is treatment which involves providing, withdrawing or withholding treatment in circumstances where—

(a) in a case where a single treatment is being proposed, there is a fine balance between its benefits to the patient and the burdens and risks it is likely to entail for him,

(b) in a case where there is a choice of treatments, a decision as to which one to use is finely balanced, or

(c) what is proposed would be likely to involve serious consequences for the patient."

These criteria, which define serious medical treatment by reference to the characteristics of the treatment, allow for a significant amount of discretion to be exercised by the treating clinician. The wording of the criteria is such that electro-convulsive therapy, a treatment that would be regarded as being "serious" by most patients, might not be regarded by the clinician as coming within the terms of reg.4 if the treatment is being provided as a final treatment option. It is also the case that relatively minor treatments could come within the scope of para.(b).

The term "likely" in para.(c) suggests a high degree of probability of serious consequences; a mere possibility would not be sufficient. Paragraph 10.44 of the *Code of Practice* states:

"'Serious consequences' are those which could have a serious impact on the patient, either from the effects of the treatment itself or its wider implications. This may include treatments which:

- cause serious and prolonged pain, distress or side effects
- have potentially major consequences for the patient (for example, stopping life- sustaining treatment or having major surgery), or
- have a serious impact on the patient's future life choices (for example, interventions for ovarian cancer)."

Paragraphs 5 to 7 of Practice Direction 9E (Applications relating to Serious Medical Treatment) which supplements Part 9 of the Court of Protection Rules 2007 read:

"Matters which should be brought to the court

5. Cases involving any of the following decisions should be regarded as serious medical treatment for the purpose of the Rules and this practice direction, and should be brought to the court:

(a) decisions about the proposed withholding or withdrawal of artificial nutrition and hydration from a person in a permanent vegetative state or a minimally conscious state;

(b) cases involving organ or bone marrow donation by a person who lacks capacity to consent; and

(c) cases involving non-therapeutic sterilisation of a person who lacks capacity to consent.

6. Examples of serious medical treatment may include:

(a) certain terminations of pregnancy in relation to a person who lacks capacity to consent to such a procedure;

(b) a medical procedure performed on a person who lacks capacity to consent to it, where the procedure is for the purpose of a donation to another person;

(c) a medical procedure or treatment to be carried out on a person who lacks capacity to consent to it, where that procedure or treatment must be carried out using a degree of force to restrain the person concerned;

(d) an experimental or innovative treatment for the benefit of a person who lacks capacity to consent to such treatment; and

(e) a case involving an ethical dilemma in an untested area.

7. There may be other procedures or treatments not contained in the list in paragraphs 5 and 6 above which can be regarded as serious medical treatment. Whether or not a procedure is regarded as serious medical treatment will depend on the circumstances and the consequences for the patient."

Subsection (7)

1–368　　For the purposes of this section and s.38, "NHS body" means a body in England which is—

  (a) [. . .];
  (b) an NHS foundation trust;
  [(ba) a clinical commissioning group;
  (bb) the National Health Service Commissioning Board;
  (bc) a local authority (within the meaning of section 2B of the National Health Service Act 2006) acting in the exercise of public health functions (within the meaning of that Act);]
  (c) [. . .];
  (d) an NHS Trust; or
  (e) a Care Trust (SI 2006/1832, reg.3).

In Wales, "NHS body" means—

(a) a Local Health Board;
(b) an NHS trust all or most of whose hospitals, establishments and facilities are situated in Wales;
(c) a Special Health Authority performing functions only or mainly in respect of Wales (SI 2007/852 (W.77), reg.3).

Provision of accommodation by NHS body

1–369　　**38.**—(1) This section applies if an NHS body proposes to make arrangements—

  (a) for the provision of accommodation in a hospital or care home for a person (P) who lacks capacity to agree to the arrangements, or
  (b) for a change in P's accommodation to another hospital or care home,

and is satisfied that there is no person, other than one engaged in providing care or treatment for P in a professional capacity or for remuneration, whom it would be appropriate for it to consult in determining what would be in P's best interests.

　　(2) But this section does not apply if P is accommodated as a result of an obligation imposed on him under the Mental Health Act.

　　[(2A) And this section does not apply if—

  (a) an independent mental capacity advocate must be appointed under section 39A or 39C (whether or not by the NHS body) to represent P, and
  (b) the hospital or care home in which P is to be accommodated under the arrangements referred to in this section is the relevant hospital or care home under the authorisation referred to in that section.]

　　(3) Before making the arrangements, the NHS body must instruct an independent mental capacity advocate to represent P unless it is satisfied that—

  (a) the accommodation is likely to be provided for a continuous period which is less than the applicable period, or
  (b) the arrangements need to be made as a matter of urgency.

　　(4) If the NHS body—

  (a) did not instruct an independent mental capacity advocate to represent P before making the arrangements because it was satisfied that subsection (3)(a) or (b) applied, but

(b) subsequently has reason to believe that the accommodation is likely to be provided for a continuous period—

  (i) beginning with the day on which accommodation was first provided in accordance with the arrangements, and

  (ii) ending on or after the expiry of the applicable period,

it must instruct an independent mental capacity advocate to represent P.

(5) The NHS body must, in deciding what arrangements to make for P, take into account any information given, or submissions made, by the independent mental capacity advocate.

(6) "Care home" has the meaning given in section 3 of the Care Standards Act 2000 (c.14).

[(7) "Hospital" means—

(a) in relation to England, a hospital as defined by section 275 of the National Health Service Act 2006; and

(b) in relation to Wales, a health service hospital as defined by section 206 of the National Health Service (Wales) Act 2006 or an independent hospital as defined by section 2 of the Care Standards Act 2000.]

(8) "NHS body" has such meaning as may be prescribed by regulations made for the purposes of this section by—

(a) the Secretary of State, in relation to bodies in England, or

(b) the National Assembly for Wales, in relation to bodies in Wales.

(9) "Applicable period" means—

(a) in relation to accommodation in a hospital, 28 days, and

(b) in relation to accommodation in a care home, 8 weeks.

[(10) For the purposes of subsection (1), a person appointed under Part 10 of Schedule A1 to be P's representative is not, by virtue of that appointment, engaged in providing care or treatment for P in a professional capacity or for remuneration.]

AMENDMENTS

Subss.(2A) and (10) were inserted by the Mental Health Act 2007 s.50(7), Sch.9, Pt.1, para.4.

Sub.(7) was substituted by SI 2010/813 art.17(3).

1–370

DEFINITIONS

"Mental Health Act": s.64(1)

"independent mental capacity act advocate": s.64(1)

1–371

GENERAL NOTE

This section applies if a NHS body intends to arrange for P to be accommodated in a hospital (either NHS or private) or a care home for a period likely to exceed 28 days (for a hospital) or eight weeks (for a care home), or for P to be moved between such accommodation, and there is no-one apart from a professional or paid carer for the NHS body to consult in determining what would be in P's best interests (subss.(1) and (9)). In this situation the NHS body must instruct an IMCA to represent P and must take into account any information given, or submissions made, by the IMCA when a decision is made about what arrangements to make for P (subss.(3) and (5)). Such consultation need not take place if the P is likely to stay in the accommodation for less than the applicable period or if the need for the move is urgent, for example, where P requires an emergency hospital admission, or where a care home place will be lost if P is not moved immediately (subs.(3)). However, the consultation must take place after the arrangements have been made if the NHS body

1–372

subsequently believes that P will be accommodated at the hospital or care home for the applicable period (subs.(4)). Subsections (3) and (4) do not apply if a person listed in s.40 is available to be consulted. This section does not apply if an IMCA has to be appointed under s.39A or 39C (subs.2A). It will also not apply if P is accommodated in the hospital or the care home as a result of an obligation imposed on him or her under the Mental Health Act 1983 (subs.(2)). It will apply to decisions about providing accommodation for P if P is about to be discharged from detention under the 1983 Act.

Where an NHS body has made arrangements as to P's accommodation under this section and it is then proposed to review those arrangements, an IMCA may (not must) be instructed to represent P at the review: see the Mental Capacity Act 2005 (Independent Mental Capacity Advocates) (Expansion of Role) Regulations 2006 (SI 2006/2883) reg.3. The equivalent provision for Wales is the Mental Capacity Act 2005 (Independent Mental Capacity Advocates) (Wales) Regulations 2007 (SI 2007/852 (W.77)) reg.8.

Proper records should be taken by the responsible authority of how the IMCA's representations have been taken into account and, where relevant, the reasons for disagreeing with or ignoring the representations. Where a disagreement arises, every effort must be made to resolve the disagreement at the earliest possible stage, where necessary using the authority's dispute resolution or complaint's procedure. If the IMCA continues to believe that either the proposed or present placement is not in the best interests of P, he or she could seek advice from a solicitor to ascertain whether the decision could be subject to a legal challenge. Under reg.7 of the Mental Capacity Act 2005 (Independent Mental Capacity Advocates) (General) Regulations 2005 (SI 2006/1832), once a decision has been made about P in a matter where an IMCA has been instructed, the IMCA "has the same rights to challenge the decision as he would have if he were a person (other than an IMCA) engaged in caring for P or interested in his welfare". Challenges can include the decision that the person lacks capacity. For Wales, see SI 2007/852 (W.77) reg.7.

The Social Care Institute for Excellence has published *Independent Mental Capacity Advocate involvement in accommodation and care reviews* (2010) which can be accessed at: *www.scie.org.uk/publications/guides/guide39/about.asp.*

Subsection (1)

1–373   NHS BODY.   See subs.(8). Paragraphs 10.10 to 10.12 of the *Code of Practice* state:

> "For decisions about admission to accommodation in hospital for 28 days or more, the responsible body will be the NHS body that manages the hospital. For admission to an independent or voluntary sector hospital for 28 days or more, the responsible body will be the NHS organisation arranging and funding the person's care. The independent or voluntary hospital must have arrangements in place with the NHS organisation to ensure that an IMCA can be appointed without delay.
>
> For decisions about moves into long term accommodation (for eight weeks or longer), or about a change of accommodation, the responsible body will be either:
>
> - the NHS body that proposes the move or change of accommodation (e.g. a nursing home), or
> - the local authority that has carried out an assessment of the person under the NHS and Community Care Act 1990 and decided the move may be necessary.
>
> Sometimes NHS organisations and local authorities will make decisions together about moving a person into long-term care. In these cases, the organisation that must instruct the IMCA is the one that is ultimately responsible for the decision to move the person. The IMCA to be instructed is the one who works wherever the person is at the time that the person needs support and representation."

HOSPITAL.   See subs.(7).

CARE HOME.   See subs.(6).

PERSON. Including a person who is in prison (*Code of Practice*, para.10.73).

PROFESSIONAL CAPACITY OR FOR REMUNERATION. See subs.(10).

APPROPRIATE. See the note to s.37(1)(b).

Subsection (2)

OBLIGATION IMPOSED ON HIM UNDER THE MENTAL HEALTH ACT. Including being **1–374** detained in hospital under the Mental Health Act 1983. Other obligations under the 1983 Act include a condition imposed by a tribunal under s.73 of the Act requiring the patient to reside at a particular place, a similar requirement imposed by the patient's guardian under s.8 of the Act, or a condition attached to the patient's leave of absence granted under s.17 of the Act requiring him to reside at a particular address. Such placements are excluded because the Mental Health Act provides its own safeguards for patients.

An IMCA should be instructed if it is proposed that P will remain in hospital for more that 28 days as an informal patient after being discharged from detention.

Subsection (3)

APPLICABLE PERIOD. See subs.(9). **1–375**

Subsection (4)

BEGINNING WITH. Including the day on which the accommodation was first provided **1–376** (*Zoan v Rouamba* [2000] 2 All E.R. 620 CA).

Subsection (8)

See the note on s.37(7). **1–377**

Provision of accommodation by local authority

39.—(1) This section applies if a local authority propose to make arrange- **1–378** ments—

(a) for the provision of residential accommodation for a person (P) who lacks capacity to agree to the arrangements, or

(b) for a change in P's residential accommodation,

and are satisfied that there is no person, other than one engaged in providing care or treatment for P in a professional capacity or for remuneration, whom it would be appropriate for them to consult in determining what would be in P's best interests.

[(1A) But this section applies only if—

(a) in the case of a local authority in England, subsection (1B) applies;

(b) in the case of a local authority in Wales, subsection (2) applies.]

[(1B) This subsection applies if the accommodation is to be provided in accordance with—

(a) Part 1 of the Care Act 2014, or

(b) section 117 of the Mental Health Act.]

(2) [This subsection applies] if the accommodation is to be provided in accordance with—

(a) section 21 or 29 of the National Assistance Act 1948 (c. 29), or

(b) section 117 of the Mental Health Act,

as the result of a decision taken by the local authority under section 47 of the National Health Service and Community Care Act 1990 (c.19).

(3) This section does not apply if P is accommodated as a result of an obligation imposed on him under the Mental Health Act.

[(3A) And this section does not apply if—

(a) an independent mental capacity advocate must be appointed under section 39A or 39C (whether or not by the local authority) to represent P, and

(b) the place in which P is to be accommodated under the arrangements referred to in this section is the relevant hospital or care home under the authorisation referred to in that section.]

(4) Before making the arrangements, the local authority must instruct an independent mental capacity advocate to represent P unless they are satisfied that—

(a) the accommodation is likely to be provided for a continuous period of less than 8 weeks, or

(b) the arrangements need to be made as a matter of urgency.

(5) If the local authority—

(a) did not instruct an independent mental capacity advocate to represent P before making the arrangements because they were satisfied that subsection (4)(a) or (b) applied, but

(b) subsequently have reason to believe that the accommodation is likely to be provided for a continuous period that will end 8 weeks or more after the day on which accommodation was first provided in accordance with the arrangements,

they must instruct an independent mental capacity advocate to represent P.

(6) The local authority must, in deciding what arrangements to make for P, take into account any information given, or submissions made, by the independent mental capacity advocate.

[(7) For the purposes of subsection (1), a person appointed under Part 10 of Schedule A1 to be P's representative is not, by virtue of that appointment, engaged in providing care or treatment for P in a professional capacity or for remuneration.]

AMENDMENTS

1–379   Subss.(1A) and (1B) were inserted, and the words in square brackets in subs.(2) were substituted, by SI 2015/914 art.2, Sch., para.79.

Subss.(3A) and (7) were inserted by the Mental Health Act 2007 s.50(7), Sch.9, Pt.1, para.5.

DEFINITIONS

1–380   "local authority": s.64(1)
"treatment": s.64(1)
"Mental Health Act": s.64(1)
"independent mental capacity act advocate": s.64(1)

GENERAL NOTE

1–381   This section applies if a local authority in England (for Wales see subs.(2)) intends to arrange for P to be provided with long-stay residential accommodation provided under Part 1 of the Care Act 2014 (c.23) or s.117 of the Mental Health Act 1983 (c.20), or for the accommodation to be changed, and there is no-one apart from a professional or paid carer for the authority to consult in determining what would be in P's best interests (subss.(1), (1A) and (1B)). In this situation the authority must instruct an IMCA to represent P and any information given, or submissions made, by the IMCA must be taken into account when a decision is made about what arrangements to make for P (subss.(4) and (6)). Such consultation need not take place if the P is likely to stay in the accommodation for less than eight weeks or if the need for the accommodation is urgent (subs.(4)). However, the consultation must take place after the placement has been effected if the authority subsequently believes that the accommodation will be provided for P for at least eight weeks (subs.(5)). Subsections (4) and (5) do not apply if a person listed in s.40 is available to be consulted. This section does not apply if an IMCA has to be appointed under s.39A or 39C (subs.(3A)) or if the accommodation is provided as a result of an obligation imposed on P under the 1983 Act (subs.(3)).

Where a local authority has made arrangements as to P's accommodation under this section and it is then proposed to review those arrangements, an IMCA may (not must) be instructed to represent P at the review: see the Mental Capacity Act 2005 (Independent Mental Capacity Advocates) (Expansion of Role) Regulations 2006 (SI 2006/2883) reg.3. The equivalent provision for Wales is the Mental Capacity Act 2005 (Independent Mental Capacity Advocates) (Wales) Regulations 2007 (SI 2007/852 (W.77)) reg.8. Department of Health guidance, *Prioritising need in the context of Putting People First* (2010), states that it is good practice for local authorities to undertake a review within three months of a person moving to new accommodation or where there have been other major changes to the support plan. Otherwise, reviews should take place at least annually (para.144). The guidance also states that adults lacking capacity are likely to need more frequent monitoring arrangements than other service users (para.146).

Proper records should be taken by the responsible authority of how the IMCA's submissions have been taken into account and, where relevant, the reasons for disagreeing with or ignoring the submissions. Where a disagreement arises, every effort must be made to resolve the disagreement at the earliest possible stage, where necessary using the authority's dispute resolution or complaint's procedure. If the IMCA continue to believe that the proposed placement is not in the best interests of P, he or she could seek advice from a solicitor to ascertain whether the decision could be subject to a legal challenge. Under reg.7 of the Mental Capacity Act 2005 (Independent Mental Capacity Advocates) (General) Regulations 2005 (SI 2006/1832), once a decision has been made about P in a matter where an IMCA has been instructed, the IMCA "has the same rights to challenge the decision as he would have if he were a person (other than an IMCA) engaged in caring for P or interested in his welfare". Challenges can include the decision that the person lacks capacity. For Wales, see SI 2007/852 (W.77) reg.7.

The Social Care Institute for Excellence has published *Independent Mental Capacity Advocate involvement in accommodation and care reviews* (2010) which can be accessed at: *www.scie.org.uk/publications/guides/guide39/about.asp.*

Subsection (1)

LOCAL AUTHORITY.   See the note on "NHS body" in s.37(1).   **1–382**

RESIDENTIAL ACCOMODATION.   In *R. (on the application of Batantu) v Islington LBC*   **1–383**
(2001) 4 C.C.L. Rep. 445, Henriques J. said that the meaning of accommodation under the 1948 Act (now see Pt 1 of the Care Act 2014) is wide and flexible and embraces care homes, ordinary and sheltered housing, housing association and other registered social housing, and private sector housing which may have been purchased by the local authority. It would also include hostel accommodation.

PERSON.   Including a person who is in prison (*Code of Practice*, para.10.73).

PROFESSIONAL CAPACITY OR FOR REMUNERATION.   See subs.(7).

APPROPRIATE.   See the note to s.37(1)(b).

Subsection (3)
See the note on s.38(2).   **1–384**

Subsection (4)
MUST INSTRUCT.   This requirement will not be satisfied in the absence of a wide range   **1–385**
of staff being aware of the local authority's duty to instruct an IMCA.

[Person becomes subject to Schedule A1

1–386   **39A.**—(1) This section applies if—

    (a) a person ("P") becomes subject to Schedule A1, and

    (b) the managing authority of the relevant hospital or care home are satisfied that there is no person, other than one engaged in providing care or treatment for P in a professional capacity or for remuneration, whom it would be appropriate to consult in determining what would be in P's best interests.

(2) The managing authority must notify the supervisory body that this section applies.

(3) The supervisory body must instruct an independent mental capacity advocate to represent P.

(4) Schedule A1 makes provision about the role of an independent mental capacity advocate appointed under this section.

(5) This section is subject to paragraph 161 of Schedule A1.

(6) For the purposes of subsection (1), a person appointed under Part 10 of Schedule A1 to be P's representative is not, by virtue of that appointment, engaged in providing care or treatment for P in a professional capacity or for remuneration.]

AMENDMENT

1–387   This section was inserted by the Mental Health Act 2007 s.50(7), Sch.9, Pt.1, para.6.

DEFINITIONS

1–388   "independent mental capacity advocate": s.64(1).
"treatment": s.64(1).

GENERAL NOTE

1–389   This section requires a supervisory body identified under the deprivation of liberty procedure set out in Sch.A1 to appoint an IMCA for P if the managing authority has notified it that: (1) P is "subject to Sch.A1" and (2) there is no appropriate person (other than one engaged in providing care or treatment for P in a professional capacity or for remuneration) to consult in determining P's best interests. The circumstances in which P becomes subject to Sch.A1 are set out in s.39B.

The general functions of an IMCA are set out in s.36 and SI 2006/1832. An IMCA who has been appointed under this section is given additional functions in paras 57, 58, 69(7)–(8), 82, 86, 90, 132, 135 and 136 of Sch.A1. With one exception, once a representative has been appointed under Pt 10 of Sch.A1 the functions imposed on the s.39A IMCA cease to apply (subs.(6)). The exception is that the power given to the IMCA to make an application to the court to exercise its jurisdiction under s.21A in connection with the giving of a standard authorisation is retained (ibid. para.161).

The duty to appoint an IMCA under this section does not apply if a person listed in s.40 is available to be consulted.

The Social Care Institute for Excellence has published *IMCA and paid relevant person's representative roles in the Mental Capacity Act Deprivation of Liberty Safeguards* (2011) which can be accessed at: *www.scie.org.uk/publications/guides/guide41/*.

[Section 39A: supplementary provision

1–390   **39B.**—(1) This section applies for the purposes of section 39A.

(2) P becomes subject to Schedule A1 in any of the following cases.

(3) The first case is where an urgent authorisation is given in relation to P under paragraph 76(2) of Schedule A1 (urgent authorisation given before request made for standard authorisation).

(4) The second case is where the following conditions are met.

(5) The first condition is that a request is made under Schedule A1 for a standard authorisation to be given in relation to P ("the requested authorisation").

(6) The second condition is that no urgent authorisation was given under paragraph 76(2) of Schedule A1 before that request was made.

(7) The third condition is that the requested authorisation will not be in force on or before, or immediately after, the expiry of an existing standard authorisation.

(8) The expiry of a standard authorisation is the date when the authorisation is expected to cease to be in force.

(9) The third case is where, under paragraph 69 of Schedule A1, the supervisory body select a person to carry out an assessment of whether or not the relevant person is a detained resident.]

AMENDMENT
This section was inserted by the Mental Health Act 2007 s.50(7), Sch.9, Pt.1, para.6.   **1–391**

GENERAL NOTE
This section identifies the three circumstances that determine when P becomes "subject   **1–392**
to Schedule A1" for the purposes of s.39A. An account of the Sch.A1 procedure can be
found in Pt 2.

[Person unrepresented whilst subject to Schedule A1
    39C.—(1) This section applies if—   **1–393**
    (a) an authorisation under Schedule A1 is in force in relation to a person ("P"),
    (b) the appointment of a person as P's representative ends in accordance with
         regulations made under Part 10 of Schedule A1, and
    (c) the managing authority of the relevant hospital or care home are satisfied
         that there is no person, other than one engaged in providing care or treatment for P in a professional capacity
or for remuneration, whom it would be appropriate to consult in determining what
would be in P's best interests.

(2) The managing authority must notify the supervisory body that this section
applies.

(3) The supervisory body must instruct an independent mental capacity advocate to represent P.

(4) Paragraph 159 of Schedule A1 makes provision about the role of an independent mental capacity advocate appointed under this section.

(5) The appointment of an independent mental capacity advocate under this
section ends when a new appointment of a person as P's representative is made in
accordance with Part 10 of Schedule A1.

(6) For the purposes of subsection (1), a person appointed under Part 10
of Schedule A1 to be P's representative is not, by virtue of that appointment,
engaged in providing care or treatment for P in a professional capacity or for
remuneration.]

AMENDMENT
This section was inserted by the Mental Health Act 2007 s.50(7), Sch.9, Pt.1, para.6.   **1–394**

DEFINITION
"independent mental capacity advocate": s.64(1).   **1–395**

GENERAL NOTE

1–396   This section requires a supervisory body identified under the deprivation of liberty procedure set out in Sch.A1 to appoint an IMCA for P if a managing authority has notified it that:
(1) P is subject to Sch.A1; (2) the appointment of P's Part 10 representative ends; and (3)
there is no appropriate person (other than one engaged in providing care or treatment for P
in a professional capacity or for remuneration) to consult in determining P's best interests.

The circumstances in which P becomes subject to Sch.A1 are set out in s.39B. An IMCA
will only be appointed under this section when a standard authorisation is in place because a
Part 10 representative is only appointed following such an authorisation (Sch.A1, para.139).
The appointment will come to an end once a new Part 10 representative has been appointed.

The general functions of an IMCA are set out in s.36 and SI 2006/1832. An IMCA who
has been appointed under this section will also perform the functions of the Part 10 representative until a new one is appointed (Sch.A1, para.159(2)).

The duty to appoint an IMCA under this section does not apply if a person listed in s.40
is available to be consulted.

[Person subject to Schedule A1 without paid representative

1–397   **39D.**—(1) This section applies if—

(a)   an authorisation under Schedule A1 is in force in relation to a person ("P"),

(b)   P has a representative ("R") appointed under Part 10 of Schedule A1, and

(c)   R is not being paid under regulations under Part 10 of Schedule A1 for
acting as P's representative.

(2) The supervisory body must instruct an independent mental capacity advocate to represent P in any of the following cases.

(3) The first case is where P makes a request to the supervisory body to instruct
an advocate.

(4) The second case is where R makes a request to the supervisory body to
instruct an advocate.

(5) The third case is where the supervisory body have reason to believe one or
more of the following—

(a)   that, without the help of an advocate, P and R would be unable to exercise
one or both of the relevant rights;

(b)   that P and R have each failed to exercise a relevant right when it would
have been reasonable to exercise it;

(c)   that P and R are each unlikely to exercise a relevant right when it would be
reasonable to exercise it.

(6) The duty in subsection (2) is subject to section 39E.

(7) If an advocate is appointed under this section, the advocate is, in particular,
to take such steps as are practicable to help P and R to understand the following
matters—

(a)   the effect of the authorisation;

(b)   the purpose of the authorisation;

(c)   the duration of the authorisation;

(d)   any conditions to which the authorisation is subject;

(e)   the reasons why each assessor who carried out an assessment in connection
with the request for the authorisation, or in connection with a review of the
authorisation, decided that P met the qualifying requirement in question;

(f)   the relevant rights;

(g)   how to exercise the relevant rights.

(8) The advocate is, in particular, to take such steps as are practicable to help
P or R—

(a) to exercise the right to apply to court, if it appears to the advocate that P or R wishes to exercise that right, or

(b) to exercise the right of review, if it appears to the advocate that P or R wishes to exercise that right.

(9) If the advocate helps P or R to exercise the right of review—

(a) the advocate may make submissions to the supervisory body on the question of whether a qualifying requirement is reviewable;

(b) the advocate may give information, or make submissions, to any assessor carrying out a review assessment.

(10) In this section—

"relevant rights" means—

(a) the right to apply to court, and

(b) the right of review;

"right to apply to court" means the right to make an application to the court to exercise its jurisdiction under section 21A;

"right of review" means the right under Part 8 of Schedule A1 to request a review.]

AMENDMENT

This section was inserted by the Mental Health Act 2007 s.50(7), Sch.9, Pt.1, para.6. **1–398**

DEFINITION

"independent mental capacity advocate": s.64(1). **1–399**

GENERAL NOTE

Where an authorisation under Sch.A1 is in force in relation to P and P has a Part 10 rep- **1–400**
resentative (R) who is not being paid for acting as such, the supervisory body must instruct
an IMCA to act for P if:

(i) either P or R make a request to the supervisory body to instruct an IMCA; or

(ii) the supervisory body have reason to believe that without the help of an advocate, P and R would be unable to exercise one or both of the relevant rights as defined in subs.(10), or have failed to exercise a relevant right when it would have been reasonable to exercise it, or would be unlikely to exercise a relevant right when it would be reasonable to exercise it.

Unlike the other circumstances under the Act in which a duty to appoint an IMCA arises, the trigger for the appointment under this section is not expressed as being the fact that there is no other person who it would be appropriate to consult in determining what would be in P's best interests.

In *AJ v A Local Authority* [2015] EWCOP 5, Baker J. said at para.138 that an IMCA appointed under this section "must act with diligence and urgency to ensure that any challenge to an authorisation under Schedule A1 is brought before the court expeditiously. Failure to do so will lead to the evaporation of P's [rights under art.5 of the European Convention on Human Rights]".

If a supervisory body has already appointed an IMCA under this provision at the request of R or because they had reason to believe one or more of the things set out in subs.(5), they must appoint a further advocate if P requests it (s.39E).

Apart from the general functions of the IMCA set out in s.36 and SI 2006/1832, an IMCA appointed under this section has the additional functions set out in subss.(7) to (9) and in Sch.A1, paras 49, 95. In *AJ*, above, Baker J. said at para.108:

"[T]he functions of a s.39D IMCA are as set out in that section, as supplemented by Sch.A1, and concern matters relating to the deprivation of liberty provisions under the Schedule. An IMCA appointed under section 39D does not have a broader, general role of representing or supporting P, and is not under a general duty to assist in determining what is in P's best interests but, rather, to perform the specific functions set out in s.39D(7), (8) and (9)."

The duty to appoint an IMCA under this section does not apply if a person listed in s.40 is available to be consulted.

Subsection (5)

1–401   REASON TO BELIEVE.   The supervisory body must assess whether P and R are able to exercise their rights to request a review of the authorisation or to make an application to the court under s.21A.

Subsection (8)

1–402   The IMCA must assist P or R to exercise their rights even if such action is not considered to be in their best interests.

[Limitation on duty to instruct advocate under section 39D

1–403   **39E.**—(1) This section applies if an advocate is already representing P in accordance with an instruction under section 39D.

(2) Section 39D(2) does not require another advocate to be instructed, unless the following conditions are met.

(3) The first condition is that the existing advocate was instructed—

(a)   because of a request by R, or

(b)   because the supervisory body had reason to believe one or more of the things in section 39D(5).

(4) The second condition is that the other advocate would be instructed because of a request by P.]

AMENDMENT

1–404   This section was inserted by the Mental Health Act 2007 s.50(7), Sch.9, Pt.1, para.6.

GENERAL NOTE

1–405   See the General Note to s.39D.

[Exceptions

1–406   **40.**—[(1)] The duty imposed by section 37(3), 38(3) or (4) [, 39(4) or (5), 39A(3), 39C(3) or 39D(2)] does not apply where there is—

(a)   a person nominated by P (in whatever manner) as a person to be consulted on matters to which that duty relates,

(b)   a donee of a lasting power of attorney created by P who is authorised to make decisions in relation to those matters, or

(c)   a deputy appointed by the court for P with power to make decisions in relation to those matters.]

[(2) A person appointed under Part 10 of Schedule A1 to be P's representative is not, by virtue of that appointment, a person nominated by P as a person to be consulted in matters to which a duty mentioned in subsection (1) relates.]

AMENDMENT

1–407   This section was substituted by the Mental Health Act 2007 s.49. The amendments to it were made by s.50(7), Sch.9, Pt 1, para.7 of that Act.

DEFINITIONS

1–408   "lasting power of attorney": s.64(1)

"deputy": s.64(1)

GENERAL NOTE

This section confirms that the independent mental advocacy scheme does not apply **1–409** where there is a suitable person who can be consulted about P's best interests. An IMCA would have to be appointed if the person had not been either nominated or authorised to be consulted about, or to make decisions in relation to, the relevant matter.

Paragraph (a)

The nomination may be written or oral. The decision-maker must be satisfied that the **1–410** nomination was made when P was mentally capable and that the nominee is willing to be consulted.

In *AJ v A Local Authority* [2015] EWCOP 5, Baker J. held at para.112 where P has executed an LPA, the duty to appoint an IMCA under s.39D is not excluded under this paragraph unless the donee of the LPA is authorised to make decisions in relation to the matters in section 39D(7) and (8). His Lordship said at para.115:

> "In my judgment, the power given under a standard form LPA giving donees the power to make decisions concerning health and welfare or property and financial affairs do not include the power to make decisions relating to the matters to which the duty under section 39D(2) relates."

Power to adjust role of independent mental capacity advocate

41.—(1) The appropriate authority may make regulations— **1–411**
(a) expanding the role of independent mental capacity advocates in relation to persons who lack capacity, and
(b) adjusting the obligation to make arrangements imposed by section 35.
(2) The regulations may, in particular—
(a) prescribe circumstances (different to those set out in sections 37, 38 and 39) in which an independent mental capacity advocate must, or circumstances in which one may, be instructed by a person of a prescribed description to represent a person who lacks capacity, and
(b) include provision similar to any made by section 37, 38, 39 or 40.
(3) "Appropriate authority" has the same meaning as in section 35.

DEFINITIONS

"independent mental capacity advocate": s.64(1) **1–412**

GENERAL NOTE

This section provides that scope of the independent mental advocacy scheme can **1–413** be extended by regulations made by the Secretary of State or the Welsh Ministers. The Mental Capacity Act 2005 (Independent Mental Capacity Advocates) (Expansion of Role) Regulations 2006 (SI 2006/2883), which are reproduced in Part 3, have been made under this section. The equivalent provision for Wales is the Mental Capacity Act 2005 (Independent Mental Capacity Advocates) (Wales) Regulations 2007 (SI 2007/852 (W.77)) regs 8 and 9. These regulations do not prevent an NHS body or local authority from instructing an IMCA in other circumstances. However, the regulations only provide authority for the Secretary of State or the Welsh Ministers to make arrangements (i.e. provide funding) for IMCAs to be available in the circumstances set out in the regulations.

The Mental Capacity Act 2005 (Independent Mental Capacity Advocates (General) Regulations 2006 (SI 2006/1832), which are considered in the notes to s.37, apply where an IMCA has been instructed under regulations made by virtue of this section (ibid., reg.2(2)).

Subsection (1)

REGULATIONS. Regulations made under this power are subject to the affirmative resolu- **1–414** tion procedure (s.65(4)).

Miscellaneous and supplementary

Codes of practice

1–415   **42.**—(1) The Lord Chancellor must prepare and issue one or more codes of practice—

(a) for the guidance of persons assessing whether a person has capacity in relation to any matter,

(b) for the guidance of persons acting in connection with the care or treatment of another person (see section 5),

(c) for the guidance of donees of lasting powers of attorney,

(d) for the guidance of deputies appointed by the court,

(e) for the guidance of persons carrying out research in reliance on any provision made by or under this Act (and otherwise with respect to sections 30 to 34),

(f) for the guidance of independent mental capacity advocates,

[(fa) for the guidance of persons exercising functions under Schedule A1,

(fb) for the guidance of representatives appointed under Part 10 of Schedule A1,]

(g) with respect to the provisions of sections 24 to 26 (advance decisions and apparent advance decisions), and

(h) with respect to such other matters concerned with this Act as he thinks fit.

(2) The Lord Chancellor may from time to time revise a code.

(3) The Lord Chancellor may delegate the preparation or revision of the whole or any part of a code so far as he considers expedient.

(4) It is the duty of a person to have regard to any relevant code if he is acting in relation to a person who lacks capacity and is doing so in one or more of the following ways—

(a) as the donee of a lasting power of attorney,

(b) as a deputy appointed by the court,

(c) as a person carrying out research in reliance on any provision made by or under this Act (see sections 30 to 34),

(d) as an independent mental capacity advocate,

[(da) in the exercise of functions under Schedule A1,

(db) as a representative appointed under Part 10 of Schedule A1,]

(e) in a professional capacity,

(f) for remuneration.

(5) If it appears to a court or tribunal conducting any criminal or civil proceedings that—

(a) a provision of a code, or

(b) a failure to comply with a code,

is relevant to a question arising in the proceedings, the provision or failure must be taken into account in deciding the question.

(6) A code under subsection (1)(d) may contain separate guidance for deputies appointed by virtue of paragraph 1(2) of Schedule 5(functions of deputy conferred on receiver appointed under the Mental Health Act).

(7) In this section and in section 43, "code" means a code prepared or revised under this section.

AMENDMENTS

1–416   The words in square brackets in subss.(1) and (4) were inserted by the Mental Health Act 2007 s.50(7), Sch.9, Pt.1, para.8.

DEFINITIONS **1–417**
  "treatment": s.64(1)
  "lasting power of attorney": s.64(1)
  "deputy": s.64(1)
  "the court": s.64(1)
  "independent mental capacity advocate": s.64(1)
  "advance decision": s.64(1)
  "Mental Health Act": s.64(1)

GENERAL NOTE

This section requires the Lord Chancellor to publish a Code of Practice (or Codes of **1–418** Practice) to address the issues set out in subs.(1). The Code can be revised (subs.(2)). These responsibilities may be delegated (subs.(3)). The Code sets out how the legal rules contained in the Act and the associated regulations should work in practice. Donees, deputies, professionals, researchers, independent mental capacity advocates and paid workers acting on behalf of a person who lacks capacity must have regard to the Code (subs.(4)) The Code can be used as evidence in court or tribunal proceedings and, if relevant, will be taken into account in the determination (subs.(5)). However, no legal liability arises from a breach of the Code itself.

A *Code of Practice* was laid before Parliament in draft in February 2007, pursuant to this section and s.43 and was approved in April 2007. The Introduction to the Code states at p.1:

> "The Act does not impose a legal duty on anyone to 'comply' with the Code – it should be viewed as guidance rather than instruction. But if they have not followed relevant guidance contained in the Code then they will be expected to give good reasons why they have departed from it."

The *Code of Practice* can be accessed at the Department of Health's website (see Appendix B). A supplement to the Code, dealing with the deprivation of liberty safeguards, was published in July 2008 and is reproduced in Part 5.

Subsection (1)

GUIDANCE. In *R. v Secretary of State for the Environment Ex p. Lancashire* CC [1994] **1–419** 4 All E.R. 165 at 173, Jowitt J. said:

> "The concept of guidance goes beyond simply providing a checklist of factors which should be taken into account. To guide someone is to lead, steer or point someone in a particular direction."

Subsection (1) para.(b)

Note the scope of this category, which includes informal and family carers. Such carers **1–420** are not placed under an obligation to "have regard" to the Code (subs.(4)). The position of informal and family carers was examined by the Joint Committee:

> "The position is different with regard to guidance issued to assist non-professional or informal decision makers, such as family members and unpaid carers acting under [s.5]. It is essential that family members and carers carrying out such responsibilities are provided with appropriate guidance and assistance, both to promote good practice and also to impress upon them the seriousness of their actions and the need to be accountable for them. We accept that it would be inappropriate to impose on them a strict requirement to act in accordance with the Code of Practice" (Vol.1, para.232).

While such an approach is understandable, the Act places unrealistic expectations on lay carers in that it does not recognise any distinction between lay and professional carers when it comes to adherence to the principles set out in s.1, the requirement to assess capacity under ss.2 and 3, and the determination of best interests under s.4. The Introduction to the Code states that lay carers "should follow the guidance in the Code as far as they are aware of it" (p.2).

Subsection (1) para.(c)

1–421   Although an attorney acting under an Enduring Power of Attorney is not placed under an obligation to have regard to the Code, he or she should use it as guidance.

Subsection (2)

1–422   The Code will "be revised fairly frequently", per the Parliamentary Under-Secretary of State (*Hansard*, HL Vol.669, col.758). To date, no revision to the Code or its supplement has been made.

Subsection (4)

1–423   HAVE REGARD TO.   The Introduction to the Code states at p.2:

> "Certain categories of people are legally required to 'have regard to' relevant guidance in the Code of Practice. That means they must be aware of the Code of Practice when acting or making decisions on behalf of someone who lacks capacity to make a decision for themselves, and they should be able to explain how they had regard to the Code when acting or making decisions."

In *R. (on the application of Munjaz) v Mersey Care National Health Service Trust* [2005] UKHL 58, the House of Lords considered the legal status of the *Code of Practice* issued pursuant to s.118 of the Mental Health Act 1983. Although there are differences in the wording of s.118 and this section, the decision in *Munjaz* can be regarded as a clear indication of the approach that a court might adopt when interpreting the status of the Code issued under the Act. This was confirmed by Roderic Wood J. in *SBC v PBA* [2011] EWHC 2580 (Fam) at para.67. In *Munjaz* it was contended that the policy of Ashworth Hospital relating to the seclusion of patients was unlawful because it provided for less frequent medical reviews, particularly after the first week of seclusion, than that laid down in the Mental Health Act *Code of Practice*. Ashworth had also adopted a definition of seclusion that differed from that set out in the Code. It was held that:

1. The Code does not have the binding effect which a statutory provision or a statutory instrument would have. It is what it purports to be, guidance and not instruction.
2. The guidance in the Code should be given great weight. Although it is not instruction, the Code is much more than mere advice which an addressee is free to follow or not as it chooses.
3. The Code contains guidance which should be considered with great care, and should be followed unless there are cogent reasons for not doing so. The requirement that cogent reasons must be shown for any departure sets a high standard which is not easily satisfied. The reasons must be spelled out clearly, logically and convincingly.
4. In reviewing any departures from the Code, the court should scrutinise the reasons given for departure with the intensity which the importance and sensitivity of the subject matters requires.
5. For the purpose of determining whether Ashworth's policy was compatible with the European Convention on Human Rights (ECHR), the Code is irrelevant: if the policy is incompatible, consistency with the Code will not save it; if it is compatible, it requires no support from the Code.

The following circumstances could provide cogent reasons for not following the guidance contained in the Code issued under this section:

1. The best interests of P (or a group of persons who share particular well-defined characteristics) would not be satisfied if the guidance was followed.
2. There has been a determination of the High Court that a particular aspect of the guidance is not legally accurate.
3. Legal advice has been received which casts a significant doubt on the legal correctness of an aspect of the guidance.
4. Following the guidance would involve breaching P's ECHR rights.

5. A judgment is taken that a particular aspect of the guidance should not be followed for safety or other legitimate reason.

If a person fails to comply with the guidance contained in the Code, he or she must be prepared to give reasons to explain the non-compliance. It would be sensible for a contemporaneous record of such reasons to be made.

Subsection (4) para.(f)

For REMUNERATION.   For example, a care assistant who works in a care home where the residents lack capacity.   **1–424**

Codes of practice: procedure

43.—(1) Before preparing or revising a code, the Lord Chancellor must consult—   **1–425**
   (a) the National Assembly for Wales, and
   (b) such other persons as he considers appropriate.
   (2) The Lord Chancellor may not issue a code unless—
   (a) a draft of the code has been laid by him before both Houses of Parliament, and
   (b) the 40 day period has elapsed without either House resolving not to approve the draft.
   (3) The Lord Chancellor must arrange for any code that he has issued to be published in such a way as he considers appropriate for bringing it to the attention of persons likely to be concerned with its provisions.
   (4) "40 day period", in relation to the draft of a proposed code, means—
   (a) if the draft is laid before one House on a day later than the day on which it is laid before the other House, the period of 40 days beginning with the later of the two days;
   (b) in any other case, the period of 40 days beginning with the day on which it is laid before each House.
   (5) In calculating the period of 40 days, no account is to be taken of any period during which Parliament is dissolved or prorogued or during which both Houses are adjourned for more than 4 days.

GENERAL NOTE

This section sets out the procedure for issuing and revising the *Code of Practice* and requires the Lord Chancellor to publish the Code in an appropriate format.   **1–426**

Subsection (1)(a)

The functions of the National Assembly for Wales are performed by the Welsh Ministers (Government of Wales Act 2006 s.162, Sch.11, para.30).   **1–427**

Subsection (2)

This procedure is known as the "negative resolution" procedure.   **1–428**

Ill-treatment or neglect

44.—(1) Subsection (2) applies if a person (D)—   **1–429**
   (a) has the care of a person (P) who lacks, or whom D reasonably believes to lack, capacity,
   (b) is the donee of a lasting power of attorney, or an enduring power of attorney (within the meaning of Schedule 4), created by P, or
   (c) is a deputy appointed by the court for P.

(2) D is guilty of an offence if he ill-treats or wilfully neglects P.

(3) A person guilty of an offence under this section is liable—

(a) on summary conviction, to imprisonment for a term not exceeding 12 months or a fine not exceeding the statutory maximum or both;

(b) on conviction on indictment, to imprisonment for a term not exceeding 5 years or a fine or both.

DEFINITIONS

1–430 "lasting power of attorney": s.64(1)
"deputy": s.64(1)
"the court": s.64(1)

GENERAL NOTE

1–431 This section creates the offence of ill-treatment or wilful neglect of a person who lacks capacity or is believed to lack capacity. Its purpose was described by Lord Judge C.J. in *R. v Nursing* [2012] EWCA Crim 2521 at para.18:

"The purpose of s.44 of the Act is clear. Those who are in need of care are entitled to protection against ill-treatment or wilful neglect. The question whether they have been so neglected must be examined in the context of the statutory provisions which provide that, to the greatest extent possible, their autonomy should be respected. The evidential difficulties which may arise when this offence is charged do not make it legally uncertain within the principles in *Mirsa* [2005] 1 Cr. App. R 328 and *R v Rimmington: R v Goldstein* [2006] 1 AC 459. On analysis, the offence created by s.44 is not vague. It makes it an offence for an individual responsible for the care of someone who lacks the capacity to care for himself to ill-treat or wilfully to neglect that person. Those in care who still enjoy some level of capacity for making their own decisions are entitled to be protected from wilful neglect which impacts on the areas of their lives over which they lack capacity. However s.44 did not create an absolute offence. Therefore, actions or omissions, or a combination of both, which reflect or are believed to reflect the protected autonomy of the individual needing care do not constitute wilful neglect. Within these clear principles, the issue in an individual prosecution is fact specific."

In its Report, the House of Lords Select Committee welcomed "the Government's commitment to discuss with the Crown Prosecution Service and the Association of Chief Police Officers the need to ensure appropriate use is made of [this section]" and recommended "that the Government initiate a review of whether the offence in [this section] meets the test of legal certainty; and if it does not, to bring forward new legislative provisions" (paras 308, 309).

The standard of proof to be applied in a prosecution under this section was considered in *R. v Hopkins* [2011] EWCA Crim 1513 where it was held that the prosecution must prove (1) to the criminal standard that the defendant ill treated or wilfully neglected a person in his care, and (2) that on a balance of probability that person was a person who at the material time lacked capacity.

In *R. v Newington (Susan)* (1990) 91 Cr. App. R. 247, a case under s.127 of the Mental Health Act 1983, the Court of Appeal said that "ill-treatment" could not be equated with "wilfully to neglect". The court therefore advised the Crown Prosecution Service that, when proceedings were brought, charges of "ill-treatment" and of "wilfully to neglect" should be put in separate counts in the indictment. This ruling applies to proceedings brought under this section. The Crown Prosecution Service has published "Guidance on Prosecuting Crimes against Older People" which can be accessed at: *www.cps.gov.uk/publications/docs/caop_guidance.pdf*.

This section is drafted in broader terms than s.127 of the 1983 Act. Section 127 creates two separate offences that could apply to incapacitated people who are also suffering from a mental disorder within the meaning of s.1 of that Act at the time when the offence was committed. Firstly, under subs.(1) it is an offence for an employee or manager of a hospital, independent hospital or care home to ill-treat or wilfully to neglect an in-patient or out-patient of that hospital or home. Secondly, under subs.(2) it is an offence for a guardian appointed under the 1983 Act or some other person who has the custody or care of a mentally disordered person who is living in the community to ill-treat or wilfully to neglect that person.

The Government rejected recommendation 80 of the Joint Committee that this section be "extended to include the misappropriation of the person's property and financial assets" on the ground that a person who uses the funds of someone who lacks capacity for his own benefit may be prosecuted for the offence of theft and that a new offence of "misappropriation" would be very similar to that offence (*The Government Response to the Scrutiny Committee's Report on the Draft Mental Incapacity Bill*, Cm 6121). A donee of a lasting power of attorney, a deputy appointed by the court or a carer who abuses his or her position could be guilty of the offence of "fraud by abuse of position" under s.4 of the Fraud Act 2006. Section 4 reads:

"(1) A person is in breach of this section if he:
 (a) occupies a position in which he is expected to safeguard, or not act against, the financial interests of another person,
 (b) intends, by means of the abuse of that position
  (i) to make a gain for himself or another, or
  (ii) to cause loss to another or to expose another to a risk of loss.
(2) A person may be regarded as having abused his position even though his conduct consisted of an omission rather than an act."

The English "No Secrets" and the Welsh "In Safe Hands" guidance set out the multi-agency procedures to be followed when a vulnerable adult is believed to be suffering abuse. Abuse is defined as "a violation of an individual's human and civil rights by any other person or persons" (*No Secrets*, para.2.5).

Sections 30 to 41 of the Sexual Offences Act 2003 create a number of offences "against persons with a mental disorder impeding choice".

Dave Sheppard and Gemma Bensley have published a comprehensive analysis of cases brought under this section. The document, "Offences of ill-treatment and/or wilful neglect under the Mental Health Act 1983 and the Mental Capacity Act 2005 in England and Wales" (March, 2014), can be obtained from Dave Sheppard at *www.mhaandmca.co.uk.*

Subsection (1) para.(a)
An offence under this section could be committed if either D is unaware of P's incapacity, or if D's belief that P lacks capacity is incorrect.   **1–432**

CARE. This is not defined. In *Minister of Health v Royal Midlands Counties Home for Incurables at Lemington Spa* [1954] Ch. 530, Denning L.J. defined care as "the homely art of making people comfortable and providing for their well being so far as their condition allows". All those who come within the scope of s.5 would have "the care of" P.

PERSON. Of any age. Incapacity arising solely from the fact that P is not old enough to be considered capable would not qualify as incapacity for the purpose of this section.

REASONABLY BELIEVES. Alison Brammer considers that "reasonably" imputes a degree of objectivity and the word "belief" suggests "more than mere suspicion but less than a requirement to be satisfied" ("Carers and the Mental Capacity Act 2005: Angels permitted, Devils Prosecuted?" [2014] Crim. L.R. 589).

CAPACITY. It was unclear what capacity meant in this context as the functional test of capacity set out in s.3 is not obviously applicable to an offence. This issue was addressed in *R. v Dunn* [2010] EWCA Crim 2935 where it was held that the matter in respect of which capacity was required to be lacking for the purposes of this section was the person's ability to make decisions concerning his or her care. *Dunn* was followed in *R. v Hopkins* [2011] EWCA Crim 1513, where Pitchford L.J. said at para.40:

> "Unconstrained by authority, this court would be minded to accept the submission made on behalf of the appellants that Section 44 (1) (a), read together with Section 2 (1) of the Mental Capacity Act 2005, is so vague that it fails the test of sufficient certainty at common law and under Article 7.1, ECHR. However this court has made a decision upon Section 44 of the Act which binds this court."

The prosecution must prove on a balance of probability that the person was a person who at the material time lacked capacity: see *R. v Hopkins*, above.

Subsection (2)

1–433   ILL-TREATS. The *Code of Practice* states that for

> "a person to be found guilty of ill treatment, they must either:

- have deliberately ill-treated the person, or
- be reckless in the way they were ill-treating the person or not.

> It does not matter whether the behaviour was likely to cause, or actually caused, harm or damage to the victim's health" (para.14.25).

There is Crown Court authority to support the proposition that it is not necessary to establish a course of conduct as a single act, such as slapping a person's face on one occasion, could constitute ill-treatment (*R. v Holmes* [1979] Crim. L.R. 52, Crown Court (Bodmin)). As it is likely that there is no need for the prosecution to show that the treatment in question caused actual injury to the victim, "ill treatment" encompasses a wide range of conduct. It is submitted that for the offence of ill-treatment to be proved, the prosecution would have to prove: (1) deliberate conduct by the accused which could properly be described as ill-treatment irrespective of whether it damaged or threatened to damage the victims health; (2) a guilty mind involving either an appreciation by the accused that he was inexcusably ill-treating a person or that he was reckless as to whether he was inexcusably acting in that way; and (3) that the victim was either a person without capacity or was believed to lack capacity (*R. v Newington* (Susan), above). In *Newington* the court disapproved of a direction given by the trial judge "that violence would inevitably amount to ill-treatment" on the ground that violence necessarily used for the reasonable control of a patient would not amount to ill-treatment.

WILFULLY NEGLECTS. The meaning to be attributed to the expression "wilful neglect" may vary according to the context but generally the expression should be taken to mean that there has been an intentional or purposive omission to do something that the person in question knows he or she has a duty to do (*De Maroussem v Commissioner of Income Tax* [2004] UKPC 43 at para.41: also see the *Code of Practice*, para.14.26). In the context of a verdict of neglect made at a Coroner's inquest, Sir Thomas Bingham MR said that neglect "means a gross failure to provide adequate nourishment or liquid, or provide or procure basic medical attention or shelter or warmth for someone in a dependent position (because of youth, age, illness or incarceration) who cannot provide it for himself. Failure to provide medical attention for a dependent person whose physical condition is such as to show that he obviously needs it may amount to neglect. So it may be if it is the dependent person's mental condition which obviously calls for medical attention (as it would, for example, if a mental nurse observed that a patient had a propensity to swallow razor blades and failed to report this propensity to a doctor, in a case where the patient had no intention to cause himself injury but did thereafter swallow razor blades with fatal results). In both cases the crucial consideration will be what the dependent person's condition, whether physical or mental, appeared to be" (*R. v Humberside and Scunthorpe Coroner, Ex p. Jamieson* [1994] 3 All E.R. 972 at 990, 991).

In *R. v Patel* [2013] EWCA Crim 965, the court held that:

1. Neglect is wilful if a nurse or medical practitioner knows that it is necessary to administer a piece of treatment and deliberately decides not to carry out that treatment, which is within their power but which they cannot face performing. If the practitioner was acting at a time of stress, that would be a matter which the judge could take into account at the time of sentence.
2. The offence can be established even if the decision of the carer not to do something which should have been done was, unknown to the carer, unlikely to have caused any adverse consequences to P.

With regard to point 1, in *R. v Hopkins*, above, the Court of Appeal said, at para.49, that neglect would be proved by a failure to act during any period embraced by the count; this section does not require proof of any particular harm or proof of the risk of any particular harm.

In *R. v Nursing*, above, at para.20, the Court of Appeal held that if a jury were to conclude that the defendant may have been motivated by the wish or sense of obligation to respect the person's autonomy, any area of apparent neglect so motivated would not be *wilful* for the purposes of this offence. The leading case on the term "wilfully" is *R. v Sheppard (James Martin)* [1981] A.C. 394, HL, a case brought under s.1(1) of the Children and Young Persons Act 1933 (c.12). Lord Keith said at 418:

"It is used here to describe the mental element, which, in addition to the fact of neglect, must be proved The primary meaning of 'wilful' is 'deliberate'. So a parent who knows that his child needs medical care and deliberately, that is by conscious decision, refrains from calling a doctor, is guilty under the sub-section. As a matter of general principle, recklessness is to be equiparated with deliberation. A parent who fails to provide medical care which his child needs because he does not care whether it is needed or not is reckless of his child's welfare. He too is guilty of an offence. But a parent who has genuinely failed to appreciate that his child needs medical care, through personal inadequacy or stupidity or both, is not guilty."

Despite the fact that in *Patel*, which was heard in May 2013, the Court of Appeal said at para.36 that "we have come to the conclusion that the decision in *Sheppard* is of no assistance to this court in construing section 44 of the 2005 Act because of the difference in wording between the two statutes", the Court of Appeal in *R. v Turnbill* [2013] EWCA Crim 1422, which was heard in July 2013, applied and quoted from *Sheppard*. Hallett L.J. said at para.19:

"In some of the passages to which we have referred, [the judge] appears to equate carelessness or negligence with wilful neglect. They are not the same. Parliament has decreed that neglect is not enough to constitute a criminal offence . . . The neglect must be 'wilful' and that means something more is required than a duty and what a reasonable person would regard as a reckless breach of that duty."

A direction of the kind suggested by Lord Keith's reasoning in *Sheppard*, suitably tailored to the facts of the case, should be given by the trial judge hearing a case under this section (*R. v Morrell (Karen Victoria)* [2002] EWCA Crim 2547). In *Morrell,* the court said that the fact that the neglect is committed by a professional cannot make it automatically "wilful", since "there is or can be a room for genuine mistake, even with an experienced practitioner".

PART 2

THE COURT OF PROTECTION AND THE PUBLIC GUARDIAN

The Court of Protection

The Court of Protection

1–434
45.—(1) There is to be a superior court of record known as the Court of Protection.

(2) The court is to have an official seal.

(3) The court may sit at any place in England and Wales, on any day and at any time.

(4) The court is to have a central office and registry at a place appointed by the Lord Chancellor [, after consulting the Lord Chief Justice].

(5) The Lord Chancellor may [, after consulting the Lord Chief Justice] designate as additional registries of the court any district registry of the High Court and any county court office.

[(5A) The Lord Chief Justice may nominate any of the following to exercise his functions under this section—

(a) the President of the Court of Protection;

(b) a judicial office holder (as defined in section 109(4) of the Constitutional Reform Act 2005).]

(6) The office of the Supreme Court called the Court of Protection ceases to exist.

AMENDMENTS

1–435
The amendments to this section were made by SI 2006/1016 art.2, Sch.1, para.32.

GENERAL NOTE

1–436
This section establishes a superior court of record called the Court of Protection which has a comprehensive jurisdiction over the health, welfare and financial affairs of people who lack capacity. As it is a superior court of record, the court is not part of the High Court and has no inherent jurisdiction. Subject to claims brought under the Human Rights Act (see below), the Court has no power to overturn or declare unlawful decisions of public authorities, including the Public Guardian, on administrative law (judicial review) grounds (*Re MN (Adult)* [2015] EWCA Civ 411). The court has the same powers, rights, privileges and authority as the High Court (s.47(1)). As a superior court of record, its decisions can be reported and used as precedents (*R. (on the application of Cart) v Upper Tribunal* [2009] EWHC 3052 (QB) at para.75).

In *Cheshire West and Chester Council v P* [2011] EWHC 1330 (Fam), a case where Baker J. was required to determine whether P was being deprived of his liberty, his Lordship said at para.52:

"The processes of the Court of Protection are essentially inquisitorial rather than adversarial. In other words, the ambit of the litigation is determined, not by the parties, but by the court, because the function of the court is not to determine in a disinterested way a dispute brought to it by the parties, but rather, to engage in a process of assessing whether an adult is lacking in capacity, and if so, making decisions about his welfare that are in his best interests. It may be that one party or another asserts a fact which, if in dispute, must be proved, to the requisite standards of the balance of probabilities, but the question of whether or not the circumstances as a whole amount to a deprivation of liberty is not one which falls to be determined by application of a burden or standard of proof."

This statement was endorsed by the President in *Re G* [2014] EWCOP 1361 at para.26.

The court is able to sit anywhere in England and Wales (subs.(3)), with the general rule being that a hearing is to be held in private (CPR 2007, Pt.13). The Explanatory Notes state, at para.130, that it "is intended that the Court of Protection will have a regional presence but will have a central office and registry as designated by the Lord Chancellor. Additional registries (being High Court district registries or county courts) may also be designated".

The address of the court is:

Court of Protection
PO Box 70185
First Avenue House
42–49 High Holborn
London WC1A 9JA
DX 160013
Kingsway 7
telephone: 0300 456 4600
emergency applications only—out of office hours telephone: 020 7947 6000

HMCTS has introduced a standardised process to ensure that the workload of the court is allocated to the regions efficiently. To this end, regional hubs to the court have been established in Birmingham, Bristol, Cardiff, Leeds, Newcastle, Manchester and Reading.

In addition to the powers contained in s.16 to make an order and to appoint a deputy and the powers contained in ss.22 and 23 relating to lasting powers of attorney, the court also has the power under s.15 to make declarations on whether a person has capacity to make a particular decision, and whether an act done, or proposed to be done, in relation to a person who lacks capacity is lawful. The court does not have jurisdiction over decisions taken by a donee which are within the scope of a lasting power of attorney or to authorise the use of powers under the Mental Health Act 1983. When reaching a decision about a mentally incapacitated person the court must apply the principles set out in s.1, in particular any decision made must be in P's best interests (s.1(5)). Provision for applications to be made to the court is made in s.50.

The vast majority of the case load of the court is made up of non-contentious property and financial affairs cases decided without formal court hearings. These constitute around 90 per cent of the work (House of Lords Select Committee, para.212).

It is prima facie a contempt of court to publish a judgment in a Court of Protection case unless either the judgment has been delivered in public or, where delivered in private, the judge has authorised publication (Administration of Justice Act 1960, s.12). On January 16, 2014, the President of the Court of Protection issued Practice Guidance on "Transparency in the Court of Protection". The guidance is "intended to bring about an immediate and significant change in practice in relation to the publication of judgments in . . . the Court of Protection" (para.1). The court has power to make an order authorising the publication of information specified in r.91(2) of the 2007 Rules.

The Human Rights Act 1998

The Court of Protection has jurisdiction to determine a human rights claim brought **1–437** under s.7 of the Human Rights Act 1998. Such a claim must be clearly identified and properly pleaded (*Re MN (Adult)*, above, at para.85).

In *Winterwerp v Netherlands* (1979) 2 E.H.R.R. 38 at para.75, the European Court of Human Rights (ECHR), in holding that the capacity to deal personally with one's property involves the exercise of private rights and hence affects "civil rights and obligations" for the purposes of Art.6(1) of the European Convention on Human Rights, said:

"Whatever the justification for depriving a person of unsound mind of the capacity to administer his property, the guarantees laid down by Art.6(1) must nevertheless be respected."

Article 6 is also applicable where the purpose of the proceedings is to determine whether or not legal capacity can be restored to the applicant to enable him to carry out certain legal acts (*Matter v Slovakia* (2001) 31 E.H.R.R. 32 at para.51).

In *Shtukaturov v Russia* (2012) 54 E.H.R.R. 27 at para.73, the ECtHR held that the decision of the judge to decide to deprive the applicant of his legal capacity on the basis of documentary evidence, without seeing or hearing the applicant, was unreasonable and in breach of the principle of adversarial proceedings enshrined in art.6.1 of the Convention.

Guidance

1–438   The Social Care Institute for Excellence has published *Good practice guidance on accessing the Court of Protection* (2011) which can be accessed at: *www.scie.org.uk/publications/guides/guide42/*.

The judges of the Court of Protection

1–439   **46.**—(1) Subject to Court of Protection Rules under section 51(2)(d), the jurisdiction of the court is exercisable by a judge nominated for that purpose by—

(a)   the [Lord Chief Justice], or

[(b)   where nominated by the Lord Chief Justice to act on his behalf under this subsection –

    (a)   the President of the Court of Protection;

    (b)   a judicial office holder (as defined in section 109(4) of the Constitutional Reform Act 2005).]

(2) To be nominated, a judge must be—

(a)   the President of the Family Division,

(b)   the [Chancellor of the High Court],

(c)   a puisne judge of the High Court,

(d)   a circuit judge, [. . .]

(e)   a district judge[,

(f)   a District Judge (Magistrates' Courts),

(g)   a judge of the First-tier Tribunal, or of the Upper Tribunal, by virtue of appointment under paragraph 1(1) of Schedule 2 or 3 to the Tribunals, Courts and Enforcement Act 2007,

(h)   a transferred-in judge of the First-tier Tribunal or of the Upper Tribunal (see section 31(2) of that Act),

(i)   a deputy judge of the Upper Tribunal (whether under paragraph 7 of Schedule 3 to, or section 31(2) of, that Act),

(j)   the Chamber President, or Deputy Chamber President, of a chamber of the First-tier Tribunal or of a chamber of the Upper Tribunal,

(k)   the Judge Advocate General,

(l)   a Recorder,

(m)   the holder of an office listed in the first column of the table in section 89(3C) of the Senior Courts Act 1981 (senior High Court Masters etc),

(n)   a holder of an office listed in column 1 of Part 2 of Schedule 2 to that Act (High Court Masters etc),

(o)   a deputy district judge appointed under section 102 of that Act or under section 8 of the County Courts Act 1984,

(p)   a member of a panel of Employment Judges established for England and Wales or for Scotland,

(q)   a person appointed under section 30(1)(a) or (b) of the Courts-Martial (Appeals) Act 1951 (assistants to the Judge Advocate General),

(r)   a deputy judge of the High Court,

(s) the Senior President of Tribunals,

(t) an ordinary judge of the Court of Appeal (including the vice-president, if any, of either division of that court),

(u) the President of the Queen's Bench Division,

(v) the Master of the Rolls, or

(w) the Lord Chief Justice].

(3) The [Lord Chief Justice, after consulting the Lord Chancellor,] must—

(a) appoint one of the judges nominated by virtue of subsection (2)(a) to (c) to be President of the Court of Protection, and

(b) appoint another of those judges to be Vice-President of the Court of Protection.

(4) The [Lord Chief Justice, after consulting the Lord Chancellor,] must appoint one of the judges nominated by virtue of subsection (2)(d) [to (q)] to be Senior Judge of the Court of Protection, having such administrative functions in relation to the court as the Lord Chancellor[, after consulting the Lord Chief Justice,] may direct.

AMENDMENTS

The amendments to this section were made by SI 2006/1016 art.2, Sch.1, para.33 and the Crime and Courts Act 2013 s.21(4), Sch.14, Pt 3, para.5.

1–440

DEFINITIONS

"the court": s.64(1)

1–441

GENERAL NOTE

The jurisdiction of the Court of Protection is exercised by judges nominated by the Lord Chancellor, or a person acting on his behalf, from the list set out in subs.(2). One of the nominated judges must be appointed as President of the Court of Protection and another to be Vice-President (subs.(3)). A judge must also be appointed to be Senior Judge of the Court of Protection (subs.(4)).

1–442

Supplementary powers

General powers and effect of orders etc

47.—(1) The court has in connection with its jurisdiction the same powers, rights, privileges and authority as the High Court.

(2) Section 204 of the Law of Property Act 1925 (c. 20) (orders of High Court conclusive in favour of purchasers) applies in relation to orders and directions of the court as it applies to orders of the High Court.

(3) Office copies of orders made, directions given or other instruments issued by the court and sealed with its official seal are admissible in all legal proceedings as evidence of the originals without any further proof.

1–443

DEFINITIONS

"the court": s.64(1)

"purchaser": s.64(1)

1–444

GENERAL NOTE

Subsection (1)

This gives the Court of Protection the same powers as the High Court, for example in relation to witnesses, injunctions, contempt, and enforcement in connection with its juris-

1–445

diction under the Act. These powers can be exercised by all of the judges who sit in the court. In *W v M* [2011] EWHC 1197 (COP) at para.21, Baker J. confirmed that the court has the power under this section and s.37(1) of the Senior Courts Act 1981 to grant injunctions. The court also has the power to award damages under the Human Rights Act 1998 (*YA(F) v A Local Authority* [2010] EWHC 2770 (Fam), and *A Local Authority v Mrs D* [2013] EWHC B34 (COP) which is noted under s.15(1)(c)). Also see CPR 2007 r.184.

Unless orders (otherwise known as Hadkinson orders), which are orders instructing a party to comply with directions specified in the order and also stating the consequences of noncompliance, can be made in the Court of Protection (*A Local Authority v B, F and G* [2014] EWCOP B18). Such orders may be made where a party is in contempt or has failed to comply with a previous order. That party may be prevented from proceeding with a subsequent application unless they comply with the original order.

Subsection (2)

1–446   Section 204 of the 1925 Act reads:

"(1) An order of the court under any statutory or other jurisdiction shall not, as against a purchaser, be invalidated on the ground of want of jurisdiction, or of want of any concurrence, consent, notice, or service, whether the purchaser has notice of any such want or not.

(2) This section has effect with respect to any lease, sale, or other act under the authority of the court, and purporting to be in pursuance of any statutory power notwithstanding any exception in such statute.

(3) This section applies to all orders made before or after the commencement of this Act."

Interim orders and directions

1–447   **48.**—The court may, pending the determination of an application to it in relation to a person (P), make an order or give directions in respect of any matter if—

(a)   there is reason to believe that P lacks capacity in relation to the matter,

(b)   the matter is one to which its powers under this Act extend, and

(c)   it is in P's best interests to make the order, or give the directions, without delay.

DEFINITIONS

1–448   "the court": s.64(1)

GENERAL NOTE

1–449   This section enables the court to make interim orders even if evidence of lack of capacity is not yet available, where there is reason for the court to believe that the person lacks capacity in respect of a particular matter within the jurisdiction of the court and it is in the best interests of the person for the court to act without delay. It provides for the court to take steps pending a formal declaration of capacity under s.15. Given the pressure that the Court of Protection is under, "it is absolutely essential that the [court] establishes a practice that . . . interim cases [concerning the appropriate placement of P] must be dealt with quickly, and, having regard to the demands on the system generally, proportionately, that is to say almost certainly without detailed oral evidence" (*FP v GM and A Health Board* [2011] EWHC 2778 (COP) at para.12, per Hedley J.).

The approach that the court should take when applying this section was identified by Judge Marshall in *F, Re* [2009] M.H.L.R. 196 at para.44:

"The proper test for the engagement of s 48 in the first instance is whether there is evidence giving good cause for concern that P may lack capacity in some relevant regard. Once that is raised as a serious possibility, the court then moves on to the second stage to decide what action, if any, it is in P's best interests to take before a final determination of his capacity can be made. Such action can include not only taking immediate safeguarding steps (which may be positive or negative) with regard to P's affairs or life decisions, but it can also include giving directions to enable evidence to resolve the issue of capacity to be obtained quickly. Exactly what direction may be appropriate will depend on the individual facts of the case, the circumstances of P, and the momentousness of the urgent decisions in question, balanced against the principle that P's right to autonomy of decision-making for himself is to be restricted as little as is consistent with his best interests. Thus, where capacity itself is in issue, it may well be the case that the only proper direction in the first place should be as to obtaining appropriate specialist evidence to enable that issue to be reliably determined."

Judge Marshall said, at para.39, that the Act "is meant to operate in a simple and practical way, and to facilitate any necessary determination about P's capacity if there is doubt. It is clearly intended at least that general medical practitioners and health professionals other than mental capacity specialists should be able to supply evidence which will enable the Court of Protection to decide whether it can or should intervene, and if so, how."

Re F was applied by Judge Cardinal in *SMBC v HSG* [2011] EWHC B13 (COP) who identified, at para.57, the following lessons that he considered should be learnt from the "difficult" application that he had considered:

"i. An expert as a matter of good practice ought in my judgement to seek clarifications and raise questions under Rule 129 Court of Protection Rules 2007 before completing a report referring to lacunae in the information before him.

ii. A social worker investigating capacity ought to keep a party's solicitor informed of his intention to interview that party and not just proceed.

iii. It is right to conclude that a party may lack capacity [and thus the test in *Re F* is met] if there are significant and important gaps in the history and therefore the knowledge of the expert examining that party and there is evidence which may well point to incapacity in the relevant regard.

iv. It is unhelpful for a doctor [in this case a GP] to descend to vague expressions such as *mental health issues* in a report he/she knows is to go to the court.

v. It is not in my judgement an improper interference with the human or common law rights of a party for a medical expert to be provided with educational health and other records to enable him to complete his inquiries.

vi. I do not accept that psychometric testing is so intrusive as to be an improper test to apply to someone on the borderline of capacity even where he is reluctant to undertake them.

vii. If a solicitor acting for the Official Solicitor discusses the case with a joint expert orally or in writing the instructing parties should be provided with a copy of that communication or attendance note of that conversation."

An application under this section must use the procedure set out in Part 10 of the CPR 2007 and Practice Direction 10B.

Without notice applications
In *B Borough Council v Mrs S and Mr S (by the Official Solicitor)* [2006] EWHC 2584 **1–450** (Fam), Charles J. provided the following guidance on without notice applications at para.38:

"Good practice, fairness and indeed common sense demand that on any such application the Applicant should provide the court with:
    (i) a balanced, fair and particularised account of the events leading up to the application and thus of the matters upon which it is based. In many cases this

should include a brief account of what the Applicant thinks the Respondent's case is, or is likely to be,

(ii) where available and appropriate, independent evidence,

(iii) a clear and particularised explanation of the reasons why the application is made without notice and the reasons why the permission to apply to vary or discharge the injunction granted should be on notice (rather than immediately or forthwith as in the standard collection and location orders) and why the return date should not be within a short period of time. As to that I accept and acknowledge that a reference to notice being given if practicable, or for a short period of notice (say two working hours or just two hours if a week end or holiday period is imminent), may often provide an appropriate balance to avoid a sequence of effectively without notice applications, and that in some cases a longer period of notice may be appropriate, and

(iv) in many cases an account of the steps the Applicant proposes concerning service, the giving of an explanation of the order and the implementation of an order. This is likely to be of particular importance in cases such as this one where emotional issues are involved and family members of a person who lacks capacity are the subject of the injunctions and orders. In such cases, as here, information as to those intentions are likely to inform issues as to the need for, and the proportionality of, the relief sought and granted."

Paragraph (a)

1–451   The test under this paragraph is lower than that of evidence sufficient, in itself, to rebut the presumption of capacity. In *F, Re,* above, at para.36, Judge Marshall said that what is required "is simply sufficient evidence to justify a reasonable belief that P *may* lack capacity in the relevant regard. There are various phrases which might be used to describe this, such as 'good' or 'serious cause for concern' or 'a real possibility' that P lacks capacity, but the concept behind each of them is the same, and is really quite easily recognised".

Power to call for reports

1–452   **49.**—(1) This section applies where, in proceedings brought in respect of a person (P) under Part 1, the court is considering a question relating to P.

(2) The court may require a report to be made to it by the Public Guardian or by a Court of Protection Visitor.

(3) The court may require a local authority, or an NHS body, to arrange for a report to be made—

(a) by one of its officers or employees, or

(b) by such other person (other than the Public Guardian or a Court of Protection Visitor) as the authority, or the NHS body, considers appropriate.

(4) The report must deal with such matters relating to P as the court may direct.

(5) Court of Protection Rules may specify matters which, unless the court directs otherwise, must also be dealt with in the report.

(6) The report may be made in writing or orally, as the court may direct.

(7) In complying with a requirement, the Public Guardian or a Court of Protection Visitor may, at all reasonable times, examine and take copies of—

(a) any health record,

(b) any record of, or held by, a local authority and compiled in connection with a social services function, and

(c) any record held by a person registered under Part 2 of the Care Standards Act 2000 (c.14) [or Chapter 2 of Part 1 of the Health and Social Care Act 2008], so far as the record relates to P.

(8) If the Public Guardian or a Court of Protection Visitor is making a visit in the course of complying with a requirement, he may interview P in private.

(9) If a Court of Protection Visitor who is a Special Visitor is making a visit in the course of complying with a requirement, he may if the court so directs carry out in private a medical, psychiatric or psychological examination of P's capacity and condition.

(10) "NHS body" has the meaning given in section 148 of the Health and Social Care (Community Health and Standards) Act 2003 (c. 43).

(11) "Requirement" means a requirement imposed under subsection (2) or (3).

AMENDMENT
The words in square brackets in subs.(7) were inserted by SI 2010/813 art.17(4).   **1–453**

DEFINITIONS
"the court": s.64(1)   **1–454**
"Court of Protection Visitor": s.64(1)
"local authority": s.64(1)
"Court of Protection Rules": s.64(1)
"social services function": s.64(1)

GENERAL NOTE
This section makes provision for reports to be made to assist the Court of Protection   **1–455**
in determining a case relating to P. The court can require either written or oral reports to be made by the Public Guardian, a Court of Protection Visitor, a local authority or a NHS body (subss.(2), (3) and (6)). The power of the court to require reports does not extend to private organisations. The report, which could assist the court in determining whether an oral hearing of a case is needed, must deal with such matters as the court and/or the Court of Protection Rules direct (subss.(4) and (5)). Although a report from a Court of Protection Visitor may be funded by the Court (*A v A Local Authority* [2011] EWHC 727 (Fam) at para.18) there is no provision within this section for the court to order payment of the fees and expenses of a public body that is ordered to produce a report (*RS v LCC* [2015] EWCOP 56 at para.27). It is the duty of the person making the report to assist the court on the matters within his or her expertise (CPR 2007 r.117(2)). Unless the court otherwise directs, the matters to be covered in the report are set out in r.117(3). Written questions may be put to the report writer (r.118(1)). The Public Guardian and a Court of Protection Visitor are given power to examine and take copies of relevant records and to interview P in private (subss.(7) and (8)). Where a Court of Protection Visitor is a Special Visitor (see s.61(2)), he or she may, on the directions of the court, carry out in private medical, psychiatric or psychological examinations of P's capacity and condition (subs.(9)).

Subsection (2)
A case heard under the Mental Health Act 1959 (c.2) suggests that in initial applications   **1–456**
for the appointment of a deputy and in applications to determine proceedings, where the ultimate issue is whether an individual should either become or remain subject to the court's jurisdiction, the court should lean towards disclosing the Visitor's report, and the individual should be permitted to test the report by putting questions to the Visitor. The court should only withhold disclosure where this is deemed to be in the person's best interests. In all other cases, the judge should only direct disclosure if he sees a positive advantage in doing so, either in the interests of the person generally, or because he feels it would assist the judge in the exercise of his functions (*WLW, Re* [1972] Ch. 456 at 457, per Goff J.).

It is a contempt of court to interfere with the discharge of a Visitor's duties (*Anon, Re* (1875–90) 18 Ch. D. 26 at 27, per James L.J.).

REPORT. Guidance on the preparation, form and structure of the report is set out in Practice Direction 14E.

Subsection (3)

1–457 Paragraph (b) covers the situation where the local authority or NHS body has subcontracted its work to someone else.

NHS BODY. See subs.(10).

Subsection (5)

1–458 See r.117 of the CPR 2007.

Subsection (6)

1–459 ORALLY. The power to receive oral reports is particularly helpful in cases of urgency.

Subsections (7), (8) and (9)

1–460 REQUIREMENT. See subs.(11)

Practice and procedure

Applications to the Court of Protection

1–461 **50.**—(1) No permission is required for an application to the court for the exercise of any of its powers under this Act—

(a) by a person who lacks, or is alleged to lack, capacity,

(b) if such a person has not reached 18, by anyone with parental responsibility for him,

(c) by the donor or a donee of a lasting power of attorney to which the application relates,

(d) by a deputy appointed by the court for a person to whom the application relates, or

(e) by a person named in an existing order of the court, if the application relates to the order.

[(1A) Nor is permission required for an application to the court under section 21A by the relevant person's representative.]

(2) But, subject to Court of Protection Rules and to paragraph 20(2) of Schedule 3 (declarations relating to private international law), permission is required for any other application to the court.

(3) In deciding whether to grant permission the court must, in particular, have regard to—

(a) the applicant's connection with the person to whom the application relates,

(b) the reasons for the application,

(c) the benefit to the person to whom the application relates of a proposed order or directions, and

(d) whether the benefit can be achieved in any other way.

(4) "Parental responsibility" has the same meaning as in the Children Act 1989 (c. 41).

AMENDMENT

1–462 Subs.(1A) was inserted by the Mental Health Act 2007 s.50(7) Sch.9, Pt 1, para.9.

DEFINITIONS

1–463 "the court": s.64(1)

"lasting power of attorney": s.64(1)
"deputy": s.64(1)
"Court of Protection Rules": s.64(1)

GENERAL NOTE

This section provides that persons listed in subs.(1) can make as application to the Court **1–464** of Protection as of right. The representative of a person detained under the authority of Sch.A1 also has such a right when making an application under s.21A (subs.(1A)). Other potential applicants have to obtain the permission of the court (subs.(2) and CPR 2007, r.50), apart from those listed in CPR 2007 rr.51 and 52. The factors that the court must have regard to when considering whether to grant permission are set out in subs.(3). They "are designed to ensure that any proposed application will promote the interests of the person concerned, rather than causing unnecessary distress or difficulty for him" (Explanatory Notes, para.136). The majority of applications to the court are decided on the basis of the judge's consideration of the papers without any of the parties attending. This is provided for in CPR 2007 r.55.

The *Code of Practice* deals with the identity of the applicant at paras 8.7–8.10:

"The person making the application will vary, depending on the circumstances. For example, a person wishing to challenge a finding that they lack capacity may apply to the court, supported by others where necessary. Where there is a disagreement among family members, for example, a family member may wish to apply to the court to settle the disagreement—bearing in mind the need, in most cases, to get permission before-hand.

For cases about serious or major decisions concerning medical treatment . . . the NHS Trust or other organisation responsible for the patient's care will usually make the application. If social care staff are concerned about a decision that affects the welfare of a person who lacks capacity, the relevant local authority should make the application.

For decisions about the property and affairs of someone who lacks capacity to manage their own affairs, the applicant will usually be the person (for example, family carer) who needs specific authority from the court to deal with the individual's money or property.

If the applicant is the person who is alleged to lack capacity, they will always be a party to the court proceedings. In all other cases, the court will decide whether the person who lacks, or is alleged to lack, capacity should be involved as a party to the case. Where the person is a party to the case, the court may appoint the Official Solicitor to act for them."

As the European Court of Human Rights has identified that the state may have positive obligations designed to secure respect for private and family life under art.8 of the European Convention on Human Rights (see, for example, *Glasser v United Kingdom* (2001) 33 E.H.R.R. 1), it is arguable that a local authority has an obligation to make an application to the court if a mentally incapacitated adult is assessed as being likely to suffer harm if he remained with his family. Also see *S (Adult Patient) (Inherent Jurisdiction; Family Life), Re* [2002] EWHC 2278; [2003] 1 F.L.R. 292, noted under s.16(2).

Subsection (1) (a)

Part 17 of CPR 2007 provides for the court to appoint a litigation friend to act for P. **1–465**

Subsection (2)

PERMISSION. In *Re S (Hospital Patient: Court's Jurisdiction)* [1995] 3 All E.R. 290 at **1–466** 302j, a case under the inherent jurisdiction, Sir Thomas Bingham M.R. said:

"It cannot of course be suggested that any stranger or officious busybody, however remotely connected with a patient or with the subject matter of proceedings, can properly seek or obtain declaratory or any other relief (in private law any more than public law proceedings). But it can be suggested that where a serious justiciable issue is brought before the court by a party with a genuine and legitimate interest in obtaining a decision . . . the court will not impose nice tests to determine the precise legal standing of that claimant."

Subsection (3)

1–467   The court will grant permission where there is a dispute, such as a contact dispute, that requires resolution: see *London Borough of Hillingdon v PS* Unreported, December 4, 2014, D.J. Marin.

In *NK v VW* (COP), October 27, 2010, Macur J. said:

"In those circumstances, I refuse NK permission to make application pursuant to the MCA 2005 in relation to his mother. In doing so I obviously consider that section 50(3) and the associated Rules require the Court to prevent not only the frivolous and abusive applications but those which have no realistic prospect of success or bear any sense of proportional response to the problem that is envisaged by NK in this case." (para.16)

Court of Protection Rules

1–468   **51.**—[(1) Rules of court with respect to the practice and procedure of the court (to be called "Court of Protection Rules") may be made in accordance with Part 1 of Schedule 1 to the Constitutional Reform Act 2003.]

(2) Court of Protection Rules may, in particular, make provision—

(a)   as to the manner and form in which proceedings are to be commenced;

(b)   as to the persons entitled to be notified of, and be made parties to, the proceedings;

(c)   for the allocation, in such circumstances as may be specified, of any specified description of proceedings to a specified judge or to specified descriptions of judges;

(d)   for the exercise of the jurisdiction of the court, in such circumstances as may be specified, by its officers or other staff;

(e)   for enabling the court to appoint a suitable person (who may, with his consent, be the Official Solicitor) to act in the name of, or on behalf of, or to represent the person to whom the proceedings relate;

(f)   for enabling an application to the court to be disposed of without a hearing;

(g)   for enabling the court to proceed with, or with any part of, a hearing in the absence of the person to whom the proceedings relate;

(h)   for enabling or requiring the proceedings or any part of them to be conducted in private and for enabling the court to determine who is to be admitted when the court sits in private and to exclude specified persons when it sits in public;

(i)   as to what may be received as evidence (whether or not admissible apart from the rules) and the manner in which it is to be presented;

(j)   for the enforcement of orders made and directions given in the proceedings.

(3) Court of Protection Rules may, instead of providing for any matter, refer to provision made or to be made about that matter by directions.

(4) Court of Protection Rules may make different provision for different areas.

AMENDMENT

1–469   Subs.(1) was substituted by SI 2006/1016 art.2, Sch.1, para.34.

DEFINITIONS
"the court": s.64(1)

1–470

GENERAL NOTE

The Court of Protection Rules 2007 (SI 2007/1744) have been made under this section. They are reproduced in Part 4 and are referred to throughout this work as "the CPR 2007".

1–471

[Practice directions

52.—(1) Directions as to the practice and procedure of the court may be given in accordance with Part 1 of Schedule 2 to the Constitutional Reform Act 2005.

(2) Practice directions given otherwise than under subsection (1) may not be given without the approval of—

(a) the Lord Chancellor, and

(b) the Lord Chief Justice.

(3) The Lord Chief Justice may nominate any of the following to exercise his functions under this section—

(a) the President of the Court of Protection;

(b) a judicial office holder (as defined in section 109(4) of the Constitutional Reform Act 2005).]

1–472

AMENDMENT

This section was substituted by SI 2006/1016 at art.2, Sch.1 para.35.

1–473

DEFINITIONS
"the court": s.64(1)

1–474

GENERAL NOTE

This section provides for practice directions to be made regarding the court's practice and procedure. Section 51(3) enables the Court of Protection Rules, instead of providing for any matter, to refer to provision made by a practice direction. The "intention is to make rules accompanied by practice directions, on the model of the Civil Procedure Rules 1998" (Explanatory Notes, para.138).

All of the practice directions that have been issued can be accessed on the website of Her Majesty's Courts Service (see Appendix B). The numbering of the practice directions indicate the Part of the CPR 2007 that they supplement.

1–475

Rights of appeal

53.—(1) Subject to the provisions of this section, an appeal lies to the Court of Appeal from any decision of the court.

[(2) Court of Protection Rules may provide that, where a decision of the court is made by a specified description of person, an appeal from the decision lies to a specified description of judge of the court and not to the Court of Appeal.]

(3) [. . .]

(4) Court of Protection Rules may make provision—

(a) that, in such cases as may be specified, an appeal from a decision of the court may not be made without permission;

(b) as to the person or persons entitled to grant permission to appeal;

(c) as to any requirements to be satisfied before permission is granted;

(d) that where a [. . .] judge of the court makes a decision on an appeal, no appeal may be made to the Court of Appeal from that decision unless the Court of Appeal considers that—

(i)   the appeal would raise an important point of principle or practice, or

1–476

        (ii) there is some other compelling reason for the Court of Appeal to hear it;

    (e) as to any considerations to be taken into account in relation to granting or refusing permission to appeal.

AMENDMENTS

1–477   The amendments to this section were made by the Criminal Justice and Courts Act 2015 s.62.

DEFINITIONS

1–478   "the court": s.64(1)

GENERAL NOTE

1–479   This section, which is supplemented by Pt 20 CPR 2007, is concerned with appeals from decisions of the Court of Protection. In order for there to be a "decision" capable of supporting an appeal there must be the determination of an issue arising between two or more parties to proceedings before the court (*Re X (Court of Protection Practice)* [2015] EWCA Civ 599).

In *Aintree University Hospitals NHS Foundation Trust v James* [2013] UKSC 67, Lady Hale said:

"[I]f the judge has correctly directed himself as to the law . . . an appellate court can only interfere with his decision if satisfied that it was wrong: *Re B (A Child) (Care Proceedings: Appeal)* [2013] UKSC 33. In a case as sensitive and difficult as this, whichever way the judge's decision goes, an appellate court should be very slow to conclude that he was wrong."

Subsection (1)

1–480   Notwithstanding the use of the words "any decision", the phrase "an appeal lies to the Court of Appeal from any decision of the court" does not include a decision made by a judge nominated under s.46(2)(a) to (c) granting or refusing permission to appeal a decision of a circuit judge under r.172 (7) of the Court of Protection Rules (*TA v AA* [2013] EWCA Civ 1661 at para.67).

Fees and costs

Fees

1–481   **54.**—(1) The Lord Chancellor may with the consent of the Treasury by order prescribe fees payable in respect of anything dealt with by the court.

(2) An order under this section may in particular contain provision as to—

    (a) scales or rates of fees;

    (b) exemptions from and reductions in fees;

    (c) remission of fees in whole or in part.

(3) Before making an order under this section, the Lord Chancellor must consult—

    (a) the President of the Court of Protection,

    (b) the Vice-President of the Court of Protection, and

    (c) the Senior Judge of the Court of Protection.

(4) The Lord Chancellor must take such steps as are reasonably practicable to bring information about fees to the attention of persons likely to have to pay them.

(5) Fees payable under this section are recoverable summarily as a civil debt.

DEFINITIONS
　"the court": s.64(1)　　　　　　　　　　　　　　　　　　　　　　**1–482**

Subsection (1)
　BY ORDER.　See the Court of Protection Fees Order 2007 (SI 2007/1745) which is　**1–483**
reproduced in Part 4.

Subsection (2)
　The principle underpinning this provision was explained by the Parliamentary Under-　**1–484**
Secretary of State: "[W]e believe that it is right that people should pay a fair price for the
court's work on their behalf, but it is also right that fee reduction and remission arrangements exist so that no one is prevented from going to court if paying the fees would cause
them financial hardship, or if there are other exceptional circumstances" (*Hansard*, HL Vol.
669, col.754).

Costs

　55.—(1) Subject to Court of Protection Rules, the costs of and incidental to all　**1–485**
proceedings in the court are in its discretion.
　(2) The rules may in particular make provision for regulating matters relating
to the costs of those proceedings, including prescribing scales of costs to be paid
to legal or other representatives.
　(3) The court has full power to determine by whom and to what extent the costs
are to be paid.
　(4) The court may, in any proceedings—
　(a)　disallow, or
　(b)　order the legal or other representatives concerned to meet,
the whole of any wasted costs or such part of them as may be determined in
accordance with the rules.
　(5) "Legal or other representative", in relation to a party to proceedings, means
any person exercising a right of audience or right to conduct litigation on his
behalf.
　(6) "Wasted costs" means any costs incurred by a party—
　(a)　as a result of any improper, unreasonable or negligent act or omission on
　　　the part of any legal or other representative or any employee of such a
　　　representative, or
　(b)　which, in the light of any such act or omission occurring after they were
　　　incurred, the court considers it is unreasonable to expect that party to pay.

DEFINITIONS
　"Court of Protection Rules": s.64(1)　　　　　　　　　　　　　　　　**1–486**
　"the court": s.64(1)

GENERAL NOTE
　See Pt 19 of the CPR 2007.　　　　　　　　　　　　　　　　　　　　**1–487**

Fees and costs: supplementary

　56.—(1) Court of Protection Rules may make provision—　　　　　　**1–488**
　(a)　as to the way in which, and funds from which, fees and costs are to be paid;
　(b)　for charging fees and costs upon the estate of the person to whom the pro-
　　　ceedings relate;
　(c)　for the payment of fees and costs within a specified time of the death of the
　　　person to whom the proceedings relate or the conclusion of the proceedings.

(2) A charge on the estate of a person created by virtue of subsection (1)(b) does not cause any interest of the person in any property to fail or determine or to be prevented from recommencing.

DEFINITIONS

1–489 "Court of Protection Rules": s.64(1)

GENERAL NOTE

1–490 See Pt 19 of the CPR 2007.

The Public Guardian

The Public Guardian

1–491 **57.**—(1) For the purposes of this Act, there is to be an officer, to be known as the Public Guardian.

(2) The Public Guardian is to be appointed by the Lord Chancellor.

(3) There is to be paid to the Public Guardian out of money provided by Parliament such salary as the Lord Chancellor may determine.

(4) The Lord Chancellor may, after consulting the Public Guardian—

(a) provide him with such officers and staff, or

(b) enter into such contracts with other persons for the provision (by them or their sub-contractors) of officers, staff or services,

as the Lord Chancellor thinks necessary for the proper discharge of the Public Guardian's functions.

(5) Any functions of the Public Guardian may, to the extent authorised by him, be performed by any of his officers.

GENERAL NOTE

1–492 This section provides the Public Guardian to be appointed by the Lord Chancellor, and for the Lord Chancellor either to provide the Public Guardian with officers and staff and/or to enter into contacts with other persons for the provision of officers, staff or services for the discharge of the Public Guardian's functions. The Public Guardian, who is supported by the Office of the Public Guardian, an executive agency of the Ministry of Justice, has both administrative and supervisory functions. These are set out in s.58. The Public Guardian is required to produce annual reports (s.60).

The address of the Public Guardian is:

Office of the Public Guardian
PO Box 16185
Birmingham
B2 2WH

tel: 0300 456 0300
fax: 0870 739 5780
The Document Exchange (DX) address is:
Office of the Public Guardian
DX 744240
Birmingham 79

Functions of the Public Guardian

1–493 **58.**—(1) The Public Guardian has the following functions—

(a) establishing and maintaining a register of lasting powers of attorney,

(b) establishing and maintaining a register of orders appointing deputies,

(c) supervising deputies appointed by the court,

(d) directing a Court of Protection Visitor to visit—
    (i) a donee of a lasting power of attorney,
    (ii) a deputy appointed by the court, or
    (iii) the person granting the power of attorney or for whom the deputy is appointed (P),
and to make a report to the Public Guardian on such matters as he may direct,
(e) receiving security which the court requires a person to give for the discharge of his functions,
(f) receiving reports from donees of lasting powers of attorney and deputies appointed by the court,
(g) reporting to the court on such matters relating to proceedings under this Act as the court requires,
(h) dealing with representations (including complaints) about the way in which a donee of a lasting power of attorney or a deputy appointed by the court is exercising his powers,
(i) publishing, in any manner the Public Guardian thinks appropriate, any information he thinks appropriate about the discharge of his functions.

(2) The functions conferred by subsection (1)(c) and (h) may be discharged in co-operation with any other person who has functions in relation to the care or treatment of P.

(3) The Lord Chancellor may by regulations make provision—
(a) conferring on the Public Guardian other functions in connection with this Act;
(b) in connection with the discharge by the Public Guardian of his functions.

(4) Regulations made under subsection (3)(b) may in particular make provision as to—
(a) the giving of security by deputies appointed by the court and the enforcement and discharge of security so given;
(b) the fees which may be charged by the Public Guardian;
(c) the way in which, and funds from which, such fees are to be paid;
(d) exemptions from and reductions in such fees;
(e) remission of such fees in whole or in part;
(f) the making of reports to the Public Guardian by deputies appointed by the court and others who are directed by the court to carry out any transaction for a person who lacks capacity.

(5) For the purpose of enabling him to carry out his functions, the Public Guardian may, at all reasonable times, examine and take copies of—
(a) any health record,
(b) any record of, or held by, a local authority and compiled in connection with a social services function, and
(c) any record held by a person registered under Part 2 of the Care Standards Act 2000 (c.14) [or Chapter 2 of Part 1 of the Health and Social Care Act 2008],
so far as the record relates to P.

(6) The Public Guardian may also for that purpose interview P in private.

AMENDMENT
The words in square brackets in subs.(5) were inserted by SI 2010/813 art.17(5).   **1–494**

DEFINITIONS

1–495   "lasting power of attorney": s.64(1)
"deputy": s.64(1)
"the court": s.64(1)
"Court of Protection Visitor": s.64(1)
"health record": s.64(1)
"local authority": s.64(1)
"social services function": s.64(1)

GENERAL NOTE

1–496   The functions of the Public Guardian listed in subs.(1) are supplemented by regs.30 to 48 of the Lasting Powers of Attorney, Enduring Powers of Attorney and Public Guardian Regulations 2007 (SI 2007/1253): see Part 3. Regulation 43 enables the Public Guardian to make applications to the Court of Protection. His functions include establishing and maintaining registers of LPAs and orders appointing deputies, supervising deputies to ensure that they exercise their responsibilities in line with the authority given to them, dealing with representations about the way both donees of LPAs and deputies are exercising their powers, and making enquiries or referring matters to the court where there are concerns that donees or deputies are not acting appropriately. The Public Guardian is given power to examine and take copies of relevant health or social services records, and also interview P in private (subss.(5) and (6)). Similar rights are provided for when the Public Guardian is reporting to the Court of Protection (s.49(7)–(8)).

The Public Guardian has no power of enforcement or sanction. An application to the court would have to be made if such power needs to be exercised.

The Public Guardian (Fees, etc) Regulations 2007 (SI 2007/2051) (see Part 3) provide for fees to be charged in connection with the functions carried out by the Public Guardian. No fee is payable by the relevant person if that person is in receipt of a benefit set out in reg.9(7). This exemption does not apply if the person has been awarded damages in excess of £16,000 which has been disregarded for the purposes of determining eligibility for any of these benefits (reg.9(2)). Under reg.10, the Public Guardian has power to reduce or remit any fee if, "owing to the exceptional circumstances of the particular case", payment of the fee would "involve undue hardship".

In May 2013, the Office of the Public Guardian published a "Safeguarding Policy".

Subsections (1)(a), (1)(b)

1–497   For the role of the Public Guardian in relation to the registers, see regs 20 to 32 of SI 2007/1253.

The Public Guardian has issued Practice Note No. 02/2011 on "Updating Public Guardian Registers: Notification of Death".

Subsection (1)(c)

1–498   After the appointment of the deputy, the Public Guardian must determine the level of supervision required. The levels of supervision are set out in SI 2007/2051 reg.8(3). Also see the General Note to s.19.

For the power of the Public Guardian to require information from deputies, see reg.41 of SI 2007/1253. A deputy can require a review of decisions made by the Public Guardian, see reg.42.

Subsection (1)(d)

1–499   For visits by the Public Guardian or by Court of Protection Visitors at his direction, see reg.44 of SI 2007/1253. The Public Guardian can direct a Visitor to visit the donor or attorney of an EPA under reg.48.

Subsection (1)(f)

For reports from deputies, see regs 38 to 40 of SI 2007/1253. The Public Guardian   **1–500**
can require the deputy to provide him with information (reg.41), and the deputy can
require the Public Guardian to reconsider any decision that he has made in respect of
him (reg.42).

Subsection (1)(h)

The Public Guardian might wish to refer a complaint concerning the personal welfare   **1–501**
of P to the relevant health or social care agency. If the complaint suggests that a criminal
offence has been committed, this will be referred to the police.

In the performance of his functions under this provision, the Public Guardian has the
power to require information from a donee or deputy under regs 46 and 47 of SI 2007/1253.

Subsection (2)

It "is intended that the Public Guardian will work closely with organisations such as   **1–502**
local authorities and NHS bodies" (Explanatory Notes, para.146). Although the Public
Guardian's supervisory function will be mainly focused on financial affairs, he "would
have a role in identifying and tackling possible abuse with other agencies by providing a focus for concerns and fielding them to the appropriate agency" (Department of
Constitutional Affairs, Oral and written evidence, Ev 265).

Subsections (3), (4)

REGULATIONS. See SI 2007/1253, noted above.   **1–503**

59.—[*Repealed by the Public Bodies (Abolition of Her Majesty's Inspectorate*   **1–504**
of Courts Administration and Public Guardian Board) Order 2012 (SI 2012/2401)
art.4(2), Sch.2, para.2.]

Annual report

60.—(1) The Public Guardian must make an annual report to the Lord   **1–505**
Chancellor about the discharge of his functions.

(2) The Lord Chancellor must, within one month of receiving the report, lay a
copy of it before Parliament.

DEFINITIONS

"Public Guardian": s.64(1)   **1–506**

Court of Protection Visitors

61.—(1) A Court of Protection Visitor is a person who is appointed by the Lord   **1–507**
Chancellor to—

(a) a panel of Special Visitors, or

(b) a panel of General Visitors.

(2) A person is not qualified to be a Special Visitor unless he—

(a) is a registered medical practitioner or appears to the Lord Chancellor to
have other suitable qualifications or training, and

(b) appears to the Lord Chancellor to have special knowledge of and experience in cases of impairment of or disturbance in the functioning of the
mind or brain.

(3) A General Visitor need not have a medical qualification.

(4) A Court of Protection Visitor—

(a) may be appointed for such term and subject to such conditions, and

(b) may be paid such remuneration and allowances,

as the Lord Chancellor may determine.

(5) For the purpose of carrying out his functions under this Act in relation to a person who lacks capacity (P), a Court of Protection Visitor may, at all reasonable times, examine and take copies of—

(a) any health record,

(b) any record of, or held by, a local authority and compiled in connection with a social services function, and

(c) any record held by a person registered under Part 2 of the Care Standards Act 2000 (c.14) [or Chapter 2 of Part 1 of the Health and Social Care Act 2008],

so far as the record relates to P.

(6) A Court of Protection Visitor may also for that purpose interview P in private.

AMENDMENT

1–508   The words in square brackets in subs.(5) were inserted by SI 2010/813 art.17(6).

DEFINITIONS

1–509   "health record": s.64(1)
"local authority": s.64(1)
"social services function": s.64(1)

GENERAL NOTE

1–510   This section provides for the Lord Chancellor to appoint Special Visitors, who will usually be experienced consultant psychiatrists, and General Visitors. Their role is to carry out visits and produce independent reports on matters relating to the exercise of powers under the Act as directed by the Court of Protection (s.49(2)) or the Public Guardian (s.58(1)(d) and reg.44 of the Lasting Powers of Attorney, Enduring Powers of Attorney and Public Guardian Regulations 2007 (SI 2007/1253)). The Visitors have the power to examine and take copies of relevant records, and to interview P in private.

PART 3

MISCELLANEOUS AND GENERAL

Declaratory provision

Scope of the Act
62.—For the avoidance of doubt, it is hereby declared that nothing in this Act **1–511**
is to be taken to affect the law relating to murder or manslaughter or the operation
of section 2 of the Suicide Act 1961 (c. 60) (assisting suicide).

GENERAL NOTE
This section, which was inserted following representations from the Catholic Bishops' **1–512**
Conference of England and Wales, seeks to address the concerns that were expressed
to the Joint Committee that this legislation might pave the way for "euthanasia by the
backdoor" (see para.196). Euthanasia, which is "a deliberate intervention with the express
aim of ending life", is illegal (*Who Decides: Making Decisions on Behalf of Mentally
Incapacitated Adults*, Cm.3803, para.1.8). Notwithstanding the declaration made in this
section, it is the case that both a valid and applicable written advance decision to refuse
life-sustaining treatment (see ss.24–26) and a refusal of such treatment by a donee under
a lasting power of attorney, if such power is granted to the donee (see s.11(8)), are lawful
and must be obeyed by healthcare professionals. A mentally capable patient can therefore
use either of these mechanisms to bring about his or her death during a subsequent mental
incapacity by refusing either the provision of nutrition and hydration by artificial means or
other potentially life saving medical interventions in specified circumstances. In such an
eventuality there can be no question of the person having committed suicide, nor therefore
of the doctor having aided and abetted him or her in doing so (*Airedale NHS Trust v Bland*
[1993] 1 All E.R. 821, HL, at 866, per Lord Goff). However, if a donee "wanted to refuse
consent to treatment and the doctors thought that this was with the intention of murder
or manslaughter then the doctor could continue to treat", per the Parliamentary Under-
Secretary of State in correspondence quoted at *Hansard*, HL Vol.688, col.1150.
Whether a decision to discontinue treatment that would inevitably lead to the patient's
death constitutes euthanasia was considered by Lord Goff in *Bland* at 867:

"[T]he law draws a crucial distinction between cases in which a doctor decides not to
provide, or continue to provide, for his patient treatment or care which could or might
prolong his life and those in which he decides, for example by administering a lethal
drug, actively to bring his patient's life to an end. As I have already indicated, the
former may be lawful, either because the doctor is giving effect to his patient's wishes
by withholding the treatment or care, even in certain circumstances in which the patient
is incapacitated from stating whether or not he gives his consent. But it is not lawful
for a doctor to administer a drug to his patient to bring about his death, even though
that course is prompted by a humanitarian desire to end his suffering, however great
that suffering may be: see *R v Cox* (September 18,1992, unreported) *per* Ognall J in the
Crown Court at Winchester. So to act is to cross the Rubicon which runs between on
the one hand the care of the living patient and on the other hand euthanasia—actively
causing his death to avoid or to end his suffering. Euthanasia is not lawful at common
law. It is, of course well known that there are many responsible members of our society
who believe that euthanasia should be made lawful; but that result could I believe, only
be achieved by legislation which expresses the democratic will that so fundamental
a change should be made in our law, and can, if enacted, ensure that such legalised
killing can only be carried out subject to appropriate supervision and control. It is true
that the drawing of this distinction may lead to a charge of hypocrisy, because it can be
asked why, if the doctor, by discontinuing treatment, is entitled in consequence to let

his patient die, it should not be lawful to put him out of his misery straight away, in a more humane manner, by a lethal injection, rather than to let him linger on in pain until he dies. But the law does not feel able to authorise euthanasia, even in circumstances such as these, for, once euthanasia is recognised as lawful in these circumstances, it is difficult to see any logical basis for excluding it in others."

In *Bland* the House of Lords held that treatment, including the provision of nutrition and hydration to the patient by artificial means, could be withheld from a mentally inca-pacitated patient who had no hope of recovery when it was known that the patient would shortly thereafter die, provided that responsible and competent medical opinion was of the view that it would be in the patient's best interests not to prolong his life by continuing the treatment because such treatment would be futile and would not confer any benefit on him.

In *Re Gardner* (COP) July 6, 2011, the donor of a lasting power of attorney included the following statement in the guidance section of the instrument: "If I am suffering from a terminal illness I would ask that my attorneys assist me in travelling to a country where it is legal for me to take my own life should I choose to do so". On the application of the Public Guardian, Senior Judge Lush severed the guidance for the following reasons: (i) s.62 provides that nothing in the Act is to be taken to affect the law relating to murder or manslaughter or the operation of s.2 of the Suicide Act 1961 (assisting suicide); (ii) the donor was purporting to authorise the attorneys to commit the criminal offence of assist-ing suicide, and the fact that a person who assists a suicide is not always prosecuted in England and Wales does not detract from the fact that it remains a criminal offence; and (iii) although the statement appeared in the guidance section, it is not open to a donor to provide guidance to the attorneys relating to the commission of a criminal offence.

Private international law

International protection of adults
1–513   63.—Schedule 3—
   (a)   gives effect in England and Wales to the Convention on the International Protection of Adults signed at the Hague on 13th January 2000 (Cm. 5881) (in so far as this Act does not otherwise do so), and
   (b)   makes related provision as to the private international law of England and Wales.

GENERAL NOTE
1–514   Schedule 3, which is considered by Alexander Ruck Keene in "An International Can of Worms? Schedule 3 to the Mental Capacity Act 2005" [2011] Eld.L.J. 77–82, makes provi-sion as to the private international law of England and Wales in relation to those who are over the age of 16 who cannot protect their interests. In particular, it gives effect in England and Wales to the Convention on the International Protection of Adults (Cm.5881) which was signed at the Hague on January 13, 2000 and entered into force on January 1, 2009. It does so on a very wide basis in that the Schedule provides for the mutual recognition of protective measures imposed by a foreign court regardless of whether that court is located in a Convention country. This means that Sch.3 comes into play whenever a cross-border incapacity issue arises. The aims of the Convention are set out in art.1. They are to:

   • provide for the protection in international situations of adults who, by reason of impairment or insufficiency in their personal faculties, are not in a position to defend their interests
   • establish rules on jurisdiction, applicable law, international recognition and enforce-ment of protective measures which are to be respected by all Contracting States, and co-operation between Contracting States.

The basis of the jurisdiction is habitual residence, not best interests: see *Re MN* [2010]

EWHC 1926 (Fam) at para.38 and the note on para.7(a) of Sch.3. In other words, the habitual residence of the person determines which State authorities have jurisdiction over his person and property.

Schedule 3 was analysed in *Health Services Executive of Ireland v PA* [2015] EWCOP 38, where Baker J. made the following findings:

1. As the Schedule implements, as a matter of domestic law, obligations in respect of the recognition, enforcement and implementation of "protective measures" imposed by a foreign court regardless of whether that court is located in a Convention country, it would not be permissible to apply one rule for Convention states and another for non-Convention states (para.39).

2. The scheme of the Convention, reflected in the Schedule, is to focus on the factual description of the adult rather than any legal test as to capacity (para.43).

3. The court must look at the order and judgment of the foreign court—and if it thinks it necessary to do so, and insofar as it is permissible to do so under para.24, the evidence before the foreign court—to establish whether the foreign court has made a finding which is binding or, if not, whether the individual comes within the meaning of "adult" under Sch.3 para.4(1) (para.44).

4. The scheme of the Convention is to facilitate the recognition and enforcement of protective measures taken by foreign courts save in the circumstances set out in paras 19(3) and (4). The measure "is to be recognised" if taken on the grounds that the individual was habitually resident in the country where the order containing the measure was made. The grounds on which a measure may be challenged may be procedural (para.19(3)) or substantive (para.19(4)). By reason of para.21, however, provides that for the purposes of paras 19 and 20 any finding of fact relied on when the measure was taken is conclusive, there is no power to challenge the finding made in the foreign court that the individual is habitually resident in that country. Accordingly, a finding of a foreign court that the individual concerned was habitually resident in that country cannot be challenged in any process to recognise or enforce a measure in this country, although the process by which the measure was ordered may be challenged (for example, if the individual was not given an opportunity to be heard) and the measure itself may be challenged (for example, if inconsistent with a mandatory provision of law of this country) (para.52).

5. Paragraph 19(3) gives the court a discretionary power to refuse to recognise a protective measure if certain procedural safeguards are not met. It is plain from the way in which that paragraph is drafted that the court only has a discretion to decline to recognise a foreign order if all three of the conditions in the subparagraph are satisfied. In other words, the court only has a discretion to disapply a measure in a foreign order if it "thinks" that the case in which the measure was taken was not urgent and the adult was not given the opportunity to be heard and that omission amounted to a breach of natural justice. "Thinks" for these purposes means "concludes on a balance of probabilities" (para.55).

6. By including Sch.3 in the Act, Parliament authorised a system of recognition and enforcement of foreign orders notwithstanding the fact that the approach of the foreign courts and laws to these issues may be different to that of the domestic court. These differences may extend not only to the way in which the individual is treated but also to questions of jurisprudence and capacity. Thus the fact that there are provisions within the Act that appear to conflict with the laws and procedures of the foreign state should not by itself lead to a refusal to recognise or enforce the foreign order. Given that Parliament has included s.63 and Sch.3 within the Act, clearly intending to facilitate recognition and enforcement in such circumstances, it cannot be the case that those other provisions within the Act that seemingly conflict with the laws and procedures of the foreign state are mandatory provisions of the laws of England and Wales so as to justify the English court refusing to recognise the foreign order on grounds of such inconsistency. In such circumstances, it is only where the

court concludes that recognition of the foreign measure would be manifestly contrary to public policy that the discretionary ground to refuse recognition will arise. Furthermore, in conducting the public policy review, the court must always bear in mind, in the words of Munby L.J. in *Re L* [2012] EWCA Civ 1157 that "the test is stringent, the bar is set high".

7. Although no wide-ranging review as to the merits of the foreign measure is either necessary or appropriate, a limited review will always be required as indicated by the European Court in *Pellegrini v Italy* (2002) 35 E.H.R.R. 2. That will be sufficient to identify any cases where the content and form of the foreign measure, and the processes by which it was taken, are objectionable.

8. The court should conduct a limited review to satisfy itself that the foreign orders comply with the ECHR, and in doing so should strive to achieve a combined and harmonious application of the provisions of the two international instruments. When considering applications to recognise and enforce compulsory psychiatric placements under Sch.3, the limited review should encompass the court being satisfied that (1) the *Winterwerp* criteria are met and (2) that the individual's right to challenge the detention under art.5(4) is effective (i.e. that they have a right to take proceedings to challenge the detention and the right to regular reviews thereafter) (para.96).

9. Baker J. agreed with the decision of Mostyn J. in *Re M* [2011] EWHC 3590 (COP) in holding that an order recognising and enforcing a foreign measure under Sch.3 is not a welfare order as defined in s.16A(4)(b). The rules as to ineligibility in s.16A therefore do not apply. This means that the court will be obliged to recognise and enforce orders of a foreign court depriving an individual of his liberty in circumstances in which it would not be able to do so under the domestic jurisdiction under the Act on the grounds that the individual is being treated or is treatable under the Mental Health Act as defined in Sch.1A. Once again, however, this is subject, to its discretion to refuse recognition and enforcement where that would be manifestly contrary to public policy (para.98).

10. As the definition of "adult" in para.4 of Sch.3 plainly extends to persons who may not be incapacitated within the meaning of s.2, it follows that the court will be obliged to recognise and enforce orders of a foreign court in terms that could not be included in an order made under the domestic jurisdiction under the Act. This is subject, however, to its discretion to refuse recognition and enforcement where that would be manifestly contrary to public policy. Baker J. agreed and adopted Hedley J.'s conclusion in *Re MN* (above) that a decision to recognise under para.19(1) or to enforce under para.22(2) is not a decision governed by the best interests of the individual so that those paragraphs are not disapplied by para.19(4)(b) and section 1(5) of the Act. Thus it follows that the Court will be obliged to recognise and enforce a measure in a foreign court order even where applying a best interests test would not be included in an order made under the domestic jurisdiction under the Act. Again, however, this is subject, to its discretion to refuse recognition and enforcement where that would be manifestly contrary to public policy (para.98).

11. It is not open to the Court of Protection to refuse recognition and enforcement of a foreign order simply because the individual may have the relevant decision-making capacity and objects to the order being recognised and enforced. Such an approach would undermine the whole purpose of Sch.3 (para.101).

In *Health Services Executive of Ireland v CNWL* [2015] EWCOP 38, Baker J. held that it would not always be necessary for P to be a party in Sch.3 cases because of the limited role of the court.

A number of European countries have ratified the Convention (Finland, France, Germany, Switzerland, Estonia, the Czech Republic, and the United Kingdom (for Scotland only)). The Convention has not been ratified in England and Wales. As Sch.3 effectively implements the Convention in English law, non-ratification has little practical effect. However, the fact that England and Wales is not yet a "Convention country" and is therefore not in a position to undertake reciprocal arrangements with other Convention countries as regards transfers of jurisdiction means that Sch.3 is not fully in force: see *JO v GO* [2013] EWHC 3932 (COP) and para.35 of Sch.3.

For the purposes of the Convention, England and Wales, Scotland and Northern Ireland are treated separately because they constitute separate jurisdictions. The provisions of Sch.3 are intended to be compatible with the provisions of Sch.3 to the Adults with Incapacity (Scotland) Act 2000 (asp 4) which provides for the private international law of Scotland in this field, and implemented the Convention in Scotland.

The Law Society has published a practice note on "Mental capacity: international aspects" which can be accessed at: *www.lawsociety.org.uk/advice/practice-notes/mental-capacity-international-aspects*.

Children

Due to the amendment made to the definition of "adult" in para.4 of Sch.3 by SI 2010/1898, a 16 or 17-year-old child who is the subject of proceedings under Council Regulation (EC) No.2201/2003 (commonly known as "Brussels II Revised") or the 1996 Hague Convention cannot be the subject of proceedings under Sch.3. A determination under Brussels II Revised can lead to a foreign child being compulsorily detained in a psychiatric hospital in England or Wales without being detained under the Mental Health Act 1983. For an example of such a case, see *HSE Ireland v SF (A Minor)* [2012] EWHC 1640 (Fam). **1–515**

General

Interpretation

64.—(1) In this Act— **1–516**

"the 1985 Act" means the Enduring Powers of Attorney Act 1985 (c. 29),

"advance decision" has the meaning given in section 24(1),

["authorisation under Schedule A1" means either—

(a)   a standard authorisation under that Schedule, or

(b)   an urgent authorisation under that Schedule.]

"the court" means the Court of Protection established by section 45, "Court of Protection Rules" has the meaning given in section 51(1), "Court of Protection Visitor" has the meaning given in section 61, "deputy" has the meaning given in section 16(2)(b),

"enactment" includes a provision of subordinate legislation (within the meaning of the Interpretation Act 1978 (c. 30)),

"health record" has the meaning given in section 68 of the Data Protection Act 1998 (c. 29) (as read with section 69 of that Act),

"the Human Rights Convention" has the same meaning as "the Convention" in the Human Rights Act 1998 (c. 42),

"independent mental capacity advocate" has the meaning given in section 35(1),

"lasting power of attorney" has the meaning given in section 9,

"life-sustaining treatment" has the meaning given in section 4(10),

"local authority" [, except in [section 35(6A)(a) and] Schedule A1,] means—

(a)   the council of a county in England in which there are no district councils,

(b)   the council of a district in England,

(c)   the council of a county or county borough in Wales,

(d)   the council of a London borough,

(e)   the Common Council of the City of London, or

(f)   the Council of the Isles of Scilly,

"Mental Health Act" means the Mental Health Act 1983 (c. 20),

"prescribed", in relation to regulations made under this Act, means prescribed by those regulations,

"property" includes any thing in action and any interest in real or personal property,

"public authority" has the same meaning as in the Human Rights Act 1998,

"Public Guardian" has the meaning given in section 57,

"purchaser" and "purchase" have the meaning given in section 205(1) of the Law of Property Act 1925 (c. 20),

"social services function" has the meaning given in section 1A of the Local Authority Social Services Act 1970 (c. 42),

"treatment" includes a diagnostic or other procedure,

"trust corporation" has the meaning given in section 68(1) of the Trustee Act 1925 (c.19), and

"will" includes codicil.

(2) In this Act, references to making decisions, in relation to a donee of a lasting power of attorney or a deputy appointed by the court, include, where appropriate, acting on decisions made.

(3) In this Act, references to the bankruptcy of an individual include a case where a bankruptcy restrictions order under the Insolvency Act 1986 (c. 45) has effect in respect of him.

[(3A) In this Act references to a debt relief order (under Part 7A of the Insolvency Act 1986) being made in relation to an individual include a case where a debt relief restrictions order under the Insolvency Act 1986 has effect in respect of him.]

(4) "Bankruptcy restrictions order" includes an interim bankruptcy restrictions order.

[(4A) "Debt relief restrictions order" includes an interim debt relief restrictions order.]

[(5) In this Act, references to deprivation of a person's liberty have the same meaning as in Article 5(1) of the Human Rights Convention.

(6) For the purposes of such references, it does not matter whether a person is deprived of his liberty by a public authority or not.]

AMENDMENTS

1–517   The amendments to this section were made by the Mental Capacity Act 2007 s.50(7), Sch.9, Pt.1, para.10, SI 2012/2404 art.3(2), Sch.1, para.53(4), and the Health and Social Care Act 2012 s.55(2), Sch.5, para.135.

GENERAL NOTE

Subsection (1)

1–518   TREATMENT.   The provision of nutrition and hydration to a patient which involves the application of a medical technique is "medical treatment" (*Airedale NHS Trust v Bland* [1993] 1 All E.R. 821, HL).

Subsection (5)

1–519   The effect of this provision is that the interpretation of the meaning of a "deprivation of liberty" will evolve with successive decisions of the European Court of Human Rights. Lady Hale has described the case law of the Court on the meaning of a deprivation of liberty as being "clear in some respects but not in others" (*P v Cheshire West and Chester Council; P and Q v Surrey CC* [2014] UKSC 19 at para.32).

Subsection (6)

This provision, which appears to remove the requirement that a deprivation of liberty for the purposes of the Act must be "imputable to the state" (see *Storck v Germany* (2006) 43 E.H.R.R. 6), has not been considered by the courts.

1–520

Rules, regulations and orders

65.—(1) Any power to make rules, regulations or orders under this Act [, other than the powers in section 21]—

    (a) is exercisable by statutory instrument;

    (b) includes power to make supplementary, incidental, consequential, transitional or saving provision;

    (c) includes power to make different provision for different cases.

1–521

(2) Any statutory instrument containing rules, regulations or orders made by the Lord Chancellor or the Secretary of State under this Act, other than—

    (a) regulations under section 34 (loss of capacity during research project),

    (b) regulations under section 41 (adjusting role of independent mental capacity advocacy service),

    (c) regulations under paragraph 32(1)(b) of Schedule 3 (private international law relating to the protection of adults),

    (d) an order of the kind mentioned in section 67(6) (consequential amendments of primary legislation), or

    (e) an order under section 68 (commencement),

is subject to annulment in pursuance of a resolution of either House of Parliament.

(3) A statutory instrument containing an Order in Council under paragraph 31 of Schedule 3 (provision to give further effect to Hague Convention) is subject to annulment in pursuance of a resolution of either House of Parliament.

(4) A statutory instrument containing regulations made by the Secretary of State under section 34 or 41 or by the Lord Chancellor under paragraph 32(1)(b) of Schedule 3 may not be made unless a draft has been laid before and approved by resolution of each House of Parliament.

[(4A) Subsection (2) does not apply to a statutory instrument containing regulations made by the Secretary of State under Schedule A1.

(4B) If such a statutory instrument contains regulations under paragraph 42(2) (b), 129, 162 or 164 of Schedule A1 (whether or not it also contains other regulations), the instrument may not be made unless a draft has been laid before and approved by resolution of each House of Parliament.

(4C) Subject to that, such a statutory instrument is subject to annulment in pursuance of a resolution of either House of Parliament.]

[(5) An order under section 21—

    (a) may include supplementary, incidental, consequential, transitional or saving provision;

    (b) may make different provision for different cases;

    (c) is to be made in the form of a statutory instrument to which the Statutory Instruments Act 1946 applies as if the order were made by a Minister of the Crown; and

    (d) is subject to annulment in pursuance of a resolution of either House of Parliament.]

AMENDMENTS

1–522   The amendments to this section were made by SI 2006/1016 art.2, Sch.1 and the Mental Capacity Act 2005 s.50(7), Sch.9, Pt.1, para.11.

Existing receivers and enduring powers of attorney etc

1–523   **66.**—(1) The following provisions cease to have effect—

(a)   Part 7 of the Mental Health Act,

(b)   the Enduring Powers of Attorney Act 1985 (c. 29).

(2) No enduring power of attorney within the meaning of the 1985 Act is to be created after the commencement of subsection (1)(b).

(3) Schedule 4 has effect in place of the 1985 Act in relation to any enduring power of attorney created before the commencement of subsection (1)(b).

(4) Schedule 5 contains transitional provisions and savings in relation to Part 7 of the Mental Health Act and the 1985 Act.

GENERAL NOTE

1–524   This section repeals Pt VII of the Mental Health Act 1983 and the whole of the Enduring Powers of Attorney Act 1985, but provides through transitional provisions contained in Schs 4 and 5 that those with valid powers as attorneys under the 1985 Act or receivers appointed under the 1983 Act do not lose their powers on the implementation of the repeals. It has not been possible to create an enduring power of attorney since the repeal of the 1985 Act took effect on October 1, 2007.

Subsection (3)

1–525   Schedule 4 has effect in relation to enduring powers of attorney created before the implementation of the Act. It ensures that such instruments will continue to have the same legal effect as they had at the time they were made. They will also continue to be governed by the same legal rules and procedures which were in place at the time they were made. The Schedule therefore reproduces, with amendments, the relevant provisions of the 1985 Act and provides that the principles set out in s.1 shall not retrospectively apply to EPAs. The amendments are directed to the way in which tasks performed by the replaced Court of Protection will, on implementation of the Act, be divided between the Court of Protection and the Office of Public Guardian.

Detailed consideration of the EPA regime, as amended by Sch.4, is to be found in *Heywood and Massey* (London: Sweet and Maxwell, 2010), Part A, Chs.11 and 12.

Subsection (4)

1–526   Schedule 5 contains transitional provisions that apply to circumstances where a receiver was appointed under the Mental Health Act 1983 before October 1, 2007. From that date, existing receivers became deputies with the functions that they had as receivers (Sch.5, para.1(2)). Where a former receiver wishes to make a decision for P, but may not be reason of s.20(1) because P retains the capacity to make the decision in question, the former receiver must make an application to the Court of Protection for directions (Sch.5, para.1(4)).

Minor and consequential amendments and repeals

1–527   **67.**—(1) Schedule 6 contains minor and consequential amendments.

(2) Schedule 7 contains repeals.

(3) The Lord Chancellor may by order make supplementary, incidental, consequential, transitional or saving provision for the purposes of, in consequence of, or for giving full effect to a provision of this Act.

(4) An order under subsection (3) may, in particular—

(a)   provide for a provision of this Act which comes into force before another provision of this Act has come into force to have effect, until the other provision has come into force, with specified modifications;

(b) amend, repeal or revoke an enactment, other than one contained in an Act or Measure passed in a Session after the one in which this Act is passed.

(5) The amendments that may be made under subsection (4)(b) are in addition to those made by or under any other provision of this Act.

(6) An order under subsection (3) which amends or repeals a provision of an Act or Measure may not be made unless a draft has been laid before and approved by resolution of each House of Parliament.

Commencement and extent

68.—(1) This Act, other than sections 30 to 41, comes into force in accordance with provision made by order by the Lord Chancellor.   **1–528**

(2) Sections 30 to 41 come into force in accordance with provision made by order by—

(a) the Secretary of State, in relation to England, and

(b) the National Assembly for Wales, in relation to Wales.

(3) An order under this section may appoint different days for different provisions and different purposes.

(4) Subject to subsections (5) and (6), this Act extends to England and Wales only.

(5) The following provisions extend to the United Kingdom—

(a) paragraph 16(1) of Schedule 1(evidence of instruments and of registration of lasting powers of attorney),

(b) paragraph 15(3) of Schedule 4(evidence of instruments and of registration of enduring powers of attorney).

(6) Subject to any provision made in Schedule 6, the amendments and repeals made by Schedules 6 and 7 have the same extent as the enactments to which they relate.

GENERAL NOTE

The Act is fully in force: see the Mental Capacity Act 2005 (Commencement No.1)   **1–529**
Order 2006 (SI 2006/2814) (as amended by SI 2006/3473), the Mental Capacity Act 2005 (Commencement No.1) (England and Wales) Order 2007 (SI 2007/563), the Mental Capacity Act (Commencement) (Wales) Order 2007 (SI 2007/856) (W.79) and the Mental Capacity (Commencement No.2) Order 2007 (SI 2007/1897).

Subsection (2)(b)

The functions of the National Assembly for Wales are performed by the Welsh Ministers   **1–530**
(Government of Wales Act 2006 s.162, Sch.11, para.30).

Short title

69. This Act may be cited as the Mental Capacity Act 2005.   **1–531**

SCHEDULES

[SCHEDULE A1

HOSPITAL AND CARE HOME RESIDENTS: DEPRIVATION OF LIBERTY

PART 1

AUTHORISATION TO DEPRIVE RESIDENTS OF LIBERTY ETC

Application of Part

1—532

1.—(1) This Part applies if the following conditions are met.

(2) The first condition is that a person ("P") is detained in a hospital or care home—for the purpose of being given care or treatment—

in circumstances which amount to deprivation of the person's liberty.

(3) The second condition is that a standard or urgent authorisation is in force.

(4) The third condition is that the standard or urgent authorisation relates—

(a) to P, and

(b) to the hospital or care home in which P is detained.

Authorisation to deprive P of liberty

1—533

2. The managing authority of the hospital or care home may deprive P of his liberty by detaining him as mentioned in paragraph 1(2).

No liability for acts done for purpose of depriving P of liberty

1—534

3.—(1) This paragraph applies to any act which a person ("D") does for the purpose of detaining P as mentioned in paragraph 1(2).

(2) D does not incur any liability in relation to the act that he would not have incurred if P—

(a) had had capacity to consent in relation to D's doing the act,

and

(b) had consented to D's doing the act.

No protection for negligent acts etc

1—535

4.—(1) Paragraphs 2 and 3 do not exclude a person's civil liability for loss or damage, or his criminal liability, resulting from his negligence in doing any thing.

(2) Paragraphs 2 and 3 do not authorise a person to do anything otherwise than for the purpose of the standard or urgent authorisation that is in force.

(3) In a case where a standard authorisation is in force, paragraphs 2 and 3 do not authorise a person to do anything which does not comply with the conditions (if any) included in the authorisation.

PART 2

INTERPRETATION: MAIN TERMS

Introduction

1—536

5.—This Part applies for the purposes of this Schedule.

Detained resident

1—537

6. "Detained resident" means a person detained in a hospital or care home—for the purpose of being given care or treatment—in circumstances which amount to deprivation of the person's liberty.

Relevant person etc

1—538

7. In relation to a person who is, or is to be, a detained resident—

"relevant person" means the person in question;

"relevant hospital or care home" means the hospital or care home in question;

"relevant care or treatment" means the care or treatment in question.

Authorisations

1—539
1—540
1—541

8. "Standard authorisation" means an authorisation given under Part 4.

9. "Urgent authorisation" means an authorisation given under Part 5.

10. "Authorisation under this Schedule" means either of the following—

(a) a standard authorisation;

(b) an urgent authorisation.

11.—(1) The purpose of a standard authorisation is the purpose which is stated in the authorisation in accordance with paragraph 55(1)(d).

(2) The purpose of an urgent authorisation is the purpose which is stated in the authorisation in accordance with paragraph 80(d).

1–542

PART 3

THE QUALIFYING REQUIREMENTS

The qualifying requirements

12.—(1) These are the qualifying requirements referred to in this Schedule—

1–543

(a) the age requirement;

(b) the mental health requirement;

(c) the mental capacity requirement;

(d) the best interests requirement;

(e) the eligibility requirement;

(f) the no refusals requirement.

(2) Any question of whether a person who is, or is to be, a detained resident meets the qualifying requirements is to be determined in accordance with this Part.

(3) In a case where—

(a) the question of whether a person meets a particular qualifying requirement arises in relation to the giving of a standard authorisation, and

(b) any circumstances relevant to determining that question are expected to change between the time when the determination is made and the time when the authorisation is expected to come into force,

those circumstances are to be taken into account as they are expected to be at the later time.

The age requirement

13. The relevant person meets the age requirement if he has reached 18.

1–544

The mental health requirement

14.—(1) The relevant person meets the mental health requirement if he is suffering from mental disorder (within the meaning of the Mental Health Act, but disregarding any exclusion for persons with learning disability).

1–545

(2) An exclusion for persons with learning disability is any provision of the Mental Health Act which provides for a person with learning disability not to be regarded as suffering from mental disorder for one or more purposes of that Act.

The mental capacity requirement

15. The relevant person meets the mental capacity requirement if he lacks capacity in relation to the question whether or not he should be accommodated in the relevant hospital or care home for the purpose of being given the relevant care or treatment.

1–546

The best interests requirement

16.—(1) The relevant person meets the best interests requirement if all of the following conditions are met.

1–547

(2) The first condition is that the relevant person is, or is to be, a detained resident.

(3) The second condition is that it is in the best interests of the relevant person for him to be a detained resident.

(4) The third condition is that, in order to prevent harm to the relevant person, it is necessary for him to be a detained resident.

(5) The fourth condition is that it is a proportionate response to—

(a) the likelihood of the relevant person suffering harm, and

(b) the seriousness of that harm,

for him to be a detained resident.

The eligibility requirement

17.—(1) The relevant person meets the eligibility requirement unless he is ineligible to be deprived of liberty by this Act.

1–548

(2) Schedule 1A applies for the purpose of determining whether or not P is ineligible to be deprived of liberty by this Act.

The no refusals requirement

1–549   18. The relevant person meets the no refusals requirement unless there is a refusal within the meaning of paragraph 19 or 20.

1–550   19.—(1) There is a refusal if these conditions are met—

(a)   the relevant person has made an advance decision;

(b)   the advance decision is valid;

(c)   the advance decision is applicable to some or all of the relevant treatment.

(2) Expressions used in this paragraph and any of sections 24, 25 or 26 have the same meaning in this paragraph as in that section.

1–551   20.—(1) There is a refusal if it would be in conflict with a valid decision of a donee or deputy for the relevant person to be accommodated in the relevant hospital or care home for the purpose of receiving some or all of the relevant care or treatment—

(a)   in circumstances which amount to deprivation of the person's liberty, or

(b)   at all.

(2) A donee is a donee of a lasting power of attorney granted by the relevant person.

(3) A decision of a donee or deputy is valid if it is made—

(a)   within the scope of his authority as donee or deputy, and

(b)   in accordance with Part 1 of this Act.

PART 4

STANDARD AUTHORISATIONS

Supervisory body to give authorisation

1–552   21. Only the supervisory body may give a standard authorisation.

1–553   22. The supervisory body may not give a standard authorisation unless—

(a)   the managing authority of the relevant hospital or care home have requested it, or

(b)   paragraph 71 applies (right of third party to require consideration of whether authorisation needed).

1–554   23. The managing authority may not make a request for a standard authorisation unless—

(a)   they are required to do so by paragraph 24 (as read with paragraphs 27 to 29),

(b)   they are required to do so by paragraph 25 (as read with paragraph 28), or

(c)   they are permitted to do so by paragraph 30.

Duty to request authorisation: basic cases

1–555   24.—(1) The managing authority must request a standard authorisation in any of the following cases.

(2) The first case is where it appears to the managing authority that the relevant person—

(a)   is not yet accommodated in the relevant hospital or care home,

(b)   is likely—at some time within the next 28 days—to be a detained resident in the relevant hospital or care home, and

(c)   is likely—

(i) at that time, or

(ii) at some later time within the next 28 days,

to meet all of the qualifying requirements.

(3) The second case is where it appears to the managing authority that the relevant person—

(a)   is already accommodated in the relevant hospital or care home,

(b)   is likely—at some time within the next 28 days—to be a detained resident in the relevant hospital or care home,

and

(c)   is likely—

(i) at that time, or

(ii) at some later time within the next 28 days,

to meet all of the qualifying requirements.

(4) The third case is where it appears to the managing authority that the relevant person—

(a)   is a detained resident in the relevant hospital or care home, and

(b)   meets all of the qualifying requirements, or is likely to do so at some time within the next 28 days.

(5) This paragraph is subject to paragraphs 27 to 29.

Duty to request authorisation: change in place of detention

25.—(1) The relevant managing authority must request a standard authorisation if it appears to them that these conditions are met.

1–556

(2) The first condition is that a standard authorisation—

(a) has been given, and

(b) has not ceased to be in force.

(3) The second condition is that there is, or is to be, a change in the place of detention.

(4) This paragraph is subject to paragraph 28.

26.—(1) This paragraph applies for the purposes of paragraph 25.

1–557

(2) There is a change in the place of detention if the relevant person—

(a) ceases to be a detained resident in the stated hospital or care home, and

(b) becomes a detained resident in a different hospital or care home ("the new hospital or care home").

(3) The stated hospital or care home is the hospital or care home to which the standard authorisation relates.

(4) The relevant managing authority are the managing authority of the new hospital or care home.

Other authority for detention: request for authorisation

27.—(1) This paragraph applies if, by virtue of section 4A(3), a decision of the court authorises the relevant person to be a detained resident.

1–558

(2) Paragraph 24 does not require a request for a standard authorisation to be made in relation to that detention unless these conditions are met.

(3) The first condition is that the standard authorisation would be in force at a time immediately after the expiry of the other authority.

(4) The second condition is that the standard authorisation would not be in force at any time on or before the expiry of the other authority.

(5) The third condition is that it would, in the managing authority's view, be unreasonable to delay making the request until a time nearer the expiry of the other authority.

(6) In this paragraph—

(a) the other authority is—

   (i) the decision mentioned in sub-paragraph (1), or

   (ii) any further decision of the court which, by virtue of section 4A(3), authorises, or is expected to authorise, the relevant person to be a detained resident;

(b) the expiry of the other authority is the time when the other authority is expected to cease to authorise the relevant person to be a detained resident.

Request refused: no further request unless change of circumstances

28.—(1) This paragraph applies if—

1–559

(a) a managing authority request a standard authorisation under paragraph 24 or 25, and

(b) the supervisory body are prohibited by paragraph 50(2) from giving the authorisation.

(2) Paragraph 24 or 25 does not require that managing authority to make a new request for a standard authorisation unless it appears to the managing authority that—

(a) there has been a change in the relevant person's case, and

(b) because of that change, the supervisory body are likely to give a standard authorisation if requested.

Authorisation given: request for further authorisation

29.—(1) This paragraph applies if a standard authorisation—

1–560

(a) has been given in relation to the detention of the relevant person, and

(b) that authorisation ("the existing authorisation") has not ceased to be in force.

(2) Paragraph 24 does not require a new request for a standard authorisation ("the new authorisation") to be made unless these conditions are met.

(3) The first condition is that the new authorisation would be in force at a time immediately after the expiry of the existing authorisation.

(4) The second condition is that the new authorisation would not be in force at any time on or before the expiry of the existing authorisation.

(5) The third condition is that it would, in the managing authority's view, be unreasonable to delay making the request until a time nearer the expiry of the existing authorisation.

(6) The expiry of the existing authorisation is the time when it is expected to cease to be in force.

Power to request authorisation

1–561 30.—(1) This paragraph applies if—

(a) a standard authorisation has been given in relation to the detention of the relevant person,

(b) that authorisation ("the existing authorisation") has not ceased to be in force,

(c) the requirement under paragraph 24 to make a request for a new standard authorisation does not apply, because of paragraph 29, and

(d) a review of the existing authorisation has been requested, or is being carried out, in accordance with Part 8.

(2) The managing authority may request a new standard authorisation which would be in force on or before the expiry of the existing authorisation; but only if it would also be in force immediately after that expiry.

(3) The expiry of the existing authorisation is the time when it is expected to cease to be in force.

(4) Further provision relating to cases where a request is made under this paragraph can be found in—

(a) paragraph 62 (effect of decision about request), and

(b) paragraph 124 (effect of request on Part 8 review).

Information included in request

1–562 31. A request for a standard authorisation must include the information (if any) required by regulations.

Records of requests

1–563 32.—(1) The managing authority of a hospital or care home must keep a written record of—

(a) each request that they make for a standard authorisation, and

(b) the reasons for making each request.

(2) A supervisory body must keep a written record of each request for a standard authorisation that is made to them.

Relevant person must be assessed

1–564 33.—(1) This paragraph applies if the supervisory body are requested to give a standard authorisation.

(2) The supervisory body must secure that all of these assessments are carried out in relation to the relevant person—

(a) an age assessment;

(b) a mental health assessment;

(c) a mental capacity assessment;

(d) a best interests assessment;

(e) an eligibility assessment;

(f) a no refusals assessment.

(3) The person who carries out any such assessment is referred to as the assessor.

(4) Regulations may be made about the period (or periods) within which assessors must carry out assessments.

(5) This paragraph is subject to paragraphs 49 and 133.

Age assessment

1–565 34. An age assessment is an assessment of whether the relevant person meets the age requirement.

Mental health assessment

1–566 35. A mental health assessment is an assessment of whether the relevant person meets the mental health requirement.

1–567 36. When carrying out a mental health assessment, the assessor must also—

(a) consider how (if at all) the relevant person's mental health is likely to be affected by his being a detained resident, and

(b) notify the best interests assessor of his conclusions.

Mental capacity assessment

1–568 37. A mental capacity assessment is an assessment of whether the relevant person meets the mental capacity requirement.

Best interests assessment

38. A best interests assessment is an assessment of whether the relevant person meets the best interests requirement.　　　**1–569**

39.—(1) In carrying out a best interests assessment, the assessor must comply with the duties in sub-paragraphs (2) and (3).　　　**1–570**

(2) The assessor must consult the managing authority of the relevant hospital or care home.

(3) The assessor must have regard to all of the following—

(a)　the conclusions which the mental health assessor has notified to the best interests assessor in accordance with paragraph 36(b);

(b)　any relevant needs assessment;

(c)　any relevant care plan.

(4) A relevant needs assessment is an assessment of the relevant person's needs which—

(a)　was carried out in connection with the relevant person being accommodated in the relevant hospital or care home, and

(b)　was carried out by or on behalf of—

　(i) the managing authority of the relevant hospital or care home, or

　(ii) the supervisory body.

(5) A relevant care plan is a care plan which—

(a)　sets out how the relevant person's needs are to be met whilst he is accommodated in the relevant hospital or care home, and

(b)　was drawn up by or on behalf of—

　(i) the managing authority of the relevant hospital or care home, or

　(ii) the supervisory body.

(6) The managing authority must give the assessor a copy of—

(a)　any relevant needs assessment carried out by them or on their behalf, or

(b)　any relevant care plan drawn up by them or on their behalf.

(7) The supervisory body must give the assessor a copy of—

(a)　any relevant needs assessment carried out by them or on their behalf, or

(b)　any relevant care plan drawn up by them or on their behalf.

(8) The duties in sub-paragraphs (2) and (3) do not affect any other duty to consult or to take the views of others into account.

40.—(1) This paragraph applies whatever conclusion the best interests assessment comes to.　　　**1–571**

(2) The assessor must state in the best interests assessment the name and address of every interested person whom he has consulted in carrying out the assessment.

41. Paragraphs 42 and 43 apply if the best interests assessment comes to the conclusion that the relevant person meets the best interests requirement.　　　**1–572**

42.—(1) The assessor must state in the assessment the maximum authorisation period.　　　**1–573**

(2) The maximum authorisation period is the shorter of these periods—

(a)　the period which, in the assessor's opinion, would be the appropriate maximum period for the relevant person to be a detained resident under the standard authorisation that has been requested;

(b)　1 year, or such shorter period as may be prescribed in regulations.

(3) Regulations under sub-paragraph (2)(b)—

(a)　need not provide for a shorter period to apply in relation to all standard authorisations;

(b)　may provide for different periods to apply in relation to different kinds of standard authorisations.

(4) Before making regulations under sub-paragraph (2)(b) the Secretary of State must consult all of the following—

(a)　each body required by regulations under paragraph 162 to monitor and report on the operation of this Schedule in relation to England;

(b)　such other persons as the Secretary of State considers it appropriate to consult.

(5) Before making regulations under sub-paragraph (2)(b) the National Assembly for Wales must consult all of the following—

(a)　each person or body directed under paragraph 163(2) to carry out any function of the Assembly of monitoring and reporting on the operation of this Schedule in relation to Wales;

(b)　such other persons as the Assembly considers it appropriate to consult.

43. The assessor may include in the assessment recommendations about conditions to which the standard authorisation is, or is not, to be subject in accordance with paragraph 53.　　　**1–574**

44.—(1) This paragraph applies if the best interests assessment comes to the conclusion that the relevant person does not meet the best interests requirement.　　　**1–575**

(2) If, on the basis of the information taken into account in carrying out the assessment, it appears

to the assessor that there is an unauthorised deprivation of liberty, he must include a statement to that effect in the assessment.

(3) There is an unauthorised deprivation of liberty if the managing authority of the relevant hospital or care home are already depriving the relevant person of his liberty without authority of the kind mentioned in section 4A.

1–576   45. The duties with which the best interests assessor must comply are subject to the provision included in appointment regulations under Part 10 (in particular, provision made under paragraph 146).

Eligibility assessment

1–577   46. An eligibility assessment is an assessment of whether the relevant person meets the eligibility requirement.

1–578   47.—(1) Regulations may—

(a) require an eligibility assessor to request a best interests assessor to provide relevant eligibility information, and

(b) require the best interests assessor, if such a request is made, to provide such relevant eligibility information as he may have.

(2) In this paragraph—

"best interests assessor" means any person who is carrying out, or has carried out, a best interests assessment in relation to the relevant person;

"eligibility assessor" means a person carrying out an eligibility assessment in relation to the relevant person;

"relevant eligibility information" is information relevant to assessing whether or not the relevant person is ineligible by virtue of paragraph 5 of Schedule 1A.

No refusals assessment

1–579   48. A no refusals assessment is an assessment of whether the relevant person meets the no refusals requirement.

Equivalent assessment already carried out

1–580   49.—(1) The supervisory body are not required by paragraph 33 to secure that a particular kind of assessment ("the required assessment") is carried out in relation to the relevant person if the following conditions are met.

(2) The first condition is that the supervisory body have a written copy of an assessment of the relevant person ("the existing assessment") that has already been carried out.

(3) The second condition is that the existing assessment complies with all requirements under this Schedule with which the required assessment would have to comply (if it were carried out).

(4) The third condition is that the existing assessment was carried out within the previous 12 months; but this condition need not be met if the required assessment is an age assessment.

(5) The fourth condition is that the supervisory body are satisfied that there is no reason why the existing assessment may no longer be accurate.

(6) If the required assessment is a best interests assessment, in satisfying themselves as mentioned in sub-paragraph (5), the supervisory body must take into account any information given, or submissions made, by—

(a) the relevant person's representative,

(b) any section 39C IMCA, or

(c) any section 39D IMCA.

(7) It does not matter whether the existing assessment was carried out in connection with a request for a standard authorisation or for some other purpose.

(8) If, because of this paragraph, the supervisory body are not required by paragraph 33 to secure that the required assessment is carried out, the existing assessment is to be treated for the purposes of this Schedule—

(a) as an assessment of the same kind as the required assessment, and

(b) as having been carried out under paragraph 33 in connection with the request for the standard authorisation.

Duty to give authorisation

1–581   50.—(1) The supervisory body must give a standard authorisation if—

(a) all assessments are positive, and

(b) the supervisory body have written copies of all those assessments.

(2) The supervisory body must not give a standard authorisation except in accordance with sub-paragraph (1).

(3) All assessments are positive if each assessment carried out under paragraph 33 has come to the conclusion that the relevant person meets the qualifying requirement to which the assessment relates.

Terms of authorisation

51.—(1) If the supervisory body are required to give a standard authorisation, they must decide the period during which the authorisation is to be in force.　　1–582

(2) That period must not exceed the maximum authorisation period stated in the best interests assessment.

52. A standard authorisation may provide for the authorisation to come into force at a time after it is given.　　1–583

53.—(1) A standard authorisation may be given subject to conditions.　　1–584

(2) Before deciding whether to give the authorisation subject to conditions, the supervisory body must have regard to any recommendations in the best interests assessment about such conditions.

(3) The managing authority of the relevant hospital or care home must ensure that any conditions are complied with.

Form of authorisation

54. A standard authorisation must be in writing.　　1–585

55.—(1) A standard authorisation must state the following things—　　1–586

(a) the name of the relevant person;

(b) the name of the relevant hospital or care home;

(c) the period during which the authorisation is to be in force;

(d) the purpose for which the authorisation is given;

(e) any conditions subject to which the authorisation is given;

(f) the reason why each qualifying requirement is met.

(2) The statement of the reason why the eligibility requirement is met must be framed by reference to the cases in the table in paragraph 2 of Schedule 1A.

56.—(1) If the name of the relevant hospital or care home changes, the standard authorisation is to be read as if it stated the current name of the hospital or care home.　　1–587

(2) But sub-paragraph (1) is subject to any provision relating to the change of name which is made in any enactment or in any instrument made under an enactment.

Duty to give information about decision

57.—(1) This paragraph applies if—　　1–588

(a) a request is made for a standard authorisation, and

(b) the supervisory body are required by paragraph 50(1) to give the standard authorisation.

(2) The supervisory body must give a copy of the authorisation to each of the following—

(a) the relevant person's representative;

(b) the managing authority of the relevant hospital or care home;

(c) the relevant person;

(d) any section 39A IMCA;

(e) every interested person consulted by the best interests assessor.

(3) The supervisory body must comply with this paragraph as soon as practicable after they give the standard authorisation.

58.—(1) This paragraph applies if—　　1–589

(a) a request is made for a standard authorisation, and

(b) the supervisory body are prohibited by paragraph 50(2) from giving the standard authorisation.

(2) The supervisory body must give notice, stating that they are prohibited from giving the authorisation, to each of the following—

(a) the managing authority of the relevant hospital or care home;

(b) the relevant person;

(c) any section 39A IMCA;

(d) every interested person consulted by the best interests assessor.

(3) The supervisory body must comply with this paragraph as soon as practicable after it becomes apparent to them that they are prohibited from giving the authorisation.

Duty to give information about effect of authorisation

59.—(1) This paragraph applies if a standard authorisation is given.　　1–590

(2) The managing authority of the relevant hospital or care home must take such steps as are practicable to ensure that the relevant person understands all of the following—

(a) the effect of the authorisation;

(b) the right to make an application to the court to exercise its jurisdiction under section 21A;

(c) the right under Part 8 to request a review;

(d) the right to have a section 39D IMCA appointed;

(e) how to have a section 39D IMCA appointed.

(3) Those steps must be taken as soon as is practicable after the authorisation is given.

(4) Those steps must include the giving of appropriate information both orally and in writing.

(5) Any written information given to the relevant person must also be given by the managing authority to the relevant person's representative.

(6) They must give the information to the representative as soon as is practicable after it is given to the relevant person.

(7) Sub-paragraph (8) applies if the managing authority is notified that a section 39D IMCA has been appointed.

(8) As soon as is practicable after being notified, the managing authority must give the section 39D IMCA a copy of the written information given in accordance with sub-paragraph (4).

Records of authorisations

1–591   **60.** A supervisory body must keep a written record of all of the following information—

(a) the standard authorisations that they have given;

(b) the requests for standard authorisations in response to which they have not given an authorisation;

(c) in relation to each standard authorisation given: the matters stated in the authorisation in accordance with paragraph 55.

Variation of an authorisation

1–592   **61.**—(1) A standard authorisation may not be varied except in accordance with Part 7 or 8.

(2) This paragraph does not affect the powers of the Court of Protection or of any other court.

Effect of decision about request made under paragraph 25 or 30

1–593   **62.**—(1) This paragraph applies where the managing authority request a new standard authorisation under either of the following—

(a) paragraph 25 (change in place of detention);

(b) paragraph 30 (existing authorisation subject to review).

(2) If the supervisory body are required by paragraph 50(1) to give the new authorisation, the existing authorisation terminates at the time when the new authorisation comes into force.

(3) If the supervisory body are prohibited by paragraph 50(2) from giving the new authorisation, there is no effect on the existing authorisation's continuation in force.

When an authorisation is in force

1–594   **63.**—(1) A standard authorisation comes into force when it is given.

(2) But if the authorisation provides for it to come into force at a later time, it comes into force at that time.

1–595   **64.**—(1) A standard authorisation ceases to be in force at the end of the period stated in the authorisation in accordance with paragraph 55(1)(c).

(2) But if the authorisation terminates before then in accordance with paragraph 62(2) or any other provision of this Schedule, it ceases to be in force when the termination takes effect.

(3) This paragraph does not affect the powers of the Court of Protection or of any other court.

1–596   **65.**—(1) This paragraph applies if a standard authorisation ceases to be in force.

(2) The supervisory body must give notice that the authorisation has ceased to be in force.

(3) The supervisory body must give that notice to all of the following—

(a) the managing authority of the relevant hospital or care home;

(b) the relevant person;

(c) the relevant person's representative;

(d) every interested person consulted by the best interests assessor.

(4) The supervisory body must give that notice as soon as practicable after the authorisation ceases to be in force.

When a request for a standard authorisation is "disposed of"

1–597   **66.**—A request for a standard authorisation is to be regarded for the purposes of this Schedule as disposed of if the supervisory body have given—

(a) a copy of the authorisation in accordance with paragraph 57, or

(b) notice in accordance with paragraph 58.

Right of third party to require consideration of whether authorisation needed

67. For the purposes of paragraphs 68 to 73 there is an unauthorised deprivation of liberty if— 1–598

(a) a person is already a detained resident in a hospital or care home, and

(b) the detention of the person is not authorised as mentioned in section 4A.

68.—(1) If the following conditions are met, an eligible person may request the supervisory body 1–599
to decide whether or not there is an unauthorised deprivation of liberty.

(2) The first condition is that the eligible person has notified the managing authority of the relevant hospital or care home that it appears to the eligible person that there is an unauthorised deprivation of liberty.

(3) The second condition is that the eligible person has asked the managing authority to request a standard authorisation in relation to the detention of the relevant person.

(4) The third condition is that the managing authority has not requested a standard authorisation within a reasonable period after the eligible person asks it to do so.

(5) In this paragraph "eligible person" means any person other than the managing authority of the relevant hospital or care home.

69.—(1) This paragraph applies if an eligible person requests the supervisory body to decide 1–600
whether or not there is an unauthorised deprivation of liberty.

(2) The supervisory body must select and appoint a person to carry out an assessment of whether or not the relevant person is a detained resident.

(3) But the supervisory body need not select and appoint a person to carry out such an assessment in either of these cases.

(4) The first case is where it appears to the supervisory body that the request by the eligible person is frivolous or vexatious.

(5) The second case is where it appears to the supervisory body that—

(a) the question of whether or not there is an unauthorised deprivation of liberty has already been decided, and

(b) since that decision, there has been no change of circumstances which would merit the question being decided again.

(6) The supervisory body must not select and appoint a person to carry out an assessment under this paragraph unless it appears to the supervisory body that the person would be—

(a) suitable to carry out a best interests assessment (if one were obtained in connection with a request for a standard authorisation relating to the relevant person), and

(b) eligible to carry out such a best interests assessment.

(7) The supervisory body must notify the persons specified in subparagraph (8)—

(a) that the supervisory body have been requested to decide whether or not there is an unauthorised deprivation of liberty;

(b) of their decision whether or not to select and appoint a person to carry out an assessment under this paragraph;

(c) if their decision is to select and appoint a person, of the person appointed.

(8) The persons referred to in sub-paragraph (7) are—

(a) the eligible person who made the request under paragraph 68;

(b) the person to whom the request relates;

(c) the managing authority of the relevant hospital or care home;

(d) any section 39A IMCA.

70.—(1) Regulations may be made about the period within which an assessment under paragraph 1–601
69 must be carried out.

(2) Regulations made under paragraph 129(3) apply in relation to the selection and appointment of a person under paragraph 69 as they apply to the selection of a person under paragraph 129 to carry out a best interests assessment.

(3) The following provisions apply to an assessment under paragraph 69 as they apply to an assessment carried out in connection with a request for a standard authorisation—

(a) paragraph 131 (examination and copying of records);

(b) paragraph 132 (representations);

(c) paragraphs 134 and 135(1) and (2) (duty to keep records and give copies).

(4) The copies of the assessment which the supervisory body are required to give under paragraph 135(2) must be given as soon as practicable after the supervisory body are themselves given a copy of the assessment.

71.—(1) This paragraph applies if— 1–602

(a) the supervisory body obtain an assessment under paragraph 69,

(b) the assessment comes to the conclusion that the relevant person is a detained resident, and

(c) it appears to the supervisory body that the detention of the person is not authorised as mentioned in section 4A.

(2) This Schedule (including Part 5) applies as if the managing authority of the relevant hospital or care home had, in accordance with Part 4, requested the supervisory body to give a standard authorisation in relation to the relevant person.

(3) The managing authority of the relevant hospital or care home must supply the supervisory body with the information (if any) which the managing authority would, by virtue of paragraph 31, have had to include in a request for a standard authorisation.

(4) The supervisory body must notify the persons specified in paragraph 69(8)—

(a) of the outcome of the assessment obtained under paragraph 69, and

(b) that this Schedule applies as mentioned in sub-paragraph (2).

1–603 72.—(1) This paragraph applies if—

(a) the supervisory body obtain an assessment under paragraph 69, and

(b) the assessment comes to the conclusion that the relevant person is not a detained resident.

(2) The supervisory body must notify the persons specified in paragraph 69(8) of the outcome of the assessment.

1–604 73.—(1) This paragraph applies if—

(a) the supervisory body obtain an assessment under paragraph 69,

(b) the assessment comes to the conclusion that the relevant person is a detained resident, and

(c) it appears to the supervisory body that the detention of the person is authorised as mentioned in section 4A.

(2) The supervisory body must notify the persons specified in paragraph 69(8)—

(a) of the outcome of the assessment, and

(b) that it appears to the supervisory body that the detention is authorised.

PART 5

URGENT AUTHORISATIONS

Managing authority to give authorisation

1–605 74. Only the managing authority of the relevant hospital or care home may give an urgent authorisation.

1–606 75. The managing authority may give an urgent authorisation only if they are required to do so by paragraph 76 (as read with paragraph 77).

Duty to give authorisation

1–607 76.—(1) The managing authority must give an urgent authorisation in either of the following cases.

(2) The first case is where—

(a) the managing authority are required to make a request under paragraph 24 or 25 for a standard authorisation, and

(b) they believe that the need for the relevant person to be a detained resident is so urgent that it is appropriate for the detention to begin before they make the request.

(3) The second case is where—

(a) the managing authority have made a request under paragraph 24 or 25 for a standard authorisation, and

(b) they believe that the need for the relevant person to be a detained resident is so urgent that it is appropriate for the detention to begin before the request is disposed of.

(4) References in this paragraph to the detention of the relevant person are references to the detention to which paragraph 24 or 25 relates.

(5) This paragraph is subject to paragraph 77.

1–608 77.—(1) This paragraph applies where the managing authority have given an urgent authorisation ("the original authorisation") in connection with a case where a person is, or is to be, a detained resident ("the existing detention").

(2) No new urgent authorisation is to be given under paragraph 76 in connection with the existing detention.

(3) But the managing authority may request the supervisory body to extend the duration of the original authorisation.

(4) Only one request under sub-paragraph (3) may be made in relation to the original authorisation.

(5) Paragraphs 84 to 86 apply to any request made under subparagraph (3).

Terms of authorisation

78.—(1) If the managing authority decide to give an urgent authorisation, they must decide the period during which the authorisation is to be in force.

(2) That period must not exceed 7 days.

1–609

Form of authorisation

79. An urgent authorisation must be in writing.

80. An urgent authorisation must state the following things—

    (a) the name of the relevant person;

    (b) the name of the relevant hospital or care home;

    (c) the period during which the authorisation is to be in force;

    (d) the purpose for which the authorisation is given.

81.—(1) If the name of the relevant hospital or care home changes, the urgent authorisation is to be read as if it stated the current name of the hospital or care home.

(2) But sub-paragraph (1) is subject to any provision relating to the change of name which is made in any enactment or in any instrument made under an enactment.

1–610
1–611

1–612

Duty to keep records and give copies

82.—(1) This paragraph applies if an urgent authorisation is given.

(2) The managing authority must keep a written record of why they have given the urgent authorisation.

(3) As soon as practicable after giving the authorisation, the managing authority must give a copy of the authorisation to all of the following—

    (a) the relevant person;

    (b) any section 39A IMCA.

1–613

Duty to give information about authorisation

83.—(1) This paragraph applies if an urgent authorisation is given.

(2) The managing authority of the relevant hospital or care home must take such steps as are practicable to ensure that the relevant person understands all of the following—

    (a) the effect of the authorisation;

    (b) the right to make an application to the court to exercise its jurisdiction under section 21A.

(3) Those steps must be taken as soon as is practicable after the authorisation is given.

(4) Those steps must include the giving of appropriate information both orally and in writing.

1–614

Request for extension of duration

84.—(1) This paragraph applies if the managing authority make a request under paragraph 77 for the supervisory body to extend the duration of the original authorisation.

(2) The managing authority must keep a written record of why they have made the request.

(3) The managing authority must give the relevant person notice that they have made the request.

(4) The supervisory body may extend the duration of the original authorisation if it appears to them that—

    (a) the managing authority have made the required request for a standard authorisation,

    (b) there are exceptional reasons why it has not yet been possible for that request to be disposed of, and

    (c) it is essential for the existing detention to continue until the request is disposed of.

(5) The supervisory body must keep a written record that the request has been made to them.

(6) In this paragraph and paragraphs 85 and 86—

    (a) "original authorisation" and "existing detention" have the same meaning as in paragraph 77;

    (b) the required request for a standard authorisation is the request that is referred to in paragraph 76(2) or (3).

85.—(1) This paragraph applies if, under paragraph 84, the supervisory body decide to extend the duration of the original authorisation.

(2) The supervisory body must decide the period of the extension.

(3) That period must not exceed 7 days.

(4) The supervisory body must give the managing authority notice stating the period of the extension.

(5) The managing authority must then vary the original authorisation so that it states the extended duration.

(6) Paragraphs 82(3) and 83 apply (with the necessary modifications) to the variation of the original authorisation as they apply to the giving of an urgent authorisation.

1–615

1–616

(7) The supervisory body must keep a written record of—

(a) the outcome of the request, and

(b) the period of the extension.

1–617   **86.**—(1) This paragraph applies if, under paragraph 84, the supervisory body decide not to extend the duration of the original authorisation.

(2) The supervisory body must give the managing authority notice stating—

(a) the decision, and

(b) their reasons for making it.

(3) The managing authority must give a copy of that notice to all of the following—

(a) the relevant person;

(b) any section 39A IMCA.

(4) The supervisory body must keep a written record of the outcome of the request.

No variation

1–618   **87.**—(1) An urgent authorisation may not be varied except in accordance with paragraph 85.

(2) This paragraph does not affect the powers of the Court of Protection or of any other court.

When an authorisation is in force

1–619   **88.** An urgent authorisation comes into force when it is given.

1–620   **89.**—(1) An urgent authorisation ceases to be in force at the end of the period stated in the authorisation in accordance with paragraph 80(c) (subject to any variation in accordance with paragraph 85).

(2) But if the required request is disposed of before the end of that period, the urgent authorisation ceases to be in force as follows.

(3) If the supervisory body are required by paragraph 50(1) to give the requested authorisation, the urgent authorisation ceases to be in force when the requested authorisation comes into force.

(4) If the supervisory body are prohibited by paragraph 50(2) from giving the requested authorisation, the urgent authorisation ceases to be in force when the managing authority receive notice under paragraph 58.

(5) In this paragraph—

"required request" means the request referred to in paragraph 76(2) or (3);

"requested authorisation" means the standard authorisation to which the required request relates.

(6) This paragraph does not affect the powers of the Court of Protection or of any other court.

1–621   **90.**—(1) This paragraph applies if an urgent authorisation ceases to be in force.

(2) The supervisory body must give notice that the authorisation has ceased to be in force.

(3) The supervisory body must give that notice to all of the following—

(a) the relevant person;

(b) any section 39A IMCA.

(4) The supervisory body must give that notice as soon as practicable after the authorisation ceases to be in force.

PART 6

ELIGIBILITY REQUIREMENT NOT MET: SUSPENSION OF STANDARD AUTHORISATION

1–622   **91.**—(1) This Part applies if the following conditions are met.

(2) The first condition is that a standard authorisation—

(a) has been given, and

(b) has not ceased to be in force.

(3) The second condition is that the managing authority of the relevant hospital or care home are satisfied that the relevant person has ceased to meet the eligibility requirement.

(4) But this Part does not apply if the relevant person is ineligible by virtue of paragraph 5 of Schedule 1A (in which case see Part 8).

1–623   **92.** The managing authority of the relevant hospital or care home must give the supervisory body notice that the relevant person has ceased to meet the eligibility requirement.

1–624   **93.**—(1) This paragraph applies if the managing authority give the supervisory body notice under paragraph 92.

(2) The standard authorisation is suspended from the time when the notice is given.

(3) The supervisory body must give notice that the standard authorisation has been suspended to the following persons—

(a) the relevant person;

(b) the relevant person's representative;

(c) the managing authority of the relevant hospital or care home.

94.—(1) This paragraph applies if, whilst the standard authorisation is suspended, the managing authority are satisfied that the relevant person meets the eligibility requirement again.

(2) The managing authority must give the supervisory body notice that the relevant person meets the eligibility requirement again.

95.—(1) This paragraph applies if the managing authority give the supervisory body notice under paragraph 94.

(2) The standard authorisation ceases to be suspended from the time when the notice is given.

(3) The supervisory body must give notice that the standard authorisation has ceased to be suspended to the following persons—

(a) the relevant person;

(b) the relevant person's representative;

(c) any section 39D IMCA;

(d) the managing authority of the relevant hospital or care home.

(4) The supervisory body must give notice under this paragraph as soon as practicable after they are given notice under paragraph 94.

96.—(1) This paragraph applies if no notice is given under paragraph 94 before the end of the relevant 28 day period.

(2) The standard authorisation ceases to have effect at the end of the relevant 28 day period.

(3) The relevant 28 day period is the period of 28 days beginning with the day on which the standard authorisation is suspended under paragraph 93.

97. The effect of suspending the standard authorisation is that Part 1 ceases to apply for as long as the authorisation is suspended.

1–625

1–626

1–627

1–628

PART 7

STANDARD AUTHORISATIONS: CHANGE IN SUPERVISORY RESPONSIBILITY

Application of this Part

98.—(1) This Part applies if these conditions are met.

(2) The first condition is that a standard authorisation—

(a) has been given, and

(b) has not ceased to be in force.

(3) The second condition is that there is a change in supervisory responsibility.

(4) The third condition is that there is not a change in the place of detention (within the meaning of paragraph 25).

99. For the purposes of this Part there is a change in supervisory responsibility if—

(a) one body ("the old supervisory body") have ceased to be supervisory body in relation to the standard authorisation, and

(b) a different body ("the new supervisory body") have become supervisory body in relation to the standard authorisation.

1–629

1–630

Effect of change in supervisory responsibility

100.—(1) The new supervisory body becomes the supervisory body in relation to the authorisation.

(2) Anything done by or in relation to the old supervisory body in connection with the authorisation has effect, so far as is necessary for continuing its effect after the change, as if done by or in relation to the new supervisory body.

(3) Anything which relates to the authorisation and which is in the process of being done by or in relation to the old supervisory body at the time of the change may be continued by or in relation to the new supervisory body.

(4) But—

(a) the old supervisory body do not, by virtue of this paragraph, cease to be liable for anything done by them in connection with the authorisation before the change; and

(b) the new supervisory body do not, by virtue of this paragraph, become liable for any such thing.

1–631

PART 8

STANDARD AUTHORISATIONS: REVIEW

Application of this Part

101.—(1) This Part applies if a standard authorisation—

(a) has been given, and

1–632

(b) has not ceased to be in force.

(2) Paragraphs 102 to 122 are subject to paragraphs 123 to 125.

Review by supervisory body

1–633

102.—(1) The supervisory body may at any time carry out a review of the standard authorisation in accordance with this Part.

(2) The supervisory body must carry out such a review if they are requested to do so by an eligible person.

(3) Each of the following is an eligible person—

(a) the relevant person;

(b) the relevant person's representative;

(c) the managing authority of the relevant hospital or care home.

Request for review

1–634

103.—(1) An eligible person may, at any time, request the supervisory body to carry out a review of the standard authorisation in accordance with this Part.

(2) The managing authority of the relevant hospital or care home must make such a request if one or more of the qualifying requirements appear to them to be reviewable.

Grounds for review

1–635

104.—(1) Paragraphs 105 to 107 set out the grounds on which the qualifying requirements are reviewable.

(2) A qualifying requirement is not reviewable on any other ground.

Non-qualification ground

1–636

105.—(1) Any of the following qualifying requirements is reviewable on the ground that the relevant person does not meet the requirement—

(a) the age requirement;

(b) the mental health requirement;

(c) the mental capacity requirement;

(d) the best interests requirement;

(e) the no refusals requirement.

(2) The eligibility requirement is reviewable on the ground that the relevant person is ineligible by virtue of paragraph 5 of Schedule 1A.

(3) The ground in sub-paragraph (1) and the ground in subparagraph (2) are referred to as the non-qualification ground.

Change of reason ground

1–637

106.—(1) Any of the following qualifying requirements is reviewable on the ground set out in sub-paragraph (2)—

(a) the mental health requirement;

(b) the mental capacity requirement;

(c) the best interests requirement;

(d) the eligibility requirement;

(e) the no refusals requirement.

(2) The ground is that the reason why the relevant person meets the requirement is not the reason stated in the standard authorisation.

(3) This ground is referred to as the change of reason ground.

Variation of conditions ground

1–638

107.—(1) The best interests requirement is reviewable on the ground that—

(a) there has been a change in the relevant person's case, and

(b) because of that change, it would be appropriate to vary the conditions to which the standard authorisation is subject.

(2) This ground is referred to as the variation of conditions ground.

(3) A reference to varying the conditions to which the standard authorisation is subject is a reference to—

(a) amendment of an existing condition,

(b) omission of an existing condition, or

(c) inclusion of a new condition (whether or not there are already any existing conditions).

Notice that review to be carried out

108.—(1) If the supervisory body are to carry out a review of the standard authorisation, they must give notice of the review to the following persons— **1–639**

(a) the relevant person;

(b) the relevant person's representative;

(c) the managing authority of the relevant hospital or care home.

(2) The supervisory body must give the notice—

(a) before they begin the review, or

(b) if that is not practicable, as soon as practicable after they have begun it.

(3) This paragraph does not require the supervisory body to give notice to any person who has requested the review.

Starting a review

109.—To start a review of the standard authorisation, the supervisory body must decide which, if any, of the qualifying requirements appear to be reviewable. **1–640**

No reviewable qualifying requirements

110.—(1) This paragraph applies if no qualifying requirements appear to be reviewable. **1–641**

(2) This Part does not require the supervisory body to take any action in respect of the standard authorisation.

One or more reviewable qualifying requirements

111.—(1) This paragraph applies if one or more qualifying requirements appear to be reviewable. **1–642**

(2) The supervisory body must secure that a separate review assessment is carried out in relation to each qualifying requirement which appears to be reviewable.

(3) But sub-paragraph (2) does not require the supervisory body to secure that a best interests review assessment is carried out in a case where the best interests requirement appears to the supervisory body to be non-assessable.

(4) The best interests requirement is non-assessable if—

(a) the requirement is reviewable only on the variation of conditions ground, and

(b) the change in the relevant person's case is not significant.

(5) In making any decision whether the change in the relevant person's case is significant, regard must be had to—

(a) the nature of the change, and

(b) the period that the change is likely to last for.

Review assessments

112.—(1) A review assessment is an assessment of whether the relevant person meets a qualifying requirement. **1–643**

(2) In relation to a review assessment—

(a) a negative conclusion is a conclusion that the relevant person does not meet the qualifying requirement to which the assessment relates;

(b) a positive conclusion is a conclusion that the relevant person meets the qualifying requirement to which the assessment relates.

(3) An age review assessment is a review assessment carried out in relation to the age requirement.

(4) A mental health review assessment is a review assessment carried out in relation to the mental health requirement.

(5) A mental capacity review assessment is a review assessment carried out in relation to the mental capacity requirement.

(6) A best interests review assessment is a review assessment carried out in relation to the best interests requirement.

(7) An eligibility review assessment is a review assessment carried out in relation to the eligibility requirement.

(8) A no refusals review assessment is a review assessment carried out in relation to the no refusals requirement.

113.—(1) In carrying out a review assessment, the assessor must comply with any duties which would be imposed upon him under Part 4 if the assessment were being carried out in connection with a request for a standard authorisation. **1–644**

(2) But in the case of a best interests review assessment, paragraphs 43 and 44 do not apply.

(3) Instead of what is required by paragraph 43, the best interests review assessment must include

recommendations about whether — and, if so, how — it would be appropriate to vary the conditions to which the standard authorisation is subject.

Best interests requirement reviewable but non-assessable

1–645   **114.**—(1) This paragraph applies in a case where—

(a) the best interests requirement appears to be reviewable, but

(b) in accordance with paragraph 111(3), the supervisory body are not required to secure that a best interests review assessment is carried out.

(2) The supervisory body may vary the conditions to which the standard authorisation is subject in such ways (if any) as the supervisory body think are appropriate in the circumstances.

Best interests review assessment positive

1–646   **115.**—(1) This paragraph applies in a case where—

(a) a best interests review assessment is carried out, and

(b) the assessment comes to a positive conclusion.

(2) The supervisory body must decide the following questions—

(a) whether or not the best interests requirement is reviewable on the change of reason ground;

(b) whether or not the best interests requirement is reviewable on the variation of conditions ground;

(c) if so, whether or not the change in the person's case is significant.

(3) If the supervisory body decide that the best interests requirement is reviewable on the change of reason ground, they must vary the standard authorisation so that it states the reason why the relevant person now meets that requirement.

(4) If the supervisory body decide that—

(a) the best interests requirement is reviewable on the variation of conditions ground, and

(b) the change in the relevant person's case is not significant,

they may vary the conditions to which the standard authorisation is subject in such ways (if any) as they think are appropriate in the circumstances.

(5) If the supervisory body decide that—

(a) the best interests requirement is reviewable on the variation of conditions ground, and

(b) the change in the relevant person's case is significant,

they must vary the conditions to which the standard authorisation is subject in such ways as they think are appropriate in the circumstances.

(6) If the supervisory body decide that the best interests requirement is not reviewable on—

(a) the change of reason ground, or

(b) the variation of conditions ground,

this Part does not require the supervisory body to take any action in respect of the standard authorisation so far as the best interests requirement relates to it.

Mental health, mental capacity, eligibility or no refusals review assessment positive

1–647   **116.**—(1) This paragraph applies if the following conditions are met.

(2) The first condition is that one or more of the following are carried out—

(a) a mental health review assessment;

(b) a mental capacity review assessment;

(c) an eligibility review assessment;

(d) a no refusals review assessment.

(3) The second condition is that each assessment carried out comes to a positive conclusion.

(4) The supervisory body must decide whether or not each of the assessed qualifying requirements is reviewable on the change of reason ground.

(5) If the supervisory body decide that any of the assessed qualifying requirements is reviewable on the change of reason ground, they must vary the standard authorisation so that it states the reason why the relevant person now meets the requirement or requirements in question.

(6) If the supervisory body decide that none of the assessed qualifying requirements are reviewable on the change of reason ground, this Part does not require the supervisory body to take any action in respect of the standard authorisation so far as those requirements relate to it.

(7) An assessed qualifying requirement is a qualifying requirement in relation to which a review assessment is carried out.

One or more review assessments negative
117.—(1) This paragraph applies if one or more of the review assessments carried out comes to a negative conclusion.
    (2) The supervisory body must terminate the standard authorisation with immediate effect.

1–648

Completion of a review
118.—(1) The review of the standard authorisation is complete in any of the following cases.
    (2) The first case is where paragraph 110 applies.
    (3) The second case is where—
    (a) paragraph 111 applies, and
    (b) paragraph 117 requires the supervisory body to terminate the standard authorisation.
    (4) In such a case, the supervisory body need not comply with any of the other provisions of paragraphs 114 to 116 which would be applicable to the review (were it not for this sub-paragraph).
    (5) The third case is where—
    (a) paragraph 111 applies,
    (b) paragraph 117 does not require the supervisory body to terminate the standard authorisation, and
    (c) the supervisory body comply with all of the provisions of paragraphs 114 to 116 (so far as they are applicable to the review).

1–649

Variations under this Part
119. Any variation of the standard authorisation made under this Part must be in writing.

1–650

Notice of outcome of review
120.—(1) When the review of the standard authorisation is complete, the supervisory body must give notice to all of the following—
    (a) the managing authority of the relevant hospital or care home;
    (b) the relevant person;
    (c) the relevant person's representative;
    (d) any section 39D IMCA.
    (2) That notice must state—
    (a) the outcome of the review, and
    (b) what variation (if any) has been made to the authorisation under this Part.

1–651

Records
121. A supervisory body must keep a written record of the following information—
    (a) each request for a review that is made to them;
    (b) the outcome of each request;
    (c) each review which they carry out;
    (d) the outcome of each review which they carry out;
    (e) any variation of an authorisation made in consequence of a review.

1–652

Relationship between review and suspension under Part 6
122.—(1) This paragraph applies if a standard authorisation is suspended in accordance with Part 6.
    (2) No review may be requested under this Part whilst the standard authorisation is suspended.
    (3) If a review has already been requested, or is being carried out, when the standard authorisation is suspended, no steps are to be taken in connection with that review whilst the authorisation is suspended.

1–653

Relationship between review and request for new authorisation
123.—(1) This paragraph applies if, in accordance with paragraph 24 (as read with paragraph 29), the managing authority of the relevant hospital or care home make a request for a new standard authorisation which would be in force after the expiry of the existing authorisation.
    (2) No review may be requested under this Part until the request for the new standard authorisation has been disposed of.
    (3) If a review has already been requested, or is being carried out, when the new standard authorisation is requested, no steps are to be taken in connection with that review until the request for the new standard authorisation has been disposed of.
    124.—(1) This paragraph applies if—
    (a) a review under this Part has been requested, or is being carried out, and
    (b) the managing authority of the relevant hospital or care home make a request under paragraph

1–654

1–655

30 for a new standard authorisation which would be in force on or before, and after, the expiry of the existing authorisation.

(2) No steps are to be taken in connection with the review under this Part until the request for the new standard authorisation has been disposed of.

1–656   125. In paragraphs 123 and 124—

(a) the existing authorisation is the authorisation referred to in paragraph 101;

(b) the expiry of the existing authorisation is the time when it is expected to cease to be in force.

PART 9

ASSESSMENTS UNDER THIS SCHEDULE

Introduction

1–657   126. This Part contains provision about assessments under this Schedule.

127. An assessment under this Schedule is either of the following—

(a) an assessment carried out in connection with a request for a standard authorisation under Part 4;

(b) a review assessment carried out in connection with a review of a standard authorisation under Part 8.

1–658   128. In this Part, in relation to an assessment under this Schedule—

"assessor" means the person carrying out the assessment;

"relevant procedure" means—

(a) the request for the standard authorisation, or

(b) the review of the standard authorisation;

"supervisory body" means the supervisory body responsible for securing that the assessment is carried out.

Supervisory body to select assessor

1–659   129.—(1) It is for the supervisory body to select a person to carry out an assessment under this Schedule.

(2) The supervisory body must not select a person to carry out an assessment unless the person—

(a) appears to the supervisory body to be suitable to carry out the assessment (having regard, in particular, to the type of assessment and the person to be assessed), and

(b) is eligible to carry out the assessment.

(3) Regulations may make provision about the selection, and eligibility, of persons to carry out assessments under this Schedule.

(4) Sub-paragraphs (5) and (6) apply if two or more assessments are to be obtained for the purposes of the relevant procedure.

(5) In a case where the assessments to be obtained include a mental health assessment and a best interests assessment, the supervisory body must not select the same person to carry out both assessments.

(6) Except as prohibited by sub-paragraph (5), the supervisory body may select the same person to carry out any number of the assessments which the person appears to be suitable, and is eligible, to carry out.

1–660   130.—(1) This paragraph applies to regulations under paragraph 129(3).

(2) The regulations may make provision relating to a person's—

(a) qualifications,

(b) skills,

(c) training,

(d) experience,

(e) relationship to, or connection with, the relevant person or any other person,

(f) involvement in the care or treatment of the relevant person,

(g) connection with the supervisory body, or

(h) connection with the relevant hospital or care home, or with any other establishment or undertaking.

(3) The provision that the regulations may make in relation to a person's training may provide for particular training to be specified by the appropriate authority otherwise than in the regulations.

(4) In sub-paragraph (3) the "appropriate authority" means—

(a) in relation to England: the Secretary of State;

(b) in relation to Wales: the National Assembly for Wales.

(5) The regulations may make provision requiring a person to be insured in respect of liabilities that may arise in connection with the carrying out of an assessment.

(6) In relation to cases where two or more assessments are to be obtained for the purposes of the relevant procedure, the regulations may limit the number, kind or combination of assessments which a particular person is eligible to carry out.

(7) Sub-paragraphs (2) to (6) do not limit the generality of the provision that may be made in the regulations.

Examination and copying of records

131. An assessor may, at all reasonable times, examine and take copies of—   **1–661**
(a) any health record,
(b) any record of, or held by, a local authority and compiled in accordance with a social services function, and
(c) any record held by a person registered under Part 2 of the Care Standards Act 2000 [or Chapter 2 of Part 1 of the Health and Social Care Act 2008],
which the assessor considers may be relevant to the assessment which is being carried out.

Representations

132. In carrying out an assessment under this Schedule, the assessor must take into account any   **1–662**
information given, or submissions made, by any of the following—
(a) the relevant person's representative;
(b) any section 39A IMCA;
(c) any section 39C IMCA;
(d) any section 39D IMCA.

Assessments to stop if any comes to negative conclusion

133.—(1) This paragraph applies if an assessment under this Schedule comes to the conclusion that   **1–663**
the relevant person does not meet one of the qualifying requirements.

(2) This Schedule does not require the supervisory body to secure that any other assessments under this Schedule are carried out in relation to the relevant procedure.

(3) The supervisory body must give notice to any assessor who is carrying out another assessment in connection with the relevant procedure that they are to cease carrying out that assessment.

(4) If an assessor receives such notice, this Schedule does not require the assessor to continue carrying out that assessment.

Duty to keep records and give copies

134.—(1) This paragraph applies if an assessor has carried out an assessment under this Schedule   **1–664**
(whatever conclusions the assessment has come to).

(2) The assessor must keep a written record of the assessment.

(3) As soon as practicable after carrying out the assessment, the assessor must give copies of the assessment to the supervisory body.

135.—(1) This paragraph applies to the supervisory body if they are given a copy of an assessment   **1–665**
under this Schedule.

(2) The supervisory body must give copies of the assessment to all of
the following—
(a) the managing authority of the relevant hospital or care home;
(b) the relevant person;
(c) any section 39A IMCA;
(d) the relevant person's representative.

(3) If—
(a) the assessment is obtained in relation to a request for a standard authorisation, and
(b) the supervisory body are required by paragraph 50(1) to give the standard authorisation,
the supervisory body must give the copies of the assessment when they give copies of the authorisation in accordance with paragraph 57.

(4) If—
(a) the assessment is obtained in relation to a request for a standard authorisation, and
(b) the supervisory body are prohibited by paragraph 50(2) from giving the standard authorisation,
the supervisory body must give the copies of the assessment when they give notice in accordance with paragraph 58.

(5) If the assessment is obtained in connection with the review of a standard authorisation, the

supervisory body must give the copies of the assessment when they give notice in accordance with paragraph 120.

1–666   **136.**—(1) This paragraph applies to the supervisory body if—

(a) they are given a copy of a best interests assessment, and

(b) the assessment includes, in accordance with paragraph 44(2), a statement that it appears to the assessor that there is an unauthorised deprivation of liberty.

(2) The supervisory body must notify all of the persons listed in subparagraph (3) that the assessment includes such a statement.

(3) Those persons are—

(a) the managing authority of the relevant hospital or care home;

(b) the relevant person;

(c) any section 39A IMCA;

(d) any interested person consulted by the best interests assessor.

(4) The supervisory body must comply with this paragraph when (or at some time before) they comply with paragraph 135.

PART 10

RELEVANT PERSON'S REPRESENTATIVE

The representative

1–667   **137.** In this Schedule the relevant person's representative is the person appointed as such in accordance with this Part.

1–668   **138.**—(1) Regulations may make provision about the selection and appointment of representatives.

(2) In this Part such regulations are referred to as "appointment regulations".

Supervisory body to appoint representative

1–669   **139.**—(1) The supervisory body must appoint a person to be the relevant person's representative as soon as practicable after a standard authorisation is given.

(2) The supervisory body must appoint a person to be the relevant person's representative if a vacancy arises whilst a standard authorisation is in force.

(3) Where a vacancy arises, the appointment under sub-paragraph (2) is to be made as soon as practicable after the supervisory body becomes aware of the vacancy.

1–670   **140.**—(1) The selection of a person for appointment under paragraph 139 must not be made unless it appears to the person making the selection that the prospective representative would, if appointed—

(a) maintain contact with the relevant person,

(b) represent the relevant person in matters relating to or connected with this Schedule, and

(c) support the relevant person in matters relating to or connected with this Schedule.

1–671   **141.**—(1) Any appointment of a representative for a relevant person is in addition to, and does not affect, any appointment of a donee or deputy.

(2) The functions of any representative are in addition to, and do not affect—

(a) the authority of any donee,

(b) the powers of any deputy, or

(c) any powers of the court.

Appointment regulations

1–672   **142.** Appointment regulations may provide that the procedure for appointing a representative may begin at any time after a request for a standard authorisation is made (including a time before the request has been disposed of).

1–673   **143.**—(1) Appointment regulations may make provision about who is to select a person for appointment as a representative.

(2) But regulations under this paragraph may only provide for the following to make a selection—

(a) the relevant person, if he has capacity in relation to the question of which person should be his representative;

(b) a donee of a lasting power of attorney granted by the relevant person, if it is within the scope of his authority to select a person;

(c) a deputy, if it is within the scope of his authority to select a person;

(d) a best interests assessor;

(e) the supervisory body.

(3) Regulations under this paragraph may provide that a selection by the relevant person, a donee or a deputy is subject to approval by a best interests assessor or the supervisory body.

(4) Regulations under this paragraph may provide that, if more than one selection is necessary in connection with the appointment of a particular representative—

(a) the same person may make more than one selection;

(b) different persons may make different selections.

(5) For the purposes of this paragraph a best interests assessor is a person carrying out a best interests assessment in connection with the standard authorisation in question (including the giving of that authorisation).

144.—(1) Appointment regulations may make provision about who may, or may not, be— **1–674**

(a) selected for appointment as a representative, or

(b) appointed as a representative.

(2) Regulations under this paragraph may relate to any of the following matters—

(a) a person's age;

(b) a person's suitability;

(c) a person's independence;

(d) a person's willingness;

(e) a person's qualifications.

145. Appointment regulations may make provision about the formalities of appointing a person as **1–675**
a representative.

146. In a case where a best interests assessor is to select a person to be appointed as a representative, appointment regulations may provide for the variation of the assessor's duties in relation to the assessment which he is carrying out.

Monitoring of representatives

147. Regulations may make provision requiring the managing authority of the relevant hospital or **1–676**
care home to—

(a) monitor, and

(b) report to the supervisory body on,

the extent to which a representative is maintaining contact with the relevant person.

Termination

148. Regulations may make provision about the circumstances in which the appointment of a **1–677**
person as the relevant person's representative ends or may be ended.

149. Regulations may make provision about the formalities of ending the appointment of a person as a representative.

Suspension of representative's functions

150.—(1) Regulations may make provision about the circumstances in which functions exercisable **1–678**
by, or in relation to, the relevant person's representative (whether under this Schedule or not) may be—

(a) suspended, and

(b) if suspended, revived.

(2) The regulations may make provision about the formalities for giving effect to the suspension or revival of a function.

(3) The regulations may make provision about the effect of the suspension or revival of a function.

Payment of representative

151. Regulations may make provision for payments to be made to, or in relation to, persons exercising functions as the relevant person's representative. **1–679**

Regulations under this Part

152. The provisions of this Part which specify provision that may be made in regulations under this **1–680**
Part do not affect the generality of the power to make such regulations.

Effect of appointment of section 39C IMCA

153. Paragraphs 159 and 160 make provision about the exercise of functions by, or towards, the **1–681**
relevant person's representative during periods when—

(a) no person is appointed as the relevant person's representative, but

(b) a person is appointed as a section 39C IMCA.

PART 11

IMCAS

Application of Part

1–682   **154.** This Part applies for the purposes of this Schedule.

The IMCAs

1–683   **155.** A section 39A IMCA is an independent mental capacity advocate appointed under section 39A.

1–684   **156.** A section 39C IMCA is an independent mental capacity advocate appointed under section 39C.

1–685   **157.** A section 39D IMCA is an independent mental capacity advocate appointed under section 39D.

1–686   **158.** An IMCA is a section 39A IMCA or a section 39C IMCA or a section 39D IMCA.

Section 39C IMCA: functions

1–687   **159.**—(1) This paragraph applies if, and for as long as, there is a section 39C IMCA.

(2) In the application of the relevant provisions, references to the relevant person's representative are to be read as references to the section 39C IMCA.

(3) But sub-paragraph (2) does not apply to any function under the relevant provisions for as long as the function is suspended in accordance with provision made under Part 10.

(4) In this paragraph and paragraph 160 the relevant provisions are—

(a) paragraph 102(3)(b) (request for review under Part 8);

(b) paragraph 108(1)(b) (notice of review under Part 8);

(c) paragraph 120(1)(c) (notice of outcome of review under Part 8).

1–688   **160.**—(1) This paragraph applies if—

(a) a person is appointed as the relevant person's representative, and

(b) a person accordingly ceases to hold an appointment as a section 39C IMCA.

(2) Where a function under a relevant provision has been exercised by, or towards, the section 39C IMCA, there is no requirement for that function to be exercised again by, or towards, the relevant person's representative.

Section 39A IMCA: restriction of functions

1–689   **161.**—(1) This paragraph applies if—

(a) there is a section 39A IMCA, and

(b) a person is appointed under Part 10 to be the relevant person's representative (whether or not that person, or any person subsequently appointed, is currently the relevant person's representative).

(2) The duties imposed on, and the powers exercisable by, the section 39A IMCA do not apply.

(3) The duties imposed on, and the powers exercisable by, any other person do not apply, so far as they fall to be performed or exercised towards the section 39A IMCA.

(4) But sub-paragraph (2) does not apply to any power of challenge exercisable by the section 39A IMCA.

(5) And sub-paragraph (3) does not apply to any duty or power of any other person so far as it relates to any power of challenge exercisable by the section 39A IMCA.

(6) Before exercising any power of challenge, the section 39A IMCA must take the views of the relevant person's representative into account.

(7) A power of challenge is a power to make an application to the court to exercise its jurisdiction under section 21A in connection with the giving of the standard authorisation.

PART 12

MISCELLANEOUS

Monitoring of operation of Schedule

1–690   **162.**—(1) Regulations may make provision for, and in connection with, requiring one or more prescribed bodies to monitor, and report on, the operation of this Schedule in relation to England.

(2) The regulations may, in particular, give a prescribed body authority to do one or more of the following things—

(a) to visit hospitals and care homes;

(b) to visit and interview persons accommodated in hospitals and care homes;

(c) to require the production of, and to inspect, records relating to the care or treatment of persons.

(3) "Prescribed" means prescribed in regulations under this paragraph.

163.—(1) Regulations may make provision for, and in connection with, enabling the National Assembly for Wales to monitor, and report on, the operation of this Schedule in relation to Wales.

(2) The National Assembly may direct one or more persons or bodies to carry out the Assembly's functions under regulations under this paragraph.

1–691

Disclosure of information

164.—(1) Regulations may require either or both of the following to disclose prescribed information to prescribed bodies—

(a) supervisory bodies;

(b) managing authorities of hospitals or care homes.

(2) "Prescribed" means prescribed in regulations under this paragraph.

(3) Regulations under this paragraph may only prescribe information relating to matters with which this Schedule is concerned.

1–692

Directions by National Assembly in relation to supervisory functions

165.—(1) The National Assembly for Wales may direct a Local Health Board to exercise in relation to its area any supervisory functions which are specified in the direction.

(2) Directions under this paragraph must not preclude the National Assembly from exercising the functions specified in the directions.

(3) In this paragraph "supervisory functions" means functions which the National Assembly have as supervisory body, so far as they are exercisable in relation to hospitals (whether NHS or independent hospitals, and whether in Wales or England).

1–693

166.—(1) This paragraph applies where, under paragraph 165, a Local Health Board ("the specified LHB") is directed to exercise supervisory functions ("delegated functions").

(2) The National Assembly for Wales may give directions to the specified LHB about the Board's exercise of delegated functions.

(3) The National Assembly may give directions for any delegated functions to be exercised, on behalf of the specified LHB, by a committee, sub-committee or officer of that Board.

(4) The National Assembly may give directions providing for any delegated functions to be exercised by the specified LHB jointly with one or more other Local Health Boards.

(5) Where, under sub-paragraph (4), delegated functions are exercisable jointly, the National Assembly may give directions providing for the functions to be exercised, on behalf of the Local Health Boards in question, by a joint committee or joint subcommittee.

1–694

167.—(1) Directions under paragraph 165 must be given in regulations.

(2) Directions under paragraph 166 may be given—

(a) in regulations, or

(b) by instrument in writing.

1–695

168. The power under paragraph 165 or paragraph 166 to give directions includes power to vary or revoke directions given under that paragraph.

1–696

Notices

169. Any notice under this Schedule must be in writing.

1–697

Regulations

170.—(1) This paragraph applies to all regulations under this Schedule, except regulations under paragraph 162, 163, 167 or 183.

(2) It is for the Secretary of State to make such regulations in relation to authorisations under this Schedule which relate to hospitals and care homes situated in England.

(3) It is for the National Assembly for Wales to make such regulations in relation to authorisations under this Schedule which relate to hospitals and care homes situated in Wales.

1–698

171. It is for the Secretary of State to make regulations under paragraph 162.

172. It is for the National Assembly for Wales to make regulations under paragraph 163 or 167.

173.—(1) This paragraph applies to regulations under paragraph 183.

1–699
1–700
1–701

(2) It is for the Secretary of State to make such regulations in relation to cases where a question as to the ordinary residence of a person is to be determined by the Secretary of State.

(3) It is for the National Assembly for Wales to make such regulations in relation to cases where a question as to the ordinary residence of a person is to be determined by the National Assembly.

PART 13

INTERPRETATION

Introduction

1–702   174. This Part applies for the purposes of this Schedule.

Hospitals and their managing authorities

1–703   175.—(1) "Hospital" means—

(a) an NHS hospital, or

(b) an independent hospital.

(2) "NHS hospital" means—

(a) a health service hospital as defined by section 275 of the National Health Service Act 2006 or section 206 of the National Health Service (Wales) Act 2006, or

(b) a hospital as defined by section 206 of the National Health Service (Wales) Act 2006 vested in a Local Health Board.

[(3) "Independent hospital"—

(a) in relation to England, means a hospital as defined by section 275 of the National Health Service Act 2006 that is not an NHS hospital; and

(b) in relation to Wales, means a hospital as defined by section 2 of the Care Standards Act 2000 that is not an NHS hospital.]

1–704   176.—(1) "Managing authority", in relation to an NHS hospital, means—

(a) if the hospital—

(i) is vested in the appropriate national authority for the purposes of its functions under the National Health Service Act 2006 or of the National Health Service (Wales) Act 2006, or

(ii) consists of any accommodation provided by a local authority and used as a hospital by or on behalf of the appropriate national authority under either of those Acts,

the [. . .], [. . .] Local Health Board or Special Health Authority responsible for the administration of the hospital;

[(aa) in relation to England, if the hospital falls within paragraph (a)(i) or (ii) and no Special Health Authority has responsibility for its administration, the Secretary of State;]

(b) if the hospital is vested in a [. . .], National Health Service trust or NHS foundation trust, that trust;

(c) if the hospital is vested in a Local Health Board, that Board.

(2) For this purpose the appropriate national authority is—

(a) in relation to England: the Secretary of State;

(b) in relation to Wales: the National Assembly for Wales;

(c) in relation to England and Wales: the Secretary of State and the National Assembly acting jointly.

1–705   [177. "Managing authority", in relation to an independent hospital, means—

(a) in relation to England, the person registered, or required to be registered, under Chapter 2 of Part 1 of the Health and Social Care Act 2008 in respect of regulated activities (within the meaning of that Part) carried on in the hospital, and

(b) in relation to Wales, the person registered, or required to be registered, under Part 2 of the Care Standards Act 2000 in respect of the hospital.]

Care homes and their managing authorities

1–706   178. "Care home" has the meaning given by section 3 of the Care Standards Act 2000.

1–707   [179. "Managing authority", in relation to a care home, means—

(a) in relation to England, the person registered, or required to be registered, under Chapter 2 of Part 1 of the Health and Social Care Act 2008 in respect of the provision of residential accommodation, together with nursing or personal care, in the care home, and

(b) in relation to Wales, the person registered, or required to be registered, under Part 2 of the Care Standards Act 2000 in respect of the care home.]

Supervisory bodies: hospitals

1–708   180.—(1) The identity of the supervisory body is determined under this paragraph in cases where the relevant hospital is situated in England.

[(2) If the relevant person is ordinarily resident in the area of a local authority in England, the supervisory body are that local authority.]

(3) If [the relevant person is not ordinarily resident in England and] the National Assembly for Wales or a Local Health Board commission the relevant care or treatment, the National Assembly are the supervisory body.

(4) In any other case, the supervisory body are [the local authority] for the area in which the relevant hospital is situated.

[(4A) "Local authority" means—

(a) the council of a county;

(b) the council of a district for which there is no county council;

(c) the council of a London borough;

(d) the Common Council of the City of London;

(e) the Council of the Isles of Scilly.]

(5) If a hospital is situated in the areas of two (or more) [local authorities], it is to be regarded for the purposes of sub-paragraph (4) as situated in whichever of the areas the greater (or greatest) part of the hospital is situated.

181.—(1) The identity of the supervisory body is determined under this paragraph in cases where the relevant hospital is situated in Wales.

1–709

(2) The National Assembly for Wales are the supervisory body.

[(3) But if the relevant person is ordinarily resident in the area of a local authority in England, the supervisory body are that local authority.

(4) "Local authority" means—

(a) the council of a county;

(b) the council of a district for which there is no county council;

(c) the council of a London borough;

(d) the Common Council of the City of London;

(e) the Council of the Isles of Scilly.]

Supervisory bodies: care homes

182.—(1) The identity of the supervisory body is determined under this paragraph in cases where the relevant care home is situated in England or in Wales.

1–710

(2) The supervisory body are the local authority for the area in which the relevant person is ordinarily resident.

(3) But if the relevant person is not ordinarily resident in the area of a local authority, the supervisory body are the local authority for the area in which the care home is situated.

(4) In relation to England "local authority" means—

(a) the council of a county;

(b) the council of a district for which there is no county council;

(c) the council of a London borough;

(d) the Common Council of the City of London;

(e) the Council of the Isles of Scilly.

(5) In relation to Wales "local authority" means the council of a county or county borough.

(6) If a care home is situated in the areas of two (or more) local authorities, it is to be regarded for the purposes of sub-paragraph (3) as situated in whichever of the areas the greater (or greatest) part of the care home is situated.

[Supervisory bodies: determination of place of ordinary residence]

183.—(1) Subsections (5) and (6) of section 24 of the National Assistance Act 1948 (deemed place of ordinary residence) apply to any determination of where a person is ordinarily resident for the purposes of paragraphs 180, 181 and 182 as those subsections apply to such a determination for the purposes specified in those subsections.

1–711

(2) In the application of section 24(6) of the 1948 Act by virtue of subparagraph (1) [to any determination of where a person is ordinarily resident for the purposes of paragraph 182], section 24(6) is to be read as if it referred to a hospital vested in a Local Health Board as well as to hospitals vested in the Secretary of State and the other bodies mentioned in section 24(6).

[(2A) Section 39(1), (2) and (4) to (6) of the Care Act 2014 and paragraphs 1(1), 2(1) and 8 of Schedule 1 to that Act apply to any determination of where a person is ordinarily resident for the purposes of paragraphs 180, 181 and 182 as they apply for the purposes of Part 1 of that Act.]

(3) Any question arising as to the ordinary residence of a person is to be determined by the Secretary of State or by the National Assembly for Wales.

(4) The Secretary of State and the National Assembly must make and publish arrangements for determining which cases are to be dealt with by the Secretary of State and which are to be dealt with by the National Assembly.

(5) Those arrangements may include provision for the Secretary of State and the National Assembly to agree, in relation to any question that has arisen, which of them is to deal with the case.

(6) Regulations may make provision about arrangements that are to have effect before, upon, or after the determination of any question as to the ordinary residence of a person.

(7) The regulations may, in particular, authorise or require a local authority to do any or all of the following things—

    (a) to act as supervisory body even though it may wish to dispute that it is the supervisory body;

    (b) to become the supervisory body in place of another local authority;

    (c) to recover from another local authority expenditure incurred in exercising functions as the supervisory body.

Same body managing authority and supervisory body

1–712   **184.**—(1) This paragraph applies if, in connection with a particular person's detention as a resident in a hospital or care home, the same body are both—

    (a) the managing authority of the relevant hospital or care home, and

    (b) the supervisory body.

(2) The fact that a single body are acting in both capacities does not prevent the body from carrying out functions under this Schedule in each capacity.

(3) But, in such a case, this Schedule has effect subject to any modifications contained in regulations that may be made for this purpose.

Interested persons

1–713   **185.** Each of the following is an interested person—

    (a) the relevant person's spouse or civil partner;

    [(b) where the relevant person and another person are not married to each other, nor in a civil partnership with each other, but are living together as if they were a married couple: that other person;]

    (d) the relevant person's children and step-children;

    (e) the relevant person's parents and step-parents;

    (f) the relevant person's brothers and sisters, half-brothers and half-sisters, and stepbrothers and stepsisters;

    (g) the relevant person's grandparents;

    (h) a deputy appointed for the relevant person by the court;

    (i) a donee of a lasting power of attorney granted by the relevant person.

1–714   **186.**—(1) An interested person consulted by the best interests assessor is any person whose name is stated in the relevant best interests assessment in accordance with paragraph 40 (interested persons whom the assessor consulted in carrying out the assessment).

(2) The relevant best interests assessment is the most recent best interests assessment carried out in connection with the standard authorisation in question (whether the assessment was carried out under Part 4 or Part 8).

1–715   **187.** Where this Schedule imposes on a person a duty towards an interested person, the duty does not apply if the person on whom the duty is imposed—

    (a) is not aware of the interested person's identity or of a way of contacting him, and

    (b) cannot reasonably ascertain it.

1–716   **188.** The following table contains an index of provisions defining or otherwise explaining expressions used in this Schedule—

age assessment	paragraph 34
age requirement	paragraph 13
age review assessment	paragraph 112(3)
appointment regulations	paragraph 138
assessment under this Schedule	paragraph 127
assessor (except in Part 9)	paragraph 33
assessor (in Part 9)	paragraphs 33 and 128
authorisation under this Schedule	paragraph 10

best interests (determination of)	section 4
best interests assessment	paragraph 38
best interests requirement	paragraph 16
best interests review assessment	paragraph 112(6)
care home	paragraph 178
change of reason ground	paragraph 106
complete (in relation to a review of a standard authorisation)	paragraph 118
deprivation of a person's liberty	section 64(5) and (6)
Deputy	section 16(2)(b)
detained resident	paragraph 6
disposed of (in relation to a request for a standard authorisation)	paragraph 66
eligibility assessment	paragraph 46
eligibility requirement	paragraph 17
eligibility review assessment	paragraph 112(7)
eligible person (in relation to paragraphs 68 to 73)	paragraph 68
eligible person (in relation to Part 8)	paragraph 102(3)
expiry (in relation to an existing authorisation)	paragraph 125(b)
existing authorisation (in Part 8)	paragraph 125(a)
Hospital	paragraph 175
IMCA	paragraph 158
in force (in relation to a standard authorisation)	paragraphs 63 and 64
in force (in relation to an urgent authorisation)	paragraphs 88 and 89
ineligible (in relation to the eligibility requirement)	Schedule 1A
interested person	paragraph 185
interested person consulted by the best interests assessor	paragraph 186
lack of capacity	section 2
lasting power of attorney	section 9
managing authority (in relation to a care home)	paragraph 179
managing authority (in relation to a hospital)	paragraph 176 or 177
maximum authorisation period	paragraph 42
mental capacity assessment	paragraph 37
mental capacity requirement	paragraph 15
mental capacity review assessment	paragraph 112(5)
mental health assessment	paragraph 35
mental health requirement	paragraph 14
mental health review assessment	paragraph 112(4)

negative conclusion	paragraph 112(2)(a)
new supervisory body	paragraph 99(b)
no refusals assessment	paragraph 48
no refusals requirement	paragraph 18
no refusals review assessment	paragraph 112(8)
non-qualification ground	paragraph 105
old supervisory body	paragraph 99(a)
positive conclusion	paragraph 112(2)(b)
purpose of a standard authorisation	paragraph 11(1)
purpose of an urgent authorisation	paragraph 11(2)
qualifying requirements	paragraph 12
refusal (for the purposes of the no refusals requirement)	paragraphs 19 and 20
relevant care or treatment	paragraph 7
relevant hospital or care home	paragraph 7
relevant managing authority	paragraph 26(4)
relevant person	paragraph 7
relevant person's representative	paragraph 137
relevant procedure	paragraph 128
review assessment	paragraph 112(1)
reviewable	paragraph 104
section 39A IMCA	paragraph 155
section 39C IMCA	paragraph 156
section 39D IMCA	paragraph 157
standard authorisation	paragraph 8
supervisory body (except in Part 9)	paragraph 180, 181or 182
supervisory body (in Part 9)	paragraph 128 and paragraph 180, 181 or 182
unauthorised deprivation of liberty (in relation to paragraphs 68 to 73)	paragraph 67
urgent authorisation	paragraph 9
variation of conditions ground	paragraph 107]

AMENDMENTS

1–717   This Schedule was inserted by the Mental Health Act 2007 s.50(5), Sch.7. The amendments to it were made by SI 2010/813 art.17, the Health and Social Care Act 2012 s.55(2), Sch.5, para.136, SI 2014/560 art.2, Sch.1, para.30 and SI 2015/914 art.2, Sch., para.80.

GENERAL NOTE

1–718   This Schedule is considered in Part 2.

SCHEDULE 1

LASTING POWERS OF ATTORNEY: FORMALITIES

PART 1

MAKING INSTRUMENTS

General requirements as to making instruments

1.—(1) An instrument is not made in accordance with this Schedule unless—   **1–719**
(a) it is in the prescribed form,
(b) it complies with paragraph 2, and
(c) any prescribed requirements in connection with its execution are satisfied.
(2) Regulations may make different provision according to whether—
(a) the instrument relates to personal welfare or to property and affairs (or to both);
(b) only one or more than one donee is to be appointed (and if more than one, whether jointly or jointly and severally).
(3) In this Schedule—
(a) "prescribed" means prescribed by regulations, and
(b) "regulations" means regulations made for the purposes of this Schedule by the Lord Chancellor.

Requirements as to content of instruments

2.—(1) The instrument must include—   **1–720**
(a) the prescribed information about the purpose of the instrument and the effect of a lasting power of attorney,
(b) a statement by the donor to the effect that he—
    (i) has read the prescribed information or a prescribed part of it (or has had it read to him), and
    (ii) intends the authority conferred under the instrument to include authority to make decisions on his behalf in circumstances where he no longer has capacity,
(c) a statement by the donor—
    (i) naming a person or persons whom the donor wishes to be notified of any application for the registration of the instrument, or
    (ii) stating that there are no persons whom he wishes to be notified of any such application,
(d) a statement by the donee (or, if more than one, each of them) to the effect that he—
    (i) has read the prescribed information or a prescribed part of it (or has had it read to him), and
    (ii) understands the duties imposed on a donee of a lasting power of attorney under sections 1(the principles) and 4 (best interests), and
(e) a certificate by a person of a prescribed description that, in his opinion, at the time when the donor executes the instrument—
    (i) the donor understands the purpose of the instrument and the scope of the authority conferred under it,
    (ii) no fraud or undue pressure is being used to induce the donor to create a lasting power of attorney, and
    (iii) there is nothing else which would prevent a lasting power of attorney from being created by the instrument.
(2) Regulations may—
(a) prescribe a maximum number of named persons;
(b) provide that, where the instrument includes a statement under sub-paragraph (1)(c)(ii), two persons of a prescribed description must each give a certificate under sub-paragraph (1)(e).
(3) The persons who may be named persons do not include a person who is appointed as donee under the instrument.
(4) In this Schedule, "named person" means a person named under sub-paragraph (1)(c).
(5) A certificate under sub-paragraph (1)(e)—
(a) must be made in the prescribed form, and
(b) must include any prescribed information.
(6) The certificate may not be given by a person appointed as donee under the instrument.

Failure to comply with prescribed form

3.—(1) If an instrument differs in an immaterial respect in form or mode of expression from the   **1–721**
prescribed form, it is to be treated by the Public Guardian as sufficient in point of form and expression.
(2) The court may declare that an instrument which is not in the prescribed form is to be treated

as if it were, if it is satisfied that the persons executing the instrument intended it to create a lasting power of attorney.

PART 2

REGISTRATION

1–722   **4.**—(1) An application to the Public Guardian for the registration of an instrument intended to create a lasting power of attorney—
  (a) must be made in the prescribed form, and
  (b) must include any prescribed information.
  (2) The application may be made—
  (a) by the donor,
  (b) by the donee or donees, or
  (c) if the instrument appoints two or more donees to act jointly and severally in respect of any matter, by any of the donees.
  (3) The application must be accompanied by—
  (a) the instrument, and
  (b) any fee provided for under section 58(4)(b).
  (4) A person who, in an application for registration, makes a statement which he knows to be false in a material particular is guilty of an offence and is liable—
  (a) on summary conviction, to imprisonment for a term not exceeding 12 months or a fine not exceeding the statutory maximum or both;
  (b) on conviction on indictment, to imprisonment for a term not exceeding 2 years or a fine or both.

1–723   **5.** Subject to paragraphs 11 to 14, the Public Guardian must register the instrument as a lasting power of attorney at the end of the prescribed period.

1–724   **6.**—(1) A donor about to make an application under paragraph 4(2)(a) must notify any named persons that he is about to do so.
  (2) The donee (or donees) about to make an application under paragraph 4(2)(b) or (c) must notify any named persons that he is (or they are) about to do so.

1–725   **7.** As soon as is practicable after receiving an application by the donor under paragraph 4(2)(a), the Public Guardian must notify the donee (or donees) that the application has been received.

1–726   **8.**—(1) As soon as is practicable after receiving an application by a donee (or donees) under paragraph 4(2)(b), the Public Guardian must notify the donor that the application has been received.
  (2) As soon as is practicable after receiving an application by a donee under paragraph 4(2)(c), the Public Guardian must notify—
  (a) the donor, and
  (b) the donee or donees who did not join in making the application,
that the application has been received.

1–727   **9.**—(1) A notice under paragraph 6 must be made in the prescribed form.
  (2) A notice under paragraph 6, 7 or 8 must include such information, if any, as may be prescribed.

1–728   **10.** The court may—
  (a) on the application of the donor, dispense with the requirement to notify under paragraph 6(1), or
  (b) on the application of the donee or donees concerned, dispense with the requirement to notify under paragraph 6(2),
  if satisfied that no useful purpose would be served by giving the notice.

1–729   **11.**—(1) If it appears to the Public Guardian that an instrument accompanying an application under paragraph 4 is not made in accordance with this Schedule, he must not register the instrument unless the court directs him to do so.
  (2) Sub-paragraph (3) applies if it appears to the Public Guardian that the instrument contains a provision which—
  (a) would be ineffective as part of a lasting power of attorney, or
  (b) would prevent the instrument from operating as a valid lasting power of attorney.
  (3) The Public Guardian—
  (a) must apply to the court for it to determine the matter under section 23(1), and
  (b) pending the determination by the court, must not register the instrument.
  (4) Sub-paragraph (5) applies if the court determines under section 23(1) (whether or not on an application by the Public Guardian) that the instrument contains a provision which—
  (a) would be ineffective as part of a lasting power of attorney, or

268

(b) would prevent the instrument from operating as a valid lasting power of attorney.

(5) The court must—

(a) notify the Public Guardian that it has severed the provision, or

(b) direct him not to register the instrument.

(6) Where the court notifies the Public Guardian that it has severed a provision, he must register the instrument with a note to that effect attached to it.

12.—(1) Sub-paragraph (2) applies if it appears to the Public Guardian that—   **1–730**

(a) there is a deputy appointed by the court for the donor, and

(b) the powers conferred on the deputy would, if the instrument were registered, to any extent conflict with the powers conferred on the attorney.

(2) The Public Guardian must not register the instrument unless the court directs him to do so.

13.—(1) Sub-paragraph (2) applies if a donee or a named person—   **1–731**

(a) receives a notice under paragraph 6, 7 or 8 of an application for the registration of an instrument, and

(b) before the end of the prescribed period, gives notice to the Public Guardian of an objection to the registration on the ground that an event mentioned in section 13(3) or (6)(a) to (d) has occurred which has revoked the instrument.

(2) If the Public Guardian is satisfied that the ground for making the objection is established, he must not register the instrument unless the court, on the application of the person applying for the registration—

(a) is satisfied that the ground is not established, and

(b) directs the Public Guardian to register the instrument.

(3) Sub-paragraph (4) applies if a donee or a named person—

(a) receives a notice under paragraph 6, 7 or 8 of an application for the registration of an instrument, and

(b) before the end of the prescribed period—

(i) makes an application to the court objecting to the registration on a prescribed ground, and

(ii) notifies the Public Guardian of the application.

(4) The Public Guardian must not register the instrument unless the court directs him to do so.

14.—(1) This paragraph applies if the donor—   **1–732**

(a) receives a notice under paragraph 8 of an application for the registration of an instrument, and

(b) before the end of the prescribed period, gives notice to the Public Guardian of an objection to the registration.

(2) The Public Guardian must not register the instrument unless the court, on the application of the donee or, if more than one, any of them—

(a) is satisfied that the donor lacks capacity to object to the registration, and

(b) directs the Public Guardian to register the instrument.

15. Where an instrument is registered under this Schedule, the Public Guardian must give notice of   **1–733**
the fact in the prescribed form to—

(a) the donor, and

(b) the donee or, if more than one, each of them.

16.—(1) A document purporting to be an office copy of an instrument registered under this   **1–734**
Schedule is, in any part of the United Kingdom, evidence of—

(a) the contents of the instrument, and

(b) the fact that it has been registered.

(2) Sub-paragraph (1) is without prejudice to—

(a) section 3 of the Powers of Attorney Act 1971 (c. 27) (proof by certified copy), and

(b) any other method of proof authorised by law.

PART 3

CANCELLATION OF REGISTRATION AND NOTIFICATION OF SEVERANCE

17.—(1) The Public Guardian must cancel the registration of an instrument as a lasting power of   **1–735**
attorney on being satisfied that the power has been revoked—

(a) as a result of the donor's bankruptcy [or a debt relief order (under Part 7A of the Insolvency Act 1986) having been made in respect of the donor], or

(b) on the occurrence of an event mentioned in section 13(6)(a) to (d).

(2) If the Public Guardian cancels the registration of an instrument he must notify—

(a) the donor, and

(b) the donee or, if more than one, each of them.

1–736 **18.** The court must direct the Public Guardian to cancel the registration of an instrument as a lasting power of attorney if it—

(a) determines under section 22(2)(a) that a requirement for creating the power was not met,

(b) determines under section 22(2)(b) that the power has been revoked or has otherwise come to an end, or

(c) revokes the power under section 22(4)(b) (fraud etc.).

1–737 **19.**—(1) Sub-paragraph (2) applies if the court determines under section 23(1) that a lasting power of attorney contains a provision which—

(a) is ineffective as part of a lasting power of attorney, or

(b) prevents the instrument from operating as a valid lasting power of attorney.

(2) The court must—

(a) notify the Public Guardian that it has severed the provision, or

(b) direct him to cancel the registration of the instrument as a lasting power of attorney.

1–738 **20.** On the cancellation of the registration of an instrument, the instrument and any office copies of it must be delivered up to the Public Guardian to be cancelled.

PART 4

RECORDS OF ALTERATIONS IN REGISTERED POWERS

Partial revocation or suspension of power as a result of bankruptcy

1–739 **21.** If in the case of a registered instrument it appears to the Public Guardian that under section 13 a lasting power of attorney is revoked, or suspended, in relation to the donor's property and affairs (but not in relation to other matters), the Public Guardian must attach to the instrument a note to that effect.

Termination of appointment of donee which does not revoke power

1–740 **22.** If in the case of a registered instrument it appears to the Public Guardian that an event has occurred—

(a) which has terminated the appointment of the donee, but

(b) which has not revoked the instrument,

the Public Guardian must attach to the instrument a note to that effect.

Replacement of donee

1–741 **23.** If in the case of a registered instrument it appears to the Public Guardian that the donee has been replaced under the terms of the instrument the Public Guardian must attach to the instrument a note to that effect.

Severance of ineffective provisions

1–742 **24.** If in the case of a registered instrument the court notifies the Public Guardian under paragraph 19(2)(a) that it has severed a provision of the instrument, the Public Guardian must attach to it a note to that effect.

Notification of alterations

1–743 **25.** If the Public Guardian attaches a note to an instrument under paragraph 21, 22, 23 or 24 he must give notice of the note to the donee or donees of the power (or, as the case may be, to the other donee or donees of the power).

AMENDMENT

1–744 The words in square brackets in para.17(1)(a) were inserted by SI 2012/2404 art.3(2), Sch.1, para.53(5).

DEFINITIONS

1–745 "lasting power of attorney": s.64(1)

"Public Guardian": s.64(1)

"the court": s.64(1)

"deputy": s.64(1)

"bankruptcy": s.64(3)

GENERAL NOTE

1–746 This Schedule sets out the requirements with regard to the formalities of a lasting power of attorney (LPA). An LPA is not created unless it is made and registered in accordance with the provisions s.9(2).

In summary, the requirements are:

Making instruments
- The LPA must be in the prescribed form.
- The form must contain statements by both the donor and donee to the effect that they have read (or in the case of the donor, had read to them) prescribed information.
- The LPA must include the names of any persons (a "named person"), not being a donee, whom the donor wishes to be notified of any application to register the LPA or a statement that there are no such persons.
- The form must include a certificate by a person of a prescribed description that, in his or her opinion, at the time when the donor executes the instrument the donor understands the purpose of the instrument and the scope of the authority conferred, that no fraud or undue pressure is being used to induce the donor to create an LPA, and that there is nothing else that would prevent an LPA being created.
- The Public Guardian may treat a LPA differing in an immaterial respect from the prescribed form as sufficient to create an LPA.
- The Court of Protection has the power to declare that an instrument not in the prescribed form is to be treated as if it were.

1–747

Registration
- The powers given in an LPA to the donee cannot be exercised until the document has been registered with the Public Guardian.
- The application, which must be in the prescribed form, can be made by the donor or donee.
- The named person must be notified of the pending registration by the donor or donee.
- The Public Guardian must notify the applicant that the application has been received unless the court has dispensed with this requirement.
- The donee or the named person may object to the LPA within a prescribed period.
- The objection is made to the either the Public Guardian or the court, depending upon the nature of the objection.
- If the LPA is registered, the Public Guardian must notify the donor and donee.

1–748

Cancellation of registration
- The Public Guardian will cancel the LPA if satisfied that the power has been revoked on the basis of the donor's bankruptcy or him being made subject to a debt relief order, the donee disclaiming the appointment, the death or bankruptcy of the donee, the dissolution or annulment of a marriage or civil partnership between the donor and donee, and the lack of capacity of the donee.
- The court must direct the Public Guardian to cancel the registration of an LPA if the court decides that a requirement for creating the LPA was not met, decides that the LPA has been revoked or otherwise come to an end, or it revokes the power on fraud or undue pressure grounds.
- On cancellation the Public Guardian will notify both the donor and donee.

1–749

Records of alterations in registered powers
- The Public Guardian must attach a note to the LPA in the circumstances set out in paras 21–24.
- The Public Guardian must give the donor and donee notice of any notes attached.

1–750

Prescribed forms
The prescribed forms for the making and registration of LPAs are set out in the Schs 1 to 5 to the Lasting Powers of Attorney, Enduring Powers of Attorney and Public Guardian Regulations 2007 (SI 2007/1253 (as amended)). For the loss or destruction of forms, see reg.19.

1–751

Paragraph 1(1)(c)
Prescribed requirements in connection with its execution. See SI 2007/1253 reg.9.

1–752

Paragraph 2(1)(c)
See SI 2007/1253, regs 6 and 7.

1–753

Paragraph 2(1)(e)

1–754   "The relevant person would interview the donor without the presence of the proposed [donee] and immediately before the signing of the LPA", per the Parliamentary Under-Secretary of State, St.Comm.A, para.142.

PERSON OF A PRESCRIBED DESCRIPTION. See SI 2007/1253 reg.8.

Paragraph 2(2)(a)

1–755   MAXIMUM NUMBER OF NAMED PERSONS. Is 5 (SI 2007/1253 reg.6).

Paragraph 2(2)(b)

1–756   See SI 2007/1253 reg.7.

Paragraph 2(3)

1–757   A "person who is appointed as donee" includes a replacement donee (*Howarth, Re* (COP) July 29, 2008, Senior Judge Lush).

Paragraph 3

1–758   Unlike the court, the Public Guardian does not have the power to declare that an instrument that is not in the prescribed form may be treated as if it were.

This paragraph applies only to an instrument that is not in the prescribed form and does not apply any prescribed requirements in connection with its execution (*Re Hurren* (COP) September 28, 2011).

In *Re Lane* (COP) January 24, 2012, the donor made an LPA on May 3, 2011 using the 2007 prescribed form. The transitional provisions of the Lasting Powers of Attorney, Enduring Powers of Attorney and Public Guardian (Amendment) Regulations 2009, which introduced new prescribed forms, provide that an instrument executed by the donor before April 1, 2011 on the 2007 prescribed form is capable of being a valid LPA. The Public Guardian made an application to the court for the severance of an invalid restriction, and drew the court's attention to the date of execution, submitting that the "old" forms were not materially different from the "new" forms. Senior judge Lush accepted that the "old" forms differed from the "new" forms in an immaterial respect and were accordingly within the scope of this paragraph.

Paragraph 5

1–759   PRESCRIBED PERIOD. See reg.12 of SI 2007/1253.

Paragraphs 6, 7 and 8

1–760   If a notified person wishes to make an objection to the registration to the Public Guardian, see regs.14 and 15 of SI 2007/1253.

An LPA is not ineffective merely because the donor has put in place complex arrangements to secure compliance with his wishes: see XY v Public Guardian [2015] EWCOP 35, where Senior Judge Lush agreed with the following submission made by counsel:

> "With respect to the Public Guardian, it is no part of his statutory duties to police the practicality or utility of individual aspects of an LPA. In the context of section 23 and Schedule 1, paragraph 11 of the MCA 2005 the phrase 'ineffective as part of a lasting power of attorney' clearly means 'not capable of taking effect, according to its legal terms as part of an LPA.' Examples of provisions which would be ineffective as part of a power of attorney would include:
>
> (a)   a provision which purported to permit the attorney to make gifts which go beyond the statutory restrictions found at section 12 MCA 2005.
>
> (b)   a provision which purported to go beyond what a person can do by an attorney (such as make a will or vote).
>
> (c)   a provision which purported to permit the attorney to consent to a marriage on behalf of the donor (see MCA section 27(1)(a)).
>
> Neither the court nor the Public Guardian are concerned with whether a restriction that does not contravene the terms of the MCA 2005 may pose practical difficulties in its operation."

Paragraph 13

1–761   OBJECTION. See SI 2007/1253 regs.14, 14A and 15.

Paragraph 15
REGISTERED. See SI 2007/1253 reg.17.

Paragraphs 21 to 24
NOTE TO THAT EFFECT. See SI 2007/1253 reg.18.

[SCHEDULE 1A

PERSONS INELIGIBLE TO BE DEPRIVED OF LIBERTY BY THIS ACT

PART 1

INELIGIBLE PERSONS

Application
1. This Schedule applies for the purposes of—
(a) section 16A, and
(b) paragraph 17 of Schedule A1.

Determining ineligibility
2. A person ("P") is ineligible to be deprived of liberty by this Act ("ineligible") if—
(a) P falls within one of the cases set out in the second column of the following table, and
(b) the corresponding entry in the third column of the table — or the provision, or one of the provisions, referred to in that entry — provides that he is ineligible.

	Status of P	*Determination of ineligibility*
Case A	P is— (a) subject to the hospital treatment regime, and (b) detained in a hospital under that regime.	P is ineligible.
Case B	P is— (a) subject to the hospital treatment regime, but (b) not detained in a hospital under that regime.	See paragraphs 3 and 4.
Case C	P is subject to the community treatment regime.	See paragraphs 3 and 4.
Case D	P is subject to the guardianship regime.	See paragraphs 3 and 5.
Case E	P is— (a) within the scope of the Mental Health Act, but (b) not subject to any of the mental health regimes.	See paragraph 5.

Authorised course of action not in accordance with regime
3.—(1) This paragraph applies in cases B, C and D in the table in paragraph 2.
(2) P is ineligible if the authorised course of action is not in accordance with a requirement which the relevant regime imposes.
(3) That includes any requirement as to where P is, or is not, to reside.
(4) The relevant regime is the mental health regime to which P is subject.

Treatment for mental disorder in a hospital
4.—(1) This paragraph applies in cases B and C in the table in paragraph 2.
(2) P is ineligible if the relevant care or treatment consists in whole or in part of medical treatment for mental disorder in a hospital.

P objects to being a mental health patient etc
5.—(1) This paragraph applies in cases D and E in the table in paragraph 2.
(2) P is ineligible if the following conditions are met.
(3) The first condition is that the relevant instrument authorises P to be a mental health patient.
(4) The second condition is that P objects—
(a) to being a mental health patient, or
(b) to being given some or all of the mental health treatment.

(5) The third condition is that a donee or deputy has not made a valid decision to consent to each matter to which P objects.

(6) In determining whether or not P objects to something, regard must be had to all the circumstances (so far as they are reasonably ascertainable), including the following—

(a) P's behaviour;

(b) P's wishes and feelings;

(c) P's views, beliefs and values.

(7) But regard is to be had to circumstances from the past only so far as it is still appropriate to have regard to them.

PART 2

INTERPRETATION

Application

1–769

6. This Part applies for the purposes of this Schedule.

Mental health regimes

1–770

7. The mental health regimes are—

(a) the hospital treatment regime,

(b) the community treatment regime, and

(c) the guardianship regime.

Hospital treatment regime

1–771

8.—(1) P is subject to the hospital treatment regime if he is subject to—

(a) a hospital treatment obligation under the relevant enactment, or

(b) an obligation under another England and Wales enactment which has the same effect as a hospital treatment obligation.

(2) But where P is subject to any such obligation, he is to be regarded as not subject to the hospital treatment regime during any period when he is subject to the community treatment regime.

(3) A hospital treatment obligation is an application, order or direction of a kind listed in the first column of the following table.

(4) In relation to a hospital treatment obligation, the relevant enactment is the enactment in the Mental Health Act which is referred to in the corresponding entry in the second column of the following table.

Hospital treatment obligation	Relevant enactment
Application for admission for assessment	Section 2
Application for admission for assessment	Section 4
Application for admission for treatment	Section 3
Order for remand to hospital	Section 35
Order for remand to hospital	Section 36
Hospital order	Section 37
Interim hospital order	Section 38
Order for detention in hospital	Section 44
Hospital direction	Section 45A
Transfer direction	Section 47
Transfer direction	Section 48
Hospital order	Section 51

Community treatment regime

1–772

9. P is subject to the community treatment regime if he is subject to—

(a) a community treatment order under section 17A of the Mental Health Act, or

(b) an obligation under another England and Wales enactment which has the same effect as a community treatment order.

Guardianship regime

1–773

10. P is subject to the guardianship regime if he is subject to—

(a) a guardianship application under section 7 of the Mental Health Act,

(b) a guardianship order under section 37 of the Mental Health Act, or

(c) an obligation under another England and Wales enactment which has the same effect as a guardianship application or guardianship order.

England and Wales enactments

11.—(1) An England and Wales enactment is an enactment which extends to England and Wales (whether or not it also extends elsewhere).

(2) It does not matter if the enactment is in the Mental Health Act or not.

    1–774

P within scope of Mental Health Act

12.—(1) P is within the scope of the Mental Health Act if—

(a) an application in respect of P could be made under section 2 or 3 of the Mental Health Act, and

(b) P could be detained in a hospital in pursuance of such an application, were one made.

(2) The following provisions of this paragraph apply when determining whether an application in respect of P could be made under section 2 or 3 of the Mental Health Act.

(3) If the grounds in section 2(2) of the Mental Health Act are met in P's case, it is to be assumed that the recommendations referred to in section 2(3) of that Act have been given.

(4) If the grounds in section 3(2) of the Mental Health Act are met in P's case, it is to be assumed that the recommendations referred to in section 3(3) of that Act have been given.

(5) In determining whether the ground in section 3(2)(c) of the Mental Health Act is met in P's case, it is to be assumed that the treatment referred to in section 3(2)(c) cannot be provided under this Act.

    1–775

Authorised course of action, relevant care or treatment & relevant instrument

13. In a case where this Schedule applies for the purposes of section 16A—

"authorised course of action" means any course of action amounting to deprivation of liberty which the order under section 16(2)(a) authorises;

"relevant care or treatment" means any care or treatment which—

(a) comprises, or forms part of, the authorised course of action, or

(b) is to be given in connection with the authorised course of action;

"relevant instrument" means the order under section 16(2)(a).

    1–776

14. In a case where this Schedule applies for the purposes of paragraph 17 of Schedule A1—

"authorised course of action" means the accommodation of the relevant person in the relevant hospital or care home for the purpose of being given the relevant care or treatment;

"relevant care or treatment" has the same meaning as in Schedule A1;

"relevant instrument" means the standard authorisation under Schedule A1.

    1–777

15.—(1) This paragraph applies where the question whether a person is ineligible to be deprived of liberty by this Act is relevant to either of these decisions—

(a) whether or not to include particular provision ("the proposed provision") in an order under section 16(2)(a);

(b) whether or not to give a standard authorisation under Schedule A1.

(2) A reference in this Schedule to the authorised course of action or the relevant care or treatment is to be read as a reference to that thing as it would be if—

(a) the proposed provision were included in the order, or

(b) the standard authorisation were given.

(3) A reference in this Schedule to the relevant instrument is to be read as follows—

(a) where the relevant instrument is an order under section 16(2)(a): as a reference to the order as it would be if the proposed provision were included in it;

(b) where the relevant instrument is a standard authorisation: as a reference to the standard authorisation as it would be if it were given.

    1–778

Expressions used in paragraph 5

16.—(1) These expressions have the meanings given—

"donee" means a donee of a lasting power of attorney granted by P;

"mental health patient" means a person accommodated in a hospital for the purpose of being given medical treatment for mental disorder;

"mental health treatment" means the medical treatment for mental disorder referred to in the definition of "mental health patient".

(2) A decision of a donee or deputy is valid if it is made—

(a) within the scope of his authority as donee or deputy, and

(b) in accordance with Part 1 of this Act.

    1–779

Expressions with same meaning as in Mental Health Act

1–780 **17.**—(1) "Hospital" has the same meaning as in Part 2 of the Mental Health Act.

(2) "Medical treatment" has the same meaning as in the Mental Health Act.

(3) "Mental disorder" has the same meaning as in Schedule A1 (see paragraph 14).]

AMENDMENT

1–781 This Schedule was inserted by the Mental Health Act 2007 s.50(6), Sch.8.

GENERAL NOTE

1–782 This Schedule is considered in Part 2.

SCHEDULE 2

PROPERTY AND AFFAIRS: SUPPLEMENTARY PROVISIONS

1–783 **1.** Paragraphs 2 to 4 apply in relation to the execution of a will, by virtue of section 18, on behalf of P.

1–784 **2.** The will may make any provision (whether by disposing of property or exercising a power or otherwise) which could be made by a will executed by P if he had capacity to make it.

1–785 **3.**—(1) Sub-paragraph (2) applies if under section 16 the court makes an order or gives directions requiring or authorising a person (the authorised person) to execute a will on behalf of P.

(2) Any will executed in pursuance of the order or direction—

(a) must state that it is signed by P acting by the authorised person,

(b) must be signed by the authorised person with the name of P and his own name, in the presence of two or more witnesses present at the same time,

(c) must be attested and subscribed by those witnesses in the presence of the authorised person, and

(d) must be sealed with the official seal of the court.

1–786 **4.**—(1) This paragraph applies where a will is executed in accordance with paragraph 3.

(2) The Wills Act 1837 (c. 26) has effect in relation to the will as if it were signed by P by his own hand, except that—

(a) section 9 of the 1837 Act (requirements as to signing and attestation) does not apply, and

(b) in the subsequent provisions of the 1837 Act any reference to execution in the manner required by the previous provisions is to be read as a reference to execution in accordance with paragraph 3.

(3) The will has the same effect for all purposes as if—

(a) P had had the capacity to make a valid will, and

(b) the will had been executed by him in the manner required by the 1837 Act.

(4) But sub-paragraph (3) does not have effect in relation to the will—

(a) in so far as it disposes of immovable property outside England and Wales, or

(b) in so far as it relates to any other property or matter if, when the will is executed—

(i) P is domiciled outside England and Wales, and

(ii) the condition in sub-paragraph (5) is met.

(5) The condition is that, under the law of P's domicile, any question of his testamentary capacity would fall to be determined in accordance with the law of a place outside England and Wales.

1–787 **5.**—(1) If provision is made by virtue of section 18 for—

(a) the settlement of any property of P, or

(b) the exercise of a power vested in him of appointing trustees or retiring from a trust,

the court may also make as respects the property settled or the trust property such consequential vesting or other orders as the case may require.

(2) The power under sub-paragraph (1) includes, in the case of the exercise of such a power, any order which could have been made in such a case under Part 4 of the Trustee Act 1925 (c.19).

1–788 **6.**—(1) If a settlement has been made by virtue of section 18, the court may by order vary or revoke the settlement if—

(a) the settlement makes provision for its variation or revocation,

(b) the court is satisfied that a material fact was not disclosed when the settlement was made, or

(c) the court is satisfied that there has been a substantial change of circumstances.

(2) Any such order may give such consequential directions as the court thinks fit.

1–789 **7.**—(1) Sub-paragraph (2) applies if the court is satisfied—

(a) that under the law prevailing in a place outside England and Wales a person (M) has been appointed to exercise powers in respect of the property or affairs of P on the ground (however formulated) that P lacks capacity to make decisions with respect to the management and administration of his property and affairs, and

(b) that, having regard to the nature of the appointment and to the circumstances of the case, it is expedient that the court should exercise its powers under this paragraph.

(2) The court may direct—

(a) any stocks standing in the name of P, or

(b) the right to receive dividends from the stocks,

to be transferred into M's name or otherwise dealt with as required by M, and may give such directions as the court thinks fit for dealing with accrued dividends from the stocks.

(3) "Stocks" includes—

(a) shares, and

(b) any funds, annuity or security transferable in the books kept by any body corporate or unincorporated company or society or by an instrument of transfer either alone or accompanied by other formalities,

and "dividends" is to be construed accordingly.

8.—(1) Sub-paragraphs (2) and (3) apply if— **1–790**

(a) P's property has been disposed of by virtue of section 18,

(b) under P's will or intestacy, or by a gift perfected or nomination taking effect on his death, any other person would have taken an interest in the property but for the disposal, and

(c) on P's death, any property belonging to P's estate represents the property disposed of.

(2) The person takes the same interest, if and so far as circumstances allow, in the property representing the property disposed of.

(3) If the property disposed of was real property, any property representing it is to be treated, so long as it remains part of P's estate, as if it were real property.

(4) The court may direct that, on a disposal of P's property—

(a) which is made by virtue of section 18, and

(b) which would apart from this paragraph result in the conversion of personal property into real property,

property representing the property disposed of is to be treated, so long as it remains P's property or forms part of P's estate, as if it were personal property.

(5) References in sub-paragraphs (1) to (4) to the disposal of property are to—

(a) the sale, exchange, charging of or other dealing (otherwise than by will) with property other than money;

(b) the removal of property from one place to another;

(c) the application of money in acquiring property;

(d) the transfer of money from one account to another;

and references to property representing property disposed of are to be construed accordingly and as including the result of successive disposals.

(6) The court may give such directions as appear to it necessary or expedient for the purpose of facilitating the operation of sub-paragraphs (1) to (3), including the carrying of money to a separate account and the transfer of property other than money.

9.—(1) Sub-paragraph (2) applies if the court has ordered or directed the expenditure of money— **1–791**

(a) for carrying out permanent improvements on any of P's property, or

(b) otherwise for the permanent benefit of any of P's property.

(2) The court may order that—

(a) the whole of the money expended or to be expended, or

(b) any part of it,

is to be a charge on the property either without interest or with interest at a specified rate.

(3) An order under sub-paragraph (2) may provide for excluding or restricting the operation of paragraph 8(1) to (3).

(4) A charge under sub-paragraph (2) may be made in favour of such person as may be just and, in particular, where the money charged is paid out of P's general estate, may be made in favour of a person as trustee for P.

(5) No charge under sub-paragraph (2) may confer any right of sale or foreclosure during P's lifetime.

10.—(1) Any functions which P has as patron of a benefice may be discharged only by a person (R) **1–792** appointed by the court.

(2) R must be an individual capable of appointment under section 8(1)(b) of the 1986 Measure (which provides for an individual able to make a declaration of communicant status, a clerk in Holy Orders, etc. to be appointed to discharge a registered patron's functions).

(3) The 1986 Measure applies to R as it applies to an individual appointed by the registered patron of the benefice under section 8(1)(b) or (3) of that Measure to discharge his functions as patron.

(4) "The 1986 Measure" means the Patronage (Benefices) Measure 1986 (No.3).

1–793
DEFINITIONS
"will": s.64(1)
"property": s.64(1)
"the court": s.64(1)

1–794
GENERAL NOTE
This Schedule contains detailed provisions relating to the court's powers in relation to property and affairs, in particular the making of wills and settlements.

1–795
Paragraph 3(2)(b)
As the authorised person is not a witness, he or she would not be precluded from benefiting under s.15 of the Wills Act 1837 (c.26).

1–796
Paragraph 3(2)(d)
"The benefit of a court seal is that it provides authentication as to the originality of a document. It helps prevent fraud, and it reassures the financial institutions that they are dealing with the right person", per the Parliamentary Under-Secretary of State, St.Comm.A, para.188.

1–797
Paragraph 4(3)
A statutory will has the same effect as a will made by a competent testator.

1–798
Paragraph 4(4)
The court has power to order the execution of a will dealing with immoveable property situated within England and Wales irrespective of the patient's domicile (*P Re* [2009] EWHC 163 (Ch); [2009] 2 All E.R. 1198).

1–799
Paragraph 7
The purpose of this provision is to enable the court to recognise judicially the operation of foreign law, whereby some form of curatorship has been constituted for a patient, without itself having to go into questions of mental status and capacity.

1–800
Paragraph 8
This paragraph ensures that those who have an interest in property that has been disposed of by virtue of s.18 of the Act should preserve that interest. To a large extent, its practical application has been superseded by the court's ability to authorise the execution of a statutory will (*Re Treadwell* [2013] EWHC 2409 (COP) at para.84).

1–801
Paragraph 10
A "benefice" is a freehold office of the Church of England, such as the vicar of a parish. The patron of a benefice has the right to appoint a cleric to that office. The representative of P "will have to be an individual who is a communicant of the Church of England or a church in communion with it or a clerk in holy orders. The representative will fulfil the patron's role not only in presenting a priest to a vacant benefice under the Patronage Benefices Measure 1986 (m.3) but also in performing the other functions of a patron such as acting as a consultee when there is a proposal to suspend presentation under s.67 of the Pastoral Measure 1983 (m.1). In discharging his or her functions the representative will be subject to the provisions of the 1986 Measure in the same way that a registered patron would be", per the Under-Secretary of State (*Hansard*, HL Vol.670, col.1496).

SCHEDULE 3

INTERNATIONAL PROTECTION OF ADULTS

PART 1

PRELIMINARY

1–802
Introduction
1. This Part applies for the purposes of this Schedule.

1–803
The Convention
2.—(1) "Convention" means the Convention referred to in section 63.

(2) "Convention country" means a country in which the Convention is in force.

(3) A reference to an Article or Chapter is to an Article or Chapter of the Convention.

(4) An expression which appears in this Schedule and in the Convention is to be construed in accordance with the Convention.

Countries, territories and nationals

3.—(1) "Country" includes a territory which has its own system of law.   **1–804**

(2) Where a country has more than one territory with its own system of law, a reference to the country, in relation to one of its nationals, is to the territory with which the national has the closer, or the closest, connection.

Adults with incapacity

4.—(1) "Adult" means [subject to sub-paragraph (2)] a person who—   **1–805**

  (a) as a result of an impairment or insufficiency of his personal faculties, cannot protect his interests, and

  (b) has reached 16.

[(2) But "adult" does not include a child to whom either of the following applies—

  (a) the Convention on Jurisdiction, Applicable Law, Recognition, Enforcement and Co-Operation in respect of Parental Responsibility and Measures for the Protection of Children that was signed at The Hague on 19 October 1996;

  (b) Council Regulation (EC) No. 2201/2003 concerning jurisdiction and the recognition and enforcement of judgments in matrimonial matters and the matters of parental responsibility.]

Protective measures

5.—(1) "Protective measure" means a measure directed to the protection of the person or property   **1–806**
of an adult; and it may deal in particular with any of the following—

  (a) the determination of incapacity and the institution of a protective regime,

  (b) placing the adult under the protection of an appropriate authority,

  (c) guardianship, curatorship or any corresponding system,

  (d) the designation and functions of a person having charge of the adult's person or property, or representing or otherwise helping him,

  (e) placing the adult in a place where protection can be provided,

  (f) administering, conserving or disposing of the adult's property,

  (g) authorising a specific intervention for the protection of the person or property of the adult.

(2) Where a measure of like effect to a protective measure has been taken in relation to a person before he reaches 16, this Schedule applies to the measure in so far as it has effect in relation to him once he has reached 16.

Central Authority

6.—(1) Any function under the Convention of a Central Authority is exercisable in England and   **1–807**
Wales by the Lord Chancellor.

(2) A communication may be sent to the Central Authority in relation to England and Wales by sending it to the Lord Chancellor.

PART 2

JURISDICTION OF COMPETENT AUTHORITY

7.—(1) The court may exercise its functions under this Act (in so far as it cannot otherwise do so)   **1–808**
in relation to—

  (a) an adult habitually resident in England and Wales,

  (b) an adult's property in England and Wales,

  (c) an adult present in England and Wales or who has property there, if the matter is urgent, or

  (d) an adult present in England and Wales, if a protective measure which is temporary and limited in its effect to England and Wales is proposed in relation to him.

(2) An adult present in England and Wales is to be treated for the purposes of this paragraph as habitually resident there if—

  (a) his habitual residence cannot be ascertained,

  (b) he is a refugee, or

  (c) he has been displaced as a result of disturbance in the country of his habitual residence.

1–809 8.—(1) The court may also exercise its functions under this Act (in so far as it cannot otherwise do so) in relation to an adult if sub-paragraph (2) or (3) applies in relation to him.

(2) This sub-paragraph applies in relation to an adult if—

(a) he is a British citizen,

(b) he has a closer connection with England and Wales than with Scotland or Northern Ireland, and

(c) Article 7 has, in relation to the matter concerned, been complied with.

(3) This sub-paragraph applies in relation to an adult if the Lord Chancellor, having consulted such persons as he considers appropriate, agrees to a request under Article 8 in relation to the adult.

1–810 9.—(1) This paragraph applies where jurisdiction is exercisable under this Schedule in connection with a matter which involves a Convention country other than England and Wales.

(2) Any Article on which the jurisdiction is based applies in relation to the matter in so far as it involves the other country (and the court must, accordingly, comply with any duty conferred on it as a result).

(3) Article 12 also applies, so far as its provisions allow, in relation to the matter in so far as it involves the other country.

1–811 10. A reference in this Schedule to the exercise of jurisdiction under this Schedule is to the exercise of functions under this Act as a result of this Part of this Schedule.

PART 3

APPLICABLE LAW

1–812 11. In exercising jurisdiction under this Schedule, the court may, if it thinks that the matter has a substantial connection with a country other than England and Wales, apply the law of that other country.

1–813 12. Where a protective measure is taken in one country but implemented in another, the conditions of implementation are governed by the law of the other country.

1–814 13.—(1) If the donor of a lasting power is habitually resident in England and Wales at the time of granting the power, the law applicable to the existence, extent, modification or extinction of the power is—

(a) the law of England and Wales, or

(b) if he specifies in writing the law of a connected country for the purpose, that law.

(2) If he is habitually resident in another country at that time, but England and Wales is a connected country, the law applicable in that respect is—

(a) the law of the other country, or

(b) if he specifies in writing the law of England and Wales for the purpose, that law.

(3) A country is connected, in relation to the donor, if it is a country—

(a) of which he is a national,

(b) in which he was habitually resident, or

(c) in which he has property.

(4) Where this paragraph applies as a result of sub-paragraph (3)(c), it applies only in relation to the property which the donor has in the connected country.

(5) The law applicable to the manner of the exercise of a lasting power is the law of the country where it is exercised.

(6) In this Part of this Schedule, "lasting power" means—

(a) a lasting power of attorney (see section 9),

(b) an enduring power of attorney within the meaning of Schedule 4, or

(c) any other power of like effect.

1–815 14.—(1) Where a lasting power is not exercised in a manner sufficient to guarantee the protection of the person or property of the donor, the court, in exercising jurisdiction under this Schedule, may disapply or modify the power.

(2) Where, in accordance with this Part of this Schedule, the law applicable to the power is, in one or more respects, that of a country other than England and Wales, the court must, so far as possible, have regard to the law of the other country in that respect (or those respects).

1–816 15. Regulations may provide for Schedule 1(lasting powers of attorney: formalities) to apply with modifications in relation to a lasting power which comes within paragraph 13(6)(c) above.

1–817 16.—(1) This paragraph applies where a person (a representative) in purported exercise of an authority to act on behalf of an adult enters into a transaction with a third party.

(2) The validity of the transaction may not be questioned in proceedings, nor may the third party be held liable, merely because—

(a) where the representative and third party are in England and Wales when entering into the transaction, sub-paragraph (3) applies;

(b) where they are in another country at that time, sub-paragraph (4) applies.

(3) This sub-paragraph applies if—

(a) the law applicable to the authority in one or more respects is, as a result of this Schedule, the law of a country other than England and Wales, and

(b) the representative is not entitled to exercise the authority in that respect (or those respects) under the law of that other country.

(4) This sub-paragraph applies if—

(a) the law applicable to the authority in one or more respects is, as a result of this Part of this Schedule, the law of England and Wales, and

(b) the representative is not entitled to exercise the authority in that respect (or those respects) under that law.

(5) This paragraph does not apply if the third party knew or ought to have known that the applicable law was—

(a) in a case within sub-paragraph (3), the law of the other country;

(b) in a case within sub-paragraph (4), the law of England and Wales.

17. Where the court is entitled to exercise jurisdiction under this Schedule, the mandatory provisions of the law of England and Wales apply, regardless of any system of law which would otherwise apply in relation to the matter.   **1–818**

18. Nothing in this Part of this Schedule requires or enables the application in England and Wales of a provision of the law of another country if its application would be manifestly contrary to public policy.   **1–819**

PART 4

RECOGNITION AND ENFORCEMENT

19.—(1) A protective measure taken in relation to an adult under the law of a country other than England and Wales is to be recognised in England and Wales if it was taken on the ground that the adult is habitually resident in the other country.   **1–820**

(2) A protective measure taken in relation to an adult under the law of a Convention country other than England and Wales is to be recognised in England and Wales if it was taken on a ground mentioned in Chapter 2 (jurisdiction).

(3) But the court may disapply this paragraph in relation to a measure if it thinks that—

(a) the case in which the measure was taken was not urgent,

(b) the adult was not given an opportunity to be heard, and

(c) that omission amounted to a breach of natural justice.

(4) It may also disapply this paragraph in relation to a measure if it thinks that—

(a) recognition of the measure would be manifestly contrary to public policy,

(b) the measure would be inconsistent with a mandatory provision of the law of England and Wales, or

(c) the measure is inconsistent with one subsequently taken, or recognised, in England and Wales in relation to the adult.

(5) And the court may disapply this paragraph in relation to a measure taken under the law of a Convention country in a matter to which Article 33 applies, if the court thinks that that Article has not been complied with in connection with that matter.

20.—(1) An interested person may apply to the court for a declaration as to whether a protective measure taken under the law of a country other than England and Wales is to be recognised in England and Wales.   **1–821**

(2) No permission is required for an application to the court under this paragraph.

21. For the purposes of paragraphs 19 and 20, any finding of fact relied on when the measure was taken is conclusive.   **1–822**

22.—(1) An interested person may apply to the court for a declaration as to whether a protective measure taken under the law of, and enforceable in, a country other than England and Wales is enforceable, or to be registered, in England and Wales in accordance with Court of Protection Rules.   **1–823**

(2) The court must make the declaration if—

(a) the measure comes within sub-paragraph (1) or (2) of paragraph 19, and

(b) the paragraph is not disapplied in relation to it as a result of sub-paragraph (3), (4) or (5).

(3) A measure to which a declaration under this paragraph relates is enforceable in England and Wales as if it were a measure of like effect taken by the court.

23.—(1) This paragraph applies where—   **1–824**

(a) provision giving effect to, or otherwise deriving from, the Convention in a country other than England and Wales applies in relation to a person who has not reached 16, and

(b) a measure is taken in relation to that person in reliance on that provision.

(2) This Part of this Schedule applies in relation to that measure as it applies in relation to a protective measure taken in relation to an adult under the law of a Convention country other than England and Wales.

1–825   **24.** The court may not review the merits of a measure taken outside England and Wales except to establish whether the measure complies with this Schedule in so far as it is, as a result of this Schedule, required to do so.

1–826   **25.** Court of Protection Rules may make provision about an application under paragraph 20 or 22.

PART 5

CO-OPERATION

1–827   **26.**—(1) This paragraph applies where a public authority proposes to place an adult in an establishment in a Convention country other than England and Wales.

(2) The public authority must consult an appropriate authority in that other country about the proposed placement and, for that purpose, must send it—

(a) a report on the adult, and

(b) a statement of its reasons for the proposed placement.

(3) If the appropriate authority in the other country opposes the proposed placement within a reasonable time, the public authority may not proceed with it.

1–828   **27.** A proposal received by a public authority under Article 33 in relation to an adult is to proceed unless the authority opposes it within a reasonable time.

1–829   **28.**—(1) This paragraph applies if a public authority is told that an adult—

(a) who is in serious danger, and

(b) in relation to whom the public authority has taken, or is considering taking, protective measures, is, or has become resident, in a Convention country other than England and Wales.

(2) The public authority must tell an appropriate authority in that other country about—

(a) the danger, and

(b) the measures taken or under consideration.

1–830   **29.** A public authority may not request from, or send to, an appropriate authority in a Convention country information in accordance with Chapter 5(co-operation) in relation to an adult if it thinks that doing so—

(a) would be likely to endanger the adult or his property, or

(b) would amount to a serious threat to the liberty or life of a member of the adult's family.

PART 6

GENERAL

1–831   **30.** A certificate given under Article 38 by an authority in a Convention country other than England and Wales is, unless the contrary is shown, proof of the matters contained in it.

1–832   **31.** Her Majesty may by Order in Council confer on the Lord Chancellor, the court or another public authority functions for enabling the Convention to be given effect in England and Wales.

1–833   **32.**—(1) Regulations may make provision—

(a) giving further effect to the Convention, or

(b) otherwise about the private international law of England and Wales in relation to the protection of adults.

(2) The regulations may—

(a) confer functions on the court or another public authority;

(b) amend this Schedule;

(c) provide for this Schedule to apply with specified modifications;

(d) make provision about countries other than Convention countries.

1–834   **33.** Nothing in this Schedule applies, and no provision made under paragraph 32 is to apply, to any matter to which the Convention, as a result of Article 4, does not apply.

1–835   **34.** A reference in this Schedule to regulations or an order (other than an Order in Council) is to regulations or an order made for the purposes of this Schedule by the Lord Chancellor.

1–836   **35.** The following provisions of this Schedule have effect only if the Convention is in force in accordance with Article 57—

(a) paragraph 8,
(b) paragraph 9,
(c) paragraph 19(2) and (5),
(d) Part 5,
(e) paragraph 30.

AMENDMENTS

The amendments to para.4 were made by the Parental Responsibility and Measures for the **1–837** Protection of Children (International Obligations) (England and Wales and Northern Ireland) Regulations 2010 (SI 2010/1898) reg.17, Sch., para.10.

DEFINITIONS

"property": s.64(1) **1–838**
"the court": s.64(1)
"Court of Protection Rules": s.64(1)

GENERAL NOTE

See the notes to s.63. This Schedule, which has been described by Alex Ruck Keene and Victoria **1–839** Butler-Cole as a "very odd piece of legislation" (Court of Protection Newsletter—August 2010: accessed at *www.39essex.co.uk*), is divided into six parts. Part 1 contains definitions and introductory provisions. Part 2 provides the grounds, based on arts 5-11 of the Hague Convention on the International Protection of Adults, on which the Court of Protection will exercise its jurisdiction under this Act when dealing with cases with an international element. Part 3 makes provision as to the law of which country is to apply in various situations. It also provides protection for a third party who enters into a transaction with a representative on behalf of a person, where that representative was actually not entitled so to act under the law of a country other than England and Wales applicable by virtue of Pt 3. Part 4 provides for the recognition and enforcement of protective measures taken in other countries. Part 5 provides for co-operation between authorities in England and Wales and authorities in other Convention countries. Part 6 includes powers to make further provision as to private international by Order in Council and regulations and provisions on commencement.

PART 1

Paragraph 4

This paragraph contains a much wider definition of capacity than the one provided for in s.2. For **1–840** the position pertaining to children, see the General Note to s.63.

PART 2

Paragraph 7(a)

In *Re MN*, above, Hedley J. said at paras 22 and 23: **1–841**

"Habitual residence is an undefined term and in English authorities it is regarded as a question of fact to be determined in the individual circumstances of the case. It is well recognised in English law that the removal of a child from one jurisdiction to another by one parent without the consent of the other is wrongful and is not effective to change habitual residence, see e.g. *Re P-J* [2009] 2 FLR 1051 (CA). It seems to me that the wrongful removal (in this case without authority under the [Healthcare Directive executed by MN in accordance with Californian Law] whether because Part 3 is not engaged or the decision was not made in good faith) of an incapacitated adult should have the same consequence and should leave the courts of the country from which she was taken free to take protective measures. Thus in this case were the removal 'wrongful', I would hold that MN was habitually resident in California at the date of Judge Cain's orders.

If, however the removal were a proper and lawful exercise of authority under the Directive, different considerations arise. The position in April 2010 was that MN had been living with her niece in England and Wales on the basis that the niece was providing her with a permanent home. There is no evidence other than that MN is content and well cared for there and indeed may lose or even have lost any clear recollection of living on her own in California. In those circumstances it seems to me most probable that MN will have become habitually resident in England and Wales and this court will be required to accept and exercise a full welfare jurisdiction under the Act pursuant to paragraph 7(l)(a) of Schedule 3. Hence my view that authority to remove is the key consideration".

Hedley J.'s judgment was approved by Sir James Munby P. in *JO v GO* [2013] EWHC 3932 (COP) at para.16. In this case the President held that:

1. Habitual residence is, in essence, a question of fact to be determined having regard to all the circumstances of the particular case. Habitual residence can in principle be lost and another habitual residence acquired on the same day.

2. In the case of an adult who lacks the capacity to decide where to live, habitual residence can in principle be lost and another habitual residence acquired without the need for any court order or other formal process, such as the appointment of an attorney or deputy.

3. The doctrine of necessity enables a relative or carer to make a decision that leads to a change of the protected person's habitual residence as long as the decision is reasonable, arrived at in good faith and taken in the best interests of that person.

4. The wrongful removal of an incapacitated adult from one jurisdiction to another is not effective to change that person's habitual residence and leaves the courts of the country from which she was taken free to take protective measures: also see *Re MN*, above, at para.22.

5. The relevant date for determining habitual residence is the date of the hearing, and at the point of issue of the relevant application.

The authorities on habitual residence were reviewed by Moylan J. in *An English Local Authority v SW* [2014] EWCOP 43 where it was held that:

1. The definition of "habitual residence" under the Act should be the same as that applied in other family law instruments, including Brussels IIa (Council Regulations (EC) No. 2201/2013) (para.64).

2. It is important that the "determination of habitual residence is kept as free as possible from analytical complexities or constructs. It is a question of fact" (para.67).

3. The degree of integration and a person's state of mind "are clearly factors to which appropriate weight must be given when the court is undertaking a broad assessment of all the circumstances of the case. The broad assessment which is required properly to determine whether the quality of residence is such that it has become habitual in that it has the necessary degree of stability in order to distinguish it from mere presence or temporary or intermittent residence. This means a sufficient, or some, degree of integration . . ." (para.72). With regard to the case before him, his Lordship said at para.75:

> "Many people would rather not be living where they are and might wish fervently to live somewhere else. However, at least after a person has been living in one place for a significant period of time it will be difficult not to come to the conclusion that they are sufficiently integrated into their environment, whatever its composition, for them to be habitually resident there [N.B. SW had been living in her current location for over four years]. In the present case, any other conclusion would, in my view, be placing far too much weight on an assessment on SW's state of mind and the extent to which she feels settled."

PART 3

Paragraph 12

1–842   The adult's best interests have to be considered in the context of implementing the enforcement of an order (*Re MN*, above, at para.28).

The "conditions of implementation" are that the requirements of the ECHR are met, in particular the *Winterwerp* criteria and reviews of sufficient regularity to satisfy art.5(4) (*Health Services Executive of Ireland v PA* [2015] EWCOP 38 at para.102).

PART 4

1–843   A principal purpose of this Part "is to ensure that a person is returned to the jurisdiction of her habitual residence so that her best interests may be protected there" (*Re MN*, above, at para.28). Under para.24, the court is prevented from examining the merits of the measure taken outside England and Wales.

Paragraph 19

1–844   An order made under this paragraph is not a welfare order under s.16(2)(a). Consequently, s.16A does not apply. Therefore the fact that the patient would almost certainly (i) be subject to a deprivation of liberty and (ii) satisfy the clinical grounds for detention under the Mental Health Act 1983 on his arrival at an

English Hospital did not have the effect of barring the court from recognising and declaring to be enforceable an order of the Irish High Court which contemplated such a result (*Re M* [2011] EWHC 3590 (COP)).

Paragraph 19(1)
In *Re MN*, above, Hedley J. held that the best interests principle in s.1(5) does not apply when the court is considering whether to recognise a foreign protective measure. His Lordship said at para.31:

    "[A] decision to recognise under para.19(1) or to enforce under para.22(2) is not a decision governed by the best interests of MN and that those paragraphs are not disapplied thereby by para. 19(4)(b) and s.1(5) of the Act. My reasons are really threefold. First, I do not think that a decision to recognise or enforce can be properly described as a decision for and on behalf of' MN. She is clearly affected by the decision but it is a decision in respect of an order and not a person. Secondly, this rather technical reason is justified as reflecting the policy of the Schedule and of Part 4 namely ensuring that persons who lack capacity have their best interests and their affairs dealt with in the country of habitual residence; to decide otherwise would be to defeat that purpose. Thirdly, best interests in the implementation of an order clearly are relevant and are dealt with by para.12 which would otherwise not really be necessary."

The term "habitually resident" is not defined: see the note on para.7(a).

1–845

Paragraph 19(4)(a)
The use of the term "manifestly" suggests circumstances in which recognition of an order "would be repellent to the judicial conscience of the court" (*Re MN*, above, para.26).

1–846

Part 6

Paragraph 32
No regulations have been made under this provision.

1–847

SCHEDULE 4

Provisions Applying to Existing Enduring Powers of Attorney

Part 1

Enduring Powers of Attorney

Enduring power of attorney to survive mental incapacity of donor
   1.—(1) Where an individual has created a power of attorney which is an enduring power within the meaning of this Schedule—
   (a) the power is not revoked by any subsequent mental incapacity of his,
   (b) upon such incapacity supervening, the donee of the power may not do anything under the authority of the power except as provided by sub-paragraph (2) unless or until the instrument creating the power is registered under paragraph 13, and
   (c) if and so long as paragraph (b) operates to suspend the donee's authority to act under the power, section 5 of the Powers of Attorney Act 1971 (c. 27) (protection of donee and third persons), so far as applicable, applies as if the power had been revoked by the donor's mental incapacity,
and, accordingly, section 1 of this Act does not apply.
   (2) Despite sub-paragraph (1)(b), where the attorney has made an application for registration of the instrument then, until it is registered, the attorney may take action under the power—
   (a) to maintain the donor or prevent loss to his estate, or
   (b) to maintain himself or other persons in so far as paragraph 3(2) permits him to do so.
   (3) Where the attorney purports to act as provided by sub-paragraph (2) then, in favour of a person who deals with him without knowledge that the attorney is acting otherwise than in accordance with sub-paragraph (2)(a) or (b), the transaction between them is as valid as if the attorney were acting in accordance with sub-paragraph (2)(a) or (b).

1–848

Characteristics of an enduring power of attorney
   2.—(1) Subject to sub-paragraphs (5) and (6) and paragraph 20, a power of attorney is an enduring power within the meaning of this Schedule if the instrument which creates the power—
   (a) is in the prescribed form,
   (b) was executed in the prescribed manner by the donor and the attorney, and

1–849

(c) incorporated at the time of execution by the donor the prescribed explanatory information.

(2) In this paragraph, "prescribed" means prescribed by such of the following regulations as applied when the instrument was executed—

    (a) the Enduring Powers of Attorney (Prescribed Form) Regulations 1986 (SI 1986/126),

    (b) the Enduring Powers of Attorney (Prescribed Form) Regulations 1987 (SI 1987/1612),

    (c) the Enduring Powers of Attorney (Prescribed Form) Regulations 1990 (SI 1990/1376),

    (d) the Enduring Powers of Attorney (Welsh Language Prescribed Form) Regulations 2000 (SI 2000/289).

(3) An instrument in the prescribed form purporting to have been executed in the prescribed manner is to be taken, in the absence of evidence to the contrary, to be a document which incorporated at the time of execution by the donor the prescribed explanatory information.

(4) If an instrument differs in an immaterial respect in form or mode of expression from the prescribed form it is to be treated as sufficient in point of form and expression.

(5) A power of attorney cannot be an enduring power unless, when he executes the instrument creating it, the attorney is—

    (a) an individual who has reached 18 and is not bankrupt [or is not subject to a debt relief order (under Part 7A of the Insolvency Act 1986)], or

    (b) a trust corporation.

(6) A power of attorney which gives the attorney a right to appoint a substitute or successor cannot be an enduring power.

(7) An enduring power is revoked by the bankruptcy of the donor or attorney [or the making of a debt relief order (under Part 7A of the Insolvency Act 1986) in respect of the donor or attorney].

(8) But where the donor or attorney is bankrupt merely because an interim bankruptcy restrictions order has effect in respect of him [or where the donor or attorney is subject to an interim debt relief restrictions order], the power is suspended for so long as the order has effect.

(9) An enduring power is revoked if the court—

    (a) exercises a power under sections 16 to 20 in relation to the donor, and

    (b) directs that the enduring power is to be revoked.

(10) No disclaimer of an enduring power, whether by deed or otherwise, is valid unless and until the attorney gives notice of it to the donor or, where paragraph 4(6) or 15(1) applies, to the Public Guardian.

Scope of authority etc. of attorney under enduring power

1–850

3.—(1) If the instrument which creates an enduring power of attorney is expressed to confer general authority on the attorney, the instrument operates to confer, subject to—

    (a) the restriction imposed by sub-paragraph (3), and

    (b) any conditions or restrictions contained in the instrument,

authority to do on behalf of the donor anything which the donor could lawfully do by an attorney at the time when the donor executed the instrument.

(2) Subject to any conditions or restrictions contained in the instrument, an attorney under an enduring power, whether general or limited, may (without obtaining any consent) act under the power so as to benefit himself or other persons than the donor to the following extent but no further—

    (a) he may so act in relation to himself or in relation to any other person if the donor might be expected to provide for his or that person's needs respectively, and

    (b) he may do whatever the donor might be expected to do to meet those needs.

(3) Without prejudice to sub-paragraph (2) but subject to any conditions or restrictions contained in the instrument, an attorney under an enduring power, whether general or limited, may (without obtaining any consent) dispose of the property of the donor by way of gift to the following extent but no further—

    (a) he may make gifts of a seasonal nature or at a time, or on an anniversary, of a birth, a marriage or the formation of a civil partnership, to persons (including himself) who are related to or connected with the donor, and

    (b) he may make gifts to any charity to whom the donor made or might be expected to make gifts,

provided that the value of each such gift is not unreasonable having regard to all the circumstances and in particular the size of the donor's estate.

PART 2

ACTION ON ACTUAL OR IMPENDING INCAPACITY OF DONOR

Duties of attorney in event of actual or impending incapacity of donor

1–851

4.—(1) Sub-paragraphs (2) to (6) apply if the attorney under an enduring power has reason to believe that the donor is or is becoming mentally incapable.

(2) The attorney must, as soon as practicable, make an application to the Public Guardian for the registration of the instrument creating the power.

(3) Before making an application for registration the attorney must comply with the provisions as to notice set out in Part 3 of this Schedule.

(4) An application for registration—

(a) must be made in the prescribed form, and

(b) must contain such statements as may be prescribed.

(5) The attorney—

(a) may, before making an application for the registration of the instrument, refer to the court for its determination any question as to the validity of the power, and

(b) must comply with any direction given to him by the court on that determination.

(6) No disclaimer of the power is valid unless and until the attorney gives notice of it to the Public Guardian; and the Public Guardian must notify the donor if he receives a notice under this subparagraph.

(7) A person who, in an application for registration, makes a statement which he knows to be false in a material particular is guilty of an offence and is liable—

(a) on summary conviction, to imprisonment for a term not exceeding 12 months or a fine not exceeding the statutory maximum or both;

(b) on conviction on indictment, to imprisonment for a term not exceeding 2 years or a fine or both.

(8) In this paragraph, "prescribed" means prescribed by regulations made for the purposes of this Schedule by the Lord Chancellor.

PART 3

NOTIFICATION PRIOR TO REGISTRATION

5. Subject to paragraph 7, before making an application for registration the attorney must give notice of his intention to do so to all those persons (if any) who are entitled to receive notice by virtue of paragraph 6. **1–852**

6.—(1) Subject to sub-paragraphs (2) to (4), persons of the following classes (relatives) are entitled to receive notice under paragraph 5— **1–853**

(a) the donor's spouse or civil partner,

(b) the donor's children,

(c) the donor's parents,

(d) the donor's brothers and sisters, whether of the whole or half blood,

(e) the widow, widower or surviving civil partner of a child of the donor,

(f) the donor's grandchildren,

(g) the children of the donor's brothers and sisters of the whole blood,

(h) the children of the donor's brothers and sisters of the half blood,

(i) the donor's uncles and aunts of the whole blood,

(j) the children of the donor's uncles and aunts of the whole blood.

(2) A person is not entitled to receive notice under paragraph 5 if—

(a) his name or address is not known to the attorney and cannot be reasonably ascertained by him, or

(b) the attorney has reason to believe that he has not reached 18 or is mentally incapable.

(3) Except where sub-paragraph (4) applies—

(a) no more than 3 persons are entitled to receive notice under paragraph 5, and

(b) in determining the persons who are so entitled, persons falling within the class in subparagraph (1)(a) are to be preferred to persons falling within the class in sub-paragraph (1)(b), those falling within the class in sub-paragraph (1)(b) are to be preferred to those falling within the class in sub-paragraph (1)(c), and so on.

(4) Despite the limit of 3 specified in sub-paragraph (3), where—

(a) there is more than one person falling within any of classes (a) to (j) of sub-paragraph (1), and

(b) at least one of those persons would be entitled to receive notice under paragraph 5, then, subject to sub-paragraph (2), all the persons falling within that class are entitled to receive notice under paragraph 5.

7.—(1) An attorney is not required to give notice under paragraph 5— **1–854**

(a) to himself, or

(b) to any other attorney under the power who is joining in making the application, even though he or, as the case may be, the other attorney is entitled to receive notice by virtue of paragraph 6.

(2) In the case of any person who is entitled to receive notice by virtue of paragraph 6, the attorney, before applying for registration, may make an application to the court to be dispensed from the requirement to give him notice; and the court must grant the application if it is satisfied—

    (a) that it would be undesirable or impracticable for the attorney to give him notice, or

    (b) that no useful purpose is likely to be served by giving him notice.

1–855   **8.**—(1) Subject to sub-paragraph (2), before making an application for registration the attorney must give notice of his intention to do so to the donor.

(2) Paragraph 7(2) applies in relation to the donor as it applies in relation to a person who is entitled to receive notice under paragraph 5.

1–856   **9.** A notice to relatives under this Part of this Schedule must—

    (a) be in the prescribed form,

    (b) state that the attorney proposes to make an application to the Public Guardian for the registration of the instrument creating the enduring power in question,

    (c) inform the person to whom it is given of his right to object to the registration under paragraph 13(4), and

    (d) specify, as the grounds on which an objection to registration may be made, the grounds set out in paragraph 13(9).

1–857   **10.** A notice to the donor under this Part of this Schedule—

    (a) must be in the prescribed form,

    (b) must contain the statement mentioned in paragraph 9(b), and

    (c) must inform the donor that, while the instrument remains registered, any revocation of the power by him will be ineffective unless and until the revocation is confirmed by the court.

1–858   **11.**—(1)Subject to sub-paragraph (2), before making an application for registration an attorney under a joint and several power must give notice of his intention to do so to any other attorney under the power who is not joining in making the application; and paragraphs 7(2) and 9 apply in relation to attorneys entitled to receive notice by virtue of this paragraph as they apply in relation to persons entitled to receive notice by virtue of paragraph 6.

(2) An attorney is not entitled to receive notice by virtue of this paragraph if—

    (a) his address is not known to the applying attorney and cannot reasonably be ascertained by him, or

    (b) the applying attorney has reason to believe that he has not reached 18 or is mentally incapable.

1–859   **12.** Despite section 7 of the Interpretation Act 1978 (c. 30) (construction of references to service by post), for the purposes of this Part of this Schedule a notice given by post is to be regarded as given on the date on which it was posted.

PART 4

REGISTRATION

Registration of instrument creating power

1–860   **13.**—(1) If an application is made in accordance with paragraph 4(3) and (4) the Public Guardian must, subject to the provisions of this paragraph, register the instrument to which the application relates.

(2) If it appears to the Public Guardian that—

    (a) there is a deputy appointed for the donor of the power created by the instrument, and

    (b) the powers conferred on the deputy would, if the instrument were registered, to any extent conflict with the powers conferred on the attorney,

the Public Guardian must not register the instrument except in accordance with the court's directions.

(3) The court may, on the application of the attorney, direct the Public Guardian to register an instrument even though notice has not been given as required by paragraph 4(3) and Part 3 of this Schedule to a person entitled to receive it, if the court is satisfied—

    (a) that it was undesirable or impracticable for the attorney to give notice to that person, or

    (b) that no useful purpose is likely to be served by giving him notice.

(4) Sub-paragraph (5) applies if, before the end of the period of 5 weeks beginning with the date (or the latest date) on which the attorney gave notice under paragraph 5 of an application for registration, the Public Guardian receives a valid notice of objection to the registration from a person entitled to notice of the application.

(5) The Public Guardian must not register the instrument except in accordance with the court's directions.

(6) Sub-paragraph (7) applies if, in the case of an application for registration—

    (a) it appears from the application that there is no one to whom notice has been given under paragraph 5, or

(b) the Public Guardian has reason to believe that appropriate inquiries might bring to light evidence on which he could be satisfied that one of the grounds of objection set out in subparagraph (9) was established.

(7) The Public Guardian—

(a) must not register the instrument, and

(b) must undertake such inquiries as he thinks appropriate in all the circumstances.

(8) If, having complied with sub-paragraph (7)(b), the Public Guardian is satisfied that one of the grounds of objection set out in sub-paragraph (9) is established—

(a) the attorney may apply to the court for directions, and

(b) the Public Guardian must not register the instrument except in accordance with the court's directions.

(9) A notice of objection under this paragraph is valid if made on one or more of the following grounds—

(a) that the power purported to have been created by the instrument was not valid as an enduring power of attorney,

(b) that the power created by the instrument no longer subsists,

(c) that the application is premature because the donor is not yet becoming mentally incapable,

(d) that fraud or undue pressure was used to induce the donor to create the power,

(e) that, having regard to all the circumstances and in particular the attorney's relationship to or connection with the donor, the attorney is unsuitable to be the donor's attorney.

(10) If any of those grounds is established to the satisfaction of the court it must direct the Public Guardian not to register the instrument, but if not so satisfied it must direct its registration.

(11) If the court directs the Public Guardian not to register an instrument because it is satisfied that the ground in sub-paragraph (9)(d) or (e) is established, it must by order revoke the power created by the instrument.

(12) If the court directs the Public Guardian not to register an instrument because it is satisfied that any ground in sub-paragraph (9) except that in paragraph (c) is established, the instrument must be delivered up to be cancelled unless the court otherwise directs.

Register of enduring powers

14. The Public Guardian has the function of establishing and maintaining a register of enduring powers for the purposes of this Schedule.

1–861

PART 5

LEGAL POSITION AFTER REGISTRATION

Effect and proof of registration

15.—(1) The effect of the registration of an instrument under paragraph 13 is that—

1–862

(a) no revocation of the power by the donor is valid unless and until the court confirms the revocation under paragraph 16(3);

(b) no disclaimer of the power is valid unless and until the attorney gives notice of it to the Public Guardian;

(c) the donor may not extend or restrict the scope of the authority conferred by the instrument and no instruction or consent given by him after registration, in the case of a consent, confers any right and, in the case of an instruction, imposes or confers any obligation or right on or creates any liability of the attorney or other persons having notice of the instruction or consent.

(2) Sub-paragraph (1) applies for so long as the instrument is registered under paragraph 13 whether or not the donor is for the time being mentally incapable.

(3) A document purporting to be an office copy of an instrument registered under this Schedule is, in any part of the United Kingdom, evidence of—

(a) the contents of the instrument, and

(b) the fact that it has been so registered.

(4) Sub-paragraph (3) is without prejudice to section 3 of the Powers of Attorney Act 1971 (c. 27) (proof by certified copies) and to any other method of proof authorised by law.

Functions of court with regard to registered power

16.—(1) Where an instrument has been registered under paragraph 13, the court has the following functions with respect to the power and the donor of and the attorney appointed to act under the power.

1–863

(2) The court may—

    (a) determine any question as to the meaning or effect of the instrument;

    (b) give directions with respect to—

        (i) the management or disposal by the attorney of the property and affairs of the donor;

        (ii) the rendering of accounts by the attorney and the production of the records kept by him for the purpose;

        (iii) the remuneration or expenses of the attorney whether or not in default of or in accordance with any provision made by the instrument, including directions for the repayment of excessive or the payment of additional remuneration;

    (c) require the attorney to supply information or produce documents or things in his possession as attorney;

    (d) give any consent or authorisation to act which the attorney would have to obtain from a mentally capable donor;

    (e) authorise the attorney to act so as to benefit himself or other persons than the donor otherwise than in accordance with paragraph 3(2) and (3) (but subject to any conditions or restrictions contained in the instrument);

    (f) relieve the attorney wholly or partly from any liability which he has or may have incurred on account of a breach of his duties as attorney.

(3) On application made for the purpose by or on behalf of the donor, the court must confirm the revocation of the power if satisfied that the donor—

    (a) has done whatever is necessary in law to effect an express revocation of the power, and

    (b) was mentally capable of revoking a power of attorney when he did so (whether or not he is so when the court considers the application).

(4) The court must direct the Public Guardian to cancel the registration of an instrument registered under paragraph 13 in any of the following circumstances—

    (a) on confirming the revocation of the power under sub-paragraph (3),

    (b) on directing under paragraph 2(9)(b) that the power is to be revoked,

    (c) on being satisfied that the donor is and is likely to remain mentally capable,

    (d) on being satisfied that the power has expired or has been revoked by the mental incapacity of the attorney,

    (e) on being satisfied that the power was not a valid and subsisting enduring power when registration was effected,

    (f) on being satisfied that fraud or undue pressure was used to induce the donor to create the power,

    (g) on being satisfied that, having regard to all the circumstances and in particular the attorney's relationship to or connection with the donor, the attorney is unsuitable to be the donor's attorney.

(5) If the court directs the Public Guardian to cancel the registration of an instrument on being satisfied of the matters specified in sub-paragraph (4)(f) or (g) it must by order revoke the power created by the instrument.

(6) If the court directs the cancellation of the registration of an instrument under sub-paragraph (4) except paragraph (c) the instrument must be delivered up to the Public Guardian to be cancelled, unless the court otherwise directs.

Cancellation of registration by Public Guardian

1–864

    17. The Public Guardian must cancel the registration of an instrument creating an enduring power of attorney—

    (a) on receipt of a disclaimer signed by the attorney;

    (b) if satisfied that the power has been revoked by the death or bankruptcy of the donor or attorney [or the making of a debt relief order (under Part 7A of the Insolvency Act 1986) in respect of the donor or attorney] or, if the attorney is a body corporate, by its winding up or dissolution;

    (c) on receipt of notification from the court that the court has revoked the power;

    (d) on confirmation from the court that the donor has revoked the power.

PART 6

PROTECTION OF ATTORNEY AND THIRD PARTIES

Protection of attorney and third persons where power is invalid or revoked

1–865

    18.—(1) Sub-paragraphs (2) and (3) apply where an instrument which did not create a valid power of attorney has been registered under paragraph 13 (whether or not the registration has been cancelled at the time of the act or transaction in question).

(2) An attorney who acts in pursuance of the power does not incur any liability (either to the donor or to any other person) because of the non-existence of the power unless at the time of acting he knows—

    (a) that the instrument did not create a valid enduring power,

    (b) that an event has occurred which, if the instrument had created a valid enduring power, would have had the effect of revoking the power, or

    (c) that, if the instrument had created a valid enduring power, the power would have expired before that time.

(3) Any transaction between the attorney and another person is, in favour of that person, as valid as if the power had then been in existence, unless at the time of the transaction that person has knowledge of any of the matters mentioned in sub-paragraph (2).

(4) If the interest of a purchaser depends on whether a transaction between the attorney and another person was valid by virtue of sub-paragraph (3), it is conclusively presumed in favour of the purchaser that the transaction was valid if—

    (a) the transaction between that person and the attorney was completed within 12 months of the date on which the instrument was registered, or

    (b) that person makes a statutory declaration, before or within 3 months after the completion of the purchase, that he had no reason at the time of the transaction to doubt that the attorney had authority to dispose of the property which was the subject of the transaction.

(5) For the purposes of section 5 of the Powers of Attorney Act 1971 (c. 27) (protection where power is revoked) in its application to an enduring power the revocation of which by the donor is by virtue of paragraph 15 invalid unless and until confirmed by the court under paragraph 16—

    (a) knowledge of the confirmation of the revocation is knowledge of the revocation of the power, but

    (b) knowledge of the unconfirmed revocation is not.

Further protection of attorney and third persons

19. (1) If—   **1–866**

    (a) an instrument framed in a form prescribed as mentioned in paragraph 2(2) creates a power which is not a valid enduring power, and

    (b) the power is revoked by the mental incapacity of the donor,

sub-paragraphs (2) and (3) apply, whether or not the instrument has been registered.

(2) An attorney who acts in pursuance of the power does not, by reason of the revocation, incur any liability (either to the donor or to any other person) unless at the time of acting he knows—

    (a) that the instrument did not create a valid enduring power, and

    (b) that the donor has become mentally incapable.

(3) Any transaction between the attorney and another person is, in favour of that person, as valid as if the power had then been in existence, unless at the time of the transaction that person knows—

    (a) that the instrument did not create a valid enduring power, and

    (b) that the donor has become mentally incapable.

(4) Paragraph 18(4) applies for the purpose of determining whether a transaction was valid by virtue of sub-paragraph (3) as it applies for the purpose or determining whether a transaction was valid by virtue of paragraph 18(3).

PART 7

JOINT AND JOINT AND SEVERAL ATTORNEYS

Application to joint and joint and several attorneys

20.—(1) An instrument which appoints more than one person to be an attorney cannot create an   **1–867** enduring power unless the attorneys are appointed to act—

    (a) jointly, or

    (b) jointly and severally.

(2) This Schedule, in its application to joint attorneys, applies to them collectively as it applies to a single attorney but subject to the modifications specified in paragraph 21.

(3) This Schedule, in its application to joint and several attorneys, applies with the modifications specified in sub-paragraphs (4) to (7) and in paragraph 22.

(4) A failure, as respects any one attorney, to comply with the requirements for the creation of enduring powers—

    (a) prevents the instrument from creating such a power in his case, but

    (b) does not affect its efficacy for that purpose as respects the other or others or its efficacy in his case for the purpose of creating a power of attorney which is not an enduring power.

(5) If one or more but not both or all the attorneys makes or joins in making an application for registration of the instrument—

- (a) an attorney who is not an applicant as well as one who is may act pending the registration of the instrument as provided in paragraph 1(2),
- (b) notice of the application must also be given under Part 3 of this Schedule to the other attorney or attorneys, and
- (c) objection may validly be taken to the registration on a ground relating to an attorney or to the power of an attorney who is not an applicant as well as to one or the power of one who is an applicant.

(6) The Public Guardian is not precluded by paragraph 13(5) or (8) from registering an instrument and the court must not direct him not to do so under paragraph 13(10) if an enduring power subsists as respects some attorney who is not affected by the ground or grounds of the objection in question; and where the Public Guardian registers an instrument in that case, he must make against the registration an entry in the prescribed form.

(7) Sub-paragraph (6) does not preclude the court from revoking a power in so far as it confers a power on any other attorney in respect of whom the ground in paragraph 13(9)(d) or (e) is established; and where any ground in paragraph 13(9) affecting any other attorney is established the court must direct the Public Guardian to make against the registration an entry in the prescribed form.

(8) In sub-paragraph (4), "the requirements for the creation of enduring powers" means the provisions of—

- (a) paragraph 2 other than sub-paragraphs (8) and (9), and
- (b) the regulations mentioned in paragraph 2.

Joint attorneys

1–868 **21.**—(1) In paragraph 2(5), the reference to the time when the attorney executes the instrument is to be read as a reference to the time when the second or last attorney executes the instrument.

(2) In paragraph 2(6) to (8), the reference to the attorney is to be read as a reference to any attorney under the power.

(3) Paragraph 13 has effect as if the ground of objection to the registration of the instrument specified in sub-paragraph (9)(e) applied to any attorney under the power.

(4) In paragraph 16(2), references to the attorney are to be read as including references to any attorney under the power.

(5) In paragraph 16(4), references to the attorney are to be read as including references to any attorney under the power.

(6) In paragraph 17, references to the attorney are to be read as including references to any attorney under the power.

Joint and several attorneys

1–869 **22.**—(1) In paragraph 2(7), the reference to the bankruptcy of the attorney is to be read as a reference to the bankruptcy of the last remaining attorney under the power; and the bankruptcy of any other attorney under the power causes that person to cease to be an attorney under the power.

[(1A)—In paragraph 2(7), the reference to the making of a debt relief order (under Part 7A of the Insolvency Act 1986) in respect of the attorney is to be read as a reference to the making of a debt relief order in respect of the last remaining attorney under the power; and the making of a debt relief order in respect of any other attorney under the power causes that person to cease to be an attorney under the power.]

(2) In paragraph 2(8), the reference to the suspension of the power is to be read as a reference to its suspension in so far as it relates to the attorney in respect of whom the interim bankruptcy restrictions order has effect.

[(2A)—In paragraph 2(8), the reference to the suspension of the power is to be read as a reference to its suspension in so far as it relates to the attorney in respect of whom the interim debt relief restrictions order has effect.]

(3) The restriction upon disclaimer imposed by paragraph 4(6) applies only to those attorneys who have reason to believe that the donor is or is becoming mentally incapable.

PART 8

INTERPRETATION

1–870 **23.**—(1) In this Schedule—

"enduring power" is to be construed in accordance with paragraph 2, "mentally incapable" or "mental incapacity", except where it refers to revocation at common law, means in relation to any person, that he is incapable by reason of mental disorder [. . .] of managing and administering his property and affairs and "mentally capable" and "mental capacity" are to be construed accordingly,

"notice" means notice in writing, and

"prescribed", except for the purposes of paragraph 2, means prescribed by regulations made for the purposes of this Schedule by the Lord Chancellor.

[(1A) In sub-paragraph (1), "mental disorder" has the same meaning as in the Mental Health Act but disregarding the amendments made to that Act by the Mental Health Act 2007.]

(2) Any question arising under or for the purposes of this Schedule as to what the donor of the power might at any time be expected to do is to be determined by assuming that he had full mental capacity at the time but otherwise by reference to the circumstances existing at that time.

DEFINITIONS
    "bankrupt": s.64(3)   **1–871**
    "trust corporation": s.64(1)
    "Public Guardian": s.64(1)
    "the court": s.64(1)
    "deputy": s.64(1)
    "property": s.64(1)
    "purchaser": s.64(1)
    "Mental Health Act": s.64(1)

AMENDMENTS
    The amendments to this Schedule were made by the Mental Health Act 2007 s.1(4), Sch.2, Pt 2,   **1–872**
para.23 and SI 2012/2404 art.3(2), Sch.1, para.53(6).

GENERAL NOTE
    The prescribed forms for the making and registration of EPAs are set out in the Schs 7 and 8 to the   **1–873**
Lasting Powers of Attorney, Enduring Powers of Attorney and Public Guardian Regulations 2007 (SI 2007/1253). For the loss or destruction of forms, see reg.29. The purpose of this Schedule is explained in the notes to s.66(3).
    A statement of the law, practice and procedure relating to the rectification of EPAs and the severance of ineffective provisions, and the circumstances in which differences from the prescribed form may be regarded as immaterial is contained in a position statement prepared on behalf of the Office of the Public Guardian which is reproduced at para.14 of *Re Newman* (COP) July 30, 2012. The statement was described by Senior Judge Lush at para.16 as being "accurate".

Paragraph 13(1)
    REGISTER THE INSTRUMENT. See regs 23 to 27 of SI 2007/1253.   **1–874**

Paragraphs 13(2), 13(5), 13(7), and 24(2)
    See reg.26 of SI 2007/1253.   **1–875**

Paragraph 13(4)
    See reg.25 of SI 2007/1253.   **1–876**

Paragraph 13(9)(a)
    Whenever possible, the donor should be given the benefit of the doubt when any question arises as   **1–877**
to the construction of an EPA (*Harries Re*, an order of the Senior Judge, June 22, 2009).

Paragraph 13(9)(d)
    FRAUD OR UNDUE PRESSURE.   See the notes to s.22(3).   **1–878**

Paragraph 16(3)
    The mental capacity required to create an LPA is not necessarily the same as the mental capacity   **1–879**
required to revoke an EPA (*Cloutt Re* (COP) November 7, 2008, Senior Judge Lush).

Paragraph 16(4)(g)

1–880   In *Re AB (Revocation of an enduring power of attorney)* [2014] EWCOP 12, Senior Judge Lush said at para.29:

> "Generally speaking, any attorney acting under an EPA who has behaved, or is behaving, or proposes to behave, in a way that contravenes his authority or is not in the donor's best interests is likely to be unsuitable to be the donor's attorney, but the converse is not necessarily true. An attorney may be unsuitable to be the donor's attorney because the attorney has fallen out with them and no longer wishes them to act, even though their conduct as attorney has been exemplary."

In the context of inter-sibling rivalry, Patten J. said in *Re F* [2004] 3 All E.R. 277, at 284:

> "It seems to me that to remove a chosen attorney because of hostility from a sibling or other relative, in the absence of any effective challenge to his competence or integrity, should require clear evidence either that the continuing hostility will impede the proper administration of the estate or will cause significant distress to the donor which would be avoided by the appointment of a receiver."

A list of signs that a donee may be exploiting the donor or failing to act in the donor's best interests appears in paragraph 7.70 of the *Code of Practice* which is reproduced in the General Note to s.10.

Paragraph 20

1–881   This paragraph should be construed as meaning that a valid enduring power of attorney must state whether, *in the event that they exercise the power,* the attorneys must exercise it jointly or jointly and severally. That construction applied whether the power of attorney purported to appoint attorneys in the alternative or in succession (*J (Enduring Power of Attorney), Re* [2009] EWHC 436 (Ch); [2009] 2 All E.R. 1051).

Paragraph 20(6), (7)

1–882   See reg.28 of SI 2007/1253.

SCHEDULE 5

TRANSITIONAL PROVISIONS AND SAVINGS

PART 1

REPEAL OF PART 7 OF THE MENTAL HEALTH ACT 1983

Existing receivers

1–883   1.—(1) This paragraph applies where, immediately before the commencement day, there is a receiver (R) for a person (P) appointed under section 99 of the Mental Health Act.

(2) On and after that day—

(a) this Act applies as if R were a deputy appointed for P by the court, but with the functions that R had as receiver immediately before that day, and

(b) a reference in any other enactment to a deputy appointed by the court includes a person appointed as a deputy as a result of paragraph (a).

(3) On any application to it by R, the court may end R's appointment as P's deputy.

(4) Where, as a result of section 20(1), R may not make a decision on behalf of P in relation to a relevant matter, R must apply to the court.

(5) If, on the application, the court is satisfied that P is capable of managing his property and affairs in relation to the relevant matter—

(a) it must make an order ending R's appointment as P's deputy in relation to that matter, but

(b) it may, in relation to any other matter, exercise in relation to P any of the powers which it has under sections 15 to 19.

(6) If it is not satisfied, the court may exercise in relation to P any of the powers which it has under sections 15 to 19.

(7) R's appointment as P's deputy ceases to have effect if P dies.

(8) "Relevant matter" means a matter in relation to which, immediately before the commencement day, R was authorised to act as P's receiver.

(9) In sub-paragraph (1), the reference to a receiver appointed under section 99 of the Mental Health Act includes a reference to a person who by virtue of Schedule 5 to that Act was deemed to be a receiver appointed under that section.

Orders, appointments etc

2.—(1) Any order or appointment made, direction or authority given or other thing done which has, **1–884**
or by virtue of Schedule 5 to the Mental Health Act was deemed to have, effect under Part 7 of the Act
immediately before the commencement day is to continue to have effect despite the repeal of Part 7.

(2) In so far as any such order, appointment, direction, authority or thing could have been made,
given or done under sections 15 to 20 if those sections had then been in force—

(a) it is to be treated as made, given or done under those sections, and

(b) the powers of variation and discharge conferred by section 16(7) apply accordingly.

(3) Sub-paragraph (1)—

(a) does not apply to nominations under section 93(1) or (4) of the Mental Health Act, and

(b) as respects receivers, has effect subject to paragraph 1.

(4) This Act does not affect the operation of section 109 of the Mental Health Act (effect and proof
of orders etc.) in relation to orders made and directions given under Part 7 of that Act.

(5) This paragraph is without prejudice to section 16 of the Interpretation Act 1978 (c. 30) (general
savings on repeal).

Pending proceedings

3.—(1) Any application for the exercise of a power under Part 7 of the Mental Health Act which **1–885**
is pending immediately before the commencement day is to be treated, in so far as a corresponding
power is exercisable under sections 16 to 20, as an application for the exercise of that power.

(2) For the purposes of sub-paragraph (1) an application for the appointment of a receiver is to be
treated as an application for the appointment of a deputy.

Appeals

4.—(1) Part 7 of the Mental Health Act and the rules made under it are to continue to apply to any **1–886**
appeal brought by virtue of section 105 of that Act which has not been determined before the commencement day.

(2) If in the case of an appeal brought by virtue of section 105(1) (appeal to nominated judge) the
judge nominated under section 93 of the Mental Health Act has begun to hear the appeal, he is to
continue to do so but otherwise it is to be heard by a puisne judge of the High Court nominated under
section 46.

Fees

5. All fees and other payments which, having become due, have not been paid to the former Court **1–887**
of Protection before the commencement day, are to be paid to the new Court of Protection.

Court records

6.—(1) The records of the former Court of Protection are to be treated, on and after the commence- **1–888**
ment day, as records of the new Court of Protection and are to be dealt with accordingly under the
Public Records Act 1958 (c. 51).

(2) On and after the commencement day, the Public Guardian is, for the purpose of exercising any
of his functions, to be given such access as he may require to such of the records mentioned in sub-
paragraph (1) as relate to the appointment of receivers under section 99 of the Mental Health Act.

Existing charges

7. This Act does not affect the operation in relation to a charge created before the commencement **1–889**
day of—

(a) so much of section 101(6) of the Mental Health Act as precludes a charge created under section
101(5) from conferring a right of sale or foreclosure during the lifetime of the patient, or

(b) section 106(6) of the Mental Health Act (charge created by virtue of section 106(5) not to cause
interest to fail etc.).

Preservation of interests on disposal of property

8. Paragraph 8(1) of Schedule 2 applies in relation to any disposal of property (within the meaning **1–890**
of that provision) by a person living on 1 st November 1960, being a disposal effected under the
Lunacy Act 1890 (c.5) as it applies in relation to the disposal of property effected under sections 16
to 20.

Accounts

1–891 9. Court of Protection Rules may provide that, in a case where paragraph 1 applies, R is to have a duty to render accounts—

(a) while he is receiver;

(b) after he is discharged.

Interpretation

1–892 10. In this Part of this Schedule—

(a) "the commencement day" means the day on which section 66(1)(a) (repeal of Part 7 of the Mental Health Act) comes into force,

(b) "the former Court of Protection" means the office abolished by section 45, and

(c) "the new Court of Protection" means the court established by that section.

PART 2

REPEAL OF THE ENDURING POWERS OF ATTORNEY ACT 1985

Orders, determinations, etc

1–893 11.—(1) Any order or determination made, or other thing done, under the 1985 Act which has effect immediately before the commencement day continues to have effect despite the repeal of that Act.

(2) In so far as any such order, determination or thing could have been made or done under Schedule 4 if it had then been in force—

(a) it is to be treated as made or done under that Schedule, and

(b) the powers of variation and discharge exercisable by the court apply accordingly.

(3) Any instrument registered under the 1985 Act is to be treated as having been registered by the Public Guardian under Schedule 4.

(4) This paragraph is without prejudice to section 16 of the Interpretation Act 1978 (c. 30) (general savings on repeal).

Pending proceedings

1–894 12.—(1) An application for the exercise of a power under the 1985 Act which is pending immediately before the commencement day is to be treated, in so far as a corresponding power is exercisable under Schedule 4, as an application for the exercise of that power.

(2) For the purposes of sub-paragraph (1)—

(a) a pending application under section 4(2) of the 1985 Act for the registration of an instrument is to be treated as an application to the Public Guardian under paragraph 4 of Schedule 4 and any notice given in connection with that application under Schedule 1 to the 1985 Act is to be treated as given under Part 3 of Schedule 4,

(b) a notice of objection to the registration of an instrument is to be treated as a notice of objection under paragraph 13 of Schedule 4, and

(c) pending proceedings under section 5 of the 1985 Act are to be treated as proceedings on an application for the exercise by the court of a power which would become exercisable in relation to an instrument under paragraph 16(2) of Schedule 4 on its registration.

Appeals

1–895 13.—(1) The 1985 Act and, so far as relevant, the provisions of Part 7 of the Mental Health Act and the rules made under it as applied by section 10 of the 1985 Act are to continue to have effect in relation to any appeal brought by virtue of section 10(1)(c) of the 1985 Act which has not been determined before the commencement day.

(2) If, in the case of an appeal brought by virtue of section 105(1) of the Mental Health Act as applied by section 10(1)(c) of the 1985 Act (appeal to nominated judge), the judge nominated under section 93 of the Mental Health Act has begun to hear the appeal, he is to continue to do so but otherwise the appeal is to be heard by a puisne judge of the High Court nominated under section 46.

Exercise of powers of donor as trustee

1–896 14.—(1) Section 2(8) of the 1985 Act (which prevents a power of attorney under section 25 of the Trustee Act 1925 (c.19) as enacted from being an enduring power) is to continue to apply to any enduring power—

(a) created before 1 st March 2000, and

(b) having effect immediately before the commencement day.

(2) Section 3(3) of the 1985 Act (which entitles the donee of an enduring power to exercise the

donor's powers as trustee) is to continue to apply to any enduring power to which, as a result of the provision mentioned in sub-paragraph (3), it applies immediately before the commencement day.

(3) The provision is section 4(3)(a) of the Trustee Delegation Act 1999 (c. 15) (which provides for section 3(3) of the 1985 Act to cease to apply to an enduring power when its registration is cancelled, if it was registered in response to an application made before 1 st March 2001).

(4) Even though section 4 of the 1999 Act is repealed by this Act, that section is to continue to apply in relation to an enduring power—

   (a) to which section 3(3) of the 1985 Act applies as a result of sub-paragraph (2), or

   (b) to which, immediately before the repeal of section 4 of the 1999 Act, section 1 of that Act applies as a result of section 4 of it.

(5) The reference in section 1(9) of the 1999 Act to section 4(6) of that Act is to be read with sub-paragraphs (2) to (4).

Interpretation
15. In this Part of this Schedule, "the commencement day" means the day on which section 66(1)(b) (repeal of the 1985 Act) comes into force.   **1–897**

DEFINITIONS   **1–898**
"Mental Health Act": s.64(1)
"deputy": s.64(1)
"the court": s.64(1)
"enactment": s.64(1)
"property": s.64(1)
"Public Guardian": s.64(1)
"Court of Protection Rules": s.64(1)
"the 1985 Act": s.64(1)

GENERAL NOTE
See the notes to s.66(4).   **1–899**

SCHEDULE 6

MINOR AND CONSEQUENTIAL AMENDMENTS

[*Not reproduced*]   **1–900**

SCHEDULE 7

REPEALS

[*Not reproduced*]   **1–901**

PART 2

THE DEPRIVATION OF LIBERTY SAFEGUARDS

Section 4A of the Mental Capacity Act (the 2005 Act) prohibits the deprivation **2–001** of the liberty of a person under the Act other than where the court has made an order under s.16(2)(a); where it is authorised for life-sustaining or other emergency treatment (s.4B); or where the deprivation is authorised under the procedures set out in Sch.A1. This Part explains the background to the deprivation of liberty procedures, describes how they are intended to operate, and considers their interface with the Mental Health Act 1983 (the 1983 Act).

The deprivation of liberty procedures are considered in the supplement to the *Code of Practice* on the Act which is reproduced in Pt.5. Developments in case law, especially with regard to the meaning of a deprivation of liberty, have diluted the helpfulness of the guidance contained in the supplement.

HL v United Kingdom (the "Bournewood" case)

In *HL v United Kingdom* (2004) 40 E.H.R.R. 761, Mr L alleged that he had **2–002** been detained at the Bournewood Hospital as an informal patient in violation of art.5(1) of the European Convention on Human Rights (ECHR) which is designed to ensure that no one should be arbitrarily deprived of his or her liberty. He also claimed that the procedures available to him for a review of the legality of his detention did not satisfy the requirements of art.5(4) which provides a person who has been deprived of his or her liberty with a right to a speedy independent legal review of the detention. The facts of the case are remarkable. From the age of 13, for a period of over 30 years, Mr L, who had a profound learning disability, was autistic and lacked the capacity to consent or dissent from being in hospital, was a resident at the Bournewood Hospital. He was eventually discharged into the community to live with carers, Mr and Mrs E. Under their care Mr L flourished for three years until an incident occurred that led to his readmission to hospital. While attending a day centre, Mr L became particularly agitated and he could not be calmed. Mr and Mrs E, who had been able to deal with such incidents successfully, could not be contacted. A doctor attended the day centre and administered a sedative to Mr L. On the advice of Mr L's social worker, he was taken to the Bournewood Hospital by which time the effect of the sedative was beginning to wear off and he was becoming increasingly agitated. Mr L was assessed by a psychiatrist as requiring inpatient treatment. On Mr L's admission, his consultant psychiatrist considered whether it was necessary to detain him under the provisions of the 1983 Act but decided that this was not necessary because he appeared fully compliant and did not resist admission to hospital. He was therefore admitted informally. Mr and Mrs E made it plain that they wanted to take Mr L back into their care. Mr L's consultant psychiatrist was not prepared to countenance this and he remained in the hospital. Proceedings were commenced in the name of Mr L against the Bournewood NHS Trust for judicial review of the trust's decision to detain him and for a writ of habeas corpus to release him from detention. It was claimed that Mr L's detention was unlawful on the ground that the 1983 Act, which had not been invoked, was the only basis for the hospital's right to detain him. The hospital claimed that Mr L was not being detained, but if he was, the detention was authorised under the common law doctrine of necessity. Subsequent to the decision of the House of Lords ([1998] 3 All E.R. 289) to dismiss Mr L's claim, an application was made to European Court of Human Rights (ECtHR).

The decision of the ECtHR focussed on the findings of the House of Lords that the detention of a compliant mentally incapacitated patient could be justified under the common law doctrine of necessity, and that Mr L had not been detained while he was a patient at the Bournewood Hospital. The ECtHR held:

1. In order to determine whether a person has been deprived of his or her liberty for the purposes of art.5(1), the starting point must be the specific situation of the individual concerned and account must be taken of a whole range of factors arising in a particular case such as the type, duration, effects and manner of implementation of the measure in question. The distinction between a deprivation of, and a restriction upon, liberty is merely one of degree or intensity and not one of nature or substance (para.89).

2. The correspondence between HL's carers and his psychiatrist reflected both the carers' wish to have HL immediately released to their care and, equally, the clear intention of the health care professionals to exercise strict control over his assessment, treatment, contacts and, notably, movement and residence: HL would only be released from the hospital to the care of his carers as and when the professionals considered it appropriate. It followed that HL was being deprived of his liberty because he "was under continuous supervision and control and was not free to leave"(para.91). The fact that HL might have been on a ward which was not "locked" or "lockable" was not determinative (para.92). With regard to HL's compliance to his admission, the Court observed that "the right to liberty is too important in a democratic society for a person to lose the benefit of Convention protection for the single reason that he may have given himself up to be taken into detention, especially when it is not disputed that that person is legally incapable of consenting to, or disagreeing with, the proposed action" (para.90). The Court found "striking the lack of any fixed procedural rules by which the admission and detention of compliant incapacitated patients is conducted" when contrasted with "the extensive network of safeguards applicable to psychiatric committals covered by the 1983 Act" (para.120). This absence of procedural safeguards in the doctrine of necessity failed to protect HL against arbitrary deprivations of his liberty. His detention therefore violated art.5(1).

3. There had also been a violation of art.5(4) of the Convention as HL did not have the opportunity to have the lawfulness of his detention reviewed by a court as neither judicial review nor other judicial remedies cited by the Government satisfied the requirements of art.5(4) (para.141).

What constitutes a "deprivation of liberty"?

2–003   Section 64(5) of the 2005 Act states that "references to deprivations of a person's liberty have the same meaning as in Article 5(1) of the Human Rights Convention". It will therefore be necessary to examine the case law of both the

ECtHR and domestic courts on the interpretation of the phrase "deprived of his liberty". The deprivation can occur in either a domestic or institutional setting.

Restrictions on a person's movements and freedom to chose his residence which do not constitute a deprivation of liberty and which are necessary "for the prevention of crime, for the protection of health or morals, or for the protection of the rights and freedom of others" are allowed for under art.2 of Protocol 4 of the Convention, which has not been ratified by the United Kingdom. According to Lord Hope, "art.2 of Protocol 4 helps to put the ambit of [art.5] into its proper perspective" (*Austin v Commissioner of Police of the Metropolis* [2009] UKHL 5 at para.15).

In *Secretary of State for the Home Department v JJ* [2007] UKHL 45, Lady Hale said at para.57:

"My Lords, what does it mean to be deprived of one's liberty? Not, we are all agreed, to be deprived of the freedom to live one's life as one pleases. It means to be deprived of one's physical liberty . . . And what does this mean? It must mean being forced or obliged to be at a particular place where one does not choose to be . . . But even that is not always enough because merely being required to live at a particular place or to keep within a particular geographical area does not, without more, amount to a deprivation of liberty. There must be a greater degree of control over one's physical ability than that. But how much?"

The Supreme Court addressed this question in *P v Cheshire West and Chester Council; P and Q v Surrey CC* [2014] UKSC 19 (*Cheshire West*), which are cases about the criteria for judging whether the living arrangements made for a mentally incapacitated person amount to a deprivation of liberty. If they do, then the deprivation has to be authorised, either by the Court of Protection or by the deprivation of liberty safeguards: see below. The following description of the situation of the individuals who were the focus of the hearing is taken from the press summary prepared by the court:

"P and Q (otherwise known as MIG and MEG) are sisters who became the subject of care proceedings in 2007 when they were respectively 16 and 15. Both have learning disabilities. MIG was placed with a foster mother to whom she was devoted and went to a further education unit daily. She never attempted to leave the foster home by herself but would have been restrained from doing so had she tried. MEG was moved from foster care to a residential home for learning disabled adolescents with complex needs. She sometimes required physical restraint and received tranquillising medication. When the care proceedings were transferred to the Court of Protection in 2009, the judge held that these living arrangements were in the sisters' best interests and did not amount to a deprivation of liberty. This finding was upheld by the Court of Appeal.

P is an adult born with cerebral palsy and Down's syndrome who requires 24 hour care. Until he was 37 he lived with his mother but when her health deteriorated the local social services authority obtained orders from the Court of Protection that it was in P's best interests to live in accommodation arranged by the authority. Since November 2009 he has lived in a staffed bungalow with other residents near his home and has one to one support to enable him to leave the house frequently for activities and visits. Intervention is sometimes required when he exhibits challenging behaviour. The judge held that these arrangements did deprive him of his liberty but that it was in P's best interests for them to continue. The Court of Appeal substituted a declaration that the arrangements did not involve a deprivation of liberty, after comparing his circumstances with another person of the same age and disabilities as P."

The scope of article 5 of the ECHR

2–004   The "first and most fundamental question" before the court in *Cheshire West* was "whether the concept of physical liberty protected by art.5 is the same for everyone, regardless of whether or not they are mentally or physically disabled" (per Lady Hale at para.33). Lady Hale, who gave the lead judgment, provided a forthright answer:

> "45. [I]t is axiomatic that people with disabilities, both mental and physical, have the same human rights as the rest of the human race. It may be that those rights have sometimes to be limited or restricted because of their disabilities, but the starting point should be the same as that for everyone else. This flows inexorably from the universal character of human rights, founded on the inherent dignity of all human beings, and is confirmed in the United Nations Convention on the Rights of Persons with Disabilities. Far from disability entitling the state to deny such people human rights: rather it places upon the state (and upon others) the duty to make reasonable accommodation to cater for the special needs of those with disabilities.

> 46. Those rights include the right to physical liberty, which is guaranteed by article 5 of the European Convention. This is not a right to do or to go where one pleases. It is a more focussed right, not to be deprived of that physical liberty. But, as it seems to me, what it means to be deprived of liberty must be the same for everyone, whether or not they have physical or mental disabilities. If it would be a deprivation of my liberty to be obliged to live in a particular place, subject to constant monitoring and control, only allowed out with close supervision, and unable to move away without permission even if such an opportunity became available, then it must also be a deprivation of the liberty of a disabled person. The fact that my living arrangements are comfortable, and indeed make my life as enjoyable as it could possibly be, should make no difference. A gilded cage is still a cage."

Although a minority of the justices could "see the attractions of a universal test, applicable to all regardless of any physical or mental disabilities", as Lady Hale proposed, they considered that "it is not a concept which we can find reflected in the Strasbourg cases" and that the ECtHR "has remained wedded to a case-specific test" (per Lord Carnwath and Lord Hodge at para.94).

How to identify a deprivation of liberty?

2–005   Lord Kerr defined liberty at para.76:

> "Liberty means the state or condition of being free from external constraint. It is predominantly an objective state. It does not depend on one's disposition to exploit one's freedom. Nor is it diminished by one's lack of capacity."

Lady Hale examined the relevant case law of the ECtHR to identify the essential character of a deprivation of liberty. Three components were identified:

(i) the objective component of confinement in a particular restricted place for a not negligible length of time;

(ii) the subjective component of lack of valid consent; and

(iii) the attribution of responsibility to the state.

Components (ii) and (iii), which are consider below, were not in issue before the court, but component (i) was. With regard to component (i), Lady Hale said at para.38:

> "Simply asking whether a person is 'confined' is not enough except in obvious cases. The 'starting point' is always upon the 'concrete situation' of the particular person concerned and 'account must be taken of a whole range of criteria such as the type, duration, effects and manner of implementation of the measures in question'. The presence or absence of coercion is also relevant. Thus there is no single 'touchstone' of what constitutes a deprivation of liberty in this or any other context."

The "starting point" identified by Lady Hale is taken from the case of *Guzzardi v Italy* (1980) 3 E.H.R.R. 33 at para.92. In *Guzzardi* it was said that the difference between "deprivation of and restriction upon liberty is . . . merely one of degree or intensity, and not one of nature or substance" (para.93). Lady Hale said that the cases before the court were not about this distinction (para.48), although it is difficult to see why this was the case.

Rather than attempt to lay down a prescriptive list of criteria for a deprivation of liberty, Lady Hale identified, at para.50, the factors that are *not* relevant to the determination. They are:

(i) the person's compliance or lack of objection;

(ii) the relative normality of the placement (whatever the comparison made); and

(iii) the reason or purpose behind a particular placement.

Lord Neuberger qualified point (i) by referring to "those rare circumstances where the absence of objection can be said to amount to consent, as in *Mihailovs v Latvia*, paras 138–139" (para.68). If a person has validly consented to his confinement, there can be no deprivation of liberty (*Stanev v Bulgaria* (2012) 55 E.H.R.R. 22 at para.117).

The consequence of point (ii) is that the court rejected the "relative normality" approach of the Court of Appeal in the *P* case, where the life which P was leading was compared with the life which another person with his disabilities might be leading. Lord Kerr said at para.77:

> "The question whether one is restricted (as a matter of actuality) is determined by comparing the extent of your actual freedom with someone of your age and station whose freedom is not limited. Thus a teenager of the same age and familial background as MIG and MEG is the relevant comparator for them. If one compares their state with a person of similar age and full capacity it is clear that their liberty is in fact circumscribed. They may not be conscious, much less resentful, of the constraint but, objectively, limitations on their freedom are in place."

The fact that all that could be done for the person is being done does not determine whether a deprivation exists. Lady Hale said at para.56:

"[T]he purpose of article 5 is to ensure that people are not deprived of their liberty without proper safeguards, safeguards which will secure that the legal justifications for the constraints which they are under are made out: in these cases, the law requires that they do indeed lack the capacity to decide for themselves where they should live and that the arrangements made for them are in their best interests. It is to set the cart before the horse to decide that because they do indeed lack capacity and the best possible arrangements have been made, they are not in need of those safeguards."

The attribution of responsibility to the state

2–006   In *P and Q v Surrey CC* [2011] EWCA 190 at para.18, Wilson L.J. said that this requirement "is the mechanism for the exclusion from the ambit of art.5 of steps taken for the protection of small or disabled children, without recourse to the state, by those with parental responsibility for them in the proper exercise of their powers".

In *A (child), Re and C (adult), Re* [2010] EWHC 978 (Fam) at para.106, Munby J. said that a local authority will only be responsible for a deprivation of liberty in a domestic setting so as to engage the state's responsibility for the deprivation under art.5 if it is "directly or actively involved in the domestic, family regime" and that the mere provision of support services for the family would not be sufficient to trigger such responsibility.

The close involvement of P's family in her care at her home led Bodey J. to reach the following conclusion in *W City Council v Mrs L* [2015] EWCOP 20 at para.27:

"This is a shared arrangement set up by agreement with a caring and pro-active family: and the responsibility of the State is, it seems to me, diluted by the strong role which the family has played and continues to play. I do not consider in such circumstances that the mischief of State interference at which Article 5 was and is directed, sufficiently exists."

These cases did not consider the effect of s.64(6) on the definition of a deprivation of liberty for the purposes of the Act.

The lack of valid consent to the deprivation of liberty

2–007   In *A Primary Care Trust v LDV* [2013] EWHC 272 (Fam), Baker J. accepted that he should proceed as if exercising the capacity test from Sch.A1 when exercising the Court of Protection jurisdiction. Without "seeking to set any sort of precedent" about the information that must be provided to a patient before he makes a decision whether to consent to a placement in a psychiatric hospital which amounts to a deprivation of liberty Baker J. said, at para.39, that

"the clinicians and the court should ask whether [the patient] has the capacity to understand, retain and weigh the following information:

(1) that she is in hospital to receive care and treatment for a mental disorder;

(2) that the care and treatment will include varying levels of supervision (including supervision in the community), use of physical restraint and the prescription and administration of medication to control her mood;

(3) that staff at the hospital will be entitled to carry out property and personal searches;

(4) that she must seek permission of the nursing staff to leave the hospital, and, until the staff at the hospital decide otherwise, will only be allowed to leave under supervision;

(5) that if she left the hospital without permission and without supervision, the staff would take steps to find and return her, including contacting the police."

This list requires the patient to possess a very high level of capacity. Indeed, some members of the hospital staff might find it difficult to satisfy such a test without the assistance of written prompts. It is suggested that a more appropriate list might be: can the patient understand, etc., that he is being admitted to hospital informally and that this means that, subject to s.5, he can leave whenever he wants, that the purpose of the admission is to treat his mental disorder, that such treatment might involve the administration of medication, that during his stay in hospital he will be subject to hospital rules, and that the rules might involve placing restrictions on him.

In the context of palliative care, the Department of Health has provided the following advice:

"[I]f the person has capacity to consent to the arrangements for their care at the time of their admission or at a time before losing capacity, and does consent, the Department considers this consent to cover the period until death and that hence there is no deprivation of liberty. (An important exception would be if the care package to which the individual consented were to change in a manner that imposed significant extra restrictions or which included care contrary to the previously expressed wishes and preferences of the individual. In such circumstances, the individual's consent is unlikely to cover the changed care and an application for a DoLS authorisation or a Court of Protection order may be required if there is or will be a deprivation of liberty.)" (Letter to DoLs Leads from Niall Fry, MCA-DoLS Lead, dated Jan.14, 2015).

In *Trust A v X* [2015] EWHC 922 (Fam), Keehan J. said that the references made by the Court of Appeal in *Re RK v BCC* [2011] EWCA Civ 1305 to the effect that an adult in the exercise of parental responsibility may not lawfully detain or authorise the deprivation of liberty of a child were made obiter, and he doubted whether they correctly stated the legal position. His Lordship held that it was possible for parents in the proper exercise of parental responsibility, to consent to the accommodation of their mentally incapacitated child in a hospital and thus render what would otherwise be a deprivation of liberty not a deprivation of liberty (i.e. the second limb in the *Cheshire West* case is not satisfied). His Lordship said at para.57:

"The decisions which might be said to come within the zone of parental responsibility for a 15 year old who did not suffer from the conditions with which D has been diagnosed will be of a wholly different order from those decisions which have to be taken by parents whose 15 year old son suffers with D's disabilities. Thus a decision to keep such a 15 year old boy under constant supervision and control would undoubtedly be considered an inappropriate exercise of parental responsibility and would probably amount to ill treatment. The decision to keep an autistic 15 year old boy who has erratic, challenging and potentially harmful behaviours under constant supervision and control is a quite different matter; to do otherwise would be neglectful. In such a case I consider the decision to keep this young person under constant supervision and control is the proper exercise of parental responsibility."

In *Birmingham City Council v D* [2016] EWCOP 8, the local authority sought to persuade Keehan J. that the arguments he accepted in *Trust A v X* in respect of a 15-year-old young person apply with equal force to a young person of 16 or 17 years. His Lordship did not agree and held "that however close the parents are to their child and however cooperative they are with treating clinicians, the parent of a 16 or 17 year old young person may not consent to their confinement which, absent a valid consent, would amount to a deprivation of that young person's liberty" (para.105). His Lordship rejected a submission made by the Official Solicitor that his decision in *Trust A v X* was wrong (para.139).

In *Re AB* [2015] EWHC 3125 (Fam), Keehan J. asked whether the considerations that he had identified in *Trust A v X*, above, apply when a child is accommodated by a local authority pursuant to s.20 of the Children Act 1989. His Lordship's conclusion on this point is set out at paras.26 and 27 of his judgment:

"The only possible answer is they may do. It will all depend on the facts of the individual case. At one extreme, an agreed reception into care of a child, that is beneficial and for a short-lived period, where the parent and the local authority are working together co-operatively in the best interests of the child, may be an appropriate exercise of parental responsibility. Thus it would be appropriate for that parent to consent to the child residing in a place (for example, a hospital) for a period and in circumstances which amount to a deprivation of liberty.

At the other extreme, there will be cases where children have been removed from their parents' care pursuant to a s.20 agreement as a prelude to the issue of care proceedings and where the local authority contend the threshold criteria of s.31(2) of the Children Act 1989 are satisfied. In such an event, I find it difficult to conceive of a set of circumstances where it could properly be said that a parent's consent to what, otherwise, would amount to a deprivation of liberty, would fall within the zone of parental responsibility of that parent. This parent's past exercise of parental responsibility will, perforce of circumstances, have been seriously called into question and it would not be right or appropriate within the spirit of the conclusion of the Supreme Court in *Cheshire West* to permit such a parent to so consent."

His Lordship confirmed at para.29 that where a child is in the care of a local authority and subject to an interim care, or a care, order, the local authority cannot in the exercise of its statutory parental responsibility consent to what would otherwise amount to a deprivation of liberty.

The "acid test"

2–008   At para.49, Lady Hale identified the "acid test" for a deprivation of liberty as being the fact that the person concerned "was under continuous supervision and control and was not free to leave" (*HL v United Kingdom*, above, at para.91). It is important to appreciate that to be deprived of his liberty the person must be under continuous supervision *and* control *and* must not be free to leave. Lord Neuberger added "area and period of confinement" to the test at para.63. The significance of the term "area" is not clear. With regard to the period of confinement, in *Storck v Germany* (2006) 43 E.H.R.R. 6 at para.74, the ECtHR held that will be no deprivation of liberty if the confinement in question is for a negligible length of time. Neither is there a deprivation of liberty if the deprivation is required for a short period in order to respond to an emergency (*X v United Kingdom* (1982) 4 E.H.R.R. 188 at para.41). However, cases are very fact sensitive and in *ZH v Commissioner of the Police of the Metropolis* [2013] EWCA Civ 69 a deprivation of liberty was found to have occurred in a situation where P had been subjected to intense restraint for approximately 40 minutes. This was a case where "the restraint of ZH was closely analogous to the classic or paradigm case of detention in prison or a police cell" (per Lord Dyson M.R. at para.83).

Lady Hale said the supervision and control is not relevant only insofar as it demonstrates that the person is not free to leave as a "person might be under constant supervision and control but still be free to leave should he express the desire so to do. Conversely, it is possible to imagine situations in which a person is not free to leave but is not under such continuous supervision and control as to lead to the conclusion that he was deprived of his liberty". For an example of the latter situation, see *W City Council v Mrs L* [2015] EWCOP 20 where, although Mrs L was prevented from leaving her home, the restrictions placed on her were not "continuous or complete" (para.26).

Continuous supervision and control

What constitutes continuous supervision and control? Although it is clearly   **2–009** something more substantial that occasional supervision and control, no guidance was provided by the court on the nature or extent of the supervision and control that must be present. This is regrettable given that a court has to consider "the degree of supervision and control over the person's movements" (*Chosta v Ukraine*, App.No. 35807/05, Jan.14, 2014). In *Guzzardi v Italy* (1981) 3 E.H.R.R. 333 at para.95, the ECtHR said that the supervision was carried out "strictly and on an almost constant basis". Lady Hale used the phrase "constant monitoring and control" at para.46 of her judgment. Given that "continuous" means "without a break" (Shorter OED), it is suggested that a significant degree of both supervision and control which is exercised on an almost constant basis has to be present before this component of the "acid test" can be satisfied. It is important to recognise that control, which involves the exercise of power to ensure that something happens to a person even if he does not want it to happen, is not the same as support, which is to help and/or encourage a person to do something for himself. It is not entirely clear what "supervision" means in this context. It probably involves both the monitoring (see Lady Hale, above) and observation of individuals. The point at which "supervision" becomes "control" was not addressed by the court. It is submitted that all mentally incapacitated hospital in-patients should be subject to continuous supervision, but that not all such patients would be the subject of continuous control.

It is important for those who are assessing whether a deprivation of liberty exists to take account of the cumulative effect of the restrictions imposed on a person (*Guzzardi v Italy*, above, at para.95), bearing in mind that the exercise of restraint which does not constitute a deprivation of liberty is authorised under s.6 of the 2005 Act.

Not free to leave

2–010   No analysis of this component of the "acid test" was provided, although in the cases before the court not free to leave meant "not free to go anywhere without permission and close supervision" (per Lady Hale at para.48). It is not a precondition of the test that the person must have expressed a desire to leave; it is sufficient for those in control to have formed the opinion that the person would be prevented from leaving if he made an attempt to leave. The vast majority of people who have a significant degree of mental incapacity are likely to come into this category. The Department of Health's Guidance on the *Cheshire West* judgment dated October 22, 2015, states at para.32:

> "[I]t may be useful to bear in mind that, just because an individual is physically unable to leave their place of care/ treatment, this does not necessarily mean the individual is 'not free to leave' under the acid test. Rather, the question is, would they be allowed to leave if they were assisted to do so e.g. by family/ friends? If the provider would facilitate the person leaving, then the individual is not deprived of their liberty."

For the application of this component of the "acid test" to patients who are being treated for physical disorders in Intensive Care Units and other hospital settings, see *R. (on the application of LF) v HM Coroner for Inner South London* which is noted below.

Deprivation of the liberty in domestic settings

2–011   With regard to the situation of MIG and MEG in *Cheshire West*, Lady Hale said at para.54:

> "If the acid test is whether a person is under the complete supervision and control of those caring for her and is not free to leave the place where she lives, then the truth is that both MIG and MEG are being deprived of their liberty. Furthermore, that deprivation is the responsibility of the state. Similar constraints would not necessarily amount to a deprivation of liberty for the purpose of article 5 if imposed by parents in the exercise of their ordinary parental responsibilities and outside the legal framework governing state intervention in the lives of children or people who lack the capacity to make their own decisions."

Lord Neuberger said at para.72:

> "In the case of children living at home, what might otherwise be a deprivation of liberty would normally not give rise to an infringement of article 5 because it will have been imposed not by the state, but by virtue of what the Strasbourg court has called 'the rights of the holder of parental authority', which are extensive albeit that they 'cannot be unlimited' (see *Nielsen v Denmark* (1988) 11 EHRR 175, para 72, a decision which, at least on its facts, is controversial, as evidenced by the strength of the dissenting opinions). However, it is fair to say that, while this point would apply to adoptive parents, I doubt that it would include foster parents (unless, perhaps, they had the benefit of a residence order). But in the great majority of cases of people other than young children living in ordinary domestic circumstances, the degree of supervision and control and the freedom to leave would take the situation out of article 5.4. And, where article 5.4 did apply, no doubt the benignly intimate circumstances

of a domestic home would frequently help to render any deprivation of liberty easier to justify" [NB It is suggested that the references to art 5.4 should be references to art.5.1].

A minority of the Justices did not agree that MIG and MEG were deprived of their liberty on the ground "that nobody using ordinary language would describe people living happily in a domestic setting as being deprived of their liberty" (per Lord Carnwath and Lord Hodge at para.99).

In *W City Council v Mrs L* [2015] EWCOP 20 at para.24, Bodey J. said that the fact that Mrs L was "capable of expressing her wishes and feelings ... in such things as for example her choice of clothes, the choice of what she does around the property, and in her going in and out of the garden at will" was "relevant" in the evaluation of whether Mrs L is being deprived of her liberty. His Lordship also made reference at para.28 to Lady Hale's reference in *Cheshire West* at para.38 to "the presence or absence of coercion" being a relevant consideration. Mostyn J. agreed with this decision in *Bournemouth Borough Council v PS* [2015] EWCOP 39, a case where his Lordship held that PS was not being deprived of his liberty for the following reasons

"First, he is not under continuous supervision. He is afforded appreciable privacy. Second, he is free to leave. Were he to do so his carers would seek to persuade him to return but such persuasion would not cross the line into coercion. The deprivation of liberty line would only be crossed if and when the police exercised powers under the Mental Health Act. Were that to happen then a range of reviews and safeguards would become operative. But up to that point [PS] is a free man. In my judgment, on the specific facts in play here, the acid test is not met. [PS] is not living in a cage, gilded or otherwise" (para.33).

These cases, which are not easy to reconcile with the decision in *Cheshire West*, illustrate the difficulties that face professionals when identifying whether a deprivation of liberty exists in the post *Cheshire West* world.

The case law of the European Court of Human Rights
The effect of s.64(5) of the 2005 Act is that the interpretation of the meaning   **2–012** of a "deprivation of liberty" will evolve with successive decisions of the ECtHR. Lady Hale described the case law of the ECtHR on the meaning of a deprivation of liberty as being "clear in some respects but not in others" (para.32).

When examining decisions of the ECtHR on the meaning of "continuous supervision and control" and "not free to leave", it should be noted that in *R. (on the application of Gillan) v Metropolitan Police Commissioner* [2006] UKHL 12, Lord Bingham said that the jurisprudence of the ECtHR on what constitutes a deprivation of liberty "is closely focused on the facts of particular cases, and this makes it perilous to transpose the outcome of one case to another where the facts are different" (para.23).

Policy
Lady Hale made the following comments at para.57 under this heading. They   **2–013** contain a thinly veiled plea for legislative reform:

"Because of the extreme vulnerability of people like P, MIG and MEG, I believe that we should err on the side of caution in deciding what constitutes a deprivation of liberty in their case. They need a periodic independent check on whether the arrangements made for them are in their best interests. Such checks need not be as elaborate as those currently provided for in the Court of Protection or in the Deprivation of Liberty safeguards (which could in due course be simplified and extended to placements outside hospitals and care homes). Nor should we regard the need for such checks as in any way stigmatising of them or of their carers. Rather, they are a recognition of their equal dignity and status as human beings like the rest of us."

Implications of the judgement

2–014   Although the judgment clarified the law by identifying the factors that are to be disregarded when determining whether a deprivation of liberty exists, practitioners will continue to be faced with the task of deciding whether a person is subject to continuous supervision and control and is free to leave the place where he is. This will not always be an easy task in the light of the Supreme Court's failure to provide guidance on the components of the "acid test".

Of particular significance are the findings of the court that (i) a deprivation of liberty can occur in a situation where P and his family are perfectly happy with the placement, (ii) the deprivation of liberty can occur in a placement which comprises living arrangements of relative normality, (iii) P does not have to try to leave in order to found to be not free to leave, (iv) the absence of an objection to the placement by P cannot be equated with consent, and (v) the fact that all that can be done for P is being done is not relevant to the existence of a deprivation of liberty. These findings have resulted in a very significant increase in the number of individuals who are assessed as being deprived of their liberty.

Given that deprivations of liberty can occur in domestic settings and in supported accommodation, commissioning bodies should seek to regularise any deprivations of liberty that may be occurring by making applications to the Court of Protection: see *The obligation of local authorities to investigate possible deprivations of liberty*, below.

As "account must be taken of a whole range of criteria such as the type, duration, effects and manner of implementation of the measures in question" (Lady Hale at para.38) before a determination is made as to whether a person is deprived of his liberty and as this formulation enables a court "to have regard to the specific context and circumstances surrounding types of restriction other than the paradigm of confinement in a cell" (*Austin v United Kingdom*, App. No.39692/09 para.59, March 15, 2012), consideration should be given to the context of the restrictions that are being imposed and whether a degree of pragmatism should be adopted when making the determination. For example, it is suggested that mentally incapacitated patients who are receiving life sustaining treatments in an intensive care unit of a hospital would not be the subject of a deprivation of liberty due to the type and manner of the restrictions that are being imposed. The contention that a degree of pragmatism may be adopted when making such determinations is supported by the following comment of Lord Hope in *Austin v Commissioner of Police of the Metropolis* [2009] UKHL 16 at para.34:

"I would hold therefore that there is room, even in a case of fundamental rights as to whose application no restriction or limitation is permitted by the Convention, for a pragmatic approach to be taken which takes full account of all the circumstances."

It is also noteworthy that Lord Neuberger said that the "acid test" proposed by Lady Hale "should be adopted unless there is good reason not to do so" (para.61).

The Law Society has published "Identifying a deprivation of liberty: a practical guide" (2015). This comprehensive guide can be accessed at the Society's website.

The application of the acid test to patients who are being treated for physical disorders in Intensive Care Units (ICU) and other hospital settings

In *R. (on the application of LF) v HM Coroner for Inner South London* [2015] EWHC 2990 (Admin), the Divisional Court had to determine whether a heavily sedated mentally incapacitated patient who had been transferred to the hospital's ICU for life saving treatment was being deprived of her liberty. This required the court to determine whether the "acid test" for the deprivation of liberty identified in the Cheshire West case was satisfied. The court noted that the context of Cheshire West was to ensure that, in circumstances where those who suffer from mental disability are deprived of their liberty for the purpose of care and treatment, such deprivation is periodically reviewed with appropriate judicial oversight. Gross L.J. said that "the question whether there has been a deprivation of liberty in any particular case is fact-sensitive and specific" (para.57 (vii)). In holding that the acid test was not satisfied in this case, his Lordship said at para.76:

2–015

"In my respectful view, the notion that *Cheshire West* requires treating all patients in an ICU (and other hospital settings) for more than a very brief period as subject to a deprivation of liberty provided only that they lacked capacity to consent to the particular stage of treatment, would involve a wholesale extension rather than an application of that authority. Again with respect, any such extension would be mechanistic, unwarranted and divorced from the mischief *Cheshire West* was seeking to address."

On making a similar finding, Charles J. said at para.145:

"[S]uch an extension of *Cheshire West* would not draw any distinction between patients with and those without any previous mental incapacity, which furnishes a stark contrast with the issue addressed in *Cheshire West*. The existence of that contrast shows that the issues at the heart of this case were not under consideration in *Cheshire West* and so provides a good reason for not applying it as if it sets out a set of statutory principles across very different concrete situations."

His Lordship said that in cases where a patient is in hospital for care and treatment for physical disorders, what is required is a fact sensitive approach which takes into account issues such as "the length of time that the relevant care and treatment has lasted, changes in it and the impact of any pre-existing lack of capacity" (para.150).

Gross L.J. said that, by contrast to the "ordinary" case of a patient with or without prior mental incapacity in an ICU, there could be other situations where the principle of *Cheshire West* may well be applicable. Examples include instances where there is a serious debate as to proper treatment or active resistance from family members to a particular course of treatment (at para.81).

With regard to the "not free to leave" component of the acid test, both Gross L.J. (at para.87) and Charles J.(at para.151) considered that it was not necessary to ask the question whether the hospital staff would have refused to allow the patient to leave if her sister pressed the issue. In making this finding, the court did not follow the approach advocated in the Law Society's Practical Guide. Gross L.J. said that "it is fanciful in this case to suppose that [the patient's sister] would have sought to remove [the patient] from the hospital while she was undergoing treatment in the ICU and therefore idle to consider what the hospital's response would have been" and that he did not accept that "the hospital's potential response to an unasked question . . . by itself constitutes or evidences a deprivation of liberty."

This important decision has significant implications not only for patients being treated in ICUs and hospices, but also to patients who have no prior history of mental incapacity who are admitted to hospital for treatment for physical disorders.

The response of the Government to the judgment in HL v United Kingdom

2–016   In order to remedy the breaches of art.5 identified by the ECtHR in *HL v United Kingdom*, the Government undertook to provide additional procedural safeguards for incapacitated people who were not subject to the 1983 Act, but whose care and treatment in a hospital or care home involved a deprivation of liberty. Accordingly, in March 2005, a consultative document (*"Bournewood" Consultation: The approach to be taken in response to the judgment of the European Court of Human Rights in the "Bournewood" case*) was issued by the Government. The following options were identified:

1.   A new form of "protective care" which would a basis for new procedures to govern admission and detention and therefore the circumstances in which a person might be lawfully deprived of liberty.

2.   Extending the use of detention under the 1983 Act to the Bournewood group of patients.

3.   Using existing arrangements for guardianship under the 1983 Act (modified as necessary).

A report of the outcome of the consultation was published in June 2006. At the same time, the Government announced its decision to proceed with the protective care option which had been favoured by the majority of respondents to the consultation, with a view to new deprivation of liberty safeguards being introduced into the 2005 Act. The Mental Health Bill (now the Mental Health Act 2007) was identified as a suitable vehicle through which to amend the Act for this purpose. The new procedures, which provide for a person's deprivation of liberty to be "authorised", are located in Schs A1 and 1A. They are extremely complex, and caused the Joint Committee on Human Rights to "question whether they will be readily understood by proprietors of residential care homes, even with the benefit of professional advice" (*Legislative Scrutiny: Mental Health Bill*, HL Paper 40; HC 288, para.90).

The House of Lords Select Committee found that the "level and breadth of criticism of the Deprivation of Liberty Safeguards, including from the judiciary, demonstrates that the legislation is not fit for purpose" and that "better implementation would not be sufficient to address the fundamental problems identified" (para.257). The Committee "therefore recommend that the Government undertake a comprehensive review of the DoLS legislation with a view to replacing it with provisions that are compatible in style and ethos with the Mental Capacity

Act" (para.258). The Committee expressed its concern that "there is a very real risk that the Deprivation of Liberty Safeguards are frequently not used when they should be, leaving individuals without the safeguards Parliament intended, and leaving care providers vulnerable to legal challenge" (para.270).

The Social Care Institute for Excellence (SCIE) report *Deprivation of Liberty Safeguards: putting them into practice* (2014) describes "good practice in the management and implementation of the Deprivation of Liberty Safeguards". The report can be accessed at: *www.scie.org.uk/publications/reports/report66.pdf*.

The obligation of local authorities to investigate possible deprivations of liberty

In *A (child), Re and C (adult), Re* [2010] EWHC 978 (Fam), Munby J. held **2–017** that where a local authority knows or ought to know that a vulnerable child or adult is subject to restrictions on their liberty by a private individual that arguably give rise to a deprivation of liberty, then its positive obligations under art.5 of the ECHR will be triggered. On the nature of these obligations, his Lordship said at para.95:

"1. They include the duty to investigate, so as to determine whether there is, in fact, a deprivation of liberty. In this context the local authority will need to consider all the factors relevant to the objective (in terms of the nature of the confinement) and subjective elements (whether the individual has validly consented to the confinement).

2. If, having carried out its investigation, the local authority is satisfied that the objective element is not present, so there is no deprivation of liberty, the local authority will have discharged its immediate obligations. However, its positive obligations may in an appropriate case require the local authority to continue to monitor the situation in the event that circumstances should change.

3. If, however, the local authority concludes that the measures imposed do or may constitute a deprivation of liberty, then it will be under a positive obligation, both under art.5 alone and taken together with art.14, to take reasonable and proportionate measures to bring that state of affairs to an end. What is reasonable and proportionate in the circumstances will, of course, depend upon the context, but it might require the local authority to exercise its statutory powers and duties so as to provide support services for the carers that will enable inappropriate restrictions to be ended, or at least minimised.

4. If, however, there are no reasonable measures that the local authority can take to bring the deprivation of liberty to an end, or if the measures it proposes are objected to by the individual or his family, then it may be necessary for the local authority to seek the assistance of the court in determining whether there is, in fact, a deprivation of liberty and, if there is, obtaining authorisation for its continuance."

His Lordship continued:

"What emerges from this is that, whatever the extent of a local authority's positive obligations under art.5, its duties, and more important its powers, are limited. In essence, its duties are threefold: a duty in appropriate circumstances to investigate; a duty in appropriate circumstances to provide supporting services; and a duty in appropriate circumstances to refer the matter to the court. But, and this is a key message, whatever the positive obligations of a local authority under article 5 may be, they do not clothe it with any power to regulate, control, compel, restrain, confine or coerce. A local authority which seeks to do so must either point to specific statutory authority for what it is doing . . . or obtain the appropriate sanction of the court. Of course if there is immediate threat to life or limb a local authority will be justified in taking protective (including compulsory) steps: *R (G) v Nottingham City Council* [2008] EWHC 152 (Admin); [2008] 1 FLR 1660, at para.21. But it must follow up any such intervention with an immediate application to the court" (para.96).

His Lordship said that investigations by local authorities must be carried out "with sensitivity and with a proper appreciation of the limited extent of their powers" (para.98) and that, "generally speaking, a local authority will only be justified in seeking a without notice order for the removal of an incapacitated or vulnerable adult in the kind of circumstances which in the case of a child would justify a without notice application for an emergency protection order" (para.99).

In the opening paragraphs of Ch.3, the supplement to the *Code of Practice* states that "in the vast majority of cases, it should be possible to plan in advance so that a standard authorisation can be obtained before the deprivation of liberty begins. There may, however, be some exceptional cases where the need for the deprivation of liberty is so urgent that it is in the best interests of the person for it to begin while the application is being considered."

The importance of this guidance was emphasised by Baker J. in *AJ v A Local Authority* [2015] EWCOP 5 at para.133. However, as it is the managing authority that instigates the authorisation procedure, an authorisation cannot be obtained until an offer of a placement has been made.

The fact that a deprivation of liberty could be authorised under Sch.A1 does not absolve the supervisory body from making an application to the court where the facts would otherwise merit it (*NHS Trusts 1 and 2 v FG* [2014] EWCOP 30 at para.101 (iii)).

The purpose of deprivation of liberty authorisations

2–018   Lady Hale has described the essence of authorisations as being "to secure professional assessment, by people independent of the hospital or care home in question, of (a) whether the person concerned lacks the capacity to make his own decision about whether to be accommodated in the hospital or care home for the purpose of care or treatment (Sch.A1, para 15), and (b) whether it is in his best interests to be detained (para 16). The procedures are administrative, but the authorisation can be challenged in the Court of Protection under section 21A" (*P v Cheshire West and Chester Council; P and Q v Surrey CC* [2014] UKSC 19 at para.9).

In *London Borough of Hillingdon v Neary* [2011] EWHC 1377 (COP) at para.33, Jackson J. said:

"The DOL scheme is an important safeguard against arbitrary detention. Where stringent conditions are met, it allows a managing authority to deprive a person of liberty at a particular place. It is not to be used by a local authority as a means of getting its own way on the question of whether it is in the person's best interests to be in the place at all. Using the DOL regime in that way turns the spirit of the Mental Capacity Act 2005 on its head, with a code designed to protect the liberty of vulnerable people being used instead as an instrument of confinement. In this case, far from being a safeguard, the way in which the

DOL process was used masked the real deprivation of liberty, which was the refusal to allow Steven to go home."

His Lordship further stated, at paras 196 and 202, that the practical and evidential burden is on a local authority to demonstrate that its arrangements are better than those that can be achieved within the family, and it was the local authority and not the individual concerned who should take the matter to court. The state has an obligation under art.5(4) of the ECHR to ensure that a person deprived of liberty is not only entitled but enabled to have the lawfulness of his detention reviewed speedily by a court. As his Lordship pointed out at para.74, a best interests assessor could propose an application to the court as a condition of the authorisation.

Safeguarding concerns should not lead to an authorisation being used improperly by failing to respect the ECHR rights of P and P's family (*Somerset v MK* [2014] EWCOP 25).

Schedule A1—authorising the deprivation of a person's liberty in a hospital or care home

Although Sch.A1 refers to the person who either is lacking capacity, or is   **2–019** thought to lack capacity as "the relevant person", to be consistent with the rest of the Act this person will be referred to here as P.

Supervisory bodies and managing authorities

For the identity of supervisory bodies and managing authorities in Sch.AI,   **2–020** see "Requests for a standard authorisation made by a managing authority to the supervisory body", below.

Forms

The Department of Health published deprivation of liberty forms developed   **2–021** for use by supervisory bodies and managing authorities. Criticism of the number and complexity of the forms led to the ADASS developing a new set of simplified forms which can be accessed at: www.adass.org.uk/mental-health-Drugs-and-Alcohol/key-documents/New-DoLS-Forms/. The Welsh Assembly Government has published a separate set of forms which can be accessed at: *www.wales.nhs. uk/sites3/page.cfm?orgid=744&pid=36053*.

In *C v Blackburn and Derwen Borough Council* [2011] EWHC 3321 (COP), Peter Jackson J. said at para.26(3):

> "The basic requirements for the form of a standard authorisation are set out at paragraph 55(1) of MCA Schedule A1. Although these are barely met in this case, one must look to the substance of these documents, and not just to their presentation. Authorisations must be founded on sound assessments. In the present case, the managing authority's request and the best interests assessment are documents of substance. The nature of the restrictions is sufficiently clear from the documentation . . .. The fact that they are inadequately summarised in the standard authorisation is unsatisfactory for a document of this importance, but not fatal to the lawfulness of the authorisation."

The requirements and procedure for requesting and granting a standard authorisation (Pts 3 and 4 of Sch.A1—paras 12–73).

2–022   Part 2 of Sch.A1 sets out the "qualifying requirements" that must be met before a standard authorisation can be given to provide legal authority to detain a person in a hospital (including an acute ward (*NHS Trust v FG* [2014] EWCOP 30)) or care home. A deprivation of liberty that occurs in other settings can only be authorised by way of an application to the Court of Protection. When making their determinations, those who assess whether the qualifying requirements are satisfied may take into account circumstances that are expected to change by the time the authorisation is expected to come into force (para.12(3)). The assessment process ends if one of the assessors concludes that the person does not meet a qualifying requirement (para.133; and see *Refusal of standard authorisation*, below).

The requirements are:

(a) *the age requirement*—the person must be aged 18 or over (para.13). For the eligibility of a person to carry out an age assessment, see reg.8 of SI 2008/1858.

(b) *the mental health requirement*—the person must be suffering from a mental disorder within the meaning of the 1983 Act (i.e. "any disorder or disability of mind") but disregarding any exclusion for persons with learning disability (para.14). This means that a person with a learning disability comes within the scope of Sch.A1 whether or not the disability is associated with abnormally aggressive or seriously irresponsible conduct. Dependence on alcohol or drugs is not considered to be a mental disorder for the purposes of the 1983 Act (see s.1(3) of that Act), although an alcoholic or a drug addict who suffers from an associated mental disorder would qualify.

The Department of Health has provided the following advice on the meaning of mental disorder:

> "It may be helpful for you to be aware that the Department of Health does not consider a state of unconsciousness in itself as being a mental disorder. As such, we would not consider that an individual who is unconscious and who does not have a mental disorder would be eligible for a standard authorisation." (Letter from Niall Fry, MCA—DoLs Policy Lead, Jan 14, 2015)

When carrying out a mental health assessment, the assessor must consider how (if at all) the person's mental health is likely to be affected by his being a detained resident, and notify the best interests assessor of his conclusions (para.36). For the eligibility of a person to carry out a mental health assessment, see reg.4 of SI 2008/1858.

(c) *the mental capacity requirement*—the person must lack the capacity to decide whether or not he should be accommodated in the hospital or care home for the purpose of being given the relevant care or treatment (para.15). The assessment should be undertaken in accordance with ss.2 and 3, and the assessor must apply the principles set out in s.1. In *A Local Authority v FG* [2011] EWHC 3932 (COP) at para.16, Hedley J. offered the following guidance on the information that should be provided to a person in order to assess his capacity where the choice is between family or local authority provision:

"That involves an ability to understand what the issues are that determine family or Local Authority provision, what the consequences of any such decision are, and how they are likely to impact on the person's emotional, physical and educational welfare. That is a relatively sophisticated process, and in the context of this case is, it seems to me, a difficult one."

For the eligibility of a person to carry out a mental capacity assessment, see reg.6 of SI 2008/1858.

(d) *the best interests requirement*—the assessor must determine whether a deprivation of liberty is occurring, or is likely to occur. If this is the case, an assessment must be made as to whether the deprivation is in the best interests of the person, is necessary to prevent harm to him, and is a proportionate response to the likelihood and seriousness of that harm (para.16). There is no appeal from an assessor's decision that P is not subject to a deprivation of liberty. Note that in relation to the prevention of harm the requirement is one of necessity, not desirability. The best interests assessor must consult with the managing authority of the hospital or care home, and that authority and the supervisory body must provide the assessor with any needs assessment or care plan that has been made by them, or on their behalf (para.39). The assessor must have regard to such documents, and of the opinion of the mental health assessor on the impact of the proposed course of action on the person's mental health. The assessor must state the maximum authorisation period (para.42), and the supervisory body may not grant an authorisation for longer than this period (para.51). The assessor may make recommendations about conditions relating to the deprivation to be attached to the authorisation (para.43), such as conditions relating to contact or cultural issues (supplement to the *Code of Practice*, para.4.74). The supervisory body must "have regard" to such recommendations and, if the supervisory body accepts them, the managing authority must ensure they are complied with (para.53). When undertaking the assessment, the assessor will be bound by the general duty regarding the determination of a person's best interests which is set out in s.4. If a person consulted by the assessor under s.4(7) is an "interested person" as defined in para.185, para.40(2) applies and the name and address of that person must be set out in the assessment. The assessor is subject to the principles set out in s.1 and should, in particular, consider whether "it is necessary for [P] to be a detained resident" (para.16(4)) or whether P's care could be provided in a less restrictive manner (s.1(6)). If the best interests assessor does not support the deprivation of liberty, it would be helpful if the assessor discussed the possibility of alternative placements, which might avoid a deprivation of liberty, with the managing authority during the assessment process (supplement to the *Code of Practice*, para.4.72). For the eligibility of a person to carry out a best interests assessment, see reg.5 of SI 2008/1858.

In *A County Council v MB* [2010] EWHC 2508 (COP) at paras 95 and 96, Charles J. said that where assessors either conclude that it is not in the best interests of P to be detained at a particular location or there are other difficulties that lead them to conclude that the court should be involved, and/or that there are strong arguments why deprivation of liberty should not continue without further and immediate assessment, they "should consider whether given the choices immediately and practicably available it would remain in the best interests of a person to be remain detained, in the short term, pursuant to a standard authorisation of limited duration. In many cases this would be likely to involve the consideration of the impact of a move that might only be for a short time or which does not satisfy the identified needs of P. Further, in my view, like the court, the best interest assessors should be considering available alternatives and thus solutions that are, or might in practice become or be made available. This will involve a consideration of the impact, difficulties and timings involved in a move and/or a change by reference to the actual alternatives available if P can no longer be lawfully deprived of his liberty at his existing placement."

His Lordship also made the following points at para.98 (iii), (iv) and (v):

"In *G v E* [2010] EWHC 1115, Baker J. ruled that a best interests approach should be adopted to govern an incapacitated person's discharge from detention. His Lordship stated that:

'. . . it would be quite contrary to [E]'s best interests to insist upon his immediate return home because of a narrow, inflexible interpretation of Article 5'.

In those circumstances, discharge was delayed in his best interests whilst preparations for his return home could be made.

To immediately discharge a detained resident from a care home, or to remove the provisions relating to his deprivation of liberty there, may engage, and risk violating, his other human rights even when the change of residence that is planned would not, when it is ready to be implemented, involve a deprivation of his liberty.

Detained residents are owed a duty of care by the relevant authority and immediate discharge or removal of the provisions relating to deprivation of liberty might expose that authority to the risk of liability in negligence for the foreseeable consequences of such actions."

The responsibility of the supervisory body to scrutinise best interests assessments is considered below.

(e) *the eligibility requirement*—the person is ineligible to be deprived of his liberty under the Act if he is, or might be, subject to the 1983 Act in one of the circumstances set out in Sch.1A (para.17). Schedule 1A is considered below. For the eligibility of a person to carry out an eligibility assessment, see reg.7 of SI 2008/1858. Where the eligibility assessor and the best interests assessor are not the same person, reg.15 applies.

(f) *the no refusals requirement*—the purpose of this requirement is to establish whether an authorisation would conflict with an existing decision relating to the person. There are refusals if: (i) the authorisation is sought for the purpose of treatment for either a mental or physical disorder which is covered, either wholly or partially, by a valid and applicable advance decision made by the person, or (ii) to place the person in a hospital or care home would conflict with a valid decision of a donee of a lasting power of attorney or a deputy appointed by the Court of Protection (paras 18–20).

The donee and the deputy would be governed by s.4 when reaching their decision. For the eligibility of a person to carry out a no refusals assessment, see reg.9 of SI 2008/1858.

The assessors

Although the person assessing the mental health requirement cannot also be the **2–023** best interests assessor (para.129(5)), the supervisory body can appoint the same assessor for other assessments. Local authorities that are both supervisory body and managing authority of a care home cannot use their own best interests assessors to carry out assessments (SI 2008/1858 reg.12(2)).

Assessors may at all reasonable times examine and take copies of relevant records (para.131) and must take into account any information given, or submissions made, by a representative or any s.39A, 39C or 39D IMCA (para.132). The general eligibility requirements of assessors are set out in SI 2008/1858 reg.3. Requirements relating to the selection of assessors are set out in regs 10–12.

Generally speaking, the assessments must be completed within 21 calendar days of the request by the managing authority. However, where the managing authority has given an urgent authorisation, the assessments must be completed before the authorisation expires (SI 2008/1858 reg.13).

The responsibilities of the supervisory body to scrutinise assessments

In *London Borough of Hillingdon v Neary* [2011] EWHC 1377 (COP) at **2–024** para.33, Jackson J. said:

"The granting of DOL standard authorisations is a matter for the local authority in its role as a supervisory body. The responsibilities of a supervisory body, correctly understood, require it to scrutinise the assessment it receives with independence and a degree of care that is appropriate to the seriousness of the decision and to the circumstances of the individual case that are or should be known to it. Where, as here, a supervisory body grants authorisations on the basis of perfunctory scrutiny of superficial best interests assessments, it cannot expect the authorisations to be legally valid."

His Lordship made further comments on the scrutiny of best interests assessments at paras 174 to 177:

"Although the framework of the Act requires the supervising body to commission a number of paper assessments before granting a standard authorisation, the best interests assessment is anything but a routine piece of paperwork. Properly viewed, it should be seen as a cornerstone of the protection that the DOL safeguards offer to people facing deprivation of liberty if they are to be effective as safeguards at all.

The corollary of this, in my view, is that the supervisory body that receives the best interests assessment must actively supervise the process by scrutinising the assessment with independence and with a degree of care that is appropriate to the seriousness of the decision and the circumstances of the individual case that are or should be known to it.

Paragraph 50 [of Schedule A1] provides that a supervisory body must give a standard authorisation if all assessments are positive. This obligation must be read in the light of the overall scheme of the schedule, which cannot be to require the supervisory body to grant an authorisation where it is not or should not be satisfied that the best interests assessment is a thorough piece of work that adequately analyses the four necessary conditions.

In support, I refer to the fact that the supervisory body has control over the terms of the authorisation in relation to its length and any conditions that should be attached. It does not have to follow the recommendations of the best interests assessor on those issues. It would not be possible for the supervisory body to make decisions of this kind rationally without having a sufficient knowledge base about the circumstances of the person affected. In all cases, it is open to the supervisory body to go back to the best interests assessor for discussion or for further enquiries to be made."

His Lordship said that if the supervisory body considers the best interests assessment to be inadequate, "it is obliged to take all necessary steps to remedy the inadequacy, and if necessary bring the deprivation of liberty to an end, including by conducting a review under Pt 8 or by applying to the court" (para.180).

Requests for a standard authorisation made by a managing authority to the supervisory body

2–025   The "managing authority" of a NHS hospital is the NHS body responsible for running the relevant hospital, and the managing authority of a private hospital or care home is the person registered, or required to be registered, in respect of that hospital or home (paras 176–179). The managing authority must request authorisation from the relevant "supervisory body" if a person who meets or is likely to meet all of the qualifying requirements is, or is likely to be during the next 28 days, accommodated in their hospital or care home in circumstances that amount to a deprivation of liberty (para.24). In *AM v South London & Maudsley NHS Foundation Trust* [2013] UKUT 0365 (AAC) at para.57, Charles J. said that "in the context of defining the duty on a managing authority to request a standard authorisation Parliament was using the word 'likely' in the sense of whether, in the period referred to, there is a real risk or possibility that the relevant person will be a 'detained resident' [as defined in para.6] and intended that the word 'likely' was to relate to both that period and that status". In the meantime, an urgent authorisation may be issued by the managing authority if certain criteria are satisfied (see below). The information to be provided in a request for a standard authorisation is set out in SI 2008/1858 reg.16. If the person who is the subject of a standard authorisation becomes a detained resident in a different hospital or care home, the managing authority of that hospital or care home must request a new standard authorisation (paras 25–26). Managing authorities must keep written records of requests for authorisation and the reasons for them (para.32), and they should have systems in place to identify when a deprivation of liberty of a mentally incapacitated person may be taking place.

The supervisory body will usually be the local authority for the area where the person is ordinarily resident. The National Assembly for Wales is the supervisory body in all cases where care and/or treatment in hospital is commissioned by the Assembly or a Local Health Board unless the person has ordinary residence in England (paras 180–183). Where a person is admitted to a care home or to an NHS hospital he continues to be ordinarily resident in the area in which he was ordinarily resident immediately before his admission (para.183). Guidance on the determination of a person's ordinary residence for the purposes of Sch.

A1 can be found in paras 51 to 63 of Annex H to *Carer support statutory guidance*, Department of Health, March 2016. If there is a dispute about the person's place of ordinary residence, this is to resolved by either the Secretary of State or the National Assembly for Wales (para.183(3)). Before referring the case to the Secretary of State, local authorities in England must comply with the Ordinary Residence Disputes (Mental Capacity Act 2005) Directions 2010 which are reproduced in Pt 6. The determination of cross-border disputes about ordinary residence is governed by arrangements made between the Secretary of State and the Welsh Ministers. These are also reproduced in Pt 6. If a local authority wishes to dispute whether it is the supervisory body, the provisions of SI 2008/1858 regs 17–19 apply. The managing authority and the supervisory body can be the same body (para.184). Schedule A1, Pt 7 (paras 98–100) applies if there is a change of supervisory body but the person does not move, for example because of changes in a local authority boundary.

The Association of Directors of Adult Social Services has published a "Protocol for the Inter-Authority Management of Deprivation of Liberty Safeguards Applications" (2009) which aims to outline the responsibilities and actions to be taken by local authorities in circumstances where a person is classified as ordinarily resident in one local authority but is residing in another local authority and deprivation of liberty assessments need to be undertaken.

A standard authorisation request must be made if an order of the Court of Protection authorising a person's deprivation of liberty is about to expire and the person will continue to be deprived of his or her liberty (para.27). Provision is also made for a request to be made where there has been a previous refusal of a request for a standard authorisation but the managing authority considers that a fresh application would succeed (para.28).

Equivalent assessments

With one exception, on a request for a standard authorisation being made to it **2–026** the supervisory body must arrange for the person to be assessed within 21 days to determine whether each of the qualifying requirements are satisfied (para.33). The exception is that a particular assessment need not be undertaken if the supervisory body has in its possession an equivalent assessment that has been carried out within the previous year (apart from the age assessment (para.49(4)) and which meets the all of the requirements of the particular assessment, and it has no reason to believe that the assessment may no longer be accurate (paras 33(5) and 49). For example, a recent assessment for detention under the 1983 Act could be considered as being the equivalent of the mental health assessment. In order to qualify as an equivalent assessment, the person who made the assessment must have been an eligible person for the purposes of SI 2008/1858. Caution should be exercised in using equivalent assessments for both the mental capacity and mental health assessments as the supervisory body would need to be assured about the person's current mental health and mental capacity status. If the previous assessment is a best interests assessment, the supervisory body must take into account any information given, or submissions made by P's representative and any s.39C or s.39D IMCA (para.49(6)).

Decision-making by managing authorities and supervisory bodies

In *London Borough of Hillingdon v Neary* [2011] EWHC 1377 (COP) at **2–027** para.33, Jackson J. said:

"Poor decision-making processes often lead to bad decisions. Where a local authority wears a number of hats, it should be clear about who is responsible for its direction. Here, one sub-department of Hillingdon's adult social services provides social work support and another is responsible for running facilities such as the support unit. At the same time, senior social workers represent the supervisory body that determines whether or not a DOL authorisation should be granted. In that situation, welfare planning should be directed by the team to which the allocated social worker belongs, although there will of course be the closest liaison with those who run the support facilities. The tail of service provision, however expert and specialised, should not wag the dog of welfare planning. Unfortunately, this case was characterised either by an absence of decision-making or by a disorganised situation where nobody was truly in charge and it was consequently possible for nobody to take responsibility."

Damages for an unlawful deprivation of liberty

2–028 In *Essex CC v RF* [2015] EWCOP 51, District Judge Mort made a distinction between cases involving procedural breaches and those involving substantive breaches. He said

"72. Procedural breaches occur where the authority's failure to secure authorisation for the deprivation of liberty or provide a review of the detention would have made no difference to P's living or care arrangements.

73. Substantive breaches occur where P would not have been detained if the authority had acted lawfully. Such breaches have more serious consequences for P."

This case involved a substantive breach of P's rights. Taking previous cases into account, Judge Mort said that "the level of damages for the unlawful deprivation of an incapacitated person's liberty is between £3000 and £4000 per month" (para.77). It is likely that only nominal damages would be payable for a procedural breech: see *Bostridge v Oxleas NHS Foundation Trust* [2015] EWCA Civ 79.

Right of third party to require consideration of whether authorisation needed (paras 67–73)

2–029 A third party, such as a member of P's family or a person inspecting the hospital or care home, can trigger the assessment process by:

(a) informing the managing authority that it appears to him that the person is being deprived of his liberty without authorisation; and

(b) asking the managing authority to request a standard authorisation.

If the managing authority does not request the authorisation, the third party can request the supervisory body to decide whether there is an unauthorised deprivation of liberty (para.68). The supervisory body must then appoint a suitable qualified person to carry out an assessment of whether or not a deprivation of liberty exists, but need not do so if either:

(a) the request appears to be either frivolous or vexatious, or

(b) the question of whether the deprivation of liberty exists has already been determined and there is no change in circumstances that would merit the question being reconsidered (para.69(3) to (5)).

Subject to para.69(3) to (5), the assessment must be completed within 7 days of the request by the supervisory body (SI 2008/1858 reg.14). The supervisory body's response to the request must be notified to the person who made it, the person to whom the request relates, the managing authority and any s.39A IMCA (para.69(7),(8)). The same notifications need to be undertaken if the assessor concludes that there has been no deprivation of liberty (para.72). If the assessor concludes that the person is being deprived of his liberty, the full assessment process is triggered (para.71(2)), and the same people must be notified of that fact (para.71(4)). The same people must also be notified if a conclusion is reached that the detention is already authorised under s.4A (para.73).

The procedure for an urgent authorisation (Sch.AI, Pt 5—paras 74–90)

Wherever possible, a request for a standard authorisation should be made   **2–030**
before the deprivation of liberty commences. However, where the deprivation of liberty starts before the authorisation can be obtained, an urgent authorisation can be given which makes the deprivation lawful for a short period of time. The Government expects that an urgent authorisation "will be issued only in rare circumstances" (Hansard, HL Vol.703, col.390, per Baroness Thornton). An urgent authorisation is, in effect, a self authorisation. The managing authority of a care home or hospital can give itself an urgent authorisation to deprive a person of their liberty in cases of urgency for a maximum period of 7 days if the qualifying requirement are, or shortly will be, met (para.78). In exceptional circumstances, this period can be extended to 14 days by the supervisory body (paras 84, 85). The Explanatory Notes to the 2007 Act state, at para.231, that an extension "might occur for example if the best interests assessor has not been able to contact someone they are required to consult and considers that they cannot reach a judgment without doing so". If the supervisory body refuse the request for an extension they must notify the managing authority and give reasons for their decision. This notice must be copied to P and any s.39A IMCA (para.86). The supervisory body must complete the eligibility assessments within the period of the urgent authorisation.

Under para.76 a managing body must give an urgent authorisation where they:

(a) believe that the need for P to be detained is so urgent that it is appropriate for the detention to begin before the request for a standard authorisation is made, or

(b) have made a request for a standard authorisation but believe that the need for P to be detained is so urgent that it is appropriate for the detention to begin before the request is disposed of.

This means that an urgent authorisation must either follow a request for a standard authorisation or must immediately be followed by such a request. A consequence of this is that an urgent authorisation should not be given where it is anticipated that the deprivation of liberty would end before the request for a standard authorisation could be processed. The supplement to the *Code of Practice* states, at para.6.3, that "it would not be appropriate to give an urgent authorisation simply to legitimise [a] short-term deprivation of liberty".

An urgent authorisation must be in writing (para.79) and must state the name of P, the name of the relevant hospital or care home, the period during which the authorisation is to be in force, and the purpose for which the authorisation is given (para.80). A copy of the authorisation must be sent to P and any s.39A IMCA (para.82(3)). The managing authority must keep a written record of their reasons for giving the authorisation (para.82(2)) and must take steps to ensure that P understands the effect of the authorisation and the right under s.21A to make an application to the Court of Protection (para.83).

The period of authorisation begins at the exact time that it was given on a particular day and does not commence at the beginning of that day: see para.88 and *A County Council v MB* [2010] EWHC 2508 (COP) at para.35. The authorisation ends at the end of the last day or earlier if a decision is reached on the application for a standard authorisation (para.89). Once an urgent authorisation has been given, detention can only lawfully be extended by a standard authorisation or by court order: a second urgent authorisation relating to an existing detention cannot be issued (*A County Council v MB*, above). If a request for a standard authorisation is refused, the urgent authorisation ceases to be in force when the managing authority receives notice of that fact under para.58 (para.89(4)). Notice that the authorisation has ended must be sent to P and any s.39A IMCA (para.90).

Appointment of an IMCA

2–031   Under s.39A, if the managing authority is satisfied that P will become subject to Sch.A1 and that P has no-one other than a paid or professional carer to be consulted with during the best interests assessment, the managing authority must notify the supervisory body which must instruct an Independent Mental Capacity Advocate (IMCA) to represent P. P becomes subject to Sch.A1 in the circumstances set out in s.39B.

An IMCA will also be appointed if P has an unpaid representative in the circumstances set out in s.39D, and if the appointment of P's representative ends and there is no other appropriate person to consult in determining P's best interests (s.39C). The appointment of a representative for P is considered below.

Refusal of standard authorisation

2–032   If any of the assessments concludes that a qualifying requirement is not met, no further assessments should be undertaken (para.133) and the authorisation cannot be given (para.50(2)). The supervisory body is then required to notify P, the relevant managing authority, any IMCA instructed under s.39A, and any interested person consulted in the assessment process (para.58). If the best interests assessor concludes that P does not meet the best interests requirement but becomes aware that P is being subjected to an unauthorised deprivation of liberty, he must include a statement to that effect in the assessment (para.44). A refusal could lead to P's detention under the 1983 Act or to an adjustment to P's care plan to avoid a deprivation of liberty.

The supervisory body is required to keep a written record of any requests for an authorisation that have not lead to authorisation being granted (para.60). A decision not to grant a request for a standard authorisation has no effect on the validity of an existing authorisation under Schedule A1 (para.62(3)). In *A County Council v MB* [2010] EWHC 2508 (COP) at para.100, Charles J. said that "the 'period of grace' or extension to the end of the existing standard authorisation (see para.62(3)) is the period provided by DOLS to take appropriate steps if the supervisory body is precluded from giving a standard authorisation if all of the assessments are not positive. It is therefore the period provided to the supervisory body and the managing authority to take the appropriate steps to address a difference of opinion with an assessment."

The authorisation

An authorisation must be given if the assessments that have been commissioned by the supervisory body conclude that all of the qualifying requirements have been satisfied (para.50). The effect of the authorisation is to provide legal authority for P's detention; it does not give authority to provide medical treatment to P, or to do anything else that would normally require P's consent. **2–033**

The supervisory body must state in the authorisation the period during which the authorisation is in force. This may not be longer than the maximum period identified in the best interests assessment (para.51), and may start after the authorisation is given (para.52). The maximum authorisation period that the assessor can identify is a year, or such shorter period as may be prescribed by regulations (para.42(2)). In *A County Council v MB,* above, at para.45, Charles J. held that the period of authorisation starts either:

(i) at the exact time on the day when it is given (see paras.54 and 63(1)), or

(ii) as provided by paras.52 and 63(2) at a later time specified in the document giving the authorisation.

His Lordship further held that the maximum period that can be included in the authorisation should be calculated by including the whole of the day on which the authorisation is given (or expressed to start) and on the basis that it ends at the end of the last day (para.47).

The authorisation must state the purpose for which authorisation is given, any conditions subject to which authorisation is given, and the reason why each qualifying requirement is met (para.55). It is submitted that the conditions that attached to the authorisation under para.53 must relate to the issue of deprivation of liberty, rather than to the general care and/or treatment that P should receiving: see the supplement to the *Code of Practice* para.4.74. The authorisation could include a condition that the managing authority makes an application to the Court of Protection for a disputed issue to be resolved.

The supervisory body must give copies of the authorisation to the relevant managing authority, P, any s.39A IMCA, and every interested person consulted by the best interests assessor (para.58(2)). It is for the managing authority to ensure that the conditions are complied with (para.53), to give relevant information to P and his representative (para.59), and to keep P's case under consideration and request a review if necessary (para.102). The information to P must be given both orally and in writing (para.59(4)).

If an authorisation is obtained, those who are carrying out the detention are protected against liability in battery or for wrongful imprisonment but not against liability in negligence, or for acting beyond the scope of the authorisation (paras 3, 4).

An alternative placement: the proactive role of the responsible authority

If all the qualifying requirements are met an authorisation must be given. In *P v Surrey CC* [2015] EWCOP 54, Judge Cushing said that if P's place of residence was not considered to be suitable, the responsible authority had the duty to investigate whether a less restrictive alternative was available. The judge said at para.32: **2–034**

"It could not delegate its responsibility in this regard to the relevant person's representative or the non-appointed advocate. It already knew that the care home was not suitable in the medium or longer term because it had been told so by the social worker undertaking the best interests assessment. Being in possession of that knowledge, the obligation was on the first respondent to be proactive, and they failed in that obligation."

Guidance on issues relating to the duration of authorisations of deprivations of liberty

2–035   The following guidance was provided by Charles J. in *A County Council v MB*, above, at para.56:

"In my view, the issues, arguments and conclusions [that are set out in my judgment] demonstrate that:

- Care needs to be taken in setting out the periods for which urgent and standard authorisations are given
- Authorisations do not run from the beginning of (or from an earlier time on) the day on which they are given
- It would be good practice to record the actual time at which an urgent authorisation and a standard authorisation (which does not run from the expiry of, or a specified time before the expiry of, an existing standard authorisation) was given on the form recording its grant
- In any event a record of the exact time on which all authorisations are given should be kept
- An approach that:

    (i) includes the whole of the day on which the relevant period starts, and
    (ii) ends at the end of the last day,

    would produce a result that the maximum period(s)

    (i) allowed for urgent authorisations and their extension of 7 days, and
    (ii) allowed for standard authorisations, if that is set by a period of days, months or a year,

    were not exceeded."

In *P v Surrey CC*, above, Judge Cushing said that it was not open to the supervisory body to do what it did, "namely to receive un-contradicted information from three separate sources that the care home was only suitable in the short term or for a short period and then proceed to grant the standard authorisation for a substantial period, i.e. 80% of the maximum permitted duration" (para.19).

The extent to which an authorisation provides authority for restrictions on P's private life

2–036   In *J Council v GU* [2012] EWHC 3531 (COP), P was the subject of a standard authorisation in a private care home. Due to the manifestations of his paedophilia, he was subjected to significant restrictions including strip-searching and monitoring of his correspondence and telephone conversations. These restrictions clearly contravened his right to respect for private life under art.8 of the ECHR. The Official Solicitor had been concerned that the arrangements whereby P had been subjected to the restrictions in question "have been insufficiently prescriptive in their content; carried insufficient safeguards; and were neither validated nor overseen by an organ of the state. He has therefore raised a doubt as to whether the arrangements are compliant with art.8. He is particularly concerned that there should be validation and oversight by a public authority. He is correctly concerned because where a private body wields coercive powers it is exercising functions of a public nature: see *YL v Birmingham* [2008] 1 AC 95 at para 63. And the state has a duty to exercise supervision and control over private psychiatric institutions: see *Storck v Germany* (2006) 43 EHRR 6 at para 150" (per Mostyn J. at para.15).

In order to meet the Official Solicitor's concerns, the parties agreed to a highly detailed 52 page policy document that included policies governing searches of P and his room, as well as monitoring of his telephone calls and correspondence. Additional layers of scrutiny were also agreed between the parties, including provision for the NHS Trust to periodically review each separate policy and receive monthly reports, and for the Care Quality Commission to seek expert advice as to the care of P and specifically case track P during the course of any compliance review. There would also be an annual review by the court of the arrangements in so far as they constituted a deprivation of liberty.

Mostyn J. accepted the submission of the Official Solicitor that the agreed policy document put beyond doubt any question of compliance with art.8. His Lordship said:

"[N]ot every case where there is some interference with Art 8 rights in the context of a deprivation of liberty authorised under the 2005 Act needs to have in place detailed policies with oversight by a public authority. Sometimes, particularly where the issue is one-off (such as authorising an operation), an order from the Court of Protection will suffice and will provide a sufficient basis in law. But where there is going to be a long-term restrictive regime accompanied by invasive monitoring of the kind with which I am concerned, it seems to me that policies overseen by the applicable NHS Trust and the CQC akin to those which have been agreed here are likely to be necessary if serious doubts as to art.8 compliance are to be avoided.

Of course all this debate would become empty were Parliament or the Executive or the CQC to promulgate rules or guidance to cover the situation which I have here" (paras 20, 21).

Duty to comply with conditions

Although para.53(3) states that managing authorities "must ensure that any **2–037** conditions are complied with", it is submitted that the obligations of managing authorities are satisfied if they use their best endeavours to ensure compliance: see *R. v Camden and Islington Health Authority Ex p. K* [2001] EWCA Civ 240 and *R. v Secretary of State for the Home Department, Ex p. IH* [2003] UKHL 59. The conditions should relate to the deprivation of liberty, not to the general care management of P: see the note on *The authorisation*, above. A failure to comply with a condition and the reason for the failure should be reported to the supervisory body.

Conveyance to the hospital or care home prior to an authorisation taking effect

An authorisation does not provide authority for depriving people of their liberty **2–038** when they are being conveyed from their home, or another location, to the hospital or care home specified in the authorisation. In *GJ v Foundation Trust* [2009]

EWHC 2972 (Fam) at para.75(c), Charles J. said that "the gap which Parliament deliberately left by not providing that authorisations . . . covered taking a person to hospital or care home can be filled by the [Court of Protection] . . .". This issue was taken up by the Joint Committee which, at para.99, recommended that a "take and convey" power be added to an authorisation. The Government responded as follows:

"We will reflect in the Code of Practice the importance of considering the impact of any transportation as part of assessing best interests. In practice, many people who will become subject to the proposed Mental Capacity Act deprivation of liberty safeguards will already be accommodated in hospitals or care homes at the time that a change in their care regime brings them within the scope of the safeguards, so the conveying issue will not arise.

We do accept, however, that, in a very few cases, there may be exceptional circumstances, for example where it is necessary to do more than persuade or restrain the person for the purpose of the conveyance, or perhaps if the journey was exceptionally long, where transportation may amount to a deprivation of liberty and it may be necessary to seek an order of the Court of Protection where additional consideration of the particular circumstances of the case would be an extra protection for the individual (or consider use of the 1983 Act). We do not therefore consider that it is desirable to extend authorisations to cover these rare cases, because we do not think it would strengthen the protections for the person concerned" (The Government's response to the report of the Joint Committee on Human Rights, Department of Health, April 13, 2007, paras 80,81).

The Joint Committee were not convinced by this response and remained of the view that in order to be compatible with art.5 of the ECHR it was necessary for the legislation "to provide a procedure which precedes detention in all cases" (*Legislative Scrutiny: Seventh Progress Report*, HL Paper 112; HC 555, para.1.29). The issue here is not solely one of strengthening the "protections of the persons concerned"; those involved in transporting the person to the hospital or care home require legal justification for their action. If the act of transporting the person merely involves restricting a person's liberty, the authorisation for the restriction is to be found in ss.5 and 6 of the 2005 Act. If, however, exceptional circumstances exist which result in a person being deprived of his liberty during the transportation in a non-emergency situation, ss.5 and 6 would not provide the necessary authority. In this situation, either the 1983 Act should be invoked or an application to authorise the deprivation be made to the Court of Protection. In *Milton Keynes Council v RR* [2014] EWCOP B19, DJ Mort severely criticised the Council for its failure to apply to the court for authority to remove P from her home. It is instructive to note that in the "Bournewood case" Lord Goff said that Mr L, who had been sedated, was detained when he was being taken by ambulance from the day centre to the hospital ([1998] 3 All E.R. 289 at 301). If the person is being transported to a care home, guardianship would provide the necessary authorisation as s.18(7) of the 1983 Act provides the applicant with a power to take and convey the person to a specified place of residence.

It is suggested that a deprivation of liberty occurs during transportation if:

(1) either force, medication, or threats have to be used to overcome P's resistance to being transported;

(2) subterfuge has to be resorted to, e.g. P is falsely informed that he will be returning to his home in the near future; or

(3) the circumstances of the transportation are very onerous for P.

Taking P from his or her home would constitute a violation of art.8(1) of the ECHR, which guarantees a right to respect for private life, family life, and one's home, unless a justification for the removal can be found under art.8(2). In the context of the removal of a child from the parental home, Munby J. held that the protection provided by art.8 is not confined to unfairness in the trial process but extends to guarantee fairness at all stages of child protection (*G (Care: Challenge to Local Authority's Decision), Re* [2003] EWHC 551, para.35). In *G v E* [2010] EWHC 621 (Fam) at para.88, Baker J. said:

> "In my judgment, precisely the same principles apply in cases concerning incapacitated adults. Article 8 gives the families of such adults (and by 'families' I include relationships between such adults and long-term foster carers) not only substantive protection against any inappropriate interference with their family life but also procedural safeguards including the involvement of the carers in the decision-making process, seen as a whole, to a degree sufficient to provide them with the requisite protection of the families' interests. If they have not, there will have been a failure to respect the family life of the incapacitated adult (and of course the carer)."

The use of restraint to take the person to the hospital or care home is considered in the supplement to the *Code of Practice* at paras 2.14 and 2.15. In *DCC v KH* (2009) COP, Case No.11729380, the court agreed with the Official Solicitor's submission that these paragraphs are addressing the situation where there is no standard authorisation in force.

Applications to the Court where police assistance may be required to remove P from premises

In *LBH v GP* (2009) COP, Case No. FD08P01058 at paras 31, 32, Coleridge J.   **2–039**
provided the following guidance, subsequently approved by the President of the Family Division and Court of Protection, on situations where someone lacking capacity or under a disability requires to be removed from premises with the help of the police:

> "In the event that it is expected that the assistance of the Police may be required to effect or assist with the removal of a vulnerable / incapacitated adult ("P") which the Court is being asked to authorise, the following steps should generally be taken:
>
> 1. the Local Authority/NHS body/other organisation/person (the Applicant) applying to the Court for an authorisation to remove P should, in advance of the hearing of the Application, discuss and, where possible, agree with the Police the way in which it is intended that the removal will be effected, to include, where applicable, the extent to which it is expected that restraint and/or force may be used and the nature of any restraint (for example, handcuffs) that may be used;
>
> 2. the Applicant should ensure that information about the way in which it is intended that removal will be effected is provided to the Court and to the

litigation friend (in cases where a person has been invited and/or appointed to act as P's litigation friend) before the Court authorises removal. In particular, the Court and the litigation friend should be informed whether there is agreement between the Applicant and the Police and, if there is not, about the nature and extent of any disagreement;

3. where the Applicant and the Police do not agree about how removal should be effected, the Court should give consideration to inviting/directing the Police to attend the hearing of the Application so that the Court can, where appropriate, determine how it considers removal should be effected and/or ensure that any authorisation for removal is given on a fully informed basis."

Powers of staff to return P to the hospital or care home subsequent to the granting of an authorisation

2–040   In *DCC v KH* (2009) COP, Case No. 11729380, an application was made by the local authority for a declaration that it would be lawful to use force on P which, if necessary, would deprive him of his liberty in order to facilitate his return to the care home where he was subject to a standard authorisation. P had indicated that he might not return to the care home from a contact visit to his mother's home. The court held that the application was not necessary as the standard authorisation provided the local authority with sufficient protection for the return of P to the care home. In the event of P resisting his return to the care home, it would be perfectly proper for appropriate restraint to be used whether with or without the assistance of the police.

This is a pragmatic decision of the court which was required because of the inadequate drafting of the legislation in that an authorisation is only stated to provide authority for a deprivation of P's liberty "in" the care home (Sch.A1, para.1(2)). The court recognised the force of the Official Solicitor's submission that it could not possibly have been in the contemplation of Parliament that care homes would need to make applications to court for declarations on every occasion that persons subject to standard authorisations need to be taken out into the community.

The December 2010 issue of the *Thirty Nine Essex Street Court of Protection Newsletter* contains a summary of an unreported decision of Mostyn J. (*Re ADE (Scope of Sch1)* (2010) COP 30/06/10) which affirms the decision in *DCC v KH*. The relevant part of the summary reads:

"Mostyn J was considering the extent of the powers granted to a local authority and a care home under existing (and any renewed) standard authorisations. He noted that it was common cause that these powers extended to a power to restrain P if he tried to leave the care home. The question for him was whether within those powers there was a power to coerce P to return if he refused to return to the care home from a period of leave. Mostyn J noted that it was understandably in P's interests that he should have access to society in the community and 'escape' the confines of the care home, and that the relevant PCT had agreed to fund 'befrienders' to encourage access to the community. Mostyn J therefore asked himself whether the powers under the existing standard authorisation extend to coercing P back to the nursing home if P refused to return. He noted that it would be little short of absurd if the local authority and care home had powers to restrain P from leaving but not to compel him to return, and that the greater power must include the lesser. Mostyn J therefore declared that the power was implicit in the current and any future standard authorisation."

Due to the fact that Sch.A1 does not cover the issue, it is suggested that power to return P identified in these cases should only be invoked if the restraint required to secure P's return comes within the scope of s.6 of the Act. In the absence of P being made the subject of a guardianship application under the Mental Health Act (guardianship provides for a specific power to return P to the specified place of residence), P's care plan should deal with the action that would need to be taken if P were to absent himself and the care plan should be authorised by the Court of Protection.

The appointment of representatives and the role of the supervisory body (Sch.A1, Pt 10—paras 137–153)

As soon as practicable after a standard authorisation is given, the super-   **2–041**
visory body must appoint a person to be P's representative (para.139). The Mental Capacity (Deprivation of Liberty: Appointment of Relevant Person's Representative) Regulations 2008 (SI 2008/1315), which are reproduced in Pt 3, provide details in relation to the selection, appointment and termination of the appointment of a representative. In most cases, the representative will be a friend, relative or informal carer of P but a paid appointment can be made where the person has no one else to fulfil the role. The supplement to the *Code of Practice* suggests, at para.4.76, that, where possible, the best interests assessor should recommend someone to be appointed as P's representative. The role of the representative is to maintain contact with P and to support and represent him in matters relating to the authorisation, including requesting a review, using the organisations complaint's procedure or applying to the Court of Protection on his behalf (para.140). In *AB v LCC* [2011] 3151 (COP) at para.26, Mostyn J. agreed with a submission that the representive's role in the deprivation of liberty process is crucial in that it provides "the relevant person with representation and support that is independent of the commissioners and providers of the services they receive". The supplement to the *Code of Practice* states at para.7.17: "It should not be assumed that the representative needs to be someone who supports the deprivation of liberty". Decisions by the representative are governed by the best interests principle set out in s.1(5). Representatives do not have a right of access to P's records. The functions of a representative are in addition to, and do not affect the authority of a donee of a lasting power of attorney or the powers of a court appointed deputy (para.141). In *AB v LCC*, at para.22, Mostyn J. thought it surprising that Pt10 does not set out the function or role of the representative (referred to as the RPR). His Lordship attempted to fill this gap at para.23:

"References are made to the RPR throughout Sch.A1 and include inter alia the following:

i.   The supervisory body must ensure the RPR is provided with a copy of the statutory assessments for a standard authorisation: para 57(2)(a) [and must be informed by the managing authority of its effect: para 59(5)].

ii. The supervisory body must inform the RPR if the supervisory body is prohibited from giving a standard authorisation: para 58(2)(b).

iii. Any written information regarding the effect of the standard authorisation, the right to apply to the Court of Protection, the right to request a review and the right to have an IMCA appointed to be given to the detained resident must be given to the RPR as soon as possible by the managing authority if the supervisory authority has granted a standard authorisation: paragraph 59(5) and (6).

iv. If a standard authorisation ceases to be in force or is suspended the RPR must be given notice: see para 65(1)(c) and para 93(3)(b).

v. A review of the standard authorisation must be carried out by the supervisory body if requested by the RPR: see para 102(3)(b).

vi. The supervisory body must inform the RPR of the outcome of the review in writing: see para 120(1)(c)."

In *AJ v A Local Authority* [2015] EWCOP 5, Baker J. made the following findings:

1. A representative should "only be selected or confirmed by a BIA where he or she satisfies not only the criteria in reg.3 of the Mental Capacity (Deprivation of Liberty: Appointment of Relevant Person's Representative) Regulations 2008 but also the requirements of para.140 of Sch.A1 of the MCA. This requires that the BIA not only checks that the facts set out in reg.3 are satisfied but also carries out an analysis and reaches a judgment as to whether the prospective representative would, if appointed, (a) maintain contact with the relevant person; (b) represent the relevant person in matters relating to or connected with the Schedule and (c) support the relevant person in matters relating to or connected with the Schedule" (para.115).

2. The "local authority is under an obligation to satisfy itself that a person selected for appointment as RPR meets the criteria in reg.3 and in para.140 of Sch.A1. If the local authority concludes that the person selected for appointment does not meet the criteria, it should refer the matter back to the BIA" (para.136).

3. It "is likely to be difficult for a close relative or friend who believes that it is in P's best interests to move into residential care, and has been actively involved in arranging such a move, into a placement that involves a deprivation of liberty, to fulfil the functions of RPR, which involve making a challenge to any authorisation of that deprivation. BIAs and local authorities should therefore scrutinise very carefully the selection and appointment of RPRs in circumstances which are likely to give rise to this potential conflict of interest" (para.137).

4. The "appointment of a RPR and IMCA does not absolve the local authority from responsibility for ensuring that P's Article 5 rights are respected. The local authority must monitor whether the RPR is representing and supporting P in accordance with the duty under paragraph 140 and, if not, consider terminating his appointment on the grounds that he is no longer eligible. The local authority must make sufficient resources available to assist an IMCA and keep in touch with the IMCA to ensure that all reasonable steps are being taken to pursue P's Article 5 rights" (para.139).

5. In "circumstances where a RPR and an IMCA have failed to take sufficient steps to challenge the authorisation, the local authority should consider bringing the matter before the court itself. This is likely, however, to be a last resort since in most cases P's Article 5 rights should be protected by the combined efforts of a properly selected and appointed RPR and an IMCA carrying out their duties with appropriate expedition" (para.140).

With regard to point 5, a local authority is far better equipped to bring an application to the court than either a RPR or an IMCA. And unlike both a RPR and an IMCA, a local authority would be in a position to act as soon as the need to make an application has been identified.

If the representative is unpaid, an IMCA must be appointed in the circumstances identified in s.39D to provide support to P and/or his representative. For the circumstances where an IMCA will be appointed when the appointment of the representative ends, see s.39C.

Transfer of authorisation

2–042   There is no power which enables a standard authorisation to be transferred from one hospital or care home to another. If P is transferred, the managing authority of the new establishment must request a new authorisation (para.25). If a new authorisation is granted, the existing authorisation terminates when the new one comes into force. If a new authorisation is refused, this does not affect the validity of the existing one (para.62).

Further authorisations

2–043   The managing authority must apply for a further authorisation to begin if the existing authorisation is about to expire (para.29) and it appears to the authority that the qualifying requirements continue to be met. Such a request will result in the full assessment process being repeated. The existing authorisation terminates at the time when the new authorisation comes into force (para.62(2)). If no request for a further authorisation is made, the authorisation will come to an end at the expiration of the authorised period.

Suspension of authorisation (Sch.AI, Pt 6—paras 91–97)

2–044   A standard authorisation may be suspended for up to 28 days if P has ceased to meet the eligibility requirement set out in Sch.1A for reasons other than his objection to becoming a mental health patient, in which case the authorisation will be reviewed (para.91(4)) The authorisation will end if P continues to be ineligible at the end of the 28 days (para.96(2)). Notice of the suspension must be sent by the supervisory body to P, his representative and the managing authority (para.93(3)), who, along with any s.39D IMCA, must also be informed when the suspension has come to an end (para.95(3)). The suspension will come to an end if during the 28 day period the managing authority are satisfied that P meets the eligibility requirement again in which case the managing authority must notify the supervisory body (para.94). The purpose of a suspension is to allow for a short period of treatment under the 1983 Act.

Review by supervisory body (Sch.AI, Pt 8—paras 101–125)

2–045   Although the supervisory body is not placed under a duty to monitor a standard authorisation, it may review the authorisation at any time and must do so if requested to do by P, his representative, an IMCA or the managing authority of the hospital or care home (para.102). The managing authority, which is required to keep the person's case under review, must request a review if one or more of the qualifying requirements appear to them to be reviewable (para.103). The qualifying requirements are reviewable if:

(a) P no longer meets the age, mental health, mental capacity, best interests or no refusals requirements, or

(b) P no longer meets the eligibility requirement because he now objects to receiving treatment for his mental health in hospital and he meets the criteria for detention under s.2 or 3 of the 1983 Act, or

(c) the reason why P meets a qualifying requirement is not the reason stated in the authorisation, or

(d) there has been a change in P's case and, because of that change, it would be appropriate to vary the conditions of the authorisation (this ground only applies to the best interests requirement) (paras 104–107).

The supervisory body, which must give notice of the review to P, his representative and to the managing authority (para.108), is not automatically obliged to re-assess all of the qualifying requirements when it receives a request for a review. Rather, it must determine which, if any, "appear to be reviewable" (para.109), and appoint assessors to review those requirements (para.111). There is no requirement to carry out a review of the best interests requirement if that requirement is only reviewable on the "variation of conditions" ground (see (d), above) and the change in P's case is not significant (para.111). If none of the requirements appear to be reviewable, no further action is required (para.110) and the review ends (para.118(2)).

The assessment process on a review is the same as applies when an application for an authorisation is made, with the exception that the best interests assessor is not obliged to include a statement that there is an unauthorised deprivation of liberty under para.44, and rather than make recommendations about what conditions should apply under para.33, the assessor must include recommendations about whether it would be appropriate to vary the conditions (para.113).

If the assessments are positive, the supervisory body must consider whether the authorisation needs to be varied on the change of reason ground or, for the best interests review only, the variation of conditions ground (paras 115–116). If the supervisory body is informed that one or more of the qualifying requirements is no longer satisfied, it must terminate the authorisation.

When the review is complete, the supervisory body must give notice to the managing authority, P, his or her representative and any s.39D IMCA. The notice must state the outcome of the review and what variation (if any) has been made to the authorisation (para.120).

As it is a review by the body that authorised the application, a review by the supervisory body is neither independent nor external and therefore does not constitute a review for the purposes of art.5(4) of the ECHR.

As an alternative to requesting a review, the managing authority could make a request for a fresh standard authorisation. Such a request would have to be made if the authorisation is about to expire (para.29). A request for a fresh authorisation may be made even if a review has already been requested or is being carried out (para.30), in which case the request for the fresh authorisation takes precedence (para.124).

Review by the Court of Protection

2–046   Neither the standard nor urgent authorisation procedure requires the approval of the Court of Protection.

Article 5(4) of the ECHR requires that everyone "who is deprived of his liberty
. . . shall be entitled to take proceedings by which the lawfulness of his detention
shall be decided speedily by a court and his release ordered if the detention is not
lawful". Section 21A gives the Court of Protection jurisdiction for this purpose.

Monitoring (paras 162, 163)

Under s.4(1) of the Health and Social Care Act 2008, the Care Quality **2–047**
Commission "must have regard to . . . the need to protect and promote the rights
of people who use health and social care services (including in particular . . .
persons who are deprived of their liberty in accordance with the Mental Capacity
Act 2005, and of other vulnerable adults)". The Commission has a duty to monitor
the operation of Sch.A1 in England (Mental Capacity (Deprivation of Liberty:
Monitoring and Reporting; and Assessments—Amendment) Regulations 2009
(SI 2009/827) regs 2 to 5). Under the Regulations, the Commission must report to
the Secretary of State on the operation of Sch.A1 when requested to do so by the
Secretary of State (reg.3). It may provide advice or information on the operation
of Sch.A1 to the Secretary of State at any time, but must do so when requested by
the Secretary of State (reg.5). In order to fulfil its monitoring or reporting responsibilities, the Commission may visit hospitals and care homes, visit and interview
residents of hospitals and care homes (the regulations do not state that this may be
in private), and require the production of, and inspect, records relating to the care
or treatment of such residents —

(i) who are the subject of an authorisation under Sch.A1; or
(ii) whom the Commission has reason to consider ought to have been or should
be the subject of an assessment under Sch.A1 (reg.4).

Regulation 18 (4A) and (4B) of the Care Quality Commission (Registration)
Regulations 2009 (SI 2009/3112) (as amended by SI 2012/921 reg.5) requires
the registered person to notify the Care Quality Commission of the outcome (or
withdrawal) of any request to a supervisory body made by the registered person
for a standard authorisation, and the outcome (or withdrawal) of any application
made to a court in relation to depriving a service user of their liberty pursuant to
s.16(2)(a).

The monitoring of the medical treatment of persons who are subject to an
authorisation is not provided for. There is therefore no equivalent to the second
opinion procedure contained in Pts 4 and 4A of the 1983 Act.

Responsibility for monitoring the operation of Sch.A1 in Wales has been given
by Welsh Ministers to Health Inspectorate Wales (HIW) and Social Services
Inspectorate for Wales (CSSIW).

Neither the Commission nor the Inspectorates are provided with a power to
enforce compliance of the deprivation of liberty procedures requirements.

Reporting the death of a person subject to an authorisation

The Department of Health published the following on January 19, 2011 **2–048**
(Gateway reference 15453):

"There is currently no statutory requirement for anyone other than the Registrar
of Births and Deaths (or a Prison Governor who has a separate statutory duty)
to refer certain deaths to a coroner. These are deaths where there is reasonable cause to suggest that the person died a violent, unnatural or sudden death

of which the cause is unknown or where the person died in prison or police custody. There is therefore no statutory requirement for the Registrar to refer deaths of those who are subject to deprivation of liberty safeguards.

However, there is a common law duty (which applies to everyone) to refer deaths to a coroner in the circumstances set out above. The subsequent action taken by the coroner will vary but could include no further action, the commissioning of a post-mortem examination or the opening of an inquest with or without a jury.

Should you wish to notify a death to a coroner, you should speak immediately to the Coroner's office covering the district where the body lies and subsequently confirm your conversation in writing.

If a death is referred to a coroner, a doctor should not issue a Medical Certificate of Cause of Death until the coroner has made a decision about whether or not to undertake further investigation. This is not a legal requirement but it avoids the family thinking they can register the death before the coroner has made his or her decision.

Care homes and hospitals who are managing authorities under the Mental Capacity Act Deprivation of Liberty Safeguards, need to know how to contact the relevant coroner's office should a person in their care who is deprived of their liberty die whilst subject to that authorisation.

Some coroners have indicated that they expect managing authorities to refer to them all deaths of those who are deprived of their liberty under the Mental Capacity Act Deprivation of Liberty Safeguards. Supervisory bodies, local authorities and Primary Care Trusts, should ascertain what their local coroners' expectations are in this regard and communicate that in turn to all the managing authorities that they liaise with.

If in doubt, it is always preferable to report the death as no harm can come from this cause of action, whereas not reporting the death can be problematic."

The Chief coroner's guidance on the deprivation of liberty safeguards is reproduced at Appendix C.

Schedule 1A—persons ineligible to be deprived of liberty by the Mental Capacity Act [The references to paragraph numbers are to the paragraphs of Sch.1A]

2–049   The Act cannot be used to deprive P of his liberty if P is "ineligible": see s.16A for the Court of Protection and Sch.A1, paras 12(e) and 17 for the authorisation procedure. P is ineligible if he falls within Cases A to E of Sch.1A. If P is ineligible, the 1983 Act must be used. In *GJ v Foundation Trust* [2009] EWHC 2972 (Fam) and *AM v South London & Maudsley NHS Foundation Trust* [2013] UKUT 365 (AAC); [2014] M.H.L.R. 181, Charles J. analysed the circumstances under which the 1983 Act has primacy over the 2005 Act. These cases are considered in the notes to Case E and under the heading "Deprivations of liberty—the Mental Capacity Act 2005 or the Mental Health Act 1983".

Case A (patients detained under the Mental Health Act 1983)

2–050   P is ineligible if he is subject to the "hospital treatment regime" and is detained under that regime in either an independent or NHS hospital. P is subject to the "hospital treatment regime" if he is subject to a "hospital treatment obligation" i.e. he is detained under ss.2, 3, 4, 35, 36, 37, 38, 44, 45A, 47, 48 or 51 of the 1983 Act or under "another England and Wales enactment which has the same effect as a hospital treatment obligation", such as the Criminal Procedure (Insanity) Act 1964 (paras 2, 8). The consequence of this is that if P is detained in hospital under the 1983 Act he is ineligible for detention under the authorisation procedure for any purpose (*A NHS Trust v Dr A* [2013] EWHC 2442 (COP) at para.87). If P requires treatment for a physical disorder in that hospital, he will be detained and treated for his mental disorder under the 1983 Act and treated for any physical disorder under the 2005 Act.

Case B (patients on leave of absence or conditional discharge)

This Case applies if P is subject to the "hospital treatment regime" (i.e. he is subject to a "hospital treatment obligation": see the note on Case A) but is not detained in hospital under that regime. This covers patients who have been granted leave of absence under s.17 of the 1983 Act or who have been granted a conditional discharge under either s.42 or 73 of that Act. P will be ineligible if: 2–051

(a) the proposed course of action under the 2005 Act is "not in accordance with a requirement" which the 1983 Act imposes, such as a requirement as to where P is, or is not, to reside (para.3). This means that P would be ineligible if, for example, there is a conflict between where P is required to reside under the conditions of a conditional discharge and where he would be required to reside under a standard authorisation; or

(b) the proposed care and treatment to be administered under the 2005 Act "consists in whole or in part of medical treatment for mental disorder in a hospital" (para.4).

In *A Hospital Trust v CD* [2015] EWCOP 74, Mostyn J. held that paras.4.50 and 4.51 of the Supplement to the Code of Practice are correct and that if P is detained under the 1983 Act and is granted leave of absence to be treated in another hospital for a physical disorder, then P will be eligible. In this case his Lordship reaffirmed the approach that he had taken in *An NHS Trust v A* [2015] EWCOP 71; *Re AB* [2015] EWCOP 31, per HHJ Parry, not followed.

Case C (patients on a community treatment order)

P is ineligible if: 2–052

(a) he is subject to a "community treatment regime", i.e. a community treatment order under s.17A of the 1983 Act or its equivalent (para.9); and

(b) either of the situations set out in paras (a) or (b) of Case B, above, apply.

Case D (patients subject to guardianship)

If P is subject to a guardianship application under s.7 of the 1983 Act, a guardianship order under s.37 of that Act, or an obligation under another England and Wales enactment which has similar effect (para.10), he will be ineligible if: 2–053

(a) the proposed course of action under the 2005 Act is not in accordance with a requirement imposed by the guardianship, including any requirement where P is to reside (para.3). This means that P would be ineligible if, for example, there is a conflict between where P is required to reside under the terms of the guardianship and where he would be required to reside under a standard authorisation; or

(b) the standard authorisation would authorise P to be a "mental health patient" (i.e. a person accommodated in a hospital for the purpose of being given medical treatment for mental disorder (para.16)), P objects (or would be likely to object if he was in a position to do so) to being a mental patient or to being given some or all of the mental health treatment, and no valid consent has been given by a donee of a lasting power of attorney or a court deputy to each matter to which P objects. The donee and the deputy will be governed by s.4 when making their decision. In determining whether P would be likely to object, regard must be had to all the circumstances, including P's behaviour, his wishes and feelings and his views values and beliefs, although circumstances from the past only need to be considered in so far as it is appropriate to consider them (para.5; also see the notes to Case E).

Case E (patients who are "within the scope" of the 1983 Act but are not subject to it)

2–054   P is "within the scope" of the 1983 Act if an application under s.2 or 3 of that Act could be made in respect of him if practitioners were minded to do so, and P could be detained in a hospital in pursuance of such an application, were one made (para.12(1)). Note that the reference is to "a hospital"; the assessor cannot restrict his or her consideration to the hospital where the patient might be receiving treatment for a physical condition. An establishment which is registered as a care home, but is neither registered as an independent hospital nor part of the NHS, is not a hospital for the purposes of Sch.1A. A person being cared for in such a home is therefore not a "mental health patient" for the purposes of this Case (see paras 5(3) and 16) and is not ineligible (*W Primary Care Trust v TB* [2009] EWHC 1737 (Fam)).

A patient will not come within the scope of the 1983 Act if it is not possible to make an application under either s.2 or s.3 in respect of him by virtue of the ruling in *R. v East London and The City Mental Health Trust Ex p. Brandenburg* [2003] UKHL 58 where it was held that a patient who had been discharged from the 1983 Act by a Mental Health Review Tribunal could not be re-detained under that Act in the absence of a "new information" test being satisfied.

If P comes within the scope of the 1983 Act, P it is to be assumed that the necessary medical recommendations are in place (para.12(3),(4)) and that the treatment referred to in s.3(2)(c) of the 1983 Act, which is treatment for mental disorder that "is necessary for the health or safety of the patient or for the protection of other persons", cannot be provided under the 2005 Act (para.12(5)). P would be ineligible if the situation set out in para.(b) of Case D, above, applies, i.e. he objects (or would be likely to object if he was in a position to do so) to being admitted to hospital or to being treated for his mental disorder there and no valid consent has been given by a donee or a deputy. If a donee or deputy consents, P will be eligible. In determining whether P objects to being a "mental health patient", regard must be had to all the circumstances, including P's behaviour, his wishes and feelings and his views values and beliefs, although circumstances from the past only need to be considered in so far as it is appropriate to consider them (para.5(6),(7)).

In *GJ v Foundation Trust* [2009] EWHC 2972 (Fam), Charles J. said that as the test in s.3(2)(c) relates to treatment rather than assessment, "an assessment can be said to be outside para.5(3) of Sch.1A to the MCA. But, as the focus of this aspect of the authorisation scheme concerning eligibility is (a) on P being detained in a hospital or in a care home for the purpose of being given care or treatment (see paras 1(2) and 2 of Sch.A1 to the MCA), and (b) arises when an application under s.2 or s.3 MHA could be made in respect of P, in my judgment the provisions looked at as a whole have the result that the assessor under the MCA should also proceed on the assumption that assessment and treatment under s.2 MHA 1983 cannot be provided under the MCA" (para.44).

His analysis of the legislation led his Lordship to reach the following conclusions:

"58. In my judgment, the MHA 1983 has primacy in the sense that the relevant decision makers under both the MHA 1983 and the MCA should approach the questions they have to answer relating to the application of the MHA 1983 on the basis of an assumption that an alternative solution is not available under the MCA.

59. [I]n my view this does not mean that the two regimes are necessarily always mutually exclusive. But it does mean . . . that it is not lawful for the medical practitioners referred to in ss.2 and 3 of the MHA 1983, decision makers under the MCA, treating doctors, social workers or anyone else to proceed on the basis that they can pick and choose between the two statutory regimes as they think fit having regard to general considerations (e.g. the preservation or promotion of a therapeutic relationship with P) that they consider render one regime preferable to the other in the circumstances of the given case".

In *AM v South London & Maudsley NHS Foundation Trust* [2013] UKUT 0365 (AAC), Charles J. revisited the primacy issue and held that although para.59 of his judgment in *GJ* is correct, para.58 is not. His Lordship said at para.78:

"(i) general propositions in respect of issues that arise concerning the inter-relationship between the MHA and the MCA are dangerous,

(ii) as a general proposition the second part of paragraph 58 in *GJ v Foundation Trust* is not correct, as in the circumstances of this case the regimes provide relevant and available alternatives,

(iii) albeit that the legislative history that the DOLS provisions were added to the MCA to fill the *Bournewood* gap and thus something not covered by the well established regime under the MHA and much of the definition of 'ineligibility' in the MCA relates to the applicability of the MHA, any analysis that is based on or includes the concept of primacy of the MHA in the sense used in paragraph 58 of *GJ v Foundation Trust* (or any other sense) should be case specific, and

(iv) I agree with the point made by the Secretary of State for Health to Upper Tribunal Judge Jacobs that my references to the MHA having primacy in *GJ v Foundation Trust* were made in and should be confined to the application of Case E in that case, and I add that even in that confined context they need some qualification to expand on the point I made that the two statutory schemes are not always mutually exclusive and so to acknowledge the point set out above that in defined circumstances Parliament has created alternatives that are factors for the relevant decision maker to take into account."

Having considered the case law and the statutory provision, Hayden J. said that "it is clear that the magnetic north when contemplating the deprivation of liberty of those who fall within Case E is and is likely to remain the Mental Health Act" (*Northampton Healthcare NHS Foundation Trust v ML* [2014] EWCOP 2 at para.76).

In determining whether the first condition of the objection test in para.5 is satisfied i.e. the relevant instrument "authorises P to be a mental health patient", his Lordship held in *GJ* that the decision maker should adopt a "but for" test if P suffers from both a mental and a physical disorder (para.87). This means that the decision maker should ask: (i) what treatment would P receive for his physical disorder which is unconnected to his mental disorder, and (ii) what treatment would P receive for his mental disorder (including treatment for a physical disorder or illness that is connected to his mental disorder and/or which is likely to directly affect his mental disorder). The decision maker should then ask whether, "but for" the need for P to have treatment for his physical disorder, should P be detained in hospital? If the answer is in the negative, P does not satisfy the test and is not ineligible. Put another way, the test is not satisfied if the need for treatment for his physical disorder is "the only effective reason" for P's detention (para.89).

His Lordship said that the second condition of the objection test (i.e. P objects), has to be looked at "without taking any fine distinctions between the potential reasons for the objection to treatment of different types, or to simply being in a hospital. As is recognised and provided for by para.5(6), this is because it is often going to be the case that the relevant person (P) does not have the capacity to make a properly informed and balanced decision. So what matters, applying the approach set out in para.5(6), is whether P will or does object to what is proposed" (para.83). This statement establishes a low threshold for establishing whether P objects in that any non compliant behaviour by P is likely to constitute evidence of an objection. The supplement to the *Code of Practice* states at para.4.46 that if there is reason to think that P would object if able to do so, then P "should be assumed to be objecting". It is not the role of the assessor to consider whether an objection is reasonable.

Research conducted by Dr I.C.H. Clare and her colleagues found that while verbal and physical challenges by patients and the use of restrictions by staff were used as indicators of a deprivation of liberty, in the context of treatment of a mental disorder the possibility that they signalled "objection", suggesting consideration of the use of the 1983 Act, was not always recognised (*Understanding the interface between the Mental Capacity Act's Deprivation of Liberty Safeguards (MCA-DOLS and the Mental Health Act (MHA)*, University of Cambridge, 2013, para.5.3.2).

Deprivations of liberty—the Mental Capacity Act 2005 or the Mental Health Act 1983?

2–055   Paragraph 13.69 of the Code of Practice on the 1983 Act states:

"In the rare cases where neither the Act nor a DoLS authorisation nor a Court of Protection order is appropriate, then to avoid an unlawful deprivation of liberty it may be necessary to make an application to the High Court to use its inherent jurisdiction to authorise the deprivation of liberty."

Deprivations of liberty in hospitals

Schedule 1A sets out the circumstances that prevent a person who is being   **2–055A**
deprived of his liberty from being the subject of a standard authorisation. If Sch.
1A applies, the 1983 Act must be used. In *AM v South London & Maudsley NHS
Foundation Trust* [2013] UKUT 0365 (AAC); [2014] M.H.L.R. 181, para.28,
Charles J. reached the following conclusions:

"(i) in the circumstances defined therein the DOLS were intended to and do
      provide an alternative basis to that provided by the MHA to authorise the
      deprivation of the liberty of an incapacitated person for a range of pur-
      poses including his or her assessment or treatment for mental or physical
      disorders in hospital, and so

(ii) a decision maker under the MHA has to consider whether that alternative is
      available and, if it is, whether it should be used when he or she applies the
      'necessity test' set by the MHA.

The qualification 'in the circumstances defined thereby' in sub-paragraph (i) is
important and means that the relevant decision maker has to consider the application of those provisions to the circumstances of the particular case."

His Lordship held that the fact that a choice has to be made between the two
statutory schemes leads to the following results:

"(i) the First-tier Tribunal (and earlier decision makers under the MHA) have
      to apply the statutory tests imposed by the MHA and the possible applica-
      tion of the MCA and its DOLS are relevant to that exercise,

(ii) the First-tier Tribunal (and the earlier decision makers under the MHA)
      have to assess whether as a result of the identified risks the relevant person
      ought to be detained, or kept in hospital in circumstances which on a
      objective assessment give rise to a risk that cannot be ignored that they
      amount to a deprivation of liberty (see for example paragraph 22 of Upper
      Tribunal Judge Jacobs decision in *DN v Northumberland & Wear NHS
      Foundation Trust* [see below]),

(iii) if the answer is 'yes', this triggers a value judgment applying the 'neces-
      sity test' as between the choices that are or will or may become available,

(iv) the search applying the MHA 'necessity test' is for the alternative that best
      achieves the objective of assessment or treatment of the type described in
      ss.2 and 3 MHA in the least restrictive way. This potentially introduces
      tensions and so a need to balance the impact of detention under the MCA
      and an authorisation under the DOLS as the means of ensuring that a
      deprivation of liberty to best achieve the desired objective is lawful and
      governed by a statutory regime, and

(v)   the theoretical and practical availability of the MCA regime and its
      DOLS is one of the factors that needs to be considered by the MHA
      decision maker in carrying out that search, as are their overall impact in
      best achieving the desired objective when compared with other available
      choices and so detention under ss. 2 or 3 MHA" (para.75).

Bearing in mind that the relevant test is which regime offers "the least restrictive way of best achieving the proposed assessment or treatment" for the patient
(para.73), the key question identified in *AM* is when can a compliant incapacitated
person be properly and lawfully detained under the 1983 Act when he could be

admitted as an informal patient pursuant to s.131 of the that Act and ss.5 and 6 of the 2005 Act and be the subject of a deprivation of liberty authorisation? Among the matters to be considered, apart from the practical availability of the DOL regime, are the likelihood of the patient's continued compliance and whether the patient's mental capacity will fluctuate (para.73). With regard to the initial admission of the patient to hospital, his Lordship agreed that such a patient could be legitimately admitted as a detained patient under the 1983 Act in the circumstances set out at para.4.21 of the *Code of Practice* on the 1983 Act and at para.4.48 of the supplement to the *Code of Practice* on the 2005 Act.

It is likely that the practical effect of the analysis undertaken by Charles J. will be largely confined to a situation where P who, subsequent to being detained under the 1983 Act, becomes compliant to both being in the hospital and being treated there for his mental disorder but continues to be subject to a deprivation of liberty because he satisfies the "acid test" set out by the Supreme Court in *Cheshire West*: see *What constitutes a "deprivation of liberty"?*, above. Decision-makers might regard continued detention under the 1983 Act as being the least restrictive option for such a patient because of the superior protections provided to P under that Act, in particular the tribunal and consent to treatment regimes. This approach is supported by the following comments made by Peter Jackson J. in *C v Blackburn and Darwen Borough Council* [2011] EWHC 3321 (COP) at para.35:

> "In my view, there are good reasons why the provisions of the MHA should prevail where they apply. It is a self-contained system with inbuilt checks and balances and it is well understood by professionals working in the field."

If an authorisation is granted, it would have to be reviewed if P subsequently objected to either receiving treatment for his mental disorder or to being in the hospital.

In *DN v Northumberland Tyne and Wear NHS Foundation Trust* [2011] UKUT 327 (AAC), UT Judge Jacobs held that there was no reason why a standard authorisation could not be made in anticipation of the patient being discharged from detention under the 1983 Act and moving to a care home (see Sch.A1, para.12(3)) as long as he was not "within the scope of the Mental Health Act" on his discharge (see Sch.1A, para.12). Such an approach would enable suitable arrangements, in particular those relating to him accessing alcohol, to be in place on his arrival at the care home. This decision follows the approach set out by the Department of Health in a letter to the tribunal about the relationship between the 1983 Act (MHA) and the 2005 Act (MCA). The letter, which is reproduced in the judgment at para.18, is set out below:

> "As the Department understands it, there is no general rule that the MHA takes precedence over the MCA (or, indeed, vice versa).
>
> In general, the possibility that a person's needs for care and treatment could be met by relying on the MCA—with or without an authorisation under the MCA DOLS—relevant to decisions that have to be made under the MHA in the same way as all alternative possibilities.
>
> Decision-makers under the MHA must, inevitably, consider what other options are available when deciding whether it is right for compulsory measures under the MHA to be used, or continue to be used. The use of the MCA (with or without an authorisation under MCA DOLS) may be one of those options.

All such alternative options must be considered on their merits. The fact that someone could be deprived of their liberty and given treatment under the MCA does not automatically mean that it is inappropriate to detain them under the MHA, any more than (say) the possibility that someone with capacity may consent to continuing treatment for their mental disorder automatically makes their continued detention under the MHA improper.

There are, however, specific circumstances in which the fact that someone is, or could be made, subject to compulsory measures under the MHA means that they cannot also be deprived of their liberty under the MCA.

Those circumstances are set out in the 'eligibility requirement' in paragraph 17 of Schedule A1 to the MCA, the meaning of which is defined by Schedule 1A to the same Act. A person who is ineligible as determined in accordance with Schedule 1A cannot be deprived of their liberty under the MCA and therefore cannot be the subject of any authorisation under the MCA DOLS.

Schedule 1A sets out five cases in which a person is ineligible.

Case A is (in summary) where a person is currently detained in hospital under the MHA. That person cannot simultaneously be subject to an authorisation under the MCA depriving them of their liberty either in that hospital or anywhere else.

However, that is not to say that a person cannot (in effect) be discharged from one regime to the other. There is nothing to prevent a prospective application being made for an MCA DOLS authorisation in anticipation of, or the expectation that, the person concerned will be discharged from detention under the MHA. Paragraph 12(3) of Schedule A1 to the MCA says, in effect, that when deciding whether the qualifying requirements for an authorisation are met, it is the circumstances which are expected to apply at the time the authorisation is expected to come into effect which are to be considered.

The main effect of Cases B, C and D is that a person who is subject to compulsory measures under the MHA which fall short of actual detention cannot be deprived of their liberty under the MCA if that would conflict with a requirement imposed on them under the MHA. So, a person who is on leave of absence from detention in hospital under the MHA can, in general, be the subject of an MCA DOLS authorisation—but not if (for example) that authorisation envisages them living in one care home when it is a condition of their leave of absence that they live in a different care home.

Cases B and C also, in effect, prevent people being made the subject of a MCA DOLS authorisation detaining them in a hospital for the purpose of mental health treatment where the same could be achieved by recalling them to hospital from leave of absence, supervised community treatment or conditional discharge under the MHA (as the case may be).

Case E concerns people who are 'within the scope' of the MHA, but not so far actually liable to be detained under it. In broad terms (and subject to certain caveats), it means that the MCA cannot be used to deprive someone of their liberty in a hospital for the purposes of mental health treatment if they are objecting to that course of action and they could instead be detained under the MHA.

It is important to note that case E only applies to detention in hospital, and only where the purpose of the proposed deprivation of liberty is treatment for mental disorder within the meaning of the MHA. It is not relevant to deprivation of liberty in other settings (eg care homes) or for other purposes (eg treatment for physical health problems, or for substance dependence by itself separately from treatment for mental disorder with the meaning of the MHA).

The Government's policy intention was that people who lack capacity to consent to being admitted to hospital, but who are clearly objecting to it, should generally be treated like people who have capacity and are refusing to consent to mental health treatment. If it is considered necessary to detain them in hospital, and they would have been detained under the MHA if they had the capacity to refuse treatment, then as a matter of policy it was thought right that the MHA should be used in preference to the MCA.

It was specifically in the context of the interpretation of Case E that Mr Justice Charles talked in [*GJ*] about the MHA having 'primacy'. Outside that context, the Department does not understand him to have been making a more general statement about the relationship between the two Acts. Indeed, as set out above, the Department does not think it would actually be possible to say, in general, which has primacy over the other."

Deprivations of liberty in care homes

2–056   In its response to the Bournewood consultation exercise, the Government rejected the option of using the guardianship provisions of the 1983 Act as a vehicle that could be used to authorise detention. This decision was partly due to the commonly held opinion that guardianship cannot be used to deprive a person of their liberty: see, for example, para.13.16 of the *Code of Practice* on the 2005 Act and the obiter comment of Peter Jackson J. in *C v Blackburn and Darwen Borough Council* [2011] EWHC 3321 (COP) at para.30. Is this opinion correct? The 1983 Act provides the guardian of a mentally incapacitated person with the following powers:

- a power to take the person to the place specified by the guardian, using force if necessary (ss.18(7) and 137).

- a power to require the person to reside at that place (s.8(1)(a)). (NB Neither the Court of Protection (*C v Blackburn and Darwen Borough Council*, above), nor a deputy appointed by the Court of Protection nor the donee of a lasting power of attorney can make a decision about the person's place of residence which conflicts with that of the guardian (s.8(1))).

- a power to return the person to that place if he leaves without authority, using force if necessary (ss.18(3), 137).

- a power to take the person to a place where he will receive medical treatment (s.8(1)(b)), using force if necessary (ss.18(3), 137).

Put bluntly, a person under guardianship, who must be over the age of 16, can be forced to leave his home to go to a place where he does not want to go to, can be required to stay at that place and can be returned to that place if he leaves without being given permission to do so. Many people would regard a person who is subject to the operation of such powers as being clearly deprived of his liberty.

In the *Cheshire West* case, the Supreme Court held that in order to be deprived of his liberty for the purposes of the 2005 Act a mentally incapacitated person must be under "continuous supervision and control and . . . not free to leave". It follows that although the guardianship provisions of the 1983 Act provide authority to convey P to a care home, to require him to remain there, and to return him if he absconds, an authorisation under Sch.A1 will be required if P is subject to a continuous supervision and control within the care home and is assessed as meeting the qualifying requirements (*C v Blackburn and Darwen Borough Council*, above, at para.30).

Although it was held in *DCC v KH* (2009) COP, Case No.11729380, that a standard authorisation provides an implied authority to use restraint on P, amounting if necessary to a deprivation of liberty, if P refused to return to the care home where the deprivation of liberty was authorised, professionals might prefer to rely on the explicit power contained in s.18(3) of the 1983 Act (see the cases noted under *Powers of staff to return P to the hospital or care home subsequent to the granting of an authorisation*, above).

This was a crucial factor in favour of guardianship in *NM v Kent CC* [2015] UKUT 125 where UT Judge Jacobs held that although a deprivation of liberty authorisation allowed the home to prevent M from leaving, it did not deal with the possibility that he might abscond.

PART 3

DELEGATED LEGISLATION

THE MENTAL CAPACITY ACT 2005 (INDEPENDENT MENTAL CAPACITY ADVOCATES) (GENERAL) REGULATIONS 2006

(SI 2006/1832)

Dated July 7, 2006 and made by the Secretary of State for Health under the Mental Capacity Act 2005 (c.9) ss.35(2), (3), 36, 37(6), (7), 38(8), 64(1) and 65(1).

GENERAL NOTE

These Regulations define "NHS body" and "serious medical treatment" for the purposes **3–001** of certain provisions the Act which deal with independent mental capacity advocates (IMCAs). The Regulations also contain provision as to who can be appointed to act as an IMCA and as to an IMCA's functions when he has been instructed to represent a person in a particular case. The provisions about the IMCA's appointment and functions apply where the IMCA is instructed under ss.37 to 39 of the Act or under regulations made by virtue of s.41 of the Act (see reg.2(2)).

Regulation 3 defines "NHS body". This term is used in ss.37 and 38. Those sections impose an obligation on NHS bodies to instruct an IMCA in certain circumstances involving acts or decisions relating to serious medical treatment or to accommodation.

Regulation 4 defines "serious medical treatment". Under s.37, an NHS body must instruct an IMCA where it is proposing to provide, or secure the provision of, such treatment.

Regulation 5 provides that a person can only act as an IMCA if he has been approved by a local authority or is a member of a class which has been so approved. For an IMCA to be appointed, he must satisfy certain requirements as to experience, training, good character and independence.

Regulation 6 sets out the steps an IMCA must take once he has been instructed to act in a particular case. He must obtain and evaluate information about the person he has been instructed to represent (P) and about P's wishes, feelings, beliefs or values. He must then report to the person who instructed him.

Under *regulation 7,* an IMCA who is instructed to represent P in relation to any matter may challenge a decision made in that matter in relation to P, including any decision as to whether P is a person who lacks capacity. The challenge may be through court proceedings. For the purpose of making a challenge, the IMCA is treated in the same way as any other person caring for P or interested in his welfare.

The equivalent to regs 3 to 7 with respect to Wales are regs 3 to 7 of the Mental Capacity Act 2005 (Independent Mental Capacity Advocates) (Wales) Regulations 2007 (SI 2007/852 (W.77)).

Citation, commencement and extent

1.—(1) These Regulations may be cited as the Mental Capacity Act 2005 **3–002** (Independent Mental Capacity Advocates) (General) Regulations 2006.

(2) These Regulations shall come into force—

(a) for the purpose of enabling the Secretary of State to make arrangements under section 35 of the Act, and for the purpose of enabling local authorities to approve IMCAs, on 1st November 2006, and

(b) for all other purposes, on 1st April 2007.

(3)   These Regulations apply in relation to England only.

Interpretation

3–003   **2.**—(1) In these Regulations—

"the Act" means the Mental Capacity Act 2005; and

"IMCA" means an independent mental capacity advocate.

(2) In these Regulations, references to instructions given to a person to act as an IMCA are to instructions given under sections 37 to 39 of the Act or under regulations made by virtue of section 41 of the Act.

Meaning of NHS Body

3–004   **3.**—(1) For the purposes of sections 37 and 38 of the Act, "NHS body" means a body in England which is—

(a)   [. . .];

(b)   an NHS foundation trust;

[(ba)   a clinical commissioning group;

(bb)   the National Health Service Commissioning Board;

(bc)   a local authority (within the meaning of section 2B of the National Health Service Act 2006) acting in the exercise of public health functions (within the meaning of that Act);]

(c)   [. . .];

(d)   an NHS Trust; or

(e)   a Care Trust.

(2) In this regulation—

"Care Trust" means a body designated as a Care Trust under section 45 of the Health and Social Care Act 2001;

["clinical commissioning group" means a body established under section 14D of the National Health Service Act 2006;]

"NHS foundation trust" has the meaning given in section 1 of the Health and Social Care (Community Health and Standards) Act 2003;

"NHS trust" means a body established under section 5 of the National Health Service and Community Care Act 1990;

[. . .]

[. . .]

AMENDMENTS

3–005   The amendments to this regulation were made by SI 2013/235 art.11, Sch.2, para.99.

Meaning of serious medical treatment

3–006   **4.**—(1) This regulation defines serious medical treatment for the purposes of section 37 of the Act.

(2) Serious medical treatment is treatment which involves providing, withdrawing or withholding treatment in circumstances where—

(a) in a case where a single treatment is being proposed, there is a fine balance between its benefits to the patient and the burdens and risks it is likely to entail for him,

(b) in a case where there is a choice of treatments, a decision as to which one to use is finely balanced, or

(c) what is proposed would be likely to involve serious consequences for the patient.

Appointment of independent mental capacity advocates

5.—(1) No person may be appointed to act as an IMCA for the purposes of sections 37 to 39 of the Act, or regulations made by virtue of section 41 of the Act, unless—   **3–007**

(a) he is for the time being approved by a local authority on the grounds that he satisfies the appointment requirements, or

(b) he belongs to a class of persons which is for the time being approved by a local authority on the grounds that all persons in that class satisfy the appointment requirements.

(2) The appointment requirements, in relation to a person appointed to act as an IMCA, are that—

(a) he has appropriate experience or training or an appropriate combination of experience and training;

(b) he is a person of integrity and good character; and

(c) he is able to act independently of any person who instructs him.

[(3) Before a determination is made in relation to any person for the purposes of paragraph (2)(b), there must be obtained, in respect of that person, an enhanced criminal record certificate issued pursuant to section 113B of the Police Act 1997 which includes—

(a) where the determination is in respect of a person's appointment as an IMCA for a person who has not attained the age of 18, suitability information relating to children (within the meaning of section 113BA of the Police Act 1997);

(b) where the determination is in respect of a person's appointment as an IMCA for a person who has attained the age of 18, suitability information relating to vulnerable adults (within the meaning of section 113BB of that Act).]

AMENDMENT

Paragraph (3) was substituted by SI 2009/2376 reg.2.   **3–008**

Functions of an independent mental capacity advocate

6.—(1) This regulation applies where an IMCA has been instructed by an authorised person to represent a person ("P").   **3–009**

(2) "Authorised person" means a person who is required or enabled to instruct an IMCA under sections 37 to 39 of the Act or under regulations made by virtue of section 41 of the Act.

(3) The IMCA must determine in all the circumstances how best to represent and support P.

(4) In particular, the IMCA must—

(a) verify that the instructions were issued by an authorised person;

   (b) to the extent that it is practicable and appropriate to do so—
     (i) interview P, and
     (ii) examine the records relevant to P to which the IMCA has access under section 35(6) of the Act;
   (c) to the extent that it is practicable and appropriate to do so, consult—
     (i) persons engaged in providing care or treatment for P in a professional capacity or for remuneration, and
     (ii) other persons who may be in a position to comment on P's wishes, feelings, beliefs or values; and
   (d) take all practicable steps to obtain such other information about P, or the act or decision that is proposed in relation to P, as the IMCA considers necessary.

(5) The IMCA must evaluate all the information he has obtained for the purpose of—
   (a) ascertaining the extent of the support provided to P to enable him to participate in making any decision about the matter in relation to which the IMCA has been instructed;
   (b) ascertaining what P's wishes and feelings would be likely to be, and the beliefs and values that would be likely to influence P, if he had capacity in relation to the proposed act or decision;
   (c) ascertaining what alternative courses of action are available in relation to P;
   (d) where medical treatment is proposed for P, ascertaining whether he would be likely to benefit from a further medical opinion.

(6) The IMCA must prepare a report for the authorised person who instructed him.

(7) The IMCA may include in the report such submissions as he considers appropriate in relation to P and the act or decision which is proposed in relation to him.

Challenges to decisions affecting persons who lack capacity

3–010   **7.**—(1) This regulation applies where—
   (a) an IMCA has been instructed to represent a person ("P") in relation to any matter, and
   (b) a decision affecting P (including a decision as to his capacity) is made in that matter.

(2) The IMCA has the same rights to challenge the decision as he would have if he were a person (other than an IMCA) engaged in caring for P or interested in his welfare.

THE MENTAL CAPACITY ACT 2005 (INDEPENDENT MENTAL CAPACITY ADVOCATES) (EXPANSION OF ROLE) REGULATIONS 2006

(SI 2006/2883)

Dated October 30, 2006 and made by the Secretary of State for Health under the Mental Capacity Act 2005 (c.9) ss.41(1), (2), 64(1) and 65(1).

GENERAL NOTE

These Regulations adjust the obligation to make arrangements as to the availability of independent mental capacity advocates (IMCAs) which is imposed by s.35 of the Act. Under the Regulations, the Secretary of State may also make arrangements to enable IMCAs to be available to represent a person (P) who lacks capacity to agree to the outcome of an accommodation review or to protective measures taken in adult protection cases. **3–011**

Regulation 2 provides that arrangements under s.35 may extend to cover IMCAs who are instructed in the circumstances specified in reg.3 or 4.

Regulation 3 specifies circumstances where an NHS body has made, or a local authority have made, arrangements as to P's accommodation and it is then proposed to review those arrangements. In addition, P must not have capacity to participate in the review and there must be no one else who can be consulted as to matters affecting his best interests.

Regulation 4 specifies circumstances where it is alleged that P is or has been abused or neglected by another person or that he is abusing or has abused another person. In addition, protective measures affecting P must have been taken, or be proposed, by an NHS body or local authority in accordance with any adult protection procedures which have been set up pursuant to statutory guidance. The current guidance is entitled "No secrets: guidance on developing and implementing multi-agency policies and procedures to protect vulnerable adults from abuse", Department of Health and Home Office. The equivalent guidance for Wales is "In Safe Hands", National Assembly for Wales.

Regulation 5 provides that an NHS body or local authority may instruct an IMCA to represent P if the NHS body considers, or the local authority consider, that that would be of particular benefit to P. The NHS body or local authority must take account of information provided by the IMCA and of any submissions made by him.

Paragraph 10.61 of the *Code of Practice* states:

"Responsible bodies are expected to take a strategic approach in deciding whether they will use IMCAs in [the situations set out in regs 3 and 4]. They should establish a policy locally for determining these decisions, setting out the criteria for appointing an IMCA including the issues to be taken into account when deciding if an IMCA will be of particular benefit to the person concerned. However, decision-makers will need to consider each case separately to see if the criteria are met. Local authorities or NHS bodies may wish to publish their approach for ease of access, setting out the ways they intend to use these additional powers and review it periodically."

The equivalent to regs 3 and 4 with respect to Wales are regs 8 and 9 of the Mental Capacity Act 2005 (Independent Mental Capacity Advocates) (Wales) Regulations 2007 (SI 2007/852 (W.77)).

Citation, commencement, extent and interpretation

1.—(1) These Regulations may be cited as the Mental Capacity Act 2005 (Independent Mental Capacity Advocates) (Expansion of Role) Regulations 2006. **3–012**

(2) These Regulations shall come into force—

(a) for the purpose of enabling the Secretary of State to make arrangements by virtue of regulation 2, on 1st November 2006, and

(b) for all other purposes, on 1st April 2007.

(3) These Regulations apply in relation to England only.

(4) In these Regulations—

"the Act" means the Mental Capacity Act 2005;

"IMCA" means an independent mental capacity advocate; and

"NHS body" means a body in England which is—

(a) [. . .];

(b) an NHS foundation trust;

[(ba) a clinical commissioning group;

(bb) the National Health Service Commissioning Board;]

(c) [. . .];

(d) an NHS Trust; or

(e) a Care Trust.

(5) In the definition of "NHS body" in paragraph (4)—

"Care Trust" means a body designated as a Care Trust under section 45 of the Health and Social Care Act 2001;

"NHS foundation trust" has the meaning given in section 1 of the Health and Social Care (Community Health and Standards) Act 2003;

"NHS trust" means a body established under section 5 of the National Health Service and Community Care Act 1990;

"Primary Care Trust" means a body established under section 16A of the National Health Service Act 1977; and

"Strategic Health Authority" means a Strategic Health Authority established under section 8 of the National Health Service Act 1977.

AMENDMENTS

3–013   The amendments to this regulation were made by SI 2013/235 art.11, Sch.2, para.101.

GENERAL NOTE

3–014   Due to the amendments made to this regulation by SI 2013/235, the definitions of Primary Care Trust and Strategic Health Authority are redundant.

Adjustment of the obligation to make arrangements imposed by section 35 of the Act

3–015   **2.** Arrangements made by the Secretary of State under section 35 of the Act may include such provision as she considers reasonable for the purpose of enabling IMCAs to be available to represent and support persons in the circumstances specified in regulation 3 or 4.

Review of arrangements as to accommodation

3–016   **3.**—(1) The circumstances specified in this regulation are where—

(a) qualifying arrangements have been made by an NHS body or local authority as to the accommodation of a person ("P") who lacks capacity to agree to the arrangements;

(b) a review of the arrangements is proposed or in progress (whether under a care plan or otherwise);

(c) the NHS body is satisfied, or the local authority are satisfied, that there is no person, other than a person engaged in providing care or treatment for P in a professional capacity or for remuneration, whom it would be appropriate to consult in determining what would be in P's best interests;

(d) none of the following exist—

  (i) a person nominated by P (in whatever manner) as a person to be consulted in matters affecting his interests,

  (ii) a donee of a lasting power of attorney created by P,

  (iii) a deputy appointed by the Court of Protection for P, or

  (iv) a donee of an enduring power of attorney (within the meaning of Schedule 4 to the Act) created by P; and

(e) sections 37, 38 and 39 of the Act do not apply.

(2) In this regulation—

"accommodation" means—

(a) accommodation in a care home or hospital, or

[(b) accommodation provided in respect of the meeting of a person's needs under section 18 or 19 of the Care Act 2014 (duty and power to meet needs for care and support), or

(c) residential accommodation provided in accordance with section 21 or 29 of the National Assistance Act 1948 as the result of a decision taken by a local authority under section 47 of the National Health Service and Community Care Act 1990;]

  as the result of a decision taken by a local authority under section 47 of the National Health Service and Community Care Act 1990;

"care home" and "hospital" have the same meaning as in section 38 of the Act; and

"qualifying arrangements" means arrangements—

(a) under which accommodation has been provided for P for a continuous period of 12 weeks or more, and

(b) which are not made as a result of an obligation imposed on P under the Mental Health Act 1983.

AMENDMENT

The amendment to para.(2) was made by SI 2015/643 art.2, Sch., para 27.   **3–017**

GENERAL NOTE

The *Code of Practice*, at para.10.61, expects local authorities and NHS bodies to have   **3–018**
a policy setting out when this discretionary power is to be used: see the General Note to these Regulations.

Adult protection cases

4.—(1) The circumstances specified in this regulation are where—   **3–019**

(a) an NHS body proposes to take or has taken, or a local authority propose to take or have taken, protective measures in relation to a person ("P") who lacks capacity to agree to one or more of the measures;

(b) the proposal is made or the measures have been taken—

  (i) following the receipt of an allegation or evidence that P is being, or has been, abused or neglected by another person or that P is abusing, or has abused, another person, and

(ii) in accordance with arrangements relating to the protection of vulnerable adults from abuse which are made pursuant to guidance issued under section 7 of the Local Authority Social Services Act 1970; and

(c) none of the following provisions apply—

(i) section 37, 38 or 39 of the Act, or

(ii) regulation 3 of these Regulations.

(2) The reference to protective measures in relation to P includes measures to minimise the risk that any abuse or neglect of P, or abuse by P, will continue.

GENERAL NOTE

3–020   Under this regulation, an IMCA may be appointed even where P has family or friends whom it might be appropriate to consult. The *Code of Practice*, at para.10.61, expects local authorities and NHS bodies to have a policy setting out when this discretionary power is to be used: see the General Note to these Regulations.

The Directors of Adult Social Services and the Social Care Institute for Excellence have published *Practice guidance on the involvement of Independent Mental Capacity Advocates (IMCAs) in safeguarding adults* (2009).

Instructing an IMCA

3–021   **5.**—(1) In the circumstances specified in regulation 3 or 4, an NHS body or local authority may instruct an IMCA to represent P if the NHS body is satisfied, or the local authority are satisfied, that it would be of particular benefit to P to be so represented.

(2) An NHS body which instructs, or a local authority which instruct, an IMCA under paragraph (1) must—

(a) in making any decision resulting from a review of arrangements as to P's accommodation, or

(b) in making any decision, or further decision, about protective measures in relation to P,

take into account any information given, or submissions made, by the IMCA.

THE MENTAL CAPACITY ACT 2005 (LOSS OF CAPACITY DURING RESEARCH PROJECT) (ENGLAND) REGULATIONS 2007

(SI 2007/679)

Dated March 3, 2007 and made by the Secretary of State for Health under the Mental Capacity Act 2005 (c.9) ss.30(6)(a), 34(1), (2) and (3)(b), 64(1) and 65(1)(c).

GENERAL NOTE

These Regulations are made under s.34 of the Act. They provide for certain research, **3–022** relating to people without capacity to consent to it, to be carried out lawfully where otherwise the requirements of s.30 would have to be complied with.

Regulation 1 provides for the Regulations to come into force on July 1, 2007 for the purpose of enabling applications for approval of research protocols under the Regulations to be made and determined and on October 1, 2007 for all other purposes.

Regulation 2 provides that the Regulations apply where a research project began before October 1, 2007 and a person (P) consented, prior to March 31, 2008, to take part in the project but has subsequently lost capacity to continue to consent.

Regulation 3 provides that research under such a project may be carried out using information or material collected prior to P's loss of capacity. The information or material must be either data within the meaning of the Data Protection Act 1998 (c. 29) or material which consists of or includes human cells or DNA. In addition the requirements of Schs 1 and 2 must be complied with.

Schedule 1 provides that an appropriate body, as defined in reg.1(3), must have approved a protocol for the project which provides for research to be carried out in relation to a person who has consented to take part and then lost capacity. The appropriate body must also be satisfied that there are reasonable arrangements for ensuring that Sch.2 will be complied with.

Schedule 2, which repeats the relevant safeguards from s.32 and 33, sets out requirements as to consultation about P's involvement in the project, as to respecting his wishes and objections and as to assuming that his interests outweigh those of science and society.

Provision for Wales, which in all material respects replicates these regulations, is contained in the Mental Capacity Act 2005 (Loss of Capacity during Research Project) (Wales) Regulations 2007 (SI 2007/837 (W.72)).

Citation, commencement, territorial application and interpretation

1.—(1) These Regulations may be cited as the Mental Capacity Act 2005 (Loss **3–023** of Capacity during Research Project) (England) Regulations 2007 and shall come into force on—

(a) 1 July 2007 for the purpose of enabling applications for approval for the purposes of Schedule 1 to be made to, and determined by, an appropriate body,

(b) 1 October 2007 for all other purposes.

(2) These Regulations apply in relation to the carrying out of research in England.

(3) In these Regulations—

"the Act" means the Mental Capacity Act 2005;

"appropriate body" has the meaning given by section 30(4) of the Act and the Mental Capacity Act 2005 (Appropriate Body) (England) Regulations 2006.

Application

3–024   **2.** These Regulations apply where—

(a) a person ("P")—

    (i) has consented before 31 March 2008 to take part in a research project ("the project") begun before 1st October 2007, but

    (ii) before the conclusion of the project, loses capacity to consent to continue to take part in it, and

    (iii) research for the purposes of the project in relation to P would, apart from these Regulations, be unlawful by virtue of section 30 of the Act.

Research which may be carried out despite a participant's loss of capacity

3–025   **3.** Despite P's loss of capacity, research for the purposes of the project may be carried out using information or material relating to him if—

(a) that information or material was obtained before P's loss of capacity,

(b) that information or material is either—

    (i) data within the meaning given in section 1(1) of the Data Protection Act 1998, or

    (ii) material which consists of or includes human cells or human DNA,

(c) the project satisfies the requirements set out in Schedule 1, and

(d) the person conducting the project ("R") takes in relation to P such steps as are set out in Schedule 2.

SCHEDULE 1   REGULATION 3(C)

REQUIREMENTS WHICH THE PROJECT MUST SATISFY

3–026   **1.** A protocol approved by an appropriate body and having effect in relation to the project makes provision for research to be carried out in relation to a person who has consented to take part in the project but loses capacity to consent to continue to take part in it.

3–027   **2.** The appropriate body is satisfied that there are reasonable arrangements in place for ensuring that the requirements of Schedule 2 will be met.

SCHEDULE 2   REGULATION 3(D)

STEPS WHICH THE PERSON CONDUCTING THE PROJECT MUST TAKE

3–028   **1.** R must take reasonable steps to identify a person who—

(a) otherwise than in a professional capacity or for remuneration, is engaged in caring for P or is interested in P's welfare, and

(b) is prepared to be consulted by R under this Schedule.

3–029   **2.** If R is unable to identify such a person he must, in accordance with guidance issued by the Secretary of State, nominate a person who—

(a) is prepared to be consulted by R under this Schedule, but

(b) has no connection with the project.

3–030   **3.** R must provide the person identified under paragraph 1, or nominated under paragraph 2, with information about the project and ask him—

(a) for advice as to whether research of the kind proposed should be carried out in relation to P, and

(b) what, in his opinion, P's wishes and feelings about such research being carried out would be likely to be if P had capacity in relation to the matter.

3–031   **4.** If, at any time, the person consulted advises R that in his opinion P's wishes and feelings would be likely to lead him to wish to withdraw from the project if he had capacity in relation to the matter, R must ensure that P is withdrawn from it.

3–032   **5.** The fact that a person is the donee of a lasting power of attorney given by P, or is P's deputy, does not prevent him from being the person consulted under paragraphs 1 to 4.

3–033   **6.** R must ensure that nothing is done in relation to P in the course of the research which would be contrary to—

(a) an advance decision of his which has effect, or

(b) any other form of statement made by him and not subsequently withdrawn,
of which R is aware.

7. The interests of P must be assumed to outweigh those of science and society.   **3–034**

8. If P indicates (in any way) that he wishes the research in relation to him to be discontinued, it   **3–035**
must be discontinued without delay.

9. The research in relation to P must be discontinued without delay if at any time R has reasonable   **3–036**
grounds for believing that the requirement set out in paragraph 1 of Schedule 1 is no longer met or
that there are no longer reasonable arrangements in place for ensuring that the requirements of this
Schedule are met in relation to P.

10. R must conduct the research in accordance with the provision made in the protocol referred to   **3–037**
in paragraph 1 of Schedule 1 for research to be carried out in relation to a person who has consented to
take part in the project but loses capacity to consent to continue to take part in it.

THE LASTING POWERS OF ATTORNEY, ENDURING POWERS OF ATTORNEY AND PUBLIC GUARDIAN REGULATIONS 2007

(SI 2007/1253)

Dated April 16, 2007 and made by the Lord Chancellor under the Mental Capacity Act 2005 (c.9) ss.13(6)(a), 58(3) and 64(1), Schs 1 and 4.

GENERAL NOTE

3–038   These Regulations supplement the requirements set out in Sch.1 to the Act which apply to the making and registration of lasting powers of attorney and the requirements set out in Sch.4 which apply to the registration of enduring powers of attorney. The Regulations also confer functions on the Public Guardian and make other provision in connection with functions conferred on him by the Act or by these Regulations.

CONTENTS

PART 1

Preliminary

PART 2

LASTING POWERS OF ATTORNEY

Instruments intended to create a lasting power of attorney

Registering the instrument

Post-registration

PART 1

PRELIMINARY

Citation and commencement

3–039   **1.**—(1) These Regulations may be cited as the Lasting Powers of Attorney, Enduring Powers of Attorney and Public Guardian Regulations 2007.

(2) These Regulations shall come into force on 1 October 2007.

Interpretation

3–040   **2.**—(1) In these Regulations—

"the Act" means the Mental Capacity Act 2005;

"court" means the Court of Protection;

"LPA certificate", in relation to an instrument made with a view to creating a lasting power of attorney, means the certificate which is required to be included in the instrument by virtue of paragraph 2(1)(e) of Schedule 1 to the Act;

"[person to notify]", in relation to an instrument made with a view to creating a lasting power of attorney, means a person who [, under Schedule 1, paragraph 2(1)(c)(i) of the Act,] is named in the instrument as being a person to be notified of any application for the registration of the instrument;

"prescribed information", in relation to any instrument intended to create a lasting power of attorney, means the information contained in the form used for the instrument which appears under the heading ["Section 8—Your legal rights and responsibilities"].

AMENDMENTS
The amendments to this rule were made by SI 2015/899 r.4.   **3–041**

Minimal differences from forms prescribed in these Regulations

3.—(1) In these Regulations, any reference to a form—   **3–042**
  (a) in the case of a form set out in Schedules 1 to 7 to these Regulations, is to be regarded as including a Welsh version of that form; and
  (b) in the case of a form set out in Schedules 2 to 7 to these Regulations, is to be regarded as also including—
     (i) a form to the same effect but which differs in an immaterial respect in form or mode of expression;
     (ii) a form to the same effect but with such variations as the circumstances may require or the court or the Public Guardian may approve; or
     (iii) a Welsh version of a form within (i) or (ii).

Computation of time

4.—(1) This regulation shows how to calculate any period of time which is   **3–043**
specified in these Regulations.

(2) A period of time expressed as a number of days must be computed as clear days.

(3) Where the specified period is 7 days or less, and would include a day which is not a business day, that day does not count.

(4) When the specified period for doing any act at the office of the Public Guardian ends on a day on which the office is closed, that act will be done in time if done on the next day on which the office is open.

(5) In this regulation—

"business day" means a day other than—
  (a) a Saturday, Sunday, Christmas Day or Good Friday; or
  (b) a bank holiday under the Banking and Financial Dealings Act 1971, in England and Wales; and

"clear days" means that in computing the number of days—
  (a) the day on which the period begins, and
  (b) if the end of the period is defined by reference to an event, the day on which that event occurs,

are not included.

PART 2

LASTING POWERS OF ATTORNEY

Instruments intended to create a lasting power of attorney

Forms for lasting powers of attorney

3–044   **5.**—(1) The forms set out in Parts 1 and 2 of Schedule 1 to these Regulations are the forms which, in the circumstances to which they apply, are to be used for instruments intended to create a lasting power of attorney.

GENERAL NOTE

3–045   The donor of an LPA and the witnesses to the signing need not be in the same room as long as they are in sight of each other (*Re Clarke* (COP) September 19, 2011).

Maximum number of [people to notify]

3–046   **6.**—The maximum number of [people to notify] that the donor of a lasting power of attorney may specify in the instrument intended to create the power is 5.

AMENDMENTS

3–047   The amendments to this rule were made by SI 2015/899 r.5.

3–047A   **7.**—[*Repealed by SI 2015/899 r.6*]

Persons who may provide an LPA certificate

3–048   **8.**—(1) Subject to paragraph (3), the following persons may give an LPA certificate—

(a) a person chosen by the donor as being someone who has known him personally for the period of at least two years which ends immediately before the date on which that person signs the LPA certificate;

(b) a person chosen by the donor who, on account of his professional skills and expertise, reasonably considers that he is competent to make the judgments necessary to certify the matters set out in paragraph (2)(1)(e) of Schedule 1 to the Act.

(2) The following are examples of persons within paragraph (1)(b)—

(a) a registered health care professional;

(b) a barrister, solicitor or advocate called or admitted in any part of the United Kingdom;

(c) a registered social worker; or

(d) an independent mental capacity advocate.

(3) A person is disqualified from giving an LPA certificate in respect of any instrument intended to create a lasting power of attorney if that person is—

(a) a family member of the donor;

(b) a donee of that power;

(c) a donee of—

    (i) any other lasting power of attorney, or

    (ii) an enduring power of attorney,

which has been executed by the donor (whether or not it has been revoked);

(d) a family member of a donee within sub-paragraph (b);

(e) a director or employee of a trust corporation acting as a donee within sub-paragraph (b);

(f) a business partner or employee of—
  (i) the donor, or
  (ii) a donee within sub-paragraph (b);
(g) an owner, director, manager or employee of any care home in which the donor is living when the instrument is executed; or
(h) a family member of a person within sub-paragraph (g).
  (4) In this regulation—
  "care home" has the meaning given in section 3 of the Care Standards Act 2000;
  "registered health care professional" means a person who is a member of a profession regulated by a body mentioned in section 25(3) of the National Health Service Reform and Health Care Professions Act 2002; and
  "registered social worker" means a person registered as a social worker in a register maintained by—
[(a) the Health and Care Professions [Council];
(b) the Care Council for Wales;
(c) the Scottish Social Services Council; or
(d) the Northern Ireland Social Care Council.

AMENDMENT
The amendment to this regulation was made by SI 2012/1479 Sch.1, Pt 1, para.81.　**3–049**

GENERAL NOTE
Paragraph (3)(a)

The term "family member" is not defined. In *Re Kittle* (COP) December 1, 2009, Senior　**3–050**
Judge Lush, in finding that a first cousin was not a member of the family of the donor,
followed the decision of the Court of Appeal in *Langdon v Horton* [1951] 1 All E.R. 60,
where, in the context of the Rent Acts, the court adopted an objective approach to deciding the meaning of "member of the tenant's family". This approach required the court to
consider whether the "ordinary man" would consider the relationship in question to fall
within the meaning of "member of the family". *Kittle* was cited in *Re Phillips* (COP) May
16, 2012, where Judge Lush said at para.28:

"In my judgment, anyone who describes himself in this context as the attorney's partner
is courting trouble and automatically disqualifies himself from being a person who can
give an LPA certificate. This applies regardless of whether he describes himself as the
attorney's partner intentionally or inadvertently, whether they live at the same address
or at separate locations, whether the relationship is intimate or platonic, and whether the
statement is true or false."

Paragraph (3)(f)

In *Re Putt* (COP), March 22, 2011 at para.13, Judge Lush said:　**3–051**

"The words 'business partner or employee' are ordinary words of the English language
and should be construed in the way that an ordinary sensible person would construe
them. The choice of the word 'business' is designed to distinguish partnership as an
economic relationship from partnership of a more personal and intimate nature. I
assume that Parliament was looking at the substance rather than the form and intended
to include all kinds of 'business partner' under this umbrella term – equity partner, sala-
ried partner, fixed-share partner, and so on – and that, if it had intended to treat business
arrangements under the Limited Liability Partnership Act 2000 any differently from
those under the Partnership Act 1890, it would have expressly said so in the regulations. The word 'employee' probably denotes no more than a person who is employed

and remunerated by the business and is generally, though not necessarily, of a junior or subordinate status to the attorney."

Judge Lush held, at para.15, that "the wording of regulation 8(3)(f) cannot be construed as making any distinction between a partnership under the Partnership Act 1890 and the Limited Liability Partnership Act 2000 for the purpose of providing an LPA certificate".

Execution of instrument

3–052 **9.**—(1) An instrument intended to create a lasting power of attorney must be executed in accordance with this regulation.

(2) The donor must read (or have read to him) all the prescribed information.

(3) As soon as reasonably practicable after the steps required by paragraph (2) have been taken, the donor must—

(a) complete the provisions of Sections 1 to 7 of the instrument that apply to him (or direct another person to do so); and

[(b) subject to paragraph (7), in the presence of a witness—

(i) sign Section 9 of the instrument if the instrument is intended to create a lasting power of attorney for property and financial affairs (Form LP1F); or

(ii) sign Sections 5 and 9 of the instrument if the instrument is intended to create a lasting power of attorney for health and welfare (Form LP1H);]

(4) As soon as reasonably practicable after the steps required by paragraph (3) have been taken—

(a) the person giving an LPA certificate, [. . .]

(b) [. . .]

must complete the LPA certificate at [Section 10] of the instrument and sign it.

(5) As soon as reasonably practicable after the steps required by paragraph (4) have been taken—

(a) the donee, or

(b) if more than one, each of the donees,

must read (or have read to him) all the prescribed information.

(6) As soon as reasonably practicable after the steps required by paragraph (5) have been taken, the donee or, if more than one, each of them—

(a) must complete the provisions of [Section 11] of the instrument that apply to him (or direct another person to do so); and

(b) subject to paragraph (7), must sign [Section 11] of the instrument in the presence of a witness.

(7) If the instrument is to be signed by any person at the direction of the donor, or at the direction of any donee, the signature must be done in the presence of two witnesses.

(8) For the purposes of this regulation—

(a) the donor may not witness any signature required for the power;

(b) a donee may not witness any signature required for the power apart from that of another donee.

(9) A person witnessing a signature must—

(a) sign the instrument; and

(b) give his full name and address.

(10) Any reference in this regulation to a person signing an instrument (however expressed) includes his signing it by means of a mark made on the instrument at the appropriate place.

3–053

Registering the instrument

Notice to be given by a person about to apply for registration of lasting power of attorney
10. Schedule 2 to these Regulations sets out the form of notice ([Form LPA3])   **3–054**
which must be given by a donor or donee who is about to make an application for
the registration of an instrument intended to create a lasting power of attorney.

3–055

[Application for registration
11.—(1) An application to the Public Guardian for the registration of an instru-   **3–056**
ment intended to create a lasting power of attorney that is in Form LP1F or LP1H
must be made by completion of Sections 12 and 13, the relevant parts of Section
14 and Section 15 of that Form.

(2) An application to the Public Guardian for the registration of an instrument
intended to create a lasting power of attorney that is in a pre-July 2015 form must
be made by using Form LP2 set out in Schedule 3 to these Regulations.

(3) An application to the Public Guardian for the registration of an instrument
intended to create a lasting power of attorney where the application is a repeat
application ("a reduced fee repeat application") may only be made if—

(a) the initial application for the registration of a lasting power of attorney is
made on or after 1st October 2011;

(b) the initial application was returned to the applicant as invalid;

(c) the reduced fee repeat application is submitted for registration within three
months of the date on which the initial application was returned to the applicant as invalid; and

(d) the reduced fee for such applications applies.

(4) Where the initial application for the registration of the lasting power of
attorney was made in accordance with paragraph (1) using Form LP1F or LP1H,
a reduced fee repeat application must also be made by the completion of Form
LP1F or LP1H as appropriate, including completion of the repeat application
option in Section 14 of that Form.

(5) Where the initial application for the registration of the lasting power of
attorney was made in accordance with paragraph (2) using a pre-July 2015 form,
a reduced fee repeat application must be made by the completion of Form LP1F
or LP1H as appropriate, including completion of the repeat application option in
Section 14 of that Form.

(6) Where the instrument to be registered which is sent with the application is
neither—

(a) the original instrument intended to create the power; nor

(b) a certified copy of it,

the Public Guardian must not register the instrument unless the court directs the
Public Guardian to do so.

(7) In this regulation—

(a) "pre-July 2015 form" means a valid instrument intended to create a lasting power of attorney that is not in Form LP1F or LP1H but that complies with these Regulations as they were in force immediately before 1st July 2015; and

(b) "certified copy" means a photographic or other facsimile copy which is certified as an accurate copy by—

(i) the donor; or

(ii) a solicitor or notary.]

AMENDMENT

3–057   This rule was substituted by SI 2015/899 r.9.

GENERAL NOTE

3–058   The fee prescribed in the Schedule to the Public Guardian (Fees, etc) Regulations 2007 (SI 2007/2051) shall be payable upon the application to register. A reduced fee is payable upon a repeat application (SI 2007/2051 regs 3, 5).

Period to elapse before registration in cases not involving objection or defect

3–059   12. The period at the end of which the Public Guardian must register an instrument in accordance with paragraph 5 of Schedule 1 to the Act is the period of [four weeks] beginning with—

(a) the date on which the Public Guardian gave the notice or notices under paragraph 7 or 8 of Schedule 1 to the Act of receipt of an application for registration; or

(b) if notices were given on more than one date, the latest of those dates.

AMENDMENT

3–060   The amendment to this regulation was made by SI 2013/506 reg.3.

Notice of receipt of application for registration

3–061   13.—(1) Part 1 of Schedule 4 to these Regulations sets out the form of notice ("LPA 003A") which the Public Guardian must give to the donee (or donees) when the Public Guardian receives an application for the registration of a lasting power of attorney.

(2) Part 2 of Schedule 4 sets out the form of notice ("LPA 003B") which the Public Guardian must give to the donor when the Public Guardian receives such an application.

(3) Where it appears to the Public Guardian that there is good reason to do so, the Public Guardian must also provide (or arrange for the provision of) an explanation to the donor of—

(a) the notice referred to in paragraph (2) and what the effect of it is; and

(b) why it is being brought to his attention.

(4) Any information provided under paragraph (3) must be provided—

(a) to the donor personally; and

(b) in a way that is appropriate to the donor's circumstances (for example using simple language, visual aids or other appropriate means).

Objection to registration: notice to Public Guardian [to be given by the donee of the power or a [person to notify]]

3–062   14.—(1) This regulation deals with any objection to the registration of an instrument as a lasting power of attorney which is to be made to the Public Guardian [by the donee of the power or a [person to notify].

(2) Where [the donee of the power or a [person to notify]

(a) is entitled to receive notice under paragraph 6, 7 or 8 of Schedule 1 to the Act of an application for the registration of the instrument, and

(b) wishes to object to registration on a ground set out in paragraph 13(1) of Schedule 1 to the Act,

he must do so before the end of the period of [three weeks] beginning with the date on which the notice is given.

(3) A notice of objection must be given in writing, setting out—

(a) the name and address of the objector;

(b) [. . .] the name and address of the donor of the power;

(c) if known, the name and address of the donee (or donees); and

(d) the ground for making the objection.

(4) The Public Guardian must notify the objector as to whether he is satisfied that the ground of the objection is established.

(5) At any time after receiving the notice of objection and before giving the notice required by paragraph (4), the Public Guardian may require the objector to provide such further information,
or produce such documents, as the Public Guardian reasonably considers necessary to enable him to determine whether the ground for making the objection is established.

(6) Where—

(a) the Public Guardian is satisfied that the ground of the objection is established, but

(b) by virtue of section 13(7) of the Act, the instrument is not revoked,

the notice under paragraph (4) must contain a statement to that effect.

(7) Nothing in this regulation prevents an objector from making a further objection under paragraph 13 of Schedule 1 to the Act where—

(a) the notice under paragraph (4) indicates that the Public Guardian is not satisfied that the particular ground of objection to which that notice relates is established; and

(b) the period specified in paragraph (2) has not expired.

AMENDMENTS

The amendments to this regulation were made by SI 2007/2161 reg.3, SI 2013/506 reg.4 and SI 2015/899 r.10.

3–063

[Objection to registration: notice to Public Guardian to be given by the donor

14A.—(1) This regulation deals with any objection to the registration of an instrument as a lasting power of attorney which is to be made to the Public Guardian by the donor of the power.

3–064

(2) Where the donor of the power—

(a) is entitled to receive notice under paragraph 8 of Schedule 1 to the Act of an application for the registration of the instrument, and

(b) wishes to object to the registration, he must do so before the end of the period of [three weeks] beginning with the date on which the notice is given.

(3) The donor of the power must give notice of his objection in writing to the Public Guardian, setting out—

(a) the name and address of the donor of the power;

(b) if known, the name and address of the donee (or donees); and

(c) the ground for making the objection.]

AMENDMENTS
3–065   This regulation was inserted by SI 2007/2161 reg.4. The amendment to it was made by SI 2013/506 reg.5.

Objection to registration: application to the court
3–066   **15.**—(1) This regulation deals with any objection to the registration of an instrument as a lasting power of attorney which is to be made to the court.

(2) The grounds for making an application to the court are—

(a) that one or more of the requirements for the creation of a lasting power of attorney have not been met;

(b) that the power has been revoked, or has otherwise come to an end, on a ground other than the grounds set out in paragraph 13(1) of Schedule 1 to the Act;

(c) any of the grounds set out in paragraph (a) or (b) of section 22(3) of the Act.

(3) Where any person—

(a) is entitled to receive notice under paragraph 6, 7 or 8 of Schedule 1 to the Act of an application for the registration of the instrument, and

(b) wishes to object to registration on one or more of the grounds set out in paragraph (2),

he must make an application to the court before the end of the period of [three weeks] beginning with the date on which the notice is given.

(4) The notice of an application to the court, which a person making an objection to the court is required to give to the Public Guardian under paragraph 13(3) (b)(ii) of Schedule 1 to the Act, must be in writing.

AMENDMENT
3–067   The amendment to this regulation was made by SI 2013/506 reg.6.

Notifying applicants of non-registration of lasting power of attorney
3–068   **16.** Where the Public Guardian is prevented from registering an instrument as a lasting power of attorney by virtue of—

(a) paragraph 11(1) of Schedule 1 to the Act (instrument not made in accordance with Schedule),

(b) paragraph 12(2) of that Schedule (deputy already appointed),

(c) paragraph 13(2) of that Schedule (objection by donee or named person on grounds of bankruptcy, disclaimer, death etc),

(d) paragraph 14(2) of that Schedule (objection by donor), or

(e) regulation 11(2) of these Regulations (application for registration not accompanied by original instrument or certified copy),

he must notify the person (or persons) who applied for registration of that fact.

Notice to be given on registration of lasting power of attorney
3–069   **17.**—(1) Where the Public Guardian registers an instrument as a lasting power of attorney, he must—

(a) retain a copy of the instrument; and

(b) return to the person (or persons) who applied for registration the original instrument, or the certified copy of it, which accompanied the application for registration.

(2) Schedule 5 to these Regulations sets out the form of notice ("LPA 004")

which the Public Guardian must give to the donor and donee (or donees) when the Public Guardian registers an instrument.

(3) Where it appears to the Public Guardian that there is good reason to do so, the Public Guardian must also provide (or arrange for the provision of) an explanation to the donor of—

(a) the notice referred to in paragraph (2) and what the effect of it is; and

(b) why it is being brought to his attention.

(4) Any information provided under paragraph (3) must be provided—

(a) to the donor personally; and

(b) in a way that is appropriate to the donor's circumstances (for example using simple language, visual aids or other appropriate means).

(5) "Certified copy" is to be construed in accordance with regulation 11(3).

Post-registration

Changes to instrument registered as lasting power of attorney

18.—(1) This regulation applies in any case where any of paragraphs 21 to 24   **3–070**
of Schedule 1 to the Act requires the Public Guardian to attach a note to an instrument registered as a lasting power of attorney.

(2) The Public Guardian must give a notice to the donor and the donee (or, if more than one, each of them) requiring him to deliver to the Public Guardian—

(a) the original [. . .] instrument which was sent to the Public Guardian for registration;

(b) any office copy of that registered instrument; and

(c) any certified copy of that registered instrument.

(3) On receipt of the document, the Public Guardian must—

(a) attach the required note; and

(b) return the document to the person from whom it was obtained.

AMENDMENT

The word omitted in para.(2)(a) was repealed by SI 2009/1884 reg.3.   **3–071**

Loss or destruction of instrument registered as lasting power of attorney

19.—(1) This regulation applies where—   **3–072**

(a) a person is required by or under the Act to deliver up to the Public Guardian any of the following documents—

   (i) an instrument registered as a lasting power of attorney;

   (ii) an office copy of that registered instrument;

   (iii) a certified copy of that registered instrument; and

(b) the document has been lost or destroyed.

(2) The person required to deliver up the document must provide to the Public Guardian in writing—

(a) if known, the date of the loss or destruction and the circumstances in which it occurred;

(b) otherwise, a statement of when he last had the document in his possession.

Disclaimer of appointment by a donee of lasting power of attorney

20.—(1) Schedule 6 to these Regulations sets out the form ("LPA 005") which   **3–073**
a donee of an instrument registered as a lasting power of attorney must use to disclaim his appointment as donee.

(2) The donee must send—

(a) the completed form to the donor; and

(b) a copy of it to—

    (i) the Public Guardian; and

    (ii) any other donee who, for the time being, is appointed under the power.

Revocation by donor of lasting power of attorney

3–074   **21.**—(1)A donor who revokes a lasting power to attorney must—

(a) notify the Public Guardian that he has done so; and

(b) notify the donee (or, if more than one, each of them) of the revocation.

(2) Where the Public Guardian receives a notice under paragraph (1)(a), he must cancel the registration of the instrument creating the power if he is satisfied that the donor has taken such steps as are necessary in law to revoke it.

(3) The Public Guardian may require the donor to provide such further information, or produce such documents, as the Public Guardian reasonably considers necessary to enable him to determine whether the steps necessary for revocation have been taken.

(4) Where the Public Guardian cancels the registration of the instrument he must notify—

(a) the donor; and

(b) the donee or, if more than one, each of them.

Revocation of a lasting power of attorney on death of donor

3–075   **22.**—(1) The Public Guardian must cancel the registration of an instrument as a lasting power of attorney if he is satisfied that the power has been revoked as a result of the donor's death.

(2) Where the Public Guardian cancels the registration of an instrument he must notify the donee or, if more than one, each of them.

PART 3

ENDURING POWERS OF ATTORNEY

Notice of intention to apply for registration of enduring power of attorney

3–076   **23.**—(1) Schedule 7 to these Regulations sets out the form of notice ("EP1PG") which an attorney (or attorneys) under an enduring power of attorney must give of his intention to make an application for the registration of the instrument creating the power.

(2) In the case of the notice to be given to the donor, the attorney must also provide (or arrange for the provision of) an explanation to the donor of—

(a) the notice and what the effect of it is; and

(b) why it is being brought to his attention.

(3) The information provided under paragraph (2) must be provided—

(a) to the donor personally; and

(b) in a way that is appropriate to the donor's circumstances (for example using simple language, visual aids or other appropriate means).

Application for registration

3–077   **24.**—(1) Schedule 8 to these Regulations sets out the form ("EP2PG") which must be used for making an application to the Public Guardian for the registration of an instrument creating an enduring power of attorney.

[(1A) The Public Guardian must not register an instrument where only a certified copy of the instrument is sent with the application, unless the applicant verifies that he cannot produce the original instrument because it has been lost or, as the case may be, destroyed.]

(2) Where the instrument to be registered which is sent with the application is neither—

(a) the original instrument creating the power, nor

(b) a certified copy of it [in relation to which paragraph (1A) has been complied with],

the Public Guardian must not register the instrument unless the court directs him to do so.

(3) "Certified copy", in relation to an enduring power of attorney, means a copy certified in accordance with section 3 of the Powers of Attorney Act 1971.

AMENDMENTS

The amendments to this regulation were made by SI 2010/1063 reg.3.　　　　**3–078**

GENERAL NOTE

The fee prescribed in the Schedule to the Public Guardian (Fees, etc) Regulations 2007 　**3–079**
(SI 2007/2051) shall be payable upon the application to register (2007/2051 regs 3, 4).

Notice of objection to registration

25.—(1) This regulation deals with any objection to the registration of an 　**3–080**
instrument creating an enduring power of attorney which is to be made to the
Public Guardian under paragraph 13(4) of Schedule 4 to the Act.

(2) A notice of objection must be given in writing, setting out—

(a) the name and address of the objector;

(b) if different, the name and address of the donor of the power;

(c) if known, the name and address of the attorney (or attorneys); and

(d) the ground for making the objection.

Notifying applicants of non-registration of enduring power of attorney

26. Where the Public Guardian is prevented from registering an instrument 　**3–081**
creating an enduring power of attorney by virtue of—

(a) paragraph 13(2) of Schedule 4 to the Act (deputy already appointed),

(b) paragraph 13(5) of that Schedule (receipt by Public Guardian of valid notice
of objection from person entitled to notice of application to register),

(c) paragraph 13(7) of that Schedule (Public Guardian required to undertake
appropriate enquiries in certain circumstances), or

(d) regulation 24(2) of these Regulations (application for registration not
accompanied by original instrument or certified copy),

he must notify the person (or persons) who applied for registration of that fact.

Registration of instrument creating an enduring power of attorney

27.—(1) Where the Public Guardian registers an instrument creating an endur- 　**3–082**
ing power of attorney, he must—

(a) retain a copy of the instrument; and

(b) return to the person (or persons) who applied for registration the original
instrument, or the certified copy of it, which accompanied the application.

(2) "Certified copy" has the same meaning as in regulation 24(3).

Objection or revocation not applying to all joint and several attorneys

3–083   **28.** In a case within paragraph 20(6) or (7) of Schedule 4 to the Act, the form of the entry to be made in the register in respect of an instrument creating the enduring power of attorney is a stamp bearing the following words (inserting the information indicated, as appropriate)—

"THE REGISTRATION OF THIS ENDURING POWER OF ATTORNEY IS QUALIFIED AND EXTENDS TO THE APPOINTMENT OF . . . . (insert name of attorney(s) not affected by ground(s) of objection or revocation) ONLY AS THE ATTORNEY(S) OF . . . . (insert name of donor)".

Loss or destruction of instrument registered as enduring power of attorney

3–084   **29.**—(1)This regulation applies where—
(a) a person is required by or under the Act to deliver up to the Public Guardian any of the following documents—
  (i) an instrument registered as an enduring power of attorney;
  (ii) an office copy of that registered instrument; or
  (iii) a certified copy of that registered instrument; and
(b) the document has been lost or destroyed.

(2) The person who is required to deliver up the document must provide to the Public Guardian in writing—
(a) if known, the date of the loss or destruction and the circumstances in which it occurred;
(b) otherwise, a statement of when he last had the document in his possession.

PART 4

FUNCTIONS OF THE PUBLIC GUARDIAN

The registers

Establishing and maintaining the registers

3–085   **30.**—(1) In this Part "the registers" means—
(a) the register of lasting powers of attorney,
(b) the register of enduring powers of attorney, and (c) the register of court orders appointing deputies,
which the Public Guardian must establish and maintain.

(2) On each register the Public Guardian may include—
(a) such descriptions of information about a registered instrument or a registered order as the
Public Guardian considers appropriate; and
(b) entries which relate to an instrument or order for which registration has been cancelled.

Disclosure of information on a register: search by the Public Guardian

3–086   **31.**—(1)Any person may, by an application made under paragraph (2), request the Public Guardian to carry out a search of one or more of the registers. (2) An application must—
(a) state—

(i) the register or registers to be searched;

(ii) the name of the person to whom the application relates; and

(iii) such other details about that person as the Public Guardian may require for the purpose of carrying out the search; and

(b) be accompanied by any fee provided for under section 58(4)(b) of the Act.

(3) The Public Guardian may require the applicant to provide such further information, or produce such documents, as the Public Guardian reasonably considers necessary to enable him to carry out the search.

(4) As soon as reasonably practicable after receiving the application—

(a) the Public Guardian must notify the applicant of the result of the search; and

(b) in the event that it reveals one or more entries on the register, the Public Guardian must disclose to the applicant all the information appearing on the register in respect of each entry.

Disclosure of additional information held by the Public Guardian

32.—(1) This regulation applies in any case where, as a result of a search made under regulation 31, a person has obtained information relating to a registered instrument or a registered order which confers authority to make decisions about matters concerning a person ("P"). **3–087**

(2) On receipt of an application made in accordance with paragraph (4), the Public Guardian may, if he considers that there is good reason to do so, disclose to the applicant such additional information as he considers appropriate.

(3) "Additional information" means any information relating to P—

(a) which the Public Guardian has obtained in exercising the functions conferred on him under the Act; but

(b) which does not appear on the register.

(4) An application must state—

(a) the name of P;

(b) the reasons for making the application; and

(c) what steps, if any, the applicant has taken to obtain the information from P.

(5) The Public Guardian may require the applicant to provide such further information, or produce such documents, as the Public Guardian reasonably considers necessary to enable him to determine the application.

(6) In determining whether to disclose any additional information [relating] to P, the Public Guardian must, in particular, have regard to—

(a) the connection between P and the applicant;

(b) the reasons for requesting the information (in particular, why the information cannot or should not be obtained directly from P);

(c) the benefit to P, or any detriment he may suffer, if a disclosure is made; and

(d) any detriment that another person may suffer if a disclosure is made.

AMENDMENT

The word in square brackets in para.(6) was inserted by SI 2009/1884 reg.4.   **3–088**

Security for discharge of functions

Persons required to give security for the discharge of their functions

33.—(1) This regulation applies in any case where the court orders a person ("S") to give to the Public Guardian security for the discharge of his functions.   **3–089**

(2) The security must be given by S—

(a) by means of a bond which is entered into in accordance with regulation 34; or

(b) in such other manner as the court may direct.

(3) For the purposes of paragraph (2)(a), S complies with the requirement to give the security only if—

(a) the endorsement required by regulation 34(2) has been provided; and

(b) the person who provided it has notified the Public Guardian of that fact.

(4) For the purposes of paragraph (2)(b), S complies with the requirement to give the security—

(a) in any case where the court directs that any other endorsement must be provided, only if—

(i) that endorsement has been provided; and

(ii) the person who provided it has notified the Public Guardian of that fact;

(b) in any case where the court directs that any other requirements must be met in relation to the giving of the security, only if the Public Guardian is satisfied that those other requirements have been met.

Security given under regulation 33(2)(a): requirement for endorsement

3–090   **34.**—(1) This regulation has effect for the purposes of regulation 33(2)(a).

(2) A bond is entered into in accordance with this regulation only if it is endorsed by—

(a) an authorised insurance company; or

(b) an authorised deposit-taker.

(3) A person may enter into the bond under—

(a) arrangements made by the Public Guardian; or

(b) other arrangements which are made by the person entering into the bond or on his behalf.

(4) The Public Guardian may make arrangements with any person specified in paragraph (2) with a view to facilitating the provision by them of bonds which persons required to give security to the Public Guardian may enter into.

(5) In this regulation—

"authorised insurance company" means—

(a) a person who has permission under Part 4 of the Financial Services and Markets Act 2000 to effect or carry out contracts of insurance;

(b) an EEA firm of the kind mentioned in paragraph 5(d) of Schedule 3 to that Act, which has permission under paragraph 15 of that Schedule to effect or carry out contracts of insurance;

(c) a person who carries on insurance market activity (within the meaning given in section 3 16(3) of that Act); and

"authorised deposit-taker" means—

(a) a person who has permission under Part 4 of the Financial Services and Markets Act 2000 to accept deposits;

(b) an EEA firm of the kind mentioned in paragraph 5(d) of Schedule 3 to that Act, which has permission under paragraph 15 of that Schedule to accept deposits.

(6) The definitions of "authorised insurance company" and "authorised deposit-taker" must be read with—

(a) section 22 of the Financial Services and Markets Act 2000;

(b) any relevant order under that section; and

(c) Schedule 2 to that Act.

GENERAL NOTE
Paragraph (4)
   This paragraph allows the Public Guardian to make arrangements to facilitate the provi-   **3–091**
sion of bonds. The arrangement is commonly called "the Scheme". The Scheme provides
suitable surety bonds for the purposes of security to all deputies appointed by the Court.
From October 2012, the Scheme is administered by Deputy Bond Services. Deputies
are not bound to enter into an arrangement within the Scheme and can seek their own
arrangements. Public Guardian Practice Note No.03/2012 sets out the Public Guardian's
expectations for any company seeking to provide bonds outside of the Scheme. It can be
accessed at: *www.justice.gov.uk/downloads/protecting-the-vulnerable/mca/pg-note-03-12-*
surety-bonds.pdf.

Security given under regulation 33(2)(a): maintenance or replacement
   35.—(1) This regulation applies to any security given under regulation 33(2)   **3–092**
(a).
   (2) At such times or at such intervals as the Public Guardian may direct by
notice in writing, any person ("S") who has given the security must satisfy the
Public Guardian that any premiums payable in respect of it have been paid.
   (3) Where S proposes to replace a security already given by him, the new
security is not to be regarded as having been given until the Public Guardian is
satisfied that—
   (a) the requirements set out in sub-paragraphs (a) and (b) of regulation 3 3(3)
       have been met in relation to it; and
   (b) no payment is due from S in connection with the discharge of his functions.
   [(4) The Public Guardian must, if satisfied as to the matters in paragraph (3),
provide written notice of that fact to S within 2 weeks of being given notification
in accordance with regulation 33(3)(b) in relation to the new security.]

AMENDMENT
   Paragraph (4) was inserted by SI 2013/506 reg.7.   **3–093**

Enforcement following court order of any endorsed security
   36.—(1) This regulation applies to any security given to the Public Guardian in   **3–094**
respect of which an endorsement has been provided.
   (2) Where the court orders the enforcement of the security, the Public Guardian
must—
   (a) notify any person who endorsed the security of the contents of the order; and
   (b) notify the court when payment has been made of the amount secured.

Discharge of any endorsed security
   37.—(1) This regulation applies to any security given by a person ("S") to the   **3–095**
Public Guardian in respect of which an endorsement has been provided.
   (2) The security may be discharged if the court makes an order discharging it.
   [(3) Otherwise the security may not be discharged—
   (a) if the person on whose behalf S was appointed to act dies, until the end of
       the period of 2 years beginning on the date of his death; or
   (b) in any other case, until the end of the period of 7 years beginning on which-
       ever of the following dates first occurs—
       (i) if S dies, the date of his death;
       (ii) if the court makes an order which discharges S but which does not also
            discharge the security under paragraph (2), the date of the order;

(iii) the date when S otherwise ceases to be under a duty to discharge the functions in respect of which he was ordered to give security.]

[(3A) Where S has replaced a security ("the original security") previously given by S and the Public Guardian has provided notice in accordance with regulation 35(4), the original security shall stand discharged 2 years from the date on which that notice was issued unless discharged by earlier order of the court upon application under paragraph (2).]

(4) For the purposes of paragraph (3), if a person takes any step with a view to discharging the security before the end of the period specified in that paragraph, the security is to be treated for all purposes as if it were still in place.

[(5) For the purposes of paragraph (3A), if a person takes any step otherwise than under paragraph (2) with a view to discharging the original security before the end of the period specified paragraph (3A), the security is to be treated for all purposes as if it were still in place.]

AMENDMENTS

3–096   The amendments to this regulation were made by SI 2010/1063 reg.4 and SI 2013/506 reg.8.

Deputies

Application for additional time to submit a report

3–097   **38.**—(1) This regulation applies where the court requires a deputy to submit a report to the Public Guardian and specifies a time or interval for it to be submitted.

(2) A deputy may apply to the Public Guardian requesting more time for submitting a particular report.

(3) An application must—

(a) state the reason for requesting more time; and

(b) contain or be accompanied by such information as the Public Guardian may reasonably require to determine the application.

(4) In response to an application, the Public Guardian may, if he considers it appropriate to do so, undertake that he will not take steps to secure performance of the deputy's duty to submit the report at the relevant time on the condition that the report is submitted on or before such later date as he may specify.

Content of reports

3–098   **39.**—(1) Any report which the court requires a deputy to submit to the Public Guardian must include such material as the court may direct.

(2) The report must also contain or be accompanied by—

(a) specified information or information of a specified description; or

(b) specified documents or documents of a specified description.

(3) But paragraph (2)—

(a) extends only to information or documents which are reasonably required in connection with the exercise by the Public Guardian of functions conferred on him under the Act; and

(b) is subject to paragraph (1) and to any other directions given by the court.

(4) Where powers as respects a person's property and affairs are conferred on a deputy under section 16 of the Act, the information specified by the Public Guardian under paragraph (2) may include accounts which—

(a) deal with specified matters; and

(b) are provided in a specified form.

(5) The Public Guardian may require—

(a) any information provided to be verified in such manner, or

(b) any document produced to be authenticated in such manner, as he may reasonably require.

(6) "Specified" means specified in a notice in writing given to the deputy by the Public Guardian.

Power to require final report on termination of appointment

40.—(1) This regulation applies where—   3–099

(a) the person on whose behalf a deputy was appointed to act has died;

(b) the deputy has died;

(c) the court has made an order discharging the deputy; or

(d) the deputy otherwise ceases to be under a duty to discharge the functions to which his appointment relates.

(2) The Public Guardian may require the deputy (or, in the case of the deputy's death, his personal representatives) to submit a final report on the discharge of his functions.

(3) A final report must be submitted—

(a) before the end of such reasonable period as may be specified; and

(b) at such place as may be specified.

(4) The Public Guardian must consider the final report, together with any other information that he may have relating to the discharge by the deputy of his functions.

(5) Where the Public Guardian is dissatisfied with any aspect of the final report he may apply to the court for an appropriate remedy (including enforcement of security given by the deputy).

(6) "Specified" means specified in a notice in writing given to the deputy or his personal representatives by the Public Guardian.

GENERAL NOTE

In circumstances where the Court has not made an Order directing a final report, this   3–100
regulation provides the Public Guardian with a legal power to require an outgoing deputy
(or his personal representative(s) in the event of the deputy's death) to provide a final report
of his activities as deputy. It gives the Public Guardian power to examine the final report
in conjunction with any existing information held by the Office of the Public Guardian
regarding the way in which the deputy had exercised his powers.

The Public Guardian has published a Practice Note on "Deputy Final Reports"
(No.01/2012) which sets out the general policy of the Public Guardian with regard to the
requesting of a final report from an outgoing Deputy. It can be accessed at: *www.gov.uk/
government/collections/public-guardian-practice-notes.*

Power to require information from deputies

41.—(1) This regulation applies in any case where—   3–101

(a) the Public Guardian has received representations (including complaints) about—

   (i) the way in which a deputy is exercising his powers; or

   (ii) any failure to exercise them; or

(b) it appears to the Public Guardian that there are other circumstances which—

   (i) give rise to concerns about, or dissatisfaction with, the conduct of the deputy (including any failure to act); or

(ii) otherwise constitute good reason to seek information about the deputy's discharge of his functions.

(2) The Public Guardian may require the deputy—
(a) to provide specified information or information of a specified description; or
(b) to produce specified documents or documents of a specified description.

(3) The information or documents must be provided or produced—
(a) before the end of such reasonable period as may be specified; and
(b) at such place as may be specified.

(4) The Public Guardian may require—
(a) any information provided to be verified in such manner, or
(b) any document produced to be authenticated in such manner,
as he may reasonably require.

(5) "Specified" means specified in a notice in writing given to the deputy by the Public Guardian.

Right of deputy to require review of decisions made by the Public Guardian

3–102   **42.**—(1) A deputy may require the Public Guardian to reconsider any decision he has made in relation to the deputy.

(2) The right under paragraph (1) is exercisable by giving notice of exercise of the right to the Public Guardian before the end of the period of 14 days beginning with the date on which notice of the decision is given to the deputy.

(3) The notice of exercise of the right must—
(a) state the grounds on which reconsideration is required; and
(b) contain or be accompanied by any relevant information or documents.

(4) At any time after receiving the notice and before reconsidering the decision to which it relates, the Public Guardian may require the deputy to provide him with such further information, or to produce such documents, as he reasonably considers necessary to enable him to reconsider the matter.

(5) The Public Guardian must give to the deputy—
(a) written notice of his decision on reconsideration, and
(b) if he upholds the previous decision, a statement of his reasons.

Miscellaneous functions

Applications to the Court of Protection

3–103   **43.** The Public Guardian has the function of making applications to the court in connection with his functions under the Act in such circumstances as he considers it necessary or appropriate to do so.

Visits by the Public Guardian or by Court of Protection Visitors at his direction

3–104   **44.**—(1) This regulation applies where the Public Guardian visits, or directs a Court of Protection Visitor to visit, any person under any provision of the Act or these Regulations.

(2) The Public Guardian must notify (or make arrangements to notify) the person to be visited of—
(a) the date or dates on which it is proposed that the visit will take place;
(b) to the extent that it is practicable to do so, any specific matters likely to be covered in the course of the visit; and

(c) any proposal to inform any other person that the visit is to take place.

(3) Where the visit is to be carried out by a Court of Protection Visitor—

(a) the Public Guardian may—

(i) give such directions to the Visitor, and

(ii) provide him with such information concerning the person to be visited, as the Public Guardian considers necessary for the purposes of enabling the visit to take place and the Visitor to prepare any report the Public Guardian may require; and

(b) the Visitor must seek to carry out the visit and take all reasonable steps to obtain such other information as he considers necessary for the purpose of preparing a report.

(4) A Court of Protection Visitor must submit any report requested by the Public Guardian in accordance with any timetable specified by the Public Guardian.

(5) If he considers it appropriate to do so, the Public Guardian may, in relation to any person interviewed in the course of preparing a report—

(a) disclose the report to him; and

(b) invite him to comment on it.

Functions in relation to persons carrying out specific transactions

45.—(1) This regulation applies where, in accordance with an order made under section 16(2)(a) of the Act, a person ("T") has been authorised to carry out any transaction for a person who lacks capacity.   **3–105**

(2) The Public Guardian has the functions of—

(a) receiving any reports from T which the court may require;

(b) dealing with representations (including complaints) about—

(i) the way in which the transaction has been or is being carried out; or

(ii) any failure to carry it out.

(3) Regulations 38 to 41 have effect in relation to T as they have effect in relation a deputy.

Power to require information from donees of lasting power of attorney

46.—(1) This regulation applies where it appears to the Public Guardian that there are circumstances suggesting that the donee of a lasting power of attorney may—   **3–106**

(a) have behaved, or may be behaving, in a way that contravenes his authority or is not in the best interests of the donor of the power,

(b) be proposing to behave in a way that would contravene that authority or would not be in the donor's best interests, or

(c) have failed to comply with the requirements of an order made, or directions given, by the court.

(2) The Public Guardian may require the donee—

(a) to provide specified information or information of a specified description; or

(b) to produce specified documents or documents of a specified description.

(3) The information or documents must be provided or produced—

(a) before the end of such reasonable period as may be specified; and

(b) at such place as may be specified.

(4) The Public Guardian may require—

(a) any information provided to be verified in such manner, or

(b) any document produced to be authenticated in such manner,

as he may reasonably require.

(5) "Specified" means specified in a notice in writing given to the donee by the Public Guardian.

GENERAL NOTE

3–107   In *Re Harcourt* (COP), July 31, 2012, Senior Judge Lush said at para.36:

> "The [Office of the Public Guardian] has no powers of enforcement and, if it considers it necessary or expedient to freeze the donor's accounts, or suspend the attorney's powers, or revoke the LPA, it must apply to the Court of Protection for an order to that effect."

Power to require information from attorneys under enduring power of attorney

3–108   **47.**—(1) This regulation applies where it appears to the Public Guardian that there are circumstances suggesting that, having regard to all the circumstances (and in particular the attorney's relationship to or connection with the donor) the attorney under a registered enduring power of attorney may be unsuitable to be the donor's attorney.

(2) The Public Guardian may require the attorney—

(a) to provide specified information or information of a specified description; or

(b) to produce specified documents or documents of a specified description.

(3) The information or documents must be provided or produced—

(a) before the end of such reasonable period as may be specified; and

(b) at such place as may be specified.

(4) The Public Guardian may require—

(a) any information provided to be verified in such manner, or

(b) any document produced to be authenticated in such manner,

as he may reasonably require.

(5) "Specified" means specified in a notice in writing given to the attorney by the Public Guardian.

Other functions in relation to enduring powers of attorney

3–109   **48.**—[(1)] The Public Guardian has the following functions—

(a) directing a Court of Protection Visitor—

(i) to visit an attorney under a registered enduring power of attorney, or

(ii) to visit the donor of a registered enduring power of attorney, and to make a report to the Public Guardian on such matters as he may direct;

(b) dealing with representations (including complaints) about the way in which an attorney under a registered enduring power of attorney is exercising his powers.

[(2) The functions conferred by paragraph (1) may be discharged in co-operation with any other person who has functions in relation to the care or treatment of P.]

AMENDMENTS

3–110   The amendments to this regulation were made by SI 2010/1063 reg.5.

SCHEDULES 1 TO 8

[Not reproduced]

THE MENTAL CAPACITY ACT 2005 (TRANSFER OF PROCEEDINGS) ORDER 2007

(SI 2007/1899)

Dated June 25, 2007 and made by the President of the Family Division of the High Court with the agreement of the Lord Chancellor under the Mental Capacity Act 2005 (c.9) ss.21 and 65(5).

GENERAL NOTE

This Order provides for transfers of proceedings between the Court of Protection and a court having jurisdiction under the Children Act 1989 (c. 41). **3–111**

Article 2 specifies the circumstances in which proceedings in the Court of Protection may be transferred to a court having jurisdiction under the Children Act and sets out how proceedings are to be dealt with when a transfer is made.

Article 3 specifies the circumstances in which proceedings in a court having jurisdiction under the Children Act may be transferred to the Court of Protection and sets out how proceedings are to be dealt with when a transfer is made.

Article 4 makes provision for treating any fee paid to start the proceedings which are transferred as if it had been the fee payable to start proceedings in the court to which the transfer is made.

Citation and commencement

1.—(1) This Order may be cited as The Mental Capacity Act 2005 (Transfer of **3–112**
Proceedings) Order 2007.

(2) This Order shall come into force on 1st October 2007.

(3) In this Order "the Children Act" means the Children Act 1989.

Transfers from the Court of Protection to a court having jurisdiction under the Children Act

2.—(1) This article applies to any proceedings in the Court of Protection which **3–113**
relate to a person under 18.

(2) The Court of Protection may direct the transfer of the whole or part of the proceedings to a court having jurisdiction under the Children Act where it considers that in all the circumstances, it is just and convenient to transfer the proceedings.

(3) In making a determination, the Court of Protection must have regard to—

(a) whether the proceedings should be heard together with other proceedings that are pending in a court having jurisdiction under the Children Act;

(b) whether any order that may be made by a court having jurisdiction under that Act is likely to be a more appropriate way of dealing with the proceedings;

(c) the need to meet any requirements that would apply if the proceedings had been started in a court having jurisdiction under the Children Act; and

(d) any other matter that the court considers relevant.

(4) The Court of Protection—

(a) may exercise the power to make an order under paragraph (2) on an application or on its own initiative; and

(b) where it orders a transfer, must give reasons for its decision.

(5) Any proceedings transferred under this article—

(a) are to be treated for all purposes as if they were proceedings under the Children Act which had been started in a court having jurisdiction under that Act; and

(b) are to be dealt with after the transfer in accordance with directions given by a court having jurisdiction under that Act.

Transfers from a court having jurisdiction under the Children Act to the Court of Protection

3–114

3.—(1) This article applies to any proceedings in a court having jurisdiction under the Children Act which relate to a person under 18.

(2) A court having jurisdiction under the Children Act may direct the transfer of the whole or part of the proceedings to the Court of Protection where it considers that in all circumstances, it is just and convenient to transfer the proceedings.

(3) In making a determination, the court having jurisdiction under the Children Act must have regard to—

(a) whether the proceedings should be heard together with other proceedings that are pending in the Court of Protection;

(b) whether any order that may be made by the Court of Protection is likely to be a more appropriate way of dealing with the proceedings;

(c) the extent to which any order made as respects a person who lacks capacity is likely to continue to have effect when that person reaches 18; and

(d) any other matter that the court considers relevant.

(4) A court having jurisdiction under the Children Act—

(a) may exercise the power to make an order under paragraph (2) on an application or on its own initiative; and

(b) where it orders a transfer, must give reasons for its decision.

(5) Any proceedings transferred under this article—

(a) are to be treated for all purposes as if they were proceedings under the Mental Capacity Act 2005 which had been started in the Court of Protection; and

(b) are to be dealt with after the transfer in accordance with directions given by the Court of Protection.

GENERAL NOTE

3–115

In *B Local Authority v RM* [2010] EWHC 3802 (Fam) at para.28, Hedley J. said:

"[This case] raises the question particularly under art 3(3)(d) as to what matters the court should take into account in deciding whether to exercise these powers and to adopt this approach. An ex tempore judgment in a case on its own facts is no basis for attempting an exhaustive analysis of these issues; nevertheless, a number of matters suggest themselves, matters which may often be relevant in the relatively small number of cases in which this issue is likely to arise. One, is the child over 16? Otherwise of course, there is no power. Two, does the child manifestly lack capacity in respect of the principal decisions which are to be made in the Children Act proceedings? Three, are the disabilities which give rise to lack of capacity lifelong or at least long-term? Four, can the decisions which arise in respect of the child's welfare all be taken and all issues resolved during the child's minority? Five, does the Court of Protection have powers or procedures more appropriate to the resolution of outstanding issues than are available under the Children Act? Six, can the child's welfare needs be fully met by the exercise of Court of Protection powers? These provisional thoughts are intended to put some flesh on to the provisions of art 3(3); no doubt, other issues will arise in other cases. The essential thrust, however, is whether looking at the individual needs of the specific young person, it can be said that their welfare will be better safeguarded within the Court of Protection than it would be under the Children Act."

Avoidance of double liability for fees

4. Any fee paid for the purpose of starting any proceedings that are transferred under article 2 or 3 is to be treated as if it were the fee that would have been payable if the proceedings had started in the court to which the transfer is made.

3–116

THE PUBLIC GUARDIAN (FEES, ETC) REGULATIONS 2007

(SI 2007/2051)

Dated June 26, 2007 and made by the Lord Chancellor under the Mental Capacity Act 2005 (c.9) sections 58(3), (4) and 65(1)(b).

Citation and commencement

3–117   1. These Regulations may be cited as the Public Guardian (Fees, etc) Regulations 2007 and shall come into force on 1 October 2007.

Interpretation

3–118   2. In these Regulations—

"the Act" means the Mental Capacity Act 2005;

"court" means the Court of Protection;

["office copy" means a true copy of the original marked by the Public Guardian as being an office copy;]

"P" means the person in respect of whom a deputy has been appointed under section 16 of the Act; and

"Public Guardian" means the officer appointed in accordance with section 57 of the Act;

"the registers" means—
(a) the register of lasting powers of attorney,
(b) the register of enduring powers of attorney, and (c) the register of court orders appointing deputies,
established and maintained by the Public Guardian under section 58(1)(a) and (b) of and paragraph 14 of Schedule 4 to the Act.

AMENDMENT

3–119   The definition of "office copy" was inserted by SI 2009/514 reg.3.

Schedule of fees

3–120   3. The fees set out in the Schedule to these Regulations shall apply in accordance with the following provisions of these Regulations.

[Fee for application to register an enduring power of attorney]

3–121   4.—(1) A fee for the registration of an enduring power of attorney shall be payable by the person seeking to register the enduring power of attorney under regulation 24 of the Lasting Powers of Attorney, Enduring Powers of Attorney and Public Guardian Regulations 2007 (application for registration).

(2) The fee prescribed by paragraph (1) shall be payable upon the application to register the enduring power of attorney.

AMENDMENT

3–122   The heading to this rule was substituted by SI 2011/2189 reg.3.

[Enduring power of attorney office copy fee

    4A.—(1) A fee for an office copy of an enduring power of attorney registered **3–123** under paragraph 13 in Part 4 of Schedule 4 to the Mental Capacity Act 2005 shall be payable by the person requesting the office copy.

    (2) The fee prescribed by paragraph (1) shall be payable at the time the request for an office copy is made.]

AMENDMENT
    This regulation was inserted by SI 2009/514 reg.4.   **3–124**

[Fees for application to register a lasting power of attorney and repeat application to register]

    5.—(1) A fee for the registration of a lasting power of attorney shall be payable **3–125** by the person seeking to register the lasting power of attorney under regulation 11 of the Lasting Powers of Attorney, Enduring Powers of Attorney and Public Guardian Regulations 2007 (application for registration).

    [(1A) A reduced fee for an application to register a lasting power of attorney shall be payable where the application is a repeat application in the following circumstances—

    (a) the initial application to register a lasting power of attorney is made on or after 1st October 2011;
    (b) the initial application is returned to the applicant as invalid; and
    (c) the repeat application to register is submitted within 3 months of the date on which the invalid application was returned to the applicant.]

    [(2) The fee prescribed by—

    (a) paragraph (1) shall be payable upon the application to register the lasting power of attorney; and
    (b) paragraph (1A) shall be payable upon the submission of the repeat application to register.]

AMENDMENTS
    The amendments to this rule were made by SI 2011/2189 reg.4.   **3–126**

[Lasting power of attorney office copy fee

    5A.—(1) A fee for an office copy of a lasting power of attorney registered under **3–127** Part 2 of Schedule 1 to the Mental Capacity Act 2005 shall be payable by the person requesting the office copy.

    (2) The fee prescribed by paragraph (1) shall be payable at the time the request for an office copy is made.]

AMENDMENT
    This regulation was inserted by SI 2009/514 reg.5.   **3–128**

Application to search the registers fee
    6. [*Omitted by SI 2011/2189 reg.5*]   **3–129**

Appointment of deputy fee
    7. [*Omitted by SI 2011/2189 reg.6*]   **3–130**

[Appointment of deputy: assessment and supervision fees]

3–131   **8.**—(1) This regulation applies where—

(a) the court has appointed a deputy under section 16 of the Act (powers to make decisions and appoint deputies: general [. . .]

(b) [. . .]

(2) Where paragraph (1) applies the Public Guardian shall [assess] the level of supervision required under section 58(1)(c) of the Act.

(3) The levels of supervision are—

(a) [general; and]

[(aa) [. . .]]

(b) [minimal.]

(c) [. . .].

[(3A) Where the Public Guardian makes an assessment in accordance with paragraph (2) a fee shall be payable by P within 30 days of the date of the invoice for the fee.]

[(4) Where the level of supervision assessed by the Public Guardian in accordance with paragraph (2) is—

(a) "general", an annual supervision fee shall be payable by P until the appointment of the deputy is terminated; and

(b) "minimal", an annual administration fee shall be payable by P until the appointment of the deputy is terminated.]

(5) Subject to paragraphs (6) and (7), the appropriate supervision fee prescribed by [paragraph (4)] shall be due on 31 March each year and shall be payable by P within 30 days of the date of the invoice for the fee.

(6) Where the period for which the fee prescribed by paragraph (4) is payable is less than one year, the amount of the fee payable shall be such proportion of the full fee as that period bears to one year.

(7) Where the deputy's appointment terminates, the appropriate fee prescribed by paragraph (4) shall be due on the date of termination and shall be payable within 30 days of the date of the invoice for the fee.

(8) In the event of termination of the appointment due to P's death, the appropriate fee prescribed by [paragraphs (3A) and (4)] shall be payable by P's estate.

AMENDMENTS

3–132   The amendments to this paragraph were made by SI 2009/514 reg.7 and SI 2011/2189 reg.7.

Exemptions

3–133   **9.**—(1) Subject to [paragraphs (2) and (2A)] no fee shall be payable under these regulations when, at the time when the fee would otherwise become payable, the relevant person is in receipt of any qualifying benefit.

(2) Paragraph (1) does not apply to a person who has an award of damages in excess of £16,000 which has been disregarded for the purposes of determining eligibility for that benefit.

[(2A) Paragraph (1) does not apply to the office copy fees prescribed by regulations 4A and 5A.]

(3) For the purposes of regulation 4 the relevant person is the donor of the enduring power of attorney.

(4) For the purposes of regulation 5 the relevant person is the donor of the lasting power of attorney.

(5) For the purposes of regulation 6 the relevant person is the person making the application.

(6) For the purposes of regulations 7 and 8 the relevant person is P.

(7) The following are qualifying benefits for the purposes of paragraph (1)—

(a) income support under the Social Security Contributions and Benefits Act 1992

(b) working tax credit, provided that—

    (i) child tax credit is being paid to the relevant person, or to a couple (as defined in section 3(5)(A) of the Tax Credits Act 2002 which includes the relevant person; or

    (ii) there is a disability element or severe disability element (or both) to the [. . .] tax credit received by the relevant person;

(c) income-based job-seeker's allowance under the Jobseekers Act 1995;

(d) guarantee credit under the State Pensions Credit Act 2002;

(e) council tax benefit under the Social Security Contributions and Benefits Act 1992; [. . .]

(f) housing benefit under the Social Security Contributions and Benefits Act 1992[; and

(g) income-related employment and support allowance under Part 1 of the Welfare Reform Act 2007]

AMENDMENTS

The amendments to this paragraph were made by SI 2007/2616 reg.2, SI 2009/514 reg.8 and SI 2011/2189 reg.8.

3–134

Reductions and remissions [. . .]

10.—[(1)] Where it appears to the Public Guardian that the payment of any fee prescribed by these Regulations would, owing to the exceptional circumstances of the particular case, involve undue hardship, he may reduce or remit the fee in that case.

3–135

[(1A) Where, at the time that a fee under these Regulations is payable, the relevant person (or a couple which includes the relevant person) is in receipt of universal credit under the Welfare Reform Act 2012(c), the Public Guardian may reduce or remit that fee.

(1B) Paragraph (1A) does not apply to the office copy fees prescribed by regulations 4A and 5A.

(1C) In paragraph (1A)—

(a) paragraphs (3) to (6) of regulation 9 apply for the purpose of determining who is the relevant person;

(b) "couple" has the meaning given in section 39 of the Welfare Reform Act 2012.]

[(2) An application for the reduction or remission of any fee paid under regulation 8 (appointment of deputy: [assessment and] supervision fees) must be made to the Public Guardian within 6 months after the date of the invoice in respect of that fee.]

AMENDMENTS

The amendments to this regulation were made by SI 2010/1062 reg.3, SI 2011/2189 reg.9 and SI 2013/1748 reg.4.

3–136

GENERAL NOTE

3–137   Applications for exemption or remission should be made to the Office of the Public Guardian using form OPG506A.

Transitional provision

3–138   **11.**—(1) In respect of the administration fee that would have been payable under rule 78 of the Court of Protection Rules 2001 on 31 March 2008, the appropriate proportion of that fee shall be due on 30 September 2007 and shall be payable within 30 days of the date of the invoice for the fee.

(2) Where the period for which the fee prescribed by paragraph (1) is payable is less than six months, the amount of the fee payable shall be such proportion of that fee as that period bears to six months.

Amendment to Schedule 7 of the Lasting Powers of Attorney, Enduring Powers of Attorney and Public Guardian Regulations 2007

12. [Not reproduced]

SCHEDULE   **Regulation 3**

FEES TO BE TAKEN

3–139

Column 1	Column 2
[Fee for application to register an enduring power of attorney (regulation 4)]	[£110.00]
[Enduring power of attorney office copy fee (regulation 4A)]	[£25]
[Fee for application to register a lasting power of attorney (regulation 5)]	[£110.00]
[Reduced fee for repeat application to register a lasting power of attorney (regulation 5)]	[£55.00]
[Lasting power of attorney office copy fee (regulation 5A)]	[£35.00]
[. . .]	[. . .]
[Deputy assessment fee (regulation 8)]	[£100]
[general supervision (regulation 8)]	[£320.00]
[. . .]	[. . .]
[minimal supervision (regulation 8)]	[£35.00]
[. . .]	[. . .]

AMENDMENTS

3–140   The amendments to this Schedule were made by SI 2009/514 reg.9, SI 2011/2189 reg.10 and SI 2013/1748 reg.5.

THE MENTAL CAPACITY (DEPRIVATION OF LIBERTY: APPOINTMENT OF REVELANT PERSON'S REPRESENTATIVE) REGULATIONS 2008

(SI 2008/1315)

Dated May 14, 2008, and made by the Secretary of State for Health under the Mental Capacity Act 2005 (c.9) s.65(1) and Sch.A1, paras 138 (1), 142 to 145, 148, 149 and 151.

GENERAL NOTE

Where the deprivation of the liberty of a mentally incapacitated person has been author- **3–141** ised under s.4A and Sch.AI to the Act, para.139 of Sch.A1 requires that the supervisory body appoint a representative to a person in respect of whom a standard authorisation has been issued. Supervisory bodies are only able to appoint representatives who have been selected for that purpose. The role of the representative is to maintain contact with the person and to support and represent them in matters relating to their deprivation of liberty.

These Regulations, which apply to England only (reg.1(2)), provide for the selection and appointment of representatives and the circumstances in which they may be paid. They were considered by Baker J. in *AJ v A Local Authority* [2015] EWCOP 5: see Pt 2 under the heading "The appointment of representatives and the role of the supervisory body".

Wales

For the equivalent Welsh Regulations, see SI 2009/266 (W.29). **3–142**

Citation, commencement and application

1.—(1) These Regulations may be cited as the Mental Capacity (Deprivation of **3–143** Liberty: Appointment of Relevant Person's Representative) Regulations 2008 and shall come into force on 3rd November 2008.

(2) These Regulations apply in relation to England only.

Interpretation

2. In these Regulations— **3–144**

"best interests assessor" means a person selected to carry out a best interests assessment under paragraph 38 of Schedule A1 to the Act;

"donee" is a person who has a lasting power of attorney conferred on them by the relevant person, giving that donee the authority to make decisions about the relevant person's personal welfare;

"the Act" means the Mental Capacity Act 2005; and

"the relevant person's managing authority" means the managing authority that has made the application for a standard authorisation in respect of the relevant person.

PART 1

SELECTION OF REPRESENTATIVES

Selection of a person to be a representative—general

3–145   **3.**—(1) In addition to any requirements in regulations 6 to 9 and 11, a person can only be selected to be a representative if they are—

(a) 18 years of age or over;

(b) able to keep in contact with the relevant person;

(c) willing to be the relevant person's representative;

(d) not financially interested in the relevant person's managing authority;

(e) not a relative of a person who is financially interested in the managing authority;

(f) not employed by, or providing services to, the relevant person's managing authority, where the relevant person's managing authority is a care home);

(g) not employed to work in the relevant person's managing authority in a role that is, or could be, related to the relevant person's case, where the relevant person's managing authority is a hospital; and

(h) not employed to work in the supervisory body that is appointing the representative in a role that is, or could be, related to the relevant person's case.

(2) For the purposes of this regulation a "relative" means—

(a) a spouse, ex-spouse, civil partner or ex-civil partner;

(b) a person living with the relevant person as if they were a spouse or a civil partner;

(c) a parent or child;

(d) a brother or sister;

(e) a child of a person falling within sub-paragraphs (a), (b) or (d);

(f) a grandparent or grandchild;

(g) a grandparent-in-law or grandchild-in-law;

(h) an uncle or aunt;

(i) a brother-in-law or sister-in-law;

(j) a son-in-law or daughter-in-law;

(k) a first cousin; or

(l) a half-brother or half-sister.

(3) For the purposes of this regulation—

(a) the relationships in paragraph (2)(c) to (k) include step relationships;

(b) references to step relationships and in-laws in paragraph (2) are to be read in accordance with section 246 of the Civil Partnership Act 2004;

(c) a person has a financial interest in a managing authority where—

(i) that person is a partner, director, other office-holder or major shareholder of the managing authority that has made the application for a standard authorisation, and

(ii) the managing authority is a care home or independent hospital; and

(d) a major shareholder means—

(i) any person holding one tenth or more of the issued shares in the managing authority, where the managing authority is a company limited by shares, and

(ii) in all other cases, any of the owners of the managing authority.

Determination of capacity

4. The best interests assessor must determine whether the relevant person has capacity to select a representative.   **3–146**

Selection by the relevant person

5.—(1) Where the best interests assessor determines that the relevant person has capacity, the relevant person may select a family member, friend or carer.   **3–147**

(2) Where the relevant person does not wish to make a selection under paragraph (1), regulation 8 applies.

Selection by a donee or deputy

6.—(1) Where—   **3–148**

(a) the best interests assessor determines that the relevant person lacks capacity to select a representative; and

(b) the relevant person has a donee or deputy and the donee's or deputy's scope of authority permits the selection of a family member, friend or carer of the relevant person,

the donee or deputy may select such a person.

(2) A donee or deputy may select himself or herself to be the relevant person's representative.

(3) Where a donee or deputy does not wish to make a selection under paragraph (1) or (2), regulation 8 applies.

Confirmation of eligibility of family member, friend or carer and recommendation to the supervisory body

7.—(1) The best interests assessor must confirm that a person selected under regulation 5(1) or 6(1) or (2) is eligible to be a representative.   **3–149**

(2) Where the best interests assessor confirms the selected person's eligibility under paragraph (1), the assessor must recommend the appointment of that person as a representative to the supervisory body.

(3) Where the best interests assessor is unable to confirm the selected person's eligibility under paragraph (1), the assessor must—

(a) advise the person who made the selection of that decision and give the reasons for it; and

(b) invite them to make a further selection.

Selection by the best interests assessor

8.—(1) The best interests assessor may select a family member, friend or carer as a representative where paragraph (2) applies.   **3–150**

(2) The best interests assessor may make a selection where—

(a) the relevant person has the capacity to make a selection under regulation 5(1) but does not wish to do so;

(b) the relevant person's donee or deputy does not wish to make a selection under regulation 6(1) or (2); or

(c) the relevant person lacks the capacity to make a selection and—

  (i) does not have a donee or deputy, or

  (ii) has a donee or deputy but the donee's or deputy's scope of authority does not permit the selection of a representative.

(3) Where the best interests assessor selects a person in accordance with

paragraph (2), the assessor must recommend that person for appointment as a representative to the supervisory body.

(4) But the best interests assessor must not select a person under paragraph (2) where the relevant person, donee or deputy objects to that selection.

(5) The best interests assessor must notify the supervisory body if they do not select a person who is eligible to be a representative.

Selection by the supervisory body

3–151   **9.**—(1)Where a supervisory body is given notice under regulation 8(5), it may select a person to be the representative, who—

(a) would be performing the role in a professional capacity;

(b) has satisfactory skills and experience to perform the role;

(c) is not a family member, friend or carer of the relevant person;

(d) is not employed by, or providing services to, the relevant person's managing authority, where the relevant person's managing authority is a care home;

(e) is not employed to work in the relevant person's managing authority in a role that is, or could be, related to the relevant person's case, where the relevant person's managing authority is a hospital; and

[(f) is not employed by the supervisory body]

(2) The supervisory body must be satisfied that there is in respect of the person—

(a) an enhanced criminal record certificate issued pursuant to section 113B of the Police Act 1997 (enhanced criminal record certificates); or

(b) if the purpose for which the certificate is required is not one prescribed under subsection (2) of that section, a criminal record certificate issued pursuant to section 113A of that Act (criminal record certificates).

AMENDMENT

3–152   Para.(1)(f) was substituted by SI 2008/2368 reg.2.

GENERAL NOTE

Paragraph (1)

3–153   The supervisory body can appoint a lay person, such as a family member or carer, to be the representative.

PERSON.   The appointee has to be a person; it is not possible to appoint either an agency or advocacy service. If the person does not want to continue to act as representative, the supervisory body should be informed (reg.13(b)).

PART 2

APPOINTMENT OF REPRESENTATIVES

Commencement of appointment procedure

3–154   **10.** The procedure for appointing a representative must begin as soon as—

(a) a best interests assessor is selected by the supervisory body for the purposes of a request for a standard authorisation; or

(b) a relevant person's representative's appointment terminates, or is to be terminated, under regulation 14 and the relevant person remains subject to a standard authorisation.

Appointment of representative

11. Except where regulation 9 applies, a supervisory body may not appoint a representative unless the person is recommended to it under regulations 7 or 8.

3–155

Formalities of appointing a representative

12.—(1) The offer of an appointment to a representative must be made in writing and state—
- (a) the duties of a representative to—
  - (i) maintain contact with the relevant person,
  - (ii) represent the relevant person in matters relating to, or connected with, the deprivation of liberty, and
  - (iii) support the relevant person in matters relating to, or connected with, the deprivation of liberty; and
- (b) the length of the period of the appointment.

(2) The representative must inform the supervisory body in writing that they are willing to accept the appointment and that they have understood the duties set out in sub-paragraph (1)(a).

(3) The appointment must be made for the period of the standard authorisation.

(4) The supervisory body must send copies of the written appointment to—
- (a) the appointed person;
- (b) the relevant person;
- (c) the relevant person's managing authority;
- (d) any donee or deputy of the relevant person;
- (e) any independent mental capacity advocate appointed in accordance with sections 37 to 39D of the Act), involved in the relevant person's case; and
- (f) every interested person named by the best interests assessor in their report as somebody the assessor has consulted in carrying out the assessment.

3–156

Termination of representative's appointment

13. A person ceases to be a representative if—
- (a) the person dies;
- (b) the person informs the supervisory body that they are no longer willing to continue as representative;
- (c) the period of the appointment ends;
- (d) a relevant person who has selected a family member, friend or carer under regulation 5(1) who has been appointed as their representative informs the supervisory body that they object to the person continuing to be a representative;
- (e) a donee or deputy who has selected a family member, friend or carer of the relevant person under regulation 6(1) who has been appointed as a representative informs the supervisory body that they object to the person continuing to be a representative;
- (f) the supervisory body terminates the appointment because it is satisfied that the representative is not maintaining sufficient contact with the relevant person in order to support and represent them;
- (g) the supervisory body terminates the appointment because it is satisfied that the representative is not acting in the best interests of the relevant person; or
- (h) the supervisory body terminates the appointment because it is satisfied that the person is no longer eligible or was not eligible at the time of appointment, to be a representative.

3–157

Formalities of termination of representative's appointment

3–158   **14.**—(1) Where a representative's appointment is to be terminated for a reason specified in paragraphs (c) to (h) of regulation 13, the supervisory body must inform the representative of—

(a) the pending termination of the appointment;

(b) the reasons for the termination of the appointment; and

(c) the date on which the appointment terminates.

    (2) The supervisory body must send copies of the termination of the appointment to—

(a) the relevant person;

(b) the relevant person's managing authority;

(c) any donee or deputy of the relevant person;

(d) any independent mental capacity advocate appointed in accordance with sections 37 to 39D of the Act, involved in the relevant person's case; and

(e) every interested person named by the best interests assessor in their report as somebody the assessor has consulted in carrying out the assessment.

Payment to a representative

3–159   **15.** A supervisory body may make payments to a representative appointed following a selection under regulation 9.

THE MENTAL CAPACITY (DEPRIVATION OF LIBERTY: STANDARD AUTHORISATIONS, ASSESSMENTS AND ORDINARY RESIDENCE) REGULATIONS 2008

(SI 2008/1858)

Dated July 9, 2008, and made by the Secretary of State for Health under s.65(1) of, and paras 31, 33(4), 47, 70, 129(3), 130 and 183(6) and (7) of Sch. A1 to, the Mental Capacity Act 2005(c.9).

GENERAL NOTE

The Act provides for the deprivation of liberty of people lacking capacity to consent **3–160** to the arrangements made for their care or treatment where authorisation under s.4A of and Sch.A1 exists. Under Sch.A1, where it appears that a person who lacks capacity is detained, or is likely to be detained, in a care home or hospital, the managing authority of the care home or hospital must request an authorisation from the supervisory body. On receiving such a request the supervisory body must ensure that various assessments are carried out in relation to the individual concerned in order to determine whether it is appropriate to grant the authorisation. The supervisory body must select people to carry out those assessments in accordance with para.129 of Sch.A1 and may only select people who are eligible in accordance with these Regulations which apply to England only (reg.1(2)) and require that—

(a) all assessors have adequate and appropriate indemnity arrangements in place and that the supervisory body is satisfied that they have suitable skills and have undergone a Criminal Record Bureau check (reg.3);

(b) mental health assessments can only be carried out by medical practitioners who have been approved under section 12 of the Mental Health Act 1983 (the 1983 Act) or registered medical practitioners who have similar mental health experience to practitioners approved under s.12 of the 1983 Act and the supervisory body is satisfied that the person has successfully completed the required training (reg.4);

(c) best interests assessments can only be carried out by mental health practitioners who have been approved under s.114(1) of the 1983 Act, certain health professionals or social workers, with specialised and relevant skills and with at least two years post registration experience. The supervisory body must be satisfied that the person has the required training (reg.5);

(d) mental capacity assessments can only be carried out by people who are eligible to carry out a mental health assessment or a best interests assessment (reg.6);

(e) eligibility assessments can only be carried out by medical practitioners who have been approved under s.12 of the 1983 Act or an approved mental health professional and the supervisory body is satisfied that the person has the required training (reg.7);

(f) age assessments and no refusals assessments can only be carried out by people who are eligible to carry out a best interests assessment (regs 8 and 9).

These Regulations provide some limitations on the ability of a supervisory body to select people to carry out assessments, even if the person meets the eligibility requirements. They do so by preventing the selection of—

(a) people who have, or are related to a person who has, a personal financial interest in the care of the individual in need of assessment or are a relative of the individual (regs 10 and 11); and

(b) a best interests assessor who is involved in the care of the individual in need of assessment, or is employed by the supervisory body where the managing authority and the supervisory body are the same (reg.12).

These Regulations also contain provisions relating to the assessments required in response to a request for—

(a) a standard authorisation by requiring that all of the required assessments be completed within 21 days from the date on which the supervisory body receives the request, except where an urgent authorisation is in force, in which case assessments must be completed during the period of the urgent authorisation (reg.13); and

(b) a decision as to whether or not there is an unauthorised deprivation of liberty by requiring that the assessment be completed within 7 days from the date the supervisory body receives the request (reg.14).

Regulation 15 enables the person carrying out the eligibility assessment to require the person conducting the best interests assessment to provide them with information relevant to their assessment.

Regulation 16 specifies the information that must be included in a request for a standard authorisation and information that must be included if it is available or could reasonably be obtained by the managing authority.

Paragraph 182 of Sch.A1 makes provision for identifying the supervisory body where the managing authority is a care home. In the case of a care home the supervisory body will be the local authority in which the person is ordinarily resident. Part 6 of these Regulations applies in specified circumstances where a local authority wishes to dispute that it is the supervisory body (reg.17). Guidance on determining ordinary residence for the purposes of Sch.A1 is contained in paras 167 to 178 of *Ordinary Residence: Guidance on the identification of the ordinary residence of people in need of community care services, England*, Department of Health, October 2013. This guidance should be read in the light of the judgment of the Supreme Court in *R. (on the application of Cornwall CC) v Somerset CC* [2015] UKSC 46.

Regulation 18 sets out who is to act as supervisory body until the question of ordinary residence is determined. *Regulation* 19 provides for the effect of a change in supervisory body following the determination of a question as to the ordinary residence of a relevant person.

Wales

3–161   For the equivalent Welsh Regulations, see SI 2009/783 (W.69).

PART 1

PRELIMINARY

Citation, commencement and application

3–162   **1.**—(1) These Regulations may be cited as the Mental Capacity (Deprivation of Liberty: Standard Authorisations, Assessments and Ordinary Residence) Regulations 2008 and shall come into force on 3rd November 2008.

(2) These Regulations apply in relation to England only.

Interpretation

3–163   **2.** In these Regulations—

"approved mental health professional" means a person approved under section 114(1) of the Mental Health Act 1983 to act as an approved mental health professional for the purposes of that Act;

"best interests assessor" means a person selected to carry out a best interests assessment under paragraph 38 of Schedule A1 to the Act;
[. . .]

"the Act" means the Mental Capacity Act 2005.

AMENDMENT
The amendment to this regulation was made by SI 2012/1479 Sch.1, Pt 1, para.85(2).   **3–164**

PART 2

ELIGIBILITY TO CARRY OUT ASSESSMENTS

Eligibility—general
   3.—(1) In addition to any requirement in regulations 4 to 9, a person is eligible   **3–165**
to carry out an assessment where paragraphs (2) to (4) are met.
   [(2) The person must satisfy the supervisory body that there is in force in relation to that person an adequate and appropriate indemnity arrangement which
provides cover in respect of any liabilities that might arise in connection with
carrying out the assessment.
   (2A) For the purposes of this regulation, an "indemnity arrangement" may
comprise—
   (a) a policy of insurance;
   (b) an arrangement made for the purposes of indemnifying a person; or
   (c) a combination of a policy of insurance and an arrangement made for the
       purposes of indemnifying a person.]
   (3) The supervisory body must be satisfied that the person has the skills and
experience appropriate to the assessment to be carried out which must include, but
are not limited to, the following—
   (a) an applied knowledge of the Mental Capacity Act 2005 and related Code of
       Practice; and
   (b) the ability to keep appropriate records and to provide clear and reasoned
       reports in accordance with legal requirements and good practice.
   (4) The supervisory body must be satisfied that there is in respect of the
person—
   (a) an enhanced criminal record certificate issued under section 113B of the
       Police Act 1997 (enhanced criminal record certificates); or
   (b) if the purpose for which the certificate is required is not one prescribed
       under subsection (2) of that section, a criminal record certificate issued pur-
       suant to section 113A of that Act (criminal record certificates).

AMENDMENT
The amendment to this regulation was made by SI 2009/827 reg.6(2).   **3–166**

Eligibility to carry out a mental health assessment
   4.—(1) A person is eligible to carry out a mental health assessment if para-   **3–167**
graphs (2) and (3) are met.
   (2) The person must be—
   (a) approved under section 12 of the Mental Health Act 1983; or
   (b) a registered medical practitioner who the supervisory body is satisfied has
       at least three years post registration experience in the diagnosis or treatment
       of mental disorder.
   (3) The supervisory body must be satisfied that the person has successfully
completed the Deprivation of Liberty Safeguards Mental Health Assessors training programme made available by the Royal College of Psychiatrists

(4) Except in the 12 month period beginning with the date the person has successfully completed the programme referred to in paragraph (3), the supervisory body must be satisfied that the person has, in the 12 months prior to selection, completed further training relevant to their role as a mental health assessor.

Eligibility to carry out a best interests assessment

3–168   **5.**—(1) A person is eligible to carry out a best interests assessment if paragraphs (2) and (3) are met.

(2) The person must be one of the following—

(a) an approved mental health professional;

(b) [. . .];

(c) a first level nurse, registered in Sub-Part 1 of the Nurses Part of the Register maintained under article 5 of the Nursing and Midwifery Order 2001;

(d) an occupational therapist registered in Part 6 [, or a social worker registered under Part 16,] of the register maintained under article 5 of the [Health and Social Work Professions Order 2001]; or

(e) a chartered psychologist who is listed in the British Psychological Society's Register of Chartered Psychologists and who holds a relevant practising certificate issued by that Society.

(3) The supervisory body must be satisfied that the person—

(a) is not suspended from the register or list relevant to the person's profession mentioned in paragraph (2);

(b) has at least two years post registration experience in one of the professions mentioned in paragraph (2);

(c) has successfully completed training that has been approved by the Secretary of State to be a best interests assessor;

(d) except in the 12 month period beginning with the date the person has successfully completed the training referred to in sub-paragraph (c), the supervisory body must be satisfied that the person has, in the 12 months prior to selection, completed further training relevant to their role as a best interests assessor; and

(e) has the skills necessary to obtain, evaluate and analyse complex evidence and differing views and to weigh them appropriately in decision making.

AMENDMENTS

3–169   The amendments to this regulation were made by SI 2012/1479 Sch.1, Pt 1, paras 55, 85(3).

Eligibility to carry out a mental capacity assessment

3–170   **6.** A person is eligible to carry out a mental capacity assessment if that person is eligible to carry out—

(a) a mental health assessment; or

(b) a best interests assessment.

Eligibility to carry out an eligibility assessment

3–171   **7.** A person is eligible to carry out an eligibility assessment if that person is—

(a) approved under section 12 of the Mental Health Act 1983 and is eligible to carry out a mental health assessment; or

(b) an approved mental health professional and is eligible to carry out a best interests assessment.

Eligibility to carry out an age assessment

8. A person is eligible to carry out an age assessment if that person is eligible to   **3–172**
carry out a best interests assessment.

Eligibility to carry out a no refusals assessment

9. A person is eligible to carry out a no refusals assessment if that person is   **3–173**
eligible to carry out a best interests assessment.

PART 3

SELECTION OF ASSESSORS

Selection of assessors—relatives

10.—(1) A supervisory body must not select a person to carry out an assess-   **3–174**
ment if the person is—
  (a) a relative of the relevant person; or
  (b) a relative of a person who is financially interested in the care of the relevant
      person.
  (2) For the purposes of this regulation a "relative" means—
  (a) a spouse, ex-spouse, civil partner or ex-civil partner;
  (b) a person living with the relevant person as if they were a spouse or a civil
      partner;
  (c) a parent or child;
  (d) a brother or sister;
  (e) a child of a person falling within sub-paragraphs (a), (b) or (d);
  (f) a grandparent or grandchild;
  (g) a grandparent-in-law or grandchild-in-law;
  (h) an uncle or aunt;
  (i) a brother-in-law or sister-in-law;
  (j) a son-in-law or daughter-in-law;
  (k) a first cousin; or
  (l) a half-brother or half-sister.
  (3) For the purposes of this regulation—
  (a) the relationships in paragraph (2)(c) to (k) include step relationships;
  (b) references to step relationships and in-laws in paragraph (2) are to be read
      in accordance with section 246 of the Civil Partnership Act 2004; and
  (c) financial interest has the meaning given in regulation 11.

Selection of assessors—financial interest

11.—(1) A supervisory body must not select a person to carry out an assessment   **3–175**
where the person has a financial interest in the case.
  (2) A person has a financial interest in a case where—
  (a) that person is a partner, director, other office-holder or major shareholder of
      the managing authority that has made the application for a standard authori-
      sation; and
  (b) the managing authority is a care home or independent hospital.
  (3) A major shareholder means—
  (a) any person holding one tenth or more of the issued shares in the managing
      authority, where the managing authority is a company limited by shares; and
  (b) in all other cases, any of the owners of the managing authority.

Selection of best interests assessors

3–176   **12.**—(1) A supervisory body must not select a person to carry out a best interests assessment if that person is involved in the care, or making decisions about the care, of the relevant person.

(2) Where the managing authority and supervisory body are both the same body, the supervisory body must not select a person to carry out a best interests assessment who is employed by it or who is providing services to it.

GENERAL NOTE
Paragraph (1)

3–177   It is submitted that a person who has undertaken a previous assessment on the relevant person is not disqualified by this provision from undertaking a further assessment.

PART 4

ASSESSMENTS

Time frame for assessments

3–178   **13.**—(1)Except as provided in paragraph (2), all assessments required for a standard authorisation must be completed within the period of 21 days beginning with the date that the supervisory body receives a request for such an authorisation.

(2) Where a supervisory body receives a request for a standard authorisation and the managing authority has given an urgent authorisation under paragraph 76 of Schedule A1 to the Act, the assessments required for that standard authorisation must be completed within the period during which the urgent authorisation is in force.

Time limit for carrying out an assessment to decide whether or not there is an unauthorised deprivation of liberty

3–179   **14.** Subject to paragraph 69(3) to (5) of Schedule A1 to the Act, an assessment required under that paragraph must be completed within the period of 7 days beginning with the date that the supervisory body receives the request from an eligible person.

Relevant eligibility information

3–180   **15.**—(1) This regulation applies where an individual is being assessed and the eligibility assessor and the best interests assessor are not the same person.

(2) The eligibility assessor must request that the best interests assessor provides any relevant eligibility information that the best interests assessor may have.

(3) The best interests assessor must comply with any request made under this regulation.

(4) In this regulation "eligibility assessor" means a person selected to carry out the eligibility assessment under paragraph 46 of Schedule A1 to the Act.

PART 5

REQUESTS FOR A STANDARD AUTHORISATION

Information to be provided in a request for a standard authorisation
    16.—(1) A request for a standard authorisation must include the following   **3–181**
information—
    (a) the name and gender of the relevant person;
    (b) the age of the relevant person or, where this is not known, whether the man-
        aging authority believes that the relevant person is aged 18 years or older;
    (c) the address and telephone number where the relevant person is currently
        located;
    (d) the name, address and telephone number of the managing authority and the
        name of the person within the managing authority who is dealing with the
        request;
    (e) the purpose for which the authorisation is requested;
    (f) the date from which the standard authorisation is sought; and
    (g) whether the managing authority has given an urgent authorisation under
        paragraph 76 of Schedule A1 to the Act and, if so, the date on which it
        expires.
    (2) Except as provided for in paragraph (3), a request for a standard authorisa-
tion must include the following information if it is available or could reasonably
be obtained by the managing authority—

    (a) any medical information relating to the relevant person's health that the
        managing authority considers to be relevant to the proposed restrictions to
        the relevant person's liberty;
    (b) the diagnosis of the mental disorder (within the meaning of the Mental
        Health Act 1983 but disregarding any exclusion for persons with learning
        disability) that the relevant person is suffering from;
    (c) any relevant care plans and relevant needs assessments;
    (d) the racial, ethnic or national origins of the relevant person;
    (e) whether the relevant person has any special communication needs;
    (f) details of the proposed restrictions on the relevant person's liberty;
    (g) whether section 39A of the Act (person becomes subject to Schedule A1)
        applies;
    (h) where the purpose of the proposed restrictions to the relevant person's
        liberty is to give treatment, whether the relevant person has made an
        advance decision that may be valid and applicable to some or all of that
        treatment;
    (i) whether the relevant person is subject to—
        (i) the hospital treatment regime,
        (ii) the community treatment regime, or
        (iii) the guardianship regime;
    (j) the name, address and telephone number of—
        (i) anyone named by the relevant person as someone to be consulted
           about his welfare,
        (ii) anyone engaged in caring for the person or interested in his welfare,
        (iii) any donee of a lasting power of attorney granted by the person,
        (iv) any deputy appointed for the person by the court, and

(v) any independent mental capacity advocate appointed in accordance with sections 37 to 39D of the Act; and

(k) whether there is an existing authorisation in relation to the detention of the relevant person and, if so, the date of the expiry of that authorisation.

(3) Where—

(a) there is an existing authorisation in force in relation to the detention of the relevant person; and

(b) the managing authority makes a request in accordance with paragraph 30 of Schedule A1 to the Act for a further standard authorisation in relation to the same relevant person,

the request need not include any of the information mentioned in paragraph (2) (a) to (j) if that information remains the same as that supplied in relation to the request for the existing authorisation.

(4) In this regulation "existing authorisation" has the same meaning as in paragraph 29 of Schedule A1 to the Act.

PART 6

[SUPERVISORY BODIES: CARE HOMES AND HOSPITALS]

Disputes about the Place of Ordinary Residence

Application and Interpretation of Part 6

3–182   **17.**—(1) This Part applies where—

(a) a local authority ("local authority A") receives a request from—

(i) a care home [or hospital] for a standard authorisation under paragraph 24, 25 or 30 of Schedule A1 to the Act, or

(ii) an eligible person to decide whether or not there is an unauthorised deprivation of liberty in a care home [or hospital] under paragraph 68 of Schedule A1 to the Act;

(b) local authority A wishes to dispute that it is the supervisory body; and

(c) a question as to the ordinary residence of the relevant person is to be determined by the Secretary of State under paragraph 183 of Schedule A1 to the Act.

(2) In this Part—

(a) "local authority A" has the meaning given in paragraph (1); and

(b) "local authority C" has the meaning given in regulation 18(2).

AMENDMENTS

3–183   The amendments to the heading of this Part and the amendments to this regulation were made by SI 2013/235 art.11 Sch.2, para.118.

Arrangements where there is a question as to the ordinary residence

3–184   **18.**—(1) Local authority A must act as supervisory body in relation to a request mentioned in regulation 17(1)(a) until the determination of the question as to the ordinary residence of the relevant person.

(2) But where another local authority ("local authority C") agrees to act as the supervisory body in place of local authority A, that local authority shall become the supervisory body until the determination of the question as to the ordinary residence of the relevant person.

(3) When the question about the ordinary residence of the relevant person has been determined, the local authority which has been identified as the supervisory body shall become the supervisory body.

Effect of change in supervisory body following determination of any question about ordinary residence

19.—(1) Where the question of ordinary residence of the relevant person is   **3–185** determined in accordance with paragraph 183(3) of Schedule A1 to the Act, and another local authority ("local authority B") becomes the supervisory body in place of local authority A or local authority C, as the case may be, [paragraphs (3) to (6A)] shall apply.

(2) Where the question of ordinary residence of the relevant person is determined in accordance with paragraph 183(3) of Schedule A1 to the Act and local authority C remains the supervisory body, [paragraphs (7) to (10)] shall apply.

(3) Local authority B shall be treated as the supervisory body that received the request mentioned in regulation 17(1)(a) and must comply with the time limits specified in—

(a) regulation 13 for carrying out the assessments required for a standard authorisation; or

(b) regulation 14 for carrying out an assessment required under paragraph 69 of Schedule A1 to the Act,

as the case may be, where the assessments have still to be completed.

(4) Anything done by or in relation to local authority A or local authority C in connection with the authorisation or request, as the case may be, has effect, so far as is necessary for continuing its effect after the change, as if done by or in relation to local authority B.

(5) Anything which relates to the authorisation or request and which is in the process of being done by or in relation to local authority A or local authority C at the time of the change may be continued by or in relation to local authority B.

(6) But—

(a) local authority A or local authority C does not, by virtue of this regulation, cease to be liable for anything done by it in connection with the authorisation or request before the change; and

(b) local authority B does not, by virtue of this regulation, become liable for any such thing.

[(6A) Local authority A or local authority C shall be entitled to recover from local authority B expenditure incurred in exercising functions as the supervisory body.]

(7) Local authority C shall be treated as the supervisory body that received the request mentioned in regulation 17(1)(a) and must comply with the time limits specified in—

(a) regulation 13 for carrying out the assessments required for a standard authorisation; or

(b) regulation 14 for carrying out an assessment required under paragraph 69 of Schedule A1 to the Act,

as the case may be, where the assessments have still to be completed.

(8) Anything done by or in relation to local authority A in connection with the authorisation or request, as the case may be, has effect, so far as is necessary for continuing its effect after the change, as if done by or in relation to local authority C.

(9) Anything which relates to the authorisation or request and which is in the process of being done by or in relation to local authority A at the time of the change may be continued by or in relation to local authority C.

(10) But—

(a) local authority A does not, by virtue of this regulation, cease to be liable for anything done by it in connection with the authorisation or request before the change; and

(b) local authority C does not, by virtue of this regulation, become liable for any such thing.

AMENDMENTS

3–186   The amendments to this regulation was made by SI 2009/827 reg.6(3).

PART 4

PRACTICE AND PROCEDURE

THE COURT OF PROTECTION RULES 2007

(SI 2007/1744)

Dated June 25, 2007 and made by the President of the Family Division of the High Court with the agreement of the Lord Chancellor under the Mental Capacity Act 2005 (c.9) ss.49(5), 50(2), 51, 53(2) and (4), 55, 56 and 65(1), and in accordance with the Constitutional Reform Act 2005 (c.4), Sch.1, Pt.1.

GENERAL NOTE

These Rules set out the practice and procedure to be followed in the Court of Protection and revoke the rules governing procedure in the former Court of Protection. **4–001**

Part 2 of the Rules sets out the overriding objective that is to be applied whenever the court exercises its powers under the Rules, or interprets any rule or practice direction. Part 3 contains provisions for interpreting the Rules and for the Civil Procedure Rules 1998 to be applied insofar as may be necessary to further the overriding objective. Part 4 makes provision as to court documents, including the requirement for certain documents to be verified by a statement of truth. Part 5 sets out the court's general case management powers, and includes the power to dispense with the requirement of any rule. The Rules provide procedures for serving documents (Part 6), notifying the person who lacks capacity and who is the subject matter of the application of certain documents and events (Part 7), seeking permission to start proceedings (Part 8), starting proceedings (Part 9), making interim applications and applications within proceedings (Part 10), procedures governing deprivations of liberty (Part 10A) as to how applications will be dealt with (Part 12) and as to hearings (Part 13), including provisions as to publication of information and as to privacy and publicity of proceedings.

The Rules set out procedures to be followed in relation to evidence (Parts 14 and 15), disclosure (Part 16), appointment of litigation friends (Part 17), change of solicitor (Part 18), costs (Part 19), appeals (Part 20), the enforcement of orders (Part 21) and transitory and transitional matters (Part 22). The detail of the transitional and transitory procedures is provided in the practice directions.

The fees to be charged in connection with the Court are set out in the Court of Protection Fees Order 2007 (SI 2007/1745) which is reproduced below.

Practice Directions

The practice directions that have been issued to supplement these Rules are noted in the General Note to the relevant Part. All of the practice directions that have been issued can be downloaded from the Ministry of Justice website at: *www.judiciary.gov.uk/publications/ court-of-protection-practice-directions.* **4–002**

Transitional provisions

Rule 66 of the Court of Protection (Amendment) Rules 2015 (SI 2015/548) states: **4–003**

"(1) The changes made by rules 8(c), 10, 11, 13, 22 to 30, 36(d) and 48 of these Rules apply only in relation to—

(a) proceedings commenced on or after 1st July 2015; and

(b) applications made on or after 1st July 2015 in existing proceedings whenever commenced.

(2) The changes made by rules 8(e), 45, 55 and 57 to 64 of these Rules apply only where the decision or order against which it is sought to appeal, or in relation to which a reconsideration is sought, was made on or after 6th April 2015.

(3) The changes made by rule 16 of these Rules apply only where service is to be effected on or after 1st July 2015.

(4) The changes made by rules 17 to 21 of these Rules apply only where the requirement for notification arises on or after 1st July 2015.

(5) The changes made by rule 31 of these Rules apply only where the application form is received on or after 1st July 2015.

(6) The changes made by rules 32 to 35 and 36(a) to (c) of these Rules apply only where the period in question starts on or after 1st July 2015.

(7) The changes made by rules 37 and 43 of these Rules apply only in relation to applications to withdraw made on or after 1st July 2015."

CONTENTS

PART 1

PRELIMINARY

PART 2

THE OVERRIDING OBJECTIVE

PART 3

INTERPRETATION AND GENERAL PROVISIONS

PART 4

COURT DOCUMENTS

PART 5

GENERAL CASE MANAGEMENT POWERS

PART 6

SERVICE OF DOCUMENTS

Service generally

Service out of the jurisdiction

PART 7

NOTIFYING P

General requirement to notify P

Circumstances in which P must be notified

Manner of notification, and accompanying documents

PART 8

PERMISSION

Evidence

Depositions

Taking evidence outside the jurisdiction

SECTION 49 REPORTS

PART 15

EXPERTS

PART 16

DISCLOSURE

[PART 17

LITIGATION FRIENDS AND RULE 3A REPRESENTATIVES

SECTION 1—LITIGATION FRIENDS

SECTION 2—RULE 3A REPRESENTATIVES

PART 18

CHANGE OF SOLICITOR

PART 19

Costs

PART 20

Appeals

Appeals to the Court of Appeal

PART 21

Enforcement

Orders for committal

PART 22

TRANSITORY AND TRANSITIONAL PROVISIONS

PART 23

MISCELLANEOUS

PART 1

PRELIMINARY

Title and commencement

1. These Rules may be cited as the Court of Protection Rules 2007 and come into force on 1 October 2007.

4–004

Revocations

2. The following rules are revoked—

4–005

(a) the Court of Protection Rules 2001; and

(b) the Court of Protection (Enduring Powers of Attorney) Rules 2001.

PART 2

THE OVERRIDING OBJECTIVE

Practice Direction
2A Participation of P

The overriding objective

3.—(1) These Rules have the overriding objective of enabling the court to deal with a case justly, having regard to the principles contained in the Act.

4–006

(2) The court will seek to give effect to the overriding objective when it—

(a) exercises any power under these Rules; or

(b) interprets any rule or practice direction.

(3) Dealing with a case justly includes, so far as is practicable—

(a) ensuring that it is dealt with expeditiously and fairly;

(b) ensuring that P's interests and position are properly considered;

(c) dealing with the case in ways which are proportionate to the nature, importance and complexity of the issues;

(d) ensuring that the parties are on an equal footing;

(e) saving expense; and

(f) allotting to it an appropriate share of the court's resources, while taking account of the need to allot resources to other cases.

GENERAL NOTE

Case management powers available to the court to facilitate the overriding objective are contained in r.25. The court can also exercise powers on its own initiative (r.27) or at the request of a party (r.85).

4–007

This rule "tends, in my judgement, to suggest that the court should be astute *in a proper case* not to overextend proceedings" (*KD v Havering LBC* [2010] 1 F.L.R. 1393, para.23, per Judge Horowitz QC).

In *NCC v PB* [2014] EWCOP 14, Parker J. said at para.127:

"All those who represent the vulnerable who cannot give them capacitous instructions have a particular responsibility to ensure that the arguments addressed are proportionate and relevant to the issues, to the actual facts with which they are dealing rather than the theory, and to have regard to the public purse, court resources, and other court users."

[Participation of P

3A.—(1) The court shall in each case, on its own initiative or on the application

4–008

of any person, consider whether it should make one or more of the directions in paragraph (2), having regard to—

   (a) the nature and extent of the information before the court;

   (b) the issues raised in the case;

   (c) whether a matter is contentious; and

   (d) whether P has been notified in accordance with the provisions of Part 7 and what, if anything, P has said or done in response to such notification.

   (2) The directions are that—

   (a) P should be joined as a party;

   (b) P's participation should be secured by the appointment of an accredited legal representative to represent P in the proceedings and to discharge such other functions as the court may direct;

   (c) P's participation should be secured by the appointment of a representative whose function shall be to provide the court with information as to the matters set out in section 4(6) of the Act and to discharge such other functions as the court may direct;

   (d) P should have the opportunity to address (directly or indirectly) the judge determining the application and, if so directed, the circumstances in which that should occur;

   (e) P's interests and position can properly be secured without any direction under sub-paragraphs (a) to (d) being made or by the making of an alternative direction meeting the overriding objective.

   (3) Any appointment or directions made pursuant to paragraph (2)(b) to (e) may be made for such period or periods as the court thinks fit.

   (4) Unless P has capacity to conduct the proceedings, an order joining P as a party shall only take effect—

   (a) on the appointment of a litigation friend on P's behalf; or

   (b) if the court so directs, on or after the appointment of an accredited legal representative.

   (5) If the court has directed that P should be joined as a party but such joinder does not occur because no litigation friend or accredited legal representative is appointed, the court shall record in a judgment or order—

   (a) the fact that no such appointment was made; and

   (b) the reasons given for that appointment not being made.

   (6) A practice direction may make additional or supplementary provision in respect of any of the matters set out in this rule.

(The appointment of litigation friends, accredited legal representatives and representatives under paragraph (2)(c) is dealt with under Part 17.)

("Accredited legal representative" is defined in rule 6.)]

AMENDMENT

4–009   This rule was inserted by SI 2015/548 r.5.

GENERAL NOTE

4–010   The purpose of this rule is to require the court to consider how best to ensure P's participation in the proceedings.

[The duty of the parties

4–011   **4.**—(1) The parties are required to help the court to further the overriding objective.

(2) Without prejudice to the generality of paragraph (1), each party is required to—
  (a) co-operate with the other parties and with the court in identifying and narrowing the issues that need to be determined by the court, and the timetable for that determination;
  (b) adhere to the timetable set by these Rules and by the court;
  (c) comply with all directions and orders of the court;
  (d) be full and frank in the disclosure of information and evidence to the court (including any disclosure ordered under Part 16);
  (e) co-operate with the other parties in all aspects of the conduct of the proceedings, including in the preparation of bundles.

(3) If the court determines that any party has failed without reasonable excuse to satisfy the requirements of this rule, it may under rule 159 depart from the general rules about costs in so far as they apply to that party.

(Rule 133(2) deals with the requirements of general disclosure.)]

AMENDMENT
This rule was substituted by SI 2015/548 r.6.   **4–012**

Court's duty to manage cases
5.—(1) The court will further the overriding objective by actively managing cases.   **4–013**
(2) Active case management includes—
  (a) encouraging the parties to co-operate with each other in the conduct of the proceedings;
  (b) identifying at an early stage—
    (i) the issues; and
    (ii) who should be a party to the proceedings;
  (c) deciding promptly—
    (i) which issues need a full investigation and hearing and which do not; and
    (ii) the procedure to be followed in the case;
  (d) deciding the order in which issues are to be resolved;
  (e) encouraging the parties to use an alternative dispute resolution procedure if the court considers that appropriate;
  (f) fixing timetables or otherwise controlling the progress of the case;
  (g) considering whether the likely benefits of taking a particular step justify the cost of taking it;
  (h) dealing with as many aspects of the case as the court can on the same occasion;
  (i) dealing with the case without the parties needing to attend at court;
  (j) Making use of technology; [. . .]
  (k) giving directions to ensure that the case proceeds quickly and efficiently;
  [(l) considering whether any hearing should be held in public; and
  (m) considering whether any document relating to proceedings should be a public document and, if so, whether and to what extent it should be redacted.

(Rules 91 to 93 make provision about the court's powers to authorise publication of information about proceedings and to order that a hearing be held in public.)

AMENDMENTS
The amendments to this rule were made by SI 2015/548 r.7.   **4–014**

PART 3

INTERPRETATION AND GENERAL PROVISIONS

Interpretation

4–015   **6.** In these Rules—

"the Act" means the Mental Capacity Act 2005;

["accredited legal representative" means a legal representative authorised pursuant to a scheme of accreditation approved by the President to represent persons meeting the definition of "P" in this rule in proceedings before the court;]

"applicant" means a person who makes, or who seeks permission to make, an application to the court;

"application form" means the document that is to be used to begin proceedings in accordance with Part 9 of these Rules or any other provision of these Rules or the practice directions which requires the use of an application form;

"application notice" means the document that is to be used to make an application in accordance with Part 10 of these Rules or any other provision of these Rules or the practice directions which requires the use of an application notice;

"attorney" means the person appointed as such by an enduring power of attorney created, or purporting to have been created, in accordance with the regulations mentioned in paragraph 2 of Schedule 4 to the Act;

"business day" means a day other than—

(a) a Saturday, Sunday, Christmas Day or Good Friday; or
(b) a bank holiday in England and Wales, under the Banking and Financial Dealings Act 1971;

"child" means a person under 18;

"court" means the Court of Protection;

"deputy" means a deputy appointed under the Act; "donee" means the donee of a lasting power of attorney;

"donor" means the donor of a lasting power of attorney, except where this expression is used in rule 68 or 201(5) (where it means the donor of an enduring power of attorney);

"enduring power of attorney" means an instrument created in accordance with such of the regulations mentioned in paragraph 2 of Schedule 4 to the Act as applied when it was executed;

"filing" in relation to a document means delivering it, by post or otherwise, to the court office; "judge" means a judge nominated to be a judge of the court under the Act;

["hearing" includes a hearing conducted by telephone, video link, or any other method permitted or directed by the court;]

"lasting power of attorney" has the meaning given in section 9 of the Act;

["legal representative" means a—

(a) barrister,
(b) solicitor,
(c) solicitor's employee,
(d) manager of a body recognised under section 9 of the Administration of Justice Act 1985, or
(e) person who, for the purposes of the Legal Services Act 2007, is an authorised person in relation to an activity which constitutes the conduct of litigation (within the meaning of that Act),

who has been instructed to act for a party in relation to any application;]

["legally aided person" means a person to whom civil legal services (within the meaning of the Legal Aid, Sentencing and Punishment of Offenders Act 2012) have been made available under arrangements made for the purposes of Part 1 of that Act);]

"order" includes a declaration made by the court;

"P" means [—

(a)] any person (other than a protected party) who lacks or, so far as consistent with the context, is alleged to lack capacity to make a decision or decisions in relation to any matter that is the subject of an application to the court[; and
(b) a relevant person as defined by paragraph 7 of Schedule A1 to the Act,]

and references to a person who lacks capacity are to be construed in accordance with the Act;

"party" is to be construed in accordance with rule 73;

[. . .]

"personal welfare" is to be construed in accordance with section 17 of the Act;

"President" and "Vice-President" refer to those judges appointed as such under section 46(3)(a) and (b) of the Act;

"property and affairs" is to be construed in accordance with section 18 of the Act;

"protected party" means a party or an intended party (other than P or a child) who lacks capacity to conduct the proceedings;

["representative" means a person appointed under rule 3A(2)(c), except where the context otherwise requires;]

"respondent" means a person who is named as a respondent in the application form or notice, as the case may be;

"Senior Judge" means the judge who has been nominated to be Senior Judge under section 46(4) of the Act, and references in these Rules to a circuit judge include the Senior Judge;

["Tier 1 Judge" means any judge nominated to act as a judge of the Court of Protection under section 46 of the Act who is neither a Tier 2 Judge nor a Tier 3 Judge;

"Tier 2 Judge" means—
(a) the Senior Judge; and
(b) such other judges nominated to act as a judge of the Court of Protection under section 46 of the Act as may be set out in the relevant practice direction;

"Tier 3 Judge" means—
(a) the President;
(b) the Vice-President; and
(c) such other judges nominated to act as a judge of the Court of Protection under section 46 of the Act as may be set out in the relevant practice direction;]

"Visitor" means a person appointed as such by the Lord Chancellor under section 61 of the Act.

AMENDMENTS

4–016   The amendments to this rule were made by SI 2009/582 r.3, SI 2009/3348 art.19 and SI 2013/534 Sch., para.17 and SI 2015/548 r.8.

GENERAL NOTE.

In *Re UF* [2013] EWHC 4289 (COP), Charles J. said:

"[O]n my reading of Rule 6 the point as to whether or not there is prima facie evidence of a lack of capacity to make the relevant decision, which is normally an issue on which the Official Solicitor seeks an interim finding before agreeing to act, is not relevant where one is dealing with an application under s.21A because, as I read Rule 6, P includes a relevant person as defined in paragraph 7 of Schedule A1, and thus the person who is the subject of the standard authorisation. That authorisation will be based on an assessment that the person lacks the capacity to make the relevant decisions on placement and that assessment may be challenged in the application made under s. 21A. Whether or not it is challenged either the underlying assessment is prima facie evidence of a lack of capacity or the issue of capacity is irrelevant to the application of the definition of P. Litigation capacity is a separate issue not mentioned in Rule 6."

4–017   RESPONDENT.   It is for the applicant to identify the correct respondent(s) on the application form. As a rule of thumb, a respondent, who will become a party to the proceedings if he files an acknowledgement of service (r.73(1)), is a person who has a material interest in the outcome of the case (*B (Court of Protection) (Notice of Proceedings), Re* [1987] 2 All E.R. 475).

Court officers

4–018   **7.**—(1) Where these Rules permit or require the court to perform an act of a purely formal or administrative character, that act may be performed by a court officer.

(2) A requirement that a court officer carry out any act at the request of any person is subject to the payment of any fee required by a fees order for the carrying out of that act.

[**7A.**—(1) The Senior Judge or the President may authorise a court officer to exercise the jurisdiction of the court in such circumstances as set out in the relevant practice direction.

(2) A court officer who has been authorised under paragraph (1)—

(a) must refer to a judge any application, proceedings or any question arising in any application or proceedings which ought, in the officer's opinion, to be considered by a judge;

(b) may not deal with any application or proceedings or any question arising in any application or proceedings by way of a hearing; and

(c) may not deal with an application for the reconsideration of an order made by that court officer or another court officer.]

AMENDMENT

This rule was inserted by SI 2011/2753 r.3. **4–019**

Computation of time

8. This rule shows how to calculate any period of time which is specified— **4–020**

(a) by these Rules;

(b) by a practice direction; or

(c) in an order or direction of the court.

(2) A period of time expressed as a number of days must be computed as clear days.

(3) In this rule "clear days" means that in computing the number of days—

(a) the day on which the period begins; and

(b) if the end of the period is defined by reference to an event, the day on which that event occurs,

are not included.

(4) Where the specified period is 7 days or less, and would include a day which is not a business day, that day does not count.

(5) When the specified period for doing any act at the court office ends on a day on which the office is closed, that act will be done in time if done on the next day on which the court office is open.

[Application of Civil Procedure Rules and Family Procedure Rules

9.—(1) In any case not expressly provided for by these Rules or the practice **4–021**
directions made under them, the court may apply either the Civil Procedure Rules 1998 or the Family Procedure Rules 2010 (including in either case the practice directions made under them) with any necessary modifications, in so far as is necessary to further the overriding objective.

(2) A reference in these Rules to the Civil Procedure Rules 1998 or to the Family Procedure Rules 2010 is to the version of those rules in force at the date specified for the purpose of that reference in the relevant practice direction.]

AMENDMENT

This rule was substituted by SI 2015/548 r.9. **4–022**

[Pilot schemes

9A.—(1) Practice directions may make provision for the operation of pilot **4–023**
schemes for assessing the use of new practices and procedures in connection with proceedings—

(a) for specified periods; and
(b) in relation to proceedings—
    (i) in specified parts of the country; or
    (ii) relating to specified types of application.
(2) Practice directions may modify or disapply any provision of these Rules during the operation of such pilot schemes.]

AMENDMENT
4–024   This rule was substituted by SI 2015/548 r.9.

PART 4

Practice Directions
    4A Court Documents
    4B Statements of Truth

COURT DOCUMENTS

Documents used in court proceedings
4–025   **10.**—(1) The court will seal or otherwise authenticate with the stamp of the court the following documents on issue—
(a) [. . .]
(b) an application form;
(c) an application notice;
(d) an order; and
(e) any other document which a rule or practice direction requires to be sealed or stamped.
(2) Where these Rules or any practice direction require a document to be signed, that requirement is satisfied if the signature is printed by computer or other mechanical means.
(3) A practice direction may make provision for documents to be filed or sent to the court by—
(a) facsimile; or
(b) other means.

AMENDMENT
4–026   The amendment to this rule was made by SI 2015/548 r.10.

Documents required to be verified by a statement of truth
4–027   **11.**—(1) The following documents must be verified by a statement of truth—
(a) [an application form, an application notice, an appellant's notice or a respondent's notice] where the applicant seeks to rely upon matters set out in the document as evidence;
(b) a witness statement;
(c) a certificate of—
    (i) service or non-service; or
    (ii) notification or non-notification;
(d) a deputy's declaration; and
(e) any other document required by a rule or practice direction to be so verified.
(2) Subject to paragraph (3), a statement of truth is a statement that—
(a) the party putting forward the document;

(b) in the case of a witness statement, the maker of the witness statement; or

(c) in the case of a certificate referred to in paragraph (1)(c), the person who signs the certificate,

believes that the facts stated in the document being verified are true.

(3) If a party is conducting proceedings with a litigation friend, the statement of truth in—

(a) [. . .]

(b) an application form; or

(c) an application notice;

[(d) an appellant's notice or a respondent's notice]

is a statement that the litigation friend believes the facts stated in the document being verified are true.

(4) The statement of truth must be signed—

(a) in the case of [an application form, an application notice, an appellant's notice or a respondent's notice]—

(i) by the party or litigation friend; or

(ii) by the legal representative on behalf of the party or litigation friend; and

(b) in the case of a witness statement, by the maker of the statement.

(5) A statement of truth which is not contained in the document which it verifies must clearly identify that document.

(6) A statement of truth in [an application form, an application notice, an appellant's notice or a respondent's notice] may be made by—

(a) a person who is not a party; or

(b) two or more parties jointly,

where this is permitted by a relevant practice direction.

AMENDMENTS

The amendments to this rule were made by SI 2015/548 r.11.   **4–028**

[Position statement not required to be verified by statement of truth

11A. Nothing in these Rules requires a position statement to be verified by a   **4–029**
statement of truth.]

AMENDMENT

This rule was inserted by SI 2015/548 r.12   **4–030**

Failure to verify a document

12. If [an application form, an application notice, an appellant's notice or a   **4–031**
respondent's notice] is not verified by a statement of truth, the applicant [(or
respondent as the case may be)] may not rely upon the document as evidence of
any of the matters set out in it unless the court permits.

AMENDMENTS

The amendments to this rule were made by SI 2015/548 r.13.   **4–032**

Failure to verify a witness statement

13. If a witness statement is not verified by a statement of truth, it shall not be   **4–033**
admissible in evidence unless the court permits.

False statements

14.—(1) Proceedings for contempt of court may be brought against a person   **4–034**

if he makes, or causes to be made, a false statement in a document verified by a statement of truth without an honest belief in its truth.

(2) Proceedings under this rule may be brought only—

(a) by the Attorney General; or

(b) with the permission of the court.

Personal details

4–035
15.—(1) Where a party does not wish to reveal—

(a) his home address or telephone number;

(b) P's home address or telephone number;

(c) the name of the person with whom P is living (if that person is not the applicant); or

(d) the address or telephone number of his place of business, or the place of business of any of the persons mentioned in sub-paragraphs (b) or (c),

he must provide those particulars to the court.

(2) Where paragraph (1) applies, the particulars given will not be revealed to any person unless the court so directs.

(3) Where a party changes his home address during the course of the proceedings, he must give notice of the change to the court.

(4) Where a party does not reveal his home address, he must nonetheless provide an address for service which must be within the jurisdiction of the court.

Supply of documents to a party from court records

4–036
16. Unless the court orders otherwise, a party to proceedings may inspect or obtain from the records of the court a copy of—

(a) any document filed by a party to the proceedings; or

(b) any communication in the proceedings between the court and—

(i) a party to the proceedings; or

(ii) another person.

Supply of documents to a non-party from court records

4–037
17.—(1) Subject to rules 20 and 92(2), a person who is not a party to proceedings may inspect or obtain from the court records a copy of any judgment or order given or made in public.

(2) The court may, on an application made to it, authorise a person who is not a party to proceedings to—

(a) inspect any other documents in the court records; or

(b) obtain a copy of any such documents, or extracts from such documents.

(3) A person making an application for an authorisation under paragraph (2) must do so in accordance with Part 10.

(4) Before giving an authorisation under paragraph (2), the court will consider whether any document is to be provided on an edited basis.

Subsequent use of court documents

4–038
18.—(1) Where a document has been filed or disclosed, a party to whom it was provided may use the document only for the purpose of the proceedings in which it was filed or disclosed, except where—

(a) the document has been read to or by the court or referred to at a public hearing; or

(b) the court otherwise permits.

(2) Paragraph (1)(a) is subject to any order of the court made under rule 92(2).

Editing information in court documents

19.—(1) A party may apply to the court for an order that a specified part of a document is to be edited prior to the document's service or disclosure.

4–039

(2) An order under paragraph (1) may be made at any time.

(3) Where the court makes an order under this rule any subsequent use of that document in the proceedings shall be of the document as edited, unless the court directs otherwise.

(4) An application under this rule must be made in accordance with Part 10.

Public Guardian to be supplied with court documents relevant to supervision of deputies

20.—(1) This rule applies in any case where the court makes an order—

4–040

(a) appointing a person to act as a deputy; or

(b) varying an order under which a deputy has been appointed.

(2) Subject to paragraphs (3) and (6), the Public Guardian is entitled to be supplied with a copy of qualifying documents if he reasonably considers that it is necessary for him to have regard to them in connection with the discharge of his functions under section 58 of the Act in relation to the supervision of deputies.

(3) The court may direct that the right to be supplied with documents under paragraph (2) does not apply in relation to such one or more documents, or descriptions of documents, as the court may specify.

(4) A direction under paragraph (3) or (6) may be given—

(a) either on the court's own initiative or on an application made to it; and

(b) either—

    (i) at the same time as the court makes the order which appoints the deputy, or which varies it; or

    (ii) subsequently.

(5) "Qualifying documents" means documents which—

(a) are filed in court in connection with the proceedings in which the court makes the order referred to in paragraph (1); and

(b) are relevant to—

    (i) the decision to appoint the deputy;

    (ii) any powers conferred on him;

    (iii) any duties imposed on him; or

    (iv) any other terms applying to those powers and duties which are contained in the order.

(6) The court may direct that any document is to be provided to the Public Guardian on an edited basis.

Provision of court order to Public Guardian

21. Any order of the court requiring the Public Guardian to do something, or not to do something, will be served by the court on the Public Guardian as soon as practicable and in any event not later than 7 days after the order was made.

4–041

Amendment of application

22.—(1) The court may allow or direct an applicant, at any stage of the proceedings, to amend his application form or notice.

4–042

(2) The amendment may be effected by making in writing the necessary altera-

tions to the application form or notice, but if the amendments are so numerous or of such a nature or length that written alteration would make it difficult or inconvenient to read, a fresh document amended as allowed or directed may be issued.

Clerical mistakes or slips

4–043   **23.** The court may at any time correct any clerical mistakes in an order or direction or any error arising in an order or direction from any accidental slip or omission.

Endorsement of amendment

4–044   **24.** Where an application form or notice, order or direction has been amended under this Part, a note shall be placed on it showing the date on which it was amended and the alteration shall be sealed.

PART 5

GENERAL CASE MANAGEMENT POWERS

The court's general powers of case management

4–045   **25.**—(1) The list of powers in this rule is in addition to any powers given to the court by any other rule or practice direction or by any other enactment or any powers it may otherwise have.

(2) The court may—

(a) extend or shorten the time for compliance with any rule, practice direction, or court order or direction (even if an application for extension is made after the time for compliance has expired);

(b) adjourn or bring forward a hearing;

(c) require P, a party, a party's legal representative or litigation friend, to attend court;

(d) hold a hearing and receive evidence by telephone or any other method of direct oral communication;

(e) stay the whole or part of any proceedings or judgment either generally or until a specified date or event;

(f) consolidate proceedings;

(g) hear two or more applications on the same occasion;

(h) direct a separate hearing of any issue;

(i) decide the order in which issues are to be heard;

(j) exclude an issue from consideration;

(k) dismiss or give judgment on an application after a decision is made on a preliminary basis;

(l) direct any party to file and serve an estimate of costs; and

(m) take any step or give any direction for the purpose of managing the case and furthering the overriding objective.

(3) A judge to whom a matter is allocated may, if he considers that the matter is one which ought properly to be dealt with by another judge, transfer the matter to such a judge.

(4) Where the court gives directions it may take into account whether or not a party has complied with any rule or practice direction.

(5) The court may make any order it considers appropriate even if a party has not sought that order.

(6) A power of the court under these Rules to make an order includes a power to vary or revoke the order;

(7) [. . .].

AMENDMENT

The amendment to this rule was made by SI 2015/548 r.14.   **4–046**

GENERAL NOTE

The principles set out in s.1 of the Act "set the context in which the case before the Court   **4–047**
of Protection proceeds but do not strictly govern its case management or other decisions
under [these Rules]" (*Re B* (2013) WL 7117512 (COP) at para.63, per D.J. Batten).

Extensive guidance on case management was provided by Parker J. in *NCC v PB* [2014]
EWCOP 14 at paras 126 to 148. In particular, her Ladyship said at para.127:

"All those who practice in the Court of Protection must appreciate that those who represent the vulnerable who cannot give them capacitous instructions have a particular
responsibility to ensure that the arguments addressed are proportionate and relevant to
the issues, to the actual facts with which they are dealing rather than the theory, and to
have regard to the public purse, court resources, and other court users."

The Court of Appeal is reluctant to interfere with case management decisions of the
court. In *NCC v MEF* [2011] EWCA Civ 1063 at para.10, Thorpe L.J. said:

"Case management decisions are for the judge in the trial court, particularly if the judge
takes control of the case at an early stage and provides for judicial continuity. Such a
judge exercises a particularly wide ambit of discretion in managing the case and it is
exceptionally rare for this court to intervene or to interfere with the case management
function of such a circuit judge to whom the case is consistently reserved."

Once findings of fact have been made following a hearing before a specific judge, the
case becomes part heard and the trial (including any subsequent "best interest" hearing)
should not resume before a different judge (*Enfield LBC v SA* [2010] EWHC 196 (Admin)
at para.113).

Paragraph (6)

In *TF v PJ* [2014] EWHC 1840 (Admin), Mostyn J. held that the identically worded   **4–048**
r.4.1(6) of the Family Procure Rules 2010 could only be invoked where there had been
non-disclosure or a significant change in circumstances.

Court's power to dispense with requirement of any rule

26. In addition to its general powers and the powers listed in rule 25, the court   **4–049**
may dispense with the requirement of any rule.

Exercise of powers on the court's own initiative

27.—(1) Except where these Rules or some other enactment make different   **4–050**
provision, the court may exercise its powers on its own initiative.

(2) The court may make an order on its own initiative without hearing the
parties or giving them the opportunity to make representations.

(3) Where the court proposes to make an order on its own initiative it may give
the parties and any person it thinks fit an opportunity to make representations and,
where it does so, it will specify the time by which, and the manner in which, the
representations must be made.

(4) Where the court proposes—

(a) to make an order on its own initiative; and

(b) to hold a hearing to decide whether to make the order,

it will give the parties and may give any other person it thinks likely to be affected by the order at least 3 days' notice of the hearing.

GENERAL NOTE

4–051   This rule enables the court to make orders on its own initiative (para.(1)), and to chose whether or not to hear representations from the parties (para.(2)). Paragraph (3) provides that where the court proposes to make an order on its own initiative it may give the parties and any person it thinks fit an opportunity to make representations laying down a timetable when it does so.

In *KD v Havering LBC* [2010] 1 F.L.R. 1393, Judge Horowitz held that the power of the court to make an order on its own initiative is a power to be exercised appropriately and with a modicum of restraint. It is a power "to be exercised as an alternative to a hearing and in the proper case such as an emergency or where there is little or no apparent contest anticipated to the exercise of the court's powers. It is not likely to be an appropriate power to be exercised where the outcome is a deprivation of liberty in circumstances where there is a serious issue or potential issue whether that is appropriate and so where Articles 5 and 6 [of the European Convention on Human Rights] are potentially both engaged" (para.28). His Honour further said that the power is "appropriate for a plain case and not where real questions are likely to be raised as to the appropriate mode of management and disposal" (para.29).

For the interaction between this rule and r.27, see the General Note to r.89.

General power of the court to rectify matters where there has been an error of procedure

4–052   **28.** Where there has been an error of procedure, such as a failure to comply with a rule or practice direction—

    (a) the error does not invalidate any step taken in the proceedings unless the court so orders; and

    (b) the court may waive the error or require it to be remedied or may make such other order as appears to the court to be just.

PART 6

Practice Directions
   6A Service
   6B Service out of Jurisdiction

SERVICE OF DOCUMENTS

Service generally

Scope

4–053   **29.**—(1) Subject to paragraph (2), the rules in this Part apply to—

    (a) the service of documents; and

    (b) to the requirement under rule 70 for a person to be notified of the issue of an application form,

and references to 'serve', 'service', 'notice' and 'notify', and kindred expressions shall be construed accordingly.

(2) The rules in this Part do not apply where—

    (a) any other enactment, a rule in another Part or a practice direction makes different provision; or

    (b) the court directs otherwise.

Who is to serve

30.—(1) The general rule is that the following documents will be served by the court—

   (a) an order or judgment of the court;

   (b) an acknowledgment of service or notification; and

   (c) except where the application is for an order for committal, a notice of hearing.

(2) Any other document is to be served by the party seeking to rely upon it, except where—

   (a) a rule or practice direction provides otherwise; or

   (b) the court directs otherwise.

(3) Where the court is to serve a document—

   (a) it is for the court to decide which of the methods of service specified in rule 31 is to be used; and

   (b) if the document is being served on behalf of a party, that party must provide sufficient copies.

4–054

Methods of service

31.—(1) A document may be served by any of the methods specified in this rule.

(2) Where it is not known whether a solicitor is acting on behalf of a person, the document may be served by—

   (a) delivering it to the person personally;

   (b) delivering it at his home address or last known home address; or

   (c) sending it to that address, or last known address, by first class post (or by an alternative method of service which provides for delivery on the next working day).

(3) Where a solicitor—

   (a) is authorised to accept service on behalf of a person; and

   (b) has informed the person serving the document in writing that he is so authorised,

the document must be served on the solicitor, unless personal service is required by an enactment, rule, practice direction or court order.

(4) Where it appears to the court that there is a good reason to authorise service by a method other than those specified in paragraphs (2) or (3), the court may direct that service is effected by that method.

(5) A direction that service is effected by an alternative method must specify—

   (a) the method of service; and

   (b) the date when the document will be deemed to be served.

(6) A practice direction may set out how documents are to be served by document exchange, electronic communication or other means.

4–055

Service of documents on children and protected parties

32.—(1) The following table shows the person on whom a document must be served if it is a document which would otherwise be served on—

   (a) a child; or

   (b) a protected party.

4–056

Type of document	Nature of party	Person to be served
Application form	Child	— A person who has parental responsibility for the child within the meaning of the Children Act 1989; or — if there is no such person, a person with whom the child resides or in whose care the child is.
Application form	Protected party	— The person who is authorised to conduct the proceedings in the protected party's name or on his behalf; or — a person who is a duly appointed attorney, donee or deputy of the protected party; or — if there is no such person, a person with whom the protected party lives or in whose care the latter is.
Application for an order appointing a litigation friend, where a child or protected party has no litigation friend	Child or protected party	— See rule 145 (appointment of litigation friend by court order—supplementary).
Any other document	Child or protected party	— The litigation friend or other duly authorised person who is conducting the proceedings on behalf of the child or protected party.

(2) The court may make an order for service on a child or a protected party by permitting the document to be served on some person other than the person specified in the table set out in paragraph (1) above (which may include service on the child or the protected party).

(3) An application for an order under paragraph (2) may be made without notice.

(4) The court may order that, although a document has been served on someone other than the person specified in the table, the document is to be treated as if it had been properly served.

(5) This rule does not apply in relation to the service of documents upon a child in any case where the court has made an order under rule 141(4) permitting the child to conduct proceedings without a litigation friend.

Service of documents on P if he becomes a party

33.—(1) If P becomes a party to the proceedings, all documents to be served   **4–057**
on him must be served on his litigation friend or [as directed by the court] on P's
behalf.

(2) The court may make an order for service on P by permitting the document to
be served on some person other than the person specified in paragraph (1) above
(which may include service on P).

(3) An application for an order under paragraph (2) may be made without
notice.

(4) The court may order that, although a document has been served on someone
other than a person specified in paragraph (1), the document is to be treated as if
it had been properly served.

(5) This rule does not apply in relation to the service of documents upon P in
any case where the court has made an order under rule [144(1)(b) (power of court
to bring to an end the appointment of a litigation friend)].

[(Rule 41A requires P to be notified where a direction has been made under rule
3A, and of the appointment of a litigation friend, accredited legal representative
or representative.)]

AMENDMENTS
The amendments to this rule were made by SI 2015/548 r.15.   **4–058**

Substituted service

34. Where it appears to the court that it is impracticable for any reason to serve   **4–059**
a document in accordance with any of the methods provided under rule 31, the
court may make an order for substituted service of the document by taking such
steps as the court may direct to bring it to the notice of the person to be served.

Deemed service

35.—(1) A document which is served in accordance with these Rules or any   **4–060**
relevant practice direction shall be deemed to be served on the day shown in the
following table—

Method of service	Deemed day of service
First class post (or other service for next-day delivery)	The second day after it was posted.
Document exchange	The second day after it was left at the document exchange.
Delivering the document to a permitted address	The day after it was delivered to that address.
Fax	If it is transmitted on a business day before 4p.m., on that day; or in any other case, on the business day after the day on which it is transmitted.
Other electronic means	The second day after the day on which it is transmitted.

(2) If a document is served personally—

(a) after 5 p.m., on a business day; or

(b) at any time on a Saturday, Sunday or a Bank Holiday,

it will be treated as being served on the next business day.

Certificate of service

4–061   **36.**—(1) Where a rule, practice direction or court order requires a certificate of service for the document, the certificate must state the details set out in the following table—

Method of service	Details to be certified
First class post (or any other service for next-day delivery)	Date of posting.
Personal service	Date of personal service.
Document exchange	Date when the document was left at the document exchange.
Delivery of document to permitted address	Date when the document was delivered to that address.
Fax	Date of transmission.
Other electronic means	Date of transmission and the means used.
Alternative method permitted by the court	As required by the court.

(2) The certificate must be filed within 7 days after service of the document to which it relates.

Certificate of non-service

4–062   **37.**—(1) Where an applicant or other person is unable to serve any document under these Rules or as directed by the court, he must file a certificate of non-service stating the reasons why service has not been effected.

(2) The certificate of non-service must be filed within 7 days of the latest date on which service should have been effected.

Power of court to dispense with service

4–063   **38.**—(1) The court may dispense with any requirement to serve a document.

(2) An application for an order to dispense with service may be made without notice.

GENERAL NOTE

4–064   The overriding objective set out in r.3(1) does not require the court to make a best interests decision pursuant to s.1(5) and s.4 of the Act when deciding whether to direct that a party shall not be served with an application to execute a statutory will (*Re B* (2013) WL 7117512 (COP) at para.63).

[Scope and interpretation

39.—(1) This rule and rules 39A to 39H make provision about—   **4–065**
(a) service of application forms and other documents out of the jurisdiction; and
(b) the procedure for service.
(2) In this rule and rules 39A to 39H—

"application form" includes an application notice;
"Commonwealth State" means a State listed in Schedule 3 to the British Nationality Act 1981(a);
"jurisdiction" means, unless the context otherwise requires, England and Wales and any part of the territorial waters of the United Kingdom adjoining England and Wales;
"Member State" means a Member State of the European Union;
"the Service Convention" means the Convention on the service abroad of judicial and extrajudicial documents in civil or commercial matters signed at the Hague on November 15, 1965;
"Service Convention country" means a country, not being a Member State, which is a party to the Service Convention; and
"the Service Regulation" means Regulation (EC) No.1393/2007 of the European Parliament and of the Council of 13 November 2007 on the service in the Member States of judicial and extra-judicial documents in civil and commercial matters (service of documents) and repealing Council Regulation (EC) No.1348/2000(b).
(3) In rules 39A to 39H, a reference to service by a party includes service by a person who is not a party where service by such a person is required under these Rules.]

AMENDMENT
    This rule was substituted by SI 2015/548 r.16.   **4–066**

[Service of application form and other documents out of the jurisdiction

39A.—(1) Subject to paragraph (2), any document to be served for the purposes   **4–067**
of these Rules may be served out of the jurisdiction without the permission of the court.
(2) An application form may not be served out of the jurisdiction unless the court has power to determine the application to which it relates under the Act.]

AMENDMENT
    This rule was substituted by SI 2015/548 r.16.   **4–068**

[Period for acknowledging service or responding to application where application is served out of the jurisdiction.]

39B.—(1) This rule applies where, under these Rules, a party is required to   **4–069**
file—
(a) an acknowledgment of service; or
(b) an answer to an application,
and sets out the time period for doing so where the application is served out of the jurisdiction.

(2) Where the applicant serves an application on a respondent in—

(a) Scotland or Northern Ireland; or

(b) a Member State or Service Convention country within Europe, the period for filing an acknowledgment of service or an answer to an application is 21 days after service of the application.

(3) Where the applicant serves an application on a respondent in a Service Convention country outside Europe, the period for filing an acknowledgment of service or an answer to an application is 31 days after service of the application.

(4) Where the applicant serves an application on a respondent in a country not referred to in paragraphs (2) and (3), the period for filing an acknowledgment of service or an answer to an application is set out in Practice Direction 6B.]

AMENDMENT

4–070   This rule was substituted by SI 2015/548 r.16.

[Method of service—general provisions

4–071   **39C.**—(1) This rule contains general provisions about the method of service of an application form or other document on a party out of the jurisdiction.

Where service is to be effected on a party in Scotland or Northern Ireland

(2) Where a party serves an application form or other document on a party in Scotland or Northern Ireland, it must be served by a method permitted by this Part.

Where service is to be effected out of the United Kingdom

(3) Where an application form or other document is to be served on a person out of the United Kingdom, it may be served by any method—

(a) provided for by—

(i) rule 39D (service in accordance with the Service Regulation); or

(ii) rule 39E (service through foreign governments, judicial authorities and British Consular authorities); or

(b) permitted by the law of the country in which it is to be served.

(4) Nothing in paragraph (3) or in any court order authorises or requires any person to do anything which is contrary to the law of the country where the application form or other document is to be served.]

AMENDMENT

4–072   This rule was substituted by SI 2015/548 r.16.

[Service in accordance with the Service Regulation

4–073   **39D.**—(1) This rule applies where an application form or other document is to be served on a person out of the United Kingdom in accordance with the Service Regulation.

(2) The person wishing to serve must file—

(a) the application form or other document;

(b) any translation; and

(c) any other documents required by the Service Regulation.

(3) When the person wishing to serve files the documents referred to in paragraph (2), the court officer must—

(a) seal, or otherwise authenticate with the stamp of the court, the copy of the application form; and

(b) forward the documents to the Senior Master of the Queen's Bench Division.

(4) In addition to the documents referred to in paragraph (2), the person wishing to serve may, if of the view that this would assist in ensuring effective service, file a photograph of the person to be served.

(The Service Regulation is annexed to Practice Direction 6B.)

(Rule 39E makes provision for service on a person in a Service Convention country.)]

AMENDMENT

This rule was substituted by SI 2015/548 r.16.   **4–074**

[Service through foreign governments, judicial authorities and British Consular authorities

39E.—(1) Where an application form or other document is to be served on a   **4–075**
person in a Service Convention country, it may be served—
  (a) through the authority designated under the Service Convention in respect of that country; or
  (b) if the law of that country permits, through—
     (i) the judicial authorities of that country; or
     (ii) a British Consular authority in that country.

(2) Where an application form or other document is to be served on a person in a country which is not a Service Convention country, it may be served, if the law of that country so permits, through—
  (a) the government of that country, where that government is willing to serve it; or
  (b) a British Consular authority in that country.

(3) Where an application form or other document is to be served in—
  (a) any Commonwealth State which is not a Service Convention country;
  (b) the Isle of Man or the Channel Islands; or
  (c) any British Overseas Territory,
the methods of service permitted by paragraphs (1)(b) and (2) are not available and the person wishing to serve, or that person's agent, must effect service direct unless Practice Direction 6B provides otherwise.

(4) This rule does not apply where service is to be effected in accordance with the Service Regulation.

(Rule 39D makes provision for service on a party in a Member State in accordance with the Service Regulation.)

(A list of British Overseas Territories is reproduced in Practice Direction 6B.)]

AMENDMENT

This rule was substituted by SI 2015/548 r.16.   **4–076**

[Procedure where service is to be through foreign governments, judicial authorities and British Consular authorities

39F.—(1) This rule applies where an application form or other document is to   **4–077**
be served under rule 39E(1) or (2).

(2) Where this rule applies, the person wishing to serve must file—
  (a) a request for service of the application form or other document, by specifying one or more of the methods in rule 39E(1) or (2);

(b) a copy of the application form or other document;

(c) any other documents or copies of documents required by Practice Direction 6B; and

(d) any translation required under rule 39G.

(3) When the person wishing to serve files the documents specified in paragraph (2), the court officer must—

(a) seal, or otherwise authenticate with the stamp of the court, the copy of the application form; and

(b) forward the documents to the Senior Master of the Queen's Bench Division.

(4) The Senior Master shall send documents forwarded under this rule—

(a) where the application form or other document is being served through the authority designated under the Service Convention, to that authority; or

(b) in any other case, to the Foreign and Commonwealth Office with a request that it arranges for the application form or other document to be served.

(5) An official certificate which—

(a) states that the method requested under paragraph (2)(a) has been performed and the date of such performance;

(b) states, where more than one method is requested under paragraph (2)(a), which method was used; and

(c) is made by—

(i) a British Consular authority in the country where the method requested under paragraph (2)(a) was performed;

(ii) the government or judicial authorities in that country; or

(iii) the authority designated in respect of that country under the Service Convention,

is evidence of the facts stated in the certificate.

(6) A document purporting to be an official certificate under paragraph (5) is to be treated as such a certificate unless it is proved not to be.]

[Translation of application form or other document

4–078   **39G.**—(1) Except where paragraphs (4) and (5) apply, every copy of the application form or other document filed under rule 39E (service through foreign governments, judicial authorities and British Consular authorities) must be accompanied by a translation of the application form or other document.

(2) The translation must be—

(a) in the official language of the country in which it is to be served; or

(b) if there is more than one official language of that country, in any official language which is appropriate to the place in the country where the application form or other document is to be served.

(3) Every translation filed under this rule must be accompanied by a statement by the person making it that it is a correct translation, and the statement must include that person's name, address and qualifications for making the translation.

(4) The applicant is not required to file a translation of the application form or other document filed under rule 39E where it is to be served in a country of which English is an official language.

(5) The applicant is not required to file a translation of the application form or other document filed under rule 39E where—

(a) the person on whom the document is to be served is able to read and understand English; and

(b) service of the document is to be effected directly on that person.

(This rule does not apply to service in accordance with the Service Regulation, which contains its own provisions about the translation of documents.)]

AMENDMENT
This rule was substituted by SI 2015/548 r.16.   **4–079**

[Undertaking to be responsible for expenses of the Foreign and Commonwealth Office

39H. Every request for service under rule 39F (procedure where service is to   **4–080**
be through foreign governments, judicial authorities, etc.) must contain an undertaking by the person making the request—

(a) to be responsible for all expenses incurred by the Foreign and Commonwealth
Office or foreign judicial authority; and

(b) to pay those expenses to the Foreign and Commonwealth Office or foreign
judicial authority on being informed of the amount.]

AMENDMENT
This rule was substituted by SI 2015/548 r.16.   **4–081**

PART 7

Practice Direction
7A Notifying P

NOTIFYING P

General requirement to notify P

General

40.—(1) Subject to paragraphs (2) and (3), the rules in this Part apply where   **4–082**
P is to be given notice of any matter or document, or is to be provided with any
document, either under the Rules or in accordance with an order or direction of
the court.

(2) [Except where rule 41A applies, if] P becomes a party, the rules in this Part
do not apply and service is to be effected in accordance with Part 6 or as directed
by the court.

(3) In any case the court may, either on its own initiative or on application,
direct that P must not be notified of any matter or document, or provided with any
document, whether in accordance with this Part or at all.

[(4) Subject to paragraph (5), where P is a child—

(a) if the person to be notified under this rule is a person with parental responsibility for the child within the meaning of the Children Act 1989(a) or, if
there is no such person, a person with whom the child resides or in whose
care the child is;

(b) all references to "P" in this Part, except that in paragraph (2), are to be read
as referring to the person notified in accordance with sub-paragraph (a).

(5) Paragraph (4) does not apply, and there is no requirement to notify P, where
the person referred to in paragraph (4)(a) has already been served or notified of the
relevant matter in accordance with another rule or practice direction.]

AMENDMENTS
4–083   The amendments to this rule were made by SI 2015/548 r.17.

Who is to notify P
4–084   **41.**—(1) Where P is to be notified under this Part, notification must be effected by—
(a) the applicant;
(b) the appellant (where the matter relates to an appeal);
(c) an agent duly appointed by the applicant or the appellant; or
(d) such other person as the court may direct.
(2) The person within paragraph (1) is referred to in this Part as "the person effecting notification".

[Notifying P of appointment of a litigation friend, etc.
4–085   **41A.** P must be notified—
(a) where a direction has been made under rule 3A; and
(b) of the appointment of a litigation friend, accredited legal representative or representative on P's behalf.]

AMENDMENT
4–085A   This rule was inserted by SI 2015/548 r.18.

Circumstances in which P must be notified

Application forms
4–086   **42.**—(1) P must be notified—
(a) that an application form has been issued by the court;
(b) that an application form has been withdrawn; and
(c) of the date on which a hearing is to be held in relation to the matter, where that hearing is for disposing of the application.
(2) Where P is to be notified that an application form has been issued, the person effecting notification must explain to P—
(a) who the applicant is;
(b) that the application raises the question of whether P lacks capacity in relation to a matter or matters, and what that means;
(c) what will happen if the court makes the order or direction that has been applied for; and
(d) where the application contains a proposal for the appointment of a person to make decisions on P's behalf in relation to the matter to which the application relates, details of who that person is.
(3) Where P is to be notified that an application form has been withdrawn, the person effecting notification must explain to P—
(a) that the application form has been withdrawn; and
(b) the consequences of that withdrawal.
(4) The person effecting notification must also inform P that he may seek advice and assistance in relation to any matter of which he is notified.

Appeals
4–087   **43.**—(1) P must be notified—
(a) that an appellant's notice has been issued by the court;
(b) that an appellant's notice has been withdrawn; and

(c) of the date on which a hearing is to be held in relation to the matter, where that hearing is for disposing of the appellant's notice.

(2) Where P is to be notified that an appellant's notice has been issued, the person effecting notification must explain to P—

(a) who the appellant is;

(b) the issues raised by the appeal; and

(c) what will happen if the court makes the order or direction that has been applied for.

(3) Where P is to be notified that an appellant's notice has been withdrawn, the person effecting notification must explain to P—

(a) that the appellant's notice has been withdrawn; and

(b) the consequences of that withdrawal.

(4) The person effecting notification must also inform P that he may seek advice and assistance in relation to any matter of which he is notified.

Final orders

44.—(1) P must be notified of [any decision of the court relating to P except for a case management decision].   **4–088**

(2) Where P is notified in accordance with this rule, the person effecting notification must explain to P the effect of the [decision].

(3) The person effecting notification must also inform P that [P] may seek advice and assistance in relation to any matter of which [P] is notified.

[(4) The person effecting notification must also provide P with a copy of any order relating to a decision of which P must be notified in accordance with paragraph (1).]

AMENDMENTS

The amendments to this rule were made by SI 2015/548 r.19.   **4–089**

Other matters

45.—(1) This rule applies where the court directs that P is to be notified of any other matter.   **4–090**

(2) The person effecting notification must explain to P such matters as may be directed by the court.

(3) The person effecting notification must also inform P that he may seek advice and assistance in relation to any matter of which he is notified.

Manner of notification, and accompanying documents

Manner of notification

46.—(1) Where P is to be notified under this Part, the person effecting notification must provide P with [, or arrange for P to be provided with] the information specified in rules [41A] to 45 in a way that is appropriate to P's circumstances (for example, using simple language, visual aids or any other appropriate means).   **4–091**

(2) The information referred to in paragraph (1) must be provided to P personally.

(3) P must be provided with the information mentioned in paragraph (1) as soon as practicable and in any event within [14] days of the date on which—

(a) the application form or appellant's notice was issued or withdrawn;

(b) the [decision] was made; [. . .]

(c) the person effecting notification received the notice of hearing from the court and in any event no later than 14 days before the date specified in the notice of the hearing, [; and]

[(d) the order referred to in rule 44(4) was served upon the person who is required to effect notification of P under that rule,]

as the case may be.

[(4) Where the provisions of rule 40(4) apply, paragraphs (1) and (2) of this rule do not apply and the person effecting notification may provide information and documents of which P must be notified to the person to be notified under rule 40(4), by any method by which service of documents would be permitted under rule 31.]

AMENDMENTS
4–092   The amendments to this rule were made by SI 2015/548 r.20.

Acknowledgment of notification
4–093   **47.** When P is notified that an application form or an appellant's notice has been issued, he must also be provided with a form for acknowledging notification.

[Certificate of notification
4–094   **48.**—(1) The person effecting notification must, within 7 days beginning with the date on which notification in accordance with this Part was given, file a certificate of notification which certifies—

(a) the date on which, and how, P was notified; and

(b) that P was notified in accordance with this Part.

(2) Subject to paragraph (3), the person effecting notification in accordance with this Part must in the certificate required by paragraph (1) describe the steps taken to enable P to understand, and the extent to which P appears to have understood, the information.

(3) Where the provisions of rule 40(4) apply, paragraph (2) does not apply.]

AMENDMENT
4–095   This rule was substituted by SI 2015/548 r.21.

Dispensing with requirement to notify, etc
4–096   **49.**—(1) The applicant, the appellant or other person directed by the court to effect notification may apply to the court seeking an order—

(a) dispensing with the requirement to comply with the provisions in this Part; or

(b) requiring some other person to comply with the provisions in this Part.

(2) An application under this rule must be made in accordance with Part 10.

PART 8

Practice Direction
8A Permission

PERMISSION

General
4–097   **50.** Subject to these Rules and to section 50(1) of, and paragraph 20 of Schedule 3 to, the Act, the applicant must apply for permission to start proceedings under the Act.

(Section 50(1) of the Act specifies persons who do not need to apply for permission. Paragraph 20 of Schedule 3 to the Act specifies an application for which permission is not needed.)

[Where the court's permission is not required

51. The permission of the court is not required—   **4–098**

(a) where an application is made by—
  (i)   the Official Solicitor; or
  (ii) the Public Guardian;
(b) where the application concerns—
  (i)   P's property and affairs;
  (ii) a lasting power of attorney which is, or purports to be, created under the Act; or
  (iii) an instrument which is, or purports to be, an enduring power of attorney;
(c) where an application is made under section 21A of the Act;
(d) where an application is made for an order under section 16(2)(a) of the Act, which is to be relied on to authorise the deprivation of P's liberty pursuant to section 4A(3) of the Act;
(e) where an application is made in accordance with Part 10;
(f) where a person files an acknowledgment of service or notification in accordance with this Part or Part 9, for any order proposed that is different from that sought by the applicant; or
(g) in any other case specified for this purpose in a practice direction.]

AMENDMENT
This rule was substituted by SI 2015/548 r.22.   **4–099**

52. [*Repealed by SI 2015/548 r.23*].   **4–100**
53. [*Repealed by SI 2015/548 r.24*].   **4–101**

[Application for permission

54. Where permission is required, the applicant must apply for permission   **4–102**
when making an application.

(Rule 84(1A) explains how the court will deal with an application for permission.)]

AMENDMENT
This rule was substituted by SI 2015/548 r.25.   **4–103**

55. [*Repealed by SI 2015/548 r.26*].   **4–104**
56. [*Repealed by SI 2015/548 r.26*].   **4–105**
57. [*Repealed by SI 2015/548 r.26*].   **4–106**
58. [*Repealed by SI 2015/548 r.23*].   **4–107**

Service of an order giving or refusing permission

59. The court [must] serve—   **4–108**
(a) the order granting or refusing permission;
(b) if refusing permission without a hearing, the reasons for its decision in summary form; and
(c) any directions,

on the applicant and on any other person [served with or notified of the application form].

AMENDMENTS

4–109   The amendments to this rule were made by SI 2015/548 r.27.

Appeal against a permission decision following a hearing

4–110   **60.** Where the court grants or refuses permission following a hearing, any appeal against the permission decision shall be dealt with in accordance with Part 20 (appeals).

[(Rule 89 deals with reconsideration of orders and decisions made without a hearing or without notice to any person who is affected by such order or decision.)]

AMENDMENT

4–111   The amendment to this rule was made by SI 2015/548 r.27.

PART 9

Practice Directions

9A The application form
9B Notification of other persons that an application has been issued
9C Responding to an application
9D Application by currently appointed Deputies, Attorneys and Donees in relation to P's property and affairs
9E Application relating to serious medical treatment
9F Applications relating to statutory wills, codicils, settlements and other dealings with P's property
9G Applications to appoint or discharge a trustee
9H Application relating to the registration of Enduring Powers of Attorney

HOW TO START PROCEEDINGS

GENERAL NOTE

Out of hours urgent medical treatment applications

4–112   Such applications must comply with Practice Directions 9E and 10B. Observations on the approach to be taken when making such applications was provided by Theis J. in *Sandwell and West Birmingham Hospitals NHS Trust v CD* [2014] EWCOP 23 at paras 35 to 41. Also see the judgment of Keehan J. in *NHS Trust v FG* [2014] EWCOP 30 which is reproduced under the heading *Best interests in cases where a pregnant woman lacks capacity to make decisions about her obstetric care* in the notes on s.4.

Initial steps

General

4–113   **61.**—(1) Applications to the court to start proceedings shall be made in accordance with this Part and, as applicable, Part 8 and the relevant practice directions.

(2) The appropriate forms must be used in the cases to which they apply, with such variations as the case requires, but not so as to omit any information or guidance which any form gives to the intended recipient.

(3) [. . .]

AMENDMENT
The amendment to this rule was made by SI 2015/548 r.29.   **4–114**

When proceedings are started
62.—(1) The general rule is that proceedings are started when the court issues   **4–115**
an application form at the request of the applicant.

(2) An application form is issued on the date entered on the application form
by the court.

Contents of the application form
63. The application form must—   **4–116**
(a) state the matter which the applicant wants the court to decide;
(b) state the order which the applicant is seeking;
(c) name—
   (i) the applicant;
   (ii) P;
   (iii) as a respondent, any person (other than P) whom the applicant rea-
        sonably believes to have an interest which means that he ought to be
        heard in relation to the application (as opposed to being notified of it in
        accordance with rule 70); and
   (iv) any person whom the applicant intends to notify in accordance with
        rule 70; and
(d) if the applicant is applying in a representative capacity, state what that
    capacity is.

Documents to be filed with the application form
64. When an applicant files his application form with the court, he must also   **4–117**
file—
(a) in accordance with the relevant practice direction, any evidence upon which
    he intends to rely;
(b) [. . .]
(c) an assessment of capacity form, where this is required by the relevant prac-
    tice direction;
(d) any other documents referred to in the application form; and
(e) such other information and material as may be set out in a practice direc-
    tion.

AMENDMENT
The amendment to this rule was made by SI 2015/548 r.30.   **4–118**

[What the court will do when an application form is filed
65. As soon as practicable after an application form is filed the court must issue   **4–119**
it and do anything else that may be set out in a practice direction.]

AMENDMENT
This rule was substituted by SI 2015/548 r.31.   **4–120**

Steps following issue of application form

Applicant to serve the application form on named respondents
66.—(1) As soon as practicable and in any event within [14] days of the date   **4–121**

on which the application form was issued, the applicant must serve a copy of the application form on any person who is named as a respondent in the application form, together with copies of any documents filed in accordance with rule 64 and a form for acknowledging service.

(2) The applicant must file a certificate of service within 7 days beginning with the date on which the documents were served.

AMENDMENT

4–122   The amendment to this rule was made by SI 2015/548 r.32.

Applications relating to lasting powers of attorney

4–123   **67.**—(1) Where the application concerns the powers of the court under section 22 or 23 of the Act (powers of the court in relation to the validity and operation of lasting powers of attorney) the applicant must serve a copy of the application form, together with copies of any documents filed in accordance with rule 64 and a form for acknowledging service—

    (a) unless the applicant is the donor or donee of the lasting power of attorney ("the power"), on the donor and every donee of the power;

    (b) if he is the donor, on every donee of the power; and

    (c) if he is a donee, on the donor and any other donee of the power,

but only if the above-mentioned persons have not been served or notified under any other rule.

(2) Where the application is solely in respect of an objection to the registration of a power, the requirements of rules 66 and 70 do not apply to an application made under this rule by—

    (a) a donee of the power; or

    (b) a person named in a statement made by the donor of the power in accordance with paragraph 2(1)(c)(i) of Schedule 1 to the Act.

(3) The applicant must comply with paragraph (1) as soon as practicable and in any event within [14] days of date on which the application form was issued.

(4) The applicant must file a certificate of service within 7 days beginning with the date on which the documents were served.

(5) Where the applicant knows or has reasonable grounds to believe that the donor of the power lacks capacity to make a decision in relation to any matter that is the subject of the application, he must notify the donor in accordance with Part 7.

AMENDMENT

4–124   The amendment to this rule was made by SI 2015/548 r.33.

Applications relating to enduring powers of attorney

4–125   **68.**—(1) Where the application concerns the powers of the court under paragraphs 2(9), 4(5)(a) and (b), 7(2), 10(c), 13, or 16(2), (3), (4) and (6) of Schedule 4 to the Act, the applicant must serve a copy of the application form, together with copies of any documents filed in accordance with rule 64 and a form for acknowledging service—

    (a) unless the applicant is the donor or attorney under the enduring power of attorney ("the power"), on the donor and every attorney of the power;

    (b) if he is the donor, on every attorney under the power; or

(c) if he is an attorney, on the donor and any other attorney under the power,
but only if the above-mentioned persons have not been served or notified under any other rule.

(2) Where the application is solely in respect of an objection to the registration of a power, the requirements of rules 66 and 70 do not apply to an application made under this rule by—

(a) an attorney under the power; or

(b) a person listed in paragraph 6(1) of Schedule 4 to the Act.

(3) The applicant must comply with paragraph (1) as soon as practicable and in any event within [14] days of the date on which the application form was issued.

(4) The applicant must file a certificate of service within 7 days beginning with the date on which the documents were served.

(5) Where the applicant knows or has reasonable grounds to believe that the donor of the power lacks capacity to make a decision in relation to any matter that is the subject of the application, he must notify the donor in accordance with Part 7.

AMENDMENT
The amendment to this rule was made by SI 2015/548 r.34.   **4–126**

Applicant to notify P of an application

69. P must be notified in accordance with Part 7 that an application form has   **4–127**
been issued, unless the requirement to do so has been dispensed with under rule 49.

Applicant to notify other persons of an application

70.—(1) As soon as practicable and in any event within [14] days of the date   **4–128**
on which the application form was issued, the applicant must notify the persons specified in the relevant practice direction—

(a) that an application form has been issued;

(b) whether it relates to the exercise of the court's jurisdiction in relation to P's property and affairs, or his personal welfare, or to both; and

(c) of the order or orders sought.

(2) Notification of the issue of the application form must be accompanied by a form for acknowledging notification.

(3) The applicant must file a certificate of notification within 7 days beginning with the date on which notification was given.

AMENDMENT
The amendment to this rule was made by SI 2015/548 r.35.   **4–129**

Requirements for certain applications

71. A practice direction may make additional or different provision in relation   **4–130**
to specified applications.

Responding to an application

Responding to an application

72.—(1) A person who is served with or notified of an application form and   **4–131**
who wishes to take part in proceedings must file an acknowledgment of service or notification in accordance with this rule.

(2) The acknowledgment of service or notification must be filed not more than [14] days after the application form was served or notification of the application was given.

(3) The court will serve the acknowledgment of service or notification on the applicant and on any other person who has filed such an acknowledgment.

(4) The acknowledgment of service or notification must—

(a) state whether the person acknowledging service or notification consents to the application;

(b) state whether he opposes the application and, if so, set out the grounds for doing so;

(c) state whether he seeks a different order from that set out in the application form and, if so, set out what that order is;

(d) provide an address for service, which must be within the jurisdiction of the court; and (e) be signed by him or his legal representative.

(5) Subject to rules 120 and 123 (restriction on filing an expert's report and court's power to restrict expert evidence), [unless the court directs otherwise,] where a person who has been served in accordance with rule 66, 67 or 68 opposes the application or seeks a different order, [that person must within 28 days of such service file] a witness statement containing any evidence upon which that person intends to rely.

(6) In addition to complying with the other requirements of this rule, an acknowledgment of notification filed by a person notified of the application in accordance with rule 67(5), 68(5), 69 or 70 must—

(a) indicate whether the person wishes to be joined as a party to the proceedings; and

(b) state the person's interest in the proceedings.

(7) Subject to rules 120 and 123 (restriction on filing an expert's report and court's power to restrict expert evidence), [unless the court directs otherwise,] where a person has been notified in accordance with rule 67(5), 68(5), 69, 70, [that person must within 28 days of such service file] a witness statement containing any evidence of his interest in the proceedings and, if he opposes the application or seeks a different order, any evidence upon which he intends to rely.

(8) The court will consider whether to join a person mentioned in paragraph (6) as a party to the proceedings and, if it decides to do so, will make an order to that effect.

(9) Where a person who is notified in accordance with rule 67(5), 68(5), 69 or 70 complies with the requirements of this rule, he need not comply with the requirements of rule 75 (application to be joined as a party).

(10) [. . .]

(11) A practice direction may make provision about responding to applications.

AMENDMENTS

4–132   The amendments to this rule were made by SI 2015/548 r.36.

The parties to the proceedings

Parties to the proceedings

4–133   **73.**—(1) Unless the court otherwise directs, the parties to any proceedings are—

(a) the applicant; and

(b) any person who is named as a respondent in the application form and who files an acknowledgment of service in respect of the application form.

(2) The court may order a person to be joined as a party if it considers that it is desirable to do so for the purpose of dealing with the application.

(3) The court may at any time direct that any person who is a party to the proceedings is to be removed as a party.

(4) Unless the court orders otherwise, P shall not be named as a respondent to any proceedings.

(5) A party to the proceedings is bound by any order or direction of the court made in the course of those proceedings.

GENERAL NOTE

Note that under para.(4) P will not necessarily be a party to the proceedings. In *Re NRA* [2015] EWCOP 59, Charles J. was faced with contradictory obiter dicta on the issue whether P must be a party to proceedings seeking welfare orders to authorise a deprivation of liberty and therefore have a litigation friend. His Lordship's judgment is summarised under the heading *Should P be a party to proceedings seeking welfare orders to authorise a deprivation of liberty?* in s.16(2)(a). **4–134**

Paragraph (2)

DESIRABLE TO DO SO FOR THE PURPOSE OF DEALING WITH THE APPLICATION. The clear import of this wording "is that the joinder of the person would be to enable the court better to deal with the substantive application (for example, by its being able to take into account and test the views of a close relative who knew the incapacitated person and was familiar with his wishes, feelings and preferences before he became incapacitated)" (*Re SK* [2012] EWHC 1990 at para.42, per Bodey J.). **4–135**

Persons to be bound as if parties

74.—(1) The persons mentioned in paragraph (2) shall be bound by any order made or directions given by the court in the same way that a party to the proceedings is so bound. **4–136**

(2) The persons referred to in paragraph (1) are—

(a) P; and

(b) any person who has been served with or notified of an application form in accordance with these Rules.

Application to be joined as a party

75.—(1) Any person with sufficient interest may apply to the court to be joined as a party to the proceedings. **4–137**

(2) An application to be joined as a party must be made by filing an application notice in accordance with Part 10 which must—

(a) state the full name and address of the person seeking to be joined as a party to the proceedings;

(b) state his interest in the proceedings;

(c) state whether he consents to the application;

(d) state whether he opposes the application and, if so, set out the grounds for doing so;

(e) state whether he proposes that an order different from that set out in the application form should be made and, if so, set out what that order is;

(f) provide an address for service, which must be within the jurisdiction of the court; and (g) be signed by him or his legal representative.

(3) Subject to rules 120 and 123 (restriction on filing an expert's report and court's power to restrict expert evidence), an application to be joined must be accompanied by—

   (a) a witness statement containing evidence of his interest in the proceedings and, if he proposes that an order different from that set out in the application form should be made, the evidence on which he intends to rely; and

   (b) a sufficient number of copies of the application notice to enable service of the application on every other party to the proceedings.

(4) The court will serve the application notice and any accompanying documents on all parties to the proceedings.

(5) The court will consider whether to join a person applying under this rule as a party to the proceedings and, if it decides to do so, will make an order to that effect.

GENERAL NOTE

4–138   The term "sufficient interest" in para.(1) should be interpreted to mean "a sufficient interest in the proceedings"' as distinct from some commercial interest of the applicant's. Such an interest in the proceedings would however exist if circumstances arose where the financial liability (or perhaps some other liability) of the applicant seeking joinder would effectively be determined once and for all in the Court of Protection proceedings. Leaving aside that possibility and the possibility of an application made by some bona fide interest group (where different considerations may apply) an applicant for joinder who or which does not have an interest in the ascertainment of the incapacitated person's best interests is unlikely to be a "person with sufficient interest"' (*Re SK* [2012] EWHC 1990 at para.41, per Bodey J.).

Applications for removal as a party to proceedings

4–139   **76.** A person who wishes to be removed as a party to the proceedings must apply to the court for an order to that effect in accordance with Part 10.

PART 10

Practice Directions
   10A Applications within proceedings
   10AA Deprivation of liberty applications
   10B Urgent and interim applications

APPLICATIONS WITHIN PROCEEDINGS

Types of applications for which the Part 10 procedure may be used

4–140   **77.**—(1) The Part 10 procedure is the procedure set out in this Part.

(2) The Part 10 procedure may be used if the application is made by any person—

   (a) in the course of existing proceedings; or

   (b) as provided for in a rule or practice direction.

(3) The court may grant an interim remedy before an application form has been issued only if—

   (a) the matter is urgent; or

   (b) it is otherwise necessary to do so in the interests of justice.

(4) An application made during the course of existing proceedings includes an application made during appeal proceedings.

[(5) Where the application seeks solely to withdraw an existing application—
  (a) the applicant must file a written request for permission setting out succinctly the reasons for the request;
  (b) the request must be in an application notice;
  (c) the court may permit an application to be made orally at a hearing or in such alternative written form as it thinks fit.

(6) Where the court deals with a written request under paragraph (5) without a hearing, rule 89 applies to any order so made.

(Rule 87A requires the court's permission to withdraw proceedings.)]

AMENDMENTS
The amendments to this rule were made by SI 2015/548 r.37.   **4–141**

Application notice to be filed
78.—(1) Subject to paragraph (5), the applicant must file an application notice   **4–142**
to make an application under this Part.

(2) The applicant must, when he files the application notice, file the evidence upon which he relies (unless such evidence has already been filed).

(3) The court will issue the application notice and, if there is to be a hearing, give notice of the date on which the matter is to be heard by the court.

(4) Notice under paragraph (3) must be given to—
  (a) the applicant;
  (b) anyone who is named as a respondent in the application notice (if not otherwise a party to the proceedings);
  (c) every party to the proceedings; and
  (d) any other person, as the court may direct.

(5) An applicant may make an application under this Part without filing an application notice if—
  (a) this is permitted by any rule or practice direction; or
  (b) the court dispenses with the requirement for an application notice.

(6) If the applicant makes an application without giving notice, the evidence in support of the application must state why notice has not been given.

What an application notice must include
79. An application notice must state—   **4–143**
  (a) what order or direction the applicant is seeking;
  (b) briefly, the grounds on which the applicant is seeking the order or direction; and (c) such other information as may be required by any rule or a practice direction.

Service of an application notice
80.—(1) Subject to paragraphs (4) and (5), the applicant must serve a copy of   **4–144**
the application notice on—
  (a) anyone who is named as a respondent in the application notice (if not otherwise a party to the proceedings);
  (b) every party to the proceedings; and
  (c) any other person, as the court may direct,
  as soon as practicable and in any event within 21 days of the date on which it was issued.

(2) The application notice must be accompanied by a copy of the evidence filed in support.

(3) The applicant must file a certificate of service within 7 days beginning with the date on which the documents were served.

(4) This rule does not require a copy of evidence to be served on a person upon whom it has already been served, but the applicant must in such a case give to that person notice of the evidence upon which he intends to rely.

(5) An application may be made without serving a copy of the application notice if this is permitted by—

(a) a rule;

(b) a practice direction; or (c) the court.

Applications without notice

4–145   **81.**—(1) This rule applies where the court has dealt with an application which was made without notice having been given to any person.

(2) Where the court makes an order, whether granting or dismissing the application, the applicant must, as soon as practicable or within such period as the court may direct, serve the documents mentioned in paragraph (3) on—

(a) anyone named as a respondent in the application notice (if not otherwise a party to the proceedings);

(b) every party to the proceedings; and

(c) any other person, as the court may direct.

(3) The documents referred to in paragraph (2) are—

(a) a copy of the application notice;

(b) the court's order; and

(c) any evidence filed in support of the application.

(Rule 89 provides for reconsideration of orders made without a hearing or without notice to a person.)

[Security for costs

4–146   **81A.**—(1) A respondent to any application may apply for security for the respondent's costs of the proceedings.

(2) An application for security for costs must be supported by written evidence.

(3) Where the court makes an order for security for costs, it must—

(a) determine the amount of security; and

(b) direct—

(i) the manner in which; and

(ii) the time within which,

the security must be given.]

AMENDMENT

4–147   This rule was inserted by SI 2015/548 r.38.

[Conditions to be satisfied

4–148   **81B.**—(1) The court may make an order for security for costs under rule 81A—

(a) if it is satisfied, having regard to all the circumstances of the case, that it is just to make such an order; and

(b) if—

(i) one or more of the conditions in paragraph (2) applies; or

(ii) an enactment permits the court to require security for costs.

(2) The conditions are—
(a) the applicant is—
  (i) resident out of the jurisdiction; but
  (ii) not resident in a Brussels Contracting State, a State bound by the Lugano Convention or a Regulation State, as defined in section 1(3) of the Civil Jurisdiction and Judgments Act 1982;
(b) the applicant is a company or other body (whether incorporated inside or outside Great Britain) and there is reason to believe that it will be unable to pay the respondent's costs if ordered to do so;
(c) the applicant has changed address since proceedings were commenced with a view to avoiding the consequences of the litigation;
(d) the applicant failed to give an address, or gave an incorrect address, in the application form commencing the proceedings;
(e) the applicant is acting as a nominal applicant and there is reason to believe that the applicant will be unable to pay the respondent's costs if ordered to do so;
(f) the applicant has taken steps in relation to the applicant's assets that would make it difficult to enforce an order for costs against the applicant.]

AMENDMENT
This rule was inserted by SI 2015/548 r.38.   **4–149**

[Security for costs other than from the applicant

81C.—(1) The respondent may seek an order against a person other than the   **4–150**
applicant, and the court may make an order for security for costs against that person, if—
(a) it is satisfied, having regard to all the circumstances of the case, that it is just to make such an order; and
(b) one or more of the conditions in paragraph (2) applies.
(2) The conditions are that the person—
(a) has assigned the right to the substantive matter to the applicant with a view to avoiding the possibility of a costs order being made against the person; or
(b) has contributed or agreed to contribute to the applicant's costs in return for a share of any money or property which the applicant may recover or be awarded in the proceedings; and
is a person against whom a costs order may be made.
(Rule 166 makes provision about costs orders against non-parties.)]

AMENDMENT
This rule was inserted by SI 2015/548 r.38.   **4–151**

[Security for costs of an appeal

81D.—(1) The court may order security for costs of an appeal against—   **4–152**
(a) an appellant;
(b) a respondent who also appeals,
on the same grounds as it may order security for costs against an applicant under rule 81A.
(2) The court may also make an order under paragraph (1) where the appellant or the respondent who also appeals is a limited company and there is reason to believe it will be unable to pay the costs of the other parties to the appeal should its appeal be unsuccessful.]

AMENDMENT

4–153   This rule was inserted by SI 2015/548 r.38.

Interim remedies

Orders for interim remedies

4–154   **82.**—(1) The court may grant the following interim remedies—

(a) an interim injunction;

(b) an interim declaration; or

(c) any other interim order it considers appropriate.

(2) Unless the court orders otherwise, a person on whom an application form is served under Part 9, or who is given notice of such an application, may not apply for an interim remedy before he has filed an acknowledgment of service or notification in accordance with Part 9.

(3) This rule does not limit any other power of the court to grant interim relief.

GENERAL NOTE

4–155   The criteria for making interim orders and declarations are set out in s.48.

[PART 10A

DEPRIVATION OF LIBERTY

4–156   **82A.** The practice direction to this Part sets out procedure governing—

(a) applications to the court for orders relating to the deprivation, or proposed deprivation, of liberty of P; and

(b) proceedings (for example, relating to costs or appeals) connected with or consequent upon such applications.]

AMENDMENT

4–157   This Part was inserted by the Court of Protection (Amendment) Rules 2009 (SI 2009/582) r.5.

Practice Direction

The following Practice Direction 10AA has been issued by the Court:

"PRACTICE DIRECTION—DEPRIVATION OF LIBERTY

This practice direction supplements Part 10A of the Court of Protection Rules 2007

PRACTICE DIRECTION A—DEPRIVATION OF LIBERTY APPLICATIONS

Introduction

4–158   1. This Practice Direction is in three parts. Part 1 addresses the procedure to be followed in applications to the court for orders under section 21A of the Mental Capacity Act 2005 relating to a standard or urgent authorisation under Schedule A1 of that Act to deprive a person of his or her liberty; or proceedings (for example, relating to costs or appeals) connected with or consequent upon such applications. Part 2 addresses the procedure to be followed in applications under s.16(2)(a) of that Act to authorise deprivation of liberty under section 4A(3) and (4) pursuant to a streamlined procedure. Part 3 makes provision common to applications under both Parts 1 and 2.

PART 1—APPLICATIONS UNDER SECTION 21A RELATING TO A STANDARD OR URGENT AUTHORISATION UNDER SCHEDULE A1

2. This Part sets out the procedure to be followed in applications to the court **4–159** for orders under section 21A of the Mental Capacity Act 2005 relating to a standard or urgent authorisation under Schedule A1 of that Act to deprive a person of his or her liberty. By their nature, such applications are of special urgency and therefore will be dealt with by the court according to the special procedure described here. Other applications may, while not being DoL applications within the meaning of the term explained above, raise issues relating to deprivation of liberty and require similarly urgent attention; and while the special DoL procedure will not apply to such applications, they should be raised with the DoL team at the earliest possible stage so that they can be handled appropriately. The key features of the special DoL procedure are:

(a) special DoL court forms ensure that DoL court papers stand out as such and receive special handling by the court office;

(b) the application is placed before a judge of the court as soon as possible— if necessary, before issue of the application—for judicial directions to be given as to the steps to be taken in the application, and who is to take each step and by when;

(c) the usual Court of Protection Rules (for example, as to method and timing of service of the application) will apply only so far as consistent with the judicial directions given for the particular case;

(d) a dedicated team in the court office ("the DoL team") will deal with DoL applications at all stages, including liaison with would-be applicants/ other parties;

(e) the progress of each DoL case will be monitored by a judge assigned to that case, assisted by the DoL team.

Before issuing an application

3. Potential applicants should contact the DoL team at the earliest possible **4–160** stage before issuing a DoL application. Where this is not possible, the applicant should liaise with the DoL team at the same time as, or as soon as possible after, lodging the application. The DoL team can be contacted by telephone in the first instance and by fax.

4. The information that the DoL team needs, with as much advance warning as possible, is (1) that a DoL application is to be made; (2) how urgent the application is (i.e., by when should the Court's decision, or interim decision, on the merits be given); and (3) when the Court will receive the application papers. In extremely urgent cases, the DoL team can arrange for a telephone application to be made to the judge for directions and/or an interim order even before the application has been issued. Further brief details should be given which may include:

(a) the parties' details

(b) where the parties live

(c) the issue to be decided

(d) the date of urgent or standard authorisation

(e) the date of effective detention

(f) the parties' legal representatives

(g) any family members or others who are involved

(h) whether there have been any other court proceedings involving the parties and if so, where.

5. Contact details for the DoL team are:

PO Box 70185

First Avenue House

42-49 High Holborn

London

WC1A 9 JA

DX: 160013 Kingsway 7

Enquiries: 0300 456 4600

6. The public counter is open between 9.30 a.m. to 4.30 p.m. on working days. The DoL team can receive telephone calls and faxes between 9.00 a.m. and 5.00 pm. Faxes transmitted after 4.30 p.m. will be dealt with the next working day.

7. When in an emergency it is necessary to make a telephone application to a judge outside normal court hours, the security office at the Royal Courts of Justice should be contacted on 020 7947 6000. The security officer should be informed of the nature of the case. In the Family Division, the out-of-hours application procedure involves the judge being contacted through a Family Division duty officer, and the RCJ security officer will need to contact the duty officer and not the judge's clerk or the judge.

8. Intending applicants/other parties may find it helpful to refer to:

(a) the Code of Practice Deprivation of Liberty Safeguards (June 2008), ISBN 978-0113228157, supplementing the main Mental Capacity Act 2005 Code of Practice: in particular Chapter 10, What is the Court of Protection and who can apply to it?; and

(b) the judgment of Mr Justice Munby in *Salford City Council v. GJ, NJ and BJ (Incapacitated Adults) [2008] EWHC 1097 (Fam); [2008] 2 FLR 1295.* Although this case was decided before the coming into force of the DoL amendments to the Mental Capacity Act 2005, it sets out helpful guidance on the appropriate court procedures for cases relating to the deprivation of liberty of adults.

9. The DoL team will be pleased to explain the court's procedures for handling DoL cases. Please note that the team (as with all court staff) is not permitted to give advice on matters of law. Please do not contact the DoL team unless your inquiry concerns a deprivation of liberty question (whether relating to a potential application, or a case which is already lodged with the Court).

DoL court forms

4–161   10. The special DoL court forms are as follows:

(a) DLA: Deprivation of Liberty Application Form: to be used for all DoL applications;

(b) DLB: Deprivation of Liberty Request for Urgent Consideration: this short form allows applicants to set out the reasons why the case is urgent, the timetable they wish the case to follow, and any interim relief sought. A draft of any order sought should be attached. Ideally, the DLB (plus any draft order) should be placed at the top of the draft application and both issued and served together;

(c) DLD: Deprivation of Liberty Certificate of Service/non-service and Certificate of notification/non-notification;

(d) DLE: Deprivation of Liberty Acknowledgement of service/notification.

These forms can be obtained from the Court of Protection office or downloaded from the court's website http://hmctsformfinder.iustice.gov.uk/HMCTS/GetForms. do7court forms category=court of protection.

11. To ensure that papers relating to DoL applications are promptly directed to the DoL team at the court, it is essential that the appropriate DoL court forms are used.

12. The DoL court forms should be used for, and only for, DoL applications. If in such a case it is anticipated that other issues may arise, the DoL forms should identify and describe briefly those issues and any relief which may be sought in respect of them: sections 3.5 and 5 of form DLA, the Deprivation of Liberty Application Form, offer an opportunity to do this. "Other issues" are perhaps most likely to arise in the event that the court decides the DoL application in the applicant's favour. In such a case, if the applicant has already identified the "other issues" in his/her DLA form, the court will be able to address these, either by dealing with them immediately or by giving directions for their future handling.

13. Accordingly, unless the court expressly directs, applicants should not issue a second and separate application (using the standard court forms) relating to any "other issues".

14. Where an application seeks relief concerning a deprivation of P's liberty other than under section 21A in respect of a standard or urgent authorisation (for example, where the application is for an order under section 16(2)(a)), the dedicated DoL court forms should not be used. Rather the standard court forms should be used for such an application, but it should be made clear on them that relief relating to a deprivation of P's liberty is being sought, and the proposed applicant should contact the DoL team to discuss handling at the earliest possible stage before issuing the application.

How to issue a DoL application

15. To issue a DoL application, the following forms should be filed at court: **4–162**

(a) form DLA

(b) form DLB (plus draft order)

(c) the appropriate court fee.

Where a draft order is lodged with the court, it would be helpful—although not compulsory—if an electronic version of the order could also be lodged on disc, if possible.

16. In cases of extreme emergency or where it is not possible to attend at the court office, for example during weekends, the court will expect an applicant to undertake to file form DLA and to pay the court fee unless an exemption applies.

Inviting the court to make judicial directions for the handling of the application

4–163   17. The following is a sample list of possible issues which the court is likely to wish to consider in judicial directions in a DoL case. It is intended as a prompt, not as a definitive list of the issues that may need to be covered:

    (a) upon whom, by when and how service of the application should be effected;

    (b) dispensing with acknowledgement of service of the application or allowing a short period of time for so doing, which in some cases may amount to a few hours only;

    (c) whether further lay or expert evidence should be obtained;

    (d) whether P/the detained person should be a party and represented by the Official Solicitor and whether any other person should be a party;

    (e) whether any family members should be formally notified of the application and of any hearing and joined as parties;

    (f) fixing a date for a First Hearing and giving a time estimate;

    (g) fixing a trial window for any final hearing and giving a time estimate;

    (h) the level of judge appropriate to hear the case;

    (i) whether the case is such that it should be immediately transferred to the High Court for a High Court Judge to give directions;

    (j) provision for a bundle for the judge at the First Hearing.

18. If you are an applicant without legal representation, and you are not sure exactly what directions you should ask for, you may prefer simply to invite the judge to make appropriate directions in light of the nature and urgency of the case as you have explained it on the DLB form. In exceptionally urgent cases, there may not be time to formulate draft directions: the court will understand if applicants in such cases (whether or not legally represented) simply ask the judge for appropriate directions.

After issue of the application

4–164   19. The DoL team will immediately take steps to ensure that the application is placed before a judge nominated to hear Court of Protection cases and DoL applications.

20. As soon as the court office is put on notice of a DoL application, the DoL team will notify a judge to put the judge on stand-by to deal with the application. The judge will consider the application on the papers and make a first order.

Steps after the judge's first order

4–165   21. The DoL team will:

    (a) action every point in the judge's note or instruction;

    (b) refer any query that arises to the judge immediately or, if not available, to another judge;

    (c) make all arrangements for any transfer of the case to another court and/or for a hearing.

22. The applicant or his/her legal representative should follow all steps in the judge's order and:

(a) form DLD should be filed with the court if appropriate; and

(b) form DLE should be included in any documents served unless ordered otherwise.

The First Hearing

23. The First Hearing will be listed for the court to fix a date for any subsequent hearing(s), give directions and/or to make an interim or final order if appropriate. The court will make such orders and give such directions as are appropriate in the case.   **4–166**

24. The court will aim to have the First Hearing before a judge of every DoL application within 5 working days of the date of issue of the application.

25. Applicants can indicate on the DLB form if they think that the application needs to be considered within a shorter timetable, and set out proposals for such a timetable. On the first paper consideration the court will consider when the First Hearing should be listed.

26. If time allows and no specific direction has been made by the court, an indexed and paginated bundle should be prepared for the judge and any skeleton arguments and draft orders given to the court as soon as they are available. A copy of the index should be provided to all parties and, where another party appears in person, a copy of the bundle should be provided.

PART 2—APPLICATIONS UNDER SECTION 16(2)(a) FOR AN ORDER AUTHORISING DEPRIVATION OF LIBERTY UNDER SECTION 4A(3) AND (4) PURSUANT TO A STREAMLINED PROCEDURE

27. This Part sets out the procedure to be followed in applications to the court under section 16(2)(a) to authorise deprivation of liberty under section 4A(3) of the Act pursuant to a streamlined procedure and applies only to such applications. Reference should be made generally to the decision of the Supreme Court in *P (by his litigation friend the Official Solicitor) v Cheshire West and Chester Council and another; P and Q (by their litigation friend the Official Solicitor) v Surrey County Council [2014] UKSC 19,* and in relation to the procedure in these cases, to the judgments of the President of the Court of Protection in *Re X and others (Deprivation of Liberty) [2014] EWCOP 25* and in *Re X and others (Deprivation of Liberty) (Number 2) [2014] EWCOP 37.*   **4–167**

Making the application

28. To bring proceedings, the applicant must file an application using form COPDOL 10, verified by a statement of truth and accompanied by all attachments and evidence required by that form and its annexes.   **4–168**

29. The application form and accompanying annexes and attachments are specifically designed to ensure that the applicant provides the court with essential information and evidence as to the proposed measures, on the basis of which the court may adjudicate as to the appropriateness of authorising a deprivation of liberty, and in particular to identify whether a case is suitable for consideration without an oral hearing. The use of the form and its annexes is mandatory and they must be provided fully completed and verified by the required statements of truth.

30. The applicant must ensure that the evidence in the application form, accompanying annexes and attachments is succinct and focussed.

31. A separate application must be made for every individual for whom the applicant requests an authorisation of deprivation of liberty. However, where there are matters in relation to which the facts are identical for a number of individuals, such as common care arrangements, the applicant may, in addition to addressing the specific issues relating to each individual, attach a generic statement dealing with the common care arrangements or other matters common to those individuals.

Deponent

4–169
32. The applicant must consider carefully who should complete the form and each annex with regard to the nature of the evidence required by each. There is no requirement that the same individual should complete and verify by statement of truth the form and each annex and indeed it might be inappropriate for this to be the case, where different people are best placed to provide evidence on different matters.

Applicant's duty of full and frank disclosure

4–170
33. The applicant has a duty of full and frank disclosure to the court of all facts and matters that may have an impact on the court's decision whether to authorise the deprivation of liberty. The applicant should therefore scrutinise the circumstances of the case and clearly identify in the evidence in support (in Annex A to form COPDOL 10) factors—

(a) needing particular judicial scrutiny;
(b) suggesting that the arrangements in relation to which authorisation is sought may not in fact be in the best interests of the person the application is about, or the least restrictive option; or
(c) otherwise tending to indicate that the order should not be made.

Pursuant to this duty, the applicant should also identify those persons, not consulted by the applicant, who are in the same category under paragraph 39 as persons with whom the applicant has consulted. Those persons must be listed in Annex B to form COPDOL 10 together with an explanation in that Annex of why they have not been consulted.

Draft order

4–171
34. The application must be accompanied by a draft of the order which the applicant seeks, including the duration of the authorisation sought, appropriate directions for review, and liberty to apply for its reconsideration.

Consultation with the person the application is about

4–172
35. Consultation with the person the application is about must take place before the application form is lodged with the court. The applicant must arrange for that person to be informed of the following matters—

(a) that the applicant is making an application to court;
(b) that the application is to consider whether the person lacks capacity to make decisions in relation to his or her residence and care, and whether to authorise a deprivation of their liberty in connection with the arrangements set out in the care plan;
(c) what the proposed arrangements under the order sought are;
(d) that the person is entitled to express his or her views, wishes and feelings

in relation to the proposed arrangements and the application, and that the person undertaking the consultation will ensure that these are communicated to the court;

(e) that the person is entitled to seek to take part in the proceedings by being joined as a party or otherwise, what that means, and that the person undertaking the consultation will ensure that any such request is communicated to the court;

(f) that the person undertaking the consultation can help him or her to obtain advice and assistance if he or she does not agree with the proposed arrangements in the application.

36. The person undertaking the consultation must complete Annex C to form COPDOL 10.

37. The applicant must confirm that the person the application is about has been supported and assisted to express his or her views, wishes and feelings in relation to the application and the arrangements proposed in it, and encouraged to take part in the proceedings to the extent that he or she wishes, in accordance with section 4(4) of the Act.

Consultation with other persons regarding the making of the application

38. The consultation required by paragraph 39 below must take place before the application is lodged with the court.   **4–173**

39. The applicant must ensure that the following people are consulted about the intention to make the application—

(a) any donee of a lasting power of attorney granted by the person;

(b) any deputy appointed for the person by the court;

together with, if possible, at least three people in the following categories—

(c) anyone named by the person the application is about as someone to be consulted on the matters raised by the application; and

(d) anyone engaged in caring for the person or interested in his or her welfare.

40. When consulting such people, the applicant must inform them of the following matters—

(a) that the applicant is making an application to court;

(b) that the application is to consider whether the person the application is about lacks capacity to make decisions in relation to his or her residence and care and whether he or she should be deprived of liberty in connection with the arrangements set out in the care plan;

(c) what the proposed arrangements under the order are; and

(d) that the applicant is under an obligation to inform the person the application is about of the matters listed in paragraph 35 above, unless in the circumstances it is inappropriate for the applicant to give that person such information.

Dispensing with notification or service of the application form

41. Provided that the court is satisfied as to the adequacy of consultation with the person the application is about in accordance with paragraphs 35 to 37, and with other persons with whom consultation should take place in accordance   **4–174**

with paragraphs 38 to 40, the court may dispense with notification of the issue of the application under rules 42, 69 and 70.

Court fees

4–175 42. An application fee is payable for all applications, and if the court decides to hold a hearing before making a decision, a hearing fee will be payable.

43. If an application is received without a fee it will be treated as incomplete and returned.

Applications suitable for the streamlined procedure

4–176 44. As soon as practicable after receipt the court officers will consider the suitability of the application to be the subject of paper determination, or to be considered at an oral hearing.

45. All applications considered suitable for the streamlined procedure will be referred to a judge for consideration without an oral hearing, as soon as practicable after receipt.

Applications not suitable for the streamlined procedure

4–177 46. If the judge considers that the application is not suitable for the streamlined process, case management directions shall be given.

Applicant to supply a copy of the order to each person consulted

4–178 47. The applicant must provide all persons consulted, including the person the application is about, with a copy of the order made pursuant to the streamlined procedure granting or refusing the authorisation of the deprivation of liberty.

Review of the authorisation

4–179 48. An application for a review of the authorisation of the deprivation of liberty must be made in accordance with the terms of the order.

PART 3—PROVISIONS COMMON TO APPLICATIONS UNDER PART 1 AND PART 2

Hearing in private

4–180 49. Part 13 of the Court of Protection Rules 2007 provides at rule 90, as supplemented by Practice Direction A to Part 13, that the general rule is that a hearing is held in private. Rule 92 allows the court to order that a hearing be in public if the criteria in rule 93 apply.

Costs

4–181 50. The general rule, in rule 157 of the Court of Protection Rules 2007, is that in a health and welfare case there will be no order as to costs of the proceedings. The general rule applies to DoL applications.

Appeals

4–182 51. Part 20 of the Court of Protection Rules 2007 applies to appeals. Permission is required to appeal (rules 171B and 172) and this will only be granted where the court considers that the appeal would have a real prospect of success or there is some other compelling reason why the appeal should be heard (rule173).

PART 11

Practice Direction
11A Human Rights Act 1998

HUMAN RIGHTS

General

83.—(1) A party who seeks to rely upon any provision of or right arising under **4–183** the Human Rights Act 1998 ("the 1998 Act") or who seeks a remedy available under that Act must inform the court in the manner set out in the relevant practice direction specifying—

(a) the Convention right (within the meaning of the 1998 Act) which it is alleged has been infringed and details of the alleged infringement; and

(b) the remedy sought and whether this includes a declaration of incompatibility under section 4 of the 1998 Act.

(2) The court may not make a declaration of incompatibility unless 21 days notice, or such other period of notice as the court directs, has been given to the Crown.

(3) Where notice has been given to the Crown, a Minister or other person permitted by the 1998 Act will be joined as a party on filing an application in accordance with rule 75 (application to be joined as a party).

PART 12

Practice Directions
12A Court's jurisdiction to be exercised by certain judges
12B Procedure for disputing the court's jurisdiction

DEALING WITH APPLICATIONS

Dealing with the application

84.—(1) As soon as practicable after any application has been issued the court **4–184** shall consider how to deal with it.

[(1A) Where permission to start proceedings is required, and whether or not it has been applied for, the court's consideration under paragraph (1) shall include whether to grant or refuse permission without a hearing, or to direct a hearing to consider whether permission should be granted.]

(2) The court may deal with an application or any part of an application at a hearing or without a hearing.

(3) In considering whether it is necessary to hold a hearing, the court shall, as appropriate, have regard to—

(a) the nature of the proceedings and the orders sought;

(b) whether the application is opposed by a person who appears to the court to have an interest in matters relating to P's best interests;

(c) whether the application involves a substantial dispute of fact;

(d) the complexity of the facts and the law;

(e) any wider public interest in the proceedings;

(f) the circumstances of P and of any party, in particular as to whether their rights would be adequately protected if a hearing were not held;

(g) whether the parties agree that the court should dispose of the application without a hearing; and

(h) any other matter specified in the relevant practice direction.

(4) Where the court considers that a hearing is necessary, it will—

(a) give notice of the hearing date to the parties and to any other person it directs; and

(b) state [what is to be dealt with at the hearing, including whether the matter is to be disposed of at that hearing]

(5) Where the court decides that it can deal with the matter without a hearing it will do so and serve a copy of its order on the parties and on any other person it directs.

AMENDMENTS

4–185   The amendments to this rule were made by SI 2015/548 r.39.

Directions

4–186   **85.**—(1) The court may—

(a) give directions in writing; or

(b) set a date for a directions hearing; and

(c) do anything else that may be set out in a practice direction.

(2) When giving directions, the court may do any of the following—

(a) require a report under section 49 of the Act and give directions as to any such report;

(b) give directions as to any requirements contained in these Rules or a practice direction for the giving of notification to any person or for that person to do anything in response to a notification;

(c) [. . .]

(d) [. . .]

(e) if the court considers that any other person or persons should be a party to the proceedings, give directions joining them as a party;

(f) if the court considers that any party to the proceedings should not be a party, give directions for that person's removal as a party;

(g) give directions for the management of the case and set a timetable for the steps to be taken between the giving of directions and the hearing;

(h) subject to rule 86, give directions as to the type of judge who is to hear the case;

(i) give directions as to whether the proceedings or any part of them are to be heard in public, or as to whether any particular person should be permitted to attend the hearing, or as to whether any publication of the proceedings is to be permitted;

(j) give directions as to the disclosure of documents, service of witness statements and any expert evidence;

(k) give directions as to the attendance of witnesses and as to whether, and the extent to which, cross-examination will be permitted at any hearing; and

(l) give such other directions as the court thinks fit.

(3) The court may give directions at any time—

(a) on its own initiative; or

(b) on the application of a party.

(4) Subject to paragraphs (5) and (6) and unless these Rules or a practice direction provide otherwise or the court directs otherwise, the time specified by a rule

or by the court for a person to do any act may be varied by the written agreement of the parties.

(5) A party must apply to the court if he wishes to vary—

(a) the date the court has fixed for the final hearing; or

(b) the period within which the final hearing is to take place.

(6) The time specified by a rule or practice direction or by the court may not be varied by the parties if the variation would make it necessary to vary the date the court has fixed for any hearing or the period within which the final hearing is to take place.

[(Participation of P in proceedings is addressed in rule 3A (participation of P) and Part 17 (litigation friends and rule 3A representatives).]

AMENDMENTS

The amendments to this rule were made by SI 2015/548 r.40.   **4–187**

Allocation of proceedings

[Court's jurisdiction in certain kinds of case to be exercised by certain judges

86.—(1) A practice direction made under this rule may specify certain   **4–188**
categories of case to be dealt with by a specific judge or a specific class of judges.

(2) Applications in any matter other than those specified in the practice direction referred to in paragraph (1) may be dealt with by any judge.]

AMENDMENT

This rule was substituted by SI 2015/548 r.41.   **4–189**

Disputing the jurisdiction of the court

Procedure for disputing the court's jurisdiction

87.—(1) A person who wishes to—   **4–190**

(a) dispute the court's jurisdiction to hear an application; or

(b) argue that the court should not exercise its jurisdiction,

may apply to the court at any time for an order declaring that it has no such jurisdiction or should not exercise any jurisdiction that it may have.

(2) An application under this rule must be—

(a) made by using the form specified in the relevant practice direction; and

(b) supported by evidence.

(3) An order containing a declaration that the court has no jurisdiction or will not exercise its jurisdiction may also make further provision, including—

(a) setting aside the application;

(b) discharging any order made [. . .]

(c) staying the proceedings [; and]

[(d) discharging any litigation friend, accredited legal representative or representative.]

AMENDMENTS

The amendments to this rule were made by SI 2015/548 r.42.   **4–191**

GENERAL NOTE

In *JO v GO* [2013] EWHC 3932 (COP), Sir James Munby P. said at para.12:   **4–192**

"Rule 87 contemplates the existence of two conceptually quite distinct powers in the Court of Protection: one, the power to determine that it 'has no jurisdiction'; the other, the power to determine that it 'should not' or 'will not' exercise its jurisdiction. The one involves the determination of what is essentially a question of law – does the court have jurisdiction? The other involves the exercise of a judicial discretion – accepting that the court has jurisdiction, should the court nonetheless decline to exercise it?"

In this case, the President held that:

1. *Forum non conveniens*, the legal doctrine whereby courts may refuse to take jurisdiction over matters where there is a more appropriate forum available to the parties, applies to cases involving incapacitated adults; and

2. A decision by the court to refuse to exercise jurisdiction on the basis of *forum non conveniens* is not a decision falling within s.1(5) of the Act, i.e. the Court is not required to treat the best interests of the adult as determinative.

[Permission required to withdraw proceedings

4–193   **87A.**—(1) Proceedings may only be withdrawn with the permission of the court.

(2) An application to withdraw proceedings must be made in accordance with Part 10.]

AMENDMENT

4–194   This rule was inserted by SI 2015/548 r.43.

Participation in hearings

Participation in hearings

4–195   **88.**—(1) The court may hear P on the question of whether or not an order should be made, whether or not he is a party to the proceedings.

(2) The court may proceed with a hearing in the absence of P if it considers that it would be appropriate to do so.

(3) A person other than P who is served with or notified of the application may only take part in a hearing if—

(a) he files an acknowledgment in accordance with the Rules and is made a party to the proceedings; or

(b) the court permits.

[(Rule 3A deals with participation of P.)]

AMENDMENT

4–196   The amendment to this rule was made by SI 2015/548 r.44.

Reconsideration of court orders

Orders made without a hearing or without notice to any person

4–197   **89.**—(1) This rule applies where the court makes an order—

(a) without a hearing; or

(b) without notice to any person who is affected by it.

(2) Where this rule applies—

(a) P;

(b) any party to the proceedings; or

(c) any other person affected by the order,

may apply to the court for reconsideration of the order made.

(3) An application under paragraph (2) must be made—

(a) within 21 days of the order being served or such other period as the court may direct; and

(b) in accordance with Part 10.

(4) The court will—

(a) reconsider the order without directing a hearing; or

(b) fix a date for the matter to be heard, and notify all parties to the proceedings and such other persons as the court may direct, of that date.

(5) Where an application is made in accordance with this rule, the court may affirm, set aside or vary any order made.

[(6) An order made by a court officer authorised under rule 7A may be reconsidered by any judge.

(6A) An order made by a Tier 1 Judge may be reconsidered by any judge.

(6B) An order made by a Tier 2 Judge may be reconsidered by any Tier 2 Judge or by a Tier 3 Judge.

(6C) An order made by a Tier 3 Judge may be reconsidered by any Tier 3 Judge.

(6D) In any case to which paragraphs (6A) to (6C) apply the reconsideration may be carried out by the judge who made the order being reconsidered.]

[(7) No application may be made seeking a reconsideration of—

(a) an order that has been made under paragraph (5); or

(b) an order granting or refusing permission to appeal.]

(8) An appeal against [an order] made under paragraph (5) may be made in accordance with Part 20 (appeals).

(9) Any order made without a hearing or without notice to any person, other than one made under paragraph (5) [or one granting or refusing permission to appeal], must contain a statement of the right to apply for a reconsideration of the decision in accordance with this rule.

(10) An application made under this rule may include a request that the court reconsider the matter at a hearing.

[(Rule 7A(2)(c) provides that a court officer authorised under that rule may not deal with an application for the reconsideration of an order made by that court officer or another court officer.)]

AMENDMENTS

The amendments to this rule were made by SI 2015/548 r.45.   **4–198**

GENERAL NOTE

On reconsideration of an order, the matter is considered afresh, there is no presumption   **4–199**
in favour of the order originally made and there is no need for the applicant to demonstrate
that the judge erred in any way when making the order, as would be necessary on an appeal
(*Baker v H* [2009] W.T.L.R. 1719 at para.18).

Judge Marshall described the purpose of this rule and the way in which it operates at
paras 61 and 62 of her judgment in *C v V* [2008] EWHC B16 (Fam):

"Such a reconsideration is not an appeal. The processes in the Court of Protection are
intended to give the court wide flexibility to reach a decision quickly, conveniently
and cost effectively when it can, whilst still preserving a proper opportunity for those
affected by its orders to have their views taken into account in full argument if necessary. To that end, on receiving an application, the court can make a decision on the
papers, or direct a full hearing, or make any order as to how the application can best be
dealt with. This will often lead to a speedy decision made solely on paper which everyone is content to accept, but any party still has the right to ask for a reconsideration.

If this occurs, the court should approach the matter as if making the decision afresh, not on the basis that the question is whether there is a justifiable attack on the first order. The party making the application has not had a proper opportunity to be heard, and should be allowed one without feeling that s/he suffers from the disadvantage of having been placed in the position of an appellant by an order made without full consideration of his points or his views".

PART 13

Practice Direction
13A Hearings (including reporting restrictions)
13B Court Bundles

HEARINGS

GENERAL NOTE
4–200   In *Re NRA* [2015] EWCOP 59, Charles J. said at para.100:

"No-one has pointed to any requirement of European law or the common law that there must be an oral hearing of a non-controversial case because it involves a deprivation of liberty or a person who lacks capacity to litigate or otherwise. Indeed, such a rigid requirement would run counter to the flexibility of the approach taken to such issues by reference to the facts and circumstances of the case."

Private hearings

General rule—hearing to be in private
4–201   **90.**—(1) The general rule is that a hearing is to be held in private.
    (2) A private hearing is a hearing which only the following persons are entitled to attend—
    (a) the parties;
    (b) P (whether or not a party);
    (c) any person acting in the proceedings as a litigation friend;
    (d) any legal representative of a person specified in any of sub-paragraphs (a) to (c); and (e) any court officer.
    (3) In relation to a private hearing, the court may make an order—
    (a) authorising any person, or class of persons, to attend the hearing or a part of it; or
    (b) excluding any person, or class of persons, from attending the hearing or a part of it.

GENERAL NOTE
4–202   "Part 13 of the CoP Rules provides that the default position is for a private hearing. This is a change for medical cases but Practice Direction 9E effectively takes one back to the previous practice that these cases were heard in public because it provides that the presumption is that such cases will be heard in public (see *Re G (Adult Patient: Publicity)* [1995] 2 FLR 528 which concluded that there was a clear balance in favour of a hearing in open court). Also applications for contempt have to be in public (Rule 188(2) and Committal for Contempt of Court (Practice Guidance – Supplemental) [2013] EWHC B7 (CoP)" (written evidence to the House of Commons Justice Committee by Munby P. and Charles J., dated March 2014, para.25).

This Rule was considered in *Independent News and Media Ltd v A* [2010] EWCA Civ 343, where the Court of Appeal made the following findings at paras 10 and 11:

"Rule 90 is clear. Hearings will normally be held in private. The court is vested with a permissive power to enable anyone, or any class of people, to be present at the hearing. The permissive power is not confined to but it includes representatives of the media. Similarly, with the court's jurisdiction to authorise the publication of information which relates to the proceedings, including, of course, the hearing itself: anyone or any class of people may apply.

None of these orders may be made unless there is 'good reason' for making it [see r.93]. We do not propose to re-write the words 'good reason'. They mean what, taken together, they say. Arguments about whether the general rule that the hearing should be in private amounts either to a presumption or to a starting point are in practice unlikely to be anything other than semantic. If in the judgment of the court there is good reason to grant the authorisation, the order may be made: otherwise not. No doubt more compelling reasons would be likely to be required in support of a full public hearing rather than a suitably anonymised publication of the court's judgment. In agreement with Hedley J, we would emphasise that, even when good reason appears, before the necessary authorisation can be granted better reasons may lead the court to refuse it. Accordingly the reality is that provided good reason appears, the court will then assess all the relevant considerations and make a balanced, fact-specific judgment whether the specific authorisation should be granted. In other words, before the court makes an order under Rules 90 to 92, a two-stage process is required; the first involves deciding whether there is 'good reason' to make an order under Rule 90(2), 91(1) or 92; if there is, then the second stage is to decide whether the requisite balancing exercise justifies the making of the order."

The Court explained at para.19:

"The new statutory structure starts with the assumption that just as the conduct of their lives by adults with the necessary mental capacity is their own affair, so too the conduct of the affairs of those adults who are incapacitated is private business. Hearings before the Court of Protection should therefore be held in private unless there is good reason why they should not. In other words, the new statutory arrangements mirror and rearticulate one long-standing common law exception to the principle that justice must be done in open court."

A was applied in *P v Independent Print Ltd* [2011] EWCA Civ 756, where it was confirmed, at para.43, that the approach that the court should adopt to the balancing exercise referred to in *A* at para.11, involving the consideration of art 8 (right to respect for family life) and art.10 (right of freedom of expression) of the European Convention of Human Rights (ECHR), "is now settled. As it was put in *Browne v Associated Newspapers Ltd* [2007] EWCA Civ 295, [2008] Q.B. 103 at para.45:

"Although the exercise upon which the judge was engaged was not the exercise of a discretion it was similar in that it involved carrying out a balancing exercise upon which different judges could properly reach different conclusions. In these circumstances it is now well settled that an appellate court should not interfere unless the judge has erred in principle or reached a conclusion which was plainly wrong or, put another way, was outside the ambit of conclusions which a judge could reasonably reach."

The Court also confirmed, at para.49, that "section 1(5) does not govern or dominate a decision to be taken under rules 90 to 93: there is no requirement for the decision to be dictated by the best interests of P. Welfare is not the paramount consideration trumping all other considerations. That is very far from saying that his best interests are ignored or are irrelevant. The impact upon him will always be *a* material factor, its weight depending on the particular facts and circumstances of the individual case. In deciding whether or not there is good reason for the media's attendance or reporting, the judge is bound to have regard to any ill-effect it may have on the person concerned. Otherwise he cannot deal with the case justly".

With regard to procedural issues, the Court said at para.25:

"An application for an order under rule 90, 91 or 92 must be commenced by filing an application notice form using COP 9 in accordance with Part 10 of the Rules. Rule 80(1)(b) provides that where an application is made, the applicant must serve the application notice on every party to the proceedings as soon as practicable and in any event within 21 days of the date on which it was issued. Having regard to the court's case management powers provided by rule 25(2)(h), the court should consider whether to direct that the application should be dealt with as a discrete issue."

In *Aidiniantz v Aidiniantz* [2015] EWCOP 65, Peter Jackson J. said at para.13:

"On the question of a public hearing, this is a question that should normally be asked and answered at the outset of proceedings. Once a hearing has taken place in private, even in the presence of the press, an application of the present type seeks to convert it into a public hearing retrospectively. This is in my view problematic. Parties and witnesses should normally know where they stand at the time that they are participating in a hearing. While the court should maintain full flexibility in the operation of Rules 90 to 93, and there may be special cases in which a decision cannot be taken until after the event, I would be cautious before following that course in any normal circumstances."

Court's general power to authorise publication of information about proceedings

4–203 **91.**—(1) For the purposes of the law relating to contempt of court, information relating to proceedings held in private [(whether or not contained in a document filed with the court) may be communicated in accordance with paragraph (2) or (2A)]

(2) The court may make an order authorising—

(a) the publication [or communication] of such information [or material] relating to the proceedings as it may specify; or

(b) the publication of the text or a summary of the whole or part of a judgment or order made by the court.

[(2A) Subject to any direction of the court, information referred to in paragraph (1) may be communicated in accordance with Practice Direction 13A.]

(3) Where the court makes an order under paragraph (2) it may do so on such terms as it thinks fit, and in particular may—

(a) impose restrictions on the publication of the identity of—
  (i) any party;
  (ii) P (whether or not a party);
  (iii) any witness; or
  (iv) any other person;

(b) prohibit the publication of any information that may lead to any such person being identified;

(c) prohibit the further publication of any information relating to the proceedings from such date as the court may specify; or

(d) impose such other restrictions on the publication of information relating to the proceedings as the court may specify.

[(4) The court may on its own initiative or upon request authorise communication—

(a) for the purposes set out in Practice Direction 13A; or

(b) for such other purposes as it considers appropriate,

of information held by it.]

AMENDMENTS

The amendments to this rule were made by SI 2015/548 r.46.

GENERAL NOTE

Paragraph (2)

In *Re DP* [2014] EWCOP 7, Sir James Munby P. was required to determine whether the anonymity of a party other than P should be preserved. At para.17, the President repeated what he said in *Re P (Enforced Caesarean: Reporting Restrictions)* [2013] EWHC 4048 (Fam) at para.26:

"So far as concerns the relationship between the media and the court I . . . merely repeat . . . , so as to emphasise, three key principles (*Re J (Reporting Restriction: Internet: Video)* [2013] EWHC 2694 (Fam), [2014] 1 FLR 523, paras 37–39). First, that 'It is not the role of the judge to seek to exercise any kind of editorial control over the manner in which the media reports information which it is entitled to publish'. Second, that 'Comment and criticism may be ill-informed and based, it may be, on misunderstanding or misrepresentation of the facts [but the] fear of such criticism, however justified that fear may be, and however unjustified the criticism, is . . . not of itself a justification for prior restraint by injunction of the kind being sought here, even if the criticism is expressed in vigorous, trenchant or outspoken terms . . . or even in language which is crude, insulting and vulgar'. Third, that 'It is no part of the function of the court exercising the jurisdiction I am being asked to apply to prevent the dissemination of material because it is defamatory . . . If what is published is defamatory, the remedy is an action for defamation, not an application in the Family Division for an injunction'."

The President said that exactly the same goes for the Court of Protection (para.26) and that what he was concerned with was "simply and solely whether JM should be identified, a matter to be determined in accordance with well established principles equally applicable in the Court of Protection as in the Family Court" (para.27).

In *Press Association v Newcastle upon Tyne Hospital Foundations Trust* [2014] EWCOP 6, Peter Jackson J. held that where a court has restricted the publication of information during proceedings that were in existence during a person's lifetime, it has not only the right but the duty to consider, when requested to do so, whether that information should continue to be protected following the person's death, and to balance the factors that arise in the particular case. His Lordship said at para.43:

"There are a number of considerations that may make it necessary and proportionate to continue to uphold after death the privacy that existed in lifetime. Two of these are referred to in *Re C [Adult Patient: Restriction of Publicity After Death* [1996] 1 F.C.R. 605]: (i) medical confidentiality, where the death of the patient does not entitle the doctor to publish her medical records: on the contrary, the doctor may only do that in prescribed circumstances; (ii) the interests of justice, which require that people should not be deterred from approaching the court out of fear that any privacy will automatically lapse on death. To these considerations, I would add the need, referred to above, to treat the rights of those who are subject to public and private hearings with consistency. The COP Rules must be read conformably with the court's obligations under the Human Rights Act and any other approach would not do this."

In *A Healthcare Trust v P* [2015] EWCOP 15, Newton J. held that information identifying P should be provided to the press (via the Injunctions Alert Service) when an application is made for a reporting restriction order under r.92(2). This enables the press to make an informed decision about whether they wished to challenge any particular application.

In *Re Treadwell* [2013] EWHC 2409 (COP), Senior Judge Lush said at para.101:

"When a deputy or attorney exceeds their authority, or behaves in a way that is not in the best interests of a person who lacks capacity, they forfeit any right to confidentiality and there is no good reason why their identity and conduct should not be made public" (*Re Treadwell* [2013] EWHC 2409 (COP) at para.101, per Senior Judge Lush).

In *Newcastle upon Tyne Hospitals Foundation Trust v LM* [2014] EWHC 454 (COP), Peter Jackson J. said at paras 26 and 27:

"The court has jurisdiction to make an order during the lifetime of a patient that will continue to have effect after death unless and until it is varied: *Re C (Adult Patient: Restriction of Publicity After Death* [1996] 1 FCR 605. The situation here is different in that the patient is no longer alive. The unusual circumstances raise interesting questions about the court's jurisdiction to restrict the reporting after a person's death of information gathered during proceedings that took place during her lifetime.

It seems to me that the proper approach is to make an order that preserves the situation until the time comes when someone seeks to present full argument on the question. I will say no more than that for the present."

In *Independent News and Media Ltd v A* [2009] EWHC 2858 (Fam) at para.12, Hedley J. said that an order under this provision disapplies s.12 of the Administration of Justice Act 1960 which reads:

"(1) The publication of information relating to proceedings before any court sitting in private shall not of itself be a contempt of course except in the following cases. . .
(b) Where the proceedings are brought under the Mental Capacity Act 2005. . .
(4) Nothing in this section shall be construed as implying that any publication is punishable as contempt of court which would not be so punishable apart from this section and in particular where the publication is not so punishable by reason of being authorised by rules of court."

Power to order a public hearing

Court's power to order that a hearing be held in public

4–206   **92.**—(1) The court may make an order—
(a) for a hearing to be held in public;
(b) for a part of a hearing to be held in public; or
(c) excluding any person, or class of persons, from attending a public hearing or a part of it.

(2) Where the court makes an order under paragraph (1), it may in the same order or by a subsequent order—
(a) impose restrictions on the publication of the identity of—
    (i)   any party;
    (ii) P (whether or not a party);
    (iii) any witness; or
    (iv) any other person;
(b) prohibit the publication of any information that may lead to any such person being identified;
(c) prohibit the further publication of any information relating to the proceedings from such date as the court may specify; or
(d) impose such other restrictions on the publication of information relating to the proceedings as the court may specify.

GENERAL NOTE
Paragraph (2)
Practice Direction 13A makes provision about hearings in the court, including report-   **4–207**
ing restriction orders. The legal test for making reporting restriction orders was identified
by Baker J. in *W v M* [2011] EWHC 1197 (COP) at paras 31 to 44 and by Keehan J. in
NHS Trust v FG [2014] EWCOP 30 at paras 20 to 29. In the latter case, Keehan J. said
at para.26:

> "A RRO should have the aim of protecting the patient rather than to confer anonymity
> on other individuals or organisations. It may do so, however, where the identification of
> doctors or hospitals, by way of example, is likely to prejudice their ability to care for the
> patient or lead to the identification and defeat the purpose of the order."

In both cases the Court said that it must undertake a balancing of rights under art.8 and
art.10 of the European Convention on Human Rights. In *The NHS Acute Trust v C* [2016]
EWCOP 17, Theis J. said at para.53:

> "The leading case on the approach to be adopted when a court is invited to make
> a reporting restriction order is the decision of the House of Lords in *Re S (a child)*
> *(Identifications: Restriction on Publication)* [2005] 1 AC 593. It was held that an intense
> focus on the comparative importance of competing rights under Articles 8 and 10 was
> required. Neither Article has presumptive weight over the other; the proportionality test
> must be applied to each."

Further guidance on undertaking the balancing exercise was given by Charles J. in
V v Associated Newspapers Ltd [2016] EWCOP 21 where it was held that the Court of
Protection has jurisdiction to extend a reporting restriction order to cover an inquest. There
is therefore no presumption that such orders should end on P's death.

In *W v M*, Baker J. confirmed that the Court has the power under s.47(1) of the Act and
s.37(1) of the Senior Courts Act 1981 to grant injunctions (para.21).

Supplementary

Supplementary provisions relating to public or private hearings
   93.—(1) An order under rule 90, 91 or 92 may be made—   **4–208**
  (a) only where it appears to the court that there is good reason for making the
      order;
  (b) at any time; and
  (c) either on the court's own initiative or on an application made by any person
      in accordance with Part 10.
   (2) A practice direction may make further provision in connection with—
  (a) private hearings;
  (b) public hearings; or
  (c) the publication of information about any proceedings.

GENERAL NOTE

Paragraph (a)
   GOOD REASON. See the General Note to r.90. In *Cheshire West and Chester Council v P*   **4–209**
[2011] EWHC 1330 (Fam) at para.89, Baker J. said:

> "In my judgment, the public interest in holding public authorities accountable for the
> actions of their employees manifestly amounts to a 'good reason' for publishing the
> judgment in an anonymised format but authorising the naming of the local authority
> in any published report of the judgment. I also endorse the submissions made by Mr.
> O'Brien that such publication will help to sustain public confidence that the Court

of Protection is carrying out its functions in the public interest within the restrictions imposed by Parliament."

PART 14

Practice Directions
14A Written evidence
14B Depositions
14C Fees for examiners of the court
14D Witness summons
14E Section 49 reports

ADMISSIONS, EVIDENCE AND DEPOSITIONS

Admissions

Making an admission

4–210   **94.**—(1) Without prejudice to the ability to make an admission in any other way, a party may
admit the truth of the whole or part of another party's case by giving notice in writing. (2) The court may allow a party to amend or withdraw an admission.

Evidence

Power of court to control evidence

4–211   **95.**—(1) The court may—
(a) control the evidence by giving directions as to—
(i) the issues on which it requires evidence;
(ii) the nature of the evidence which it requires to decide those issues; and
(iii) the way in which the evidence is to be placed before the court;
(b) use its power under this rule to exclude evidence that would otherwise be admissible;
(c) allow or limit cross-examination; [. . .]
[(d) admit such evidence, whether written or oral, as it thinks fit; and
(e) admit, accept and act upon such information, whether oral or written, from P, any protected party or any person who lacks competence to give evidence, as the court considers sufficient, although not given on oath and whether or not it would be admissible in a court of law apart from this rule.]

AMENDMENTS

4–212   The amendments to this rule were made by SI 2015/548 r.47.

GENERAL NOTE

4–213   *Paragraph (d)*
In *Enfield LBC v SA* [2010] EWHC 196 (Admin) McFarlane J. held that:
1. This paragraph gives the Court power to admit hearsay evidence which originates from a person who is not competent as a witness and which would otherwise be inadmissible under the Civil Evidence Act 1995 s.5. The weight to be attached to any particular piece of hearsay evidence will be a matter for specific evaluation in each individual case and in undertaking that evaluation regard must be had to s.4 of the 1995 Act. Within that evaluation, the fact that the individual from whom

the evidence originated is not a competent witness will no doubt be an important factor, just as it is, in a different context, when the family court has to evaluate what has been said by a very young child (paras 36, 95). Baker J. agreed with this finding in *G v E* [2010] EWHC 621 (Fam), para.121.

2. In the absence of an 'absolutely pressing emergency' (in an extreme sense given the availability of a High Court judge every day of the year), where there are extant Court of Protection proceedings relating to an individual's capacity and best interests, any question of whether or not there should be an "Achieving Best Evidence" (ABE) interview must be raised with the Court and be subject to direction from a judge. Where the substance of the interview may relate to allegations that another party to the proceedings (or someone closely connected to a party) has harmed the interviewee, then there will be good grounds for the matter being raised, at least initially, without notice to that party, but in every case notice should be given to the Official Solicitor or any other person acting as P's litigation friend. His Lordship commented obiter that for his part, where there are pending proceedings, even if the local authority and litigation friend take the view that P has capacity to consent to such an interview, if the proposal if the interview is to take place without the knowledge of another party to the proceedings, it would nevertheless 'be wise if not necessary' for the Court to be informed of the situation (paras 46, 47).

3. In order to ensure that is effective equivalence in procedures between Court of Protection proceedings and family proceedings, in such cases in the future it would be justified for the Court to make an order for specific disclosure under r.133(3) requiring all parties to give full and frank disclosure of all relevant material, including DVD recordings of ABE interviews (para.58).

In *AVS v NHS Foundation Trust* [2010] EWHC 2746 (COP) at para.28, Sir Nicholas Wall P. said:

"As I understand the Court of Protection Rules 2007, (COPR) I have the power, under COPR rule 95(a) to control the evidence that is called by giving directions as to the issues on which I require evidence, the nature of the evidence I require and the way in which evidence is to be placed before the court. I can also use my power under rule COPR 95(b) to exclude evidence that would otherwise be admissible. I can allow or limit cross-examination (COPR 95(c) and I can admit such evidence whether written or oral, as I think fit. The rules relating to experts (COPR 119 et seq) are stricter—see, for example, COPR 123."

Evidence of witnesses—general rule

96.—(1) The general rule is that any fact which needs to be proved by evidence **4–214** of a witness is to be proved—

(a) where there is a final hearing, by their oral evidence; or

(b) at any other hearing, or if there is no hearing, by their evidence in writing.

(2) Where a witness is called to give oral evidence under paragraph (1)(a), his witness statement shall stand as his evidence in chief unless the court directs otherwise.

(3) A witness giving oral evidence at the final hearing may, if the court permits—

(a) amplify his witness statement; and

(b) give evidence in relation to new matters which have arisen since the witness statement was made.

(4) The court may so permit only if it considers that there is good reason not to confine the evidence of the witness to the contents of his witness statement.

(5) This rule is subject to—

(a) any provision to the contrary in these Rules or elsewhere; or

(b) any order or direction of the court.

Written evidence—general rule

4–215   **97.** A party may not rely upon written evidence unless—

(a) it has been filed in accordance with these Rules or a practice direction;

(b) it is expressly permitted by these Rules or a practice direction; or

(c) the court gives permission.

Evidence by video link or other means

4–216   **98.** The court may allow a witness to give evidence through a video link or by other communication technology.

Service of witness statements for use at final hearing

4–217   **99.**—(1) A witness statement is a written statement which contains the evidence which that person would be allowed to give orally.

(2) The court will give directions about the service of any witness statement that a party intends to rely upon at the final hearing.

(3) The court may give directions as to the order in which witness statements are to be served. (Rules 11 and 100 require witness statements to be verified by a statement of truth.)

Form of witness statement

4–218   **100.** A witness statement must contain a statement of truth and comply with the requirements set out in the relevant practice direction.

Witness summaries

4–219   **101.**—(1) A party who wishes to file a witness statement for use at final hearing, but is unable to do so, may apply, without notice, to be permitted to file a witness summary instead.

(2) A witness summary is a summary of—

(a) the evidence, if known, which would otherwise be included in a witness statement; or

(b) if the evidence is not known, the matters about which the party filing the witness summary proposes to question the witness.

(3) Unless the court directs otherwise, a witness summary must include the name and address of the intended witness.

(4) Unless the court directs otherwise, a witness summary must be filed within the period in which a witness statement would have had to be filed.

(5) Where a party files a witness summary, so far as practicable, rules 96(3)(a) (amplifying witness statements) and 99 (service of witness statements for use at a final hearing) shall apply to the summary.

Affidavit evidence

4–220   **102.** Evidence must be given by affidavit instead of or in addition to a witness statement if this is required by the court, a provision contained in any rule, a practice direction or any other enactment.

Form of affidavit

4–221   **103.** An affidavit must comply with the requirements set out in the relevant practice direction.

Affidavit made outside the jurisdiction

104. A person may make an affidavit outside the jurisdiction in accordance with—

    (a) this Part; or

    (b) the law of the place where he makes the affidavit.

4–222

Notarial acts and instruments

105. A notarial act or instrument may, without further proof, be received in evidence as duly authenticated in accordance with the requirements of law unless the contrary is proved.

4–223

Summoning of witnesses

106.—(1) The court may allow or direct any party to issue a witness summons requiring the person named in it to attend before the court and give oral evidence or produce any document to the court.

(2) An application by a party for the issue of a witness summons may be made by filing an application notice which includes—

    (a) the name and address of the applicant and of his solicitor, if any;

    (b) the name, address and occupation of the proposed witness;

    (c) particulars of any document which the proposed witness is to be required to produce; and

    (d) the grounds on which the application is made.

(3) The general rule is that a witness summons is binding if it is served at least 7 days before the date on which the witness is required to attend before the court, and the requirements of paragraph (6) have been complied with.

(4) The court may direct that a witness summons shall be binding although it will be served less than 7 days before the date on which the witness is required to attend before the court.

(5) Unless the court directs otherwise, a witness summons is to be served by the person making the application.

(6) At the time of service the witness must be offered or paid—

    (a) a sum reasonably sufficient to cover his expenses in travelling to and from the court; and

    (b) such sum by way of compensation for loss of time as may be specified in the relevant practice direction.

(7) The court may order that the witness is to be paid such general costs as it considers appropriate.

4–224

Power of court to direct a party to provide information

107.—(1) Where a party has access to information which is not reasonably available to the other party, the court may direct that party to prepare and file a document recording the information.

(2) The court will give directions about serving a copy of that document on the other parties.

4–225

Depositions

Evidence by deposition

108.—(1) A party may apply for an order for a person to be examined before the hearing takes place.

4–226

(2) A person from whom evidence is to be obtained following an order under this rule is referred to as a 'deponent' and the evidence is referred to as a 'deposition'.

(3) An order under this rule shall be for a deponent to be examined on oath before—

    (a) a circuit judge or a district judge, whether or not nominated as a judge of the court;

    (b) an examiner of the court; or

    (c) such other person as the court appoints.

(4) The order may require the production of any document which the court considers is necessary for the purposes of the examination.

(5) The order will state the date, time and place of the examination.

(6) At the time of service of the order, the deponent must be offered or paid—

    (a) a sum reasonably sufficient to cover his expenses in travelling to and from the place of examination; and

    (b) such sum by way of compensation for loss of time as may be specified in the relevant practice direction.

(7) Where the court makes an order for a deposition to be taken, it may also order the party who obtained the order to file a witness statement or witness summary in relation to the evidence to be given by the person to be examined.

Conduct of examination

4–227
109.—(1) Subject to any directions contained in the order for examination, the examination must be conducted in the same way as if the witness were giving evidence at a final hearing.

(2) If all the parties are present, the examiner may conduct the examination of a person not named in the order for examination if all the parties and the person to be examined consent.

(3) The examiner must ensure that the evidence given by the witness is recorded in full.

(4) The examiner must send a copy of the deposition—

    (a) to the person who obtained the order for the examination of the witness; and

    (b) to the court.

(5) The court will give directions as to the service of a copy of the deposition on the other parties.

Fees and expenses of examiners of the court

4–228
110.—(1) An examiner of the court may charge a fee for the examination and he need not send the deposition to the court until the fee is paid, unless the court directs otherwise.

(2) The examiner's fees and expenses must be paid by the party who obtained the order for examination.

(3) If the fees and expenses due to an examiner are not paid within a reasonable time, he may report that fact to the court.

(4) The court may order the party who obtained the order for examination to deposit in the court office a specified sum in respect of the examiner's fees and, where it does so, the examiner will not be asked to act until the sum has been deposited.

(5) An order under this rule does not affect any decision as to the person who is ultimately to bear the costs of the examination.

Examiners of the court

111.—(1) The Lord Chancellor shall appoint persons to be examiners of the court.   **4–229**

(2) The persons appointed shall be barristers or solicitor-advocates who have been practising for a period of not less than 3 years.

(3) The Lord Chancellor may revoke an appointment at any time.

(4) In addition to appointing persons in accordance with this rule, examiners appointed under rule 34.15 of the Civil Procedure Rules 1998 may act as examiners in the court.

Enforcing attendance of a witness

112.—(1) If a person served with an order to attend before an examiner—   **4–230**

(a) fails to attend; or

(b) refuses to be sworn for the purpose of the examination or to answer any lawful question or produce any document at the examination,

a certificate of his failure or refusal, signed by the examiner, must be filed by the party requiring the deposition.

(2) On the certificate being filed, the party requiring the deposition may apply to the court for an order requiring that person to attend or to be sworn or to answer any question or produce any document, as the case may be.

(3) An application for an order under this rule may be made without notice.

(4) The court may order the person against whom an order is sought or made under this rule to pay any costs resulting from his failure or refusal.

Use of deposition at a hearing

113.—(1) A deposition ordered under rule 108, 115 or 116 may be put in evidence at a hearing unless the court orders otherwise.   **4–231**

(2) A party intending to put a deposition in evidence at a hearing must file notice of his intention to do so on the court and serve the notice on every other party.

(3) Unless the court directs otherwise, he must file the notice at least 14 days before the day fixed for the hearing.

(4) The court may require a deponent to attend the hearing and give evidence orally.

Taking evidence outside the jurisdiction

Interpretation

114. In this Section—   **4–232**

(a) "Regulation State" has the same meaning as "Member State" in the Taking of Evidence Regulation, that is all Member States except Denmark; and

(b) "the Taking of Evidence Regulation" means Council Regulation (EC) No. 1206/200 1 of 28 May 2001 on co-operation between the courts of Member States in the taking of evidence in civil and commercial matters.

Where a person to be examined is in another Regulation State

115.—(1) This rule applies where a party wishes to take a deposition from a person who is—   **4–233**

(a) outside the jurisdiction; and

(b) in a Regulation State.

(2) The court may order the issue of the request to a designated court ("the requested court") in the Regulation State in which the proposed deponent is.

(3) If the court makes an order for the issue of a request, the party who sought the order must file—

  (a) a draft Form A as set out in the annex to the Taking of Evidence Regulation (request for the taking of evidence);

  (b) except where paragraph (4) applies, a translation of the form;

  (c) an undertaking to be responsible for the costs sought by the requested court in relation to—

    (i) fees paid to experts and interpreters; and

    (ii) where requested by that party, the use of special procedure or communications technology; and

  (d) an undertaking to be responsible for the court's expenses.

(4) There is no need to file a translation if—

  (a) English is one of the official languages of the Regulation State where the examination is to take place; or

  (b) the Regulation State has indicated, in accordance with the Taking of Evidence Regulation, that English is a language which it will accept.

(5) Where article 17 of the Taking of Evidence Regulation (direct taking of evidence by the requested court) allows evidence to be taken directly in another Regulation State, the court may make an order for the submission of a request in accordance with that article.

(6) If the court makes an order for the submission of a request under paragraph (5), the party who sought the order must file—

  (a) draft Form I as set out in the annex to the Taking of Evidence Regulation (request for direct taking of evidence);

  (b) except where paragraph (4) applies, a translation of the form; and

  (c) an undertaking to be responsible for the requested court's expenses.

Where a person to be examined is out of the jurisdiction—letter of request

4–234   **116.**—(1) This rule applies where a party wishes to take a deposition from a person who is—

  (a) out of the jurisdiction; and

  (b) not in a Regulation State within the meaning of rule 114.

(2) The court may order the issue of a letter of request to the judicial authorities of the country in which the proposed deponent is.

(3) A letter of request is a request to a judicial authority to take the evidence of that person, or arrange for it to be taken.

(4) If the government of a country permits a person appointed by the court to examine a person in that country, the court may make an order appointing a special examiner for that purpose.

(5) A person may be examined under this rule on oath or affirmation in accordance with any procedure permitted in the country in which the examination is to take place.

(6) If the court makes an order for the issue of a letter of request, the party who sought the order must file—

  (a) the following documents and, except where paragraph (7) applies, a translation of them—

    (i) a draft letter of request;

    (ii) a statement of the issues relevant to the proceedings; and

(iii) a list of questions or the subject matter of questions to be put to the person to be examined; and

(b) an undertaking to be responsible for the Secretary of State's expenses.

(7) There is no need to file a translation if—

(a) English is one of the official languages of the country where the examination is to take place; or

(b) a practice direction has specified that country is a country where no translation is necessary.

Section 49 reports

Reports under section 49 of the Act

117.—(1) This rule applies where the court requires a report to be made to it under section 49 of the Act.

4–235

(2) It is the duty of the person who is required to make the report to help the court on the matters within his expertise.

(3) Unless the court directs otherwise, the person making the report must—

(a) contact or seek to interview such persons as he thinks appropriate or as the court directs;

(b) to the extent that it is practicable and appropriate to do so, ascertain what P's wishes and feelings are, and the beliefs and values that would be likely to influence P if he had the capacity to make a decision in relation to the matter to which the application relates;

(c) describe P's circumstances; and

(d) address such other matters as are required in a practice direction or as the court may direct.

(4) The court will send a copy of the report to the parties and to such persons as the court may direct.

(5) Subject to paragraphs (6) and (7), the person who is required to make the report may examine and take copies of any document in the court records.

(6) The court may direct that the right to inspect documents under this rule does not apply in relation to such documents, or descriptions of documents, as the court may specify.

(7) The court may direct that any information is to be provided to the maker of the report on an edited basis.

Written questions to person making a report under section 49

118.—(1) Where a report is made under section 49 the court may, on the application of any party, permit written questions relevant to the issues before the court to be put to the person by whom the report was made.

4–236

(2) The questions sought to be put to the maker of the report shall be submitted to the court, and the court may put them to the maker of the report with such amendments (if any) as it thinks fit and the maker of the report shall give his replies in writing to the questions so put.

(3) The court will send a copy of the replies given by the maker of the report under this rule to the parties and to such other persons as the court may direct.

PART 15

Practice Direction
15A Expert evidence

EXPERTS

References to expert
4–237   119. A reference to an expert in this Part—
(a) is to an expert who has been instructed to give or prepare evidence for the purpose of court proceedings; but
(b) does not include any person instructed to make a report under section 49 of the Act.

GENERAL NOTE
4–238   When appointing an expert to report on capacity, care should be taken to ensure that the expert has sufficient experience of assessing capacity under the Act rather than in a more general sense (*SC v BS* (COP), October 7, 2011).

Restriction on filing an expert's report
4–239   120.—(1) No person may file expert evidence unless the court or a practice direction permits, or if it is filed with the [. . .] application form and is evidence—
(a) that P is a person who lacks capacity to make a decision or decisions in relation to the matter or matters to which the application relates;
(b) as to P's best interests; or
(c) that is required by any rule or practice direction to be filed with the [. . .] application form.

(2) An applicant may only rely upon any expert evidence so filed in support of the [. . .] application form to the extent and for the purposes that the court allows.

(Rule 64(a) requires the applicant to file any evidence upon which he wishes to rely with the application form [. . .].)

AMENDMENTS
4–240   The amendments to this rule were made by SI 2015/548 r.48.

Duty to restrict expert evidence
4–241   121. Expert evidence shall be restricted to that which is reasonably required to resolve the proceedings.

GENERAL NOTE
4–242   Paragraphs 8 and 9 of "Guidance in cases involving protected parties in which the Official Solicitor is being invited to act as guardian ad litem or litigation friend" [2011] All E.R.(D) 26 (Jan)), drafted by Pauffley J. and endorsed by the President and the Official Solicitor, December 2010, state:

"The Court of Protection Rules make clear that the judge is under a duty to restrict expert evidence to that which is reasonably required to resolve the proceedings. The explanatory note to r.121 states that the court will consider what 'added value' expert evidence will give to the case. Unnecessary expert assessments must be avoided. It will be rare indeed for the court to sanction the instruction of more than one expert to advise in relation to the same issue.

The Practice Direction—Experts (PD15A) specifies that the expert should assist by 'providing objective, unbiased opinion on matters within his expertise, and should not assume the role of advocate'. The form and content of the expert's report are prescribed, in detail, by paragraph 9 of the Practice Direction. It is no part of the expert's function to analyse or summarise the evidence. Focussed brevity in report writing is to be preferred over discussion."

Experts—overriding duty to the court

122. It is the duty of the expert to help the court on the matters within his expertise.

4–243

Court's power to restrict expert evidence

123.—(1) Subject to rule 120, no party may file or adduce expert evidence unless the court or a practice direction permits.

4–244

(2) When a party applies for a direction under this rule he must—

(a) identify the field in respect of which he wishes to rely upon expert evidence;

(b) where practicable, identify the expert in that field upon whose evidence he wishes to rely;

(c) provide any other material information about the expert; and

(d) provide a draft letter of instruction to the expert.

(3) Where a direction is given under this rule, the court shall specify the field or fields in respect of which the expert evidence is to be provided.

(4) The court may specify the person who is to provide the evidence referred to in paragraph (3).

(5) Where a direction is given under this rule for a party to call an expert or put in evidence an expert's report, the court shall give directions for the service of the report on the parties and on such other persons as the court may direct.

(6) The court may limit the amount of the expert's fees and expenses that the party who wishes to rely upon the expert may recover from any other party.

General requirement for expert evidence to be given in a written report

124. Expert evidence is to be given in a written report unless the court directs otherwise.

4–245

Written questions to experts

125.—(1) A party may put written questions to—

4–246

(a) an expert instructed by another party; or

(b) a single joint expert appointed under rule 130,

about a report prepared by such person.

(2) Written questions under paragraph (1)—

(a) may be put once only;

(b) must be put within 28 days beginning with the date on which the expert's report was served; and

(c) must be for the purpose only of clarification of the report.

(3) Paragraph (2) does not apply in any case where—

(a) the court permits it to be done on a further occasion;

(b) the other party or parties agree; or

(c) any practice direction provides otherwise.

(4) An expert's answers to questions put in accordance with paragraph (1) shall be treated as part of the expert's report.

(5) Paragraph (6) applies where—

(a) a party has put a written question to an expert instructed by another party in accordance with this rule; and

(b) the expert does not answer that question.

(6) The court may make one or both of the following orders in relation to the party who instructed the expert—

(a) that the party may not rely upon the evidence of that expert; or

(b) that the party may not recover the fees and expenses of that expert, or part of them, from any other party.

(7) Unless the court otherwise directs, and subject to any final costs order that may be made, the instructing party is responsible for the payment of the expert's fees and expenses, including the expert's costs of answering questions put by any other party.

Contents of expert's report

4–247   **126.**—(1) The court may give directions as to the matters to be covered in an expert's report.

(2) An expert's report must comply with the requirements set out in the relevant practice direction.

(3) At the end of an expert's report there must be a statement that—

(a) the expert understands his duty to the court; and

(b) he has complied with that duty.

(4) The expert's report must state the substance of all material instructions, whether written or oral, on the basis of which the report was written.

(5) The instructions to the expert shall not be privileged against disclosure.

Use by one party of expert's report disclosed by another

4–248   **127.** Where a party has disclosed an expert's report, any party may use that expert's report as evidence at any hearing in the proceedings.

Discussions between experts

4–249   **128.**—(1) The court may, at any stage, direct a discussion between experts for the purpose of requiring the experts to—

(a) identify and discuss the expert issues in the proceedings; and

(b) where possible, reach an agreed opinion on those issues.

(2) The court may specify the issues which the experts must discuss.

(3) The court may direct that following a discussion between the experts they must prepare a statement for the court showing—

(a) those issues on which they agree; and

(b) those issues on which they disagree and a summary of their reasons for disagreeing.

(4) Unless the court otherwise directs, the content of the discussions between experts may be referred to at any hearing or at any stage in the proceedings.

Expert's right to ask court for directions

4–250   **129.**—(1) An expert may file a written request for directions to assist him in carrying out his function as an expert.

(2) An expert must, unless the court directs otherwise, provide a copy of any proposed request for directions under paragraph (1)—

(a) to the party instructing him, at least 7 days before he files the request; and

(b) to all other parties, at least 4 days before he files it.

(3) The court, when it gives directions, may also direct that a party be served with a copy of the directions.

Court's power to direct that evidence is to be given by a single joint expert

130.—(1) Where two or more parties wish to submit expert evidence on a particular issue, the court may direct that the evidence on that issue is to be given by one expert only.

(2) The parties wishing to submit the expert evidence are called 'the instructing parties'.

(3) Where the instructing parties cannot agree who should be the expert, the court may—

(a) select the expert from a list prepared or identified by the instructing parties; or

(b) direct the manner by which the expert is to be selected.

Instructions to a single joint expert

131.—(1) Where the court gives a direction under rule 130 for a single joint expert to be used, each party may give instructions to the expert.

(2) Unless the court otherwise directs, when an instructing party gives instructions to the expert he must, at the same time, send a copy of the instructions to the other instructing parties.

(3) The court may give directions about—

(a) the payment of the expert's fees and expenses; and

(b) any inspection, examination or experiments which the expert wishes to carry out.

(4) The court may, before an expert is instructed, limit the amount that can be paid by way of fees and expenses to the expert.

(5) Unless the court otherwise directs, and subject to any final costs order that may be made, the instructing parties are jointly and severally liable for the payment of the expert's fees and expenses.

4–251

4–252

PART 16

DISCLOSURE

GENERAL NOTE

In *RC v CC* [2013] EWHC 1424 (COP), Judge Cardinal accepted that "in principle cases should proceed on the basis of disclosure but any presumption in favour of such disclosure must be tempered by the court's paramount duty to address the best interests of [P] and the need to weigh up the Article 6 and 8 rights engaged in answering the question as to what must be disclosed" (para.22). Adopting the stance taken in *Durham CC v Dunn* [2012] EWCA Civ 1654 that the refusal of disclosure should only be permitted when it was "strictly necessary", Judge Cardinal held that the following approach should be taken:

4–253

"i. The Rules and the decided cases clearly point to a presumption that there should be disclosure of all documents unless good reason to the contrary are shown- is the withholding of disclosure strictly necessary?

ii. Applying the test of strict necessity involves the Judge who is to decide the case reading the unredacted documents and deciding for himself whether or not the documents can be withheld.

iii. In deciding whether or not documents should be so withheld the Judge should bear in mind the best interests of [P].

iv. In determining best interests the Judge should conduct a balancing act, weighing up [as I have done] the competing rights of the parties under Articles 6 and 8 of the European Convention.

v. Having done so the Court will direct accordingly but should as in public interest immunity cases keep the matter under constant review and invite further submissions if he deems it necessary.

vi. . . . .

vii. If the Judge determines as here that some documents can be disclosed to the advocate and not the party bringing the application he should direct/injunct counsel accordingly . . .".

On an appeal against Judge Cardinal's decision that three social worker statements should not be disclosed to P's birth mother who was seeking contact with her, Sir James Munby P. said that in the passage set out above the judge had "correctly identified the legal principles he had to apply and the approach he should adopt (*RC v CC* [2014] EWHC 131 (COP) at para.26). In this case, Sir James confirmed the principles that had been identified by the courts relating to the disclosure of documents in cases involving children also apply to cases in the Court of Protection relating to adults (para.20).

With regard to point vii of Judge Cardinal's approach, in *R (on the application of Mohamed) v SSD* [2012] EWHC 3454 (Admin), Moses L.J. said at para.28:

"The free and unencumbered ability to give and receive instructions is an important facet of open and fair trials. That ability is hampered if in some respects the lawyer is unable to disclose all the relevant evidence and material and, in that respect, the client is deprived of the opportunity to give informed instructions. But the degree to which that is of importance will vary from case to case. No lawyers should consent to such a [confidentiality] ring unless they are satisfied they can do so without harming their client's case. But provided the legal advisers are satisfied they can safely continue to act under a restriction, the inability to communicate fully with the client will not in such circumstances undermine the fundamental principles on which a fair application for judicial review depends."

Sir James, having made reference to this passage in his judgment, said at para.38:

"As Moses LJ made clear, this is a process dependent upon counsel's agreement an agreement which counsel for the reasons given by Moses LJ may feel unable to give and which in any event the instructions from his lay client may prevent him giving. Judge Cardinal does not seem to have explored these aspects of the matter. Nor, for that matter, does he consider other possible solutions: allowing RC to read, but not to borrow or copy, suitably redacted copies of the documents, or directing that there be disclosure to her of a document setting out the gist of what is being said by the social workers."

Meaning of disclosure

4–254   **132.** A party discloses a document by stating that the document exists or has existed.

General or specific disclosure

4–255   **133.**—(1) The court may either on its own initiative or on the application of a party make an order to give general or specific disclosure.

(2) General disclosure requires a party to disclose—

(a) the documents on which he relies; and

(b) the documents which—

(i) adversely affect his own case;

(ii) adversely affect another party's case; or

(iii) support another party's case.

(3) An order for specific disclosure is an order that a party must do one or more of the following things—

(a) disclose documents or classes of documents specified in the order;

(b) carry out a search to the extent stated in the order; or

(c) disclose any document located as a result of that search.

(4) A party's duty to disclose documents is limited to documents which are or have been in his control.

(5) For the purpose of paragraph (4) a party has or has had a document in his control if—

(a) it is or was in his physical possession;

(b) he has or has had possession of it; or

(c) he has or has had a right to inspect or take copies of it.

Procedure for general or specific disclosure

134.—(1) This rule applies where the court makes an order under rule 133 to give general or specific disclosure. **4–256**

(2) Each party must make, and serve on every other party, a list of documents to be disclosed.

(3) A copy of each list must be filed within 7 days of the date on which it is served.

(4) The list must identify the documents in a convenient order and manner and as concisely as possible.

(5) The list must indicate—

(a) the documents in respect of which the party claims a right or duty to withhold inspection (see rule 138); and

(b) the documents that are no longer in his control, stating what has happened to them.

Ongoing duty of disclosure

135.—(1) Where the court makes an order to give general or specific disclosure under rule 133, any party to whom the order applies is under a continuing duty to provide such disclosure as is required by the order until the proceedings are concluded. **4–257**

(2) If a document to which the duty of disclosure imposed by paragraph (1) extends comes to a party's notice at any time during the proceedings, he must immediately notify every other party.

Right to inspect documents

136.—(1) A party to whom a document has been disclosed has a right to inspect any document disclosed to him except where— **4–258**

(a) the document is no longer in the control of the party who disclosed it; or

(b) the party disclosing the document has a right or duty to withhold inspection of it.

(2) The right to inspect disclosed documents extends to any document mentioned in—

(a) a document filed or served in the course of the proceedings by any other party; or

(b) correspondence sent by any other party.

Inspection and copying of documents

4–259   **137.**—(1) Where a party has a right to inspect a document, he—

(a) must give the party who disclosed the document written notice of his wish to inspect it; and

(b) may request a copy of the document.

(2) Not more than 14 days after the date on which the party who disclosed the document received the notice under paragraph (1)(a), he must permit inspection of the document at a convenient place and time.

(3) Where a party has requested a copy of the document, the party who disclosed the document must supply him with a copy not more than 14 days after the date on which he received the request.

(4) For the purposes of paragraph (2), the party who disclosed the document must give reasonable notice of the time and place for inspection.

(5) For the purposes of paragraph (3), the party requesting a copy of the document is responsible for the payment of reasonable copying costs, subject to any final costs order that may be made.

Claim to withhold inspection or disclosure of document

4–260   **138.**—(1) A party who wishes to claim that he has a right or duty to withhold inspection of a document, or part of a document, must state in writing—

(a) that he has such a right or duty; and

(b) the grounds on which he claims that right or duty.

(2) The statement must be made in the list in which the document is disclosed (see rule 134(2)).

(3) A party may, by filing an application notice in accordance with Part 10, apply to the court to decide whether the claim made under paragraph (1) should be upheld.

Consequence of failure to disclose documents or permit inspection

4–261   **139.** A party may not rely upon any document which he fails to disclose or in respect of which he fails to permit inspection unless the court permits.

[PART 17

LITIGATION FRIENDS AND RULE 3A REPRESENTATIVES

SECTION 1—LITIGATION FRIENDS

Practice Directions
17A Litigation friend
17B Rule 3A representatives

[Who may act as a litigation friend

4–262   **140.**—(1) A person may act as a litigation friend on behalf of a person mentioned in paragraph (2) if that person—

(a) can fairly and competently conduct proceedings on behalf of that person; and

(b) has no interests adverse to those of that person.

(2) The persons for whom a litigation friend may act are—

(a) P;

(b) a child;

(c) a protected party.]

AMENDMENT
This rule was substituted by SI 2015/548 r.49, Sch.   **4–263**

GENERAL NOTE
The test of litigation capacity is to be found in *Masterman-Lister v Brutton & Co*   **4–264**
[2002] EWCA Civ 1889 which is considered in the General Note to s.3 under the heading
"Capacity to conduct litigation".
The role of the litigation friend is to conduct the proceedings on behalf of the person
for whom the litigation friend acts and in the best interests of that person. He or she must
have no interest in the proceedings adverse to that of P. Alex Ruck Keene has written a
comprehensive guidance note on "Acting as a litigation friend in the Court of Protection"
which can be accessed on the University of Manchester website at: www.law.manches-
ter.ac.uk/medialibrary/Main%20site/LAC/Acting-as-a-Litigation-Friend-in-the-Court-of-
Protection-October-2014.pdf. In *Cases A and B* [2014] EWCOP 48, Peter Jackson J. said
at para.16:

> "The role of the litigation friend in representing P's interests is not merely a passive
> one, discharged by critiquing other peoples' efforts. Where he considers it in his client's
> interest, he is entitled to research and present any realistic alternatives."

The Official Solicitor is the litigation friend of last resort. No person, including the
Official Solicitor, can be appointed as litigation friend without their consent. The Official
Solicitor will not accept appointment where there is another person who is suitable and
willing to act as litigation friend. Such a person could be a family member, a close friend,
an IMCA, P's representative appointed under Pt 10 of Sch.A1, or a deputy. The advantages
of appointing family or friends who have been closely involved with P as P's litigation
friend were identified by Charles J. in *Re NRA*, below, at para.161 et seq.
In *Re UF* [2013] EWHC 4289 (COP), Charles J. said that this rule must be read and
applied in the context of the overriding objective set out at r.3, and that if there was a
dispute between family members as to what course of action would be in the best interests
of P, it would rarely be appropriate for a family member to be appointed as P's litigation
friend in proceedings relating to that dispute. Prior to such an appointment, he or she would
need to demonstrate that he or she can, as P's litigation friend, take a balanced and even-
handed approach to the relevant issues (at paras 21 and 23).
A litigation friend who is not a lawyer does not need to instruct solicitors in order to
act as a litigation friend and to conduct proceedings on behalf of P (*Re X (Deprivation of
Liberty)* [2014] EWCOP 25 and 37; also see *Re NRA*, below, at para.133 et seq.).
In *Re NRA* [2015] EWCOP 59, Charles J. said at para.128 that it

> "is common ground that if and when the court appoints such a litigation friend:
>
> (i) it can also give him or her a right of audience and the right to conduct litigation in
> relation to those proceedings (see Paragraphs 1(2)(b) and 2(1)(b) of Schedule 3 to the
> 2007 Act),
> (ii) it can remove those rights, and further and alternatively
> (iii) it can end the appointment of the litigation friend (see COP Rules 144 and 140)".

In *Re NRA,* Charles J. was faced with contradictory obiter dicta on the issue whether P
must be a party to proceedings seeking welfare orders to authorise a deprivation of liberty
and therefore have a litigation friend. His Lordship's judgment is summarised under the
heading *Should P be a party to proceedings seeking welfare orders to authorise a deprivation of liberty?* in s.16(2)(a).
In *RP v United Kingdom* [2013] 1 F.L.R. 744, the European Court of Human Rights
held that art.6 of the European Convention of Human Rights was not breeched by virtue
of the Official Solicitor being appointed to be P's litigation friend on the basis of an expert
report that had been prepared on P's litigation capacity. The Court placed emphasis on
the fact that the Official Solicitor had taken steps to explain to P the ways in which she

could challenge his appointment (paras 72 to 74). The Court said that it did not consider that "acting in P's best interests" required the Official Solicitor to advance any argument P wished (para.76).

In *AB v LCC* [2011] 3151 (COP), Mostyn J. said at para.17 that in addition to the factors set out in para.(1), any putative litigation friend should also be required to confirm that he will act in P's best interests. His Lordship also gave guidance as the circumstances under which a Pt 10 representative can be appointed as P's litigation friend.

The Official Solicitor issued the following Note on February 21, 2012, explaining his current position when invited to act as litigation friend in the Court of Protection in health-care and welfare cases:

"Cases will be accepted only when his long-standing acceptance criteria (applicable in all courts) are met. Those are

- that there is evidence (or the court has made a finding) that the party (or intended party) lacks capacity to conduct the proceedings or is a child (or in Court of Protection proceedings evidence or a finding with regard to P's lack of relevant decision making capacity)
- that, on the basis of the information available to him, there is no one else suitable and willing to act as litigation friend
- that there is security for the costs of legal representation of the protected party or P or the case falls in one of the classes in which, exceptionally, he funds the litigation services out of, or partially out of, his budget, in accordance with long standing practice."

Paragraphs 6 and 7 of "Guidance in cases involving protected parties in which the Official Solicitor is being invited to act as guardian ad litem or litigation friend" ([2011] All E.R.(D) 26 (Jan)), drafted by Pauffley J. and endorsed by the President and the Official Solicitor state:

"The number of welfare cases brought under the provisions of the Mental Capacity Act 2005 is rising exponentially with concomitant resource implications for the Official Solicitor.

Judges should be alert to the problems the Official Solicitor may have in attending at each and every preliminary hearing. Consideration should be given, in appropriate cases, to dispensing with the requirement that he should be present at a time when he is unable to contribute meaningfully to the process. In circumstances where his position has been/will be communicated in writing it may be particularly appropriate for the judge to indicate that the Official Solicitor's attendance at the next directions' hearing is unnecessary."

[Requirement for a litigation friend

4–265   **141.**—(1) This rule does not apply to P (whether P is an adult or a child).

(2) A protected party (if a party to the proceedings) must have a litigation friend.

(3) A child (if a party to the proceedings) must have a litigation friend to conduct those proceedings on that child's behalf unless the court makes an order under paragraph (4).

(4) The court may make an order permitting a child to conduct proceedings without a litigation friend.

(5) An application for an order under paragraph (4)—

(a) may be made by the child;

(b) if the child already has a litigation friend, must be made on notice to the litigation friend; and

(c) if the child has no litigation friend, may be made without notice.

(6) Where—
(a) the court has made an order under paragraph (4); and
(b) it subsequently appears to the court that it is desirable for a litigation friend
    to conduct the proceedings on behalf of the child,
the court may appoint a person to the child's litigation friend.]

AMENDMENT
    This rule was substituted by SI 2015/548 r.49, Sch.   **4–266**

GENERAL NOTE
    This rules requires a protected party (see r.6) and, unless the court otherwise directs, a   **4–267**
child to have a litigation friend if they are a party to the proceedings.

[Litigation friend without a court order
    142.—(1) This rule does not apply—   **4–268**
(a) in relation to P;
(b) where the court has appointed a person under rule 143 or 144; or
(c) where the Official Solicitor is to act as a litigation friend.
    (2) A deputy with the power to conduct legal proceedings in the name of a pro-
tected party or on the protected party's behalf is entitled to be a litigation friend
of the protected party in any proceedings to which the deputy's power relates.
    (3) If no-one has been appointed by the court or, in the case of a protected party,
there is no deputy with the power to conduct proceedings, a person who wishes to
act as a litigation friend must—
(a) file a certificate of suitability stating that they satisfy the conditions in rule
    140(1); and
(b) serve the certificate of suitability on—
    (i) the person on whom an application form is to be served in accordance
        with rule 32 (service on children and protected parties); and
    (ii) every other person who is a party to the proceedings.
    (4) If the person referred to in paragraph (2) wishes to act as a litigation friend
for the protected party, that person must file and serve on the persons mentioned in
paragraph (3)(b) a copy of the court order which appointed that person.]

AMENDMENT
    This rule was substituted by SI 2015/548 r.49, Sch.   **4–269**

[Litigation friend by court order
    143.—(1) The court may make an order appointing—   **4–270**
(a) the Official Solicitor; or
(b) some other person,
to act as a litigation friend for a protected party, a child or P.
    (2) The court may make an order under paragraph (1)—
(a) either on its own initiative or on the application of any person; but
(b) only with the consent of the person to be appointed.
    (3) An application for an order under paragraph (1) must be supported by
evidence.
    (4) The court may not appoint a litigation friend under this rule unless it is
satisfied that the person to be appointed satisfies the conditions in rule 140(1).
    (5) The court may at any stage of the proceedings give directions as to the
appointment of a litigation friend.

(Rule 3A requires the court to consider how P should participate in the proceedings, which may be by way of being made a party and the appointment of a litigation friend under this Part.)]

AMENDMENT

4–271   This rule was substituted by SI 2015/548 r.49, Sch.

GENERAL NOTE

4–272   In *G v E* [2010] EWHC 2512 (COP) at para.574, Baker J. said that the Official Solicitor is not a litigation friend of last resort: the use of the term "may" in para.(1) demonstrates that the court has a complete discretion on the matter.

[Court's power to prevent a person from acting as a litigation friend or to bring an end to an appointment of a person as a litigation friend or to appoint another one

4–273   **144.**—(1) The court may either on its own initiative or on the application of any person—

   (a) direct that a person may not act as a litigation friend;

   (b) bring to an end a litigation friend's appointment; or

   (c) appoint a new litigation friend in place of an existing one.

   (2) If an application for an order under paragraph (1) is based on the conduct of the litigation friend, it must be supported by evidence.

   (3) The court may not appoint a litigation friend under this rule unless it is satisfied that the person to be appointed satisfies the conditions in rule 140(1).

   (4) The appointment of a litigation friend continues until brought to an end by court order.

   (Rule 87 applies if P has capacity in relation to the matter or matters to which the application relates.)]

AMENDMENT

4–274   This rule was substituted by SI 2015/548 r.49, Sch

[Appointment of litigation friend by court order—supplementary

4–275   **145.** The applicant must serve a copy of an application for an order under rule 143 or 144 on—

   (a) the person on whom an application form is to be served in accordance with rule 32 (service on children and protected parties);

   (b) every other person who is a party to the proceedings;

   (c) any person who is the litigation friend, or who is purporting to act as the litigation friend, when the application is made; and

   (d) unless that person is the applicant, the person who it is proposed should be the litigation friend,

   as soon as practicable and in any event within 14 days of the date on which the application was issued.]

AMENDMENT

4–276   This rule was substituted by SI 2015/548 r.49, Sch.

[Procedure where appointment of a litigation friend comes to an end for a child

4–277   **145A.** When a child reaches 18, provided the child is neither—

(a) P; nor

(b) a protected party,

the litigation friend's appointment ends and the child must serve notice on every other party—

  (i) stating that the child has reached full age;

  (ii) stating that the appointment of the litigation friend has ended; and

  (iii) providing an address for service.]

AMENDMENT

This rule was substituted by SI 2015/548 r.49, Sch.   **4–278**

[Practice direction in relation to litigation friends

146. A practice direction may make additional or supplementary provision in   **4–279**
relation to litigation friends.]

AMENDMENT

This rule was substituted by SI 2015/548 r.49, Sch.   **4–280**

[SECTION 2—RULE 3A REPRESENTATIVES

Interpretation

146A. In this Section, references to "rule 3A representatives" are references to   **4–281**
both accredited legal representatives and representatives.

("Accredited legal representative" and "representative" are defined in rule 6.)]

AMENDMENT

This rule was substituted by SI 2015/548 r.49, Sch.   **4–282**

[Who may act as a rule 3A representative for P

147. A person may act as an accredited legal representative, or a representative,   **4–283**
for P, if that person can fairly and competently discharge his or her functions on
behalf of P.]

AMENDMENT

This rule was substituted by SI 2015/548 r.49, Sch.   **4–284**

[Rule 3A representative by court order

148.—(1) The court may make an order appointing a person to act as a repre-   **4–285**
sentative, or an accredited legal representative, for P.

(2) The court may make an order under paragraph (1)—

(a) either of its own initiative or on the application of any person; but

(b) only with the consent of the person to be appointed.

(3) The court may not appoint a representative or an accredited legal representative under this rule unless it is satisfied that the person to be appointed satisfies
the conditions in rule 147.

(4) The court may at any stage of the proceedings give directions as to the terms
of appointment of a representative or an accredited legal representative.

(Rule 3A requires the court to consider how P should participate in the proceedings, which may be by way of the appointment of a representative or accredited
legal representative under this Part.)]

AMENDMENT

4–286   This rule was substituted by SI 2015/548 r.49, Sch.

[Application by rule 3A representative or by P for directions

4–287   **148A.** A representative, an accredited legal representative or P may, at any time and without giving notice to the other parties, apply to the court for directions relating to the performance, terms of appointment or continuation of the appointment of the representative or accredited legal representative.]

AMENDMENT

4–288   This rule was substituted by SI 2015/548 r.49, Sch.

[Court's power to prevent a person from acting as a rule 3A representative or to bring an end to an appointment of a person as a rule 3A representative or appoint another one

4–289   **148B.**—(1) The court may, either of its own initiative or on the application of any person—

(a) direct that a person may not act as a representative or accredited legal representative;

(b) bring to an end a representative's or accredited legal representative's appointment;

(c) appoint a new representative or accredited legal representative in place of an existing one; or

(d) vary the terms of a representative's or accredited legal representative's appointment.

(2) If an application for an order under paragraph (1) is based on the conduct of the representative or accredited legal representative, it must be supported by evidence.

(3) The court may not appoint a representative or accredited legal representative under this rule unless it is satisfied that the person to be appointed satisfies the conditions in rule 147.

(4) The appointment of a representative or accredited legal representative continues until brought to an end by court order.

(5) The court must bring to an end the appointment of a representative or an accredited legal representative if P has capacity to appoint such a representative and does not wish the appointment by the court to continue.]

AMENDMENT

4–290   This rule was substituted by SI 2015/548 r.49, Sch.

[Appointment of rule 3A representative by court order—supplementary

4–291   **148C.** The applicant must serve a copy of an application for an order under rule 148 or rule 148B on—

(a) the person on whom an application form is to be served in accordance with rule 32 (service on children and protected parties);

(b) every other person who is a party to the proceedings;

(c) any person who is the representative, or accredited legal representative, purporting to act as such representative, when the application is made; and

(d) unless that person is the applicant, the person who it is proposed should be the representative or accredited legal representative, as soon as practicable and in any event within 14 days of the date on which the application was issued.]

AMENDMENT
This rule was substituted by SI 2015/548 r.49, Sch.   **4–292**

[Practice direction in relation to rule 3A representatives
149. A practice direction may make additional or supplementary provision in   **4–293** relation to representatives or accredited legal representatives.]

AMENDMENT
This rule was substituted by SI 2015/548 r.49, Sch.   **4–294**

PART 18

Practice Direction
18A Change of solicitor

CHANGE OF SOLICITOR

Change of solicitor
150.—(1) This rule applies where a party to proceedings—   **4–295**
(a) for whom a solicitor is acting wants to change his solicitor or act in person; or
(b) after having conducted the proceedings in person, appoints a solicitor to act on his behalf (except where the solicitor is appointed only to act as an advocate for a hearing).
(2) The party proposing the change must—
(a) file a notice of the change with the court; and
(b) serve the notice of the change on every other party to the proceedings and, if there is one, on the solicitor who will cease to act.
(3) The notice must state the party's address for service.
(4) The notice filed at court must state that it has been served as required by paragraph (2)(b).
(5) Where there is a solicitor who will cease to act, he will continue to be considered the party's solicitor unless and until—
(a) the notice is filed and served in accordance with paragraphs (2), (3) and (4); or
(b) the court makes an order under rule 152 and the order is served in accordance with that rule.

[Legally aided person]
151.—(1) Where the certificate of any person ("A") [who is a legally aided   **4–296** person is revoked or withdrawn]—
(a) the solicitor who acted for A will cease to be the solicitor acting in the case as soon as his retainer is determined [under regulation 24 or 41 of the Civil Legal Aid (Procedure) Regulations 2012]; and
(b) if A wishes to continue and appoints a solicitor to act on his behalf, rule 150(2), (3) and (4) will apply as if A had previously conducted the application in person.
[(2) In this rule, "certificate" means a certificate issued under the Civil Legal Aid (Procedure) Regulations 2012.]

AMENDMENTS
4–297   The amendments to this rule were made by SI 2013/534 Sch., para.17.

Order that a solicitor has ceased to act
4–298   **152.**—(1) A solicitor may apply for an order declaring that he has ceased to be the solicitor acting for a party.

(2) Where an application is made under this rule—

(a) the solicitor must serve the application notice on the party for whom the solicitor is acting, unless the court directs otherwise; and

(b) the application must be supported by evidence.

(3) Where the court makes an order that a solicitor has ceased to act, the solicitor must—

(a) serve a copy of the order on every other party to the proceedings; and

(b) file a certificate of service.

Removal of solicitor who has ceased to act on application of another party
4–299   **153.**—(1) Where—

(a) a solicitor who has acted for a party—

    (i) has died;

    (ii) has become bankrupt;

    (iii) has ceased to practice; or

    (iv) cannot be found; and

(b) the party has not served a notice of a change of solicitor or notice of intention to act in person as required by rule 150,

any other party may apply for an order declaring that the solicitor has ceased to be the solicitor acting for the other party in the case.

(2) Where an application is made under this rule, the applicant must serve the application on the party to whose solicitor the application relates, unless the court directs otherwise.

(3) Where the court makes an order under this rule—

(a) the court will give directions about serving a copy of the order on every other party to the proceedings; and

(b) where the order is served by a party, that party must file a certificate of service.

Practice direction relating to change of solicitor
4–300   **154.** A practice direction may make additional or different provision in relation to change of solicitor.

PART 19

Practice Directions
19A Costs in the Court of Protection
19B Fixed costs in the Court of Protection

COSTS

Interpretation
4–301   **155.**—[(1) In this Part—

"authorised court officer" means any officer of the Senior Courts Costs Office whom the Lord Chancellor has authorised to assess costs;

"costs" include fees, charges, disbursements, expenses, remuneration and any reimbursement allowed to a litigant in person;

"costs judge" means a taxing Master of the Senior Courts;

"costs officer" means a costs judge or an authorised court officer;

"detailed assessment" means the procedure by which the amount of costs or remuneration is decided by a costs officer in accordance with Part 47 of the Civil Procedure Rules 1998 (which are applied to proceedings under these Rules, with modifications, by rule 160);

"fixed costs" are to be construed in accordance with the relevant practice direction;

"fund" includes any estate or property held for the benefit of any person or class of persons, and any fund to which a trustee or personal representative is entitled in that capacity;

"paying party" means a party liable to pay costs;

"pro bono representation" means representation provided free of charge;

"receiving party" means a party entitled to be paid costs;

"summary assessment" means the procedure by which the court, when making an order about costs, orders payment of a sum of money instead of fixed costs or detailed assessment.]

(2) The costs to which the rules in this Part apply include—

(a) where the costs may be assessed by the court, costs payable by a client to [their legal representative]; and

(b) costs which are payable by one party to another party under the terms of a contract, where the court makes an order for an assessment of those costs.

(3) Where advocacy or litigation services are provided to a client under a conditional fee agreement, costs are recoverable under this Part notwithstanding that the client is liable to pay his legal representative's fees and expenses only to the extent that sums are recovered in respect of the proceedings, whether by way of costs or otherwise.

(4) In paragraph (3), the reference to a conditional fee agreement [means an agreement enforceable under] section 58 of the Courts and Legal Services Act 1990.

AMENDMENTS

The amendments to this rule were made by SI 2015/548 r.50.   **4–302**

Property and affairs—the general rule

156. Where the proceedings concern P's property and affairs the general rule is   **4–303**
that the costs of the proceedings or of that part of the proceedings that concerns P's property and affairs, shall be paid by P or charged to his estate.

Personal welfare—the general rule

157. Where the proceedings concern P's personal welfare the general rule is   **4–304**
that there will be no order as to the costs of the proceedings or of that part of the proceedings that concerns P's personal welfare.

GENERAL NOTE

The rules relating to costs in the Court of Protection do not apply on an appeal from that   **4–305**
court to the Court of Appeal. In the Court of Appeal the general rule is that the unsuccessful party will be ordered to pay the costs (*Cheshire West and Chester Council v P* [2011] EWCA Civ 1330).

These Rules have not changed the long-standing practice of the court exercising its discretion to share the Official Solicitor's costs across the public bodies in personal welfare cases (*An NHS Trust v D* [2012] EWHC 886 (COP)). A costs order may be made against the Public Guardian (*The Public Guardian v CT* [2014] EWCOP 51).

In *Re G (Adult)* [2014] EWCOP 5, a preliminary question for determination was whether a costs application was governed by this rule and r.159, or whether it was regulated, pursuant to r.9, by CPR 1998 r.44.3(2), (4) and (5). The President said at para.5:

"The difference, of course, and the reason for the controversy is that whereas under CoPR 2007 rule 157 'the general rule is that there will be no order as to the costs', under CPR 1998 rule 44.3(2)(a) 'the general rule is that the unsuccessful party will be ordered to pay the costs of the successful party.' In each case (see CoPR 2007 rule 159 and CPR 1998 rule 44.3(2)(b) respectively) the court 'may' make a different order, having regard to all the circumstances, including in the one case those referred to in rule 159 and in the other those referred to in the very similarly expressed rules 44.3(4) and (5). So the essential difference is in the 'starting point' or 'default position'."

The President resolved the question by holding that the application fell to be determined in accordance with this rule and r.159. He said at para.9:

"The overall scheme of rules 156-157 is, first, the drawing of a distinction between proceedings which 'concern P's property and affairs' and those which 'concern P's personal welfare' and, secondly, the principle that, where the proceedings concern both, the costs should be apportioned between 'that part of the proceedings that concerns' the one and 'that part of the proceedings that concerns' the other. It is for this reason, and not as suggested by Mr Patel, that rule 157 contains the words upon which he relies. The key word in each of rules 156, 157 and 158 is 'proceedings' and not, it may be noted, some other word, for example, 'application'. The use of the word 'proceedings' invites two questions: What are the proceedings? Do they concern property and affairs or personal welfare? In the present case there can only be one answer: the 'proceedings' concern G's personal welfare. The fact that G's best interests are not determinative of this particular application does not bear on the fact that the application was . . . an application made in personal welfare proceedings and made for the purpose of enabling ANL to participate in personal welfare proceedings."

The court has power to make a costs order when the substantive proceedings have been resolved without a trial, but when the parties have not agreed about costs. In *M v Croydon LBC* [2012] EWCA Civ 595, the Master of The Rolls said at paras 50 and 51:

"The outcome will normally be different in cases where the consent order does not involve the claimant getting all, or substantively all, the relief which he has claimed. In such cases, the court will often decide to make no order for costs, unless it can, without much effort decide that one of the parties has clearly won, or has won to a sufficient extent to justify some order for costs in its favour. Thus, the fact that the claimant has succeeded in obtaining part of the relief he sought may justify his recovering some of his costs, for instance where the issue on which the claimant succeeded was clearly the most important and/or expensive issue. But in many such cases, the court may consider that it cannot fairly award the claimant any costs because, for instance, it is not easy to assess whether the defendants should have their costs of the issue on which the claimant did not succeed, and whether that would wipe out the costs which the claimant might recover in relation to the issue on which he won.

In many cases which are settled on terms which do not accord with the relief which the claimant has sought, the court will normally be unable decide who has won, and therefore will not make any order for costs. However, in some cases, the court may be able to form a tolerably clear view without much effort. In a number of such cases, the court may well be assisted by considering whether it is reasonably clear from the available material whether one party would have won if the case had proceeded to trial. If, for instance, it is clear that the claimant would have won, that would lend considerable support to his argument that the terms of settlement represent success such that he should be awarded his costs."

In *Re RC (deceased)* [2010] EWHC B29 (COP), a case where the applicant was asking the court to direct the Public Guardian to cancel the registration of a Lasting Power of Attorney for health and welfare, Senior Judge Lush said:

"In my judgment, because the format, the procedures for both execution and registration, and the grounds of objection are identical in relation to both types of instrument, as a general rule, the incidence of costs in cases where there is an LPA for health and welfare should not necessarily differ from the general rule in property and affairs cases, subject of course to the provisions of r.159, which allows the court to depart from the general rule if the circumstances so justify."

Apportioning costs—the general rule

158. Where the proceedings concern both property and affairs and personal   **4–306** welfare the court, insofar as practicable, will apportion the costs as between the respective issues.

Departing from the general rule

159.—(1) The court may depart from rules 156 to 158 if the circumstances so   **4–307** justify, and in deciding whether departure is justified the court will have regard to all the circumstances, including—

(a) the conduct of the parties;

(b) whether a party has succeeded on part of his case, even if he has not been wholly successful; and

(c) the role of any public body involved in the proceedings.

(2) The conduct of the parties includes—

(a) conduct before, as well as during, the proceedings;

(b) whether it was reasonable for a party to raise, pursue or contest a particular issue;

(c) the manner in which a party has made or responded to an application or a particular issue; [. . .]

(d) whether a party who has succeeded in his application or response to an application, in whole or in part, exaggerated any matter contained in his application or response [; and]

[(e) any failure by a party to comply with a rule, practice direction or court order.]

(3) Without prejudice to rules 156 to 158 and the foregoing provisions of this rule, the court may permit a party to recover their fixed costs in accordance with the relevant practice direction.

AMENDMENTS

The amendments to this rule were made by SI 2015/548 r.51.   **4–308**

GENERAL NOTE

An appeal against the exercise by a judge of his discretion under this rule faces a high   **4–309** hurdle (*Re G (An Adult)(Costs)* [2015] EWCA Civ 446 at para.22).

For the court to discern whether a departure from the general rule set out in r.157 is appropriate, it may examine all of the circumstances, not simply the items contained in sub-rule (1)(a) to (c) of this rule (*EG v RS* [2010] EWHC 3073 (COP) at para.25).

In *London Borough of Hillingdon v Steven Neary* [2011] EWHC 3522 (COP), Peter Jackson J. summarised the decision on this rule in an Appendix to his judgment. His Lordship said, at paras 7 and 8:

"[The decisions] do not purport to give any guidance over and above the words in the Rules themselves . . . Where there is a general rule from which one can depart where the circumstances justify, it adds nothing definitional to describe a case as exceptional or atypical. Instead, the decisions represent useful examples of the manner in which the court has exercised its powers."

Each application for costs must therefore be considered on its own merit or lack of merit with the clear appreciation that there must be a good reason before the court will contemplate departure from the general rule. Beyond that, as MCA s. 55(3) . . . makes plain, the court has 'full power' to make the appropriate order."

In *D v R (Deputy of S)* [2010] EWHC 3748 (COP) at para.9, Henderson J. said that the general rule "is the starting point and a good case has to be made out for departing from it. It is not the case that the court has an entirely unfettered discretion. On the contrary, there is a prescribed starting point and a discretion to depart from it in appropriate circumstances". In this case the judge departed from the general rule on the ground that the litigant's conduct had led to the hearing being substantially longer and more complicated than it should have been.

The circumstances that would justify the court from departing from the general rule "include conduct where the person against whom it is proposed to award costs is clearly acting in bad faith. Even then, there should be a carefully worded warning that costs could be awarded against them, and a consideration of their ability to pay" (*Re RC (deceased)* [2010] EWHC B29 (COP), per the Senior Judge). In *VA v Hertfordshire Partnership NHS Foundation Trust* [2011] EWHC 3524 (COP), Peter Jackson J. ordered a partial departure from the general rule in a case "where there has been no bad faith or flagrant misconduct, but there has been substandard practice and a failure by the public bodies to recognise the weakness of their own cases and the strength of the cases against them" (para.69). In *WBC v CP* [2012] EWHC 1944 (Fam) Ryder J. departed from the general rule and awarded costs against the local authority where:

(a) the authority's actions were tainted with illegality;

(b) the authority's decision making was impoverished and disorganised;

(c) the authority was responsible for the delay in referring CP's circumstances to the Court of Protection and/or the High Court in its children and inherent jurisdictions; and

(d) the authority could have arrived at the position concluded by the court many months earlier (para.17).

The "reprehensible" conduct of the local authority led Judge Marston to award indemnity costs against the authority in *Somerset CC v MK* [2015] EWCOP B1.

In *Manchester City Council v G* [2011] EWCA Civ 939 the Court of Appeal confirmed that it would only interfere with a cost decision if it could be shown that the judge had gone "seriously wrong". The court approved, at paras 16 and 17, the following passage of the judgment of Baker J. at first instance *G v E* ([2010] EWHC 3385 (Fam) at para.40):

"Of course, it is right that the Court should follow the general rule where appropriate. Parties should be free to bring personal welfare issues to the Court of Protection without fear of a costs sanction. Local authorities and others who carry out their work professionally have no reason to fear that a costs order will be made. The submission that local authorities will be discouraged from making applications to the Court of Protection if a costs order is made in this case is a thoroughly bad argument. The opposite is, in fact, the truth. It is only local authorities who break the law, or who are guilty of misconduct that falls within the meaning of rule 159, that have reason to fear a costs order. Local authorities who do their job properly and abide by the law have nothing to fear. In particular, the Court of Protection recognises that professional work in this very difficult field often involves very difficult judgments and decisions. The Court is not going to impose a costs burden on a local authority simply because hindsight demonstrates that it got those judgments wrong."

[Rules about costs in the Civil Procedure Rules to apply

160.—(1) Subject to the provisions of these Rules, Parts 44, 46 and 47 of the **4–310**
Civil Procedure Rules 1998 ("the 1998 Rules") apply with the modifications in
this rule and such other modifications as may be appropriate, to costs incurred in
relation to proceedings under these Rules as they apply to costs incurred in relation to proceedings in the High Court.

(2) Rules 3.12 to 3.18 of the 1998 Rules and Practice Direction 3E supporting
those Rules do not apply in relation to proceedings under these Rules.

(3) The provisions of Part 47 of the 1998 Rules apply with the modifications in
this rule and such other modifications as may be appropriate, to a detailed assessment of the remuneration of a deputy under these Rules as they apply to a detailed
assessment of costs in proceedings to which the 1998 Rules apply.

(4) Where the definitions in Part 44 (referred to in Parts 44, 46 and 47) of the
1998 Rules are different from the definitions in rule 155 of these Rules, the latter
definitions prevail.

(5) Rules 44.2(1) to (5), 44.5, 44.6, 44.9 and 44.13 to 44.18 of the 1998 Rules
do not apply.

(6) For rule 46.1(1) of the 1998 Rules there is substituted—

"(1) This paragraph applies where a person applies for an order for specific
disclosure before the commencement of proceedings.".

(7) Rules 46.2, 46.5 and 46.10 to 46.14 of the 1998 Rules do not apply.

(8) In rule 47.3(1)(c) of the 1998 Rules, the words "unless the costs are being
assessed under rule 46.4 (costs where money is payable to a child or protected
party)" are omitted.

(9) In rule 47.3(2) of the 1998 Rules, the words "or a District Judge" are
omitted.

(10) Rule 47.4(3) and (4) of the 1998 Rules do not apply.

(11) Rules 47.9(4), 47.10 and 47.11 of the 1998 Rules do not apply where the
costs are to be paid by P or charged to P's estate.]

AMENDMENT
This rule was substituted by SI 2015/548 r.52.   **4–311**

GENERAL NOTE
This rule should be read with r.9.   **4–312**
By virtue of para.(1), the principles regarding the awarding of wasted costs orders in the
Court of Protection are the same as in the High Court. The relevant rules can therefore be
found in CPR r.48.7 and para.53 of the Costs Practice Direction (*Sharma and Judkins v
Hunters* [2011] EWHC 2546 (COP)).

Detailed assessment of costs

161.—(1) Where the court orders costs to be assessed by way of detailed assess- **4–313**
ment, the detailed assessment proceedings shall take place in the High Court.

(2) A fee is payable in respect of the detailed assessment of costs and on an
appeal against a decision made in a detailed assessment of costs.

(3) Where a detailed assessment of costs has taken place, the amount payable
by P is the amount which the court certifies as payable.

Employment of a solicitor by two or more persons

162. Where two or more persons having the same interest in relation to a matter **4–314**

act in relation to the proceedings by separate legal representatives, they shall not be permitted more than one set of costs of the representation unless and to the extent that the court certifies that the circumstances justify separate representation.

Costs of the Official Solicitor
4–315   **163.** Any costs incurred by the Official Solicitor in relation to proceedings under these Rules or in carrying out any directions given by the court and not provided for by remuneration under rule 167 shall be paid by such persons or out of such funds as the court may direct.

Procedure for assessing costs
4–316   **164.** Where the court orders a party, or P, to pay costs to another party it may either—
  (a) make a summary assessment of the costs; or
  (b) order a detailed assessment of the costs by a costs officer,
unless any rule, practice direction or other enactment provides otherwise.

Costs following P's death
4–317   **165.** An order or direction that costs incurred during P's lifetime be paid out of or charged on his estate may be made within 6 years after P's death.

Costs orders in favour of or against non-parties
4–318   **166.**—(1) Where the court is considering whether to make a costs order in favour of or against a person who is not a party to proceedings [, that person must be]—
  (a) [. . .] added as a party to the proceedings for the purposes of costs only; [. . .]
[(aa) served with such documents as the court may direct; and]
  (b) [. . .] given a reasonable opportunity to attend [any hearing] at which the court will consider the matter further.
(2) This rule does not apply where the court is considering whether to make an order against the [Lord Chancellor in proceedings in which the Lord Chancellor has provided legal aid to a party to the proceedings].

AMENDMENTS
4–319   The amendments to this rule were made by SI 2015/548 r.51.

Remuneration of a deputy, donee or attorney
4–320   **167.**—(1) Where the court orders that a deputy, donee or attorney is entitled to remuneration out of P's estate for discharging his functions as such, the court may make such order as it thinks fit, including an order that—
  (a) he be paid a fixed amount;
  (b) he be paid at a specified rate; or
  (c) the amount of the remuneration shall be determined in accordance with the schedule of fees set out in the relevant practice direction.
(2) Any amount permitted by the court under paragraph (1) shall constitute a debt due from P's estate.
(3) The court may order a detailed assessment of the remuneration by a costs officer, in accordance with rule 164(b).

Practice direction as to costs

168. A practice direction may make further provision in respect of costs in proceedings.

4–321

PART 20

Practice Directions
20A Appeals
20B Allocation of Appeals

APPEALS

[Scope of this Part

169. This Part applies to an appeal against any decision of the court.]

4–322

AMENDMENT
This rule was substituted by SI 2015/548 r.54.

4–323

Interpretation

170.—(1) In the following provisions of this Part—

4–324

(a) "appeal judge" means a judge of the court to whom an appeal is made;
(b) "first instance judge" means the judge of the court from whose decision an appeal is brought;
(c) "appellant" means the person who brings or seeks to bring an appeal;
(d) "respondent" means—
   (i) a person other than the appellant who was a party to the proceedings before the first instance judge and who is affected by the appeal; or
   (ii) a person who is permitted or directed by the first instance judge or the appeal judge to be a party to the appeal [; and]
[(e) "a second appeal" means an appeal from a decision of a judge of the court which was itself made on appeal from a judge of the court.]

(2) In this Part, where the expression "permission" is used it means "permission to appeal" unless otherwise stated.

AMENDMENTS
The amendments to this rule were made by SI 2015/548 r.55.

4–325

Dealing with appeals

171.—(1) The court may deal with an appeal or any part of an appeal at a hearing or without a hearing.

4–326

(2) In considering whether it is necessary to hold a hearing, the court shall have regard to the matters set out in rule 84(3).

[(3) Any person bound by an order of the court by virtue of rule 74 (persons to be bound as if parties) may seek permission under this Part.

(4) All parties to an appeal must comply with any relevant practice direction.

(5) Where permission is required, it is to be granted or refused in accordance with this Part.]

(Rule 89 provides for reconsideration of orders made without a hearing or without notice to a person.)

AMENDMENTS

4–327   The amendments to this rule were made by SI 2015/548 r.56.

[Destination of appeals

4–328   **171A.**—(1) An appeal from a decision of a judge of the court shall lie to the Court of Appeal in the following cases—

(a) where it is an appeal from a decision of a Tier 3 Judge; or

(b) where it is a second appeal.

(2) Subject to paragraph (1) and to any alternative provision made by the relevant practice direction—

(a) where the first instance judge was a Tier 1 Judge, any appeal shall be heard by a Tier 2 Judge;

(b) where the first instance judge was a Tier 2 Judge, any appeal shall be heard by a Tier 3 Judge.

(3) No appeal may be made against a decision of a court officer authorised under rule 7A.

(A decision of a court officer authorised under rule 7A can be reconsidered by a judge under rule 89.)]

AMENDMENT

4–329   This rule was inserted by SI 2015/548 r.57.

[Permission to appeal—appeals to the Court of Appeal

4–330   **171B.**—(1) Subject to rule 172A, an appeal to the Court of Appeal against a decision of a judge of the court may not be made without permission.

(2) Where an appeal to the Court of Appeal is made from a decision of a Tier 3 Judge, permission may be granted by the first instance judge or by the Court of Appeal, unless the appeal is a second appeal.

(3) Where an appeal to the Court of Appeal is a second appeal, permission may only be granted by the Court of Appeal.

(4) No appeal shall lie against—

(a) the granting or refusal of permission under this rule; or

(b) an order allowing an extension of time for appealing from an order.

(The procedure for an appeal from a decision of a judge of the court to the Court of Appeal, including requirements for permission, is governed by the Civil Procedure Rules 1998.)]

AMENDMENT

4–331   This rule was inserted by SI 2015/548 r.57.

[Permission to appeal—other cases

4–332   **172.**—(1) Subject to rules 171B and 172A, an appeal against a decision of the court may not be made without permission.

(2) An application for permission to appeal may be made to—

(a) the first instance judge; or

(b) another judge who satisfies the relevant condition in paragraph (4) or (5).

(3) Where an application for permission is refused by the first instance judge, a further application for permission may be made to a judge who satisfies the relevant condition in paragraph (4) or (5).

(4) Where the decision sought to be appealed is a decision of a Tier 1 Judge, permission may also be granted or refused by—

(a) a Tier 2 Judge; or

(b) a Tier 3 Judge.

(5) Where the decision sought to be appealed is a decision of a Tier 2 Judge, permission may also be granted or refused by a Tier 3 Judge.

(6) Subject to paragraph (7) and except where another rule or a practice direction provides otherwise, where a judge who satisfies the relevant condition in paragraph (4) or (5), without a hearing, refuses permission to appeal against the decision of the first instance judge, the person seeking permission may request the decision to be reconsidered at a hearing.

(7) Where a Tier 3 Judge or the Senior Judge refuses permission to appeal without a hearing and considers that the application is totally without merit, that judge may order that the person seeking permission may not request the decision to be reconsidered at a hearing.

(8) Subject to paragraph (6), no appeal shall lie against—

(a) the granting or refusal of permission under this rule; or

(b) an order allowing an extension of time for appealing from an order.]

AMENDMENT

    This rule was substituted by SI 2015/548 r.58.   **4–333**

[Appeal against an order for committal to prison

    172A. Permission is not required to appeal against an order for committal to   **4–334**
prison.]

AMENDMENT

    This rule was substituted by SI 2015/548 r.54.   **4–335**

Matters to be taken into account when considering an application for permission

    173.—(1) Permission to appeal shall be granted only where—   **4–336**

(a) the court considers that the appeal would have a real prospect of success; or

(b) there is some other compelling reason why the appeal should be heard.

(2) An order giving permission may—

(a) limit the issues to be heard; and

(b) be made subject to conditions.

[(3) Paragraphs (1) and (2) do not apply to second appeals.]

AMENDMENT

    The amendment to this rule was made by SI 2015/548 r.59.   **4–337**

GENERAL NOTE

    If permission to appeal is granted, r.179 applies.   **4–338**

[Power to treat application for permission to appeal as application for reconsideration under rule 89

    174.—(1) Where a person seeking permission to appeal a decision would be   **4–339**
entitled to seek reconsideration of that decision under rule 89 (or would have
been so entitled had the application been made within 21 days of the date of that
decision)—

(a) a practice direction may provide; or

(b) the court may direct,

that an application for permission shall be treated as an application for reconsideration under rule 89.

(2) In any case where paragraph (1) applies, the decision in question shall be reconsidered in accordance with the provisions of rule 89.]

AMENDMENT

4–340   This rule was substituted by SI 2015/548 r.60.

Appellant's notice

4–341   **175.**—(1) Where the appellant seeks permission from [a judge other than the first instance judge], it must be requested in the appellant's notice.

(2) The appellant must file an appellant's notice at the court within—
- (a) such period as may be directed or specified in the order of the first instance judge; or
- (b) where that judge makes no such direction or order, 21 days after the date of the decision being appealed.

(3) The court will issue the appellant's notice and unless it orders otherwise, the appellant must serve the appellant's notice on each respondent and on such other persons as the court may direct, as soon as practicable and in any event within 21 days of the date on which it was issued.

(4) The appellant must file a certificate of service within 7 days beginning with the date on which he served the appellant's notice.

AMENDMENT

4–342   The amendment to this rule was made by SI 2015/548 r.59.

Respondent's notice

4–343   **176.**—(1) A respondent who—
- (a) is seeking permission from [a judge other than the first instance judge]; or
- (b) wishes to ask the appeal judge to uphold the order of the first instance judge for reasons different from or additional to those given by the first instance judge,

must file a respondent's notice.

(2) Where the respondent seeks permission from [a judge other than the first instance judge], permission must be requested in the respondent's notice.

(3) A respondent's notice must be filed within—
- (a) such period as may be directed by the first instance judge; or
- (b) where the first instance judge makes no such direction, 21 days beginning with the date referred to in paragraph (4).

(4) The date is the soonest of—
- (a) the date on which the respondent is served with the appellant's notice where—
    (i) permission [. . .] was given by the first instance judge; or
    (ii) permission [. . .] is not required;
- (b) the date on which the respondent is served with notification that [a judge other than the first instance judge] has given the appellant permission [. . .]; or
- (c) the date on which the respondent is served with the notification that the application for permission [. . .] and the appeal itself are to be heard together.

(5) The court will issue a respondent's notice and, unless it orders otherwise, the respondent must serve the respondent's notice on the appellant, any other respondent and on such other parties as the court may direct, as soon as practicable and in any event within 21 days of the date on which it was issued.

(6) The respondent must file a certificate of service within 7 days beginning with the date on which the copy of the respondent's notice was served.

AMENDMENTS
The amendments to this rule were made by SI 2015/548 r.62.   **4–344**

Variation of time
177.—(1) [*Repealed by SI 2015/548 r.63*].   **4–345**
(2) The parties may not agree to extend any date or time limit for or in respect of an appeal set by—
(a) these Rules;
(b) the relevant practice direction; or
(c) an order of the appeal judge or the first instance judge.

Power of appeal judge on appeal
178.—(1) In relation to an appeal, an appeal judge has all the powers of the first instance judge whose decision is being appealed.   **4–346**
(2) In particular, the appeal judge has the power to—
(a) affirm, set aside or vary any order made by the first instance judge;
(b) refer any claim or issue to that judge for determination;
(c) order a new hearing;
(d) make a costs order.
(3) The appeal judge may exercise his powers in relation to the whole or part of an order made by the first instance judge.

Determination of appeals
179.—(1) An appeal will be limited to a review of the decision of the first instance judge unless—   **4–347**
(a) a practice direction makes different provision for a particular category of appeal; or
(b) the appeal judge considers that in the circumstances of the appeal it would be in the interests of justice to hold a re-hearing.
(2) Unless he orders otherwise, the appeal judge will not receive—
(a) oral evidence; or
(b) evidence that was not before the first instance judge.
(3) The appeal judge will allow an appeal where the decision of the first instance judge was—
(a) wrong; or
(b) unjust, because of a serious procedural or other irregularity in the proceedings before the first instance judge.
(4) The appeal judge may draw any inference of fact that he considers justified on the evidence.
(5) At the hearing of the appeal a party may not rely upon a matter not contained in his appellant's or respondent's notice unless the appeal judge gives permission.

180. [*Repealed by SI 2015/548 r.64*]   **4–348**

4–349   **181.–182.** [*Repealed by SI 2015/548 r.64*].

PART 21

Practice Direction
21A Contempt of Court

ENFORCEMENT

Enforcement methods—general
4–350   **183.**—(1) The rules in this Part make provision for the enforcement of judgments and orders.

(2) The relevant practice direction may set out methods of enforcing judgments or orders.

(3) An application for an order for enforcement may be made on application by any person in accordance with Part 10.

Application of the Civil Procedure Rules 1998 [. . .]
4–351   **184.**—(1) The following provisions apply, as far as they are relevant and with such modifications as may be necessary, to the enforcement of orders made in proceedings under these Rules—

(a) Parts 70 (General Rules about Enforcement of Judgments and Orders), 71 (Orders to Obtain Information from Judgment Debtors), 72 (Third Party Debt Orders) [,] 73 (Charging Orders, Stop Orders and Stop Notices) [, 83 (Writs and Warrants—General Provisions) and 84 (Enforcement by Taking Control of Goods)] of the Civil Procedure Rules 1998 [.]

(b) [. . .]

AMENDMENTS
4–352   The amendments to this rule were made by SI 2015/548 r.65.

Orders for committal

GENERAL NOTE
4–353   On March 26, 2015, the Lord Chief Justice issued a Practice Direction on Contempt of Court which applies to all proceedings for committal for contempt including those before the Court of Protection. This Practice Direction supplements Practice Direction 21A.

In *Re Leslie Whiting* [2013] EWHC B27 (Fam) at para.12, Hayden J. noted "some crucial features" of the committal process:

"(1) the procedure has an essentially criminal law complexion. That is to say, contempt of court must be proved to the criminal standard, i.e. so that the judge is sure. The burden of proof rests throughout on the applicant (see: *Mubarak v Mubarak* [2001] 1 FLR 698);

(2) contempt of court involves a deliberate contumelious disobedience to the court (see: *Re A (A Child)* [2008] EWCA Civ 1138);

(3) it is not enough to suspect recalcitrance; it must be proved (see: *London Borough of Southwark v B* [1993] 2 FLR 559);

(4) committal is not the automatic consequence of a contempt, though the options before

the court are limited—for example: (a) do nothing; (b) adjourn where appropriate; (c) levy a fine; (d) sequester assets; (e) where relevant, make orders under the Mental Health Act (see: *Jamie Malcolm Hale v Rachel Tanner* [2000] 2 FLR 879);

(5) the objectives of the application are usually dual, i.e. to punish for the breach and to ensure future compliance;

(6) bearing in mind the dual purpose of many committal proceedings, they should be brought expeditiously, whilst primary evidence is available and the incidents are fresh in the mind of the relevant witness. This is particularly important in the Court of Protection where there may be reliance on a vulnerable witness and where capacity might have to be assessed."

His Lordship said that it follows "that where injunctive orders are made, they should be clear, unambivalent and drafted with care. In my judgment, simplicity should be the guide. Similarly, where breaches are alleged, they should be particularised with care, both so that the alleged contemnor knows exactly what, where, when and how it is contended that he is in breach, so as to be able to marshal his defence, but also to help the applicant focus on what evidence is likely to be required to establish the breach to the requisite standard of proof" (para.13).

Unless orders (otherwise known as Hadkinson orders) can be made in the Court of Protection (*A Local Authority v B,F and G* [2014] EWCOP B18) Such orders may be made where a party is in contempt or has failed to comply with a previous order. That party may be prevented from proceeding with a subsequent application unless they comply with the original order.

Contempt of court—generally

185. An application relating to the committal of a person for contempt of court shall be made to a judge and the power to punish for contempt may be exercised by an order of committal.

4–354

Application for order of committal

186.—(1) An application for an order of committal must be made by filing an application notice, stating the grounds of the application, and must be supported by an affidavit made in accordance with the relevant practice direction.

4–355

(2) Subject to paragraph (3), the application notice, a copy of the affidavit in support thereof and notice of the date of the hearing of the application must be served personally on the person sought to be committed.

(3) Without prejudice to its powers under Part 6, the court may dispense with service under this rule if it thinks it just to do so.

Oral evidence

187.—(1) If on the hearing of the application the person sought to be committed expresses a wish to give oral evidence on his own behalf, he shall be entitled to do so.

4–356

Hearing for committal order

188.—(1) Except where the court permits, no grounds shall be relied upon at the hearing except the grounds set out in the application notice.

4–357

(2) Notwithstanding rule 90(1) (general rule—hearing to be in private), when determining an application for committal the court will hold the hearing in public unless it directs otherwise.

(3) If the court hearing an application in private decides that a person has committed a contempt of court, it shall state publicly—

(a) the name of that person;

(b) in general terms the nature of the contempt in respect of which the order of committal is being made; and

(c) any punishment imposed.

(4) If the person sought to be committed does not attend the hearing, the court may fix a date and time for the person to be brought before the court.

GENERAL NOTE

Paragraph (2)

4–358   The discretion to hear contempt proceedings in private "should be exercised only in exceptional cases where it is necessary in the interests of justice" ([2013] 1 W.L.R. 1753, above, at para.3).

Power to suspend execution of committal order

4–359   **189.**—(1) A judge who has made an order of committal may direct that the execution of the order of committal shall be suspended for such period or on such terms and conditions as may be specified.

(2) Where an order is suspended under paragraph (1), the applicant for the order of committal must, unless the court otherwise directs, serve on the person against whom it was made a notice informing him of the making and terms of the direction under that paragraph.

Warrant for arrest

4–360   **190.** A warrant for the arrest of a person against whom an order of committal has been made shall not, without further order of the court, be enforced more than 2 years after the date on which the warrant is issued.

Discharge of person committed

4–361   **191.**—(1)The court may, on the application of any person committed to prison for contempt of court, discharge him.

(2) Where a person has been committed for failing to comply with a judgment or order requiring him to deliver any thing to some other person or to deposit it in court or elsewhere, and a writ of sequestration has also been issued to enforce that judgment or order, then, if the thing is in the custody or power of the person committed, the commissioners appointed by the writ of sequestration may take possession of it as if it were the property of that person and, without prejudice to the generality of paragraph (1), the court may discharge the person committed and may give such directions for dealing with the thing taken by the commissioners as it thinks fit.

Penal notices

4–362   **192.**—(1) The court may direct that a penal notice is to be attached to any order warning the person on whom the copy of the order is served that disobeying the order would be a contempt of court punishable by imprisonment or a fine.

(2) Unless the court gives a direction under paragraph (1), a penal notice may not be attached to any order.

(3) A penal notice is to be in the following terms: "You must obey this order. If you do not, you may be sent to prison for contempt of court.".

Saving for other powers

4–363   **193.** The rules in this Part do not limit the power of the court to make an order requiring a person guilty of contempt to pay a fine or give security for his good behaviour and those rules, so far as applicable, shall apply in relation to an application for such an order as they apply in relation to an application for an order of committal.

Power of court to commit on its own initiative

194. The preceding provisions of these Rules shall not be taken as affecting the power of the court to make an order for committal on its own initiative against a person guilty of contempt of court.

4–364

PART 22

Practice Directions
    22A Transitional provisions
    22B Transitory provisions
    22C Appeals against decisions made under Part 7 of the Mental Health Act 1983 or under the Enduring Powers of Attorney Act 1985 which are brought on or after commencement

TRANSITORY AND TRANSITIONAL PROVISIONS

Transitory provision: applications by former receivers

195.—(1) This rule and rule 196—

4–365

(a) apply in any case where a person becomes a deputy by virtue of paragraph 1(2) of Schedule 5 to the Act; but

(b) shall cease to have effect at the end of the period specified in the relevant practice direction.

(2) The deputy may make an application to the court in connection with—

(a) any decision in connection with the day-to-day management of P's property and affairs; or

(b) any supplementary decision which is necessary to give full effect to any order made, or directions given, before 1st October 2007 under Part 7 of the Mental Health Act 1983.

(3) Decisions within paragraph (2) include those that may be specified in the relevant practice direction.

(4) An application—

(a) may relate only to a particular decision or decisions to be made on P's behalf;

(b) must specify details of the decision or decisions to be made; and

(c) must be made using the application form set out in the relevant practice direction.

Transitory provision: dealing with applications under rule 195

196.—(1) The court may, in determining an application under rule 195, treat the application as if it were an application to vary the functions of the deputy which is made in accordance with the relevant practice direction made under rule 71, and dispose of it accordingly.

4–366

(2) In any other case, an application under rule 195 may be determined by an order made or directions given by—

(a) the court; or

(b) a person nominated under paragraph (3).

(3) The Senior Judge or the President may nominate an officer or officers of the court for the purpose of determining applications under rule 195.

509

(4) Where an officer has been nominated under paragraph (3) to determine an application, he may refer to a judge any proceedings or any question arising in any proceedings which ought, in the officer's opinion, to be considered by a judge.

Appeal against a decision of a nominated officer

4–367   **197.**—(1) This rule applies in relation to decisions made under rules 195 and 196 by a nominated officer.

(2) An appeal from a decision to which this rule applies lies to a judge of the court nominated by virtue of section 46(2)(e) of the Act.

(3) No permission is required for an appeal under paragraph (2).

(4) A judge determining an appeal under paragraph (2) has all the powers that an appeal judge on appeal has by virtue of rule 178.

(5) An appeal from a decision made under paragraph (2) ("a second appeal") lies to a judge of the court nominated by virtue of section 46(2)(d) of the Act.

(6) A second appeal may be made from a decision of a nominated officer, and a judge to whom such an appeal is made may, if he considers the matter is one which ought to be heard by a judge of the court nominated by virtue of section 46(2)(a) to (c), transfer the matter to such a judge.

(7) An appeal from a decision made on a second appeal lies to the Court of Appeal.

Application of Rules to proceedings within paragraphs 3 and 12 of Schedule 5 to the Act

4–368   **198.**—(1) In this rule, "pending proceedings" means proceedings on an application within paragraph 3 or 12 of Schedule 5 to the Act.

(2) A practice direction shall make provision for the extent to which these Rules shall apply to pending proceedings.

Practice direction

4–369   **199.** A practice direction may make additional or different provision in relation to transitory and transitional matters.

PART 23

Practice Directions

23A Request for directions where notice of objection prevents Public Guardian from registering Enduring Power of Attorney

23B Where P ceases to lack capacity or dies

MISCELLANEOUS

Order or directions requiring a person to give security for discharge of functions

4–370   **200.**—(1) This rule applies where the court makes an order or gives a direction—

(a) conferring functions on any person (whether as deputy or otherwise); and

(b) requiring him to give security for the discharge of those functions.

(2) The person on whom functions are conferred must give the security before he undertakes to discharge his functions, unless the court permits it to be given subsequently.

(3) Paragraphs (4) to (6) apply where the security is required to be given before any action can be taken.

(4) Subject to paragraph (5), the security must be given in accordance with the requirements of regulation 33(2)(a) of the Public Guardian Regulations (which makes provision about the giving of security by means of a bond that is endorsed by an authorised insurance company or deposit-taker).

(5) The court may impose such other requirements in relation to the giving of the security as it considers appropriate (whether in addition to, or instead of, those specified in paragraph (4)).

(6) In specifying the date from which the order or directions referred to in paragraph (1) are to take effect, the court will have regard to the need to postpone that date for such reasonable period as would enable the Public Guardian to be satisfied that—

(a) if paragraph (4) applies, the requirements of regulation 34 of the Public Guardian Regulations have been met in relation to the security; and

(b) any other requirements imposed by the court under paragraph (5) have been met.

(7) "The Public Guardian Regulations" means the Lasting Powers of Attorney, Enduring Powers of Attorney and Public Guardian Regulations 2007.

Objections to registration of an enduring power of attorney: request for directions

201.—(1) This rule applies in any case where—   **4–371**

(a) the Public Guardian (having received a notice of objection to the registration of an instrument creating an enduring power of attorney) is prevented by paragraph 13(5) of Schedule 4 to the Act from registering the instrument except in accordance with the court's directions; and

(b) on or before the relevant day, no application for the court to give such directions has been made under Part 9 (how to start proceedings).

(2) In paragraph (1)(b) the relevant day is the later of—

(a) the final day of the period specified in paragraph 13(4) of Schedule 4 to the Act; or

(b) the final day of the period of 14 days beginning with the date on which the Public Guardian receives the notice of objection.

(3) The Public Guardian may seek the court's directions about registering the instrument by filing a request in accordance with the relevant practice direction.

(4) As soon as practicable and in any event within 21 days of the date on which the request was made, the court will notify—

(a) the person (or persons) who gave the notice of objection; and

(b) the attorney or, if more than one, each of them.

(5) As soon as practicable and in any event within 21 days of the date on which the request is filed, the Public Guardian must notify the donor of the power that the request has been so filed.

(6) The notice under paragraph (4) must—

(a) state that the Public Guardian has requested the court's directions about registration;

(b) state that the court will give directions in response to the request unless an application under Part 9 is made to it before the end of the period of 21 days commencing with the date on which the notice is issued; and

(c) set out the steps required to make such an application.

(7) "Notice of objection" means a notice of objection which is made in accordance with paragraph 13(4) of Schedule 4 to the Act.

Disposal of property where P ceases to lack capacity

4–372   **202.**—(1) This rule applies where P ceases to lack capacity.

(2) In this rule, "relevant property" means any property belonging to P and forming part of his estate, and which—

(a) remains under the control of anyone appointed by order of the court; or

(b) is held under the direction of the court.

(3) The court may at any time make an order for any relevant property to be transferred to P, or at P's direction, provided that it is satisfied that P has the capacity to make decisions in relation to that property.

(4) An application for an order under this rule is to be made in accordance with Part 10.

THE COURT OF PROTECTION FEES ORDER 2007

(SI 2007/1745)

Dated July 26, 2007 and made by the Lord Chancellor under the Mental Capacity Act 2005 (c.9) ss.54(1) and (2), 65(1), with the consent of the Treasury and after consulting in accordance with s.54(3) of that Act.

GENERAL NOTE

This Order provides for fees to be charged in connection with the Court of Protection.   **4–373**

Citation and commencement

1. This Order may be cited as the Court of Protection Fees Order 2007 and comes into force on 1 October 2007.   **4–374**

Interpretation

2. In this Order—   **4–375**

"the Act" means the Mental Capacity Act 2005;

"appellant" means the person who brings or seeks to bring an appeal; "court" means the Court of Protection;

"P" means any person (other than a protected party) who lacks or, so far as consistent with the context, is alleged to lack capacity to make a decision or decisions in relation to any matter that is the subject of an application to the court and references to a person who lacks capacity are to be construed in accordance with the Act;

"protected party" means a party or an intended party (other than P or a child) who lacks capacity to conduct the proceedings;

"the Regulations" means the Lasting Powers of Attorney, Enduring Powers of Attorney and Public Guardian Regulations 2007; and

"the Rules" means the Court of Protection Rules 2007.

Schedule of fees

3. The fees set out in [Schedule 1] to this Order shall apply in accordance with the following provisions of this Order.   **4–376**

AMENDMENT

This article was amended by SI 2013/2302 art.5(2).   **4–377**

Application fee

4.—(1) An application fee shall be payable by the applicant on making an application under Part 9 of the Rules (how to start proceedings) in accordance with the following provisions of this article.   **4–378**

(2) Where permission to start proceedings is required under Part 8 of the Rules (permission), the fee prescribed by paragraph (1) shall be payable on making an application for permission.

(3) The fee prescribed by paragraph (1) shall not be payable where the application is made under—

(a) rule 67 of the Rules (applications relating to lasting powers of attorney) by—

    (i) the donee of a lasting power of attorney, or

    (ii) a person named in a statement made by the donor of a lasting power of attorney in accordance with paragraph 2(1)(c)(i) of Part 1 of Schedule 1 to the Act,

and is solely in respect of an objection to the registration of a lasting power of attorney; or

(b) rule 68 of the Rules (applications relating to enduring powers of attorney) by—

    (i) a donor of an enduring power of attorney,

    (ii) an attorney under an enduring power of attorney, or

    (iii) a person listed in paragraph 6(1) of Part 3 of Schedule 4 to the Act,

and is solely in respect of an objection to the registration of an enduring power of attorney.

(4) The fee prescribed by paragraph (1) shall not be payable where the application is made by the Public Guardian.

(5) Where a fee has been paid under paragraph (1) it shall be refunded where P dies within five days of the application being filed.

Appeal fee

4–379   **5.**—(1) An appeal fee shall be payable by the appellant on the filing of an appellant's notice under Part 20 of the Rules (appeals) in accordance with the following provisions of this article.

(2) The fee prescribed by paragraph (1) shall not be payable where the appeal is—

(a) brought by the Public Guardian; or

(b) an appeal against a decision of a nominated officer made under rule 197 of the Rules (appeal against a decision of a nominated officer).

(3) The fee prescribed by paragraph (1) shall be refunded where P dies within five days of the appellant's notice being filed.

Hearing fees

4–380   **6.**—(1) A hearing fee shall be payable by the applicant where the court has—

(a) held a hearing in order to determine the case; and

(b) made a final order, declaration or decision.

(2) A hearing fee shall be payable by the appellant in relation to an appeal where the court has—

(a) held a hearing in order to determine the appeal; and

(b) made a final order, declaration or decision in relation to the appeal.

(3) The fees prescribed by paragraphs (1) and (2) shall not be payable where the hearing is in respect of an application or appeal brought by the Public Guardian.

(4) The fee prescribed by paragraph (2) shall not be payable where the hearing is in respect of an appeal against a decision of a nominated officer made under rule 197 of the Rules (appeal against a decision of a nominated officer).

(5) The fee prescribed by paragraph (1) shall not be payable where the applicant was not required to pay an application fee under Article 4(1) by virtue of Article 4(3).

(6) The fees prescribed by paragraphs (1) and (2) shall be payable by the appli-

cant or appellant as the case may be within 30 days of the date of the invoice for the fee.

Fee for request for copy of court document
7.—(1) A fee for a copy of a court document shall be payable by the person requesting the copy of the document. **4–381**
(2) [. . .]
(3) The [fee prescribed by paragraph (1)] shall be payable at the time the request for the copy is made to the court.

AMENDMENTS
The amendments to this article where made by SI 2009/513 art.3. **4–382**

[Remissions and part remissions
8. Schedule 2 applies for the purpose of ascertaining whether a party is entitled **4–383**
to a remission or part remission of a fee prescribed by this Order.]

AMENDMENT
This article was substituted by SI 2013/2302 art.5(3). **4–384**

9. *[Repealed by SI 2013/2302 art.5(4)]* **4–385**

Transitional provision
10.—(1) In this article "Court of Protection" means the office of the Supreme **4–386**
Court called the Court of Protection which ceases to exist under section 45(6) of the Act.
(2) Where a hearing that takes place on or after 1 October 2007 was listed by the Court of Protection before 1 October 2007, no hearing fee shall be payable under Article 6.

SCHEDULE [1] **Article 3**

FEES TO BE TAKEN

Column 1	Column 2	
Application fee (Article 4)	£400.00	**4–387**
Appeal fee (Article 5)	£400.00	
Hearing fees (Article 6)	£500.00	
Copy of a document fee (Article 7(1))	£5.00	
[. . .]	[. . .]	

AMENDMENTS
The amendments to this Schedule where made by SI 2009/513 art.5 and SI 2013/2302 **4–388**
art.5(5).

[SCHEDULE 2

REMISSIONS AND PART REMISSIONS

Interpretation

4–389   **1.**—(1) In this Schedule—

"child" means a person—

(a) whose main residence is with a party and who is aged—

　　(i) under 16 years; or

　　(ii) 16 to 19 years; and is—

　　　　(aa) not married or in a civil partnership; and

　　　　(bb) enrolled or accepted in full-time education that is not advanced education, or approved training; or

(b) in respect of whom a party or their partner pays child support maintenance or periodic payments in accordance with a maintenance agreement,

and "full-time education", "advanced education" and "approved training" have the meaning given by the Child Benefit (General) Regulations 2006;

"child support maintenance" has the meaning given in section 3(6) of the Child Support Act 1991;

"couple" has the meaning given in section 3(5A) of the Tax Credits Act 2002;

"disposable capital" has the meaning given in paragraph 5;

["excluded benefits" means any of the following—

(a) any of the following benefits payable under the Social Security Contributions and Benefits Act 1992 or the corresponding provisions of the Social Security Contributions and Benefits (Northern Ireland) Act 1992—

　　(i) attendance allowance under section 64;

　　(ii) severe disablement allowance;

　　(iii) carer's allowance;

　　(iv) disability living allowance;

　　(v) constant attendance allowance under section 104 as an increase to a disablement pension;

　　(vi) any payment made out of the social fund;

　　(vii) housing benefit;

　　(viii) widowed parents allowance;

(b) any of the following benefit payable under the Tax Credits Act 2002—

　　(i) any disabled child element or severely disabled child element of the child tax credit;

　　(ii) any childcare element of the working tax credit;

(c) any direct payment made under the Community Care, Services for Carers and Children's Services (Direct Payments) (England) Regulations 2009, the Community Care, Services for Carers and Children's Services (Direct Payments) (Wales) Regulations 2011, the Carers and Direct Payments Act (Northern Ireland) 2002, or section 12B(1) of the Social Work (Scotland) Act 1968;

(d) a back to work bonus payable under section 26 of the Jobseekers Act 1995, or article 28 of the Jobseekers (Northern Ireland) Order 1995;

(e) any exceptionally severe disablement allowance paid under the Personal Injuries (Civilians) Scheme 1983;

(f) any payments from the Industrial Injuries Disablement Benefit;

(g) any pension paid under the Naval, Military and Air Forces etc (Disablement and Death) Service Pension Order 2006;

(h) any payment made from the Independent Living Funds;

(i) any payment made from the Bereavement Allowance;

(j) any financial support paid under an agreement for the care of a foster child;

(k) any housing credit element of pension credit;

(l) any armed forces independence payment;

(m) any personal independence payment payable under the Welfare Reform Act 2012;

(n) any payment on account of benefit as defined in the Social Security (Payments on Account of Benefit) Regulations 2013;

(o) any of the following amounts, as defined by the Universal Credit Regulations 2013, that make up an award of universal credit—

　　(i) an additional amount to the child element in respect of a disabled child;

　　(ii) a housing costs element;

　　(iii) a childcare costs element;

(iv) a carer element;

(v) a limited capability for work or limited capacity for work and work-related activity element.]

"family help (higher)" has the meaning given in paragraph 15(3) of the Civil Legal Aid (Merits Criteria) Regulations 2013;

"family help (lower)" has the meaning given in paragraph 15(2) of the Civil Legal Aid (Merits Criteria) Regulations 2013;

"gross monthly income" has the meaning given in paragraph 13;

"Independent Living Funds" means the funds listed at regulation 20(2)(b) of the Criminal Legal Aid (Financial Resources) Regulations 2013;

"legal representation" has the meaning given in paragraph 18(2) of the Civil Legal Aid (Merits Criteria) Regulations 2013;

"maintenance agreement" has the meaning given in subsection 9(1) of the Child Support Act 1991;

"partner" means a person with whom the party lives as a couple and includes a person with whom the party is not currently living but from whom the party is not living separate and apart;

"party" means the individual who would, but for this Schedule, be liable to pay a fee under this Order;

"restraint order" means—

(a) an order under section 42(1A) of the Senior Courts Act 1981;

(b) an order under section 33 of the Employment Tribunals Act 1996;

(c) a civil restraint order made under rule 3.11 of the Civil Procedure Rules 1998, or a practice direction made under that rule; or

(d) a civil restraint order under rule 4.8 of the Family Procedure Rules 2010, or the practice direction referred to in that rule.

(2) References to remission of a fee are to be read as including references to a part remission of a fee as appropriate and remit and remitted shall be construed accordingly.

Fee remission

2. If a party satisfies the disposable capital test, the amount of any fee remission is calculated by applying the gross monthly income test. **4–390**

Disposable capital test

Disposable capital test

3.—(1) Subject to paragraph 4, a party satisfies the disposable capital test if— **4–391**

(a) the fee payable by the party and for which an application for remission is made, falls within a fee band set out in column 1 of Table 1; and

(b) the party's disposable capital is less than the amount in the corresponding row of column 2.

Table 1

Column 1 (fee band)	Column 2 (disposable capital)
Up to and including £1,000	£3,000
£1,001 to £1,335	£4,000
£1,336 to £1,665	£5,000
£1,666 to £2,000	£6,000
£2,001 to £2,330	£7,000
£2,331 to £4,000	£8,000
£4,001 to £5,000	£10,000
£5,001 to £6,000	£12,000
£6,001 to £7,000	£14,000
£7,001 or more	£16,000

4. Subject to paragraph 14, if a party or their partner is aged 61 or over, that party satisfies the disposable capital test if that party's disposable capital is less than £16,000. **4–392**

Disposable capital

5. Subject to paragraph 14, disposable capital is the value of every resource of a capital nature belonging to the party on the date on which the application for remission is made, unless it is treated as income by this Order, or it is disregarded as excluded disposable capital. **4–393**

Disposable capital—non-money resources

4–394

6. The value of a resource of a capital nature that does not consist of money is calculated as the amount which that resource would realise if sold, less—

(a) 10% of the sale value; and

(b) the amount of any borrowing secured against that resource that would be repayable on sale.

Disposable capital—resources held outside the United Kingdom

4–395

7.—(1) Capital resources in a country outside the United Kingdom count towards disposable capital.

(2) If there is no prohibition in that country against the transfer of a resource into the United Kingdom, the value of that resource is the amount which that resource would realise if sold in that country, in accordance with paragraph 6.

(3) If there is a prohibition in that country against the transfer of a resource into the United Kingdom, the value of that resource is the amount that resource would realise if sold to a buyer in the United Kingdom.

Disposable capital—foreign currency resources

4–396

8. Where disposable capital is held in currency other than sterling, the cost of any banking charge or commission that would be payable if that amount were converted into sterling, is deducted from its value.

Disposable capital—jointly owned resources

4–397

9. Where any resource of a capital nature is owned jointly or in common, there is a presumption that the resource is owned in equal shares, unless evidence to the contrary is produced.

Excluded disposable capital

4–398

10. The following things are excluded disposable capital—

(a) a property which is the main or only dwelling occupied by the party;

(b) the household furniture and effects of the main or only dwelling occupied by the party;

(c) articles of personal clothing;

(d) any vehicle, the sale of which would leave the party, or their partner, without motor transport;

(e) tools and implements of trade, including vehicles used for business purposes;

(f) the capital value of the party's or their partner's business, where the party or their partner is self-employed;

(g) the capital value of any funds or other assets held in trust, where the party or their partner is a beneficiary without entitlement to advances of any trust capital;

(h) a jobseeker's back to work bonus;

(i) a payment made as a result of a determination of unfair dismissal by a court or tribunal, or by way of settlement of a claim for unfair dismissal;

(j) any compensation paid as a result of a determination of medical negligence or in respect of any personal injury by a court, or by way of settlement of a claim for medical negligence or personal injury;

(k) the capital held in any personal or occupational pension scheme;

(l) any cash value payable on surrender of a contract of insurance;

(m) any capital payment made out of the Independent Living Funds;

(n) any bereavement payment;

(o) any capital insurance or endowment lump sum payments that have been paid as a result of illness, disability or death;

(p) any student loan or student grant;

(q) any payments under the criminal injuries compensation scheme.

Gross monthly income test

Remission of fees—gross monthly income

4–399

11.—(1) If a party satisfies the disposable capital test, no fee is payable under this Order if, at the time when the fee would otherwise be payable, the party or their partner has the number of children specified in column 1 of Table 2 and—

(a) if the party is single, their gross monthly income does not exceed the amount set out in the appropriate row of column 2; or

(b) if the party is one of a couple, the gross monthly income of that couple does not exceed the amount set out in the appropriate row of column 3.

Table 2

Column 1 Number of children of party	Column 2 Single	Column 3 Couple
no children	£1,085	£1,245
1 child	£1,330	£1,490
2 children	£1,575	£1,735

(2) If a party or their partner has more than 2 children, the relevant amount of gross monthly income is the appropriate amount specified in Table 2 for 2 children, plus the sum of £245 for each additional child.

(3) For every £10 of gross monthly income received above the appropriate amount in Table 2, including any additional amount added under sub-paragraph (2), the party must pay £5 towards the fee payable, up to the maximum amount of the fee payable.

(4) This paragraph is subject to paragraph 12.

Gross monthly income cap

12.—(1) No remission is available if a party or their partner has the number of children specified in column 1 of Table 3 and—   **4–400**

(a) if the party is single, their gross monthly income exceeds the amount set out in the appropriate row of column 2 of Table 3; or

(b) if the party is one of a couple, the gross monthly income of that couple exceeds the amount set out in the appropriate row of column 3 of Table 3.

Table 3

Column 1 Number of children of party	Column 2 Single	Column 3 Couple
no children	£5,085	£5,245
1 child	£5,330	£5,490
2 children	£5,575	£5,735

(2) If a party or their partner has more than 2 children, the relevant amount of gross monthly income is the appropriate amount specified in Table 3 for 2 children, plus the sum of £245 for each additional child.

Gross monthly income

13.—(1) Subject to paragraph 14, gross monthly income means the total monthly income, for the month preceding that in which the application for remission is made, from all sources, other than receipt of any of the excluded benefits.   **4–401**

(2) Income from a trade, business or gainful occupation other than an occupation at a wage or salary is calculated as—

(a) the profits which have accrued or will accrue to the party; and

(b) the drawings of the party;

in the month preceding that in which the application for remission is made.

(3) In calculating profits under sub-paragraph (2)(a), all sums necessarily expended to earn those profits are deducted.

General

[Resources and income treated as the party's resources and income

14.—(1) Subject to sub-paragraphs (2) to (5), the disposable capital and gross monthly income of a partner is to be treated as disposable capital and gross monthly income of the party.   **4–402**

(2) Where the partner of the party has a contrary interest to the party in the matter to which the fee relates, the disposable capital and gross monthly income of that partner is not treated as the disposable capital and gross monthly income of the party.

(3) Where proceedings are brought concerning the property and affairs of 'P', for the purpose of determining whether a party is entitled to a remission or part remission of a fee in accordance with this Schedule—

(a) the disposable capital and gross monthly income of the person bringing those proceedings is not treated as the disposable capital and gross monthly income of the party;

(b) the disposable capital and gross monthly income of 'P' is to be treated as the disposable capital of the party; and

(c) the disposable capital and gross monthly income of the partner of 'P', if any, is not treated as the disposable capital and gross monthly income of the party.

(4) Where proceedings are brought concerning the personal welfare of 'P', for the purpose of determining whether a party is entitled to a remission or part remission of a fee in accordance with this Schedule, the disposable capital and gross monthly income of a partner, if any, is not treated as the disposable capital and gross monthly income of the party, where that partner is 'P' who is the subject of those proceedings in which the fee is payable.

(5) Where proceedings concern both the property and affairs of 'P' and their personal welfare, their disposable capital and gross monthly income shall be treated in accordance with sub-paragraph (3).]

Application for remission of a fee

4-403

15.—(1) An application for remission of a fee must be made at the time when the fee would otherwise be payable.

(2) Where an application for remission of a fee is made, the party must—

(a) indicate the fee to which the application relates;

(b) declare the amount of their disposable capital; and

(c) provide documentary evidence of their gross monthly income and the number of children relevant for the purposes of paragraphs 11 and 12.

(3) Where an application for remission of a fee is made on or before the date on which a fee is payable, the date for payment of the fee is disapplied.

(4) Where an application for remission is refused, or if part remission of a fee is granted, the amount of the fee which remains unremitted must be paid within the period notified in writing to the party.

Remission in exceptional circumstances

4-404

16. A fee specified in this Order may be remitted where the Lord Chancellor is satisfied that there are exceptional circumstances which justify doing so.

Refunds

4-405

17.—(1) Subject to sub-paragraph (3), where a party pays a fee at a time when that party would have been entitled to a remission if they had provided the documentary evidence required by paragraph 15, the fee, or the amount by which the fee would have been reduced as the case may be, must be refunded if documentary evidence relating to the time when the fee became payable is provided at a later date.

(2) Subject to sub-paragraph (3), where a fee has been paid at a time when the Lord Chancellor, if all the circumstances had been known, would have remitted the fee under paragraph 15, the fee or the amount by which the fee would have been reduced, as the case may be, must be refunded to the party.

(3) No refund shall be made under this paragraph unless the party who paid the fee applies within 3 months of the date [of the order of the court which finally disposed of the proceedings].

(4) The Lord Chancellor may extend the period of 3 months mentioned in sub-paragraph (3) if the Lord Chancellor considers that there is a good reason for a refund being made after the end of the period of 3 months.

Legal Aid

4-406

18. A party is not entitled to a fee remission if, under Part 1 of the Legal Aid, Sentencing and Punishment of Offenders Act 2012(a), they are in receipt of the following civil legal services—

(a) Legal representation; or

(b) Family help (higher); or

(c) Family help (lower) in respect of applying for a consent order.

Vexatious litigants

4-407

19.—(1) This paragraph applies where—

(a) a restraint order is in force against a party; and

(b) that party makes an application for permission to—

(i) issue proceedings or take a step in proceedings as required by the restraint order;

(ii) apply for amendment or discharge of the order; or

(iii) appeal the order.

(2) The fee prescribed by this Order for the application is payable in full.

(3) If the party is granted permission, they are to be refunded the difference between—
(a) the fee paid; and
(b) the fee that would have been payable if this Schedule had been applied without reference to this paragraph.

Exceptions

20. No remissions or refunds are available in respect of the fee payable for—   **4–408**
(a) copy or duplicate documents;
(b) searches.]

AMENDMENTS

This Schedule was inserted by SI 2013/2302 art.5(6). The amendments to it were made by *ibid.*   **4–409**
art.5(7) and SI 2014/1590 art.3(3).

DEPRIVATION OF LIBERTY SAFEGUARDS

CODE OF PRACTICE TO SUPPLEMENT THE MAIN MENTAL CAPACITY ACT 2005 CODE OF PRACTICE

This Code of Practice has been prepared and laid before Parliament by the **5–001** Lord Chancellor in accordance with sections 42 and 43 of the Mental Capacity Act 2005, after having consulted Welsh Ministers and such other persons as he considered appropriate.

London: TSO

FOREWORD BY IVAN LEWIS AND EDWINA HART MBE

The Mental Capacity Act 2005 ('the Act') provides a statutory framework for acting and making decisions on behalf of individuals who lack the mental capacity to do so for themselves. It introduced a number of laws to protect these individuals and ensure that they are given every chance to make decisions for themselves. The Act came into force in October 2007.

The Government has added new provisions to the Act: the deprivation of liberty safeguards. The safeguards focus on some of the most vulnerable people in our society: those who for their own safety and in their own best interests need to be accommodated under care and treatment regimes that may have the effect of depriving them of their liberty, but who lack the capacity to consent.

The deprivation of a person's liberty is a very serious matter and should not happen unless it is absolutely necessary, and in the best interests of the person concerned. That is why the safeguards have been created: to ensure that any decision to deprive someone of their liberty is made following defined processes and in consultation with specific authorities.

The new provisions in the Act set out the legal framework of the deprivation of liberty safeguards. This Code of Practice is formally issued by the Lord Chancellor as a Code of Practice under the Mental Capacity Act 2005. It provides guidance and information for those implementing the deprivation of liberty safeguards legislation on a daily basis. In some cases, this will be paid staff, in others those who have been appointed in law to represent individuals who lack capacity to make decisions for themselves (such as deputies or donees of a Lasting Power of Attorney).

Because of this broad audience, the Code of Practice has been written so as to make it as user-friendly as possible—like the main Mental Capacity Act 2005 Code of Practice, issued in April 2007. We are grateful to all those who commented on earlier drafts of the Code to help it achieve that goal.

INTRODUCTION

5–002   The Mental Capacity Act 2005 ('the Act'), covering England and Wales, provides a statutory framework for acting and making decisions on behalf of people who lack the capacity to make those decisions for themselves. These can be small decisions—such as what clothes to wear—or major decisions, such as where to live.

In some cases, people lack the capacity to consent to particular treatment or care that is recognised by others as being in their best interests, or which will protect them from harm. Where this care might involve depriving vulnerable people of their liberty in either a hospital or a care home, extra safeguards have been introduced, in law, to protect their rights and ensure that the care or treatment they receive is in their best interests.

This Code of Practice helps explain how to identify when a person is, or is at risk of, being deprived of their liberty and how deprivation of liberty may be avoided. It also explains the safeguards that have been put in place to ensure that deprivation of liberty, where it does need to occur, has a lawful basis. In addition, it provides guidance on what someone should do if they suspect that a person who lacks capacity is being deprived of their liberty unlawfully.

These safeguards are an important way of protecting the rights of many vulnerable people and should not be viewed negatively. Depriving someone of their liberty can be a necessary requirement in order to provide effective care or treatment. By following the criteria set out in the safeguards, and explained in this Code of Practice, the decision to deprive someone of their liberty can be made lawfully and properly.

HOW DOES THIS CODE OF PRACTICE RELATE TO THE MAIN MENTAL CAPACITY ACT 2005 CODE OF PRACTICE?

5–003   This document adds to the guidance in the main Mental Capacity Act 2005 Code of Practice ('the main Code'), which was issued in April 2007, and should be used in conjunction with the main Code. It focuses specifically on the deprivation of liberty safeguards added to the Act. These can be found in sections 4A and 4B of, and Schedules A1 and 1A to, the Act.

Though these safeguards were mentioned in the main Code (particularly in chapters 6 and 13), they were not covered in any detail. That was because, at the time the main Code was published, the deprivation of liberty safeguards were still going through the Parliamentary process as part of the Mental Health Bill.[1]

Although the main Code does not cover the deprivation of liberty safeguards, the principles of that Code, and much of its content, are directly relevant to the deprivation of liberty safeguards. It is important that both the Act and the main Code are adhered to whenever capacity and best interests issues, and the deprivation of liberty safeguards, are being considered. The deprivation of liberty safeguards are in addition to, and do not replace, other safeguards in the Act.

---

[1]   The Mental Health Bill was used as a vehicle to amend the Mental Capacity Act 2005 in order to introduce the deprivation of liberty safeguards. The Bill became the Mental Health Act 2007 following completion of its Parliamentary passage.

HOW SHOULD THIS CODE OF PRACTICE BE USED?

This Code of Practice provides guidance to anyone working with and/or caring   **5–004**
for adults who lack capacity, but it particularly focuses on those who have a 'duty
of care' to a person who lacks the capacity to consent to the care or treatment that
is being provided, where that care or treatment may include the need to deprive
the person of their liberty. This Code of Practice is also intended to provide information for people who are, or could become, subject to the deprivation of liberty
safeguards, and for their families, friends and carers, as well as for anyone who
believes that someone is being deprived of their liberty unlawfully.

In this Code of Practice, as throughout the main Code, references to 'lack of
capacity' refer to the capacity to make a particular decision at the time it needs
to be made. In the context of the deprivation of liberty safeguards, the capacity
is specifically the capacity to decide whether or not to consent to care or treatment which involves being kept in a hospital or care home in circumstances that
amount to a deprivation of liberty, at the time that decision needs to be made.

WHAT IS THE LEGAL STATUS OF THIS CODE OF PRACTICE?

As with the main Code, this Code of Practice is published by the Lord   **5–005**
Chancellor, under sections 42 and 43 of the Mental Capacity Act 2005. The
purpose of the main Code is to provide guidance and information about how the
Act works in practice.

Both this Code and the main Code have statutory force, which means that
certain people are under a legal duty to have regard to them. More details can be
found in the Introduction to the main Code, which explains the legal status of the
Code and who should have regard to it.

In addition to those for whom the main Code is intended, this Code of Practice
specifically focuses on providing guidance for:

- people exercising functions relating to the deprivation of liberty safeguards, and

- people acting as a relevant person's representative[1] under the deprivation
  of liberty safeguards (see chapter 7).

SCENARIOS USED IN THIS CODE OF PRACTICE

This Code of Practice includes boxes within the main text containing scenarios,   **5–006**
using imaginary characters and situations. These are intended to help illustrate
what is meant in the main text. They should not in any way be taken as templates
for decisions that need to be made in similar situations. Decisions must always be
made on the facts of each individual case.

ALTERNATIVE FORMATS AND FURTHER INFORMATION

This Code of Practice is also available in Welsh and can be made available in   **5–007**
other formats on request.

---

[1] A 'relevant person' is a person who is, or may become, deprived of their liberty in accordance with
the deprivation of liberty safeguards.

CONTENTS

What are the responsibilities of the managing authority and the commissioners of care if a request for an authorisation is turned down?

6. **When can urgent authorisations of deprivation of liberty be given? (5–191)**

   When can an urgent authorisation be given?

   What records should be kept about urgent authorisations?

   Who should be consulted before giving an urgent authorisation?

   Can a person be moved into care under an urgent authorisation?

   What happens at the end of an urgent authorisation period?

   How and when can an urgent authorisation be extended?

7. **What is the role of the relevant person's representative? (5–222)**

   What is the role of the relevant person's representative?

   How should managing authorities work with the relevant person's representative?

   Who can be the relevant person's representative?

   When should the relevant person's representative be identified?

   How should the relevant person's representative be selected?

   How should the relevant person's representative be appointed?

   How should the work of the relevant person's representative be supported and monitored?

   When can the appointment of the relevant person's representative be terminated?

   What happens when there is no relevant person's representative available?

   When should an IMCA be instructed?

8. **When should an authorisation be reviewed and what happens when it ends? (5–264)**

   When should a standard authorisation be reviewed?

   What happens when a review is going to take place?

   How should standard authorisations be reviewed?

   What happens if any of the requirements are not met?

   Is a review necessary when the relevant person's capacity fluctuates?

   What happens when an authorisation ends?

9. **What happens if someone thinks a person is being deprived of their liberty without authorisation? (5–295)**

   What action should someone take if they think a person is being deprived of their liberty without authorisation?

   What happens if somebody informs the supervisory body directly that they think a person is being deprived of their liberty without authorisation?

   How will the assessment of unlawful deprivation of liberty be conducted?

   What happens once the assessment has been conducted?

10. **What is the Court of Protection and when can people apply to it? (5–310)**

    When can people apply to the Court of Protection about the deprivation of liberty safeguards and who can apply?

    How should people apply to the Court of Protection?

    What orders can the Court of Protection make?

    What is the role of the Court of Protection in respect of people lacking capacity who are deprived of their liberty in settings other than hospitals or care homes?

Is legal aid available to support applications to the Court of Protection in deprivation of liberty safeguards cases?

11. How will the safeguards be monitored? (5–324)
Who will monitor the safeguards?
What will the inspection bodies do and what powers will they have?

Checklists (5–333)

Key points for care homes and hospitals (managing authorities)

Key points for local authorities and NHS bodies (supervisory bodies)

Key points for managing authorities and supervisory bodies

Annexes (5–336)

Annex 1—Overview of the deprivation of liberty safeguards process

Annex 2—What should a managing authority consider before applying for authorisation of deprivation of liberty?

Annex 3—Supervisory body action on receipt of a request for a standard deprivation of liberty authorisation or to determine whether there is an unauthorised deprivation of liberty

Annex 4—Standard authorisation review process

Key words and phrases used in the Code of Practice (5–340)

1. WHAT ARE THE DEPRIVATION OF LIBERTY SAFEGUARDS AND WHY WERE THEY INTRODUCED?

5–008   The deprivation of liberty safeguards were introduced to provide a legal framework around the deprivation of liberty. Specifically, they were introduced to prevent breaches of the European Convention on Human Rights (ECHR) such as the one identified by the judgment of the European Court of Human Rights (ECtHR) in the case of *HL v the United Kingdom*[2] (commonly referred to as the 'Bournewood' judgment). The case concerned an autistic man (HL) with a learning disability, who lacked the capacity to decide whether he should be admitted to hospital for specific treatment. He was admitted on an informal basis under common law in his best interests, but this decision was challenged by HL's carers. In its judgment, the ECtHR held that this admission constituted a deprivation of HL's liberty and, further, that:

- the deprivation of liberty had not been in accordance with 'a procedure prescribed by law' and was, therefore, in breach of Article 5(1) of the ECHR, and

---

[2]   (2004) Application No: 00045508/99.

- there had been a contravention of Article 5(4) of the ECHR because HL had no means of applying quickly to a court to see if the deprivation of liberty was lawful.

To prevent further similar breaches of the ECHR, the Mental Capacity Act 2005 has been amended to provide safeguards for people who lack capacity specifically to consent to treatment or care in either a hospital or a care home[3] that, in their own best interests, can only be provided in circumstances that amount to a deprivation of liberty, and where detention under the Mental Health Act 1983 is not appropriate for the person at that time. These safeguards are referred to in this Code of Practice as 'deprivation of liberty safeguards'.

What are the deprivation of liberty safeguards?

1.1 The deprivation of liberty safeguards provide legal protection for those vulnerable people who are, or may become, deprived of their liberty within the meaning of Article 5 of the ECHR in a hospital or care home, whether placed under public or private arrangements. They do not apply to people detained under the Mental Health Act 1983. The safeguards exist to provide a proper legal process and suitable protection in those circumstances where deprivation of liberty appears to be unavoidable, in a person's own best interests.　**5–009**

1.2 Every effort should be made, in both commissioning and providing care or treatment, to prevent deprivation of liberty. If deprivation of liberty cannot be avoided, it should be for no longer than is necessary.　**5–010**

1.3 The safeguards provide for deprivation of liberty to be made lawful through 'standard' or 'urgent' authorisation processes. These processes are designed to prevent arbitrary decisions to deprive a person of liberty and give a right to challenge deprivation of liberty authorisations.　**5–011**

1.4 The deprivation of liberty safeguards mean that a 'managing authority' (i.e. the relevant hospital or care home—see paragraph 3.1) must seek authorisation from a 'supervisory body' in order to be able lawfully to deprive someone of their liberty. Before giving such an authorisation, the supervisory body must be satisfied that the person has a mental disorder[4] and lacks capacity to decide about their residence or treatment. The supervisory body could be a primary care trust, a local authority, Welsh Ministers or a local health board (LHB) (see paragraph 3.3).　**5–012**

1.5 A decision as to whether or not deprivation of liberty arises will depend on all the circumstances of the case (as explained more fully in chapter 2). It is neither necessary nor appropriate to apply for a deprivation of liberty authorisation for everyone who is in hospital or a care home simply because the person concerned lacks capacity to decide whether or not they should be there. In deciding whether or not an application is　**5–013**

---

[3] Throughout this document, the term 'care home' means a care home registered under the Care Standards Act 2000.

[4] As defined in section 1 of the Mental Health Act 1983, a mental disorder is any disorder or disability of the mind, apart from dependence on alcohol and drugs. This includes all learning disabilities. The distinction in the Mental Health Act 1983 between learning disabilities depending on whether or not they are associated with abnormally aggressive or seriously irresponsible behaviour is not relevant.

necessary, a managing authority should carefully consider whether any restrictions that are, or will be, needed to provide ongoing care or treatment amount to a deprivation of liberty when looked at together.

5–014   1.6 The deprivation of liberty safeguards cover:

- how an application for authorisation should be applied for
- how an application for authorisation should be assessed
- the requirements that must be fulfilled for an authorisation to be given
- how an authorisation should be reviewed
- what support and representation must be provided for people who are subject to an authorisation, and
- how people can challenge authorisations.

Who is covered by these safeguards?

5–015   1.7 The safeguards apply to people in England and Wales who have a mental disorder and lack capacity to consent to the arrangements made for their care or treatment, but for whom receiving care or treatment in circumstances that amount to a deprivation of liberty may be necessary to protect them from harm and appears to be in their best interests. A large number of these people will be those with significant learning disabilities, or older people who have dementia or some similar disability, but they can also include those who have certain other neurological conditions (for example as a result of a brain injury).

5–016   1.8 In order to come within the scope of a deprivation of liberty authorisation, a person must be detained in a hospital or care home, for the purpose of being given care or treatment in circumstances that amount to a deprivation of liberty. The authorisation must relate to the individual concerned and to the hospital or care home in which they are detained.

5–017   1.9 For the purposes of Article 5 of the ECHR, there is no distinction in principle between depriving a person who lacks capacity of their liberty for the purpose of treating them for a physical condition, and depriving them of their liberty for treatment of a mental disorder. There will therefore be occasions when people who lack capacity to consent to admission are taken to hospital for treatment of physical illnesses or injuries, and then need to be cared for in circumstances that amount to a deprivation of liberty. In these circumstances, a deprivation of liberty authorisation must be applied for. Consequently, this Code of Practice must be followed and applied in acute hospital settings as well as care homes and mental health units.

5–018   1.10 It is important to bear in mind that, while the deprivation of liberty might be for the purpose of giving a person treatment, a deprivation of liberty authorisation does not itself authorise treatment. Treatment that is proposed following authorisation of deprivation of liberty may only be given with the person's consent (if they have capacity to make the decision) or in accordance with the wider provisions of the Mental Capacity Act 2005. More details of this are contained in paragraphs 5.10 to 5.13 of this Code.

5–019   1.11 The safeguards cannot apply to people while they are detained in hospital under the Mental Health Act 1983. The safeguards can, however, apply to a person who has previously been detained in hospital under the Mental Health Act 1983. There are other cases in which people who are—or could be—subject to the Mental Health Act 1983 will not meet the eligibility requirement for the safeguards. Chapter 13 of the main Code contains guidance on the relationship between the Mental Capacity Act 2005 and the Mental Health Act 1983 generally, as does the Code of Practice to the Mental Health Act 1983 itself. Paragraphs 4.40 to 4.57 of the present Code explain the relationship of the deprivation of liberty safeguards to the Mental Health Act 1983, and in particular how to assess if a person is eligible to be deprived of their liberty under the safeguards.

1.12 The safeguards relate only to people aged 18 and over. If the issue of depriving a person under the age of 18 of their liberty arises, other safeguards must be considered—such as the existing powers of the court, particularly those under section 25 of the Children Act 1989, or use of the Mental Health Act 1983. **5–020**

When can someone be deprived of their liberty?

1.13 Depriving someone who lacks the capacity to consent to the arrangements made for their care or treatment of their liberty is a serious matter, and the decision to do so should not be taken lightly. The deprivation of liberty safeguards make it clear that a person may only be deprived of their liberty: **5–021**
- in their own best interests to protect them from harm
- if it is a proportionate response to the likelihood and seriousness of the harm, and
- if there is no less restrictive alternative.

1.14 Under no circumstances must deprivation of liberty be used as a form of punishment, or for the convenience of professionals, carers or anyone else. Deprivation of liberty should not be extended due to delays in moving people between care or treatment settings, for example when somebody awaits discharge after completing a period of hospital treatment. **5–022**

Are there any cultural considerations in implementing the safeguards?

1.15 The deprivation of liberty safeguards should not impact in any different way on different racial or ethnic groups, and care should be taken to ensure that the provisions are not operated in a manner that discriminates against particular racial or ethnic groups. It is up to managing authorities and supervisory bodies to ensure that their staff are aware of their responsibilities in this regard and of the need to ensure that the safeguards are operated fairly and equitably. **5–023**

1.16 Assessors who carry out deprivation of liberty assessments to help decide whether a person should be deprived of their liberty (see chapter 4) should have the necessary skills and experience to take account of people's diverse backgrounds. Accordingly, they will need to have an understanding of, and respect for, the background of the relevant person. Supervisory bodies must take these factors into account when appointing assessors and must seek to appoint the most suitable available person for each case. **5–024**

1.17 Interpreters should be available, where necessary, to help assessors to **5–025** communicate not only with the relevant person but also with people with an interest in their care and treatment. An interpreter should be suitably qualified and experienced to enable them to provide effective language and communication support in the particular case concerned, and to offer appropriate assistance to the assessors involved. Information should be made available in other languages where relevant.

5–026   1.18 Any decision about the instruction of Independent Mental Capacity Advocates (see paragraphs 3.22 to 3.28) or relevant person's representatives (see chapter 7) should take account of the cultural, national, racial or ethnic background of the relevant person.

Where do the safeguards apply?

5–027   1.19 Although the Bournewood judgment was specifically about a patient who lacked capacity to consent to admission to hospital for mental health treatment, the judgment has wider implications that extend to people who lack capacity and who might be deprived of their liberty either in a hospital or in a care home.

5–028   1.20 It will only be lawful to deprive somebody of their liberty elsewhere (for example, in their own home, in supported living arrangements other than in a care home, or in a day centre) when following an order of the Court of Protection on a personal welfare matter. In such a case, the Court of Protection order itself provides a legal basis for the deprivation of liberty. This means that a separate deprivation of liberty authorisation under the processes set out in this Code of Practice is not required. More information about applying to the Court of Protection regarding personal welfare matters is given in chapter 10.

How do the safeguards apply to privately arranged care or treatment?

5–029   1.21 Under the Human Rights Act 1998, the duty to act in accordance with the ECHR applies only to public authorities. However, all states that have signed up to the ECHR are obliged to make sure that the rights set out in the ECHR apply to all of their citizens. The Mental Capacity Act 2005 therefore makes it clear that the deprivation of liberty safeguards apply to both publicly and privately arranged care or treatment.

How do the safeguards relate to the rest of the Mental Capacity Act 2005?

5–030   1.22 The deprivation of liberty safeguards are in addition to, and do not replace, other safeguards in the Mental Capacity Act 2005. This means that decisions made, and actions taken, for a person who is subject to a deprivation of liberty authorisation must fulfil the requirements of the Act in the same way as for any other person. In particular, any action taken under the deprivation of liberty safeguards must be in line with the principles of the Act:

- A person must be assumed to have capacity to make a decision unless it is established that they lack the capacity to make that decision.
- A person is not to be treated as unable to make a decision unless all practicable steps to help them to do so have been taken without success.

- A person is not to be treated as unable to make a decision merely because they make an unwise decision.
- An act done, or decision made, under the Act for or on behalf of a person who lacks capacity must be done, or made, in their best interests.
- Before the act is done, or the decision is made, regard must be had to whether the purpose for which it is needed can be as effectively achieved in a way that is less restrictive of the person's rights and freedom of action.

These principles are set out in chapter 2 of the main Code and explained in more detail in chapters 3 to 6 of the same document. Paragraph 5.13 of the main Code contains a checklist of factors that need to be taken into account in determining a person's best interests.

2. WHAT IS DEPRIVATION OF LIBERTY?

There is no simple definition of deprivation of liberty. The question of whether   **5–031** the steps taken by staff or institutions in relation to a person amount to a deprivation of that person's liberty is ultimately a legal question, and only the courts can determine the law. This guidance seeks to assist staff and institutions in considering whether or not the steps they are taking, or proposing to take, amount to a deprivation of a person's liberty. The deprivation of liberty safeguards give best interests assessors the authority to make recommendations about proposed deprivations of liberty, and supervisory bodies the power to give authorisations that deprive people of their liberty.

This chapter provides guidance for staff and institutions on how to assess whether particular steps they are taking, or proposing to take, might amount to a deprivation of liberty, based on existing case law. It also considers what other factors may be taken into account when considering the issue of deprivation of liberty, including, importantly, what is permissible under the Mental Capacity Act 2005 in relation to restraint or restriction. Finally, it provides a summary of some of the most important cases to date.

Further legal developments may occur after this guidance has been issued, and healthcare and social care staff need to keep themselves informed of legal developments that may have a bearing on their practice.

What does case law say to date?

2.1   The European Court of Human Rights (ECtHR) has drawn a distinction   **5–032** between the deprivation of liberty of an individual (which is unlawful, unless authorised) and restrictions on the liberty of movement of an individual.

2.2   The ECtHR made it clear that the question of whether someone has been   **5–033** deprived of liberty depends on the particular circumstances of the case. Specifically, the ECtHR said in its October 2004 judgment in *HL v the United Kingdom:*

> "to determine whether there has been a deprivation of liberty, the starting-point must be the specific situation of the individual concerned and account must be taken of a whole range of factors arising

in a particular case such as the type, duration, effects and manner of implementation of the measure in question. The distinction between a deprivation of, and restriction upon, liberty is merely one of degree or intensity and not one of nature or substance."

5–034 2.3 The difference between deprivation of liberty and restriction upon liberty is one of degree or intensity. It may therefore be helpful to envisage a scale, which moves from 'restraint' or 'restriction' to 'deprivation of liberty'. Where an individual is on the scale will depend on the concrete circumstances of the individual and may change over time. For more information on how the Act defines restraint, see paragraphs 2.8–2.12.

5–035 2.4 Although the guidance in this chapter includes descriptions of past decisions of the courts, which should be used to help evaluate whether deprivation of liberty may be occurring, each individual case must be assessed on its own circumstances. No two cases are likely to be identical, so it is important to be aware of previous court judgments and the factors that the courts have identified as important.

5–036 2.5 The ECtHR and UK courts have determined a number of cases about deprivation of liberty. Their judgments indicate that the following factors can be relevant to identifying whether steps taken involve more than restraint and amount to a deprivation of liberty. It is important to remember that this list is not exclusive; other factors may arise in future in particular cases.

- Restraint is used, including sedation, to admit a person to an institution where that person is resisting admission.
- Staff exercise complete and effective control over the care and movement of a person for a significant period.
- Staff exercise control over assessments, treatment, contacts and residence.
- A decision has been taken by the institution that the person will not be released into the care of others, or permitted to live elsewhere, unless the staff in the institution consider it appropriate.
- A request by carers for a person to be discharged to their care is refused.
- The person is unable to maintain social contacts because of restrictions placed on their access to other people.
- The person loses autonomy because they are under continuous supervision and control.

There is more information on some relevant cases at the end of this chapter (paragraphs 2.17–2.23).

How can deprivation of liberty be identified?

5–037 2.6 In determining whether deprivation of liberty has occurred, or is likely to occur, decision-makers need to consider all the facts in a particular case. There is unlikely to be any simple definition that can be applied in every case, and it is probable that no single factor will, in itself, determine whether the overall set of steps being taken in relation to the relevant person amount to a deprivation of liberty. In general, the decision-maker should always consider the following:

- All the circumstances of each and every case
- What measures are being taken in relation to the individual? When are they required? For what period do they endure? What are the effects of any restraints or restrictions on the individual? Why are they necessary? What aim do they seek to meet?
- What are the views of the relevant person, their family or carers? Do any of them object to the measures?
- How are any restraints or restrictions implemented? Do any of the constraints on the individual's personal freedom go beyond 'restraint' or 'restriction' to the extent that they constitute a deprivation of liberty?
- Are there any less restrictive options for delivering care or treatment that avoid deprivation of liberty altogether?
- Does the cumulative effect of all the restrictions imposed on the person amount to a deprivation of liberty, even if individually they would not?

What practical steps can be taken to reduce the risk of deprivation of liberty occurring?

2.7 There are many ways in which providers and commissioners of care can reduce the risk of taking steps that amount to a deprivation of liberty, by minimising the restrictions imposed and ensuring that decisions are taken with the involvement of the relevant person and their family, friends and carers. The processes for staff to follow are:
  5–038
- Make sure that all decisions are taken (and reviewed) in a structured way, and reasons for decisions recorded.
- Follow established good practice for care planning.
- Make a proper assessment of whether the person lacks capacity to decide whether or not to accept the care or treatment proposed, in line with the principles of the Act (see chapter 3 of the main Code for further guidance).
- Before admitting a person to hospital or residential care in circumstances that may amount to a deprivation of liberty, consider whether the person's needs could be met in a less restrictive way. Any restrictions placed on the person while in hospital or in a care home must be kept to the minimum necessary, and should be in place for the shortest possible period.
- Take proper steps to help the relevant person retain contact with family, friends and carers. Where local advocacy services are available, their involvement should be encouraged to support the person and their family, friends and carers.
- Review the care plan on an ongoing basis. It may well be helpful to include an independent element, possibly via an advocacy service, in the review.

What does the Act mean by 'restraint'?

2.8 Section 6(4) of the Act states that someone is using restraint if they:
  5–039
- use force—or threaten to use force—to make someone do something that they are resisting, or

- restrict a person's freedom of movement, whether they are resisting or not.

5–040 2.9 Paragraphs 6.40 to 6.48 of the main Code contain guidance about the appropriate use of restraint. Restraint is appropriate when it is used to prevent harm to the person who lacks capacity and it is a proportionate response to the likelihood and seriousness of harm. Appropriate use of restraint falls short of deprivation of liberty.

5–041 2.10 Preventing a person from leaving a care home or hospital unaccompanied because there is a risk that they would try to cross a road in a dangerous way, for example, is likely to be seen as a proportionate restriction or restraint to prevent the person from coming to harm. That would be unlikely, in itself, to constitute a deprivation of liberty. Similarly, locking a door to guard against immediate harm is unlikely, in itself, to amount to a deprivation of liberty.

5–042 2.11 The ECtHR has also indicated that the duration of any restrictions is a relevant factor when considering whether or not a person is deprived of their liberty. This suggests that actions that are immediately necessary to prevent harm may not, in themselves, constitute a deprivation of liberty.

5–043 2.12 However, where the restriction or restraint is frequent, cumulative and ongoing, or if there are other factors present, then care providers should consider whether this has gone beyond permissible restraint, as defined in the Act. If so, then they must either apply for authorisation under the deprivation of liberty safeguards (as explained in chapter 3) or change their care provision to reduce the level of restraint.

How does the use of restraint apply within a hospital or when taking someone to a hospital or a care home?

Within a hospital

5–044 2.13 If a person in hospital for mental health treatment, or being considered for admission to a hospital for mental health treatment, needs to be restrained, this is likely to indicate that they are objecting to treatment or to being in hospital. The care providers should consider whether the need for restraint means the person is objecting (see paragraph 4.46 of this Code for guidance on how to decide whether a person is objecting for this purpose). A person who objects to mental health treatment, and who meets the criteria for detention under the Mental Health Act 1983, is normally ineligible for an authorisation under the deprivation of liberty safeguards. If the care providers believe it is necessary to detain the person, they may wish to consider use of the Mental Health Act 1983.

Taking someone to a hospital or a care home

5–045 2.14 Transporting a person who lacks capacity from their home, or another location, to a hospital or care home will not usually amount to a deprivation of liberty (for example, to take them to hospital by ambulance in an emergency.) Even where there is an expectation that the person will be deprived of liberty within the care home or hospital, it is unlikely that the journey itself will constitute a deprivation of liberty so that an authorisation is needed before the journey commences. In almost all cases, it is likely that a person can be lawfully taken to a hospital or a care home under the wider provisions of the Act, as long as it is considered that being in the hospital or care home will be in their best interests.

2.15 In a very few cases, there may be exceptional circumstances where taking a person to a hospital or a care home amounts to a deprivation of liberty, for example where it is necessary to do more than persuade or restrain the person for the purpose of transportation, or where the journey is exceptionally long. In such cases, it may be necessary to seek an order from the Court of Protection to ensure that the journey is taken on a lawful basis.

5–046

How should managing authorities avoid unnecessary applications for standard authorisations?

2.16 While it is unlawful to deprive a person of their liberty without authorisation, managing authorities should take into consideration that unnecessary applications for standard authorisations in cases that do not in fact involve depriving a person of liberty may place undue stress upon the person being assessed and on their families or carers. Moreover, consideration must always be given to the possibility of less restrictive options for delivering care or treatment that avoid deprivation of liberty altogether.

5–047

Examples of case law

2.17 To provide further guidance, the following paragraphs contain short descriptions of what appear to be the significant features of recent or important cases in England and Wales and the ECtHR dealing with deprivation of liberty. Remember that:

- these descriptions are for guidance only
- only the courts can authoritatively determine the law; and
- the courts are likely to give judgments in cases after this guidance is issued. Staff will need to keep up to date and take account of further relevant legal developments.

5–048

Cases where the courts found that the steps taken did not involve a deprivation of liberty

2.18 *LLBC v TG* (judgment of High Court of 14 November 2007)

5–049

TG was a 78-year-old man with dementia and cognitive impairment. TG was resident in a care home, but was admitted to hospital with pneumonia and septicaemia. While he was in hospital, there was a dispute between the local authority and TG's daughter and granddaughter about TG's future. The daughter and granddaughter wanted TG to live with them, but the local authority believed that TG needed 24-hour care in a residential care home.

The council obtained an order from the court, directing that TG be delivered to the care home identified as appropriate by the council. Neither the daughter nor granddaughter was informed that a court hearing was taking place. That order was subsequently changed and TG was able to live with his daughter and granddaughter.

TG's daughter and granddaughter claimed that the period of time he had spent at the care home amounted to a deprivation of his liberty.

The judge considered that there was no deprivation of liberty, but the case was borderline. The key factors in his decision included:

- The care home was an ordinary care home where only ordinary restrictions of liberty applied.
- The family were able to visit TG on a largely unrestricted basis and were entitled to take him out from the home for outings.
- TG was personally compliant and expressed himself as happy in the care home. He had lived in a local authority care home for over three years and was objectively content with his situation there.
- There was no occasion where TG was objectively deprived of his liberty.

The judge said:

"Whilst I agree that the circumstances of the present case may be near the borderline between mere restrictions of liberty and Article 5 detention, I have come to the conclusion that, looked at as a whole and having regard to all the relevant circumstances, the placement of TG in Towerbridge falls short of engaging Article 5."

5–050   2.19 *Nielsen v Denmark (ECtHR; (1988) 11 EHRR 175)*

The mother of a 12-year-old boy arranged for his admission to the state hospital's psychiatric ward. The boy had a nervous disorder and required treatment in the form of regular talks and environmental therapy. The treatment given, and the conditions under which it was administered, was appropriate. The duration of treatment was 51/2 months. The boy, however, applied to the ECtHR, feeling that he had been deprived of his liberty.

The restrictions placed on the applicant's freedom of movement and contacts with the outside world were not much different from restrictions that might be imposed on a child in an ordinary hospital. The door of the ward was locked to prevent children exposing themselves to danger or running around disturbing other patients. The applicant was free to leave the ward with permission and to go out if accompanied by a member of staff. He was able to visit his family and friends, and towards the end of his stay to go to school.

The Court held:

"The restrictions imposed on the applicant were not of a nature or degree similar to the cases of deprivation of liberty specified in paragraph (1) of Article 5. In particular, he was not detained as a person of unsound mind. . . . .. Indeed, the restrictions to which the applicant was subject were no more than the normal requirements for the care of a child of 12 years of age receiving treatment in hospital. The conditions in which the applicant stayed thus did not, in principle, differ from those obtaining in many hospital wards where children with physical disorders are treated."

It concluded:

"the hospitalisation of the applicant did not amount to a deprivation of liberty within the meaning of Article 5, but was a responsible exercise by his mother of her custodial rights in the interests of the child."

2.20   *HM v Switzerland (ECtHR; (2004) 38 EHRR 17)*   **5–051**

An 84-year-old woman was placed indefinitely in a nursing home by state authorities. She had had the possibility of staying at home and being cared for there, but she and her son had refused to co-operate with the relevant care association, and her living conditions had subsequently deteriorated. The state authorities placed her in the home in order to provide her with necessary medical care and satisfactory living conditions and hygiene.

The woman was not placed in the secure ward of the home but was free to move within the home and to have social contacts with the outside world. She was initially undecided as to what solution she preferred and, after moving into the home, the applicant had agreed to stay there. However, she subsequently applied to the courts saying that she had been deprived of her liberty.

The Court held that she had not been deprived of her liberty:

"Bearing these elements in mind, in particular the fact that [the authorities] had ordered the applicant's placement in the nursing home in her own interests in order to provide her with the necessary medical care and satisfactory living conditions and standards of hygiene, and also taking into consideration the comparable circumstances of *Nielsen v Denmark* [see case summary above], the Court concludes that in the circumstances of the present case the applicant's placement in the nursing home did not amount to a deprivation of liberty within the meaning of Article 5(1), but was a responsible measure taken by the competent authorities in the applicant's best interests."

Cases where the courts have found that the steps taken involve a deprivation of liberty

2.21   *DE and JE v Surrey County Council (SCC)* (High Court judgment of 29   **5–052**
December 2006)

DE was a 76-year-old man who, following a major stroke, had become blind and had significant short-term memory impairment. He also had dementia and lacked capacity to decide where he should live, but was still often able to express his wishes with some clarity and force.

DE was married to JE. In August 2003, DE was living at home with JE. There was an occasion when JE felt that she could not care for DE, and placed him on a chair on the pavement in front of the house and called the police. The local authority then placed him in two care homes, referred to in the judgment of the court as the X home and the Y home.

Within the care homes, DE had a very substantial degree of freedom and lots of contact with the outside world. He was never subject to physical or chemical restraint.

DE repeatedly expressed the wish to live with JE, and JE also wanted DE to live with her. SCC would not agree to DE returning to live with, or visit, JE and made it clear that if JE were to persist in an attempt to remove DE, SCC would contact the police. DE and JE applied to the courts that this was a deprivation of his liberty.

In his judgment, Justice Munby said:

"The fundamental issue in this case . . . is whether DE has been and is deprived of his liberty to leave the X home and whether DE has been and is deprived of his liberty to leave the Y home. And when I refer to leaving the X home and the Y home, I do not mean leaving for the purpose of some trip or outing approved by SCC or by those managing the institution; I mean leaving in the sense of removing himself permanently in order to live where and with whom he chooses, specifically removing himself to live at home with JE."

He then said:

"DE was not and is not "free to leave", and was and is, in that sense, completely under the control of [the local authority], because, as [counsel for DE] put it, it was and is [the local authority] who decides the essential matters of where DE can live, whether he can leave and whether he can be with JE."

He concluded:

"The simple reality is that DE will be permitted to leave the institution in which [the local authority] has placed him and be released to the care of JE only as and when,—if ever; probably never,—[the local authority] considers it appropriate. [The local authority's] motives may be the purest, but in my judgment, [it] has been and is continuing to deprive DE of his liberty."

5–053   2.22   *HL v United Kingdom (ECtHR; (2004) 40 EHRR 761)*

A 48-year-old man who had had autism since birth was unable to speak and his level of understanding was limited. He was frequently agitated and had a history of self-harming behaviour. He lacked the capacity to consent to treatment.

For over 30 years, he was cared for in Bournewood Hospital. In 1994, he was entrusted to carers and for three years he lived successfully with his carers. Following an incident of self-harm at a day centre on 22 July 1997, the applicant was taken to Bournewood Hospital where he was re-admitted informally (not under the Mental Health Act 1983).

The carers wished to have the applicant released to their care, which the hospital refused. The carers were unable to visit him.

In its judgment in *HL v the United Kingdom,* the ECtHR said that:

"the key factor in the present case [is] that the health care professionals treating and managing the applicant exercised complete and effective control over his care and movements from the moment he presented acute behavioural problems on July 22, 1997 to the date when he was compulsorily detained on October 29, 1997."

"His responsible medical officer (Dr M) was clear that, had the applicant resisted admission or tried to leave thereafter, she would have prevented him from doing so and would have considered his involuntary committal under s.3 of the 1983 Act; indeed, as soon as the Court of Appeal indicated that his appeal would be allowed, he was compulsorily detained under the 1983 Act. The correspondence between the applicant's carers and Dr M reflects both the carer's wish to have the applicant immediately released to their care and, equally, the clear intention of Dr M and the other relevant health care professionals to exercise strict control over his assessment, treatment, contacts and, notably, movement and residence; the applicant would only be released from hospital to the care of Mr and Mrs E as and when those professionals considered it appropriate. . . . it was clear from the above noted correspondence that the applicant's contact with his carers was directed and controlled by the hospital, his carers visiting him for the first time after his admission on 2 November 1997."

"Accordingly, the concrete situation was that the applicant was under continuous supervision and control and was not free to leave."

2.23 *Storck v Germany (ECtHR; (2005) 43 EHRR 96)*   **5–054**

A young woman was placed by her father in a psychiatric institution on occasions in 1974 and 1975. In July 1977, at the age of 18, she was placed again in a psychiatric institution. She was kept in a locked ward and was under the continuous supervision and control of the clinic personnel and was not free to leave the clinic during her entire stay of 20 months. When she attempted to flee, she was shackled. When she succeeded one time, she was brought back by the police. She was unable to maintain regular contact with the outside world.

She applied to the courts on the basis that she had been deprived of her liberty. There was a dispute about whether she consented to her confinement.

The Court noted:

"the applicant, on several occasions, had tried to flee from the clinic. She had to be shackled in order to prevent her from absconding and had to be brought back to the clinic by the police when she managed to escape on one occasion. Under these circumstances, the Court is unable to discern any factual basis for the assumption that the applicant—presuming that she had the capacity to consent—agreed to her continued stay in the clinic. In the alternative, assuming that the applicant was no longer capable of consenting following her treatment with strong medication, she cannot, in any event, be considered to have validly agreed to her stay in the clinic."

2.24 These cases reinforce the need to carefully consider all the specific   **5–055** circumstances of the relevant individual before deciding whether or not a person is being deprived of their liberty. They also underline the vital importance of involving family, friends and carers in this decision-making process: a significant feature of a number of the cases that have come before the courts is a difference of opinion or communication issue between the commissioners or providers of care and family members and carers.

3. HOW AND WHEN CAN DEPRIVATION OF LIBERTY BE APPLIED FOR AND AUTHORISED?

5–056   There are some circumstances in which depriving a person, who lacks capacity to consent to the arrangements made for their care or treatment, of their liberty is necessary to protect them from harm, and is in their best interests.

Deprivation of liberty can be authorised by supervisory bodies (primary care trusts (PCTs), local authorities, Welsh Ministers or local health boards (LHBs). To obtain authorisation to deprive someone of their liberty, managing authorities have to apply for an authorisation following the processes set out in this chapter.[5] Once an application has been received, the supervisory body must then follow the assessment processes set out in chapter 4 before it can authorise deprivation of liberty. It should be borne in mind that a deprivation of liberty authorisation does not, in itself, give authority to treat someone. This issue is covered in paragraphs 5.10 to 5.13.

In the vast majority of cases, it should be possible to plan in advance so that a standard authorisation can be obtained before the deprivation of liberty begins. There may, however, be some exceptional cases where the need for the deprivation of liberty is so urgent that it is in the best interests of the person for it to begin while the application is being considered. In that case, the care home or hospital may give an urgent authorisation for up to seven days (see chapter 6).

How, in summary, can deprivation of liberty be authorised?

5–057   3.1   A **managing authority** has responsibility for applying for authorisation of deprivation of liberty for any person who may come within the scope of the deprivation of liberty safeguards:
- In the case of an NHS hospital, the managing authority is the NHS body responsible for the running of the hospital in which the relevant person is, or is to be, a resident.
- In the case of a care home or a private hospital, the managing authority will be the person registered, or required to be registered, under part 2 of the Care Standards Act 2000 in respect of the hospital or care home.

5–058   3.2   If a healthcare or social care professional thinks that an authorisation is needed, they should inform the managing authority. This might be as a result of a care review or needs assessment but could happen at any other time too. (See chapter 9 for guidance on action to take if there is a concern that a person is already being deprived of their liberty, without authorisation.)

5–059   3.3   A **supervisory body** is responsible for considering requests for authorisations, commissioning the required assessments (see chapter 4) and, where all the assessments agree, authorising the deprivation of liberty:
- Where the deprivation of liberty safeguards are applied to a person in a hospital situated in England, the supervisory body will be:

---

[5]   If a person is lawfully deprived of liberty in a care home or hospital as **a consequence of an order of the Court of Protection,** there is no need to apply for an authorisation. However, once the order of the Court of Protection has expired, for lawful deprivation of liberty to continue authorisation must be obtained by following the processes set out in this chapter.

—if a PCT commissions[6] the relevant care or treatment (or it is commissioned on the PCT's behalf), that PCT

—if the Welsh Ministers or an LHB commissions the relevant care and treatment in England, the Welsh Ministers, or

—in any other case, the PCT for the area in which the hospital is situated.

- Where the deprivation of liberty safeguards are applied to a person in a hospital situated in Wales, the supervisory body will be the Welsh Ministers or an LHB **unless** a PCT commissions the relevant care and treatment in Wales, in which case the PCT will be the supervisory body.

- Where the deprivation of liberty safeguards are applied to a person in a care home, whether situated in England or Wales, the supervisory body will be the local authority for the area in which the person is ordinarily resident. However, if the person is not ordinarily resident in the area of any local authority (for example a person of no fixed abode), the supervisory body will be the local authority for the area in which the care home is situated.[7]

3.4 There are two types of authorisation: standard and urgent. A managing authority must request a standard authorisation when it appears likely that, at some time during the next 28 days, someone will be accommodated in its hospital or care home in circumstances that amount to a deprivation of liberty within the meaning of article 5 of the European Convention on Human Rights. The request must be made to the supervisory body. Whenever possible, authorisation should be obtained in advance. Where this is not possible, and the managing authority believes it is necessary to deprive someone of their liberty in their best interests **before** the standard authorisation process can be completed, the managing authority must itself give an urgent authorisation and then obtain standard authorisation within seven calendar days (see chapter 6). **5–060**

3.5 The flowchart at Annex 1 gives an overview of how the deprivation of liberty safeguards process should operate. **5–061**

How should managing authorities decide whether to apply for an authorisation?

3.6 Managing authorities should have a procedure in place that identifies: **5–062**

---

[6] Guidance on establishing the responsible commissioner can be found at *http://www.dh.gov.uk/en/ Publicationsandstatistics/Publications / PublicationsPolicyAndGuidance/DH_078466.*

[7] To work out the place of ordinary residence, the usual mechanisms under the National Assistance Act 1948 apply (see *http://www.dh.gov.uk/en/SocialCare/Deliveringadultsocialcare / Ordinaryresidence / DH_079346*). Any unresolved questions about the ordinary residence of a person will be handled by the Secretary of State or by the Welsh Ministers. Until a decision is made, the local authority that received the application must act as the supervisory body. After the decision is made, the local authority of ordinary residence must become the supervisory body. Regulations 17 to 19 of the Mental Capacity (Deprivation of Liberty: Standard Authorisations, Assessments and Ordinary Residence) Regulations 2008 set out, for England, arrangements that are to have effect while any question as to the ordinary residence of a person is determined in a case in which a local authority has received a request for a standard authorisation or a request to decide whether there is an unauthorised deprivation of liberty.

- whether deprivation of liberty is or may be necessary in a particular case
- what steps they should take to assess whether to seek authorisation
- whether they have taken all practical and reasonable steps to avoid a deprivation of liberty
- what action they should take if they do need to request an authorisation
- how they should review cases where authorisation is or may be necessary, and
- who should take the necessary action.

A flowchart that can be used to help develop such a procedure is at Annex 2.

What is the application process?

5–063 3.7 A managing authority must apply for a standard authorisation. The application should be made in writing to the supervisory body. A standard form is available for this purpose.

5–064 3.8 In England, the request from a managing authority for a standard authorisation must include:

- the name and gender of the relevant person
- the age of the relevant person or, where this is not known, whether the managing authority reasonably believes that the relevant person is aged 18 years or older
- the address at which the relevant person is currently located, and the telephone number at the address
- the name, address and telephone number of the managing authority and the name of the person within the managing authority who is dealing with the request
- the purpose for which the authorisation is requested
- the date from which the authorisation is sought, and
- whether the managing authority has given an urgent authorisation and, if so, the date on which it expires.

5–065 3.9 A request for a standard authorisation must also include, if it is available or could reasonably be obtained by the managing authority:

- any medical information relating to the relevant person's health that the managing authority reasonably considers to be relevant to the proposed restrictions to their liberty
- the diagnosis of the mental disorder (within the meaning of the Mental Health Act 1983 but disregarding any exclusion for persons with learning disability) from which the relevant person is suffering
- any relevant care plans and needs assessments
- the racial, ethnic or national origins of the relevant person
- whether the relevant person has any special communication needs
- details of the proposed restrictions on the relevant person's liberty
- whether it is necessary for an Independent Mental Capacity Advocate (IMCA) to be instructed
- where the purpose of the proposed restrictions to the relevant person's liberty is to give treatment, whether the relevant person has made an advance decision that may be valid and applicable to some or all of that treatment

- whether there is an existing standard authorisation in relation to the detention of the relevant person and, if so, the date of the expiry of that authorisation
- whether the relevant person is subject to any requirements of the Mental Health Act 1983, and
- the name, address and telephone number of:
  —anyone named by the relevant person as someone to be consulted about their welfare
  —anyone engaged in caring for the person or interested in their welfare any donee of a Lasting Power of Attorney ('donee') granted by the person
  —any deputy appointed for the person by the court, and
  —any IMCA who has already been instructed.

If there is an existing authorisation, information that has not changed does not have to be resupplied.

3.10 In Wales, the request from a managing authority for a standard authorisation must include: **5–066**
- the name of the relevant person
- the name, address and telephone number of the managing authority
- the reasons why the managing authority considers that the relevant person is being or will be detained in circumstances which amount to a deprivation of liberty
- the reasons why the managing authority considers that the relevant person satisfies the qualifying requirements
- details of any urgent authorisation
- information or documents in support of why the relevant person satisfies the qualifying requirements
- the name, address and telephone number of any person who has an interest in the welfare of the relevant person, and
- details of any relevant valid and applicable advance decision.

Where should applications be sent?

3.11 If the application is being made by a care home, the application must be sent to the local authority for the area in which the relevant person is ordinarily resident. If the relevant person is not ordinarily resident in the area of any local authority (for example, is of no fixed abode), if the care home does not know where the person currently lives, or if the person does not live in England or Wales, the application should be sent to the local authority in whose area the care home is located.   **5–067**

3.12 When the application is being made by a hospital: **5–068**
- if the care is commissioned by a PCT, the application should be sent to that PCT
- if the care is commissioned by the Welsh Ministers, the application should be sent to the LHB for the area in which the relevant person is ordinarily resident
- if the care is commissioned by an LHB, the application should be sent to that LHB, and
- in any other case (for example, care that is commissioned privately),

the application should be sent to the PCT for the area in which the relevant hospital is situated.

5–069   3.13 An application sent to the wrong supervisory body can be passed on to the correct supervisory body without the managing authority needing to reapply. But the managing authority should make every effort to establish which is the correct supervisory body to minimise delays in handling the application. (Footnote 8 explains how place of ordinary residence is determined and how disputes about the place of ordinary residence will be resolved.)

5–070   3.14 The managing authority must keep a written record of each request made for a standard authorisation and the reasons for making the request.

Who should be informed that an application has been made?

5–071   3.15 The managing authority should tell the relevant person's family, friends and carers, and any IMCA already involved in the relevant person's case, that it has applied for an authorisation of deprivation of liberty, unless it is impractical or impossible to do so, or undesirable in terms of the interests of the relevant person's health or safety. Anyone who is engaged in caring for the relevant person or interested in their welfare, or who has been named by them as a person to consult, must be given the opportunity to input their views on whether deprivation of liberty is in the best interests of the relevant person, as part of the best interests assessment (see paragraphs 4.58 to 4.76), as far as is practical and appropriate. The views of the relevant person about who to inform and consult should be taken into account.

5–072   3.16 The managing authority must notify the supervisory body if it is satisfied that there is no one who should be consulted in determining the relevant person's best interests, except those providing care and treatment for the relevant person in a professional capacity or for remuneration. In such a case, the supervisory body must instruct an IMCA to represent and support the relevant person before any assessments take place (see paragraphs 3.22 to 3.27 regarding the rights and role of an IMCA instructed in these circumstances).

What action does the supervisory body need to take when it receives an application for authorisation?

5–073   3.17 When it receives an application for authorisation of deprivation of liberty, the supervisory body must, as soon as is practical and possible:
- consider whether the request is appropriate and should be pursued, and
- seek any further information that it requires from the managing authority to help it with the decision.

If the supervisory body has any doubts about proceeding with the request, it should seek to resolve them with the managing authority.

5–074   3.18 Supervisory bodies should have a procedure in place that identifies the action they should take, who should take it and within what timescale. As far as practical and possible, they should communicate the procedure to managing authorities and give them the relevant contact details for making an application. The flowchart at Annex 3 summarises the process that a supervisory body should follow on receipt of a request from a managing authority for a standard deprivation of liberty authorisation.

Can an application for authorisation be made in advance?

3.19 A standard authorisation comes into force when it is given, or at any later **5–075** time specified in the authorisation. Paragraph 3.4 refers to the timescales for initially applying for authorisations: 28 days are allowed so that authorisations can usually be sought as part of care planning (such as planning of discharge from hospital). There is no statutory limit on how far in advance of the expiry of one authorisation a fresh authorisation can be sought. Clearly, however, an authorisation should not be applied for too far in advance as this may prevent an assessor from making an accurate assessment of what the person's circumstances will be at the time the authorisation will come into force.

3.20 If a supervisory body considers that an application for an authorisation **5–076** has been made too far in advance, it should raise the matter with the managing authority. The outcome may be an agreement with the managing authority that the application should be withdrawn, to be resubmitted at a more appropriate time.

What happens when the managing authority and the supervisory body are the same organisation?

3.21 In some cases, a single organisation will be both supervisory body and **5–077** managing authority—for example, where a local authority itself provides a residential care home, rather than purchasing the service from another organisation. This does not prevent it from acting in both capacities. However, in England the regulations specify that in such a situation the best interests assessor cannot be an employee of the supervisory body/ managing authority, or providing services to it. For example, in a case involving a local authority care home, the best interests assessor could be an NHS employee or an independent practitioner. (See paragraphs 4.13 and 4.60 for full details of who can be a best interests assessor.) There are similar provisions for Wales.

When should an IMCA be instructed?

3.22 If there is nobody appropriate to consult, other than people engaged **5–078** in providing care or treatment for the relevant person in a professional capacity[8] or for remuneration, the managing authority must notify the supervisory body when it submits the application for the deprivation of liberty authorisation. The supervisory body must then instruct an IMCA straight away to represent the person. It is particularly important that the IMCA is instructed quickly if an urgent authorisation has been given, so that they can make a meaningful input at a very early stage in the process.

---

[8] A friend or family member is **not** considered to be acting in a professional capacity simply because they have been appointed as the person's representative for a previous authorisation.

(See paragraph 3.28 for other stages in the deprivation of liberty safeguards process when an IMCA must or may be instructed.)

5–079   3.23 Chapter 10 of the main Code ('What is the new Independent Mental Capacity Advocate service and how does it work?') describes the wider rights and role of an IMCA. Supervisory bodies should follow the guidance in that chapter in identifying an IMCA who is suitably qualified to represent the relevant person. However, it is also important to note that an IMCA instructed at this initial stage of the deprivation of liberty safeguards process has additional rights and responsibilities compared to an IMCA more generally instructed under the Mental Capacity Act 2005. IMCAs in this context have the right to:

- as they consider appropriate, give information or make submissions to assessors, which assessors must take into account in carrying out their assessments
- receive copies of any assessments from the supervisory body
- receive a copy of any standard authorisation given by the supervisory body
- be notified by the supervisory body if they are unable to give a standard authorisation because one or more of the deprivation of liberty assessments did not meet the qualifying requirements
- receive a copy of any urgent authorisation from the managing authority
- receive from the managing authority a copy of any notice declining to extend the duration of an urgent authorisation
- receive from the supervisory body a copy of any notice that an urgent authorisation has ceased to be in force, and
- apply to the Court of Protection for permission to take the relevant person's case to the Court in connection with a matter relating to the giving or refusal of a standard or urgent authorisation (in the same way as any other third party can).

The assessment and authorisation processes are described in chapters 4 and 5.

5–080   3.24 IMCAs will need to familiarise themselves with the relevant person's circumstances and to consider what they may need to tell any of the assessors during the course of the assessment process. They will also need to consider whether they have any concerns about the outcome of the assessment process.

5–081   3.25 Differences of opinion between an IMCA and an assessor should ideally be resolved while the assessment is still in progress. Where there are significant disagreements between an IMCA and one or more of the assessors that cannot be resolved between them, the supervisory body should be informed before the assessment is finalised. The supervisory body should then consider what action might be appropriate, including perhaps convening a meeting to discuss the matter. Wherever possible, differences of opinion should be resolved informally in order to minimise the need for an IMCA to make an application to the Court of Protection. However, an IMCA should not be discouraged from making an application to the Court of Protection should they consider it necessary. (Chapter 15 of the main Code ('What are the best ways to settle disagreements and disputes about issues covered in the Act?') contains general guidance about the resolution of disputes arising under the Act.)

3.26 An IMCA will also need to consider whether they have any concerns about the giving of an urgent authorisation (see chapter 6), and whether it would be appropriate to challenge the giving of such an authorisation via the Court of Protection.   **5–082**

3.27 Once a relevant person's representative is appointed (see chapter 7), the duties imposed on the IMCA cease to apply. The IMCA may, however, still apply to the Court of Protection for permission to take the relevant person's case to the Court in connection with the giving of a standard authorisation; but, in doing so, the IMCA must take account of the views of the relevant person's representative.   **5–083**

Other circumstances in which an IMCA must or may be instructed

3.28 An IMCA must also be instructed during gaps in the appointment of a relevant person's representative (for instance, if a new representative is being sought—see paragraphs 7.34 to 7.36). In addition, an IMCA may be instructed at any time where: **5–084**
- the relevant person does not have a paid 'professional' representative
- the relevant person or their representative requests that an IMCA is instructed to help them, or
- a supervisory body believes that instructing an IMCA will help to ensure that the person's rights are protected (see paragraphs 7.37 to 7.41).

4.   WHAT IS THE ASSESSMENT PROCESS FOR A STANDARD AUTHORISATION OF DEPRIVATION OF LIBERTY?

When a supervisory body gives a standard authorisation of deprivation of liberty, the managing authority may lawfully deprive the relevant person of their liberty in the hospital or care home named in the authorisation.   **5–085**

This chapter describes the assessments that have to be undertaken in order for a standard authorisation to be given. It also sets out who is eligible to undertake the assessments.

What assessments are required before giving a standard authorisation?

4.1 As soon as the supervisory body has confirmed that the request for a standard authorisation should be pursued, it must obtain the relevant assessments to ascertain whether the qualifying requirements of the deprivation of liberty safeguards are met. The supervisory body has a legal responsibility to select assessors who are both suitable and eligible. Assessments must be completed within 21 days for a standard deprivation of liberty authorisation, or, where an urgent authorisation has been given, before the urgent authorisation expires.   **5–086**

4.2 The assessments (described in paragraphs 4.23 to 4.76) are: **5–087**
- age assessment (paragraphs 4.23 and 4.24)
- no refusals assessment (paragraphs 4.25 to 4.28).
- mental capacity assessment (paragraphs 4.29 to 4.32)
- mental health assessment (paragraphs 4.33 to 4.39)
- eligibility assessment (paragraphs 4.40 to 4.57), and
- best interests assessment (paragraphs 4.58 to 4.76).

Standard forms are available for completion by each of the assessors.

5–088   4.3 If the person being assessed is not currently in the supervisory body's area, the supervisory body should seek, as far as is practical and possible, to arrange to use assessors based near where the person currently is.

Using equivalent assessments

5–089   4.4 The Act states that where an 'equivalent assessment' to any of these assessments has already been obtained, it may be relied upon instead of obtaining a fresh assessment.

5–090   4.5 An equivalent assessment is an assessment:

- that has been carried out in the last 12 months, not necessarily for the purpose of a deprivation of liberty authorisation (where the required assessment is an age assessment, there is no time limit on the use of an equivalent assessment)
- that meets all the requirements of the deprivation of liberty assessment,
- of which the supervisory body is satisfied that there is no reason to believe that it is no longer accurate, and
- of which the supervisory body has a written copy.

An example would be a recent assessment carried out for the purposes of the Mental Health Act 1983, which could serve as an equivalent to a mental health assessment.

5–091   4.6 Great care should be taken in deciding to use an equivalent assessment and this should not be done routinely. The older the assessment is, even if it took place within the last 12 months, the less likely it is to represent a valid equivalent assessment (unless it is an age assessment). For example, only a very recent mental capacity assessment would be appropriate where capacity is known to fluctuate, since one of the principles of the Act is that a person must be assumed to have capacity unless it is established that they lack capacity.

5–092   4.7 If an equivalent best interests assessment is used, the supervisory body must also take into account any information given, or submissions made, by the relevant person's representative or an Independent Mental Capacity Advocate (IMCA) instructed under the deprivation of liberty safeguards.

5–093   4.8 Supervisory bodies should record the reasons why they have used any equivalent assessment. A standard form is available for this purpose.

When must assessments take place?

5–094   4.9 The regulations for England[9] specify that all assessments required for a standard authorisation must be completed within 21 calendar days from the date on which the supervisory body receives a request from a managing authority. The regulations for Wales specify that all assessments required for a standard authorisation must be completed within 21 days from the date the assessors were instructed by the supervisory body.

---

[9] The Mental Capacity (Deprivation of Liberty: Standard Authorisations, Assessments and Ordinary Residence) Regulations 2008.

4.10 However, if an urgent authorisation is already in force, the assessments must be completed before the urgent authorisation expires. The regulations for Wales specify that, where the managing authority has given itself an urgent authorisation and applies for a standard authorisation, the assessors must complete the assessments within five days of the date of instruction. **5–095**

4.11 Urgent authorisations may be given by managing authorities for an initial period not exceeding seven days. If there are exceptional reasons why it has not been possible to deal with the request for a standard authorisation within the period of the urgent authorisation, they may be extended **by the supervisory body** for up to a further seven days. It is for the supervisory body to decide what constitutes an 'exceptional reason', taking into account all the circumstances of an individual case. **5–096**

4.12 Supervisory bodies must keep a record of all requests for standard authorisations that they receive and should acknowledge the receipt of requests from managing authorities for standard authorisations. **5–097**

How should assessors be selected?

4.13 The six assessments do not have to be completed by different assessors. In fact, it is highly unlikely that there will be six separate assessors—not least because it is desirable to minimise the burden on the person being assessed. However, each assessor must make their own decisions, and to ensure that an appropriate degree of objectivity is brought to the assessment process: **5–098**

- there **must** be a minimum of two assessors
- the mental health and best interests assessors **must** be different people
- the best interests assessor can be an employee of the supervisory body or managing authority, but **must not** be involved in the care or treatment of the person they are assessing nor in decisions about their care
- a potential best interests assessor should not be used if they are in a line management relationship with the professional proposing the deprivation of liberty or the mental health assessor
- none of the assessors may have a financial interest in the case of the person they are assessing (a person is considered to have a financial interest in a case where that person is a partner, director, other office-holder or major shareholder of the managing authority that has made the application for a standard authorisation)
- an assessor **must not** be a relative of the person being assessed, nor of a person with a financial interest in the person's care. For this purpose, a 'relative' is:
    a. a spouse, ex-spouse, civil partner or ex-civil partner
    b. a person living with the relevant person as if they were a spouse or a civil partner
    c. a parent or child
    d. a brother or sister
    e. a child of a person falling within definitions a, b or d
    f. a grandparent or grandchild
    g. a grandparent-in-law or grandchild-in-law
    h. an aunt or uncle

    i. a sister-in-law or brother-in-law

    j. a son-in-law or daughter-in-law

    k. a first cousin, or

    l. a half-brother or half-sister.

These relationships include step-relationships

- where the managing authority and supervisory body are both the same body (see paragraph 3.21), the supervisory body may not select to carry out a best interests assessment a person who is employed by the body, or providing services to it, and

- the supervisory body should seek to avoid appointing assessors in any other possible conflict of interests situations that might bring into question the objectivity of an assessment.

5–099   4.14 Other relevant factors for supervisory bodies to consider when appointing assessors include:

- the reason for the proposed deprivation of liberty

- whether the potential assessor has experience of working with the service user group from which the person being assessed comes (for example, older people, people with learning disabilities, people with autism, or people with brain injury)

- whether the potential assessor has experience of working with people from the cultural background of the person being assessed, and

- any other specific needs of the person being assessed, for example communication needs.

5–100   4.15 Supervisory bodies should ensure that sufficient assessors are available to meet their needs, and must be satisfied in each case that the assessors have the skills, experience, qualifications and training required by regulations to perform the function effectively. The regulations also require supervisory bodies to be satisfied that there is an appropriate criminal record certificate issued in respect of an assessor. It will be useful to keep a record of qualified assessors and their experience and availability. Supervisory bodies should consider making arrangements to ensure that assessors have the necessary opportunities to maintain their skills and knowledge (of legal developments, for example) and share, audit and review their practice.

5–101   4.16 Assessors act as individual professionals and are personally accountable for their decisions. Managing authorities and supervisory bodies must not dictate or seek to influence their decisions.

5–102   4.17 There is no reason in principle why interviews, examinations and fact-finding required as part of any deprivation of liberty safeguards assessment cannot serve more than one purpose, in order to avoid unnecessary burdens both on the person being assessed and on staff. However, if this does happen, all purposes of the interview or examination should be made clear to the relevant person, and to any family members, friends, carers or advocates supporting them.

Protection against liability

5–103   4.18 Nobody can or should carry out an assessment unless they are protected against any liabilities that might arise in connection with carrying out the assessment. Individual assessors will need to satisfy themselves, and any supervisory body that selects them as an assessor, that they are appropriately covered by either employers' or personal insurance.

What is the assessment process?

4.19 As indicated in paragraph 4.2, there are six assessments that must be conducted before a supervisory body can give an authorisation.   **5–104**

4.20 The assessments are set out in the order in which it will normally be most appropriate to complete them. In particular, it is recommended that the best interests assessment, which is likely to be the most time-consuming, is not started until there is a reasonable expectation that the other five qualifying requirements will be met.   **5–105**

4.21 But, ultimately, it is for the supervisory body to decide on the order in which the assessments should be undertaken and, in the light of the time available to complete the overall assessment process, the extent to which they should be undertaken to separate or simultaneous timescales. The supervisory body's decision about how many assessors will undertake the assessments (see paragraph 4.13) will also be a relevant factor.   **5–106**

4.22 The following paragraphs explain the assessment process.   **5–107**

Age assessment

4.23 The purpose of the age assessment is simply to confirm whether the relevant person is aged 18 or over. This is because, as paragraph 1.12 explains, the deprivation of liberty safeguards apply only to people aged 18 or over. For people under the age of 18, a different safeguards process applies. In most cases, this is likely to be a fairly straightforward assessment. If there is any doubt, age should be established by a birth certificate or other evidence that the assessor considers reliable. Where it is not possible to verify with any certainty whether a person is aged 18 or over, the assessor should base the assessment on the best of their knowledge and belief.   **5–108**

4.24 This assessment can be undertaken by anybody whom the supervisory body is satisfied is eligible to be a best interests assessor.   **5–109**

No refusals assessment

4.25 The purpose of the no refusals assessment is to establish whether an authorisation to deprive the relevant person of their liberty would conflict with other existing authority for decision-making for that person.   **5–110**

4.26 The following are instances of a conflict that would mean that a standard authorisation could not be given: **5–111**
   - If the relevant person has made **an advance decision to refuse treatment** that remains valid and is applicable to some or all of the treatment that is the purpose for which the authorisation is requested, then a standard authorisation cannot be given. See sections 24 to 26 of the Mental Capacity Act 2005 and chapter 9 of the main Code ('What does the Act say about advance decisions to refuse treatment?') for more information about advance decisions and when they are valid and applicable. Remember too that the deprivation of liberty authori-

sation does not, in itself, provide authority to treat the person (see paragraphs 5.10 to 5.13 of this Code).

- If any part of the proposal to deprive the person of their liberty (including any element of the care plan) would be in conflict with a **valid decision of a donee or a deputy** made within the scope of their authority, then a standard authorisation cannot be given. For example, if a donee or deputy decides that it would not be in the best interests of the relevant person to be in a particular care home, and that decision is within the scope of their authority, then the care plan will need to be reviewed with the donee or deputy.

5–112   4.27 If there is any such conflict, the no refusals assessment qualifying requirement will not be met and a standard authorisation for deprivation of liberty cannot be given.

5–113   4.28 The no refusals assessment can be undertaken by anybody that the supervisory body is satisfied is eligible to be a best interests assessor.

Mental capacity assessment

5–114   4.29 The purpose of the mental capacity assessment is to establish whether the relevant person lacks capacity to decide whether or not they should be accommodated in the relevant hospital or care home to be given care or treatment. The assessment refers specifically to the relevant person's capacity to make this decision at the time it needs to be made. The starting assumption should always be that a person has the capacity to make the decision.

5–115   4.30 Sections 1 to 3 of the Act set out how a person's capacity to make decisions should be determined. Chapter 4 of the main Code ('How does the Act define a person's capacity to make a decision and how should capacity be assessed?') gives further guidance on ways to assess capacity. When assessing the capacity of a person being considered for the deprivation of liberty safeguards, these guidelines should be followed.

5–116   4.31 The regulations for England specify that the mental capacity assessment can be undertaken by anyone who is eligible to act as a mental health or best interests assessor. In deciding who to appoint for this assessment, the supervisory body should take account of the need for understanding and practical experience of the nature of the person's condition and its impact on decision-making.

5–117   4.32 Supervisory bodies may wish to consider using an eligible assessor who already knows the relevant person to undertake this assessment, if they think it would be of benefit. This will primarily arise if somebody involved in the person's care is considered best placed to carry out a reliable assessment, using their knowledge of the person over a period of time. It may also help in reducing any distress that might be caused to the person if they were assessed by somebody they did not know.

Mental health assessment

5–118   4.33 The purpose of the mental health assessment is to establish whether the relevant person has a mental disorder within the meaning of the Mental Health Act 1983. That means any disorder or disability of mind, apart from dependence on alcohol or drugs. It includes all learning disabilities. This is not an assessment to determine whether the person requires mental health treatment.

4.34 A distinction can be drawn between the mental health assessment and the mental capacity assessment: **5–119**

- Although a person must have an impairment or disturbance of the functioning of the mind or brain in order to lack capacity, it does not follow that they automatically have a mental disorder within the meaning of the Mental Health Act 1983.
- The objective of the mental health assessment is to ensure that the person is medically diagnosed as being of 'unsound mind' and so comes within the scope of Article 5 of the European Convention on Human Rights.

4.35 In both England and Wales, the regulations specify that: **5–120**

- the mental health assessment must be carried out by a doctor, and
- the assessing doctor has to either be approved under section 12 of the Mental Health Act 1983, or be a registered medical practitioner with at least three years' post-registration experience in the diagnosis or treatment of mental disorder, such as a GP with a special interest. This includes doctors who are automatically treated as being section 12 approved because they are approved clinicians under the Mental Health Act 1983.

4.36 To be eligible to undertake assessments, in England a doctor will need to have completed the standard training for deprivation of liberty mental health assessors. Except in the 12 month period beginning with the date the doctor has successfully completed the standard training, the regulations for England also require the supervisory body to be satisfied that the doctor has, in the 12 months prior to selection, completed further training relevant to their role as a mental health assessor. In Wales, a doctor will need to have completed appropriate training and have appropriate skills and experience.   **5–121**

4.37 Supervisory bodies must consider the suitability of the assessor for the particular case (for example, whether they have experience relevant to the person's condition).   **5–122**

4.38 As with the mental capacity assessment, supervisory bodies may wish to consider using an eligible assessor who already knows the relevant person to undertake this assessment, if they think it would be of benefit.   **5–123**

4.39 The mental health assessor is required to consider how the mental health of the person being assessed is likely to be affected by being deprived of their liberty, and to report their conclusions to the best interests assessor. The mental health and best interests assessments cannot be carried out by the same person.   **5–124**

Eligibility assessment

4.40 This assessment relates specifically to the relevant person's status, or potential status, under the Mental Health Act 1983.   **5–125**

4.41 A person is not eligible for a deprivation of liberty authorisation if: **5–126**

- they are detained as a hospital in-patient under the Mental Health Act 1983, or

- the authorisation, if given, would be inconsistent with an obligation placed on them under the Mental Health Act 1983, such as a requirement to live somewhere else. This will only affect people who are on leave of absence from detention under the Mental Health Act 1983 or who are subject to guardianship, supervised community treatment or conditional discharge.

5–127 4.42 Where the proposed authorisation relates to a care home, or to deprivation of liberty in a hospital for non-mental health treatment, the eligibility assessment will simply be a matter of checking that authorisation would not be inconsistent with an obligation placed on the person under the Mental Health Act 1983.

5–128 4.43 When a person is subject to guardianship under the Mental Health Act 1983, their guardian can decide where they are to live, but cannot authorise deprivation of liberty and cannot require them to live somewhere where they are deprived of liberty unless that deprivation of liberty is authorised.

5–129 4.44 Occasionally, a person who is subject to guardianship and who lacks capacity to make the relevant decisions may need specific care or treatment in a care home or hospital that cannot be delivered without deprivation of liberty. This may be in a care home in which they are already living or in which the guardian thinks they ought to live, or it may be in a hospital where they need to be for physical health care. It may also apply if they need to be in hospital for mental health care. The process for obtaining a deprivation of liberty authorisation and the criteria to be applied are the same as for any other person.

5–130 4.45 If the proposed authorisation relates to deprivation of liberty in a hospital **wholly or partly for the purpose of treatment of mental disorder,** then the relevant person will not be eligible if:

- they object to being admitted to hospital, or to some or all the treatment they will receive there for mental disorder, **and**
- they meet the criteria for an application for admission under section 2 or section 3 of the Mental Health Act 1983 (unless an attorney or deputy, acting within their powers, had consented to the things to which the person is objecting).

5–131 4.46 In many cases, the relevant person will be able to state an objection. However, where the person is unable to communicate, or can only communicate to a limited extent, assessors will need to consider the person's behaviour, wishes, feelings, views, beliefs and values, both present and past, so far as they can be ascertained (see paragraphs 5.37 to 5.48 of the main Code for guidance on how to do this). If there is reason to think that a person would object if able to do so, then the person should be assumed to be objecting. Occasionally, it may be that the person's behaviour initially suggests an objection, but that this objection is in fact not directed at the treatment at all. In that case, the person should **not** be taken to be objecting.

5–132 4.47 Assessors should always bear in mind that their job is simply to establish whether the person objects to treatment or to being in hospital: whether that objection is reasonable or not is not the issue.

5–133 4.48 Even where a person does not object and a deprivation of liberty authorisation is possible, it should not be assumed that such an authorisation is invariably the correct course. There may be other factors that suggest that the Mental Health Act 1983 should be used (for example, where it is thought likely that the person will recover relevant capacity and will then refuse to consent to treatment, or where it is important for the hospital managers to have a formal power to retake a person who goes absent without leave). Further guidance on this is given in the Mental Health Act 1983 Code of Practice.

4.49 The eligibility assessor is not required to decide (or even consider) whether an application under the Mental Health Act 1983 would be in the person's best interests.   **5–134**

4.50 If the proposed authorisation relates to deprivation of liberty in a hospital **wholly or partly for the purpose of treatment of mental disorder,** then the person will also not be eligible if they are: **5–135**
- currently on leave of absence from detention under the Mental Health Act 1983
- subject to supervised community treatment, or
- subject to conditional discharge,

in which case powers of recall under the Mental Health Act 1983 should be used.

4.51 People on leave of absence from detention under the Mental Health Act 1983 or subject to supervised community treatment or conditional discharge are, however, eligible for the deprivation of liberty safeguards if they require treatment in hospital for a physical disorder.   **5–136**

Who can conduct an eligibility assessment?

4.52 The regulations for England specify that the eligibility assessment must be completed by: **5–137**
- a mental health assessor who is also a section 12 doctor, or
- a best interests assessor who is also an approved mental health professional (AMHP).

4.53 The assessment cannot be carried out by a non-section 12 doctor, even if they are qualified to be a mental health assessor, nor by a nonAMHP, even if they are qualified to be a best interests assessor. This will ensure that the eligibility assessor is sufficiently familiar with the Mental Health Act 1983, which will be particularly important in cases in which it appears that the powers available under the Mental Health Act 1983 may be more appropriate than the deprivation of liberty safeguards.   **5–138**

4.54 The eligibility assessment will often be carried out by the best interests assessor but, where this is not the case, the eligibility assessor must request the best interests assessor to provide any relevant eligibility information that the best interests assessor may have, and the best interests assessor must comply with this request.   **5–139**

What happens when people are assessed as ineligible?

4.55 If the eligibility assessor believes that the relevant person is not eligible, but (on the basis of the report of the best interests assessor) that they should nevertheless be deprived of liberty in their best interests, the eligibility assessor should immediately inform the supervisory body.   **5–140**

5–141   4.56 In the case of someone already subject to the Mental Health Act 1983, the eligibility assessor should inform the supervisory body with a view to contact being made with the relevant responsible clinician (i.e. the clinician in overall charge of the person's treatment) or, if the person is subject to guardianship, the relevant local social services authority. Otherwise, the assessor or supervisory body should take steps to arrange for the person to be assessed further with a view to an application being made for admission to hospital under the Mental Health Act 1983. Assessors will need to be familiar with local arrangements for doing this.

5–142   4.57 In some cases, even before the eligibility assessment is undertaken, it may be known that there is a chance that the person will have to be assessed with a view to an application under the Mental Health Act 1983 because the eligibility assessment might conclude that they are ineligible for a deprivation of liberty authorisation. In such cases, steps should be taken, where practical and possible, to arrange assessments in a way that minimises the number of separate interviews or examinations the person has to undergo.

Best interests assessment

5–143   4.58 The purpose of the best interests assessment is to establish, firstly, whether deprivation of liberty is occurring or is going to occur and, if so, whether:

- it is in the best interests of the relevant person to be deprived of liberty
- it is necessary for them to be deprived of liberty in order to prevent harm to themselves, and
- deprivation of liberty is a proportionate response to the likelihood of the relevant person suffering harm and the seriousness of that harm.

5–144   4.59 The best interests assessor is the person who is responsible for assessing what is in the best interests of a relevant person.

5–145   4.60 In both England and Wales, the best interests assessment must be undertaken by an AMHP, social worker, nurse, occupational therapist or chartered psychologist with the skills and experience specified in the regulations. In England, this includes at least two years' post-registration experience. In England, the supervisory body must also be satisfied that the assessor:

- is not suspended from the register or list relevant to the person's profession
- has successfully completed training that has been approved[10] by the Secretary of State to be a best interests assessor
- except in the 12 month period beginning with the date the person has successfully completed the approved training, has, in the 12 months prior to selection, completed further training relevant to their role as a best interests assessor, and
- has the skills necessary to obtain, evaluate and analyse complex evidence and differing views and to weigh them appropriately in decision-making.

---

[10] Approved courses can be found at: *http://www.dh.gov.uk/en/SocialCare/Deliveringadultsocialcare/ MentalCapacity / MentalCapacityActDeprivationofLibertySafeguards/index.htm.*

4.61 Section 4 of the Mental Capacity Act 2005 sets out the best interests   **5–146**
principles that apply for the purpose of the Act. Chapter 5 of the main
Code ('What does the Act mean when it talks about "best interests"?')
explains this in more detail, and, in particular, paragraph 5.13 of the main
Code includes a checklist of factors that need to be taken into account
in working out what is in a person's best interests. These principles and
guidance apply equally to working out a person's best interests for the
purpose of the deprivation of liberty safeguards. However, when it comes
to best interests around deprivation of liberty, additional factors apply,
including:

- whether any harm to the person could arise if the deprivation of liberty
  does not take place
- what that harm would be
- how likely that harm is to arise (i.e. is the level of risk sufficient to
  justify a step as serious as depriving a person of liberty?)
- what other care options there are which could avoid deprivation of
  liberty, and
- if deprivation of liberty is currently unavoidable, what action could be
  taken to avoid it in future.

Establishing whether deprivation of liberty is occurring

4.62 The first task of a best interests assessor is to establish whether depriva-   **5–147**
tion of liberty is occurring, or is likely to occur, since there is no point
in the assessment process proceeding further if deprivation of liberty is
not at issue. If the best interests assessor concludes that deprivation of
liberty is **not** occurring and is not likely to occur, they should state in their
assessment report to the supervisory body that deprivation of liberty is
not in the person's best interests because there is obviously a less restrictive option available. The best interests requirement will therefore not be
met in such a case.

4.63 To establish whether deprivation of liberty is occurring, or is likely to   **5–148**
occur, the best interests assessor must consult the managing authority of
the hospital or care home where the person is, or will be, accommodated
and examine any relevant needs assessments and care plans prepared
for the person. The best interests assessor must consider whether the
care plan and the manner in which it is being, or will be, implemented
constitutes a deprivation of liberty. If not, then no deprivation of liberty
authorisation is required for that care plan.

4.64 The managing authority and supervisory body must provide the best   **5–149**
interests assessor with any needs assessments or care plans that they have
undertaken or which have been undertaken on their behalf.

The best interests assessment process

4.65 If the best interests assessor considers that deprivation of liberty is occur-   **5–150**
ring, or is likely to occur, they should start a full best interests assessment.
In line with section 4(7) of the Act this involves seeking the views of a
range of people connected to the relevant person to find out whether they
believe that depriving the relevant person of their liberty is, or would be,

in the person's best interests to protect them from harm or to enable them to follow the care plan proposed. The best interests assessor should, as far as is practical and possible, seek the views of:

- anyone the person has previously named as someone they want to be consulted
- anyone involved in caring for the person
- anyone interested in the person's welfare (for example, family carers, other close relatives, or an advocate already working with the person), and
- any donee or deputy who represents the person.

5–151   4.66 This may mean that the best interests assessor needs to explain key aspects of the care plan and what it aims to do to the people being consulted. The best interests assessor should then take the views received into account as far as is practical and appropriate. It is essential that the best interests assessor provides an independent and objective view of whether or not there is a genuine justification for deprivation of liberty, taking account of all the relevant views and factors.

5–152   4.67 The best interests assessor must state in their assessment the name and address of every interested person whom they have consulted in carrying out the assessment.

5–153   4.68 Family and friends may not be confident about expressing their views: it is the responsibility of the best interests assessor to enable them to do so—using support to meet communication or language needs as necessary.

5–154 | **Scenario: Consulting around best interests**

Mr Simpson is 60 and has dementia with particularly poor short-term memory, which clinicians agree is most likely to be related to chronic excessive alcohol intake. After initial treatment in hospital, he has been admitted to a care home—a decision which he consented to.

However, though he had the mental capacity to consent to hospital admission, he has no insight into his dementia. He is unable to understand the health and safety implications of continuing to drink, and will do so heavily whenever he has access to alcohol and the money to buy it.

Although Mr Simpson had no access to alcohol in hospital, there is a pub within walking distance of the care home, which he visits and drinks in. When he returns to the home intoxicated, his behaviour can be very distressing and potentially dangerous to other residents. The care home staff believe that if this continues, there may be no other option than to return him to hospital under the Mental Health Act 1983.

The care home staff have asked Mr Simpson to drink only in moderation, but this has not proved successful; and the landlord has been asked not to serve him more than one drink but has refused to do so. The manager of the home is now considering a care plan to prevent Mr Simpson from leaving the home without an escort, and to prevent visits from friends who bring alcohol. He believes this would be in Mr Simpson's best interests.

Scenario: Consulting around best interests *(continued)*

As the pub is open all day, if this new care plan was adopted, Mr Simpson would be stopped from going out at all without an escort, even though he often goes to the shops and the park as well as the pub. Staffing levels are such that an escort would only be available on some days and for limited periods.

Mr Simpson's daughter, his closest relative, is concerned that these restrictions are excessive and would amount to a deprivation of liberty. She believes that having a drink and socialising in the pub is her father's 'only remaining pleasure', and is sure that, if he still had capacity, he would choose to carry on drinking, regardless of the health risks.

She requests a best interests meeting to consider whether a less restrictive care plan could still meet his needs.

At this meeting, Mr Simpson's community mental health nurse confirms that Mr Simpson is likely to lack capacity in relation to this particular issue, and advises that if he continues to drink to excess his dementia is likely to advance rapidly and his life expectancy will be reduced. However, small amounts of alcohol will not be significantly harmful.

The consensus is that the proposed restrictions would severely limit Mr Simpson's ability to maintain social contact and to carry on the life he has been used to, and that this would amount to deprivation of liberty. Bearing in mind his daughter's view, it is felt that it would not be in Mr Simpson's best interests to prevent him from having any alcohol at all. However, in view of the health risks and the likelihood that he would otherwise have to be detained in hospital, it would be in Mr Simpson's best interests to ensure that he does not get intoxicated. (The possibility of limiting his access to his money would be unacceptable since he retains the capacity to decide how to spend it in other ways.)

Discussion then focuses on ways of minimising restrictions so that he is still able to visit the pub, but drinks in moderation. The care home key worker says that when she has gone to the pub with Mr Simpson he has been fully co-operative and has had just one drink before coming back with her. It is therefore agreed that the home will provide an escort for him to visit the pub at least three times a week, and the shops and the park at other times, and that his daughter will be able to take him out at any time.

It is agreed that care home staff (in consultation with his daughter) will review Mr Simpson's care plan in two months' time and, if it is felt that increased restrictions are required, consider whether it is then necessary to request an authorisation for deprivation of liberty.

4.69   The best interests assessor must involve the relevant person in the assessment process as much as is possible and practical, and help them to participate in decision-making. The relevant person should be given the support needed to participate, using non-verbal means of communication where needed (see paragraphs 3.10 and 3.11 of the main Code) or the support of speech and language therapists. It may also help to involve others whom the relevant person already trusts and who are used to communicating with the relevant person.   **5–155**

4.70   The best interests assessor will need to consider the conclusions of the mental health assessor about how the person being assessed is likely to be affected by being deprived of their liberty. If the proposed care would   **5–156** involve the person being moved, then the assessor should consider the impact of the upheaval and of the journey itself on the person.

5–157 4.71 If the best interests assessment supports deprivation of liberty in the care home or hospital in question, the assessor must state what the maximum authorisation period should be in the case concerned. This must not exceed 12 months. The assessor should set out the reasons for selecting the period stated. This decision will be based on the information obtained during the consultation process—but should also reflect information from the person's care plan about how long any treatment or care will be required in circumstances that amount to a deprivation of liberty. It should also take into account any available indication of how likely it is that the relevant person's circumstances will change, including the expected progression of the illness or disability. The underlying principle is that deprivation of liberty should be for the minimum period necessary so, for the maximum 12-month period to apply, the assessor will need to be confident that there is unlikely to be a change in the person's circumstances that would affect the authorisation within that timescale.

The report of the best interests assessor

5–158 4.72 The best interests assessor must provide a report that explains their conclusion and their reasons for it. If they do not support deprivation of liberty, then their report should aim to be as useful as possible to the commissioners and providers of care in deciding on future action (for example, recommending an alternative approach to treatment or care in which deprivation of liberty could be avoided). It may be helpful for the best interests assessor to discuss the possibility of any such alternatives with the providers of care **during the assessment process**.

5–159 4.73 If the best interests assessor does not support deprivation of liberty, it would be good practice for their report to be included in the relevant person's care plan or case notes, to ensure that any views about how deprivation of liberty can be avoided are made clear to the providers of care and all relevant staff on an ongoing basis.

5–160 4.74 The best interests assessor may recommend that conditions should be attached to the authorisation. For example, they may make recommendations around contact issues, issues relevant to the person's culture or other major issues related to the deprivation of liberty, which—if not dealt with—would mean that the deprivation of liberty would cease to be in the person's best interests. The best interests assessor may also recommend conditions in order to work towards avoiding deprivation of liberty in future. But it is not the best interests assessor's role to specify conditions that do not directly relate to the issue of deprivation of liberty.

5–161 4.75 Conditions should not be a substitute for a properly constructed care plan (see paragraph 2.7 on good practice for care planning). In recommending conditions, best interests assessors should aim to impose the minimum necessary constraints, so that they do not unnecessarily prevent or inhibit the staff of the hospital or care home from responding appropriately to the person's needs, whether they remain the same or vary over time. It would be good practice for the best interests assessor to discuss any proposed conditions with the relevant personnel at the home or hospital before finalising the assessment, and to make clear in their report whether the rejection or variation of recommended conditions by the supervisory body would significantly affect the other conclusions they have reached.

4.76 Where possible, the best interests assessor should recommend someone to be appointed as the relevant person's representative (see chapter 7). The assessor should be well placed, as a result of the consultation process, to identify whether there is anybody suitable to take on this role. The appointment of the relevant person's representative cannot take place unless and until an authorisation is given. However, by identifying someone to take on this role at an early stage, the best interests assessor can help to ensure that a representative is appointed as soon as possible.   **5–162**

Scenario: Application for standard authorisation   **5–163**

Mrs Jackson is 87 years old and lives by herself in an isolated bungalow in a rural area. Over the past few years, staff at her local health centre have become increasingly concerned about her wellbeing and ability to look after herself. Her appearance has become unkempt, she does not appear to be eating properly and her house is dirty.

The community mental health team have attempted to gain her trust, but she is unwilling to engage with them. She has refused care workers entry to her home and declined their help with personal hygiene and household chores.

Because it is believed that she is a potential risk to herself, she is admitted to psychiatric hospital under section 2 of the Mental Health Act 1983 for assessment of her mental disorder.

Following the assessment, it is felt that Mrs Jackson requires further treatment for mental disorder. An application is made for her detention to be continued under section 3 of the Mental Health Act 1983. She is prescribed antipsychotic medication, but this seems to have little effect on her behaviour. She remains extremely suspicious of people to the point of being delusional. She is assessed as potentially having mild dementia, most probably of the Alzheimer type, but because there is no obvious benefit from anti-dementia medication, further treatment for mental disorder is felt unnecessary.

Mrs Jackson insists that she wishes to return to her own home, but given past failed attempts to gain her acceptance of support at home and her likely future mental deterioration, transfer to a care home is believed to be most appropriate.

A best interests meeting is held by the mental health team to consider her future care and placement, and the team's approved social worker and the instructed IMCA are invited. The meeting concludes that Mrs Jackson does not have sufficient mental capacity to make an informed decision on her stated wish to return home. There is no advance decision in existence, no Lasting Power of Attorney or court deputy appointed and no practical way of contacting her immediate family.

Scenario: Application for standard authorisation *(continued)*

An appropriate care home is identified. A care plan is developed to give Mrs Jackson as much choice and control over her daily living as possible. However, it is felt that the restrictions still necessary to ensure Mrs Jackson's wellbeing will be so intense and of such duration that a request for a standard deprivation of liberty authorisation should be made by the care home manager (the relevant managing authority).

The best interests assessor agrees that the proposed course of action is in Mrs Jackson's best interests and recommends a standard authorisation for six months in the first instance.

What guidelines are there relating to the work of assessors?

Access to records

5–164   4.77 All assessors may, at any reasonable time, examine and take copies of:
- any health record
- any record of, or held by, a local authority that was compiled in accordance with a social services function, and
- any record held by a care home

which they consider may be relevant to their assessment. Assessors should list in their assessment report what records they examined.

Recording and reporting assessments

5–165   4.78 As soon as possible after carrying out their assessments, assessors must keep a written record of the assessment and must give copies of their assessment report(s) to the supervisory body. The supervisory body must in turn give copies of the assessment report(s) to:
- the managing authority
- the relevant person and their representative, and
- any IMCA instructed

at the same time that it gives them copies of the deprivation of liberty authorisation or notification that an authorisation is not to be given (see paragraphs 5.7 and 5.18 respectively).

5.   WHAT SHOULD HAPPEN ONCE THE ASSESSMENTS ARE COMPLETE?

5–166   If all the assessments in the standard authorisation assessment process indicate that the relevant person meets all the qualifying requirements, then the supervisory body will give a deprivation of liberty authorisation. If any of the qualifying requirements are not met, however, different actions will need to be taken, depending on the circumstances of the individual case.

This chapter identifies potential outcomes of the assessment process and offers guidance on what should happen next.

What action should the supervisory body take if the assessments conclude that the person meets the requirements for authorisation?

5.1   If all the assessments conclude that the relevant person meets the require-   **5–167** ments for authorisation, and the supervisory body has written copies of all the assessments, it must give a standard authorisation. A standard form is available for this purpose.

5.2   The supervisory body cannot give a standard authorisation if any of the   **5–168** requirements are not fulfilled.

5.3   The supervisory body must set the period of the authorisation, which may   **5–169** not be longer than that recommended by the best interests assessor (see paragraph 4.71).

5.4   When the supervisory body gives a standard authorisation, it must do so   **5–170** in writing and must state the following:
- the name of the relevant person
- the name of the relevant hospital or care home
- the period during which the authorisation is to be in force (which may not exceed the period recommended by the best interests assessor)
- the purpose for which the authorisation is given (i.e. why the person needs to be deprived of their liberty)
- any conditions subject to which the authorisation is given (see paragraph 5.5), and
- the reason why each qualifying requirement is met.

5.5   The supervisory body may attach conditions to the authorisation. Before   **5–171** deciding whether to give the authorisation subject to conditions, the supervisory body must consider any recommendations made by the best interests assessor (see paragraph 4.74). Where the supervisory body does not attach conditions as recommended by the best interests assessor, it should discuss the matter with the best interests assessor in case the rejection or variation of the conditions would significantly affect the other conclusions the best interests assessor reached in their report.

5.6   It is the responsibility of the supervisory body to appoint a representative   **5–172** for the relevant person (see chapter 7).

5.7   As soon as possible after giving the authorisation, the supervisory body   **5–173** must give a copy of the authorisation to:
- the managing authority
- the relevant person
- the relevant person's representative
- any Independent Mental Capacity Advocate (IMCA) involved, and
- every interested person named by the best interests assessor in their report as somebody they have consulted in carrying out their assessment.

The supervisory body must also keep a written record of any standard authorisation that it gives and of the matters referred to in paragraph 5.4.

5.8   The managing authority must take all practical and possible steps to   **5–174** ensure that the relevant person understands the effect of the authorisation and their rights around it. These include their right to challenge the authorisation via the Court of Protection, their right to request a review, and their right to have an IMCA instructed, along with the process for doing so (see paragraphs 7.37 to 7.41). Appropriate information must be given to the relevant person both orally and in writing. Any written information must also be given to the relevant person's representative. This must happen as soon as possible and practical after the authorisation is given.

How long can an authorisation last?

5–175   5.9   A deprivation of liberty should last for the shortest period possible. The best interests assessor should only recommend authorisation for as long as the relevant person is likely to meet all the qualifying requirements. The authorisation may be for quite a short period. A short period may, for example, be appropriate if:
- the reason that the deprivation of liberty is in the person's best interests is because their usual care arrangements have temporarily broken down, or
- there are likely to be changes in the person's mental disorder in the relatively near future (for example, if the person is in rehabilitation following brain injury).

What restrictions exist on authorisations?

5–176   5.10 A deprivation of liberty authorisation—whether urgent or standard—relates solely to the issue of deprivation of liberty. It does not give authority to treat people, nor to do anything else that would normally require their consent. The arrangements for providing care and treatment to people in respect of whom a deprivation of liberty authorisation is in force are subject to the wider provisions of the Mental Capacity Act 2005.

5–177   5.11 This means that any treatment can only be given to a person who has not given their consent if:
- it is established that the person lacks capacity to make the decision concerned
- it is agreed that the treatment will be in their best interests, having taken account of the views of the person and of people close to them, and, where relevant in the case of serious medical treatment, of any IMCA involved
- the treatment does not conflict with a valid and applicable advance decision to refuse treatment, and
- the treatment does not conflict with a decision made by a donee of Lasting Power of Attorney or a deputy acting within the scope of their powers.

5–178   5.12 In deciding what is in a person's best interests, section 4 of the Act applies in the same way as it would if the person was not deprived of liberty. The guidance in chapter 5 of the main Code on assessing best interests is also relevant.

5–179   5.13 Life-sustaining treatment, or treatment to prevent a serious deterioration in the person's condition, may be provided while a decision in respect of any relevant issue is sought from the Court of Protection. The need to act in the best interests of the person concerned will continue to apply in the meantime.

Can a person be moved to a different location under a standard authorisation?

5.14 If a person who is subject to a standard authorisation moves to a different hospital or care home, the managing authority of the new hospital or care home must request a new standard authorisation. The application should be made **before** the move takes place. **5–180**

5.15 If the move has to take place so urgently that this is impossible, the managing authority of the new hospital or care home will need to give an urgent authorisation (see chapter 6). **5–181**

5.16 The only exception is if the care regime in the new facility will not involve deprivation of liberty. **5–182**

5.17 These arrangements are not an alternative to applying the provisions of sections 38 and 39 of the Act regarding change of residence. **5–183**

What happens if an assessment concludes that one of the requirements is not met?

5.18 If any of the assessments conclude that one of the requirements is not met, then the assessment process should stop immediately and authorisation may not be given. The supervisory body should: **5–184**
  • inform anyone still engaged in carrying out an assessment that they are not required to complete it
  • notify the managing authority, the relevant person, any IMCA involved and every interested person consulted by the best interests assessor that authorisation has not been given (a standard form is available for this purpose), and
  • provide the managing authority, the relevant person and any IMCA involved with copies of those assessments that have been carried out. This must be done as soon as possible, because in some cases different arrangements will need to be made for the person's care.

5.19 If the reason the standard authorisation cannot be given is because the eligibility requirement is not met, it may be necessary to consider making the person subject to the Mental Health Act 1983. If this is the case, it may be possible to use the same assessors to make that decision, thereby minimising the assessment processes. **5–185**

What are the responsibilities of the managing authority and the commissioners of care if a request for an authorisation is turned down?

5.20 The managing authority is responsible for ensuring that it does not deprive a person of their liberty without an authorisation. The managing authority must comply with the law in this respect: where a request for an authorisation is turned down, it will need to review the relevant person's actual or proposed care arrangements to ensure that a deprivation of liberty is not allowed to either continue or commence. **5–186**

5.21 Supervisory bodies and other commissioners of care will need to purchase care packages in a way that makes it possible for managing authorities to comply with the outcome of the deprivation of liberty safeguards assessment process when a request for a standard authorisation is turned down. **5–187**

5–188   5.22 The actions that both managing authorities and commissioners of care should consider if a request for an authorisation is turned down will depend on the reason why the authorisation has not been given:

- If the best interests assessor concluded that the relevant person was not in fact being, or likely to be, deprived of liberty, no action is likely to be necessary.
- If the best interests assessor concluded that the proposed or actual deprivation of liberty was not in the relevant person's best interests, the managing authority, in conjunction with the commissioner of the care, will need to consider how the care plan could be changed to avoid deprivation of liberty. (See, for example, the guidance on practical ways to reduce the risk of deprivation of liberty in paragraph 2.7.) They should examine carefully the reasons given in the best interests assessor's report, and may find it helpful to discuss the matter with the best interests assessor. Where appropriate, they should also discuss the matter with family and carers. If the person is not yet a resident in the care home or hospital, the revised care plan may not involve admission to that facility unless the conditions of care are adapted to be less restrictive and deprivation of liberty will not occur.
- If the mental capacity assessor concluded that the relevant person **has** capacity to make decisions about their care, the care home or hospital will need to consider, in conjunction with the commissioner of the care, how to support the person to make such decisions.
- If the relevant person was identified as not eligible to be subject to a deprivation of liberty authorisation, it may be appropriate to assess whether an application should be made to detain the person under the Mental Health Act 1983.
- If the relevant person does not have a mental disorder as defined in the Mental Health Act 1983, the care plan will need to be modified to avoid a deprivation of liberty, since there would be no lawful basis for depriving a person of liberty in those circumstances.
- Where there is a valid refusal by a donee or deputy, or an applicable and valid advance decision (see paragraphs 4.25 to 4.28), alternative care arrangements will need to be made. If there is a question about the refusal, a decision may be sought from the Court of Protection.
- If the person is under 18, use of the Children Act 1989 may be considered.

5–189   5.23 Working out what action should be taken where a request for a standard deprivation of liberty authorisation is turned down in respect of a 'self-funder' may present particular problems, because the managing authority may not be able to make alternative care arrangements without discussing them with those controlling the funding, whether relatives of the person concerned or others. The desired outcome should be the provision of a care regime that does not constitute deprivation of liberty.

5–190   5.24 Where the best interests assessor comes to the conclusion that the best interests requirement is not met, but it appears to the assessor that the person being assessed is already being deprived of their liberty, the assessor must inform the supervisory body and explain in their report why they have reached that conclusion. The supervisory body must then inform the managing authority to review the relevant person's care plan immediately so that unauthorised deprivation of liberty does not continue. Any necessary changes must be made urgently to stop what would be an unlawful deprivation of liberty. The steps taken to stop the deprivation of liberty should be recorded in the care plan. Where possible, family, friends and carers should be involved in deciding how to prevent the unauthorised deprivation of liberty from continuing. If the supervisory body has any doubts about whether the matter is being satisfactorily resolved within an appropriately urgent timescale, it should alert the inspection body (see chapter 11).

6. WHEN CAN URGENT AUTHORISATIONS OF DEPRIVATION OF LIBERTY BE GIVEN?

Wherever possible, applications for deprivation of liberty authorisations should be made before the deprivation of liberty commences. However, where deprivation of liberty unavoidably needs to commence before a standard authorisation can be obtained, an urgent authorisation can be given which will make the deprivation of liberty lawful for a short period of time. **5–191**

This chapter contains guidance on the rules around urgent authorisations.

When can an urgent authorisation be given?

6.1 A managing authority can itself give an urgent authorisation for deprivation of liberty where: **5–192**
- it is required to make a request to the supervisory body for a standard authorisation, but believes that the need for the person to be deprived of their liberty is so urgent that deprivation needs to begin before the request is made, or
- it has made a request for a standard authorisation, but believes that the need for a person to be deprived of liberty has now become so urgent that deprivation of liberty needs to begin before the request is dealt with by the supervisory body.

This means that an urgent authorisation can never be given without a request for a standard authorisation being made simultaneously. Therefore, before giving an urgent authorisation, a managing authority will need to have a reasonable expectation that the six qualifying requirements for a standard authorisation are likely to be met.

6.2 Urgent authorisations should normally only be used in response to sudden unforeseen needs. However, they can also be used in care planning (for example, to avoid delays in transfer for rehabilitation, where delay would reduce the likely benefit of the rehabilitation). **5–193**

6.3 However, an urgent authorisation should not be used where there is no expectation that a standard deprivation of liberty authorisation will be needed. Where, for example: **5–194**
- a person who lacks capacity to make decisions about their care and treatment has developed a mental disorder as a result of a physical illness, and
- the physical illness requires treatment in hospital in circumstances that amount to a deprivation of liberty, and
- the treatment of that physical illness is expected to lead to rapid resolu-

tion of the mental disorder such that a standard deprivation of liberty authorisation would not be required,

it would not be appropriate to give an urgent authorisation simply to legitimise the short-term deprivation of liberty.

5–195 6.4 Similarly, an urgent deprivation of liberty authorisation should not be given when a person is, for example, in an accident and emergency unit or a care home, and it is anticipated that within a matter of a few hours or a few days the person will no longer be in that environment.

5–196 6.5 Any decision to give an urgent authorisation and take action that deprives a person of liberty must be in the person's best interests, as set out in section 4 of the Mental Capacity Act 2005. Where restraint is involved, all actions must comply with the additional conditions in section 6 of the Act (see chapter 6 of the main Code).

5–197 6.6 The managing authority must decide the period for which the urgent authorisation is given, but this must not exceed seven days (see paragraphs 6.20 to 6.28 regarding the possible extension of the seven-day period). The authorisation must be in writing and must state:

- the name of the relevant person
- the name of the relevant hospital or care home
- the period for which the authorisation is to be in force, and
- the purpose for which the authorisation is given.

A standard form is available for a managing authority to use to notify a supervisory body that it has given an urgent authorisation.

5–198 6.7 Supervisory bodies and managing authorities should have a procedure in place that identifies:

- what actions should be taken when an urgent authorisation needs to be made
- who should take each action, and
- within what timescale.

What records should be kept about urgent authorisations?

5–199 6.8 The managing authority must keep a written record of any urgent authorisations given, including details of why it decided to give an urgent authorisation. They must give a copy of the authorisation to the relevant person and any IMCA instructed, and place a copy in the relevant person's records. The managing authority must also seek to ensure that, as far as possible, the relevant person understands the effect of the authorisation and the right to challenge the authorisation via the Court of Protection. Appropriate information must be given both orally and in writing.

5–200 6.9 The managing authority should, as far as possible and appropriate, notify the relevant person's family, friends and carers when an urgent authorisation is given in order to enable them to offer informed support to the person.

5–201 6.10 The processes surrounding the giving and receiving of urgent authorisations should be clearly recorded, and regularly monitored and audited, as part of a managing authority's or supervisory body's governance structure.

Who should be consulted before giving an urgent authorisation?

6.11 If the managing authority is considering depriving a person of liberty in 5–202
an emergency and giving an urgent authorisation, they must, as far as
is practical and possible, take account of the views of anyone engaged
in caring for the relevant person or interested in their welfare. The aim
should be to consult carers and family members at as early a stage as
possible so that their views can be properly taken into account before a
decision to give an urgent authorisation is taken.

6.12 The steps taken to involve family, friends or carers should be recorded 5–203
in the relevant person's records, along with their views. The views of the
carers will be important because their knowledge of the person will put
them in a good position to gauge how the person will react to the deprivation of their liberty, and the effect it will have on their mental state. It may
also be appropriate to consult any staff who may have some involvement
in the person's case.

6.13 The ultimate decision, though, will need to be based on a judgement of 5–204
what is in the relevant person's best interests. The decision-maker from
the managing authority will need to be able to show that they have made
a reasonable decision based on their professional judgement and taking
account of all the relevant factors. This is an important decision, because
it could mean the deprivation of a person's liberty without, at this stage,
the full deprivation of liberty safeguards assessment process having taken
place. The decision should therefore be taken at a senior level within the
managing authority.

Scenario: Urgent authorisation followed by short-term standard authori- 5–205
sation

Mr Baker is 75, widowed and lives near his only family—his daughter. He is
admitted to hospital having been found by his daughter on his kitchen floor. He
is uncharacteristically confused and is not able to give a reliable history of what
has happened. He has a routine physical examination, as well as blood and urine
investigations, and is diagnosed as having a urinary tract infection. He is given
antibiotics, but his nursing care is complicated by his fluctuating confusion. Once
or twice he removes his clothes and walks through the ward naked, and at times he
tries to leave the ward, unaware that he is in hospital, and believing that he is late
for an important work meeting. During more lucid moments, however, he knows
where he is and accepts the need for investigation and treatment in hospital.

The responsible consultant, in consultation with ward nursing staff and
Mr Baker's daughter, feels that it would be in his best interests to place him
in a side room to protect his dignity, and restrict his movements to ensure he
remains on the ward.

However, after two days, his confusion appears to worsen: he starts having
hallucinations and has to be restrained more often by staff to prevent him
leaving the ward. After assessment by a doctor from the liaison psychiatry team,
Mr Baker is prescribed antipsychotic medication for his own and other patients'
safety. He does not resist taking this medication. The likely benefits and possible
side effects are discussed with his daughter and, on balance, the medication is
felt to be in his best interests in order to continue his medical investigations.

Scenario: Urgent authorisation followed by short-term standard authorisation *(continued)*

Staff become concerned about the level of restriction of liberty Mr Baker is now subject to. In particular, they are concerned about the duration of the restrictions; the fact that Mr Baker no longer has lucid intervals when he can give his consent to ongoing care and treatment in hospital; and the physical restraint that is still being required on occasion.

After discussion between the ward manager and Mr Baker's daughter, the managing authority gives an urgent authorisation and submits a request for a standard authorisation to the supervisory body (PCT). A best interests assessor is appointed, and the liaison psychiatrist provides the mental health and mental capacity assessments. In making all the deprivation of liberty safeguards assessments to see whether the qualifying requirements are met, it is considered that although restraint is being used, this does not mean he is objecting having regard to all the circumstances, so he is not ineligible and a standard authorisation is given.

Can a person be moved into care under an urgent authorisation?

5–206   6.14 There may be cases in which managing authorities are considering giving an urgent authorisation to enable them to move the relevant person to a new type of care. This may occur, for example, when considering whether to admit a person living at home or with relatives into a hospital care regime that would deprive them of their liberty, and when the need for admission appears to be so urgent that there would not be enough time to follow the standard authorisation process.

5–207   6.15 For some people, such a change of location may have a detrimental effect on their mental health, which might significantly distort the way they come across during any assessment process. In such a case, managing authorities should consider whether giving the urgent authorisation and admitting the person to hospital would outweigh the benefits of leaving the person in their existing location, where any assessment of their needs might be more accurate. This will involve looking carefully at the existing care arrangements and consulting with any carers involved, to establish whether or not the person could safely and beneficially be cared for in their home environment while the assessment process takes place. Where the relevant person is already known to statutory care providers, for example the community mental health team or social services, it will be important to involve them in this decision-making process. The relevant person's GP may also be an important source of knowledge about the person's situation, and may be able to offer a valuable opinion when the appropriateness of moving the person into a different care setting is under consideration.

What happens at the end of an urgent authorisation period?

5–208   6.16 An urgent authorisation will terminate at the end of the period for which it is given. As noted above, this is normally a maximum of seven days, but in exceptional circumstances an urgent authorisation can be extended to a maximum of 14 days **by the supervisory body,** as explained in paragraphs 6.20 to 6.28.

6.17 An urgent authorisation will terminate before this time if the standard authorisation applied for is given.   **5–209**

6.18 An urgent authorisation will also terminate if a managing authority receives notice from the supervisory body that the standard authorisation will not be given. It will not then be lawful to continue to deprive the relevant person of their liberty.   **5–210**

6.19 The supervisory body must inform the relevant person and any IMCA instructed that the urgent authorisation has ended. This notification can be combined with the notification to them of the outcome of the application for standard authorisation.   **5–211**

Scenario: Considering an urgent authorisation   **5–212**

Mr Watson is 35. He has autism and learning disabilities. He lives in the family home with his parents. Although he is well settled and generally calm at home, Mr Watson sometimes becomes disturbed when in an unfamiliar and crowded environment.

While his parents are away for a couple of days, and Mr Watson is in the care of a paid carer, he has an accident at home. His carer is concerned that he may have broken his arm and takes him to the A&E department at the local hospital, where it is decided that his arm needs to be X-rayed to check for a break. The outcome is that there is no break, just bad bruising, so there is no medical need to admit him.

However, because of the pain he is in and the crowded environment, Mr Watson has become very agitated to the extent that hospital security personnel feel a need to control him physically. The carer tries to restrain him and lead him outside where she says he is likely to be more settled and calm down.

Because restraint is being used, the A&E doctor wonders whether it his duty to use an urgent authorisation or other measure to detain Mr Watson in hospital if he believes it is in his best interests.

He consults a liaison psychiatry nurse, who reassures him that such restraint is permitted under the Mental Capacity Act 2005 where it is necessary to prevent harm to the person himself and so long as it is a proportionate response. The nurse assists the carer with gentle restraint to take Mr Watson to a quieter area. She suggests the doctor phone Mr Watson's parents for further information, and obtains painkillers for Mr Watson.

The doctor speaks to Mr Watson's parents, who believe that Mr Watson does not have the mental capacity to decide on his care and treatment in the current circumstances. They have experienced similar situations many times, and are confident that Mr Watson will calm down once he is back in his home environment. They state that if any more detailed assessment of his mental state is required it should take place there, in the company of the carer whom they know and trust. They reassure the doctor that Mr Watson is highly unlikely to present a danger to himself, his carer or the general public.

The doctor decides that it will be in Mr Watson's best interests to return home with his carer.

How and when can an urgent authorisation be extended?

5–213   6.20 If there are exceptional reasons why the request for a standard authorisation cannot be dealt with within the period of the original urgent authorisation, the managing authority may ask the supervisory body to extend the duration of the urgent authorisation for a maximum of a further seven days. The managing authority must keep a written record of the reason for making the request and must notify the relevant person, in writing, that they have made the request. Standard forms are available for managing authorities to request the extension of an urgent authorisation from a supervisory body and for supervisory bodies to record their decision in response to such a request.

5–214   6.21 Unless the duration of the urgent authorisation is extended by the supervisory body, or a standard authorisation is given before the urgent authorisation expires, the authority to deprive the person of liberty will cease once the urgent authorisation period has expired. It is therefore essential that any request for an extension of an urgent authorisation is made promptly. This will necessitate good communication between the managing authority and the supervisory body regarding the progress of the standard authorisation assessment process. Particular care may need to be taken where an urgent authorisation is due to expire over the weekend or on a bank holiday, when appropriate people at the managing authority and supervisory body may not be immediately available.

5–215   6.22 The supervisory body may only extend the duration of the urgent authorisation if:
- the managing authority has made a request for a standard authorisation
- there are exceptional reasons why it has not yet been possible to make a standard authorisation, and
- it is essential for the deprivation of liberty to continue while the supervisory body makes its decision.

5–216   6.23 Extensions can only be granted for exceptional reasons. An example of when an extension would be justified might be where:
- it was not possible to contact a person whom the best interests assessor needed to contact
- the assessment could not be relied upon without their input, and
- extension for the specified period would enable them to be contacted.

5–217   6.24 It is for the supervisory body to decide what constitutes an 'exceptional reason', but because of the seriousness of the issues involved, the supervisory body's decision must be soundly based and defensible. It would not, for example, be appropriate to use staffing shortages as a reason to extend an urgent authorisation.

5–218   6.25 An urgent authorisation can only be extended once.

5–219   6.26 The supervisory body must notify the managing authority of the length of any extension granted and must vary the original urgent authorisation so that it states the extended duration. The supervisory body must also keep a written record of the outcome of the request and the period of the extension.

5–220   6.27 The managing authority must give a copy of the varied urgent authorisation to the relevant person and any IMCA instructed, and must seek to ensure that, as far as possible, the relevant person understands the effect of the varied authorisation and the right to challenge the authorisation via the Court of Protection. The appropriate information must be given both orally and in writing.

6.28 If the supervisory body decides not to extend the urgent authorisation, it must inform the managing authority of its decision and the reasons for it. The managing authority must give a copy of the notice to the relevant person and any IMCA involved.   **5–221**

7. WHAT IS THE ROLE OF THE RELEVANT PERSON'S REPRESENTATIVE?

Once a standard deprivation of liberty authorisation has been given, supervisory bodies must appoint the relevant person's representative as soon as possible and practical to represent the person who has been deprived of their liberty.   **5–222**

This chapter explains the role of the relevant person's representative and gives guidance on their selection and appointment.

What is the role of the relevant person's representative?

7.1 The supervisory body must appoint a relevant person's representative for every person to whom they give a standard authorisation for deprivation of liberty. It is important that the representative is appointed at the time the authorisation is given or as soon as possible and practical thereafter.   **5–223**

7.2 The role of the relevant person's representative, once appointed, is: **5–224**
- to maintain contact with the relevant person, and
- to represent and support the relevant person in all matters relating to the deprivation of liberty safeguards, including, if appropriate, triggering a review, using an organisation's complaints procedure on the person's behalf or making an application to the Court of Protection.

This is a crucial role in the deprivation of liberty process, providing the relevant person with representation and support that is independent of the commissioners and providers of the services they are receiving.

7.3 The best interests principle of the Act applies to the relevant person's representative in the same way that it applies to other people acting or making decisions for people who lack capacity.   **5–225**

How should managing authorities work with the relevant person's representative?

7.4 As soon as possible and practical after a standard deprivation of liberty authorisation is given, the managing authority must seek to ensure that the relevant person and their representative understand: **5–226**
- the effect of the authorisation
- their right to request a review (see chapter 8)
- the formal and informal complaints procedures that are available to them
- their right to make an application to the Court of Protection to seek variation or termination of the authorisation (see chapter 10), and
- their right, where the relevant person does not have a paid 'professional' representative, to request the support of an Independent Mental Capacity Advocate (IMCA) (see paragraphs 7.37 to 7.41).

5–227   7.5   When providing information to the person and their representative, the managing authority should take account of the communication and language needs of both the person and their representative. Provision of information should be seen as an ongoing responsibility, rather than a one-off activity.

Who can be the relevant person's representative?[11]

5–228   7.6   To be eligible to be the relevant person's representative, a person must be:
- 18 years of age or over
- able to keep in contact with the relevant person, and
- willing to be appointed.

The person must not be:
- financially interested in the relevant person's managing authority (a person is considered to be financially interested where that person is a partner, director, other office-holder or major shareholder of the managing authority)
- a relative of a person who has a financial interest in the relevant person's managing authority (paragraph 4.13 explains what is meant by 'relative')
- employed by, or providing services to, the care home in which the person relevant person is residing
- employed by the hospital in a role that is, or could be, related to the treatment or care of the relevant person, or
- employed to work in the relevant person's supervisory body in a role that is, or could be, related to the relevant person's case.

5–229   7.7   The appointment of the relevant person's representative is in addition to, and does not affect, any appointment of a donee or deputy. Similarly, the functions of the representative are in addition to, and do not affect, the authority of any donee, the powers of any deputy or any powers of the court. A donee or deputy may themselves be appointed as the relevant person's representative if they meet the eligibility criteria set out in paragraph 7.6.

5–230   7.8   There is no presumption that the relevant person's representative should be the same as the person who is their nearest relative for the purposes of the Mental Health Act 1983, even where the relevant person is likely to be subject simultaneously to an authorisation under these safeguards and a provision of the Mental Health Act 1983. This is because the relevant person's representative is not selected in the same way as the nearest relative under the Mental Health Act 1983, nor do they perform the same role. However, there is nothing to stop the relevant person's representative being the same as their nearest relative under the Mental Health Act 1983.

---

[11] Requirements relating to the eligibility, selection and appointment of relevant person's representatives are covered in regulations. The regulations for England are The Mental Capacity (Deprivation of Liberty: Appointment of Relevant Person's Representative) Regulations 2008. The regulations for Wales are The Mental Capacity (Deprivation of Liberty: Appointment of Relevant Person's Representative) (Wales) Regulations 2008.

When should the relevant person's representative be identified?

7.9 The process of identifying a representative must begin as soon as possible. **5–231**

7.10 Normally, this should be when the best interests assessor is appointed—even if one or more of the other assessments has not yet been completed. This is because the best interests assessor must, as part of the assessment process, identify if there is anyone they would recommend to become the relevant person's representative. The best interests assessor should discuss the representative role with the people interviewed as part of the assessment. **5–232**

7.11 This does leave a risk that the process to identify a representative might begin in cases where authorisation is not given. Nevertheless, it is important that the process begins, so that the representative can be appointed immediately the authorisation is given or as soon as possible and practical thereafter. **5–233**

How should the relevant person's representative be selected?

7.12 The best interests assessor should first establish whether the relevant person has the capacity to select their own representative and, if so, invite them to do so. If the relevant person has capacity and selects an eligible person (according to the criteria set out in paragraph 7.6), the best interests assessor must recommend that person to the supervisory body for appointment. **5–234**

7.13 Alternatively, if the relevant person lacks capacity and there is a donee or deputy with the appropriate authority, the donee or deputy may select the person to be recommended as the relevant person's representative, again subject to the criteria set out in paragraph 7.6.
If a donee or deputy selects an eligible person, then the best interests assessor must recommend that person to the supervisory body for appointment. **5–235**

7.14 It is up to the best interests assessor to confirm whether any representative proposed by the relevant person, a donee or a deputy is eligible. If the best interests assessor decides that a proposed representative is not eligible, they must advise the person who made the selection and invite them to make a further selection. **5–236**

7.15 If neither the relevant person, nor a donee or deputy, selects an eligible person, then the best interests assessor must consider whether they are able to identify someone eligible who could act as the relevant person's representative. **5–237**

7.16 In making a recommendation, the assessor should consider, and balance, factors such as: **5–238**
- Does the relevant person have a preference?
- If they do not have the capacity to express a preference now, is there any written statement made by the relevant person when they had capacity that indicates who they may now want to be their representative?
- Will the proposed representative be able to keep in contact with the relevant person?

- Does the relevant person appear to trust and feel comfortable with the proposed representative?
- Would the proposed representative be able to represent the relevant person effectively?
- Is the proposed representative likely to represent the relevant person's best interests?

In most cases, the best interests assessor will be able to check at the same time that the proposed representative is willing to take on the role.

5–239   7.17 It should not be assumed that the representative needs to be someone who supports the deprivation of liberty.

5–240   7.18 The best interests assessor must not select a representative where the relevant person, if they have the capacity to do so, or a donee or a deputy acting within the scope of their authority, states they are not content with that selection.

5–241   7.19 If the best interests assessor is unable to recommend anybody to be the relevant person's representative, they must notify the supervisory body accordingly. The supervisory body must then itself identify an eligible person to be appointed as the representative. In doing so, the supervisory body may select a person who:

- would be performing the role in a professional capacity
- has satisfactory skills and experience to perform the role
- is not a family member, friend or carer of the relevant person
- is not employed by, or providing services to, the relevant person's managing authority, where the relevant person's managing authority is a care home
- is not employed to work in the relevant person's managing authority in a role that is, or could be, related to the relevant person's case, where the relevant person's managing authority is a hospital
- is not employed to work in the supervisory body that is appointing the representative in a role that is, or could be, related to the relevant person's case, and
- the supervisory body is satisfied that an appropriate criminal record certificate has been issued in respect of.

5–242   7.20 The supervisory body may pay a person they select to be the relevant person's representative in the circumstances set out in paragraph 7.19. This service could be commissioned, for example, through an advocacy services provider, ensuring that the service provides effective independent representation for the relevant person.

5–243   7.21 When selecting a suitable representative for the relevant person, the best interests assessor or supervisory body should pay particular attention to the communication and cultural needs of the relevant person.

How should the relevant person's representative be appointed?

5–244   7.22 The supervisory body must invite, in writing, the person recommended by the best interests assessor to become the relevant person's representative. If the best interests assessor does not recommend anyone, then the supervisory body should identify and appoint someone to undertake the role. If the person is willing to become the representative, the supervisory body must formally appoint them. If the person refuses, a further eligible person must be identified and invited to become the representative. This process must continue until an eligible person is appointed.

7.23 The appointment of the relevant person's representative by the supervisory body must be in writing and set out the role and responsibilities of the relevant person's representative. The letter of appointment should also state the name of the appointed person and the date of expiry of the appointment, which must be for the period of the standard authorisation that has been given. The supervisory body must send copies of the written appointment to: **5–245**

- the appointed person
- the relevant person
- any donee or deputy of the relevant person
- any IMCA involved
- every interested person named by the best interests assessor in their report as somebody they have consulted in carrying out their assessment, and
- the managing authority of the relevant hospital or care home.

7.24 The relevant person's representative must confirm to the supervisory body in writing that they are willing to accept the appointment and have understood their roles and responsibilities in respect of the relevant person. **5–246**

How should the work of the relevant person's representative be supported and monitored?

7.25 It is important that the representative has sufficient contact with the relevant person to ensure that the relevant person's best interests are being safeguarded. In order to fulfil their role, therefore, the representative will need to be able to have face-to-face contact with the relevant person. That means that the care home or hospital should accommodate visits by the representative at reasonable times. The name of the person's representative should be recorded in the person's health and social care records. **5–247**

7.26 Managing authorities and supervisory bodies should inform the relevant person's representative about sources of support and information available to help them in the role, including how to access the support of an IMCA (see paragraphs 7.37 to 7.41). **5–248**

7.27 If the representative has insufficient contact with the relevant person, for whatever reason, the person may effectively be unable to access important review and appeal rights. For this reason, if the representative does not maintain an appropriate level of contact with the person, the managing authority will need to consider informing the supervisory body. When the managing authority is reviewing the person's care plan, it should consider whether the representative is in sufficient contact with the relevant person to offer effective support. Records kept by managing authorities about frequency of contact will support this consideration. **5–249**

7.28 Because the appropriate levels and methods of contact between a relevant person and their representative will vary from case to case, this is a matter about which the managing authority will need to exercise discretion. If the managing authority has any concerns, it may be best to raise the **5–250** matter with the representative initially to see whether any perceived problems can be resolved informally. If after this the representative still does not maintain what the managing authority considers to be an appropriate level of contact with the relevant person, then the managing authority should notify the supervisory body.

When can the appointment of the relevant person's representative be terminated?

5–251   7.29 The appointment of the relevant person's representative will be terminated in any of the following circumstances:
- The standard authorisation comes to an end and a new authorisation is not applied for or, if applied for, is not given.
- The relevant person, if they have capacity to do so, objects to the representative continuing in their role and a different person is selected to be their representative instead.
- A donee or deputy, if it is within their authority to do so and the relevant person lacks the capacity to decide, objects to the representative continuing in their role and a different person is selected to be the representative instead.
- The supervisory body becomes aware that the representative is no longer willing or eligible to continue in the role.
- The supervisory body becomes aware that the relevant person's representative is not keeping in touch with the person, is not representing and supporting them effectively or is not acting in the person's best interests.
- The relevant person's representative dies.

5–252   7.30 If the supervisory body becomes aware that the representative may not be keeping in touch with the person, is not acting in the relevant person's best interests, or is no longer eligible, it should contact the representative to clarify the position before deciding whether to terminate the appointment.

5–253   7.31 When the appointment of the relevant person's representative ends, the supervisory body must give notice to all those listed in paragraph 7.23. This notice should be given as soon as possible, stating when the appointment ended and the reason why.

5–254   7.32 When the appointment of a relevant person's representative ends but the lawful deprivation of liberty continues, the supervisory body must appoint a suitable replacement to be the relevant person's representative as soon as possible and practical after they become aware of the vacancy. As before, a person qualified to be a best interests assessor should make a recommendation to the supervisory body and the supervisory body should take account of any such recommendations.

5–255   7.33 If the reason for the termination of the former representative's appointment is that they are no longer eligible, the views of the former representative on who might replace them should be sought. The person identified as most suitable should then be invited to accept the appointment. This process should continue until an eligible person is willing to accept appointment.

What happens when there is no relevant person's representative available?

7.34 A person who is being deprived of their liberty will be in a particularly **5–256** vulnerable position during any gaps in the appointment of the relevant person's representative, since there may be nobody to represent their interests or to apply for a review on their behalf. In these circumstances, if there is nobody who can support and represent the person (other than a person engaged in providing care and treatment for the relevant person in a professional capacity or for remuneration), the managing authority must notify the supervisory body, who must instruct an IMCA to represent the relevant person until a new representative is appointed.

7.35 The role of an IMCA instructed in these circumstances is essentially the **5–257** same as that of the relevant person's representative. The role of the IMCA in this situation ends when the new relevant person's representative is appointed.

7.36 At any time when the relevant person does not have a representative, it **5–258** will be particularly important for supervisory bodies to consider exercising their discretion to carry out a review if there is any significant change in the person's circumstances.

When should an IMCA be instructed?

7.37 Both the person who is deprived of liberty under a standard authorisation **5–259** and their representative have a statutory right of access to an IMCA. It is the responsibility of the supervisory body to instruct an IMCA if the relevant person or their representative requests one. The intention is to provide extra support to the relevant person or a family member or friend acting as their representative if they need it, and to help them make use of the review process or access the Court of Protection safeguards. Where the relevant person has a paid 'professional' representative (see paragraphs 7.19 and 7.20), the need for additional advocacy support should not arise and so there is no requirement for an IMCA to be provided in those circumstances.

7.38 The role of the IMCA is to help represent the relevant person and, in par- **5–260** ticular, to assist the relevant person and their representative to understand the effect of the authorisation, what it means, why it has been given, why the relevant person meets the criteria for authorisation, how long it will last, any conditions to which the authorisation is subject and how to trigger a review or challenge in the Court of Protection. The IMCA can also provide support with a review (see chapter 8) or with an application to the Court of Protection (see chapter 10), for example to help the person to communicate their views.

7.39 The IMCA will have the right to make submissions to the supervisory **5–261** body on the question of whether a qualifying requirement should be reviewed, or to give information, or make submissions, to any assessor carrying out a review assessment. Both the person and their representative must be told about the IMCA service and how to request an IMCA.

7.40 An IMCA must be instructed whenever requested by the relevant person **5–262** or their representative. A request may be made more than once during the period of the authorisation. For example, help may be sought at the start of the authorisation and then again later in order to request a review.

5–263 7.41 In addition, if the supervisory body has reason to believe that the review and Court of Protection safeguards might not be used without the support of an IMCA, then they must instruct an IMCA. For example, if the supervisory body is aware that the person has selected a representative who needs support with communication, it should consider whether an IMCA is needed.

8. WHEN SHOULD AN AUTHORISATION BE REVIEWED AND WHAT HAPPENS WHEN IT ENDS?

5–264 When a person is deprived of their liberty, the managing authority has a duty to monitor the case on an ongoing basis to see if the person's circumstances change—which may mean they no longer need to be deprived of their liberty.

The managing authority must set out in the care plan clear roles and responsibilities for monitoring and confirm under what circumstances a review is necessary. For example, if a person's condition is changing frequently, then their situation should be reviewed more frequently.

This chapter explains the duties of managing authorities and supervisory bodies in relation to reviewing cases, and what happens when an authorisation ends. The review process is set out in flowchart form at Annex 4.

When should a standard authorisation be reviewed?

5–265 8.1 A standard authorisation can be reviewed at any time. The review is carried out by the supervisory body.

8.2 There are certain statutory grounds for carrying out a review. If the statutory grounds for a review are met, the supervisory body must carry out a review. If a review is requested by the relevant person, their representative or the managing authority, the supervisory body must carry out a review. Standard letters are available for the relevant person or their representative to request a review. There is also a standard form available for the managing authority to request a review. A supervisory body can also decide to carry out a review at its own discretion.

5–266 8.3 The statutory grounds for a review are:

- The relevant person no longer meets the age, no refusals, mental capacity, mental health or best interests requirements.
- The relevant person no longer meets the eligibility requirement because they now object to receiving mental health treatment in hospital and they meet the criteria for an application for admission under section 2 or section 3 of the Mental Health Act 1983 (see paragraphs 4.45 to 4.48).
- There has been a change in the relevant person's situation and, because of the change, it would be appropriate to amend an existing condition to which the authorisation is subject, delete an existing condition or add a new condition.
- The reason(s) the person now meets the qualifying requirement(s)

582

is(are) different from the reason(s) given at the time the standard authorisation was given.

8.4 Different arrangements apply if the person no longer meets the eligibility requirement because they have been detained under the Mental Health Act, or become subject to a requirement under that Act that conflicts with the authorisation. (See paragraphs 8.19 to 8.21 regarding the short-term suspension of a standard authorisation.)   **5–267**

8.5 A managing authority must request a review if it appears to it that one or more of the qualifying requirements is no longer met, or may no longer be met.   **5–268**

What happens when a review is going to take place?

8.6 The supervisory body must tell the relevant person, their representative and the managing authority if they are going to carry out a review. This must be done either before the review begins or as soon as possible and practical after it has begun. A standard form is available for this purpose.   **5–269**

8.7 The relevant person's records must include information about any formal reviews that have been requested, when they were considered, and the outcome. These records must be retained by the supervisory body.   **5–270**

8.8 Deprivation of liberty can be ended before a formal review. An authorisation only **permits** deprivation of liberty: it does not mean that a person **must be** deprived of liberty where circumstances no longer necessitate it. If a care home or hospital decides that deprivation of liberty is no longer necessary then they must end it immediately, by adjusting the care regime or implementing whatever other change is appropriate. The managing authority should then apply to the supervisory body to review and, if appropriate, formally terminate the authorisation.   **5–271**

How should standard authorisations be reviewed?

8.9 When a supervisory body receives a request for a review, it must first decide which, if any, of the qualifying requirements need to be reviewed. A standard form is available for recording this decision.   **5–272**

8.10 If the supervisory body concludes that none of the qualifying requirements need to be reviewed, no further action is necessary. For example, if there has been a very recent assessment or review and no new evidence has been submitted to show that the relevant person does not meet the criteria, or that circumstances have changed, no review is required.   **5–273**

8.11 If it appears that one or more of the qualifying requirements should be reviewed, the supervisory body must arrange for a separate review assessment to be carried out for each of these requirements.   **5–274**

8.12 The supervisory body must record when a review is requested, what it decides to do (whether it decides to carry out a review or not) and the reasons for its decision.   **5–275**

8.13 In general, review processes should follow the standard authorisation processes—so supervisory bodies should conduct the assessments outlined in chapter 4 of this Code of Practice for each of the qualifying requirements that need to be reviewed.   **5–276**

5–277   8.14 Where the supervisory body decides that the best interests requirement should be reviewed solely because details of the **conditions** attached to the authorisation need to be changed, and the review request does not include evidence that there is a significant change in the relevant person's overall circumstances, there is no need for a full reassessment of best interests. The supervisory body can simply vary the conditions attached to the authorisation as appropriate. In deciding whether a full reassessment is necessary, the supervisory body should consider whether the grounds for the authorisation, or the nature of the conditions, are being contested by anyone as part of the review request.

5–278   8.15 If the review relates to any of the other requirements, or to a significant change in the person's situation under the best interests requirement, the supervisory body must obtain a new assessment.

5–279   8.16 If the assessment shows that the requirement is still met, the supervisory body must check whether the reason that it is met has changed from the reason originally stated on the authorisation. If it has, the supervisory body should make any appropriate amendments to the authorisation. In addition, if the review relates to the best interests requirement, the supervisory body must consider whether any conditions should be changed following the new assessment.

5–280   **Scenario: The review process**

Jo is 29 and sustained severe brain damage in a road traffic collision that killed her parents. She has great difficulty in verbal and written communication. Jo can get very frustrated and has been known to lash out at other people in the nursing care home where she now lives. At first, she regularly attempted to leave the home, but the view of the organisation providing Jo's care was that such a move would place her at serious risk, so she should be prevented from leaving.

Jo was assessed under the deprivation of liberty safeguards and an authorisation was made for six months. That authorisation is not due to end for another three months. However, Jo has made huge progress at the home and her representative is no longer sure that the restrictions are necessary. Care home staff, however, do not think that her improvement reduces the best interests requirement of the deprivation of liberty authorisation.

Jo is assisted by her representative to request a review, in the form of a letter with pictures. The pictures appear to describe Jo's frustration with the legal processes that she perceives are preventing her from moving into her own accommodation.

The supervisory body appoints a best interests assessor to coordinate the review. The best interests assessor considers which of the qualifying requirements needs to be reviewed and by whom. It appears that the best interests assessment, as well as possibly the mental health and mental capacity assessments, should be reviewed.

To assess Jo's mental capacity and her own wishes for the best interests assessment, the best interests assessor feels that specialist help would be beneficial. A speech and language therapist meets with Jo and uses a visual communication system with her. Using this system, the therapist is able to say that in her view Jo is unlikely to have capacity to make the decision to leave the care home. The mental health assessment also confirmed that Jo was still considered to have a mental disorder.

Scenario: The review process *(continued)*

The best interests assessor was uncertain, however, whether it was still in Jo's best interests to remain under the deprivation of liberty authorisation. It was not possible to coordinate full updated assessments from the rehabilitation team, who knew her well, in the time limits required. So, because the care home believed that the standard authorisation was still required, and it was a complex case, the best interests assessor recommended to the supervisory body that two conditions should be applied to the standard authorisation:

- assessments must be carried out by rehabilitation specialists on Jo's clinical progress, and
- a full case review should be held within one month.

At this review meeting, to which Jo's representative and the best interests assessor were invited, it was agreed that Jo had made such good progress that deprivation of liberty was no longer necessary, because the risks of her having increased freedom had reduced. The standard authorisation was therefore terminated, and a new care plan was prepared which focused on working towards more independent living.

What happens if any of the requirements are not met?

8.17 If any of the requirements are not met, then the authorisation must be terminated immediately. **5–281**

8.18 The supervisory body must give written notice of the outcome of a review and any changes that have been made to the deprivation of liberty authorisation to: **5–282**

- the managing authority and the care home or hospital itself
- the relevant person
- the relevant person's representative, and
- any Independent Mental Capacity Advocate (IMCA) involved.

Short-term suspension of authorisation

8.19 There are separate review arrangements for cases in which the eligibility requirement ceases to be met for a short period of time for reasons other than that the person is objecting to receiving mental health treatment in hospital. For example, if the relevant person is detained as a hospital in-patient under the Mental Health Act 1983, the managing authority must notify the supervisory body, who will suspend the authorisation. **5–283**

8.20 If the relevant person then becomes eligible again within 28 days, the managing authority must notify the supervisory body who will remove the suspension. If no such notice is given within 28 days, then the authorisation will be terminated. Standard forms are available for managing authorities to notify supervisory bodies about the need for suspension of an authorisation, or that a suspension should be lifted. **5–284**

8.21 If the person ceases to meet the eligibility requirement because they begin to object to receiving mental health treatment in hospital and they meet the criteria for an application for admission under section 2 or section 3 of the Mental Health Act 1983, a review should be started immediately (see paragraph 8.3). **5–285**

Is a review necessary when the relevant person's capacity fluctuates?

5–286   8.22 Guidance about people with fluctuating or temporary capacity is contained in paragraphs 4.26 and 4.27 of the main Code. In the context of deprivation of liberty safeguards, where a relevant person's capacity to make decisions about the arrangements made for their care and treatment fluctuates on a short-term basis, a balance needs to be struck between:
- the need to review and terminate an authorisation if a person regains capacity, and
- spending time and resources constantly reviewing, terminating and then seeking fresh deprivation of liberty authorisations as the relevant person's capacity changes.

5–287   8.23 Each case must be treated on its merits. Managing authorities should keep all cases under review: where a person subject to an authorisation is deemed to have regained the capacity to decide about the arrangements made for their care and treatment, the managing authority must assess whether there is consistent evidence of the regaining of capacity on a longer-term basis. This is a clinical judgement that will need to be made by a suitably qualified person.

5–288   8.24 Where there is consistent evidence of regaining capacity on this longer-term basis, deprivation of liberty should be lifted immediately, and a formal review and termination of the authorisation sought. However, it should be borne in mind that a deprivation of liberty authorisation carries with it certain safeguards that the relevant person will lose if the authorisation is terminated. Where the regaining of capacity is likely to be temporary, and the authorisation will be required again within a short period of time, the authorisation should be left in place, but with the situation kept under ongoing review.

5–289 | **Scenario: Fluctuating capacity**

Walter, an older man with severe depression, is admitted to hospital from a care home. He seems confused and bewildered, but does not object. His family are unable to look after him at home, but they would prefer him to go into a different care home rather than stay in hospital. However, there is no alternative placement available, so when the assessment concludes that Walter lacks capacity to make decisions about his care and treatment, the only option seems to be that he should stay on the ward.

Because the care regime in the ward is extremely restrictive—Walter is not allowed to leave the hospital and his movement within the hospital is restricted for his own safety—ward staff think that they need to apply for a deprivation of liberty authorisation which is subsequently given.

However, over time Walter starts to experience lucid passages, during which he expresses relief at being on the ward rather than in the care home. A review meeting is convened and the participants agree that Walter now sometimes has capacity to make decisions about the arrangements made for his care and treatment. As this capacity fluctuates, it is decided, in consultation with his family, that the deprivation of liberty authorisation should remain in place for the time being.

Scenario: Fluctuating capacity *(continued)*

Walter remains on the ward and his progress is such that his family feel they could look after him at home. Walter seems happy with this proposal and the consultant psychiatrist with responsibility for his care agrees to this. The deprivation of liberty authorisation is reviewed and terminated.

What happens when an authorisation ends?

8.25 When an authorisation ends, the managing authority cannot lawfully continue to deprive a person of their liberty. **5–290**

8.26 If the managing authority considers that a person will still need to be deprived of liberty after the authorisation ends, they need to request a further standard authorisation to begin immediately after the expiry of the existing authorisation. **5–291**

8.27 There is no statutory time limit on how far in advance of the expiry of one authorisation the managing authority can apply for a renewal authorisation. It will need to be far enough in advance for the renewal authorisation to be given before the existing authorisation ends (but see paragraphs 3.19 and 3.20 about not applying for authorisations too far in advance). **5–292**

8.28 Once underway, the process for renewing a standard authorisation is the same as that for obtaining an original authorisation, and the same assessment processes must take place. However, the need to instruct an IMCA will not usually arise because the relevant person should at this stage have a representative appointed. **5–293**

8.29 When the standard authorisation ends, the supervisory body must inform in writing: **5–294**
- the relevant person
- the relevant person's representative
- the managing authority, and
- every interested person named by the best interests assessor in their report as somebody they have consulted in carrying out their assessment.

9. WHAT HAPPENS IF SOMEONE THINKS A PERSON IS BEING DEPRIVED OF THEIR LIBERTY WITHOUT AUTHORISATION?

It is a serious issue to deprive someone of their liberty without authorisation if they lack the capacity to consent. If anyone believes that a person is being deprived of their liberty without authorisation, they should raise this with the relevant authorities. **5–295**

If the conclusion is that the person is being deprived of their liberty unlawfully, this will normally result in a change in their care arrangements, or in an application for a deprivation of liberty authorisation being made.

This chapter explains the process for reporting concerns and for assessing whether unauthorised deprivation of liberty is occurring. The flowchart at Annex 3 summarises the process that a supervisory body should follow when it receives a request from somebody other than the managing authority to examine whether or not there is a current unauthorised deprivation of liberty.

What action should someone take if they think a person is being deprived of their liberty without authorisation?

5–296   9.1   If the relevant person themselves, any relative, friend or carer or any other third party (such as a person carrying out an inspection visit or a member of an advocacy organisation) believes that a person is being deprived of liberty without the managing authority having applied for an authorisation, they should draw this to the attention of the managing authority. A standard letter is available for this purpose. In the first instance, they should ask the managing authority to apply for an authorisation if it wants to continue with the care regime, or to change the care regime immediately. Given the seriousness of deprivation of liberty, a managing authority must respond within a reasonable time to the request. This would normally mean within 24 hours.

5–297   9.2   It may be possible for the managing authority to resolve the matter informally with the concerned person. For example, the managing authority could discuss the case with the concerned person, and perhaps make some adjustment to the care arrangements so that concerns that a deprivation of liberty may be occurring are removed. However, if the managing authority is unable to resolve the issue with the concerned person quickly, they should submit a request for a standard authorisation to the supervisory body.

5–298   9.3   If the concerned person has raised the matter with the managing authority, and the managing authority does not apply for an authorisation within a reasonable period, the concerned person can ask the supervisory body to decide whether there is an unauthorised deprivation of liberty. They should:

- tell the supervisory body the name of the person they are concerned about and the name of the hospital or care home, and
- as far as they are able, explain why they think that the person is deprived of their liberty.

A standard letter is available for this purpose.

5–299   9.4   In such circumstances, the supervisory body must select and appoint a person who is suitable and eligible to carry out a best interests assessment to consider whether the person is deprived of liberty.

5–300   9.5   The supervisory body does not, however, need to arrange such an assessment where it appears to the supervisory body that:

- the request they have received is frivolous or vexatious (for example, where the person is very obviously not deprived of their liberty) or where a very recent assessment has been carried out and repeated requests are received, or
- the question of whether or not there is an unauthorised deprivation of liberty has already been decided, and since that decision, there has been no change of circumstances that would merit the question being considered again.

The supervisory body should record the reasons for their decisions. A standard form is available for this purpose.

5–301   9.6   The supervisory body must notify the person who raised the concern, the relevant person, the managing authority of the relevant hospital or care home and any IMCA involved:

- that it has been to asked to assess whether or not there is an unauthorised deprivation of liberty
- whether or not it has decided to commission an assessment, and
- where relevant, who has been appointed as assessor.

What happens if somebody informs the supervisory body directly that they think a person is being deprived of their liberty without authorisation?

9.7 If a person raises concerns about a potential unauthorised deprivation of **5–302** liberty directly with the supervisory body, the supervisory body should immediately arrange a preliminary assessment to determine whether a deprivation of liberty is occurring. The supervisory body should then immediately notify the managing authority, rather than asking the concerned person to contact the managing authority themselves, to ask them to request a standard authorisation in respect of the person who is possibly deprived of liberty. The supervisory body should agree with the managing authority what is a reasonable period within which a standard authorisation should be requested (unless the managing authority is able to resolve the matter informally with the concerned person as described in paragraph 9.2). If the managing authority does not submit an application within the agreed period, and the matter has not been resolved informally, the supervisory body should follow the process set out in paragraphs 9.3 to 9.6 to assess whether unlawful deprivation of liberty is occurring. Even if the concerned person prefers to deal directly with the managing authority, the supervisory body should monitor what happens very closely to ensure that no unlawful deprivation of liberty may be occurring without proper action being taken.

How will the assessment of unlawful deprivation of liberty be conducted?

9.8 An assessment of whether an unlawful deprivation of liberty is occurring **5–303** must be carried out within seven calendar days. Although the assessment must be completed by somebody who is suitable and eligible to carry out a best interests assessment, it is not a best interests assessment as such. The purpose of the assessment is simply to establish whether unlawful deprivation of liberty is occurring.

9.9 The person nominated to undertake the assessment must consult the **5–304** managing authority of the relevant hospital or care home, and examine any relevant needs assessments and care plans to consider whether they constitute a deprivation of liberty. They should also speak to the person who raised the concern about why they believe that the relevant person is being deprived of their liberty and consult, as far as is possible, with the relevant person's family and friends. If there is nobody appropriate to consult among family and friends, they should inform the supervisory body who must arrange for an IMCA to be instructed to support and represent the person. A standard form is available for the assessor to record the outcome of their assessment.

What happens once the assessment has been conducted?

5–305   9.10 There are three possible outcomes of this assessment. The assessor may conclude that:

- the person is not being deprived of their liberty
- the person is being lawfully deprived of their liberty because authorisation exists (this, though, is an unlikely outcome since the supervisory body should already be aware if any authorisation exists, thus rendering any assessment in response to a third party request unnecessary), or
- the person is being deprived of their liberty unlawfully.

5–306   9.11 The supervisory body must notify the following people of the outcome of the assessment:

- the concerned third party who made the request
- the relevant person
- the managing authority of the relevant hospital or care home, and
- any IMCA involved. A standard form is available for this purpose.

5–307   9.12 If the outcome of the assessment is that there is an unauthorised deprivation of liberty, then the full assessment process should be completed as if a standard authorisation for deprivation of liberty had been applied for—unless the managing authority changes the care arrangements so that it is clear that there is no longer any deprivation of liberty.

5–308   9.13 If, having considered what could be done to avoid deprivation of liberty, the managing authority decides that the need to continue the deprivation of liberty is so urgent that the care regime should continue while the assessments are carried out, it must give an urgent authorisation and seek a standard authorisation within seven days. The managing authority must supply the supervisory body with the same information it would have had to include in a request for a standard authorisation.

5–309   9.14 If the concerned person does not accept the outcome of their request for assessment, they can apply to the Court of Protection to hear their case. See chapter 10 for more details of the role of the Court of Protection.

10.   WHAT IS THE COURT OF PROTECTION AND WHEN CAN PEOPLE APPLY TO IT?

5–310   To comply with Article 5(4) of the European Convention on Human Rights, anybody deprived of their liberty in accordance with the safeguards described in this Code of Practice is entitled to the right of speedy access to a court that can review the lawfulness of their deprivation of liberty. The Court of Protection, established by the Mental Capacity Act 2005, is the court for this purpose. Chapter 8 of the main Code provides more details on its role, powers and responsibilities.

When can people apply to the Court of Protection about the deprivation of liberty safeguards and who can apply? Applying before an authorisation is given

5–311   10.1 The relevant person, or someone acting on their behalf, may make an application to the Court of Protection **before** a decision has been reached on an application for authorisation to deprive a person of their liberty. This might be to ask the court to declare whether the relevant person has capacity, or whether an act done or proposed to be done in relation to that person is lawful (this may include whether or not the act is or would be in the best interests of the relevant person). It is up to the Court of Protection to decide whether or not to consider such an application in advance of the decision on authorisation.

Applying after an authorisation has been given

10.2 Once a standard authorisation has been given, the relevant person or their representative has the right to apply to the Court of Protection to determine any question relating to the following matters: **5–312**
   - whether the relevant person meets one or more of the qualifying requirements for deprivation of liberty
   - the period for which the standard authorisation is to be in force
   - the purpose for which the standard authorisation is given, or
   - the conditions subject to which the standard authorisation is given.

10.3 Where an urgent authorisation has been given, the relevant person or certain persons acting on their behalf, such as a donee or deputy, has the right to apply to the Court of Protection to determine any question relating to the following matters: **5–313**
   - whether the urgent authorisation should have been given
   - the period for which the urgent authorisation is to be in force, or
   - the purpose for which the urgent authorisation has been given.

10.4 Where a standard or urgent authorisation has been given, any other person may also apply to the Court of Protection for permission to take the relevant person's case to court to determine whether an authorisation should have been given. However, the Court of Protection has discretion to decide whether or not to consider an application from these people. **5–314**

10.5 Wherever possible, concerns about the deprivation of liberty should be resolved informally or through the relevant supervisory body's or managing authority's complaints procedure, rather than through the Court of Protection. Chapter 15 of the main Code ('What are the best ways to settle disagreements and disputes about issues covered in the Act?') contains general guidance on how to settle disputes about issues covered in the Mental Capacity Act 2005. The review processes covered in chapter 8 of this Code also provide a way of resolving disputes or concerns, as explained in that chapter. **5–315**

10.6 The aim should be to limit applications to the Court of Protection to cases that genuinely need to be referred to the court. However, with deprivation of liberty at stake, people should not be discouraged from making an application to the Court of Protection if it proves impossible to resolve concerns satisfactorily through other routes in a timely manner. **5–316**

How should people apply to the Court of Protection?

10.7 Guidance on the court's procedures, including how to make an application, is given in the Court of Protection Rules and Practice Directions issued by the court.[12] **5–317**

---

[12] There will usually be a fee for applications to the court. Details of the fees charged by the court

5–318 10.8 The following people have an automatic right of access to the Court of Protection and do not have to obtain permission from the court to make an application:

- a person who lacks, or is alleged to lack, capacity in relation to a specific decision or action
- the donor of a Lasting Power of Attorney to whom an application relates, or their donee
- a deputy who has been appointed by the court to act for the person concerned
- a person named in an existing court order[13] to which the application relates, and
- the person appointed by the supervisory body as the relevant person's representative.

5–319 10.9 All other applicants must obtain the permission of the court before making an application. (See section 50 of the Mental Capacity Act 2005, as amended.) This can be done by completing the appropriate application form.

What orders can the Court of Protection make?

5–320 10.10 The court may make an order:

- varying or terminating a standard or urgent authorisation, or
- directing the supervisory body (in the case of a standard authorisation) or the managing authority (in the case of an urgent authorisation) to vary or terminate the authorisation.

What is the role of the Court of Protection in respect of people lacking capacity who are deprived of their liberty in settings other than hospitals or care homes?

5–321 10.11 The deprivation of liberty safeguards relate only to circumstances where a person is deprived of their liberty in a hospital or care home. Depriving a person who lacks capacity to consent to the arrangements made for their care or treatment of their liberty in other settings (for example in a person's own home, in supported living arrangements other than in care homes or in a day centre) will only be lawful following an order of the Court of Protection on a best interests personal welfare matter (see paragraph 6.51 of the main Code).

5–322 10.12 In such a case, application to the Court of Protection should be made before deprivation of liberty begins. A Court of Protection order will then itself provide a legal basis for the deprivation of liberty. A separate deprivation of liberty authorisation under the processes set out in this Code will not be required.

---

and the circumstances in which fees may be waived or remitted are available from the Office of the Public Guardian (*http://www.publicguardian.gov.uk/*).

[13] Examples of existing court orders include orders appointing a deputy or declarations made by the court in relation to treatment issues.

Is legal aid available to support applications to the Court of Protection in deprivation of liberty safeguards cases?

10.13 Legal aid will be available both for advice and representation before the   **5–323**
Court of Protection.

11.   HOW WILL THE SAFEGUARDS BE MONITORED?

The deprivation of a person's liberty is a significant issue. The deprivation   **5–324**
of liberty safeguards are designed to ensure that a person who lacks capacity to
consent to the arrangements made for their care or treatment is suitably protected
against arbitrary detention. In order to provide reassurance that the safeguards
processes are being correctly operated, it is important for there to be an effective
mechanism for monitoring the implementation of the safeguards.

Who will monitor the safeguards?

11.1 Regulations ill confer the responsibility for the inspection process of the   **5–325**
operation of the deprivation of liberty safeguards in England on a new
regulator, the Care Quality Commission, bringing together functions
from the existing Commission for Social Care Inspection, the Healthcare
Commission and the Mental Health Act Commission. The new body
will be established during 2008, subject to the passage of the relevant
legislation through Parliament, and is expected to be fully operational
by 2009/10 in line with the deprivation of liberty safeguards coming into
force.

11.2 In Wales, the functions of monitoring the operation of the deprivation of   **5–326**
liberty safeguards will fall to Welsh Ministers. These functions will be
performed on their behalf by Healthcare Inspectorate Wales and the Care
and Social Services Inspectorate Wales.

What will the inspection bodies do and what powers will they have?

11.3 The inspection bodies for care homes and hospitals will be expected to: **5–327**
  • monitor the manner in which the deprivation of liberty safeguards are
    being operated by:
    —visiting hospitals and care homes in accordance with their existing
      visiting programme
    —interviewing people accommodated in hospitals and care homes to
      the extent that they consider it necessary to do so, and
    —requiring the production of, and inspecting, relevant records relat-
      ing to the care or treatment of people accommodated in hospitals
      and care homes
  • report annually, summarising their activity and their findings about
    the operation of the deprivation of liberty safeguards. In England this
    report will be made to the Secretary of State for Health, and in Wales
    the report will be made to the Welsh Ministers. It will be for each
    monitoring body to decide whether there should be a deprivation of
    liberty safeguards specific report or whether the report should form
    part of a wider report on the monitoring body's activities.

5–328   11.4 The inspection bodies will have the power to require supervisory bodies and managing authorities of hospitals or care homes to disclose information to them.

5–329   11.5 The inspection process will not cover the revisiting of individual assessments (other than by way of a limited amount of sampling).

5–330   11.6 The inspection process will not constitute an alternative review or appeal process. However, if the inspection body comes across a case where they believe deprivation of liberty may be occurring without an authorisation, they should inform the supervisory body in the same way as any other third party may do.

5–331   11.7 The inspection bodies will look at the deprivation of liberty protocols and procedures in place within managing authorities and supervisory bodies. The aim is to use a small amount of sampling to evaluate the effect of these protocols and procedures on individual cases. Monitoring should take place at a time when the monitoring body is visiting the care home or in-patient setting as part of routine operations, not as an exception.

5–332   11.8 Supervisory bodies and managing authorities should keep their protocols and procedures under review and supervisory bodies should assess the nature of the authorisations they are giving in light of their local population. This information may be relevant to policy decisions about commissioning care and support services.

CHECKLISTS

Key points for care homes and hospitals (managing authorities)

5–333

- Managing authorities need to adapt their care planning processes to incorporate consideration of whether a person has capacity to consent to the services which are to be provided and whether their actions are likely to result in a deprivation of liberty.
- A managing authority must not, except in an urgent situation, deprive a person of liberty unless a standard authorisation has been given by the supervisory body for that specific situation, and remains in force.
- It is up to the managing authority to request such authorisation and implement the outcomes.
- Authorisation should be obtained from the supervisory body in advance of the deprivation of liberty, except in circumstances considered to be so urgent that the deprivation of liberty needs to begin immediately. In such cases, authorisation must be obtained within seven calendar days of the start of the deprivation of liberty.
- A managing authority must ensure that they comply with any conditions attached to the authorisation.
- A managing authority should monitor whether the relevant person's representative maintains regular contact with the person.
- Authorisation of deprivation of liberty should only be sought if it is genuinely necessary for a person to be deprived of liberty in their best interests in order to keep them safe. It is not necessary to apply for authorisations for all admissions to hospitals and care homes simply because the person concerned lacks capacity to decide whether to be admitted.

Key points for local authorities and NHS bodies (supervisory bodies)

- Supervisory bodies will receive applications from managing authori- **5–334**
ties for standard authorisations of deprivation of liberty. Deprivation
of liberty cannot lawfully begin until the supervisory body has given
authorisation, or the managing authority has itself given an urgent
authorisation.

- Before an authorisation for deprivation of liberty may be given, the
supervisory body must have obtained written assessments of the relevant person in order to ensure that they meet the qualifying requirements (including that the deprivation of liberty is necessary to protect
them from harm and will be in their best interests).

- Supervisory bodies will need to ensure that sufficient assessors are
available to meet the needs of their area and that these assessors have
the skills, qualifications, experience and training to perform the function.

- Authorisation may not be given unless all the qualifying requirements
are met.

- In giving authorisation, the supervisory body must specify its duration, which may not exceed 12 months and may not be for longer than
recommended by the best interests assessor. Deprivation of liberty
should not continue for longer than is necessary.

- The supervisory body may attach conditions to the authorisation if it
considers it appropriate to do so.

- The supervisory body must give notice of its decision in writing to
specified people, and notify others.

- The supervisory body must appoint a relevant person's representative
to represent the interests of every person for whom they give a standard authorisation for deprivation of liberty.

- When an authorisation is in force, the relevant person, the relevant
person's representative and any IMCA representing the individual
have a right at any time to request that the supervisory body reviews
the authorisation.

Key points for managing authorities and supervisory bodies

- In addition to the above, both managing authorities and supervisory **5–335**
bodies should be aware of the following key points:

- An authorisation may last for a maximum period of 12 months.

- Anyone engaged in caring for the person, anyone named by them as a
person to consult, and anyone with an interest in the person's welfare
must be consulted in decision-making.

- Before the current authorisation expires, the managing authority may
seek a fresh authorisation for up to another 12 months, provided it is
established, on the basis of further assessment, that the requirements
continue to be met.

- The authorisation should be reviewed, and if appropriate revoked,
before it expires if there has been a significant change in the person's
circumstances. To this end, the managing authority will be required to
ensure that the continued deprivation of liberty of a person remains
necessary in the best interests of the person.

- A decision to deprive a person of liberty may be challenged by the relevant person, or by the relevant person's representative, by an application to the Court of Protection. However, managing authorities and supervisory bodies should always be prepared to try to resolve disputes locally and informally. No one should be forced to apply to the court because of failure or unwillingness on the part of a managing authority or supervisory body to engage in constructive discussion.
- If the court is asked to decide on a case where there is a question about whether deprivation of liberty is lawful or should continue to be authorised, the managing authority can continue with its current care regime where it is necessary:
  —for the purpose of giving the person life-sustaining treatment, or
  —to prevent a serious deterioration in their condition while the court makes its decision.
- The complete process of assessing and authorising deprivation of liberty should be clearly recorded, and regularly monitored and audited, as part of an organisation's governance structure.
- Management information should be recorded and retained, and used to measure the effectiveness of the deprivation of liberty processes. This information will also need to be shared with the inspection bodies.

Overview of the deprivation of liberty safeguards process

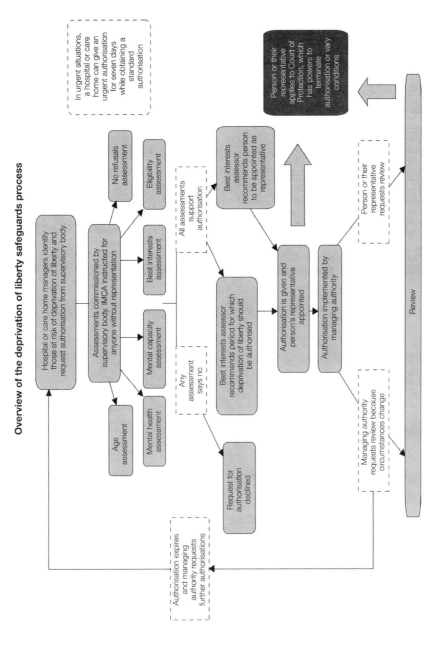

ANNEX 2

5–337

What should a managing authority consider before applying for authorisation of deprivation of liberty?

These questions are relevant **both** at admission **and** when reviewing the care of patients and residents. By considering the following questions in the following order, a managing authority will be helped to know whether an application for authorisation is required.

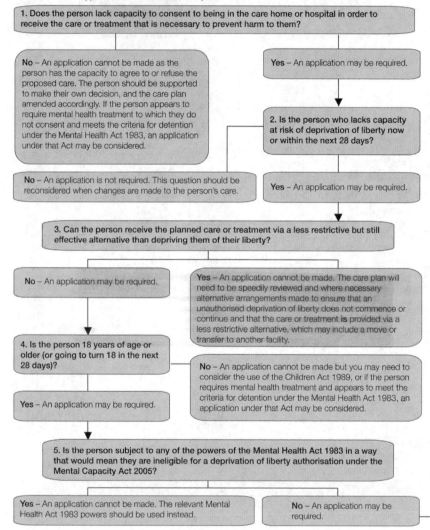

1. Does the person lack capacity to consent to being in the care home or hospital in order to receive the care or treatment that is necessary to prevent harm to them?

No – An application cannot be made as the person has the capacity to agree to or refuse the proposed care. The person should be supported to make their own decision, and the care plan amended accordingly. If the person appears to require mental health treatment to which they do not consent and meets the criteria for detention under the Mental Health Act 1983, an application under that Act may be considered.

Yes – An application may be required.

2. Is the person who lacks capacity at risk of deprivation of liberty now or within the next 28 days?

No – An application is not required. This question should be reconsidered when changes are made to the person's care.

Yes – An application may be required.

3. Can the person receive the planned care or treatment via a less restrictive but still effective alternative than depriving them of their liberty?

No – An application may be required.

Yes – An application cannot be made. The care plan will need to be speedily reviewed and where necessary alternative arrangements made to ensure that an unauthorised deprivation of liberty does not commence or continue and that the care or treatment **is** provided via a less restrictive alternative, which may include a move or transfer to another facility.

4. Is the person 18 years of age or older (or going to turn 18 in the next 28 days)?

No – An application cannot be made but you may need to consider the use of the Children Act 1989, or if the person requires mental health treatment and appears to meet the criteria for detention under the Mental Health Act 1983, an application under that Act may be considered.

Yes – An application may be required.

5. Is the person subject to any of the powers of the Mental Health Act 1983 in a way that would mean they are ineligible for a deprivation of liberty authorisation under the Mental Capacity Act 2005?

Yes – An application cannot be made. The relevant Mental Health Act 1983 powers should be used instead.

No – An application may be required.

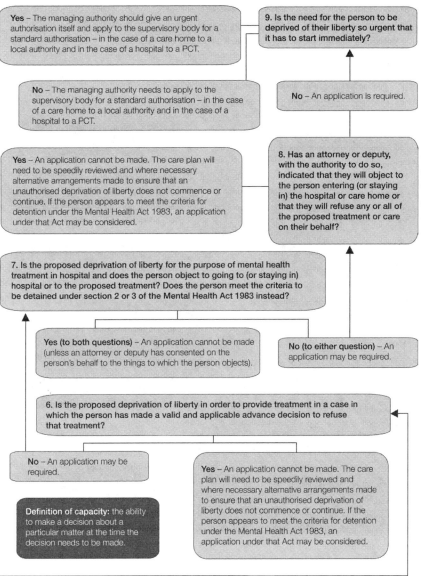

Yes – The managing authority should give an urgent authorisation itself and apply to the supervisory body for a standard authorisation – in the case of a care home to a local authority and in the case of a hospital to a PCT.

9. Is the need for the person to be deprived of their liberty so urgent that it has to start immediately?

No – The managing authority needs to apply to the supervisory body for a standard authorisation – in the case of a care home to a local authority and in the case of a hospital to a PCT.

No – An application is required.

Yes – An application cannot be made. The care plan will need to be speedily reviewed and where necessary alternative arrangements made to ensure that an unauthorised deprivation of liberty does not commence or continue. If the person appears to meet the criteria for detention under the Mental Health Act 1983, an application under that Act may be considered.

8. Has an attorney or deputy, with the authority to do so, indicated that they will object to the person entering (or staying in) the hospital or care home or that they will refuse any or all of the proposed treatment or care on their behalf?

7. Is the proposed deprivation of liberty for the purpose of mental health treatment in hospital and does the person object to going to (or staying in) hospital or to the proposed treatment? Does the person meet the criteria to be detained under section 2 or 3 of the Mental Health Act 1983 instead?

Yes (to both questions) – An application cannot be made (unless an attorney or deputy has consented on the person's behalf to the things to which the person objects).

No (to either question) – An application may be required.

6. Is the proposed deprivation of liberty in order to provide treatment in a case in which the person has made a valid and applicable advance decision to refuse that treatment?

No – An application may be required.

Yes – An application cannot be made. The care plan will need to be speedily reviewed and where necessary alternative arrangements made to ensure that an unauthorised deprivation of liberty does not commence or continue. If the person appears to meet the criteria for detention under the Mental Health Act 1983, an application under that Act may be considered.

Definition of capacity: the ability to make a decision about a particular matter at the time the decision needs to be made.

NB: An authorisation only relates to deprivation of liberty and does not give authority for any course of treatment.

ANNEX 3

5–338

Supervisory body action on receipt of a request from:

a) a managing authority for a standard deprivation of liberty authorisation
b) somebody other than a managing authority (an eligible person) to determine whether or not there is a current unauthorised deprivation of liberty

Standard authorisation review process

Valid standard deprivation of liberty safeguard authorisation in force

Supervisory body may carry out review at any time

Eligible person (the relevant person, relevant person's representative or managing authority) may at any time ask the supervisory body to carry out a review. Managing authority must request a review if one or more of the qualifying requirements appear to them to be reviewable

Supervisory body must carry out a review if asked by an eligible person

Supervisory body to notify the relevant person, the relevant person's representative and the managing authority that a review is to take place (either before the review starts or as soon as practicable thereafter). The supervisory body does not need to give notice to any person who has requested the review

Supervisory body to decide whether any qualifying requirement is reviewable on either non-qualification, change of reason or variation of conditions grounds

One or more qualifying requirements appear to be reviewable

No qualifying requirement reviewable

Supervisory body needs take no action in respect of the standard authorisation

Supervisory body to arrange a separate review assessment in relation to each qualifying requirement that appears to be reviewable, except where the best interests requirement appears to the supervisory body to be non-assessable or not reviewable on the change of reason ground or the variation of conditions ground

Best interests assessment reviewable but non-assessable

Best interests review assessment positive

Best interests requirement not reviewable on the change of reason ground or the variation of conditions ground

On change of reason ground

On variation of conditions ground

Any other review assessment negative

Every other review assessment positive

Supervisory body to decide whether any of the assessed qualifying requirements are reviewable on the change of reason ground

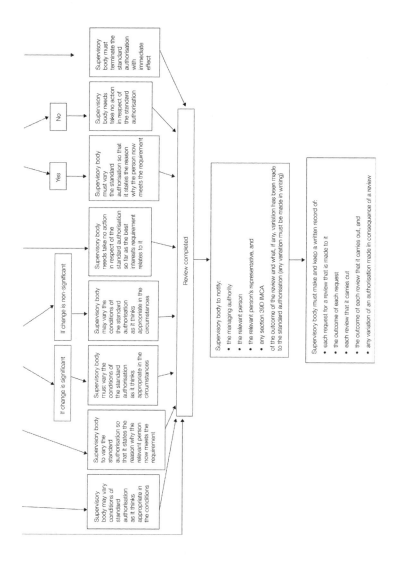

KEY WORDS AND PHRASES USED IN THE CODE OF PRACTICE

5–340   The table below is not a full index or glossary. Instead, it is a list of key terms used in this Code of Practice. References in bold indicate particularly valuable content for that term.

Advance decision to refuse treatment	A decision to refuse specified treatment made in advance by a person who has capacity to do so. This decision will then apply at a future time when that person lacks capacity to consent to, or refuse, the specified treatment. Specific rules apply to advance decisions to refuse life sustaining treatment.	4.26
Advocacy	Independent help and support with understanding issues and putting forward a person's own views, feelings and ideas.	2.7
Age assessment	An assessment, for the purpose of the deprivation of liberty safeguards, of whether the relevant person has reached age 18.	**4.23–4.24**
Approved mental health professional	A social worker or other professional approved by a local social services authority to act on behalf of a local social services authority in carrying out a variety of functions.	4.52, 4.53, 4.60
Assessor	A person who carries out a deprivation of liberty safeguards assessment	**Chapter 4 (all)** 1.16–1.17, 3.21, 5.22, 9.10 Best interests, and appointing a relevant person's representative: 7.10–7.23
Best interests assessment	An assessment, for the purpose of the deprivation of liberty safeguards, of whether deprivation of liberty is in a detained person's best interests, is necessary to prevent harm to the person and is a proportionate response to the likelihood and seriousness of that harm.	**4.58–4.76** Best interests, and appointing a relevant person's representative: 7.10–7.23
Bournewood judgment	The commonly used term for the October 2004 judgment by the European Court of Human Rights in the case of *HL v the United Kingdom* that led to the introduction of the deprivation of liberty safeguards.	**Introduction to chapter 1** 1.19, 2.2, 2.22

Capacity	Short for mental capacity. The ability to make a decision about a particular matter at the time the decision needs to be made. A legal definition is contained in section 2 of the Mental Capacity Act 2005.	Throughout
Care home	A care facility registered under the Care Standards Act 2000.	Throughout
Care Quality Commission	The new integrated regulator for health and adult social care that, subject to the passage of legislation, will take over regulation of health and adult social care from 1 April 2009.	Chapter 11
Carer	Someone who provides unpaid care by looking after a friend or neighbour who needs support because of sickness, age or disability. In this document, the term carer does not mean a paid care worker.	Throughout
Children Act 1989	A law relating to children and those with parental responsibility for children.	1.12, 5.22
Conditions	Requirements that a supervisory body may impose when giving a standard deprivation of liberty authorisation, after taking account of any recommendations made by the best interests assessor.	**4.74–4.75** 5.5 Review of: 8.14, 8.16
Consent	Agreeing to a course of action—specifically in this document, to a care plan or treatment regime. For consent to be legally valid, the person giving it must have the capacity to take the decision, have been given sufficient information to make the decision, and not have been under any duress or inappropriate pressure.	Throughout
Court of Protection	The specialist court for all issues relating to people who lack capacity to make specific decisions.	**Chapter 10**

Deprivation of liberty	Deprivation of liberty is a term used in the European Convention on Human Rights about circumstances when a person's freedom is taken away. Its meaning in practice is being defined through case law.	**Chapter 2** Throughout
Deprivation of liberty safeguards	The framework of safeguards under the Mental Capacity Act 2005 for people who need to be deprived of their liberty in a hospital or care home in their best interests for care or treatment and who lack the capacity to consent to the arrangements made for their care or treatment.	Throughout
Deprivation of liberty safeguards assessment	Any one of the six assessments that need to be undertaken as part of the standard deprivation of liberty authorisation process.	**Chapter 4**
Deputy	Someone appointed by the Court of Protection with ongoing legal authority, as prescribed by the Court, to make decisions on behalf of a person who lacks capacity to make particular decisions.	4.26, 4.65, 5.11, 5.22, 7.7, 7.13–7.15, 7.18, 7.23, 7.29, 10.3, 10.8
Donee	Someone appointed under a Lasting Power of Attorney who has the legal right to make decisions within the scope of their authority on behalf of the person (the donor) who made the Lasting Power of Attorney.	3.9, 4.26, 4.65, 5.11, 5.22, 7.7, 7.13–7.15, 7.18, 7.23, 7.29, 10.3, 10.8
Eligibility assessment	An assessment, for the purpose of the deprivation of liberty safeguards, of whether or not a person is rendered ineligible for a standard deprivation of liberty authorisation because the authorisation would conflict with requirements that are, or could be, placed on the person under the Mental Health Act 1983.	**4.40–4.57**
European Convention on Human Rights	A convention drawn up within the Council of Europe setting out a number of civil and political rights and freedoms, and setting up a mechanism for the enforcement of the obligations entered into by contracting states.	Chapter 1, Chapter 2

European Court of Human Rights	The court to which any contracting state or individual can apply when they believe that there has been a violation of the European Convention on Human Rights.	Introduction to Chapter 1, 2.1–2.2
Guardianship under the Mental Health Act 1983	The appointment of a guardian to help and supervise patients in the community for their own welfare or to protect other people. The guardian may be either a local authority or a private individual approved by the local authority.	4.43, 4.44
Independent Mental Capacity Advocate (IMCA)	Someone who provides support and representation for a person who lacks capacity to make specific decisions, where the person has no-one else to support them. The IMCA service was established by the Mental Capacity Act 2005 and is not the same as an ordinary advocacy service.	**3.22–3.28, 7.34–7.41** 3.16, 4.7, 5.7–5.8, 5.18, 6.8, 6.19, 6.27–6.28, 7.4, 7.23, 7.26, 8.18, 8.28, 9.6, 9.9
Lasting Power of Attorney	A Power of Attorney created under the Mental Capacity Act 2005 appointing an attorney (donee), or attorneys, to make decisions about the donor's personal welfare, including health care, and/or deal with the donor's property and affairs.	10.8
Life-sustaining treatment	Treatment that, in the view of the person providing health care, is necessary to keep a person alive.	5.13
Local authority	In the deprivation of liberty safeguards context, the local council responsible for social services in any particular area of the country.	1.4, 2.18, 2.21, 3.3, 3.11, 3.21, 4.77
Local health board (LHB)	Local health boards cover the same geographic areas as local authorities in Wales. They work alongside their respective local authorities in planning long-term strategies for dealing with issues of health and wellbeing in their areas.	1.4, 3.3
Main Code	The Code of Practice for the Mental Capacity Act 2005.	Throughout

Managing authority	The person or body with management responsibility for the hospital or care home in which a person is, or may become, deprived of their liberty.	**1.4–1.5, 3.1** Throughout
Maximum authorisation period	The maximum period for which a supervisory body may give a standard deprivation of liberty authorisation, which must not exceed the period recommended by the best interests assessor, and which cannot be for more than 12 months.	4.71
Mental Capacity Act 2005	Legislation that governs decision-making for people who lack capacity to make decisions for themselves or who have capacity and want to make preparations for a time when they may lack capacity in the future. It sets out who can take decisions, in which situations, and how they should go about this.	Throughout
Mental capacity assessment	An assessment, for the purpose of the deprivation of liberty safeguards, of whether a person lacks capacity in relation to the question of whether or not they should be accommodated in the relevant hospital or care home for the purpose of being given care or treatment.	4.29–4.32
Mental disorder	Any disorder or disability of the mind, apart from dependence on alcohol or drugs. This includes all learning disabilities.	1.4, 1.7, 1.9, 3.9, 4.33–4.35, 4.45, 4.50, 5.9, 5.22, 6.3
Mental Health Act 1983	Legislation mainly about the compulsory care and treatment of patients with mental health problems. It covers detention in hospital for mental health treatment, supervised community treatment and guardianship.	**4.33–4.57** 1.1, 1.11–1.12, 2.13, 4.5, 5.19, 5.22, 7.8, 8.3, 8.19–8.21
Mental health assessment	An assessment, for the purpose of the deprivation of liberty safeguards, of whether a person has a mental disorder.	**4.33–4.39**

No refusals assessment	An assessment, for the purpose of the deprivation of liberty safeguards, of whether there is any other existing authority for decision-making for the relevant person that would prevent the giving of a standard deprivation of liberty authorisation. This might include any valid advance decision, or valid decision by a deputy or donee appointed under a Lasting Power of Attorney.	**4.25–4.28**
Qualifying requirement	Any one of the six qualifying requirements (age, mental health, mental capacity, best interests, eligibility and no refusals) that need to be assessed and met in order for a standard deprivation of liberty authorisation to be given.	4.1
Relevant hospital or care home	The hospital or care home in which the person is, or may become, deprived of their liberty.	Throughout
Relevant person	A person who is, or may become, deprived of their liberty in a hospital or care home.	Throughout
Relevant person's representative	A person, independent of the relevant hospital or care home, appointed to maintain contact with the relevant person, and to represent and support the relevant person in all matters relating to the operation of the deprivation of liberty safeguards.	**Chapter 7**
Restraint	The use or threat of force to help carry out an act that the person resists. Restraint may only be used where it is necessary to protect the person from harm and is proportionate to the risk of harm.	2.8–2.15
Restriction of liberty	An act imposed on a person that is not of such a degree or intensity as to amount to a deprivation of liberty.	Chapter 2

Review	A formal, fresh look at a relevant person's situation when there has been, or may have been, a change of circumstances that may necessitate an amendment to, or termination of, a standard deprivation of liberty authorisation.	**Chapter 8**
Standard authorisation	An authorisation given by a supervisory body, after completion of the statutory assessment process, giving lawful authority to deprive a relevant person of their liberty in the relevant hospital or care home.	**Chapter 4** Throughout
Supervised community treatment	Arrangements under which people can be discharged from detention in hospital under the Mental Health Act 1983, but remain subject to the Act in the community rather than in hospital. Patients on supervised community treatment can be recalled to hospital if treatment in hospital is necessary again.	4.41, 4.50, 4.51
Supervisory body	A primary care trust, local authority, Welsh Ministers or a local health board that is responsible for considering a deprivation of liberty request received from a managing authority, commissioning the statutory assessments and, where all the assessments agree, authorising deprivation of liberty.	**1.4, 3.3** Throughout
Unauthorised deprivation of liberty	A situation in which a person is deprived of their liberty in a hospital or care home without the deprivation being authorised by either a standard or urgent deprivation of liberty authorisation.	Chapter 9
Urgent authorisation	An authorisation given by a managing authority for a maximum of seven days, which may subsequently be extended by a maximum of a further seven days by a supervisory body, that gives the managing authority lawful authority to deprive a person of their liberty in a hospital or care home while the standard deprivation of liberty authorisation process is undertaken.	**Chapter 6** Throughout

DIRECTIONS AND ARRANGEMENTS

THE ORDINARY RESIDENCE DISPUTES (MENTAL CAPACITY ACT 2005) DIRECTIONS 2010

The Secretary of State for Health makes the following directions in exercise of the power conferred by section 7A of the Local Authority Social Services Act 1970.

6–001

Commencement and interpretation

1. (1) These directions come into force on 19th April 2010 and are addressed to every local authority in England.

6–002

(2) In these directions—

"the 2005 Act" means the Mental Capacity Act 2005;

"lead local authority" means the local authority which is acting, in accordance with regulation 18 of the Mental Capacity (Deprivation of Liberty: Standard Authorisations, Assessments and Ordinary Residence) Regulations 2008 (SI 2008/1858)(arrangements where there is a question as to ordinary residence), as the supervisory body in relation to P;

"local authorities in dispute" means the local authorities which are party to an ordinary residence dispute;

"ordinary residence dispute" means any question arising under Schedule A1 to the 2005 Act (hospital and care home residents: deprivation of liberty) in relation to the ordinary residence of P; and

"P" means a relevant person within the meaning of paragraph 7 of Schedule A1 to the 2005 Act (relevant person etc).

(3) References in these directions to the date on which an ordinary residence dispute arises are references to the first date on which a written communication is sent by one of the local authorities in dispute to one or more of the other authorities in dispute, notifying that other authority or those other authorities that it does not accept that it is liable for acting as the supervisory body in relation to P.

Steps to be taken before referring a dispute to the Secretary of State

2. (1) Before they may refer an ordinary residence dispute to the Secretary of State for determination in accordance with paragraph 183(3) of Schedule A1 to the 2005 Act, the local authorities in dispute must ensure that they have taken all reasonable steps to resolve the dispute between themselves, and in particular that they have complied with the following provisions of this direction.

6–003

(2) As soon as reasonably practicable after the date on which the dispute arises, the lead local authority must identify all the local authorities in dispute and co-ordinate discussions between those authorities in an attempt to resolve the dispute.

(3) As soon as reasonably practicable after the date on which the dispute arises, each local authority in dispute must nominate a named contact within the authority who will take the lead in discussions about the dispute on behalf of the authority.

(4) Each local authority in dispute must engage in constructive dialogue with the others, with a view to the speedy resolution of the dispute.

(5) The lead local authority must gather from the other local authorities in dispute any information which may help to resolve the dispute and those other authorities must comply without delay with any reasonable request by the lead local authority to provide such information.

(6) The lead local authority must provide to P, or P's representatives, such information as appears to it to be appropriate about progress in resolving the dispute.

Stage at which dispute must be referred to Secretary of State

6–004 **3.** If the local authorities in dispute cannot resolve the ordinary residence dispute within four months of the date on which the dispute arose, they must refer the dispute to the Secretary of State in accordance with direction 4.

Documents to be sent with referral to Secretary of State

6–005 **4.** (1) The local authorities in dispute must send to the Secretary of State the following documents within 28 days of the expiry of the period mentioned in direction 3—

    (a) a covering letter signed by the lead local authority requesting the Secretary of State to determine the ordinary residence dispute;

    (b) a statement of facts signed by each of the local authorities in dispute which includes–

        (i) details of the care home in which P is, is to be or was detained;

        (ii) details of where P is residing and any former places of residence which are relevant to the ordinary residence dispute;

        (iii) a chronology of relevant events leading up to the request for a determination of the dispute, including the date on which the dispute arose;

        (iv) details of the steps that the local authorities in dispute have taken to resolve the dispute themselves; and

        (v) any other factual information which is relevant to the ordinary residence dispute; and

    (c) copies of all correspondence between the local authorities in dispute relating to the dispute.

(2) Each of the local authorities in dispute may in addition send to the Secretary of State legal submissions concerning the ordinary residence dispute.

(3) If a local authority in dispute sends legal submissions to the Secretary of State as described in paragraph (2), it must –

    (a) send these to the Secretary of State within 14 days of the date on which the documents referred to in paragraph (1) are sent; and

    (b) provide evidence that the submissions have been sent to the other local authority or authorities in dispute.

(4) The documents referred to in paragraphs (1) to (3) must be submitted to the Secretary of State at the following address—

    Department of Health
    Dignity and Safety Policy Management Unit
    Social Care Policy and Innovation Division

Wellington House
133–155 Waterloo Road
London
SE1 8UG.

(5) If, during the determination of the ordinary residence dispute by the Secretary of State, a local authority in dispute is asked to provide further information to the Secretary of State, that local authority must provide that information without delay.

CROSS-BORDER ARRANGEMENTS

The Secretary of State and the Welsh Ministers have made the following **6–006** arrangements under para.183(4):

1. The Secretary of State and the Welsh Ministers make the following arrangements under paragraph 183(4) of Schedule A1 to the Mental Capacity Act 2005 for determining which questions about a person's ordinary residence for the purposes of paragraph 182 of that Schedule are to be dealt with by the Secretary of State and which are to be dealt with by the Welsh Ministers.

2. In these arrangements—

"care home" has the meaning given by paragraph 178 of the Schedule;

"cross-border ordinary residence dispute" means an ordinary residence dispute between one or more English local authorities and one or more Welsh local authorities;

"ordinary residence dispute" means a question about a person's ordinary residence for the purposes of paragraph 182 of the Schedule ;

"the Schedule" means Schedule A1 to the Mental Capacity Act 2005.

3. The Secretary of State will determine ordinary residence disputes which involve two or more English local authorities only.

4. The Welsh Ministers will determine ordinary residence disputes which involve two or more Welsh local authorities only.

5. The Secretary of State will determine cross-border ordinary residence disputes where the person to whom the dispute relates is accommodated in a care home in England at the time the dispute is referred.

6. The Welsh Ministers will determine cross-border ordinary residence disputes where the person to whom the dispute relates is accommodated in a care home in Wales at the time the dispute is referred.

7. In the case of cross-border ordinary residence disputes, the Welsh Ministers and the Secretary of State (each referred to in this paragraph as an "authority") agree that each will –

(a) notify the other authority immediately on being made aware of the dispute;

(b) agree in accordance with these arrangements which authority will determine the dispute, as soon as details of the current accommodation of the person to whom the dispute relates are known;

(c) consult the other authority and take its views into account, prior to determining the dispute; and

(d) notify the other authority of the outcome of the determination, prior to notifying the local authorities involved in the dispute.

APPENDIX A

APPLICATIONS TO THE COURT OF PROTECTION IN RELATION TO TENANCY AGREEMENTS

Introduction

The Association of Public Authority Deputies (APAD), and other court users **A–001** have asked the court to issue guidance about applications in relation to signing or terminating tenancy agreements on behalf of adults who lack the mental capacity to understand or sign the agreement themselves. Often this is where adults with learning disabilities are moved from hospital or care home settings into supported living arrangements in the community, that allow greater autonomy and independent decision making. Many of the adults will have the capacity to make certain decisions, such as dealing with social security benefit payments, but will lack the capacity deal with the tenancy arrangement.

This guidance has been drawn up with the approval of the senior judge of the Court of Protection, and sets out the circumstances when it may be necessary to make an application, and puts in place streamlined procedures for receiving applications relating to more than one person, thereby simplifying some parts of the court procedure.

When is it necessary to apply to the Court of Protection?

If a person lacks the mental capacity to make his or her own informed deci- **A–002** sion about whether or not to accept a tenancy offer, then an appropriate person can make the decision through the best interest process outlined in the Mental Capacity Act 2005.

Alternatively, if there is a registered enduring or lasting power of attorney in place; or a deputy for property and affairs has already been appointed, then the attorney or deputy would usually make that decision (see below).

Although the Mental Capacity Act 2005 enables the making of certain decisions without the need to obtain any formal authority to act, it does not extend to *signing* legal documents, such as tenancy agreements. Someone can only sign a tenancy agreement on the person's behalf if they are:

- An attorney under a registered lasting power of attorney (LPA) or enduring power of attorney (EPA);
- A deputy appointed by the Court of Protection; or
- Someone else authorised to sign by the Court of Protection.

In some circumstances, landlords may be willing to accept unsigned tenancies, but this guidance applies to the situation where the landlord wants the tenancy to be signed. Even if the landlord will accept an unsigned agreement, it would also be appropriate to make an application where there is a dispute or if it is not clear whether the tenancy offer is in the person's best interests.

Can a deputy or attorney sign or terminate the tenancy agreement?

A–003   If the person has a registered attorney under an EPA or LPA, or has a deputy appointed to make decisions on their behalf, then the deputy or attorney can terminate or enter into a tenancy agreement without further authorisation from the court. Please note, however that deputies acting under an old style short order or receivership order made before the Mental Capacity Act came into force, may not have sufficient authority to sign the agreement, and it may be necessary to apply for 'reappointment' with the full powers of a deputy.

Does a deputy need to be appointed in all cases?

A–004   No, if the sole purpose of the application is to sign or terminate the tenancy, then the application should be for an order that specifically deals with the tenancy matter (see how to make an application, below). If, however, the adult lacks capacity to manage other aspects of their property and affairs and they have assets and income other than social security benefits then it will usually be necessary to appoint a deputy to deal with all these decisions.

What if the person lacking capacity is under 18 years of age?

A–005   Section 18(3) Mental Capacity Act enables the court to make decisions about a child's property or finances (or appoint a deputy to make these decisions) if the child lacks capacity to make such decisions and is likely to still lack capacity to make financial decisions when they reach the age of 18.

These provisions do not extend to tenancies because a person under 18 cannot legally enter into a contract, because in law, a child is deemed to lack capacity because of their age. In addition, a tenancy is a legal estate and a child cannot hold a legal estate.

As the tenant is under 18 and cannot legally sign a contract, the Court of Protection cannot appoint a deputy or authorise someone else to sign the agreement on behalf of the child. This is because the court could not authorise a transaction that would not be legal, even if the person had mental capacity. The only option here would be for someone with parental responsibility to sign, although this would have the effect of making the parent the tenant.

How to make an application

A–006   The court is prepared to deal with all of the adults required to sign the tenancy agreement(s) in a single application. This is on the understanding that the only order required from the court relates to the tenancy agreement and no further directions, for example the appointment of a deputy, are necessary.

The court will require:

- A single COP1 Application form setting out the order or declaration required with a list of all the adults required to sign the agreement annexed;
- A COP3 Assessment of capacity for **each** adult. The assessment should deal specifically with the adult's capacity to sign or terminate the agreement;
- A COP24 Witness statement for **each** person setting out the circumstances behind the moves and confirming that a best interests assessment has been

carried out, including consultation with close family members, or people in close contact with the person, where applicable.

- An application fee.
- A covering letter clearly stating that the applications relates to tenancy agreements in respect of more than one person.

The application form should request the court to make a single order or declaration that it is in all the adult service users' best interests for the tenancy arrangement to be signed or terminated on their behalf.

The procedure above can also be adapted for applications relating to individuals.

How will the court deal with the application?

When the court issues the application, the applicant will notify each adult **A–007** personally using form COP14 and provide evidence that they have done on form COP20A. Once notified, the person will have 21days to object or respond to the application.

If the court receives an objection to the application it will deal with it as a discrete issue, in accordance with the usual procedure.

Once the 21 day time limit expires, the court will issue a single order that deals with the tenancy matter for all the service users.

Will the court remit the fee?

No. The court is only charging a single fee for an application that relates to **A–008** more than one person and will not remit fees in relation to bulk applications. The applicant is responsible for paying the fee, which must accompany the application.

If the application relates to a single individual only, then the usual policy on fee remissions and exemption will apply.

Further help and information

If you need any further help or information about making an application, please **A–009** contact:

web: *courtofprotectionenquiries@hmcts.gsi.gov.uk*
telephone: 0300 456 4600

Please note that while court staff can provide guidance about making an application, they cannot give legal advice. We recommend that you seek independent legal advice where appropriate.

APPENDIX B

APPLICATIONS TO THE COURT OF PROTECTION IN CASES WHERE A PREGNANT WOMAN LACKS CAPACITY TO MAKE DECISIONS ABOUT HER OBSTETRIC CARE

The following guidance is set out in the Annex of the judgment of Keehan J. in **B–001**
NHS Trust v FG [2014] EWCOP 30.

"Guidance

Introduction: **B–002**

1. In this guidance the following terminology will be used:

'P' the pregnant woman who lacks, or may lack, the capacity to take decisions in relation to her antenatal, perinatal and postnatal care as a result of an impairment of, or a disturbance in, the functioning of her mind or brain resulting from her psychiatric illness;
'obstetric care' all care and treatment needs brought about by P's pregnancy including antenatal care, management of labour and delivery, and postnatal care;
'Mental Health Trust' the NHS Trust responsible for P's psychiatric care, whether in the community or in a psychiatric hospital;
'psychiatric hospital' any mental health unit at which P resides, whether detained pursuant to statutory powers or as a voluntary patient;
'acute hospital' a hospital other than the psychiatric hospital at which it is intended that P will receive obstetric care and deliver her child;
'Acute Trust' the NHS Trust responsible for the acute hospital;
'Court' either the Court of Protection or the Family Division of the High Court.

2. This Guidance applies in cases where a pregnant woman who lacks, or may lack, the capacity to make decisions about her obstetric care (see paragraph 1 above) resulting from a diagnosed psychiatric illness, falls within one of the four categories of cases set out in paragraph 3 below.
3. An Acute Trust and/or Mental Health trust should make an application to seek orders in relation to P's obstetric care to the Court of Protection or to the Family Division of the High Court if the case falls within any of the following four categories, namely where:

Category 1—the interventions proposed by the Trust(s) probably amount to serious medical treatment within the meaning of COP Practice Direction 9E, irrespective of whether it is contemplated that the obstetric treatment would otherwise be provided under the MCA or MHA; or
Category 2—there is a real risk that P will be subject to more than transient forcible restraint; or
Category 3—there is a serious dispute as to what obstetric care is in P's best inter-

ests whether as between the clinicians caring for P, or between the clinicians and P and/or those whose views must be taken into account under s.4(7) of the MCA; *or* Category 4—there is a real risk that P will suffer a deprivation of her liberty which, absent a Court order which has the effect of authorising it, would otherwise be unlawful (i.e. not authorised under s4B of or Schedule A1 to the MCA).

4. In relation to category 1, it is recommended that the following categories of case should be the subject of an application to the court, namely:

    i.   delivery by caesarean section is proposed in circumstances where the merits of that proposal are finely balanced; or

    ii.   delivery by caesarean section is proposed and is likely to involve more than transient forcible restraint of P.

5. It may be appropriate to make an application to the court in cases which do not fall within the categories set out in paragraph 3 above; it will depend on the facts of the case. If an application is so made, the provisions of this Guidance should be followed.

Assessment:

6. The early identification of an individual in respect of whom an application might have to be made is essential. In the case where P is detained under the provisions of the Mental Health Act 1983, the lead professional is likely to be a treating psychiatrist at the hospital where P is detained. In the case where P is living in the community the lead professional is likely to be a member of P's midwifery team.

7. Once P has been so identified, the Acute and Mental Health Trusts should liaise to assess P's capacity to make decisions in respect of her obstetric care and to plan how and when such care is to be delivered in her best interests.

8. An assessment of P's capacity to litigate should be undertaken; this will usually be performed by P's treating psychiatrist.

9. Capacity may, of course, fluctuate and it is extremely important to keep the issue of capacity under regular review.

10. Where there are concerns about P's ability to care for her unborn child the Acute and/or Mental Health Trusts should notify the relevant social services department of P's case if social workers are not already involved with her. The local authority should commence child protection procedures immediately upon receipt of a referral. Thereafter, there should be regular liaison and co-operation between the Acute Trust, the Mental Health Trust and the local authority.

11. The Acute and Mental Health Trusts, together with the relevant local authority, should hold regular planning and review meetings ('professionals meetings'). Those meetings should be minuted. Multi-agency co-operation is likely to be an essential feature of the planning process to achieve the best outcome for P and her unborn child.

12. An identified clinician from the Acute Trust or the Mental Health Trust should be appointed to chair the planning and review meetings.

13. Part of the planning process should involve identifying whether and, if so, when a decision by the Court will be required to authorise obstetric care or any deprivation of liberty to facilitate its provision.

14. The planning process should include consideration of an assessment of the

risk of harm, if any, which P poses to herself, to her unborn child or to others. Where any professional considers such a risk exists that assessment must be recorded in writing and presented at the next professionals meeting.

15. If as a result of the risk assessment the local authority proposes to make an application under the inherent jurisdiction for permission to withhold the care plan for the unborn child from P, the application should be made, save in the case of a genuine emergency, no later than 4 weeks before the expected date of delivery. (The threshold for the granting of such an application is high and applications will not be granted routinely).

16. If an application is made by either the Trusts or by the local authority for permission not to notify P of the application(s) and it is thought appropriate to apply for a Reporting Restrictions Order, the applicant(s) must give full and proper notice to the print and broadcast media of the same.

17. A decision by one agency to withhold information from any other agency must be recorded identifying the cogent reasons for the decision. The agency, from whom information is to be withheld, must be notified of the same at the earliest opportunity.

Application:

18. Where it is decided that P's case falls within one of the four categories set out in paragraph 3 above or it is otherwise decided to make an application, an application should be made to the court at the earliest opportunity.   **B–003**

19. Save in a case of genuine medical emergency, any application should be made no later than 4 weeks before the expected date of delivery. This time frame is required for the following reasons:

   i. where P is assessed as lacking capacity to litigate, it will enable the Official Solicitor to undertake any necessary investigations;

   ii. to ensure the final hearing is listed and heard at least a few days before the proposed interventions; and

   iii. to enable a directions hearing to be held around 2 weeks before the final hearing. The court and the parties will then have the opportunity to ensure the court has all the relevant and necessary evidence at the final hearing.

20. In compliance with the timetable set out above, the Trusts should in a timely manner, take the following steps:

   i. issue the application;

   ii. notify the Official Solicitor of the application;

   iii. disclose any evidence to the Official Solicitor which they consider appropriate;

   iv. seek an urgent directions hearing, preferably around two weeks before the final hearing, at which disclosure and the scope of the evidence can be determined;

   v. liaise with the Clerk of the Rules to list the substantive hearing at an early stage.

21. It is important that the Trusts should seek early advice and input from their legal advisers.

22. Late applications are to be avoided save in a case of genuine medical emergency. They have four very undesirable consequences:

i.   the application is more likely to be dealt with by the out of hours judge and without a full hearing in public;

ii.   the available written evidence is more likely to be incomplete and necessitate substantial oral evidence;

iii. it seriously undermines the role that the Official Solicitor can and should properly play in the proceedings; and

iv.   it deprives the court of the opportunity to direct that further evidence, including independent expert evidence, if necessary, is obtained in relation to the issue of capacity or best interests.

This approach is dictated by P's Article 5, 6 and 8 rights and best interests.

23. The following evidence should be filed and served in every application:

(a) In the event that P is to be transferred from a psychiatric hospital to an acute hospital for her obstetric care, a care plan from the Mental Health Trust for that transfer, to include

  (i)   when and, if not at a defined time, the circumstances in which P is to be transferred;

  (ii) the form of transport (ambulance, secure taxi etc.);

  (iii) which members of staff are to accompany P;

  (iv) an assessment of the prospects of P not co-operating with the transfer;

  (v)   whether any specialist advice has been obtained in relation to the restraint of pregnant women and, if it has, the nature of that advice;

  (vi) the plans for any restraint that may be used to facilitate the transfer, including who is to undertake the restraint, at whose direction, and with a description of the techniques to be used;

  (vii) a clear description of what P's status will be under the MHA during transfer and whilst at the acute hospital.

(b) A care plan from the Acute Trust for P's obstetric care, including:

  (i)   the obstetric interventions and care that are proposed;

  (ii) what anaesthesia is planned, or may be required;

  (iii) when, where and by whom the interventions, care and anaesthesia are to be delivered;

  (iv) what further interventions may become necessary and in what circumstances.

(c) A care plan from the Acute Trust relating to the issue of restraint at the acute hospital, including:

  (i)   an assessment of the prospects of P not complying with the obstetric interventions and care that is proposed;

  (ii) in a stepwise and escalating fashion, a description of the measures and techniques to be used;

  (iii) who is to undertake the physical or chemical restraint;

  (iv) whether any specialist advice in relation to the restraint of pregnant women has been obtained and, if so, the nature of that advice.

(d) A witness statement from P's responsible clinician (or to the extent that he/she cannot deal with the issues, from others) which:

  (i)   contains an overview of P's psychiatric history;

(ii)   details the liaison between the psychiatric and obstetric teams caring for P;

(iii) includes a focused assessment of P's capacity to consent to the obstetric treatment which is proposed;

(iv)   sets out the duration for which P's lack of capacity is likely to persist despite any steps that can reasonably be taken to help her regain capacity;

(v)   contains an assessment of the prospects of P not co-operating with the obstetric care that is proposed and its alternatives;

(vi)   endorses the plan for transfer and any restraint during it;

(vii) compares the impact upon her mental health of the proposed obstetric treatment and restraint and any alternatives;

(viii) assesses what obstetric treatment is in P's best interests from a psychiatric perspective.

(e) A witness statement from a consultant obstetrician (or to the extent that he/she cannot deal with the issues, from others) which:

(i)   contains an overview of P's obstetric history so far as it is known;

(ii)   reviews the obstetric care already provided in the present pregnancy;

(iii) details the liaison between the obstetric and psychiatric teams caring for P;

(iv)   explains what obstetric treatment and interventions are proposed;

(v)   identifies what alternative management strategies exist;

(vi)   deals with the anaesthesia which may be used and its risks/benefits;

(vii) refers to the obstetric care plan;

(viii) contains an assessment of the prospects of P not co-operating with the obstetric care that is proposed and its alternatives;

(ix)   endorses the care plan for restraint at the acute hospital;

(x)   compares the risks and benefits to P of the proposed obstetric treatment and interventions versus the alternatives and justification as to why the plan proposed is in P's best interests;

(xi)   explains why the proposed obstetric treatment and interventions are in P's best interests.

(f) Witness evidence, which may be contained in the witness statements from the consultant psychiatrist and obstetrician, which:

(i)   sets out, insofar as they are able, P's past and present wishes and feelings and beliefs and values in relation to
   (1)   the pregnancy;
   (2)   obstetric care, including the proposed obstetric care and interventions;
   (3)   the importance of minimising the risk to her own health during pregnancy and delivery of her baby;
   (4)   the importance of maximising the prospects of safe delivery of the baby;

(ii) explains whether P knows of the application and, if not sets out the cogent reasons why P has not and should not be informed of the application;

(iii) identifies the individuals whose views should be taken into account in accordance with s.4(7) of the MCA and sets out the gist of their views as to

(1) whether the obstetric care that is proposed is in P's best interests and, if not, what care they consider would be;

(2) P's own past and present wishes and feelings and beliefs and values in relation to the matters in (i) above.

Any orders authorising medical intervention, restraint and/or a deprivation of liberty are, of course, permissive and not mandatory. P's capacity to make decisions and/or the need to take any of the measures authorised by the court must be kept under close review by her treating clinicians and medical professions throughout P's antenatal, perinatal and postnatal care.

B–004 *Documents Checklist.*

1. Application notice
2. Transfer Care Plan (where relevant)
3. Obstetric care plan
4. Restraint care plan
5. Witness statement from the responsible consultant psychiatrist
6. Witness statement from the responsible consultant obstetrician"

APPENDIX C

CHIEF CORONER

CHIEF CORONER'S GUIDANCE NO. 16
DEPRIVATION OF LIBERTY SAFEGUARDS (DOLS)

Introduction   C–001

1. This guidance concerns persons who die at a time when they are deprived of their liberty under the Mental Capacity Act 2005 (MCA 2005). Under the MCA 2005 a person who lacks capacity and is in a hospital or care home for the purpose of being given care or treatment may be detained in circumstances which amount to deprivation of liberty.

2. No detention amounting to deprivation of liberty may be permitted without authorisation under the statutory scheme. It would amount otherwise to false imprisonment. The scheme, set out in Schedule A1 to the MCA 2005, provides safeguards known as Deprivation of Liberty Safeguards (DoLS).

3. The questions which are raised for coroners and must be answered are:
   - Are these persons in state detention for the purposes of the Coroners and Justice Act 2009 (the 2009 Act)?
   - Should an inquest be held into their death?
   - If so, must there be an inquest in all cases, even when they die of natural causes?
   - Should there be a jury inquest?
   - Will it be an Article 2 inquest?

4. These questions arise urgently since the use of DoLS in hospitals and care homes is now widespread and increasing. The Department of Health (DH) and Care Quality Commission (CQC) expect applications for DoLS to rise from 13,000 a year to over 100,000. Most cases concern vulnerable people with dementia. Others may have a severe learning disability or acquired brain injury.

5. For the future the Law Commission has commenced a fundamental review of DoLS provisions in the MCA 2005. It will report in 2017 with recommendations for reform and a draft Bill.

6. But for now the purpose of this guidance is to give coroners a steer on the application of DoLS in the context of coroner work. It will of course be a matter for coroners in the exercise of their independent judgment, and subject to any subsequent ruling of the High Court, to decide each case for themselves.

7. For the purpose of simplicity, the statutory authorisation for deprivation of liberty of a person in a hospital or care home will be referred to in this guidance as a DoL.

C–002 **What are DoLS? How is deprivation of liberty authorised?**

8. Following the decision in *R v Bournewood Community and Mental Health NHS Trust, ex p L* [1999] 1 AC 458 and its reconsideration at Strasbourg in *HL v UK* (2004) 40 EHRR 761, it became necessary for the UK to introduce machinery for the protection of the thousands of mentally incapacitated people who were regularly deprived of their liberty in hospitals and care homes (and elsewhere).

9. Accordingly the MCA 2005 was amended by the Mental Health Act 2007 so as to provide a new statutory scheme for persons in hospitals or care homes who were proved on a balance of probabilities to lack capacity.

C–003 **Lack of capacity**

10. Under the MCA 2005 lack of capacity is expressed in this way. A person lacks capacity in relation to a matter if he or she is unable to make a decision for himself or herself in relation to the matter because of an impairment (permanent or temporary) of, or a disturbance in the functioning of, the mind or brain: sections 1 and 2, MCA 2005.

11. Persons who lack capacity may be subject to deprivation of liberty, but only by authorisation under Schedule A1 of the MCA 2005 or by order of the Court of Protection (section 4A).

C–004 **Meaning of 'deprivation of liberty'**

12. Section 64(5) of the MCA 2005, the interpretation section, provides that references in the Act to deprivation of a person's liberty have the same meaning as in Article 5(1) of the European Convention on Human Rights. Article 5(1) of the Convention provides:

> "Everyone has the right to liberty and security of person. No one shall be deprived of his liberty save in the following cases and in accordance with a procedure prescribed by law) **the lawful detention** of persons for the prevention of the spreading of infectious diseases, **of persons of unsound mind**, alcoholics or drug addicts, or vagrants."

13. In *P v Cheshire West and Cheshire Council; P and Q v Surrey County Council* [2014] UKSC 19 (a DoLS case but not a coroner case) the Supreme Court stated that the purpose of Article 5 was to ensure that people were not deprived of their liberty without proper safeguards.

14. The Supreme Court decided (by a majority), citing *HL v UK* (above), that deprivation of liberty arose when the person concerned 'was under continuous supervision control and was not free to leave' [49], [63] and [87]. This should be determined 'primarily on an objective basis' [76]–[87].

15. It did not matter that the patient in hospital or the resident of a care home was content or compliant or voiced no objection. As Lady Hale said at [46], 'A gilded cage is still a cage.'

16. Accordingly, once there is, or is likely to be, deprivation of liberty, the detention must be authorised under the DoLS scheme in the MCA 2005.

Authorisation   **C–005**

17.   An authorisation which deprives a person of his or her liberty is obtained
      in the following way. The 'managing authority' of the hospital or care
      home (public or private) may request authorisation from the 'supervisory
      body'. There must be a request **and** an authorisation before a person is
      lawfully deprived of his or her liberty.

The managing authority   **C–006**

18.   The managing authority of an NHS hospital is the health trust, board or
      special health authority. For independent (private) hospitals the manag-
      ing authority is the person registered or required to be registered by
      statute. For care homes the managing authority is the person registered
      or required to be registered by statute. See paragraphs 175–178, Schedule
      A1.

The supervisory body

19.   Since 2009 the supervisory body for all hospitals and care homes, both   **C–007**
      public and private, is the local authority.

Standard and urgent authorisations   **C–008**

20.   There are two types of authorisation: standard authorisations and urgent
      authorisations.
21.   The DH has issued forms and guidance: see *https://www.gov.uk/govern-
      ment/collections/dh-mental-capacity-act-2005-deprivation-of-liberty-
      safeguards*. Form No.1 is for urgent authorisations, Form No.12 for
      standard authorisations.
22.   The *DoLS Code of Practice* issued by the DH can be found at *http://
      webarchive.nationalarchives.gov.uk/20130107105354/http://www.
      dh.gov.uk /prod consum dh/groups/dh digitalassets/@dh/@en/docu-
      ments/digitalasset/dh 087309.pdf*
23.   Standard authorisations are made by the local authority. They must state
      in writing (amongst other things) the name of the person to be detained,
      the hospital or care home at which deprivation of liberty is authorised,
      the duration of the authorisation, the purpose for which it was given,
      the reason why each qualifying requirement (see below) was met, and
      'any conditions' subject to which the authorisation is given. It may be
      renewed. See paragraphs 21-73, Schedule A1.
24.   There is a statutory duty upon the managing authority of a hospital or
      care home to apply for authorisation where the qualifying requirements
      are likely to be met within the following 28 days. See paragraphs 24–26,
      Schedule A1.
25.   Urgent authorisations are made by the managing authority of the hospital
      or care home in urgent cases only, for a period of seven days, pending a
      request for a standard authorisation. They do not involve recourse to the
      supervisory body. See paragraphs 74–90, Schedule A1.
26.   Once the authorisation is given (standard or urgent), the hospital or care

home may deprive the person of their liberty by detaining the person for the purpose of their being given care or treatment. See paragraph 1 (2), Schedule A1.

C–009   Safeguards

27. Safeguards (as in the phrase Deprivation of Liberty Safeguards) are provided by Schedule A1 of the MCA 2005. They involve a rigorous procedure of assessment and authorisation, independent of the hospital or home.

28. Safeguards are provided by the precondition of six qualifying requirements having to be met. These are the age, mental health, mental capacity, best interests, eligibility and no refusals requirements. See paragraph 12, Schedule A1.

29. Following a request the supervisory body must carry out assessments of all qualifying requirements before granting an authorisation: paragraph 33, Schedule A1. The six assessments must be completed by a minimum of two assessors, usually including a social worker or care worker, sometimes a psychiatrist or other medical person (see *DoLS Code of Practice* 4.13–4.57). If all assessments are in writing and 'positive', ie all qualifying requirements are met, the supervisory body must give a standard authorisation: paragraph 50, Schedule A1. This authorisation may be 'reviewed' by the supervisory body later.

30. As one would expect, where the liberty of the subject is at stake, the provisions are detailed and extensive. There are 188 paragraphs in Schedule A1. It is not the purpose of this guidance to detail all the requirements and conditions.

C–010   Court of Protection

31. The Court of Protection may make a similar order authorising deprivation of liberty in a domestic setting (outside hospitals and care homes) in relation to personal welfare: see sections 4A and 16 of the MCA 2005. This will include a placement in a supported living arrangement.

32. The authorisation of any DoL may be challenged in the Court of Protection: section 21A, MCA 2005. See, for example, *RB (by his Litigation Friend, the Official Solicitor) v Brighton and Hove City Council* [2014] EWCA Civ 561 (unsuccessful application to terminate a standard authorisation).

C–011   No challenge to validity of DoLS before coroner

33. Where an authorisation to deprive a person of liberty has been given, its validity cannot be challenged by or before a coroner.

C–012   The Coroners and Justice Act 2009: 'in state detention'

34. In order to decide whether a coroner must investigate the death of a person who was subject to a DoL, it is necessary to consider the relevant provisions of the 2009 Act. Has a person who was subject to a DoL died in state detention for the purposes of the 2009 Act?

35. A coroner must commence an investigation into a person's death under the relevant wording of section 1 of the 2009 Act where the coroner has reason to suspect that 'the deceased died while in custody **or otherwise in state detention**': section 1(2)(c). The Explanatory Notes to section 1 suggest that state detention includes persons 'held under mental health legislation': paragraph 61.

36. '**State detention**' is defined in section 48(2). 'A person is in state detention if he or she is compulsorily detained by a public authority within the meaning of section 6 of the Human Rights Act 1998.' Section 6 is headed 'Acts of public authorities'.

37. If a duty to investigate arises under section 1, the investigation may not be discontinued if the coroner has reason to suspect that the deceased 'died while in custody **or otherwise in state detention**': section 4(2)(b). In those circumstances the coroner must therefore hold an inquest: section 6.

Two opposing views

C–013

38. Two alternative views have been expressed about DoLS and whether they are included within the phrase 'in state detention'.

39. The first view is that the deprivation of liberty of DoLS extends more widely than cases of ordinary physical detention, for example to cases of persons living in relative normality, not seeking to leave or complaining about being restrained, but would be restrained if they sought to leave. See *Jervis on Coroners* 13th Edn. (2014) at paragraph 5-85.

40. In addition *Jervis* suggests that the restraint, such as it is, is outside the scope of the definition of state detention in section 48(2) (above) when it is not by a 'public authority' for the purposes of the Human Rights Act 1998, as for example in the case of a private care home.

41. On this view the death of a person in hospital or a care home who was subject to a DoL would not automatically require a coroner's investigation. Indeed in most cases there would be no need for an investigation, although the coroner would have to decide on a case by case basis whether one was necessary.

42. The second and opposing view is that a person subject to a DoL falls squarely within the 2009 Act's definition of 'in state detention'. However quiet and comfortable the person may be in, say, a care home, the reality of their position is that they have been deprived of their liberty by the authority of the state and are being held in detention under that authority—as in 'the gilded cage' referred to by Lady Hale.

43. On this view, whether intended by Parliament or not, all persons who die subject to a DoL must be the subject of a coroner investigation, whether the death was from natural causes or not. For the purposes of the 2009 Act they were 'in state detention', therefore section 1 is triggered.

44. These two competing views are not easily reconciled. They may ultimately be a matter for decision of the High Court. The former view, for example, may require coroners to consider every DoLS death on a case by case basis to see if an investigation is required. Some coroners say that the burden of doing so would be immense. The latter view, for example, may cause local authorities great concern over additional and unexpected expenditure by the coroner service as a result of many extra inquests.

C–014   The Chief Coroner's view

45.   The Chief Coroner favours the second view. It is his opinion that, on the law as it now stands, the death of a person subject to a DoL should be the subject of a coroner investigation because that person was in state detention within the meaning of the Coroners and Justice Act 2009.

46.   The Chief Coroner, who sits in the High Court on coroner cases, is not providing a judgment or ruling. This guidance is no more than the expression of an opinion, subject to the ruling of the High Court. Coroners, who are of course entitled to make their own independent judicial decisions, will do as they see fit in any particular case. But they are invited to take this guidance into account.

47.   The Chief Coroner's view is the view which was expressed in the Chief Coroners Guide to the Coroners and Justice Act 2009 Act at paragraph 54:

> "This [the definition of 'state detention' in section 48(2)], in effect, extends the definition of state detention to institutions such as immigration detention and secure mental health hospitals. It would also appear to extend to deprivation of liberty orders (Schedule A1, Mental Capacity Act 2005)."

48.   The Ministry of Justice collaborated with the Chief Coroner on the Guide and approved this wording.

49.   The Department of Health also shares this view.

50.   It was also the view of the Government in 2009 as expressed during the passage of the Coroners and Justice Bill. In response to questions from the Joint Parliamentary Committee on Human Rights, the then Government acknowledged that 'in state detention' would include the following circumstances:

    (a)   detention by a constable or other public authority pursuant to statutory or common law powers;

    (b)   **detention or deprivation of liberty pursuant to the requirements of mental health legislation, including the Mental Health Act 1983 and the Mental Capacity Act 2005, as amended by the Mental Health Act 2007**;

    (c)   the placement of a child in secure accommodation;

    (d)   detention pursuant to immigration and asylum legislation; and

    (e)   the detention of any person in custody or otherwise detained while he or she is being transported from one place to another.".

51.   In accepting that the examples in the above list would come under the definition of state detention, the then Government considered that listing them in the Bill was unnecessary. On this basis it could be said that the wording of the 2009 Act, which makes no reference to DoLS, was clearly intended by the drafters of the 2009 Act to include DoLS in the meaning of 'in state detention'.

52.   This view appears to accord with the Explanatory Notes to section 1 of the 2009 Act (see paragraph 35 above).

53.   It should of course be noted that the High Court may be less willing to resort to some of these extra-statutory materials in interpreting relevant

provisions of the 2009 Act.

54. This view may be further supported by the language used in Schedule A1 of the MCA 2005 which refers to a person 'detained in a hospital or care home' and 'place of detention'. In short once the relevant conditions are satisfied, the person is detained by operation of law. This appears to be consistent with 'compulsorily detained' in section 48(2) of the 2009 Act.

55. This view suggests that those subject to DoLS are subject in plain language to the restrictions of state detention. They are detained compulsorily under the statutory framework of the state. There should therefore be a coroner's investigation (including inquest: section 6) in all cases.

Public authority   C–015

56. On the 'public authority' point, it is certainly arguable that all hospitals and care homes are public authorities for the purposes of the Human Rights Act (see section 48(2) above). Those in public ownership clearly are. Those in private ownership will be if they are carrying out 'functions of a public nature', so as to fall within the meaning of 'public authority' in section 6(3)(b) of the Human Rights Act 1998.

57. On this point see, for example, *R (A) v Partnerships in Care Ltd* [2002] 1 WLR 2610, in which a private provider of mental health care was held to be a functional public authority, performing public functions within the meaning of section 6(3)(b) of the Act. By contrast the decision in *YL v Birmingham City Council* [2008] 1 AC 95 decided on its particular facts that the private care home was not a public body, but was providing a service for which it charged the local authority a fee for some of its residents but not all. However, the decision in *YL* has been reversed since by statute. Section 145 of the Health and Social Care Act 2008 states that where accommodation, together with nursing or personal care, is provided by a private care home and the local authority are paying for it, the care home is deemed to be a 'public authority' for the purposes of section 6(3)(b) of the Human Rights Act.

58. There is also an argument that the local authority, which as the supervisory body authorises a person to be deprived of their liberty by a DoL, is the relevant public authority. On the other hand section 64(6) of the MCA 2005 provides that for the purposes of references to deprivation of a person's liberty 'it does not matter whether a person is deprived of his liberty by a public authority or not'. That suggests that the detention is the act of the managing authority, not the supervisory body.

59. The ultimate question might therefore be: Is the detention by the managing authority in the case of a private care home a public function? The answer to that question may well be Yes. The detention is a public function because of the detailed statutory scheme which permits it. The exercise of powers of compulsory detention could therefore be considered a public function for the purposes of section 6 of the Human Rights Act.

Inquest with jury?   C–016

60. In many cases there will be no need for a jury inquest. The mandatory requirement for an inquest to be held with a jury where 'the deceased died

in custody or otherwise in state detention' does not apply to deaths from natural causes. It only applies where the death is a violent or unnatural one or the cause of death is unknown: section 7(2)(a) of the 2009 Act.

C–017   **Article 2**

61.   The mere fact that the inquest will be concerned with a death 'in state detention' does not mean that it will necessarily be an Article 2 inquest. In some cases it may be. But in many cases, particularly those where the death is from natural causes, there will be no arguable breach of the state's general duty to protect life. Nor will there be any arguable breach of the *Osman* test that the state knew or ought to have known of a real or immediate risk to the life of the deceased and failed to take measures within the scope of their powers: *Osman v UK* [1998] 29 EHRR 245.

62.   Accordingly, in most cases the procedural duty to hold a *Middleton* inquest and ascertain under section 5(2) of the 2009 Act 'in what circumstances' the deceased came by his or her death will not apply.

63.   The Article 2 procedural duty may, however, arguably arise where the death is not from natural causes and/or the fact of detention under DoLS may be a relevant factor in the cause of death.

C–018   **Conclusions**

64.   The Chief Coroner's present view, subject to a decision of the High Court, is that any person subject to a DoL is 'in state detention' for the purposes of the 2009 Act.

65.   When that person dies the death should therefore be reported to the coroner and the coroner should commence an investigation under section 1.

66.   The person is not 'in state detention' for these purposes until the DoL is authorised.

67.   Where the authorisation relates to a care home and the person is removed to a hospital and dies there (or in transit), coroners should err on the side of caution in deciding that the DoL may extend from the care home to the hospital in cases of medical necessity and therefore an investigation must be commenced. Even if the DoL is strictly place-specific (see paragraphs 25-26, Schedule A1), the law of necessity may allow the hospital to 'detain' the person, therefore an inquest would be necessary.

68.   The investigation cannot be discontinued: section 4(2)(b). There must be an inquest.

69.   There is no requirement for a jury where the death was from natural causes: section 7(2)(a).

70.   In many cases the inquest will not be an Article 2 inquest.

71.   In many cases of this kind which are uncontroversial the inquest may be a 'paper' inquest, decided in open court but on the papers without witnesses having to attend. Intelligent analysis of relevant information (without the need for a postmortem examination) may be the best approach. Bereaved families should have all of this explained to them in advance.

72.   Nevertheless, there will always be a public interest in the careful scrutiny

of any death in state detention. As in all cases there must be sufficiency of coroner inquiry.

73. Senior coroners should maintain close liaison with the DoLS lead in their local authority, working together to deal with this extra activity.

HH JUDGE PETER THORNTON QC
CHIEF CORONER
5 December 2014

APPENDIX D

CONTACT DETAILS

The following list provides contact details for relevant organisations.   **D–001**

Action on Elder Abuse

web: *www.elderabuse.org.uk*
telephone helpline: 0808 808 8141
switchboard: 020 8835 9280

Age UK

web: *www.ageuk.org.uk*
telephone helpline: 0800 169 2081

Alzheimers Society

web: *www.alzheimers.org.uk*
telephone: 020 7423 3500
telephone helpline: 0300 222 1122

British Banking Association

web: *www.bba.org.uk*
telephone: 020 7216 8800

British Institute of Learning Disabilities

web: *www.bild.org.uk*
telephone: 0121 415 6960

British Psychological Society

web: *www.bps.org.uk*
telephone: 0116 254 9568

Care Quality Commission

web: *www.cqc.org.uk*
telephone: 03000 616161

Carers UK

web: *www.carersuk.org*
telephone advice line: 0808 808 7777
switchboard: 020 7378 4999

Department of Health

web: *www.gov.uk/government/organisations/department-of-health*

Department for Work and Pensions

web: *www.gov.uk/government/organisations/department-for-work-pensions*

Down's Syndrome Association

web: *www.downs-syndrome.org.uk*
switchboard: 0333 1212 300

Headway—the Brain Injury Association

web: *www.headway.org.uk*
telephone helpline: 0808 800 2244
switchboard: 0115 924 0800

Healthcare Inspectorate for Wales

web: *www.hiw.org.uk*
telephone: 0300 062 8163

Her Majesty's Courts and Tribunals Service

web: *www.gov.uk/government/organisations/hm-courts-and-tribunals-service*

Information Commissioner's Office

web: *www.ico.gov.uk*
helpline: 0303 123 1113

Local Government Ombudsman

web: *www.lgo.org.uk*
telephone advice line: 0300 061 0614

Mencap

web: *www.mencap.org.uk*
telephone: 020 7454 0454
Mencap Direct: 0808 808 1111

Mind

web: *www.mind.org.uk*
telephone infoline: 0300 123 3393
switchboard: 020 8519 2122

Ministry of Justice

web: *www.justice.gov.uk*

National Autistic Society

web: *www.autism.org.uk*
telephone helpline: 0800 800 4104
switchboard: 020 7833 2299

Office of the Public Guardian

web: *www.justice.gov.uk/about/opg.htm*
switchboard: 0300 456 0300

Official Solicitor

web: *www.justice.gov.uk/about/ospt.htm*

Parliamentary and Health Service Ombudsman

web: *www.ombudsman.org.uk*
complaints helpline: 0345 015 4033

Public Service Ombudsman for Wales

web: *www.ombudsman-wales.org.uk*
telephone: 01656 641150

Rethink

web: *www.rethink.org*
telephone: 0300 5000 927

Royal College of Psychiatrists

web: *www.rcpsych.ac.uk*
telephone: 020 7235 2351

Solicitors for the Elderly

web: *www.solicitorsfortheelderly.com*
telephone: 0844 567 6173

Young Minds

web: *www.youngminds.org.uk*
telephone: 020 7089 5050

INDEX

(All references are to paragraph number)

Index